*The Reformation
in Historical Thought*

The Reformation
in Historical Thought

A. G. Dickens
and John Tonkin
with Kenneth Powell

Harvard University Press
Cambridge, Massachusetts   1985

This book is printed on acid-free paper, and
its binding materials have been chosen for
strength and durability.

Library of Congress Cataloging in Publication Data

Dickens, A. G. (Arthur Geoffrey), 1910–
    The Reformation in historical thought.

    Bibliography: p.
    Includes index.
    1. Reformation—Historiography.   I. Tonkin, John.
II. Powell, Kenneth.   III. Title.
BR307.D47 1985   270.6'072   85-5842
ISBN 0-674-75311-9 (alk. paper)

Preface

The broad concept of this book, including its title, was derived in the early 1970s from the example of that admirable survey by Wallace K. Ferguson, *The Renaissance in Historical Thought* (Cambridge, Mass., 1948). From the beginning it was clear that the historiography of the Reformation represents an even more complex element in Western intellectual history. Across more than four centuries one would need to review the literature concerning not one Reformation but many, each with its leaders, churches, opponents, theological refinements, and political and social backgrounds. That literature would prove immense and seldom adequately digested in secondary works. Nineteenth-century interpretations, which broadened into multiple disciplines, would pose an even more formidable task. To "cover" this spate of writings and opinions, one would ideally need to work full-time for twenty years, learn new languages, and produce at least three ponderous volumes. Even had other obligations permitted so gargantuan a project, it would nowadays prove unacceptable to publishers and readers alike. Given the need for ruthless compromise and selection, nothing like a definitive book could yet be written. Yet surely someone should start breaking the ground, secure at least in the knowledge that no attempt had yet been made, even on a moderate scale. It seemed high time to begin. As the quincentenary of Martin Luther's birth approached, the volume of historical writing on the Reformation was still growing and was far from becoming repetitive.

The gestation of this book has been complex, prolonged, and sometimes painful. It had its origins in two separate scholarly projects, each pursued for some years in blissful ignorance of the other—one at the Institute of Historical Research, with the able collaboration of Research Assistant Kenneth Powell; the other across the world in Western Australia, interrupted by two valuable periods of study at the University of Cambridge, the first in 1973 under a Nuffield Commonwealth Travelling Fellowship, and the second on a period of study leave in 1977, both periods in close association with Professor Gordon Rupp, Dixie Professor of Ecclesiastical History.

The two authors met for the first time at the end of 1977, more by chance than by deliberate planning. In sharing our experiences of the research we had each done and our perceptions of the task ahead, we soon became aware of common approaches and complementary areas of strength, and we resolved to collaborate in some way. It was not long before that collaboration developed from separate responsibility for individual chapters to joint authorship in the fullest sense.

After a period of heavy postal exchanges, the generous grant to Dickens of a Misha Strassberg Visiting Research Professorship at the University of Western Australia in 1981 allowed us to teach and write together for three months. Since then we have not only burdened the postal service further but have also passed several invaluable periods together in London. Discovering a spontaneous capacity for thinking together, we have expanded and deepened our earlier concepts, added several new chapters, and restructured the whole work several times in the light of our continuing research.

The continual discovery of fresh data and new dimensions exacerbated an already acute problem of selecting material, and it soon became clear that our purposes would not be served by awarding places in the text only to the most meritorious and deserving authors. The everextending boundaries of the subject could be marked out only at the price of including some odd fish while excluding certain more shapely and normal specimens. With some salutary guidance from Aida Donald of Harvard University Press, we have struggled hard to prevent this book from developing that monstrous corpulence which seemed all too inevitable, given its genes, metabolism, and all-too-plentiful diet. In this regard, one feature of the final version may occasion misunderstanding. The chapters on early historians of the Reformation are less rigorously selective than later chapters, perhaps suggesting that the task was begun on a larger scale than we could sustain. In fact, the ostensibly "early" chapters were among the last to be written, and at this stage we were discovering in the sixteenth century many ideas more diverse and interesting than we had anticipated. Moreover, in an age when ideologies tend to stop us seeing the trees for the wood, it seemed more important than ever to stress conscious motivation and individual contributions. These early historians stand among the makers of the Reformation: was it not essential to let them tell us at least what they thought was happening around them? At no stage could historiography contribute more to actual historical knowledge.

Each of the authors has his own personal debts to acknowledge, yet so close has the collaboration been that these may properly be recognized as common debts. Kenneth Powell's initial contribution to the project clearly demanded the inclusion of his name on the title page, although his demanding employment in another capacity prevented him from participating in the crucial and even more laborious later phases of extension and revision. Gordon Rupp's profound knowledge of the Reformation theological tradition and his lively wit have left an indelible imprint on several chapters. The Australian Research Grants Scheme awarded a substantial grant which not only facilitated an extended period of research in London but also provided the invaluable research assistance of Joan Wardrop, whose gift for analytical and critical thought was a constant stimulus. Special thanks are due to Michael Thompson, Director of the Institute of Historical Research, who has tolerated the continuing presence of his predecessor and, with his colleagues, accorded innumerable kindnesses and special facilities to both authors. Of the many friends and colleagues whose suggestions have been gratefully received, special mention must be made of Bob Scribner, who drew our attention to a number of very recent books and articles which we might otherwise have missed.

The preparation of the typescript was carried out entirely in Perth, where Phyllis Langley ably marshaled the hard-pressed secretarial resources of the History Department toward the massive task, most of which was carried through by Nancy McKenzie with great speed and expertise.

To Barbara, Kati, and Christopher Tonkin, we both acknowledge an immeasurable debt; they not only put up with periods of absence every year, but also transformed this necessity into an opportunity for cementing new and rewarding friendships across the world and across generations.

A. G. D.
J. M. T.

Contents

The Reformation
in Historical Thought

Introduction

Beginning with Luther's contemporaries and arriving finally at the quincentenary of his birth, this book will discuss the changing historical evaluations of a major episode in modern civilization. Already in its early years, the Protestant Reformation was seen as something more than a religious dispute, and the sheer diversity of its effects has since been observed with ever-increasing coverage and precision. Helped by many able witnesses, we hope to throw light not only on the movement itself but also on Western activities and values over the last four centuries. Here we have a classic test case, an exceptionally broad entrance into the palace of modern thought.

We shall not contrast the social sciences and theology as two mutually exclusive spheres, for after all religion exists within actual human societies, not within some spiritual stratosphere. Religion has been—and still remains in many communities—a dynamic of immense power. Historians who exclude theology from their inquiries are usually committing a supreme act of folly, an act even more perverse than the exclusion of individual human motivation from the list of historical causes. Again, we should not too rigorously limit our purview to the sixteenth century. Any analysis of the movements associated with Luther, Zwingli, Calvin, and the Anabaptists would be defective without some reference to their predecessors, Wycliffe, Huss, and Valla, or to the multilateral consequences of these movements between 1600 and the present. By the same token, although we are primarily concerned with the historiography of

Protestantism, we may not wholly exclude that of its opposing context, the Catholic Counter-Reformation, which, springing from a preexistent, theologically conservative reformism, arose in force well within Luther's lifetime and set bounds to Protestant expansion.

Over and above these obvious parameters, a far larger dimension appears when we envisage Reformation beside Renaissance as a recurrent historical theme rather than a single episode. Reformation occurs at various periods of Christian history, as it does in Judaism, Islam, and other institutional religions. Regarding these universal aspects we may indeed find most of our witnesses distinctly inadequate: few historians of the Reformation have thought enough about the early centuries of Christianity, while the broader perspectives afforded by comparative religion have seldom been extended to the Reformation. Perhaps our authors should have dwelt on the Old Testament image of the prophet upbraiding a backsliding leadership, and especially the priesthood. The great Protestant Reformers showed themselves to be well aware of the striking parallels between their own functions and those of the ancient prophets. Moreover, they recognized Jesus not only as Redeemer and Lord but as the last and greatest of the prophets, denouncing the hardened legalism of the Pharisees, who seemed to have such obvious successors among the clerical hierarchy of the sixteenth century.

Like a good many of our predecessors in Reformation historiography, we recognize the most basic origins of the Protestant Reformation in the clash between churchly innovation and scriptural authority. The primary aim of the Reformation was to restore the true and ancient face of the Church and to cancel the gratuitous additions imposed upon the faith by imaginative theologians, enthusiastic fundraisers, and illiterate laymen. Its especial bête noire was the host of practices and institutions arising from the nonscriptural invention of Purgatory, and regarded as exploiting the people's deep, natural affections toward deceased kinsfolk. These and other sub-Christian cults, the Reformers believed, had become ever stronger during the preceding two centuries and should once and for all be excised or at least rectified through consistent reference to the fountainhead, the Gospel of Christ enshrined in the primal documents of the faith.

Around 1500 the task appeared more feasible because of the great advances made by Greek and Hebrew studies in Western Europe and because of the textual and historical techniques of humanist scholars, which Valla, and more recently Erasmus, had already transferred from the pagan classics to the New Testament. Logical enough in principle, this resolute return to the sources was swiftly menaced by snares and illusions which most Reformers were slow to recognize. Subjective thinking and impulsive judgments soon obtruded on a public opinion by no means equipped either to assess novel interpretations of the scriptural texts or to tolerate and control such unparalleled demands for intellectual freedom. Moreover, the Scriptures, although they did indeed contain virtually all the hard evidence on Christ's teaching, presented knottier problems than the optimistic Erasmus had been willing to acknowledge in his seminal *Enchiridion* of 1503. A couple of decades later numerous scholars questioned Luther's stringent deductions from Pauline theology; still more of them, overcome by worldly prudence and the dread of social chaos, took a firm line against all risky and divisive speculation. Already both the claims and the perils of intellectual liberty beset a generation anxious for certitude, in fear of an approaching Apocalypse, and without any map of the long roads toward tolerance which lay ahead.

Nevertheless, the dark dilemmas inside the Catholic Church would not go away of their own accord. To many observers they seemed even more menacing than the threat of heresy, and they were far from being confined to recent clerical abuses and popular superstitions. Their causes were seen to extend far back into the ancient world. From the Roman Empire the Latin Church had inherited the ideal of a universal autocracy, which punished dissentients without permitting any two-way arguments. Equally characteristic of that empire was the demotic religiosity which threatened to take over Christianity and had caused the priesthood to authorize something very like a syncretic polytheism, complete with shrines, demigods, and miracles. A third and more exotic inheritance of Latin Catholicism derived from Hellenistic philosophy, which had formed the basis of the scholastic systems of the High Middle Ages. At first seeking in Thomist scholasticism a unique alliance of all sacred and profane knowledge, the method had during the fourteenth century collapsed into rival schools in which Nominalists like Ockham and Realists like Wycliffe could expose accepted Catholic doctrines to a variety of perils.

In this brief introduction we have deliberately sprinted ahead of the field to forewarn the critical reader of our own views and prejudices concerning the religious and ecclesiastical causes of the Reformation. We shall shortly trace similar analyses as claiming priority in the minds of its early historians. Yet after our first four chapters these will noticeably recede—without ever vanishing—as we move into the increasingly secular attitudes of the eighteenth, nineteenth, and twentieth centuries.

It remains to profess ourselves responsive to the demands of historical objectivity, particularly as applied to the tensions between Catholic and Protestant interpretations. The effort to be in some sense objective began among the earliest historians of the Reformation and has steadily developed ever since. Yet here we must frankly confess to participating in a general inadequacy which still persists. Despite their endeavors to break free, even modern historians remain to some extent the prisoners of their educational, social, and ecclesiastical environments. While rejoicing in the new wave of ecumenism, we do not believe ourselves capable of a superhuman detachment from the opposed confessional ideals. On the other hand, we cannot envy historians who are totally skeptical about religion; their perspective entails such obvious shortcomings in regard to sensibility and intimacy of contact with what was without question a *religious* past. Above all, our limitations must not result in a timid and boring retreat from any opinion or verdict on the contentious issues. Yet at no stage can we afford to relax our steady determination to see both sides and assimilate "new" evidence, however much it may conflict with our former judgments and prejudices. Such vigilance remains, for us and for every other historian of the Reformation, a heart-searching struggle which produces many losers and no outright winners.

Part One

LAYING THE FOUNDATIONS
The First Century

I

Views from Within: Early Historians and Controversialists

The Reformation inherited a mature world of humanism, aspiring not merely to eloquence but also to broad visions and periodizations of human history. To an ever-increasing extent, men of the sixteenth century became devoted to the search for evidence and the conquest of anachronism. In particular, gaining an authentic knowledge of the teaching and the personalities of Christ and Saint Paul was primarily a historical task, in which a return to the text of the New Testament took precedence over ecclesiastical tradition. The earliest champions of the Reformation were trying to define the historical bases and contexts of their battle even as it was being fought.

Protestantism soon thought of itself as operating within certain preexistent historical patterns, and of these two predominated. The first, derived in part from the Jewish Talmud, in part from Paul and Augustine, was thought to govern ecclesiastical history. The details show some differences, but are most typically displayed in the highly popular *Chronica* of Johann Carion (1532), a work heavily revised by Philipp Melanchthon, whose name might more appropriately have appeared on its title page.[1] It accepted a scheme embracing some six thousand years of history, divided into three equal periods, the first that of primitive man, the second governed by the Mosaic Law, and the third under the Gospel of Christ, ushered in by the Incarnation but not yet completed. In fact, many religious thinkers doubted whether God would suffer sinful man to survive until the year 2000. Luther, Melanchthon, and their followers thought it likely that the end of the world was imminent. The second major scenario, also reflected in Carion, could readily be reconciled with this religious scheme because it involved the political leadership of humanity, a separate and subordinate, but still God-created, mechanism based on the succession of world empires announced in the Book of Daniel and culminating in the Roman Empire. Contemporary thinkers, especially among the Germans, saw no need to regard this succession as mere antiquarian fiction. Like Dante two centuries earlier, they accepted that the empire—now called the Holy Roman Empire—continued in all its divine legitimacy under Maximilian I and his grandson Charles V.

Both schemes had something to offer Lutheranism, and behind them stood a formidable factor: the intensive antipapal and proimperial traditions inherited by the Germans from the long struggles between medieval popes and emperors and from that patriotic humanism which proclaimed the unique valor, piety, and inventiveness of the German nation.[2] Convinced by Luther that the popes had exceeded their spiritual authority and set Christ at defiance, the Protestants readily accepted that the tragic deviation had begun quite early in the Christian Era, possibly as late as the age of Constantine, but perhaps very soon after apostolic times. These notions were neither the cool, retrospective verdicts of second-generation Reformers nor the white-hot inventions of propagandists: they were venerable myths which the Reformers found irresistible because they defended the Reformation against the charge of irresponsible novelty. Although Luther himself did not assemble these historical patterns in any single work, John Headley's laborious survey of his writings shows that all the essential components appeared spasmodically, although with some variations; these include Luther's preference for one-thousand-year periods, each symbolized by a dominant figure, the most recent being that of the pope.[3] Luther accepted the normality of persecution and martyrdom in the early Church, followed by a spiritual downfall procured by the papacy, the canonists, and later an erroneous scholasticism. He also believed that throughout the disastrous reign of papalism there persisted a true but hidden Church, personified by a series of so-called heretics like Wycliffe and Huss and culminating in those more recent movements, including his own, which sought to recover Gospel Christianity. Despite his great familiarity with the biblical narrative, Luther sometimes regretted his limited knowledge of other aspects of history, which he valued as a source of important moral lessons, including those of patriotism. Melanchthon, whose knowledge of pagan and postbiblical history was far more extensive, produced not only the Carion chronicle of 1532 but also the revised Latin editions of 1558 and 1566. These editions, together with further versions edited by Peucer, attracted a growing readership in Germany and abroad.

Inspired by such divinely ordained schemes, the Melanchthonian school purported to be something more than a continuation of Italianate humanist historiography, with its earthy delineation of all-too-human motives. It believed in the possibility of tracing and setting forth the operations of God's Providence, and it added stature to the work of Sleidan, the first major historian of the Reformation. We should nevertheless add that Sleidan remained fortunate in having Commines and other pedestrians to bring him to earth! Still more potently, Melanchthon's outlook and the schemes behind it exercised no little influence on John Foxe, whose *Acts and Monuments* was to exercise a commanding role in Protestant ecclesiastical history (see Chapter 2). Yet as we shall shortly indicate, by 1600 these ambitious exploits were already being abandoned outside the Lutheran world in favor of a return to a more human analysis in the Italian style.

Histories of the Reformation were being written even before Luther's death. What we now call contemporary history was the norm of that period, and well before 1550 a number of German and Swiss authors were already at work on narratives which, although by modern standards far from objective, are nevertheless broader in form and purpose than the fleeting polemical literature of previous decades. The Germans of the empire, whether Catholic or Protestant, found their central theme in Luther's revolt, the politicoreligious conflicts in the diets, and the gradual establishment of a coherent Evangelical church which successfully weathered a Hapsburg reaction. Indeed, many of their modern countrymen still find it hard to conceive of a national Reformation occurring along any other lines! The death of Luther, followed in less than a decade by the Peace of Augsburg, suggested a terminus for this story, and the 1550s duly produced a crop of Reformation writings of various types. The whole period 1517–1555 was canonized as a self-sufficient phase of history, which tended to make people overlook the Bohemian Reformation of the fifteenth century and to undervalue not only the radical sects, but also the Reformed churches of Switzerland, France, and England.

Until some years after the midcentury, the historians of the movement were thus mostly Lutheran Protestants; yet during the subsequent two decades the action itself—not merely geographic but also ideological—moved elsewhere, especially to France and the Netherlands. The clash of rival religions became still further politicized, while the writers soon found themselves in intellectual atmospheres very different from those of Luther's Saxony. During the last three decades of the century, the world of Mornay, Montaigne, and Bodin would have seemed distinctly sub-Christian to most contemporaries of Luther and Melanchthon. Despite the continuance of persecution—whether Catholic, Calvinist, or political—many publicists of the later period were openly demanding toleration, while some managed with impunity to express various brands of philosophical radicalism, to argue the merits of non-Christian religions, and to think well outside the bounds of any ecclesiastical orthodoxy. Even histories defending the Catholic standpoint became more sophisticated than that of Luther's archenemy Cochlaeus, who had published his main work in 1549. In crude but convenient terms, we might postulate a century of change divisible into two main phases, not unlike those into which the seventeenth century is often divided. Thus, in the 1550s new philosophies and literary genres appeared beside the merely repetitive arguments. The martyrologies brought the manual workers and petit bourgeois into the picture. Bodin broadened the concept of religious change by developing ideas of multiple causation, which included the economic and sociological categories. Meanwhile, Montaigne invented the essay, with its temperamental, quasi-private musing, an informal utterance allowing the author some apparent inconsistencies of viewpoint and values.

Both these phases of a remarkably progressive century will be examined in our first four chapters, but we shall begin with the solid figure of Johannes Sleidan (1506–1566), author of *Commentaries on Religion and the State in the reign of Emperor Charles V* (1555).[4] Few would dispute his claim to be the most accomplished and useful contemporary historian of the Reformation. Until the early nineteenth century, his data and ideals were destined to influence the historiography of the movement throughout Europe and to dominate its progress in the Protestant lands. Sleidan's upbringing and career conferred upon him that most essential basis for the historian of a great international movement: knowledge and enthusiasm unconfined by national boundaries and cultures. In their School of Saint Jerome at Liège, the Brethren of the Common Life trained him in the sound and sober tradition of northern humanist studies. Then in 1524 he proceeded to a more advanced academy, the Trilingual College at Louvain, which was dedicated to teaching the three languages demanded by biblical studies, and had recently been defended by Erasmus against its obvious enemies, the scholastic theologians. These the great scholar dismissed as "the faded old parrots [*vetuli psitaci*] with no hope of learning a new language."[5]

At Louvain in 1530 Sleidan wrote his earliest surviving letter, and it reveals him as an enthusiastic admirer of Philipp Melanchthon, the already-famous lieutenant of Luther and the leading humanist teacher at the crowded University of Wittenberg. The letter also shows that Sleidan was a student of earlier French historians and a keen observer of contemporary affairs. In the manner of the period, he had changed his family name of Philippson to Sleidanus, referring to his birthplace: Schleiden in the northern Eifel, where the local overlord had been his benefactor. Still calling himself *homo Germanus,* Sleidan migrated in 1533 to Paris and then to Orléans, where he obtained the law degree demanded of lay aspirants to courtly or high municipal office. By 1537 he had become secretary to Cardinal Jean du Bellay, bishop of Paris, who, along with his brothers Guillaume and Martin, confirmed Sleidan's deep interest in French studies.[6] Guillaume du Bellay was then planning an extended history of France on the model of Livy, but he and his brothers were no mere academics. On the one hand, they headed a patriotic faction opposing Hapsburg expansion. On the other, they patronized the Erasmian scholars and reformists, including Rabelais; and despite the growing enmity of King Francis toward Lutheranism, they kept in touch with Protestant moderates such as Melanchthon and Martin Bucer. In this international world, Sleidan began his correspondence with Calvin, joining the network which kept the Genevan Reformer so fully informed on European affairs.

Having in 1540–1541 personally witnessed the failure of the Catholic-Protestant conferences at Hagenau and Regensburg, Sleidan settled at Strasbourg, the most liberal of the German cities, where his influential friends included the prominent lay Reformer Jakob Sturm, leader of the city council. At this stage he published two orations (1541–1544) calling on the emperor and the Protestant princes to reunite on the basis of a breach with Rome.[7] He greeted the Reformation as a miraculous work of God, and he steadily maintained this verdict while acknowledging the constitutional authority of the emperor Charles V. Soon afterward he enlarged his horizons by joining a mission from the Lutheran princes and cities to Henry VIII at Windsor, the main objective of which was to reconcile that moribund monarch with Francis I and so to prevent the emperor from making war on the Schmalkaldic League.

Meanwhile, Sleidan was developing his own historical techniques by reference not only to the ancient classics but also to French literature. Having published a Latin translation of Froissart in 1537, he completed a parallel translation of Commines in two volumes (1545–1548), respectively dedicated to Edward VI and to Protector Somerset.[8] There soon followed a Latin version of Claude de Seyssel, *La Monarchie de France,* which Sleidan probably valued not so much as absolutist theory but as a work which stressed the obligation of godly princes to protect true religion. As a diplomat and scholar Sleidan wanted to emulate Commines most especially by providing a realistic and veracious history of his own times, which he took to be a unique age of "mighty changes."

When in 1545 Sleidan accepted the office of historiographer to the Schmalkaldic League, he had already for several years been collecting materials for his *Commentaries,* beginning with the revolt of Martin Luther. And despite the growing volume of vernacular writing, such a magnum opus intended as serious study for an international readership naturally went into Latin. Sleidan's writing might be judged serious to the point of stodginess, but he enjoyed the actual labor more than most historians if we credit his letter of July 1545 to Sturm: "You would not believe how much this work delights me; it demands great industry and diligence, but since I have a natural leaning in this direction, I find it a wonderful pleasure."

By October 1547 Sleidan had completed the first four books, covering the period 1517–1525. Four years later Strasbourg sent him to the Council of Trent, where his task profited from witnessing the discussions of that motley concourse of ecclesiastics and ministers. In March 1553 he reported to his English friends John Cheke and William Cecil that his *Commentaries* had reached the year 1536. Thereafter he must have increased the pace, because by 1554 he had brought the book up to date, and early the following year a folio volume of 940 pages, the text divided into twenty-five books, was being distributed. A second edition came in 1557, and numerous others followed, including translations into German, French, and Italian, and then by 1560 into the mediocre English prose of John Daus.

At first, Sleidan's *Commentaries* were regarded by both sides as controversial. Assailed as heretical and unscholarly by Catholic polemicists, they also incurred Protestant criticism on the grounds that their attitude toward the Romanists was too moderate and that they revealed too many Protestant weaknesses. Even Melanchthon joined this chorus: "He narrates many things which I should prefer to be hidden in eternal silence."[9] Sleidan's own ideals appear not only in the preface to the first edition, but in an apologia, a vigorous rejoinder to his early critics written shortly before his death in 1556 and included in subsequent issues.

Alongside the sumptuous *Commentaries* Sleidan had also been writing another book—slighter, yet destined to exercise a considerable vogue, eventually attaining about seventy editions.[10] Its title, *Of the Four Greatest Empires,* refers to the Assyrian, Persian, Greek, and Roman empires, described in Daniel 7–12 and already approved by Melanchthon for teaching purposes. Although much nearer to Daniel than to Spengler and Toynbee, it sought to impose a cyclic pattern on Western historiography. Essentially a school textbook, it enjoyed high esteem among sixteenth-

and seventeenth-century pedagogues, some of whom, both Catholic and Protestant, published expanded versions. It appealed also to German patriotism because it gave the Holy Roman Empire an organic continuity with the ancient Roman Empire. Thus German humanists depicted their own empire as no mere chance survival, but the authentic successor to world dominion, all the more so because it had been providentially strengthened by God through the great inheritance of Hapsburg Charles V. For the German Protestants of the Reformation, one question remained: how could Evangelical freedom be preserved without breaking up the empire, managed as it was by this stubborn Catholic dynasty?

For historiography of the Reformation, however, Sleidan's substantial, fact-laden *Commentaries* matter more than this antiquarian concept of world history, and they too were based on a carefully preconceived scale of values. In the apologia his insistence on solid evidence prefigures that of Ranke: "Nothing adorns the writing of history more than truth and candour. Indeed, I have taken the utmost care that neither of these may here be wanting. To that end I have assumed nothing upon surmise or light report, but I have studiously collected what I have written from the public records and papers, the faithfulness of which can be questioned by no man."[11]

Sleidan acknowledges his debt to the advice of Jakob Sturm, whose experience of international affairs encompassed thirty years. On the other hand, his information concerning France was gathered personally during his nine years of residence there. But always, he claims, he has tried to achieve impartiality by refusing to follow personal affections and by turning to the recorded sources, so many of which were already in print. He has related events barely, simply, in good faith, just as each thing took place—*prout quaeque res acta fuit,* an almost exact anticipation of Ranke's famous phrase, *als es eigentlich gewesen!* He makes "no rhetorical flourishes" but "digests everything, putting it in its proper place, as it came to be done in order and time."

Highly conscious of the unique character of the Reformation and rejoicing in his allegiance to the Protestant cause, Sleidan remains equally aware that it would be self-defeating to traduce his opponents unjustly or to misrepresent transactions still fresh in the memory of all. Moreover, historians cannot isolate religious affairs from their secular context:

> In this history of religion, I could not omit what concerned civil government, because . . . they are interwoven the one with the other, especially in our own times, so that it was impossible to separate them. This union of the sacred and civil state is sufficiently revealed in the Scriptures, and is the reason why the change of religion in

any nation is always inevitably accompanied by offences, contentions, strikes, tumults, factions and warfare.[12]

Christ's teaching, as he himself foretold, would bring not peace but a
sword. Here Sleidan was to prove a true prophet, especially with regard
to France. Again, prophetically in another sense, was he not also condemning "ecclesiastical history" as a self-sufficient subject of study?
    Largely in terms of its secular consequences, Sleidan then sums up
the course of the Reformation. No sooner had the Gospel been preached
against papal indulgences and other human traditions than the whole of
society, especially the clergy, fell into tumult, ensuring that the matter
would be brought before the Imperial Diet. Thereupon some princes and
cities embraced the teachings of the Reformers, and the fire spread which
would ultimately blaze into open war. At this point the author pleads
for the reader's indulgence. If he be honest, which historian can avoid
making some critical admissions about his own side? Which can ignore
facts and opinions displeasing to one person or another? As examples
Sleidan cites the offenses of Commines, Platina, Bembo, Jovius, and Reginald Pole. Yet, renouncing bitter exchanges, he delares his resolve to
write "the story of that wonderful blessing God has been pleased to
bestow upon the men of this age." And to set an example of political
propriety, he ends his apologia by acknowledging the Catholic emperor
Charles and his brother King Ferdinand as divinely appointed magistrates, to whom he owes entire obedience "in all things which are not
against God." In effect, he foretells that the imperial structure can only
survive on the twin bases of traditional loyalties and religious toleration.
    Unlike so many of his countrymen, Sleidan was far from seeing the
Reformation as a purely German event. In addition to his French experience, he also understood the movement's importance in England. In
May 1548, when dedicating to Protector Somerset the second volume of
the Latin Commines, he combined the roles of religious and secular
observer in remarkably ambivalent terms. On the one hand, he sees
Somerset—who did in fact aspire to figure as a Maecenas[13]—as charged
by God to carry through a holy Reformation in England. But from a
very different viewpoint he adjures the duke to nourish the young King
Edward on a diet of Commines as a sure method to foster wisdom and
teach a realistic statecraft, at once ethical and profitable.
    Reverting to the problems of presentation, Sleidan couples his pref-
erence for the plain style of Caesar with his admiration of Commines,
"a man not very well versed in the Latin tongue, but having great dexterity
of mind." He exalts the hard factual substance as opposed to the Florentine oratorical humanism of the previous century. On this basis he

believes ancient models can be used for a historical subject as modern and multilateral as the Reformation. Independently and for different reasons the great Italians of recent years, especially Machiavelli, had moved in a similar direction. Yet Sleidan owed little to these near-contemporaries, and he died too early to have read Guicciardini, whose *History of Italy* was finished by 1540 but lay unpublished until 1561–1567. In addition to his expressed tastes, both ancient and modern, Sleidan had probably absorbed a number of relevant ideas from Polybius, the Greek historian of the emergent Roman world, whose work he certainly knew and admired. Polybius proclaimed that historical knowledge contributes to the right conduct of life, provided the historian shuns fables, marvels, and the emotionalism appropriate to dramatists. He must conduct painful research, weighing his evidence in a spirit of calm impartiality. Consciously, it would seem, Sleidan embraced Polybian precepts even to the point of deploring the fictitious speeches put by rhetoric-loving historians into the mouths of their heroes.

So much for methods and ideals; how thoroughly did Sleidan follow them in his *Commentaries*? Certainly he is a model of balance and good manners in comparison with the muckraking antipapal passages of the Protestant *Magdeburg Centuries* (1559–1574) or with the calumnies brought by Cochlaeus against Luther. And he rejects the romantic, legend-loving nonsense of the earlier German humanists. When unsure of a fact, he uses qualifying expressions: "it is believed," "as it is supposed," "there are those who think this, for reasons of which I am uncertain." He conscientiously follows the archival sources to which he had easy access during the later years at Strasbourg. He even reduces Luther's hymn *Ein' feste Burg* to Latin prose, almost treating it as documentary proof of the Reformer's steadfast courage! While he seems to imply that he seldom used anything but recorded sources, it has been demonstrated that Sleidan also was indebted to a number of narratives, such as Heinrich Dorpius's eyewitness account of Anabaptist excesses at Münster, Georg Sabinus on the election and coronation of Charles V, and Luis de Avila y Zúñiga's 1547 *Comentario* on the Schmalkaldic War between Charles and the Protestant princes.

At the same time, Sleidan's claim to impartiality concerning the Catholic-versus-Protestant struggle deserves rather less applause than his temperate manner might suggest. Although he avoids factual untruths and violent condemnations, his selections and omissions end by creating a uniformly antipapal and antiprelatical atmosphere. In the apologia he cites only Catholic examples of slanderous history, and although he exposes the sins of the Farnese family, he fails to praise the encouragement of Catholic reform by the Farnese pope, Paul III. While sparing secular rulers he misses few opportunities to report the harshness of German bishops toward rebels and heretics. In a lighter vein he relates how a Catholic prince, Henry, duke of Brunswick, faked the death of his mistress, Eva von Trott (*Eva Trottina*), and then spirited her away to a remote castle where he could visit her in privacy. Meanwhile, as official historian of the league, he naturally avoids regaling his readers with the sexual lapses of its leader, Philip of Hesse. Needless to add, Sleidan was a Reformer of the "magisterial" school, with no sympathies toward Anabaptists and religious radicals in general. He implies that the horrors of Münster typified Anabaptist behavior, which in fact they did not.

By the best modern standards, we might charge Sleidan with overestimating the superficial virtues of polite language and factual correctness, as opposed to that deeper impartiality which selects with fairness and strives to understand the viewpoint of a religious or political opponent. Nevertheless, he made immense advances on the polemical partisans of the day, and it would be difficult to parallel his restraint and good sense among the writers of the sixteenth century. All in all, Sleidan remains the most judicious as well as the broadest and best informed among contemporary historians of the Reformation. And surely he sustained honorable scars when he became a target of both parties to the conflict.

Despite his half-concealed partialities, Sleidan largely keeps his promise to avoid moralizing strictures and black-and-white verdicts. Often we sense the hand of the trained jurist. We hear the advocates for plaintiff and defendant, only to find the author consciously renouncing the office of judge as contrary to the historian's function. He shows a similar reluctance to make conjectures outside the bounds of written evidence. Although he fails to rival Guicciardini's subtle and tireless search for political motive, Sleidan runs less risk of attributing to politicians imaginatively conceived yet undocumented aims. Considering the sources available to the Italians—even to Sarpi, who boasted a certain discipleship to Sleidan (see Chapter 5)—it is hard to avoid the conclusion that they too often presented their shrewd conjectures as if these were the diarized intentions of their heroes and antiheroes. So much can be said of Sleidan's inhibited caution and scruple, even though such qualities sometimes diminish the readability and human excitement of his work.

We have already praised Sleidan's almost uniquely international range: he constantly breaks out of the German lands, not only into France and England, but also into the Netherlands, the Swiss confederation, the Turkish front, and the Council of Trent. Likewise, he is not so exclusively the Protestant humanist as to forget the medieval matrices of the Reformation. For instance, he mentions the introduction of Peter's pence into England, the impact of the Teutonic Order, the Ottoman conquests from the early fourteenth century, and the tragic visit of John Huss to the Council of Constance. More expectedly, the *Commentaries* display urbane values, including a dimension which might without anachronism be called cultural history. Literacy and learning largely determine Sleidan's overall estimate of a character: from time to time he turns aside to praise the writings of Erasmus, Hutten, Lefèvre, Marot, Guillaume du Bellay, and Budé. Likewise, he praises the enlightened patronage of sovereigns from Francis I to Edward VI. Luther he admires as much for his great literary gifts as for his steadfastness of character.

Despite the breadth of his interests, Sleidan's concept of historical causes seems nowadays too exclusively related to princes and major politicians. Like nearly all humanists, he would have accepted Guicciardini's phrase for the common people, "that foolish animal," and one would not gather from his pages that these same people were beginning to contribute—especially as martyrs—to a major historical movement. He died a little too early to understand the force of that contribution where it mattered most: in England and the Netherlands. For Germans of his day the issue was clouded by the close intermingling of religious with socioeconomic discontents in the restless minds of both peasants and townsmen. Although Sleidan provides a sustained account of the Peasants' War, he naturally finds no defense for popular revolts. He duly relates atrocities committed by the insurgents, but with characteristic moderation he does emit a note of pity when describing the ghastly slaughter of barely resisting peasants at Frankenhausen. He recounts the personal adventures of Thomas Münzer; however, he does not seriously analyze the relations between secular sedition and the new religious beliefs: we have already noticed similar limitations in his account of the Anabaptist seizure of Münster a decade later. The historians of Renaissance and Reformation, even Sleidan, were still more at home narrating events than exploring causation—unless, of course, causes could be ascribed to great personages. This propensity sprang from an externalizing habit, which had its source in the models set by the most admired Roman historians such as Livy and Caesar, who never had to cope with any theme so demanding, so multilateral, so deeply fraught with spiritual experiences and mass emotions as the Protestant Reformation.

We may praise Sleidan for rising above the polemical hurly-burly of Luther and Cochlaeus, yet at this point might not our approval come dangerously near to praising a modern historian of socialism for recoiling in pained gentility from the crude facts of street-level suffering and unrest? Can any historian afford to practice this cloistered refinement? To fish in the troubled waters of vulgar polemics has become routine for historians, yet it was hardly a task in the classical tradition as followed by Renaissance scholars. By contrast, to the calm eyes of these legists and diplomats, state papers and doctrinal formularies remained acceptable. Unashamedly armed with scissors and paste, Sleidan was prepared to incorporate these sources in summary or even in their raw texts. On the other hand, he either neglected the popular, passionate, self-revealing sources or subdued them in accordance with a Roman *gravitas*. The tradition he so largely created in Reformation studies took relatively little interest in the niceties of theology or religious experience; neither did it reconstruct the Reformation in terms of biblical and philosophical humanism. Not without justice—for the movement became increasingly political—historians tended to see the whole phenomenon as a result of the actions of princes, diets, state parliaments, and church councils. No doubt it was also a new species of church history, in which popes, missioners, and martyrs jostled with the more and more masterful lay politicians and bureaucrats.

The influence of Sleidan and other contemporary historians did not spring from a few isolated individuals. Their work coincided with a general apotheosis of historical studies throughout northern Europe, which came to have a special importance in the appeal and self-assessment of the Protestant movement. This development had already become apparent in political and secular milieus, for example with Sleidan's own patrons the du Bellays, earlier with Commines, and earlier still with the historiographers supported by the kings of France. In fact, Sleidan himself seems at once a product and an inspirer of this cumulative process, his disciples and his critics stretching toward the centuries ahead.

Formerly identified with the oratorical arts in Italy, history was now increasingly discussed as the dominant *scientia* of the age, having special value for the practicing politician. Historical lectures were frequently delivered in German and Italian universities. From the 1520s onward, chairs of history were founded at Marburg, Tübingen, Strasbourg, Heidelberg, Jena, and elsewhere.[14] As the subject expanded in the academic world, the demands of propaganda encouraged appointments of official and semiofficial historiographers by rulers, cities, and, as in Sleidan's case, confederacies. While source collections and pertinent works of reference such as Gesner's *Bibliotheca universalis* (Zurich, 1545) came from laborious scholars, historical monographs of varied merit emerged in rising numbers to form a large component of both public and private libraries. History won mounting acclaim as people understood that the Reformers' search for legitimate authority demanded not so much philosophical or theological ratiocination as an effective historical appeal to the literal sense of the New Testament—the recorded teachings of Christ, the Apostles, and the early fathers. And after those initial doubts about Sleidan, he was seen to support Melanchthon's grandiose claim that the hand of God could plainly be observed in recent history, most plainly of all in the unique changes already brought about through Luther and his allies. As a species of sacred history, the new Evangelical products thus assumed a significance above that of the classical and Italianate models. By the same process, German nationalism itself, no longer so dependent on Tacitus, Teutonic legend, and monkish annalists, claimed preternatural importance in the long story of Christendom.

Among the other contemporaries, who can be called formal historians of the Reformation in the Germanic lands? Sleidan's most important rival is the zealous yet humane and statesmanlike Heinrich Bullinger (1504–1575), patriarch of the Swiss Reformation and adviser to most of the Protestant rulers of Europe.[15] Though Swiss by birth, Bullinger began his academic career in backgrounds similar to those of Sleidan and Cochlaeus. A pupil of the Brethren at Emmerich on the lower Rhine, he proceeded as a student to the highly conservative University of Cologne. Despite being an admitted disciple of Sleidan, Bullinger was called into the polemical world to assume the mantle of Zwingli at Zurich and the leadership with Calvin of the Reformed churches. For example, as host and adviser to many exiled English Reformers, he exercised a decisive influence on that country. Thus, when he observed the Helvetic confederation, it was with a far broader vision than that of any ordinary Swiss pastor.

Two of Bullinger's several historical works have special value: his general history of the confederation up to 1519 and his narrative of the Swiss Reformation covering the momentous years from 1519 to 1532.[16] Unfortunately, the latter was not substantially printed until 1838–1840, and to this day a modern critical edition remains a desideratum for Reformation history, if only because the sources are complex and the facts not invariably accurate.

It seems obvious that the Protestant clerical controversialist Bullinger cannot be expected to write as impartially as the lay diplomat Sleidan. Nevertheless, the man from Zurich begins by independently enunciating ideals almost identical with those of the Strasbourger. He also accepts Melanchthon's raison d'être for such labors: men readily forget the teachings of God through history, so history should be written with directly religious and ethical motives. Bullinger is writing Swiss history from a Zurich standpoint, and he stresses the enormous trouble, cost, and anxiety borne by that city, which first set forth the true religion not only within its own territory but in effect for the whole confederation. Here, he believes, all will recognize the wondrous work of God in the great contest between the false religion and the true. All the same, he traces with insight the rise of the Reformation in Bern, Basel, Geneva, Glarus, and Schaffhausen, even in external but theologically related places like the city of Strasbourg and the duchy of Württemberg. Moreover, in the background one senses his mastery over French, imperial, and papal affairs, insofar as they affected the actions of Swiss statesmen. As in Sleidan's pages, the Reformation seems by no means a localizing episode because in the cities of the confederation, as in those of the empire, it brought civic minds into stimulating contact with the wide and perilous world of monarchical politics.

Apart from the fact that Bullinger wrote not in Latin but in Swiss German, his methodological principles closely resemble Sleidan's. A historian and not a mere annalist, he remarks that unless the causes of all events are depicted, whatever one writes is not merely blind but incomplete and altogether false. We must closely investigate our sources, because truth not hearsay remains the objective. Bullinger claims to have worked hard over thirty years to obtain the best evidence, laboriously acquiring and copying innumerable documents. Indeed, his text shows that these were no idle boasts; it is richly furnished with documentary evidence, together with a careful correlation of the many earlier chroniclers of his country: Utinger, Wyss, Sprüngli, Edlibach, and especially the popular Johannes Stumpf, whose chronicles were published in Zurich in 1548 and in several later editions.

Not without justice, it has been claimed that Bullinger broke away from the chronological mosaic more courageously and selectively than Sleidan had done. On the other hand, this apparent virtue could enhance his prejudices, which were not merely antipapal but non-Lutheran. Accordingly, his first five chapters cover the religious state of the confederation in 1519 and the epoch-making arrival of Zwingli in Zurich. Only in chapter 6 are we made aware that in far-off Saxony a hitherto obscure cleric called Martin Luther was at about this time having a clash with Tetzel! In other words, Bullinger's idealization of Zwingli extends to supporting Zwingli's dubious claims to total independence and even temporal priority over the Saxon Reformer: "I did not learn Christ's teaching from Luther, but from the very word of God."[17] This same tension between Zurich and Wittenberg appears in Bullinger's writings concerning Anabaptism, by modern standards unfair and superficial, yet containing informative passages which show an inquiring attitude regrettably lacking in Lutheran, Zwinglian, Calvinist, and Anglican circles. Unlike the rest of this generation, all too frightened by the horrors of Anabaptism at Münster, Bullinger at least set out to discover what the sectarians really believed.[18] In his *Der Wiedertäufer Ursprung* of 1560, he again attacks the Anabaptists, yet he also tries to classify them and grasp the interrelatedness of various branches of radicalism. He knew that they had a large pacific wing as well as a dangerously violent one. Indeed, back in 1530 he had admitted that some Anabaptists led devout and virtuous lives: he even wrote moving accounts of the sufferings of Mantz and Blaurock. On the other hand, both Wittenberg and Zurich wanted to push the radicals off their historical doorsteps. The Lutherans, including Melanchthon, depicted Anabaptism as growing up under the shadow of Zwingli, while Bullinger defends his predecessor by arguing that religious radicalism had a Saxon origin, being the offspring of Münzer and the picturesque but dangerous prophets of Zwickau. The irony would seem to lie in the odd fact that both were right, for the hydra had two heads of exceptional size.

Among the earliest attempts to write a general history of the Lutheran Reformation was that of Luther's most persistent adversary, Johannes Cochlaeus (1479–1552), who published at Mainz his *Commentaries on the acts and writings of Luther* six years before the appearance of Sleidan's great work.[19] Though unacceptable as a biography, it remains a year-by-year record of both events and controversies from Luther's initial revolt until his death. It takes Luther as archvillain and constantly turns aside to examine his writings together with the Catholic counterattacks, especially those previously delivered by Cochlaeus himself. To this central theme the period's more disastrous events are related by this highly prejudiced yet factually informed observer. Though only four years older than Luther (and likewise of peasant stock), Cochlaeus preserved faithfully the outlook of "official" fifteenth-century reformism. A strong believer in revival through general councils of the Church, he provides a significant link between the earlier conciliarism and its renewal in the Council of Trent. His tireless zeal to cleanse the Church, including the Roman Curia, of abuses is counterbalanced by his complete refusal to entertain any revision of doctrine. He represents that numerous portion of Luther's generation which saw the gravest dangers in the Protestant claim that many "accepted" developments from Christ's doctrine had themselves created major abuses. Such Catholic reformists often conceded that there had been bad popes, worldly bishops, grasping and lecherous priests, yet they could not bring themselves to believe that God would have suffered papacy and hierarchy to diverge on vital issues from the recorded gospel. They were also reluctant to admit that recent studies of Greek texts, older and more authentic than the Vulgate, might demand some revised interpretations.

These conservatives were also realistic observers of mankind, who soon perceived that bounds could scarcely be set to doctrinal reformism: once started, it would not be confined to the religious sphere but might well endanger the whole social structure of Europe. Perhaps they exaggerated the fragility of that structure, yet the twin growths of religious radicalism and social rebellion during the years 1521–1535 provided them with stong arguments. At first Cochlaeus and his friend Girolamo Aleandro thought it possible to advise and control Luther, but having seen him defy pope and emperor at Worms, they realized that he threatened no less than a major doctrinal reconstruction, and so they joined his severest enemies. Already deeply conscious of moral decline throughout Church and society, Cochlaeus identified Luther not merely as a product but as an active continuator of that decline.[20] Had not he proclaimed that all men, and even more astonishingly all women, were priests?[21] Had he not thrust aside his own indelible religious vows to contract an "incestuous" marriage ceremony with a nun?[22] Above all, whatever his own disclaimers, had he not imposed his false biblical doctrines upon craftsmen, women, and other *idiotae* ignorant of Latin, and so created the sects which endangered the cohesion of Christendom?

Cochlaeus refused to recognize Luther's apparent gifts, for what was zeal worth if misused for evil? Luther's vigor had simply sprung from his bitter hatred of the papacy. Having deceptively led the peasants into rebellious courses, he had then demanded the shedding of their blood.[23] He turned the nobility against the priests, the peasants against the princes, the estates of the empire against the emperor.[24] At the height of the Turkish menace, Luther deliberately tore apart central Europe, the guardian of the gate. Many of these charges had appeared in the long series of Cochlaeus's pamphlets, before he began in the later 1530s to compile his *Commentaries*. Their total impact remains hard to assess, but they contained enough truths, near-truths, and half-truths to convince many anxious minds of that period.

In view of Luther's own stories about encounters with the Devil, it is by no means surprising that Cochlaeus wanted to believe the legend that Luther had made a pact with Satan, or even that he had been begotten by the latter in person.[25] Year after year, like a self-appointed hound of heaven, Cochlaeus read and counterblasted Luther's writings, and by the time he came to summarize the story in his *Commentaries,* he also considered himself a prime figure in this cosmic duel, upon which hung the eternal fate of millions of souls. On only one occasion did Luther reply directly to Cochlaeus, whom he regarded, or affected to regard, as an irritating mediocrity. But in Cochlaeus as in Luther, anger invoked a heroic pertinacity. He felt himself endowed with special gifts, not only to rebut his enemy but also to commend the Catholic cause to the masses. In one amusing passage of the *Commentaries* he contrasts his own popularizing style with that of the more subtle and prolix champion of orthodoxy, Johann Eck: *Eckius prolixius ac subtilis: Cochlaeus brevius ac simplicius pro captu laicorum.*[26] Had he written more in German, the claim in the last three words might have looked more impressive.

There remains rather more to say about Cochlaeus than criticisms such as those by Adolf Herte, who has justifiably displayed Cochlaeus as the source of so many fallacies regarding Luther which have survived in popular propaganda into our own century.[27] In that age of superstition wild stories spread rapidly, and the more absurd of them Cochlaeus did not need to invent. He sometimes repeated them not as verified facts but as common beliefs. On the other hand, he made not a few penetrating observations, which may be balanced against his negative prejudices.[28] Above all, a most commendable example for our own age, he presented the Reformation as essentially a battle of ideas! And if we discuss his broader merits as a historian, these should be judged not solely by the *Commentaries* but also by his substantial history of the Hussites, based on his own researches in Bohemia and published in the same year, 1549.[29] By no means unreasonably, he also used the *Commentaries* to draw close parallels between Luther and Huss, and then between Germany's present troubles and the miseries brought by Hussitism over a century ago to the hitherto prosperous kingdom of Bohemia.[30]

On closer examination, Cochlaeus's life and personality thus prove somewhat different from the simple and disagreeable impressions one would derive from modern champions of Luther. Though educated at the University of Cologne, and in matters of theology and philosophy respectful toward his early teachers,[31] Cochlaeus should not be closely related to those archconservatives the Cologne Dominicans, the "Obscure Men" ridiculed by the humanists Hutten and Crotus Rubianus. On the contrary, he had undergone the humanist disciplines, had been a friend of both these men, and in later years remained an intimate correspondent of the distinguished Willibald Pirkheimer, anticlerical satirist and eventual Protestant. During his earlier career Cochlaeus worked as a schoolmaster at Nuremberg, published textbooks, and advocated reforms in the teaching of the classics. He corresponded also with foreign humanists like Thomas More and Richard Morison, and he consistently referred with deep respect to the prince of the tribe: *Erasmus Roterodamus, vir summae eloquentiae eruditusque, et auctoritas in Germania.*[32]

After the clash of 1524–1546 between Erasmus and Luther, Cochlaeus could represent the former as a major opponent of the latter, and to an exaggerated extent he manipulated the message of Erasmus and used it as a heavy club to beat Luther. On the other hand, around the midcentury other Catholic writers began to see through this idealization and to denounce Erasmus as a harsh anticlerical and a crypto-Protestant predecessor of Luther.[33] On second thought they realized that ever since the *Enchiridion* of 1503 he had advocated a closely scriptural Christianity and had then savagely criticized hypocritical monks, worldly popes, and pharisaical religion based on mere observances. Yet Cochlaeus died without changing his Erasmian stance. On the contrary, as late as 1549 he was still condemning the older Catholic clergy for neglecting their literary studies and so yielding public admiration to their younger (and usually Protestant) rivals, whose proficiency in the scriptural texts made their seniors appear fools in the eyes of the people.[34] In particular, Cochlaeus's attitudes toward the religious orders were by no means subservient, and he did not hesitate to present the affair of Tetzel and the indulgences as an undignified squabble over prestige and proceeds between the Augustinians and the Dominicans.[35]

Like any humanist—or for that matter any Protestant—Cochlaeus retained and frequently reiterated a strong belief in the immense influence of printing, and he blamed the greed of the printers for the huge circulation of Luther's writings.[36] While claiming to be a succinct writer, and frequently denouncing the prolixity of Luther, he nevertheless contributed some two hundred works—mainly but not entirely of pamphlet length—to the Catholic cause. All this zeal did not go unacknowledged by the higher powers. Duke George of the Albertine Saxon branch, the German ruler most zealous and energetic in the Catholic cause, supported Cochlaeus as his chaplain and secretary throughout the later years, and this connection helped Cochlaeus (who often praised the duke and defended him against Luther) to figure at diets and religious conferences with some prestige. Even the Hapsburgs displayed a little gratitude, and in 1547 King Ferdinand referred to Cochlaeus as "Counsellor of a Christian Reformation."[37] Everywhere he used his opportunities to acquire that broad knowledge of European affairs which he displayed in the *Commentaries* but which we tend to undervalue because we know it was soon to be eclipsed by a far better historian, Sleidan.

As a historian of the Reformation, Cochlaeus has nevertheless been condemned by serious historians because he continued to be bemused by his own incessant pamphleteering. At heart, he was expressing the hatred of the faithful priest for the uncanonical renegade who had summarily thrown off the sacerdotal office and with it all traces of ecclesiastical discipline.[38] In his comprehensive vision of clerical professionalism, Cochlaeus attached weight not merely to the major breaches like Luther's marriage but also to his failure to celebrate mass at an ordination and to his alleged habit of mumbling a fragmentary prayer when, distended by food and wine, he gazed out of a window, admiring the view.[39] Cochlaeus's favorite label for Luther was *jactantia*—bragging, display, ostentation—and, seen from so external a vantage point, Luther's power of projection must have seemed to reveal not a little of the proud showman. Yet the sheer superficiality of this verdict must surely occur to any attentive modern reader. One need not accept Luther's theology to perceive that he conveyed his view not as a poseur but as a man of natural charisma, profound convictions, and remarkable literary gifts. If Cochlaeus misled posterity, it was far less by his repetition of the vulgar legends than by this honest yet gigantic miscalculation.

These things said, when we have penetrated behind the offensive persona of the textbook, we still recognize in Cochlaeus a real man armed with a moral and even a religious life. He became an enthusiastic practitioner of Loyola's *Spiritual Exercises,* and he remained conscious of the dangers to which his pugnacious career exposed his own soul. As early as 1528 he remarked, "I have written enough but I have not prayed enough, and have not directed my heart to heavenly things."[40] Because he well understood that above all else history should aim at "the truth"—however defined—he should doubtless also have prayed for a better grasp of its differences from the approaches of inquisitors and hostile pamphleteers. In his day, and indeed throughout the next hundred years, men could exalt this new "science" of history without understanding what heavy claims it could make in its own right, independently of the theologians.

Around the midcentury, apart from the modest cases of Sleidan and Bullinger, it would not be easy to illustrate any noticeable growth of objectivity in the minds of European historians of any religious persuasion, but least of all among the early epigoni of Cochlaeus, such as Simon Fontaine. Fontaine, a Franciscan and a Parisian doctor of theology, had predeceased the publication in 1558 of his *Catholic History of Our Times.*[41] Arranged in seventeen books and covering some five hundred small pages, this work is written in readable French: it must have enjoyed some success, because by 1562 two more editions had appeared, one in Paris and one in Antwerp. An Italian translation followed in Venice in 1563. Five years later in Cologne the Carmelite Roverus Pontanus produced the first part of a Latin translation, which reached the year 1525.[42] Then Pontanus discovered how much of the work was mere translation from Cochlaeus and decided not to proceed. Fontaine does in fact continually praise Cochlaeus in general terms, although he makes few precise allusions to his own indebtedness. In fact, the plagiarism appears less total than presumed by some critics, even though in his obvious haste

Fontaine translated long passages of Cochlaeus sentence by sentence. Inevitably some ludicrous legends appear. Luther enters the monastery after a companion has been struck by lightning, and at the end he retires to bed with his nun and is discovered dead the next morning! The author calmly accepts the probability that Hans Luther rather than the Devil was Martin's natural father. He almost invariably spells German names wrongly, and his attempts to prove Sleidan inaccurate or self-contradictory do not impress.

As one would expect, Fontaine interpolates a few original passages concerning the Reformation in France: for example, on Lefèvre's influence on Bishop Briçonnet and on the Protestant placards and the demonstrations of 1534 against heresy in Paris.[43] Apparently lively passages often prove to be adaptations or even close translations from Cochlaeus: for example, the one describing bibliolatry among "the tailors, shoemakers and other artisans, along with the women and those who know how to read a little."[44] From their fanatical reading these lowly people gained such biblical knowledge that they dared to dispute in public not only with laymen but with priests, monks, even with licentiates and doctors of theology.

Following Cochlaeus, Fontaine shows special indignation against those women who disputed religious issues in defiance of Saint Paul's strictures on female modesty and insisted that the Apostle meant women to indoctrinate men whenever the latter proved negligent or ignorant. Having stressed the Protestants' tendency to select books of the Bible that supported their own views, Fontaine again reproduces Cochlaeus by exposing the linguistic ignorance of the older clergy, whose Greek and Hebrew were even worse than their Latin. And, he notes, although Melanchthon, Zwingli, Oecolampadius, and Bucer disagreed with one another and with Luther, they all promoted the education of the young by competent humanists, with the result that the young innovators triumphed over the old conservatives, who by their own negligence had allowed the wild boars to enter the vineyard of Christ.[45] On the other hand, Fontaine cites Sleidan himself on the rise of extravagant sects in Saxony and the involvement of both Karlstadt and Münzer. Reverting to Cochlaeus, he again shows how "printing had promoted Luther's error," because the printers soon discovered that Luther's books made them great profits, selling in vast numbers at the fairs of Frankfurt and elsewhere.[46]

As a Parisian, Fontaine had slight regard for the German magistrates and inquisitors, who for example showed little concern even when an offensive book appeared, announcing that sex was as necessary and natural as food and sleep, and advising clergy and nuns to abandon their vows of celibacy.[47] Of more importance is his full-fledged attack on Erasmus, by which Fontaine departed from Cochlaeus and anticipated the action of Pope Paul IV, who in 1558 placed that great scholar's works on the Index.[48] Erasmus, urges Fontaine, had shown irreverence toward the time-honored Vulgate text when he replaced it with his Latin translation from Greek texts, themselves also fallible and differing from one another. Fontaine concedes that Erasmus's theology on the freedom of the will proves he was not a thoroughgoing adherent of Luther; nevertheless, he insists that the Lutheran Reformation would have spread less easily had Erasmus in earlier years not so ruthlessly assaulted ecclesiastical traditions. In other words, Fontaine illustrates the spread into France of hard-line Counter-Reformation ideas, strengthened by the monarchical persecution under Henry II and using the weapons fashioned by Cochlaeus.

A German annalist with tendencies similar to Fontaine's is the far better known Laurentius Surius (Lorenz Sauer, 1522–1578), a Lübecker who appears to have been converted to Catholicism by Saint Peter Canisius.[49] Having graduated from the University of Cologne, Surius joined the Carthusians of that city in 1541, and he continued there busily editing and writing until his death. Like many of his colleagues in that order, he became heavily engaged in editing and translating works of the Rhenish mystics and the pietists of the *Devotio Moderna,* such as Tauler, Ruysbroeck, and Suso. A far wider readership, however, was attracted by his voluminous collection of saints' lives, which, after many editions and revisions by others, contributed notably to the definitive enterprise of the Bollandists.[50]

The reputation of Surius would indeed stand higher had he confined himself to these traditional tasks in preference to the hazardous duties of a contempory historian. The dedicatory epistle to his *Short Commentary* (1566, 1568) shows that it was conceived as an extension, covering the period from 1500, of the chronicle of Johannes Nauclerus.[51] More significant is the fact that he intended it as a counterblast to Sleidan. This function he discharged with more zeal than success; the name of Sleidan recurs with great frequency, almost always accompanied by abusive expressions. Surius accuses this "pernicious" historian of calumny, fraudulence, bad faith, imprudence, and other vices,[52] yet his criticism is directed not toward the facts but toward Sleidan's Protestant opinions, thus reducing his own role to that of a polemicist. Similarly, the long catalog of Luther's shortcomings is clearly based on the one by the author's neighbor Cochlaeus.[53] Having made a pact with the Devil, Luther is said to have pursued a career marked by pride, levity, opportunism, and double standards. He sought to run simultaneously with the princes and the rebellious peasants; and, in the eyes of Surius, one of Sleidan's worst offenses was his transfer of blame for the great revolt from the real culprit, Luther, to Thomas Münzer.[54]

A judgment of more historiographic interest is the condemnation of Erasmus for his lamentable failure to combat the Protestants sooner and more resolutely,[55] an attitude far from original because in Rome and at Trent Erasmus's reputation had fallen under serious attack several years earlier. Coming from a monk of unimpeachable orthodoxy, this judgment seems more understandable than the ugly and remorseless campaign against Sleidan. On the other hand, the author's well-maintained interest in the advances of the Turks must command some sympathy, together with his criticism of Luther's pacifist resignation in the face of this scourge supposedly sent by God. Surius's orthodoxy is far from being narrowly German: he deplored the ironic fact that Catholicism was being overthrown in Europe just when "the barbarous nations at the Antipodes and hitherto unknown regions are receiving the old religion and the most holy sacrifice of the Mass with the highest alacrity and devotion."[56] Naturally enough, his heroes were Thomas More, Duke George of Saxony, and the emperor Charles V. Despite, or perhaps because of, its partisan violence, Surius's chronicle appears to have been widely read in Europe. Translated into German in 1568 by Heinrich Fabricius, suffragan bishop of Speyer, and into French in 1571 by Jacques Estourneau, it reappeared with additions by Michael van Isselt in 1586 and 1601. Certainly it affected religious emotions more than the cause of historiography.

Not all the historical writers of the midcentury were marching precisely behind one or other of the rival banners of Sleidan or Cochlaeus. An event of major importance was the publication, beginning in 1559, of the massive compilation known as the *Magdeburg Centuries*,[57] the product of a small team of Lutheran scholars under Matthias Flacius Illyricus (1520–1575), an Istrian befriended by Luther at Wittenberg, where he later taught Old Testament. Flacius was a contentious theologian and eventually fell out so dramatically with Melanchthon and many others that he had to withdraw to Magdeburg, Frankfurt, and finally Jena, where he completed most of his work. The *Centuries* did not affect Reformation historiography through their factual content, because their narrative did not penetrate beyond the thirteenth century. Despite its intent to build on primary sources, the book is tainted by propagandist aims; its consistent purpose was to create an arsenal of Protestant polemic and thereby destroy the whole historical basis of papal claims to the government of the Church. In the eyes of posterity it also damaged itself by accepting miracles only when they seemed to support its own viewpoint and by incorporating along with rational arguments tiresome calumnies like the legend of "Pope Joan." No small share of the *Centuries'* original reputation came from their political acceptability to the German Protestant princes, yet in most respects they remained a backward-looking survey which impeded the development of historical writing. They stuck to a rigid and often meaningless periodization, allotting one volume to each century. And, most predictably, their widespread acclaim lent support to Melanchthon's contention that history is written to record God's inexorable will.

In two respects the Centuriators achieved some positive results. They stimulated medieval studies, already developing in Germany, as with the volumes called *Scriptores rerum Germanicarum* (Basel, 1532; Frankfurt, 1566). And, by their attempt to overthrow the documents basic to the Roman claims—a task long since undertaken with some success by Valla and Erasmus—they also helped transfer the Reformation dispute to the historical forum. Unfortunately, they did not modify Luther's pugnacious expressions, and the continuing identification of the papacy with the Antichrist ensured that little beyond a similar partisanship would be forthcoming from their Catholic opponents (see Chapter 5).

Of more direct historiographic interest are the works of certain independents, who wrote from their personal standpoints but did not circulate widely among their contemporaries. Indeed, like Bullinger, some of them remained unprinted until later. One of the very first was Friedrich Myconius (Mekum, 1491–1546), who composed a modest sketch in German covering the period 1517–1542 in twenty-four short chapters, now occupying some 128 pages of print.[58] Because Myconius died only four years after its terminal date, his work forms in an almost literal sense contemporary history, being too early to depend in any way on either Sleidan or Cochlaeus. Unfortunately, it was not published until 1718, when the manuscript was discovered and edited by the historian E. S. Cyprian and printed at Leipzig.[59]

Although it thus exerted no contemporary literary influence, Myconius's work deserves study because its approach is fresh and original, revealing the personal experiences of a cleric who became one of Luther's most effective lieutenants. Born the son of a pious burgher of Lichtenfels, the young Myconius received from 1503 on a sound schooling at the mining boomtown of Annaberg, later associated with the exploits of Tetzel. He claimed that his own father had held many Evangelical views long before Luther's emergence. After being refused an indulgence because of his inability to pay for it, he entered the local Franciscan house in 1510. While thus, in his own words, "fumbling in the shadows," he had a dream which displayed to him the biblical road to salvation. His full enlightenment came when, soon after his ordination as priest in 1516, he read Luther's Ninety-five Theses. At this point, he recalled, "God opened my eyes and ears." He first met the Reformer in person when Luther called at Weimar on his way to face Cajetan at Augsburg, and again when he stayed at Myconius's convent during his journey to the famous confrontation at Worms. At last the unsettled young Franciscan fled to Zwickau, then under the sympathetic rule of the elector Frederick. When it became safe to do so, he settled at Gotha, married the daughter of a citizen, and served for most of his remaining life as pastor of that town, although with some prolonged missionizing in Leipzig and other Saxon cities. In the 1530s he attained recognition as one of the main pillars of the movement; Luther himself wrote a preface for one of his minor works.

Myconius's practical experience of politics developed at the Marburg Conference with Zwingli, then at the crucial assembly of the princes at Schmalkalden, and eventually on the embassy sent in 1535 to Henry VIII. The conservative "tyranny" of this monarch induced Myconius to compare him with Herod and Nero,[60] even though the people of England seemed well disposed and were already producing Protestant martyrs. During the same year he heard Luther himself recalling the old adventures at Worms and in the Wartburg, "and specially how the Devil came to him in the Wartburg in the form of a great dog, seeking to slay him, though by Christ's power he was overcome."[61] Myconius heard these reminiscences when, along with Jonas, Bugenhagen, and others, he attended a party for Luther at the house of a locksmith in Gotha.

Myconius's *History of the Reformation,* which he also called a *summarium,* illustrates to perfection the attitudes of those who matured under Luther's shadow and became participants in the action they described. Everywhere he condemns the "Antichrist" papacy, the Dominicans, the saint cults, the pilgrimages, the outworn concept of Christ not as a loving savior but as a grim judge of the human race. Reverting to his own early experiences, he provides a long account of the indulgence campaign, culminating in the scandalous sales talk of Tetzel, who had asserted that even if a man had slept with his mother, God must nevertheless pardon him in return for buying an indulgence.[62] Like Cochlaeus on the other side, Myconius shows more concern for moral rearmament than for philosophical generalization or highbrow theology. He writes with great severity about the sexual vices and hypocrisy of the "celibate" clergy and about the misrepresentations of his Catholic adversaries. He expresses the belief that an avenging God struck down Emser just as he was working on a mendacious pamphlet.[63] With more humor he describes

Cochlaeus as "this bad, angry little fighting-cock of a man" (*dies böess, zornig Göckelmännlein*), who concocted untrue stories and took pains to avoid uttering a single favorable sentence regarding Luther.[64] Although Myconius's coverage of Europe does not begin to compare with that of Sleidan—or even that of Cochlaeus—he includes some exotic highlights, such as the horrifying massacre of weeping victims when the Turks took Budapest,[65] or the scenes at the sack of Rome when the German soldiers "knew that the Pope was an enemy of Luther, and had put them all under the ban as if they were Lutherans; so that they burst in, continually yelling Luther! Luther!"[66] Certainly Myconius wanted to personalize the German struggle; he halts his narrative to insert a long and useful list, city by city, region by region, of the local Reformation leaders, including rulers and city politicians, scholars and missionary preachers.[67] In addition, he gives a much shorter list of "the bitterest enemies" of the movement.[68] Even so, the lively realism of this little book owes much to its predominant emphasis on central Germany, the area which formed the hub of the original conflict and in which the author's deeper experiences had been gained.

One of the unusual yet attractive features of this work is that its last nine chapters plunge into urban history, giving firsthand accounts of various events and institutions in the city of Gotha. The passages most valuable to modern historians are those describing the clash between the city council and the common people and the anticlerical riots, which were similar to those in Erfurt.[69] Whereas more formal histories tend to find inspiration in high politics and classical models, Myconius's homespun narrative appeals to our recent interest in the varied impact of the Reformation on local communities and traditions. His strong emphasis on local history and affairs seems quite characteristic of the early humanist Reformers of central Europe. Another obvious example is Vadianus (Joachim von Watt, 1484–1551), who came back from the University of Vienna in 1518 to serve at Saint Gall as town physician. Only seven years later he was burgomaster, organizing the takeover by the Protestant party while maintaining all his admiration for Erasmus. But in the succeeding years he wrote an erudite chronicle of the abbots of the great monastery of Saint Gall from its foundation to recent times.[70] During its composition he took an active part in dissolving this ancient institution, doubtless with mixed feelings, for he was no fanatic and had made himself the prime authority on the history of Swiss monasticism.

A third historian with tenacious local roots was Matthäus Ratzeberger (1501–1559), whose involvement was with Saxony, and whose historical memoirs likewise went unpublished in his lifetime.[71] This fact does not reflect adversely on their quality, rather the reverse: their initial restriction to the ducal archives was probably because of their many "secret" passages. Though initially a medical student at Wittenberg, Ratzeberger also joined that remarkable group of young men who developed an allegiance to Luther which was both personal and permanent. Through courtly channels he reached a position which enabled him to participate in, and eventually to record, some confidential episodes of Reformation history. But his rise from medical doctor to political agent and lay theologian occurred not merely because of his professional access to rulers but because of his good sense and reliability. After serving for some years at the court of Brandenburg, Ratzeberger became in 1538 *Leibartzt* (general physician) to the elector John Frederick of Saxony. A pious daily reader of Luther's Bible, he found himself increasingly trusted with ecclesiastical negotiations, which could scarcely have occurred without Luther's advice. Both Luther and his elector appear to have seen advantages in employing this clearheaded physician instead of the tormented and pliable theologians. Certainly Ratzeberger himself felt this same antithesis about Melanchthon, whom he admired as a scholar but found lacking in staunch loyalty to Luther's principles.

The personal tensions which underlay their apparent friendship became a factor in the emergence of the two opposing groups within the Evangelical church: the orthodox rigorists, later called Gnesio-Lutherans, and the Philippists, who followed Melanchthon in allowing man a slightly larger share in the process of his own salvation. Unlike Melanchthon, Ratzeberger did not develop ecumenical emotions in conversation with liberal Catholics. Even within the divided Lutheran world his forthright advice to the elector incurred much resentment. As Catholic forbearance wore thin, Ratzeberger stood close to Luther, who never mellowed on the main issue and in 1545 dedicated to the physician one of his most violent works, *Against the Papacy at Rome, Founded by the Devil.* He also appointed Ratzeberger to the rather onerous guardianship of his children.

The disastrous political sequel has become a familiar story. The elector, contrary to the warnings of both Luther and Ratzeberger, blundered into that tragic war with the emperor Charles V which nearly destroyed the religious independence of central and northern Germany. By the end of 1547 Ratzeberger saw his beloved sovereign defeated and imprisoned and his own political influence undeservedly ruined. Philosophically retiring to Erfurt, where he served as city physician, he organized his personal records and composed the historical memoranda which have survived in the ducal library at Gotha. The most informative of these writings, often called *Luther and His Times,* was partially published from corrupt transcripts in 1704 and again in 1770, but not until the scholarly edition of 1850 by C. G. Neudecker did its true value emerge.[72] Belatedly it provided historians with an insider's knowledge of political and religious affairs at the Saxon court, together with much information on officialdom and scholars during the years that Saxony attained its greatest importance in German and European history. Ratzeberger's writings, admittedly those of a partisan in the religious struggle, nevertheless come from an observer of unusual integrity, by no means a careerist and unswerving through dark times in his loyalty to both the electoral house and the memory of Luther.

The Gotha manuscript edited by Neudecker has two distinct parts.[73] The first begins with an account of Luther's early life up to his involvement in the Diet of Worms. Then the author discusses the lives of the recent electors; the intrigues which divided the House of Wettin; the University of Wittenberg and its teachers, including Melanchthon and Luther; and the major Reformers, jurists, and humanists, such as Johannes Agricola, Bonifacius Amerbach, and Bugenhagen. After some account of the political opposition comes a separate chapter on the Sacramentarians and Schwenkfeldians, following which the narrative returns to Luther, his later life and death.

Ratzeberger is by no means a dull narrator: he relishes the dramatic and revealing occurrences, as when Luther chalked on the wall by his deathbed *Pestis eram vivus, moriens ero mors tua papa*.[74] In truth, much of his material is anecdotal rather than analytical, yet the author seems intent on achieving a series of insights which could be provided only by an observer at the center of the action. Naturally enough, his selection is that of a former participant looking back at the glorious years through the murk of the calamities which had followed Luther's death. For example, he gives in detail Luther's last admonitions to his preachers, wherein the Reformer dismissed the papalists as mere donkeys and epicureans while prophesying that the dangers would not come from them, but from factions within the Lutheran body itself.[75] Luther had foreseen that his supposed brothers would damage the Gospel, "since they have sprung from us, but were not of us." Wise after the event, Ratzeberger now sees these words as referring not to the radical sectarians but to Melanchthon and the "respectable" modifiers of "true" doctrine.

The second part of the manuscript is a memorandum, occupying nearly a hundred pages in Neudecker's edition and concerned with the dramatic sequels to Luther's death. In considerable detail the writer analyzes the pressures which drew the elector John Frederick into his ill-starred conflict with the emperor. Behind it all, in Ratzeberger's view, stood the sinister figure of Philip of Hesse, whose constant stream of rash letters gave John Frederick no rest.[76] Likewise, the elector granted too much influence to that even more suspect character, his young cousin Duke Maurice, who aspired to snatch the Saxon electorate itself, and who therefore needed to ingratiate himself with the emperor. These princes, we are told, harnessed even the theologians of Wittenberg to their chariot. Some of the young men most devoted to the idea of war had been clients of Duke Maurice; so had certain officers in the electoral army who later committed treason. Prominent also among the tools of Philip and Maurice stood the court preacher Hoffmann, together with a number of the Saxon councillors themselves.[77] Even Melanchthon, in his ambivalence and weakness, had failed to arrest the slide into disaster. Whereas Luther, alleges the author, had always heartily loved Melanchthon, the latter had long nursed a secret grudge against his leader, largely because of their varying emphases on eucharistic and other doctrines. Although there was nothing fictitious about the plotting by Duke Maurice, Ratzeberger no doubt allowed the conspiracy theme to capture him unduly, and he distributed the charges of treason with too little discrimination. He also permitted John Frederick to escape due criticism for his political and military errors. Yet it seems totally in character that, even after John Frederick's death, Ratzeberger's love and reverence for his sovereign should have overruled his critical sense. This hero worship appealed to the popular media, and the elector appears in several cartoons as a companion figure to Luther himself, a confessor of the faith.[78]

In defeat the Lutherans' chief problem lay in the tenacity with which the emperor sought to impose upon them his harsh Interim. Not altogether unjustly, Ratzeberger identifies the same courtiers and divines at Wittenberg and Leipzig as guilty, those who had precipitated the war but then relapsed into a craven acceptance of the Interim, seeking to regain the emperor's forgiveness.[79] Once more he assigns a somewhat sinister role to Melanchthon, and in particular to his unoriginal yet ecumenical doctrine concerning *adiaphora,* "things indifferent."[80] By this important concept Melanchthon had drawn a distinction between the basic ideas of Christianity and those nonessentials which over the centuries churchmen had superimposed upon the scriptural evidence. In the long run this differentiation has appeared a constructive path toward some sort of agreement between liberal Catholics and liberal Protestants. Yet around 1550 it became divisive among the Lutherans themselves, being identified with surrender by Ratzeberger and the rigorists. On the other hand, when he castigated Melanchthon's apparent submissiveness to the Interim, Ratzeberger did scant justice to the agonizing dilemma confronting his colleague, who advocated passive resistance and thereby avoided needless bloodshed. It has long been apparent that Melanchthon openly accepted the provisions of the Interim while secretly counseling resistance, and that many people followed his private precept rather than his public example. These tactics won the survival of Lutheranism far more surely and painlessly than any display of heroic defiance. What Ratzeberger could not foretell still seems a strange anomaly: that the sheer confusion of German and international politics proved sufficient to prevent Charles V from exploiting his military success and creating an imperial absolutism. As the emperor's plans sank into this quagmire, the less courageous of the Lutherans proved to have been the more realistic.

Ratzeberger's memoirs do not merely expose the state of Saxony: they also focus our attention on some of the gravest problems of the Reformation and show just how closely religion and politics were entwined. Above all, the internal conflicts among Lutherans assume a certain ironical flavor when we recall the outcome and realize that both these godly parties were in fact enabling the territorial princes to cash in on Luther's career by rejecting German unity and riveting their own governments on a divided nation. Here it seems reasonable to mention a most important aspect of Reformation history, concerning which the contempory historians have left us only minimal information. Modern research, mainly into recorded sources, has at least begun to reveal concrete links between the strengthening of states and Protestantism. Wherever the latter triumphed, ecclesiastical estates and revenues became redundant on a large scale. In many German states a sizable proportion of such resources went to charity and education, but almost everywhere the large portion that fell into governmental hands enabled the princes to survive both their immense military expenditures and the universal inflation of the 1550s. Even Catholic rulers were able in lesser measure to draw on heavy material support from the wealthy Church they were defending. German research is still advancing slowly on this subject, for the tasks remain immensely more complex than those involving the records of a unitary national state like Tudor England.

Among the literary sources for German Reformation history, we cannot afford to overlook the biographies, many of them depicting eminent leaders and written by their close collaborators.[81] Others concern relatively minor figures, in general university professors. Most such essays follow similar patterns and show common literary characteristics, enabling us to examine them as a distinct genre. The vast majority are succinct, ranging from a dozen to fifty pages. Eulogistic but not markedly polemical, they are nearly all written in the sound but unpedantic Latin of midcentury German humanism. Melanchthon contributed two of the most elegant, on Luther—written in 1546 as a preface to the second volume of the Latin works—and on Bugenhagen, the apostle of Lutheranism in northern Germany and Denmark—written in 1558.[82] In 1566 Joachim Camerarius (1500–1574), perhaps the most accomplished classicist trained by Melanchthon, issued the best life of his former master; he also preserved recollections of his distinguished friends Eobanus Hessus and Albrecht Dürer. Without his *Melanchthon* (1566), a substantial work in 123 short chapters, studies of the Reformation would be materially poorer. Although based on a long and intimate friendship, it constitutes a "life and times," for it affords a picture of the Reformer's associates and intellectual background, viewing the Reformation as the cooperative effort of a large group of Christian humanists. It also contains Melanchthon's recollection of the struggle between the Realists and the Nominalists in his early days at Tübingen.[83]

In Switzerland the biographical tradition became established in the 1530s, when Wolfgang Capito and Grynaeus wrote essays respectively on the life and the death of the major Swiss Reformer Oecolampadius.[84] Among the earliest Swiss examples is the brief biography of Zwingli by Oswald Myconius (1488–1552) published in 1532, shortly after Zwingli's death in battle.[85] Eight years later Beatus Rhenanus (1485–1547) was commissioned by the publisher Froben to enlarge an earlier sketch of the life of Erasmus to accompany the new edition of his works. As one would expect, Rhenanus produced a stylish and readable essay, which is now easily accessible in a modern English translation.[86]

Among the voluminous papers of Luther's ally Georg Spalatin (1482–1545) is a life and times of his master, Frederick the Wise: for the most part annalistic, it belongs to a different genre, and its interest arises solely from Spalatin's confidential relationship with three successive electors.[87] The familiar life of Luther by Johann Mathesius (1504–1565) was originally delivered in 1565 in the form of seventeen sermons to the author's congregation of miners at Saint Joachimsthal in Bohemia.[88] With an almost neurotic patriotism, Mathesius declares his intention, as a native German, to preach German doctrine issued by a German prophet, and to preach it to German parishioners in the German language. Though the work of a somewhat naive hero worshiper, this account is lively, anecdotal, and chronological like the rest, despite its origins in the pulpit. Not undeservedly, it soon became a well-loved item of Lutheran pietistic literature.

Of course, biography was not limited to German lands or to German subjects. Beza wrote lives, including a famous one of his predecessor Calvin;[89] while at Wittenberg the historian of Saxony, Cyriacus Spangenberg (1528–1604), published in 1556 a well-researched "history" of Savonarola,[90] by that time a patriarch of the Reformation because (in the writer's view) he had been martyred by the pope for upholding the cause of truth. A related phenomenon is the advent of mass biography with the *Prosopographiae heroum atque illustrium virorum* (1565–1566), a huge German national biography by Heinrich Pantaleon of Zurich (1522–1595), who also translated numerous contemporary authors into German. These included Sleidan and that cultural chauvinist Johannes Nauclerus (c. 1425–1519), whose zeal seems to underlie the prosopography.[91]

Especially in regard to the intensively documented Luther, it has sometimes been said that the early lives are slight and superficial, adding mere fragments to the huge factual corpus. Nevertheless, the true value of this biographical activity cannot with justice be assessed in these terms. The biographies provide authentic atmosphere: they depict background features all too neglected by more recent lives, especially by those which see the Reformers too purely in a later Lutheran theological setting. Quite vividly and with some unexpected emphases, they tell us what leading figues of the Reformation most esteemed in their colleagues. Here and there new facts and perspectives arise—for example, the snapshot of Pomeranian society provided by Melanchthon as Bugenhagen's home background; and in his *Luther* a spare yet lucid summary of the theological issues, which helps to illuminate that curious relationship between himself and the hero.

What are the common influences behind the lives? In the first place, Plutarch was universally admired by these scholars and all their educated contemporaries. Myconius wrote that a life of Zwingli called not merely for a Plutarch but for a Cicero; Melanchthon edited the *Moralia* of Plutarch,[92] who appealed to him and his sententious followers as the ancient moralist par excellence. Whereas they saw history as teaching morality by example, Plutarch had seen biography in the same light; and, like the Protestant biographers, he had interpreted the illustrious figures of the past to a lesser and more commonplace generation. Another apparent influence on this type of biography was the *Leichenrede* or *Leichenpredigt,* the funeral encomium pronounced by a colleague over the body of a deceased scholar or other celebrity. Of these, many have survived.[93] In some cases we find the *Leichenrede* appended to the printed life, which usually follows a rigid sequence: birth and origins, learning and works, death. For example, Melanchthon's *Luther,* from the edition of 1549 on, includes the famous oration delivered by Melanchthon himself, and from 1555 the one spoken by Bugenhagen on the same occasion. Very clearly, most of these biographies have their roots far less in dogmatic Lutheranism than in academic humanism, in what Luther called "The Languages," the classical studies which had recently breathed life into the universities and especially into the new German foundations of the early sixteenth century.

Here as elsewhere, one cannot but feel that the heart of the Reformation movement lies by no means exclusively in Luther's Pauline doctrine of salvation. It also has its basis in the creative relationship of Greek linguistic studies with the elucidation of the New Testament. The new textual criticism meant the transference of religious leadership from unlearned ecclesiastical "ordinaries," including bishops, to professional, full-time men of learning. Quite explicitly Melanchthon said this in his *Leichenrede* over Luther. God "calls not only to spiritual warfare those . . . who have 'ordinary' power, but he also makes war against these through Doctors chosen from other orders."[94] After all, the only possible authority for religious change had to lie in the New Testament text duly reinterpreted by the experts in Greek, as distinct from the Vulgate, which had come to be regarded as a far from impeccable version that had been misused under papal and scholastic influences. Luther himself was highly aware of this priority, and it seems unfortunate that his modern theological commentators so often fail to grasp—or at least to stress—its indispensability to the Reformation. The biographies, humanist and nonmystical in contrast with those which emanated from the Catholic Reformation, nevertheless lead us into the innermost world of early Protestantism, a movement still close to Erasmus and arising in large part from the brave new world of the universities. The notion that Lutheranism destroyed Erasmian classical studies can hardly be sustained,[95] because the latter gravitated toward Wittenberg itself, where (despite Melanchthon's fears) they retained much of the Erasmian spirit.

2

Weapons of Propaganda: The Martyrologies

The concept of martydom is central to Christianity, and when the Protestant Reformation acquired martyrs its propagandists could hardly fail to exploit this basic theme. The historians of the early Church had used the term *martyr* to signify a witness, one who throughout his life and death testified to the reality of Christian revelation. Although actual death for the faith was not an indispensable element of martyrdom, there remained something uniquely holy about such an outcome. The faith had originated on the cross and had multiplied under the persecutions of the third and fourth centuries, when, in the words of Tertullian, every convert became a candidate for martyrdom. Each death represented a victory over the hostile world, and the great narrative of Eusebius, the "Father of Church History," is imbued with a spirit of triumph, as martyrs, strengthened by divine grace, pass gladly to their gruesome fate. Thus the martyrs became educators, providing reserves of strength for future generations through the pages of historians and, increasingly, through their personal relics.

The Protestants of the mid–sixteenth century were confronted by a somewhat ambivalent situation. The calendars of saints and martyrs, integrated with the record of Christ's own life, had over the earlier centuries become the framework of liturgical observances, while the triumph of the Church within a still half-barbarian society had been accompanied by a superstitious emphasis on the material aspects of faith—an obsessive interest in miracles and an increased veneration for the physical remains of saints, which tended to exalt the shrine above the high altar. These elements, incompatible with a Christocentric and scriptural faith, flourished until eradicated throughout half of Europe by the Reformation. Ironically, Luther's first protector, Frederick the Wise of Saxony, had previously been famous as the greatest relic collector of the day. *The Golden Legend* of Jacobus de Voragine, printed by Caxton in 1483, assured English readers that God had allowed martyrs to suffer "for to enseygne and teche us . . . He breketh theym for to gadre us."[1] This and other books, with their full details of lingering deaths, suggested that the efficacy of martyrdom was not unrelated to the amount of pain suffered. Nevertheless, the more fraudulent aspects of saint cults had repelled even conservative reformists and had been exploited by anticlericals and satirists. In his Injunctions of 1536 Henry VIII, who was no Protestant, commanded the clergy that they should not "set forth or extol any images, relics, or miracles for any superstition or lucre, nor allure the people by any enticements to the pilgrimage of any saint . . . as though it were proper or peculiar to that saint to give this commodity or that, seeing all goodness, health and grace ought to be both asked for and looked for only to God."[2]

Throughout important areas of Europe Protestants were spurred on to iconoclasm by the conviction that true biblical religion was being restored after many centuries of corruption and superstition. When, however, the new movement started to acquire its own martyrs, their potential as posthumous Christian teachers had to be preserved in a new context, and the reliquary was duly replaced by a new species of martyr book. After all, the martyrs were an indispensable weapon of the Protestant cause.

Even before the development of the major books of martyrs, some individual stories had been broadcast in popular pamphlets. Among the earliest was that published by Luther himself in 1525, to commemorate his fellow Augustinian and friend at Wittenberg, Heinrich of Zutphen: *The Burning of Brother Henry in Dithmarschen*.[3] The title page shows the victim tied to a short ladder, the foot of which has been planted in the fire. He is being raised by two men, while two others are tormenting him, one using a partisan, the other an ax hammer with multiple spikes. Behind them two fat and grinning monks are observing the scene, while to the left a soldier is kicking a sympathizer, who has fallen to the ground. Thus we see Luther already utilizing the visual aids to martyrology which Foxe and others were to employ on a larger scale forty years later.

Among the most important forerunners of Protestant martyrology was the passionate and vituperative Englishman John Bale (1495–1563), a learned Carmelite scholar who came to be associated with Thomas

Cromwell and the early Lutheran group in England. Bale did not, however, initiate the English martyrological tradition; his predecessor William Tyndale (1492?–1536) had furnished prototypes. In *The Obedience of a Christian Man* (1528) Tyndale sketched the portrait of a quasi-Protestant royal martyr from the highly dubious model of King John, persecuted and humiliated by the papacy. Bale later used this material in his polemical drama *King Johan*. Tyndale also dwelled on the martyr figures of the Bible and edited the Lollard *Examination of Thorpe and Oldcastle* and *The Testament of William Tracie* (1535). The testament concerns the Gloucestershire squire of ancient lineage whose body had recently been exhumed and burned because of his Lutheran will, later a "sacred" document among the Protestants.[4]

Bale's broader impact as a historical ideologist will be discussed in Chapter 3; here we present him as a direct inspirer of John Foxe and of Continental writers such as the Magdeburg Centuriators and the German martyrologist Ludwig Rabus, who reproduced Bale's writings on the Lollard martyrs Sir John Oldcastle and William Thorpe and on the contemporary Protestant heroine Anne Askew. Everywhere the exchange of information concerning Protestant martyrs crossed state boundaries. Like Rabus, Jean Crespin used both Bale and Foxe, while Foxe and Haemstede used Crespin, the most important of the Continental martyrologists. All of them began publishing almost contemporaneously with Sleidan, thus filling the chief gap Sleidan left by discounting the popular religious movement which had produced the bulk of the martyrs and which now came to life in these writers' hands. Nevertheless, they used Sleidan as background support: indeed, Crespin translated him into French in 1556.

Crespin's *History of the Martyrs . . . since John Huss*—a title he kept modifying in later editions—was first published at Geneva in 1554.[5] Born at Arras about 1520, Crespin received legal training at Louvain and Paris. Returning to his native town, he came under suspicion of heresy and fled to Strasbourg. Subsequently he made the acquaintance of Beza and in 1548 moved on to Geneva, where he set up a printing shop to produce religious and classical works, received citizenship in 1553, and died of the plague in 1572.[6] The first French edition of his martyrology was followed by Latin versions in 1556 and 1560, by six further French editions from 1555 to 1619, and by translations into German and English. The earlier French editions show a steady enlargement by the author; those of the seventeenth century were considerably expanded by the Genevan pastor Simon Goulart and other editors.

Together with his fellow Protestant martyrologists, Crespin promoted what has been described as "the martyr complex":[7] a strong sense of the peculiar blessings conferred on a minority of true believers, an elite among the elect. In his original preface to the *History* he asserted that "among the marks of the true Church of God one of the chief has always been that through all time she has sustained the attacks of persecution."[8] Martyrs afforded a glorious example to the living, and since the time of the Apostles there had been "almost no nation or country, not even among the Turks and other barbarous peoples, where God has not placed martyrs to render to each region testimony of his truth."[9] The Roman Church might claim miracles from the dead bones of saints, but the real miracle had come from those living members of the true Church who had been given divine strength to face death unflinchingly and even with joy. Of course, Crespin anticipated constant attacks on the veracity of his work and claimed to possess documentary evidence for all his narratives.

Crespin's martyrology is divided into twelve books. The first briefly sketches the history of the Church from the time of the Apostles to the fourteenth century, seeking to trace the growth of papal despotism and the corruption of Christian doctrine. The second book outlines the reform movements of the later Middle Ages; it includes a number of early French martyrs, of whom Denis de Rieux, executed at Meaux in 1528 for repudiating the Mass, is typical.[10] Huss and John of Wesel find their proper places as "forerunners." Especially interesting is the broad coverage given to Wycliffe and the Lollards, although this element was mostly added after the 1554 edition, with the aid of Bale's *Brefe Chronicle* (1554) and Foxe's martyrology. Books 3 and 4 similarly contain much on English events under Henry VIII and Edward VI, along with the early persecution in France. The Marian martyrs also receive attention; the accounts of John Rogers, Bishop Hooper, and others are much expanded in the second edition, on the basis of Foxe.

The second half of Crespin's martyrology chiefly concerns later events in France, where the author lived long enough to witness the early Wars of Religion. The typical figure is no longer necessarily a passive victim, although the bloody massacres which punctuated the French Reformation counted as acts of collective martyrdom. That of Saint Bartholomew was the climax which stunned Europe, but the massacres in Provence in the 1530s and 1540s and Vassy in 1562 had already established the pattern.[11] Crespin himself died just before the catastrophe of 1572, which was elaborately recorded by many successors. As with Foxe's in England, Crespin's book remained a spearhead of Protestant resistance and continued to sustain the attacks of Catholic writers in the seventeenth century.[12]

Meanwhile, Crespin's martyrology inspired many a Huguenot fighter with its stories of heroic resistance to persecution. Among its readers was the major poet Théodore d'Aubigné (1551–1630), who had been converted to Calvinism after witnessing the executions of Protestants as a small boy. D'Aubigné served for many years in the Huguenot forces, and his *Histoire Universelle* is the record of his own perilous lifetime. After a period of retirement in the country, he was forced into exile in Switzerland, where he spent the last ten years of his life.[13]

D'Aubigné's epic *Les Tragiques* is a masterwork of both French literature and European Protestant literature. Although it was not published until 1616, its main structure had been completed some decades earlier. D'Aubigné tells us he began the work in 1577 when recovering from wounds received at the battle of Casteljaloux—a time of pain and reappraisal which confirmed his personal faith but deepened his remorse over the years he had wasted in the entourage of Henry of Navarre.[14] The poem begins with an eloquent tirade on the desolation of France; in Books 2 (*Princes*) and 3 (*The Gilded Room*) the author expresses his hatred of the Valois monarchy and the governmental apparatus.[15] Book 3 ends with a powerful call for vengeance, imploring the Lord to turn on those who ravage his Church. Book 4 (*Fires*) is d'Aubigné's own martyrology—derived partly from Crespin—of those who died for the true Church. The martyrs are ranged in glory around the feet of God, where Huss, Jerome of Prague, Wycliffe, the Albigensians, and the Lollards are all accorded places. Even the relatively obscure James Bainham, executed in London in 1532, appears in this catalog, which tells how he

> with open arms
> Embraced the faggots; who, dying, embraced
> The instruments of his death, instruments of his glory.[16]

Addressing the French people, d'Aubigné writes:

> O you French and Flemings (because I do not count you
> Only a nation, but a spirit, a sweet and happy race),
> Of your brave deeds our histories are full!
> Antwerp, Cambrai, Tounai, Mons and Valenciennes,
> Can I describe your deaths, your burnings,
> Your pincers of fire, your living burials![17]

Throughout Europe the witnesses of the truth glorify God in their happy deaths, and d'Aubigné's heroes are those true martyrs who chose death freely:

> You are offered life at the cost of honour;
> But your honour marches under that of the Lord
> In immortal triumph.[18]

D'Aubigné shared with other martyrologists a strong conviction that the true religion had become an international crusade. He pauses in his attack on evil rulers to praise Elizabeth of England and to contrast her with Philip of Spain and Catherine de Médicis. *Les Tragiques* is a bitter and often gloomy work, but it is deeply marked by an element of optimism concerning the renewal of faith. Probably inspired by Bullinger's exegetical work on the Apocalypse, it envisions a world on the verge of a new age.[19]

Far from being an insular Englishman, John Foxe (1516–1587) exemplifies the close relationship among the martyrologists, all members of an international movement and in most cases forced into exile by religious persecution. The form and standpoint of his work closely resemble those of Crespin, and certain detailed debts are clear. For example, Foxe's account of the Waldensians is largely drawn from those of his French equivalent; the description of the massacres at Mérindol and Cabières is also modeled on that in Crespin's *History*.[20] Foxe had been well known as a Protestant preacher and pamphleteer before the accession of Mary. His activity as a writer continued unabated, and in 1556 Oporinus of Basel printed his moralistic drama *Christus Triumphans*.[21]

Foxe had begun to gather material about the earliest English Protestant martyrs a year or two before his flight from England. At Basel he resumed work on his collection, which he intended to cover the Lollard movement as well as Protestantism proper, and to demonstrate the links between the two. The sections on Wycliffe and the Lollards were printed in 1554 in Latin as *Commentarii rerum in ecclesia gestarum*.[22] But the first edition of the *Acts and Monuments*, still unfinished and in Latin, appeared in Basel in 1559 under the title *Rerum in ecclesia gestarum . . . narratio;* it was a substantial collection covering events in England up to the execution of Cranmer. In March 1559 Foxe began revising, extending, and translating the work; the first English edition was published by John Day in 1563. Whereas the Latin version of 1559 had numbered 732 pages, this formidable volume contained no fewer than 1,800. Including further expansions, the nineteenth-century edition fills eight substantial volumes.

In a preface addressed to Queen Elizabeth, Foxe apologizes for presenting to her a work in the vulgar tongue, but goes on to state his firm belief that the contents have as much interest for the ignorant as for the learned.[23] The principal object of the work, he claims, is to demonstrate the power of God in preserving his Church amid many centuries of persecution, a task not without its secular blessings. The need is to know the acts of Christ's martyrs now, since the time of the apostles, besides other manifold examples and experiments of God's great mercies and judgments in preserving his church, in overthrowing tyrants, in confounding pride, in altering states and kingdoms, in conserving religion against errors and dissensions, in relieving the godly, in bridling the wicked, loosing and tying up again of Satan the disturber of common-weals, in punishing transgressions ... wherein is to be seen idolatry punished, blasphemy plagued, contempt of God's holy name and religion revenged, murder with murder rewarded, adulterers and wedlock-breakers destroyed, perjuries, extortions, covetous oppression, and fraudulent counsels come to nought, with other excellent works of the Lord.[24]

Foxe invokes Eusebius to remind the reader that the Church has always been subjected to bitter persecution. Comparing the martyrs of the Protestant Reformation with those of the early Church, he sees no reason to believe that the Protestants are less worthy of commendation. Have not both died for the same faith?[25] The faith of the Protestants is that of the Apostles: "If it be heresy not to acknowledge the pope as supreme head of the church, then St. Paul was a heretic, and a stark lutheran, which, having the scriptures, yet never attributed that to the pope, nor to Peter himself, to be supreme head of the church."[26]

Foxe's *Acts and Monuments* might be seen as a Protestant *Golden Legend,* yet the contrast between the "large, easy serenity" of the *Golden Legend* and the "passionately controversial excitement" of Foxe's work has been rightly emphasized.[27] His book typifies the attacking spirit of early Protestantism and was devised from the first as legitimate propaganda, intended to strengthen the converted and convert the unenlightened. Even so, Foxe clearly saw the parallels with the old martyrologies, as well as the advantages of reusing a familiar format to achieve new objectives. Thus he furnished the *Acts and Monuments* with a "Kalender" of Protestant martyrs and confessors as a deliberate rejoinder to the Roman version. Among the surviving feasts of the Church were those of Wycliffe, Cranmer, Latimer, foreign heroes like Luther and Huss, and many humbler people, mostly victims of the Marian persecution. Foxe obviously understood the value of such a device in instructing the unlearned, to whom his book was primarily addressed.

The feasibility of a Protestant calendar of saints had in fact already been demonstrated by Thomas Brice (d. 1570), whose *Compendious Register in Metre,* a verse account of the Marian victims, was published in 1559. This work, claims Brice, contains "the names of divers (although not all) bothe men, women and virgins, which for the protection of Christ their capitaine, have been most miserablie afflicted, tormented, and prisoned." The deaths are recorded, in order of month and day of occurrence, in trite six-line stanzas:

> When John Horne with a woman wise
> At Newton under Hedge were kilde,
> Stretching their hands with lifted eyes,
> And so ther yeares in earth fulfilde,
> When these with violence were put to death,
> We wisht for our Elizabeth.[28]

This final patriotic line is repeated at the close of each stanza. Brice's naive work remained sufficiently in demand to justify a second edition in 1599, when it was expanded by the addition of further martyrs.

The second English edition of the *Acts and Monuments* in 1570 was considerably longer and contained much more material on the history of the early Church. Nevertheless, its popular appeal was increased by many realistic woodcut illustrations showing the pains of martyrs at the stake. The next edition, that of 1576, was deliberately produced at lower cost to bring it within reach of a wider public. In 1589, two years after Foxe's death, Timothy Bright's *Abridgement of the Book of the Acts and Monuments of the Church* appeared. The forerunner of numerous cheap, abridged editions, it consisted of no fewer than 792 pages. In one form or another Foxe's work was absorbed by all classes of English society during the seventeenth century, and its contribution to the Great Rebellion can scarcely be doubted. It incited militant Puritan resistance and seemed to advocate something more than the passive acceptance of ungodly persecution.

The fact that the *Acts and Monuments* came to be known as the "Book of Martyrs" has tended to obscure the work's overt claim to be a general history of the Church. In fact, less than half the book concerns the sixteenth-century martyrs. Foxe claims that his intentions are fully commensurate with the profession of historian, that he has stayed "within the compass of historiographer, declaring what had been done before, and comparing things done with things now present, the like whereof . . . is not to be found lightly in chronicles before."[29] His whole view of ecclesiastical history had revolutionary overtones similar to those already accepted by German Protestants. The English Church was pure, he claims, until the arrival of Augustine. "After that began the Christian faith to enter and spring among the Saxons, after a certain Romish sort."[30] The churchmen Thomas à Becket and Stephen Langton became "traitors," while the anticlerical rulers Henry II and John, whom Bale had already tried to rehabilitate, emerged as herioc defenders of English freedom.

Foxe's view of history—of the whole background to "these latter and perilous days"—was essentially millenarian, similar in its periodization to those we have already encountered, and related to the vision of Joachim of Floris (1145–1202), which was derived from the Book of Revelation and had remained influential. Joachim had divided history into three "ages"—the age of the law, the age of the gospel, and the age of the Spirit, yet to come. Foxe improved on this scheme by seeing five ages. During the first, the apostolic period, the Church had been persecuted and pure. The second age saw the Church fully embrace the Gentiles and experience the beginning of strife within its ranks. The third age was one of corruption, encompassing more than four centuries of papal oppression and superstition, until the revival of the true Gospel by Wycliffe and Huss. During the fourteenth century the rule of the Antichrist was challenged and an era of conflict ushered in the age of Reformation, which would lead to the age of Christ.

Foxe thus shared with Melanchthon, Sleidan, Crespin, and other Protestant historians the belief that divine Providence was strongly at work, guiding the operations of the world of men. As befitted a member of the Protestant "international," he also saw the movement in its European context, yet within that framework he believed that England had been especially blessed, most remarkably of all in her deliverance from the horrors of Marian misrule. Foxe never declared (with John Aylmer) that "God is English,"[31] and Haller may have overemphasized the extent to which he felt that the English nation held a special place in God's plan. Yet Foxe did proclaim that God had preserved Queen Elizabeth from constant dangers so that she could restore the English Church.[32] The "woeful adversity" of Queen Mary proved "what the Lord can do, when man's wilfulness will needs resist him, and will not be ruled."[33] Innumerable examples of the horrible and mysterious deaths of individual persecutors demonstrated how God punished those who attacked his Church. Foxe, who could not bear to see even animals slaughtered, maintained total disapproval of violence as a tool of religious conformity, and he even pleaded for the reprieve of condemned Anabaptists.[34] Despite his Protestant one-sidedness, he played his limited role among the sincere ancestors of toleration when he wrote, "It is tyrannical to constrain by faggots. Consciences love to be taught, and religion wants to teach . . . the most effective master-teacher is love."[35] He envisaged the Gospel as triumphing through the freedom of the spirit and through toleration, which he saw as the mark of a true church, whereas persecution denoted an apostate power.[36]

Foxe was not alone in recognizing the hand of God in human technology. Echoing Luther, he gave thanks to divine Providence "for the excellent art of printing, most happily of late found out, and now commonly practised everywhere to the singular benefit of Christ's Church."[37] But perhaps the English martyrologist's greatest achievement, both as propagandist and as historian, was his insistence on the continuity of biblicism in Christian history. So effectively did he stress the degree of agreement between late medieval heresy and Protestantism that their points of divergence tended to disappear. Foxe characterized (and simplified) the English Lollards as "fierce bible-men . . . ready enough to go behind the Church, but not behind the written word."[38] On the other hand, these "advanced" elements of idealism do not greatly soften an essentially didactic intention. Although Foxe had good reason to avoid conscious falsification concerning such recent events, he remained a propagandist, sparing the reader no circumstance calculated to heighten revulsion and provoke zeal. When the dogmatic and historical basis of the *Acts and Monuments* is put aside, the terrible deaths remain in the mind: "He did knock his breast with his hands until one of his arms fell off, and then knocked still with the other, and what time the fat, water, and blood dropped out at his fingers' ends, until by renewing of the fire, his strength was gone and his hand did cleave fast in knocking, to the iron on his breast. So immediately bowing forwards, he yielded up his spirit."[39]

Foxe's martyrology provoked a vigorous response from his Catholic opponents, who drew the contrary lessons from early ecclesiastical history. James Brooks, preaching in 1553 at Paul's Cross, London, compared the rise of Protestantism with the heresies of the Church's early years, likening Queen Mary to a Judith or a Helena.[40] A sermon preached at Gloucester in 1558 denounced the popular glorification of those recently punished for heresy: "In the opinion of their favourers, they are taken for very holy martyrs."[41] Nicholas Harpsfield, writing as Alan Cope, attacked Foxe's "false martyrs" in his *Dialogi Sex* (1566). The basis of the Catholic attacks was the same as that on which Foxe denied the martyr status of Thomas à Becket and Thomas More. What made men martyrs was *non poena, sed causa*. In response to Harpsfield's criticisms, Foxe admitted that there were errors in his book: given more time, he could have done better, but the need for the work was urgent.[42]

Needless to add, Foxe's critics were by no means limited to his contemporaries. Although he was no Romanist, Archbishop Laud did not want to see Foxe's work republished, and several Tractarians of the nineteenth century not only rejected his spirit but sought to impugn his facts. Among these later adversaries the most energetic was S. R. Maitland (d. 1866), who also condemned "that jeering, mocking spirit which so strongly characterises his martyrology."[43] Maitland considered Foxe an extremest rabble-rouser who did not fit into the Anglican tradition and whose attacks on Gardiner, Bonner, and others were motivated by partisan spite. In *Six Letters on Fox's Acts and Monuments* (1837), Maitland demonstrated certain errors by reference to the recent edition of the work produced by George Townsend. He evidently regarded the very notion of a new edition of Foxe as a disservice to the Church. Still later historians of similar views included James Gairdner, who badly wanted to sever the Lollard episode, so admired by Foxe, from the Anglican sequel. J. S. Brewer also criticized Foxe as dishonest in his use of documents, but Canon Dixon, always among the more objective historians in the High Church tradition, offered a solid defense. Although not denying an element of partiality and prejudice, he noted how much Foxe had suffered from "sham editions and inefficient editors" and exonerated him from the charge of dishonesty.[44]

J. F. Mozley's *John Foxe and His Book* (1940) represents an important landmark in Foxe's rehabilitation as a major historian. Mozley found Foxe no more partisan than the much-revered Thomas More and attributed his fierce words not to theological dogma but to his advanced views on toleration and persecution together with his "deep and spontaneous human sympathy" in the face of suffering.[45] Most important, Mozley suggested that in general Foxe was an industrious historian who did not invent evidence for partisan ends, that he deserved attention as a historical source rather than as a propagandist. Realizing that Foxe had used recorded sources when he could find them, Mozley went to diocesan registers and to the *significavits* of excommunication in the Public Record Office to verify Foxe's accounts of the Lollard martyrs in the Lincoln diocese under Bishop Longland.[46] He argued convincingly that the account of the horrific martyrdom of Perotine Massey of Guernsey printed in the *Acts and Monuments* was largely accurate; the criticisms of Robert Parsons, Thomas Harding, and others were unfounded.[47] As research proceeds into the regional history of the English Reformation, Mozley's conclusions encounter support. In several areas the surviving manuscript records now being rediscovered tend to corroborate and seldom to impugn Foxe's essential accuracy.[48]

In contrast to the *Acts and Monuments*, which was assembled in the safety of exile and after the Protestant triumph in England, the martyrology of Adriaen Cornelis van Haemstede (1525?–1562), historian of the Protestant movement in the Netherlands, was written in the midst of persecution.[49] From a well-to-do merchant family of Zeeland, Haemstede was educated at Louvain as a lawyer and, about 1552, underwent a dramatic conversion. He then traveled to Emden, entered the ministry of the Reformed Church, and from 1556 to 1559 ministered to a Protestant congregation in Antwerp, by then a major center of Calvinism.

In the years preceding the revolt of the Netherlands, the Hapsburg government in Brussels had been striving in vain to extirpate Protestantism, and Haemstede's account of this period forms the most important part of his martyrology. He wrote the bulk of this work during the persecutions at Antwerp, from which in 1559 he fled, first to Ostfriesland and then to England, where he found the Protestant Church just being triumphantly restored. Haemstede's tolerant attitudes toward the sectarians had already estranged him from his elders and deacons in Antwerp; during his two years in England he fell out with the other ministers of the Dutch Reformed Church in London as well as Bishop Grindal, who had general charge over the congregations of foreign refugees in that city.

After his refusal to condemn sectarian believers in the Melchiorite teaching on the Incarnation, Haemstede was compelled to leave London. He fled with his family to Emden, where the Calvinist consistory gave him some support. His reappearance in England in the summer of 1562 led immediately to a second expulsion, and he died obscurely before the end of that year. Officially a Calvinist minister, Haemstede nevertheless believed that individuals' consciences should not be violated, and that in the effort toward unity Christian dogmas should be reduced to the most essential elements. It seems highly likely that he was influenced by so-called libertines, ultraliberals like Jacopo Aconzio, his friend and champion in England. On the other hand, we should discount the sensational stories that Haemstede was a crypto-Mennonite Anabaptist—or even a secret member of the Family of Love. The evidence seems clear that he rejected such groups for the same reason that he rejected Catholicism: because they were intolerant. It is hardly imaginable that a concealed sectarian would have compiled this capacious martyr book which rigorously excluded all sectarians, who in the Netherlands constituted most of the actual martyrs. Like Augustine, Haemstede did not believe that the mere fact of capital punishment constituted true martyrdom, although he placed a high value on the martyr's death, rating *successio martyrum* above *successio apostolorum* in the history of the Church, and greeting his own experience of suffering as his "supreme joy."[50]

Haemstede's *History and Death of the Pious Martyrs,* the earliest Netherlandish martyrology, was published in 1559, probably at Antwerp.[51] Its popularity ensured a second edition in 1565, on the eve of the Netherlands Revolt against Spanish overlordship, and at a time when some measure of religious toleration was being seriously canvassed. About twenty editions appeared by the end of the seventeenth century, and several later. The greater part of the collection—259 pages in the first edition—relates to the 1550s. The earlier sixteenth century receives under 150 pages; the martyrs of the fourteenth and fifteenth centuries are dealt with in a bare third of that space. Again, less than one-third of the whole book is devoted to the Netherlands, where the Anabaptists started issuing martyrologies of their own in 1562. These accounts begin with *The Sacrifice of the Lord* (*Het Offer des Heeren*), which by 1599 had gone through eleven editions, printed in Emden or Amsterdam. The most comprehensive and definitive Netherlandish collection was *The Bloody Theatre* (*Het bloedigh Tooneel*) in 1660 (Dordrecht) and 1685 (Amsterdam) editions, compiled by Tielman Jans van Braght.[52]

On the other hand, nearly half of Haemstede's work is devoted to France, on which Crespin's collection of 1554 was his chief source. For example, Haemstede's account of the martyrdom of Pierre Brully at Tournai in 1545 is a literal translation from the 1556 Latin text of Crespin. All the Netherlands martyrs mentioned by Crespin are duly included, many in identical order and strikingly similar terms. Haemstede had comparatively little to say about either Germany or England, and it does not appear that he used the 1554 *Commentaries* of John Foxe. He did consult the martyrology compiled by Ludwig Rabus and issued between 1554 and 1558, but it gave little help because its primary focus was on the early Church. Although Haemstede often figures as a compiler rather than an original informant, he remains a significant and independent authority on southern Netherlandish Protestantism and especially on Antwerp, where he figures as an eyewitness.

Ludwig Rabus (1524–1592) was born at Memmingen in Swabia and educated at Strasbourg, where he lodged with the leading Reformer Matthäus Zell.[53] After further study at Tübingen, he moved north to Wittenberg, where in 1543 he took his master's degree. As a committed Lutheran he was then recalled to Strasbourg to serve as Zell's lieutenant. When Zell died in 1548, Rabus succeeded him as cathedral preacher and, although removed from that office by the emperor's Interim decree, he stayed on in the city preaching and teaching until he was appointed Lutheran superintendent at Ulm. There he battled against Catholicism, Zwinglianism, Anabaptism, and other hostile forces, obtained the backing of the city authorities, and completed the local Reformation begun some thirty years earlier by Heinrich von Kettenbach and Konrad Sam. The only remaining Catholic church at Ulm was closed down, sectarian preachers were ejected, and Zwingli's works were proscribed. Rabus also enthusiastically expanded the city's educational provisions, bringing in Peter Agricola as rector of the school. He retired in 1590, after nearly thirty-five years of work in the city.

Apart from a great number of devotional works, sermons, and catechisms, Rabus's most important writings were his martyrologies. A history of the early Church (*Liber de Dei confessoribus et martyribus veteris ecclesiae*) was followed by a *History of the Martyrs*, first published at Strasbourg in 1554 and reprinted several times before the end of the sixteenth century.[54] The 1561–1562 edition was issued in two folio volumes. The first, some seven hundred pages in length, traces the history of true religion from the time of Adam—Abel being the first martyr—to the early Church. The second volume, of similar bulk, recounts in over two hundred pages the history of the medieval Church up to the time of Huss and the Lollards; its later sections are taken with due acknowledgment from Bale. The remainder of the volume is devoted to the history of contemporary Protestantism. There are lengthy biographies of the chief Reformers, including Luther and Zell, who are included among the "witnesses," a category of heroism mentioned on the title page itself. This broad criterion reflects the fact the genuine Lutheran martyrs had not been numerous in the German lands. The stabilization of the rival religions at the Peace of Augsburg in 1555 also diminished the subsequent impact of Rabus, as compared with that of Foxe and Crespin. After all, the most significant martyrologies were those which served as weapons in a continuing religious conflict.

The Roman Church, which had been pictured as the persecuting Antichrist in Protestant collections, was meanwhile renewing its own stock of martyrs both in Protestant Europe and beyond, with the heroic deaths of Francis Xavier and other missionaries of a revived Catholicism (see Chapter 5). In Protestant England it was inevitable that the reviving Roman Church should create its own new martyrology, following the imposition of the Royal Supremacy in the 1530s, which ushered in a long though intermittent era of persecution.[55] The London Carthusian martyrs of 1535 were the subject of Maurice Chauncy's *Passio XVIII Carthusianorum in regno Angliae*, first published in 1550 in a general Carthusian history.[56] Chauncy wrote an intensely emotional account—in Latin and intended for circulation within the religious orders—of the heroic witness of Prior John Houghton and his brethren. Bishop John Fisher, also executed for denying the Royal Supremacy in that year, was the subject of a contemporary manuscript life, *A Treatis contayninge the Lyfe and Maner of Death of that most holy Prelat and constant martyr of Christ John Fysher*. Not unlike Foxe but in the opposite cause, Fisher's anonymous biographer carefully pointed out the workings of Providence in the horrible ends of Henry VIII, Anne Boleyn, Cromwell, Cranmer, and other persecutors.[57]

The leading Henrician chronicler Edward Hall found the chief Catholic martyr difficult to understand. Of Thomas More he wrote in misguided partisanship: "I cannot tell whether I should call him a foolishe wyseman, or a wise foolishman, for undoubtedly he beside his learnyng, had a great witte, but it was so myngled with tauntyng and mockyng, that it seemed to them that best knew him, that he thought nothyng to be wel spoken except he had ministered some mocke in the communication."[58] *The Life of Sir Thomas More* by his own son-in-law William Roper circulated in manuscript among faithful Catholics before its first printing (1626) in Paris. Meanwhile, this moving document formed the basis of the lives by Harpsfield and Stapleton. Writing long after More's death, Roper modestly aimed to set forth "such matters touching his life as I could at the present call to remembrance." At the same time, his hagiographic intentions are clear. Many years before, More had spoken of the Christian's duty to suffer for his faith: "We may not look, at our pleasure, to go to heaven in featherbeds: it is not the way, for our Lord himself went thither with great pain and by many tribulations, which was the path wherein he walked thither; for the servant may not look to be in better case than his master."[59] Roper also relates how More "would talk unto his wife and children of the joys of heaven and the pains of hell, of the lives of holy martyrs, of their grievous martyrdoms, of their marvellous patience."[60] The claim that More foresaw his own martyrdom recurs throughout the account, in which his austerity is balanced by ample evidence of his humanity. On the other hand, now that modern scholarship has illuminated so many other aspects of More's career and ideas, it would be impossible to regard Roper's *Life* as anything like a rounded biography.

Such a description would apply even less to the *Life and Death of Sir Thomas Moore, knight* by Dr. Nicholas Harpsfield, the archdeacon of Canterbury who served as a prominent agent of the Marian reaction in Kent. A zealous and sincere persecutor, Harpsfield set More's death in the wider contexts of Catholic suffering and persecution throughout the history of the Church.[61] Thomas Stapleton, an English Catholic exile who as a boy had been inspired by accounts of More's execution, published a life of More at Douai in 1588 which drew from both Roper and Harpsfield.[62] Stapleton's work forms part of his *Tres Thomae*—the other Thomases being the Apostle and Thomas à Becket—and his aim in writing was naturally hagiographic: "Not to draw his portrait as a man of rank, learning, wit, or high position, not as a good father, a wise ruler of a household, a just judge, or a man of letters, but above all as a saint and a glorious martyr for truth and right."[63]

The continued and ever-increasing popularity of saints' lives on the eve of the Reformation had produced numerous editions of *The Golden Legend* and other established collections: it moved the Brigittine monk Richard Whitford to publish his *Martiloge* as late as 1526. The Elizabethan Cornish recusant Nicholas Roscarrock compiled his own collection of saints' lives while attacking Foxe's "huge heap" of saints and martyrs "of his own making."[64] The eminent Jesuit missionary Robert Parsons (1546–1610) published in 1603–1604 his *Treatise of Three Conversions of England,* which strove to refute Foxe and redefine martyrdom in the light of Christian history. Many of those (like Sir John Oldcastle) whom Foxe had identified as "forerunners" of the Reformation and sometimes included in his "Kalender" Parsons regarded as traitors, rogues, or plain madmen. He did not fail to enlarge on the internal divisions and warring sects which had sprung up in the wake of Luther's movement. According to Parsons, most Protestant victims had been seditious and ignorant fanatics, justly condemned and therefore by no means to be accounted true martyrs: "Fox and his fellows do jump with old heretiques, and to play catte after kind in falsifying the true storyes of Catholike Martyrs."[65]

Even Thomas Bilney, claimed by Foxe as the first English Protestant martyr, became for Parsons (with some justification) no Protestant at all, but a confused Catholic. In an earlier work, *An Epistle of the Persecution of Catholickes in Englande* (1582), Parsons had compared the sufferings of Protestants under Queen Mary with the Elizabethan persecution of the Roman faith. Again, he concluded that the Protestants were justly condemned for obstinate heresies, whereas the Catholics suffered under a novel and heretical law: "They [the Protestant martyrs] were punished by an auncient generall lawe, for brynginge in of new opinions, neuer hard of in England before, and condemned by the highe Consistorie and parlament of Christiandome, gathered together for the same purpose. We are persecuted by new nationall statutes, for holdinge the auncient faith of Christianitie, and onelie religion of our forefathers in England."[66]

The old formula *non poena, sed causa* had been invoked by all and sundry, but Parsons asserted that true martyrs were distinguished by their adherence to ancient custom. He dismissed as patently spurious the Elizabethan government's claims that it punished for treason and not for religion. Parsons, continuing the struggle to strengthen Catholic resistance in his native land, pointed out that the faith was growing in strength as persecution became more bloody. Often accused of sensationalism, Parsons nevertheless remains a persuasive and memorable writer. His description of the ultimate penalty inflicted on many Catholic missionary priests is as vivid and horrifying as anything in Foxe: "They are no soner hanged, than the hangman enforceth hym selfe in a furiose maner of haste to cut the haulter in sunder, & whiles thei are yet alive and alyve lyke, yea and of perfect sense and felyng, he bringeth them to the other torments."[67]

As a fortunate survivor of the perils of the English Mission, Parsons wrote with natural intensity; the execution in 1581 of his saintly comrade Edmund Campion had engendered much controversial literature. Campion, the most venerated of all Elizabethan Catholic martyrs, had himself written in his *Rationes Decem* a staunch defense of the mission. Although Foxe consistently pleaded for Campion's life, other Protestant divines frantically strove to demolish Campion's theological arguments and his reputation as a martyr. Their claims that he had died for treason, not for religion, are too formal to be convincing, yet there remain two sides to the argument.[68] Amid invasion threats and several genuine murder plots against Elizabeth backed by deposition in the papal bull *Regnans in Excelsis,* the politicians could hardly be expected to make nice distinctions between political and religious emissaries. Indeed, in some cases the distinction did not exist.

Manuscript accounts of Campion's execution circulated among Catholics very soon after the event. Immediately afterward William Allen (d. 1594) gave Campion detailed coverage in his *Briefe Historie of the Glorious Martyrdom of xii Reverend Priests* (1582).[69] Written in English by popular demand and then translated into Latin, Spanish, and Italian, Allen's book was a hastily compiled report on events in England. The treatments of Campion, Mayne, Thomas Sherwood, and other priests consist of brief lives with full details of their trials and executions. Campion receives special prominence; many details of his ordeal were drawn from a manuscript account compiled by the priest Thomas Alfield, a Gloucester man and himself a martyr. Allen could not resist contrasting the "few apostates and cobblers" burned by Mary with the noble army of Catholic martyrs since the 1530s, which included bishops, lords, and learned men.[70] Allen's *True, sincere, and modest defence of the English Catholiques,* published in 1584 as an answer to William Cecil's anonymous *Execution of justice in England* (1583), contains many brief accounts of martyrs, priests, and laypeople who suffered on the scaffold and rotted in prison.[71] Similar tales were printed in the *Concertatio ecclesiae catholicae in Anglia,* a collection assembled by Jesuit editors (Trier, 1583 and 1588). This can hardly have been a popular work, but its analytical table, listing over twelve hundred sufferers for the faith, demonstrates the strength and cohesion of Catholicism in England.

These early records of the Elizabethan persecution inevitably tended to focus on the martyr-priests, but it was also necessary to show that Catholicism was a popular faith, that humble laymen and women had also suffered in varying degrees. Certain Catholic propagandists had taken delight in exposing the lowly origins of most of Foxe's martyrs and had charged Protestantism with being a lower-class, uninstructed, and subversive faith. But Nicholas Sander had perceptively noted that its special strength was among the artisans.[72] Initially at least, popular Catholicism also thrived on persecution, a fact attested to by the witness of innumerable laypeople. Catholicism had been largely a hierarchical religion, and the Elizabethan authorities aimed to destroy it by removing the priests and coercing the Catholic nobility into submission, thus destroying its traditional leadership. "The clerical enterprise," argued John Bossy, "redrew the map of English Catholicism."[73] The old religion, it would seem, became less dependent on the seigneurial household and more of a genuinely popular faith. This was the achievement of the missionary priests, especially the Jesuits, who argued against any compromise with a heretical state. Yet by the early seventeenth century, social order and the demands of family, household, and class had come to count decisively more among the Catholic gentry than unrealistic calls for sacrifice in a struggle led by foreign-trained and perhaps lowborn priests.

The moving narrative of the life and execution of the York martyr Margaret Clitherow written by Father John Mush (d. 1617) was not printed until the 1870s. Mush presented her as a specimen of those who "by rare godliness did shine above the rest, or by their patient deaths most stoutly overcame all barbarous cruelty."[74] Clitherow was not the only female martyr of the Elizabethan period, although her singular qualities and the unusual manner of her death gave her special fame. Robert Southwell (1561–1595), the Jesuit poet, truly prophesied that the sites of such executions would become places of pilgrimage.[75] *Southwell's Humble Supplication to her Majestie* (written about 1593, published 1600) contains a vivid picture of the sufferings of priests and proclaims the martyr's mystical union with God:

> O life-containing Tombe of my dead Lord,
> From thee no chaunce shall hale me hence away,
> Ile linger here while death doth life affourd,
> And being dead, my twining arms shall stay,
> And cleave unto thee; nor alive or dead
> Will I be drawne from where my Lord is laid.[76]

The striking if belated efflorescence of Catholic martyrology in the last two centuries owed much to the pioneering work of Richard Challoner (1691–1781), bishop of Debra and vicar apostolic of the London District from 1758. He assured readers that his *Memoirs of Missionary Priests* (2 vols., 1741–1742) were soundly based on written evidence, including the accounts of eyewitnesses. Indeed, although somewhat un-critical by modern standards, it covered the whole period 1577–1684 and broke new ground. A century later the great volume of unpublished Catholic records known to exist in Victorian Britain caused Lord Acton to suggest the establishment of a "Lingard Club" to organize publication, but this aim was not realized on any large scale until 1904, with the foundation of the productive and scholarly Catholic Record Society. Meanwhile, the Jesuit John Morris had published his three volumes of narrative sources, *The Trouble of Our Catholic Forefathers* (1872–1877), and Henry Foley the inadequately edited yet still indispensable *Records of the English Province of the Society of Jesus* (7 vols., 1877–1884). In the twentieth century another Jesuit, J. H. Pollen, who discovered further unpublished materials in the Vatican archives and elsewhere abroad, enlarged the picture by industrious researches into the political aspects of post-Reformation English Catholiism.[77] Lately a substantial literature has further illuminated the experiences of English Catholics during penal times: its approaches have become steadily less emotional, its judgments more objective, and its interests directed more to Catholic society as a whole than to martyrology.[78]

3

A Middle Way: Tudor Historians and Politicians

As islanders with their own historical traditions, and with good reasons for gratitude to a dynasty which had overcome prolonged civil war, Tudor Englishmen made some very individual responses to the Reformation. Whether arising from foreign or internal sources, neither extremist Protestantism nor hostile Catholicism ever fully escaped the control of government. Even so, the English Reformation never became a simple act of State. On the one hand, the nation was severed from papal jurisdiction and the Church deprived of its monasteries by a ruler whose own doctrinal views remained Catholic, even though the most crucial actions were administered by his crypto-Protestant minister Thomas Cromwell. On the other hand, the religious Reformation—the actual implanting of Protestant doctrines—had started over a decade earlier, when Lutheranism began to attract groups of sympathizers first in Cambridge, then in Oxford, London, and elsewhere in southern England.

Another national peculiarity lay in the fact that Lollardy—an indigenous and primitive Church reform movement dating from John Wycliffe (d. 1384)—had survived in many areas, denouncing clerical lordship and wealth and demanding a scriptural religion while omitting the scholastic philosophy on which Wycliffe himself had originally based his structures. On the popular level Lollard criticisms spread outside the organized groups, helped prepare the ground for Lutheranism, and then merged gradually into the new movement.[1]

Great as their theological debts to the German and Swiss Reformers were, English Protestants frequently spoke of their own Reformation in narrow national terms. Yet as much as any others they considered the change a historical event, writing what they regarded as its history and prehistory even as they were executing the political and religious processes. In fact, historical theory often seems to have been excogitated simultaneously with the events, as if the actors wrote the script while treading the stage.[2]

The English Reformation was founded on historical traditions which then won acceptance as the essence of its history. An official example occurs in the Act in Restraint of Appeals (1533), which cut off all jurisdictional appeals to the Roman Curia, enunciating a bold, quasi-historical claim to total independence in both Church and State. The act opens, "Where by divers sundry old authentic histories and chronicles it is manifestly declared and expressed that this realm of England is an empire, and so hath been accepted in the world, governed by one Supreme Head and King . . . unto whom a body politic, compact of all sorts and degrees of people divided in terms and by names of Spirituality and Temporalty be bounden and owe to bear next to God a natural and humble obedience."[3] It then states that all causes affecting English subjects shall be finally determined within the kingdom: it cites numerous statutes passed by medieval kings, duly named, to limit papal jurisdiction, which had occasioned "enormities, dangers, long delays and hurts" to the kings and their subjects.

In the context of the English "myth," the claim to be an empire did not merely exclude pope and Hapsburg: by implication it also ranked Henry VIII with the first great Christian emperor, Constantine, who had long been claimed to have been of British origin.[4] It is scarcely surprising that historical arguments and legends appeared at this juncture, because the story could boast a certain antiquity. Ever since the reign of Edward III, papal jurisdiction in England had been reduced by a long succession of statutes; more recently, Henry VIII's minister Edmund Dudley probably spoke for not a few critical subjects when he called on the king to be not merely protector but active overseer of the English Church.[5] Moreover, during the harsh quarrel of 1515 between the judges and the clergy in convocation, the king, instead of remitting the dispute to Rome as his minister Wolsey advised, had asserted the Crown's freedom from any earthly superior.

The rising tide of feeling against Wolsey and clerical pretensions in general did not lack a prefabricated ideology. Champions of the State had long sought inspiration from the fourteenth-century Erastian Marsilius of Padua, whose *Defender of the Peace* (1324) had argued that the pope was not head of the Church by any divine right and that both reason and Scripture opposed his claim to a "plenitude of power over any ruler, community or individual."[6] In the 1530s Marsilius's bold arguments were familiar to all the major defenders of Henry VIII's antipapal proceedings. Among these were three well-known clerics: Edward Fox, the king's almoner; Richard Sampson, dean of the chapel royal; and Stephen Gardiner, Cambridge academic, canon lawyer, secretary to both Wolsey and the king, and since 1531 bishop of Winchester. These men probably believed what they wrote, although it is fair to add that the first two were speedily rewarded with bishoprics. There were rumors that Gardiner supported the royal case out of fear, but if so, he performed the task with unnecessary power and thoroughness in his *Oration of the True Obedience* (1535): "I see no cause why any man should be offended that the King is called Head of the Church of England rather than Head of the realm of England . . . the Church of England consisteth of the same sorts of people at this day that are comprised in this word realm, of whom the King is called the Head. Shall he not . . . be the Head of the same men when they are named the Church of England?"[7]

Here is the authentic Marsilian note, yet if public opinion were to be stabilized on the king's side, these Latin-writing clerics needed to be followed by popular expositions in English. Almost simultaneously several suitable authors offered their services to Thomas Cromwell, who had acquired the power and resources to employ an effective team of talented humanists.[8] They included William Marshall, Thomas Starkey, Richard Morison, and Richard Taverner. In 1533 Marshall, given a loan to cover expenses, was commissioned to translate Marsilius. He published his work in 1535, having carefully cut out some "dangerous" passages which alleged the popular—as opposed to divine—origins of monarchical authority.

Meanwhile, his colleagues evolved a historical ideology flexible enough to last into our century. Their analysis of the English Reformation was based on two related historical doctrines, usually known by titles respectively Latin and Greek: *via media* and *adiaphora*. *Via media* meant that an independent national Church, reformed by royal authority along scriptural lines yet retaining an organic connection with the Church Universal, should steer a middle course between stiff Romanist reaction and presumptuous Protestant innovation. *Adiaphora*, or "things indifferent," arising proximately from Melanchthon, signified that the various national churches held many observances and traditions not actually advocated by Christ and the Apostles, and therefore unessential to salvation. Some of these appeared seemly and conducive to good order, but others might become imbued with superstition. Consequently, it lay within the discretion of every national church to abandon or retain these "indifferent" practices. Originally appearing in Stoic philosophy, the broad notion of *adiaphora* was consecrated by numerous texts from Saint Matthew and the Pauline Epistles.[9] It had been most clearly restated by Augustine in his *Letter to Januarius,* where he cited the Saturday fast and daily communion as examples. Although Erasmus had welcomed the principle as consonant with a simplified and scriptural Christianity, Melanchthon had fully realized its potential to unite the opinionated rulers and city councils of Germany against Rome.

One of the earliest commendations of *adiaphora* in Henrician propaganda occurs in the tractates of Thomas Starkey (1499?–1538), who at the end of 1534 left the service of Reginald Pole in Italy and approached Pole's enemy Thomas Cromwell for patronage.[10] In his roughly contemporaneous *Dialogue between Reginald Pole and Thomas Lupset,* Starkey used these interlocutors to illustrate in detail his views on the working of a "politic mean" in the governance of Church and State, concerning which he was also deeply influenced by Marsilius. By the summer of 1535 Starkey had coupled *adiaphora* and *via media* in his work *An Exhortation to the People,* which he presented to Henry VIII at Winchester, while the court was in progress. Starkey argues that the contemporary disorders in Germany had arisen over "things in no point necessary to man's salvation, but about ceremonies and traditions," and that some people superstitiously mistook convenient practices for immutable laws of Christ and others overzealously denounced every practice not warranted by Scripture—such as pilgrimages, fasting, holy days, the veneration of saints, and even the nonscriptural sacraments, which Luther had already discarded. Starkey blandly concludes that on these matters even learned men have never fully agreed. Though much more of a Henrician Catholic than a Protestant, Starkey accepted Cromwell's politic stance by urging the people to stick to a middle path, avoiding the extremes of irrational superstition and arrogant new opinions.

Richard Taverner (1505–1575), another of Cromwell's protégés and the chief translator of Erasmus into English, enunciated a similar viewpoint, although he was clearly a Protestant humanist. Indeed, on occasion Taverner does not scruple to "bend" the sense of Erasmus, presenting him as a moderate with distinctly Protestant leanings. He constantly refers to the great humanist as providing authority for a middle way, which he himself defines: "Some we call Pharisees, we beknave, we defye as naughty papists with other like approbrious words unmete for

Christian men's ears . . . Again, other some we beheretick, we call Lutherans, and all that naught [wicked] is, but to show them charitably where they err and rightly to instruct them, we will not."[11]

The significance of Cromwell's men in preparing England for the Anglicanism of Edward VI and Elizabeth I seems marked. They were at work from the mid-1530s, not from the late 1540s, and despite the concealed clash between the religious perspectives of Cromwell and Henry VIII, their viewpoint effectively squared with that of English governments until the Catholic reaction under Queen Mary. The adiaphorist basis of the official position is illustrated by the Ten Articles, issued in 1536 under royal authority: these distinguish several times between "certain articles necessary to our salvation" and "certain other honest and commendable ceremonies, rites and usages now of long time used and accustomed in our churches, for conservation of an honest policy and decent and seemly order to be had therein."[12]

Cromwell, who had not merely accepted but also inspired this program, expressed it in his last speech to Parliament in April 1540, when, having arranged Henry's catastrophic marriage to Anne of Cleves, he stood on the brink of disaster. Cromwell denounced the extremists who called one another "papist" or "heretic." The king, he said, favored neither right nor left, but kept one object in view, the pure word of God, the Gospel.[13] The minister then announced the appointment of the commission, which in 1543 was to produce the so-called *King's Book,* a formulary far more conservative than he would have approved had he survived.

Although Cromwell's fall preceded sterner measures against Protestant heresy, the notion of a *via media* clearly survived. It has not been sufficiently noticed how closely the king's own last speech to Parliament, in December 1545, repeated Cromwell's philosophy:

> One thing, which surely is amiss, and far out of order, to the which I most heartily require you, which is, that charity and concord is not amongst you . . . Behold then what love and charity is amongst you, when the one calleth the other Heretic and Anabaptist, and he calleth him again Papist, Hypocrite and Pharisee . . . few or none preach truly and sincerely the word of God . . . Amend these crimes . . . or else I whom God hath appointed his Vicar, and high minister here, will see these divisions extinct and these enormities corrected, according to my very duty.[14]

To this situation Archbishop Thomas Cranmer contributed another distinctly historical factor, which was of long-term importance to English intellectual and social history because his two Edwardian prayer books served the Elizabethans with minimal changes and became the Prayer Book of 1662, still used in the Church of England and in modernized versions in Episcopal churches throughout the English-speaking world. Cranmer brought into felicitous harmony seemingly disparate elements: the "Use of Sarum," inherited from the medieval Church, was distinctly modernized by reference to recent Catholic and Lutheran sources.[15] With the accession of Elizabeth, the restored Church of England was still steering a middle course, now between Tridentine Catholicism and "Puritanism," a stance modeled on the views of the Swiss Reformers, who regarded bishops and vestments not as *adiaphora*, but as unwelcome signs of an incomplete Reformation.

Meanwhile, since the middle years of Henry VIII, a number of "unofficial" observers had been writing an English scenario more radical than the official one, yet likewise largely based on historical considerations. Some of these men we have already encountered among the founders of the powerful martyrological tradition. Once again the writings of William Tyndale must be regarded as setting the stage,[16] yet Tyndale made no sustained attempt to assume the mantle of ecclesiastical historian. Although in the manner of his Lutheran friends he sternly exposed the Christian Church's historical decline, he took little interest in precise details and elaborate schemes of history.

Soon after, Robert Barnes (1495–1540),[17] also among the earliest leaders of English Lutheranism, wrote the *Lives of the Roman Pontiffs*, published in Wittenberg, where Barnes associated closely with Luther.[18] This collection is based on fairly wide reading in early and medieval sources ranging from Eusebius to antipapal writers like Platina and Carion. Barnes's main aim was undisguisedly polemical: he wanted to prove the Roman Church guilty not merely of moral offenses but of doctrinal innovations contrary to the Scriptures and the primitive Church. He thus selected, often quite uncritically, anything which appeared to suit these purposes. Already with somewhat more historical skill, in his *Supplication unto Henry VIII* (1534), Barnes had manipulated the English chronicles to prove the inordinate growth of papal power and of a subversive clerical estate in medieval England.[19] This book was probably commissioned by Cromwell, and its contentions were followed by several anonymous hack writers.

John Bale must be taken more seriously as a church historian, despite his equally violent partisanship.[20] From his earlier years as a historian of the Carmelite order, his literary output became remarkably varied; his knowledge of sources—including many in manuscript—was erudite and versatile. His work on early English authors, based on his passion for preserving manuscripts from the monastic dissolution, has contributed to modern scholarship. With prejudices similar to those of Barnes but with superior scholarship, Bale compiled his *Acta Romanorum Pontificum* (1558), usually known from its English translation (1574) as *The Pageant of the Popes*.[21] Elsewhere he described most graphically his experiences as bishop of Ossory among the uncomprehending Irish.[22] For a contemporary ultra-Protestant version of church history we turn to his *Image of bothe churches* (1548) and *Actes of Englysh votaryes* (1546), which—with special attention to immorality in the monasteries—recounts the parallel tragedy Bale claimed had befallen the Church in his own country.[23]

Broadly speaking, Bale's historical scheme resembles Melanchthon's, yet it seems largely original and based more closely on the Book of Revelation. Bale believed that corruption of the Church began very soon after apostolic times and accelerated from the year 666, the Mark of the Beast. In particular, Pope Gregory VII occasioned two disasters: he busily sought to manipulate secular states and he forced celibacy on the priesthood, a step fatal to chastity and conducive to homosexuality, which was always a favorite theme of Bale's thunderous moralizing. Like many other Protestant historians, Bale rejoiced in the long-term survival of an informed opposition to Rome. Berenger had attacked false eucharistic belief; Marsilius had denounced papal claims to secular power; Wycliffe, Huss, and Luther had maintained the cause of apostolic reform into present times and seemed obvious forerunners of a mighty impending revolution.

Meanwhile, Bale thought the English experience had been similar but less disastrous, perhaps because its faith allegedly derived from Joseph of Arimathea, more likely because the Anglo-Saxon kings had kept the churchmen under firm control. Nevertheless, the mission of Augustine of Canterbury had made England subservient to superstitious monasticism, which eventually led to the triumph over scriptural Christianity by "Aristotle's artillery, as with logic, philosophy and other crafty sciences." Bale then gives the usual demonology represented by the assault of ambitious medieval churchmen—Lanfranc, Anselm, and Becket—on English kings and virtuous traditions. He had already sought to popularize this view in his play *King John*, and in another play (since lost) concerning Thomas à Becket, and Tyndale had anticipated the general theme. When his protector, Thomas Cromwell, fell, Bale fled the realm and wrote several important works on the Continent, including those on the Lollard martyrs and Anne Askew, which ultimately inspired the martyrological labors of his friend John Foxe.[24] In addition, the Centuriators of Magdeburg and other Continental historians were indebted to this learned but too often scurrilous partisan.

Gathered at Frankfurt during the Marian exile, the leading English Reformers had already split into two militant camps. The cautious men of the *via media* demanded what one of them called "the face of an English Church," as represented in Cranmer's liturgy and in the situation which had existed under Edward VI. The Protestant hard-liners, inspired by Zurich and Geneva, regarded this solution as a Reformation at best half-finished; on their return in 1558–1559 they initiated the Puritan pressure group within the Elizabethan Church (see Appendix). Their deductions from history suggested no compromises: the medieval rebels against the Church of Rome had been—and still seemed—orthodox, apostolic Christians, although that Church had long been heretical. In the words of John Foxe:

> What, say they [the Romanists], where was this church of yours before these fifty years? To whom briefly to answer, first we demand what they mean by this, which they call *our* church? If they mean the ordinance and institution of doctrine and sacraments now received of us, and differing from the church of Rome, we affirm and say, that our church was, when this church of theirs was not yet hatched out of the shell, nor did yet ever see any light: that is in the time of the apostles, in the primitive age . . . when as yet no universal pope was received publicly, but repelled in Rome, nor this fullness of plenary power yet known; nor this doctrine and abuse of sacraments yet heard of.[25]

The Puritan element in the Church did not become any less radical than it had been at Frankfurt, but it encountered a far stronger barrier: the conservative instincts of the new monarch, who could not be displaced or ignored without risking political as well as religious anarchy. Fortunately, Elizabeth and her chief ministers were cautious politicians who wanted reasonable order without anything like a religious persecution. Under these circumstances, the Thirty-nine Articles of 1563 represented a pragmatic compromise, based on only slight modifications of the highly Protestant Forty-two Articles of the Edwardian Reformers and retaining the principles of *via media* and *adiaphora* (the concept of *adiaphora* was expressed with great clarity in Articles 20 and 34). The second Edwardian Prayer Book survived with few modifications, although it was stripped of its merely Zwinglian presentation of the Eucharist. On the other hand, the 1563 articles by no means abandoned the principles of Swiss theology. Their repressive clauses are anti-Anabaptist rather than anti-Puritan; their theology of justification and predestination represents a strict rather than modified Calvinism.[26]

Early defenders of the settlement continued to define the English Reformation in terms of both biblical theology and history. Chief among them was John Jewel, bishop of Salisbury (1522–1571), whose *Apologia* of 1562, commissioned by Elizabeth's government, was directed more fiercely against the Romanist champion Thomas Harding than against the Puritans.[27] Jewel's apparent emphasis on the authority of the early church fathers was merely intended to supplement the Scriptures in demonstrating the novelty and error of many teachings that had been adopted by the Roman Church: private masses, communion in one kind, image worship, transubstantiation, and, of course, the bishop of Rome's claim to be a universal bishop or the head of a universal Church. Many aspects of Jewel's thought were marked by eclecticism: his eucharistic doctrine almost certainly came straight from his Italian friend Peter Martyr, the recent Edwardian Regius Professor of Divinity at Oxford.[28] In pleading for a general reform of church government, Jewel cited Erasmus.[29] Following Alexander Nowell, dean of Saint Paul's, he accepted the historical argument that whereas world sovereignty had never proved effective, national sovereignty certainly had; and this principle was applicable to both ecclesiastical and secular government.[30]

Such "official" Reformers tended more readily than the Puritans to follow Lutheran tradition in calling for passive obedience to the godly prince, and Jewel agreed. When his Catholic adversary Harding also resorted to history, pointing out that John Knox had not conspicuously displayed this virtue, Jewel had to allow that there must be exceptions; the subject was bound to obey his prince only "so far as God's glory is not touched."[31] All the Elizabethan protagonists had to be mindful that they already possessed a "godly prince" in the person of the queen, who as Supreme Governor of the Church of England could (and often did) intervene in its government, even to the extent of suspending Edmund Grindal, archbishop of Canterbury, for undue sympathy toward Puritan practices. Following Peter Martyr, Jewel took a more explicit stance on princely authority than that of Luther, accepting princes not as mere keepers of worldly order but as guardians over the religious lives of their subjects.[32]

Jewel and his successors Whitgift and Bancroft combated the Puritans less about fundamental dogma than is generally realized. Instead, they spoke in historical accents concerning church discipline, episcopacy, and even such ostensible *adiaphora* as the wearing of traditional vestments. In these matters the Puritans desired a strict Calvinist discipline, but many of their adversaries—and even their most active persecutor,

Archbishop Whitgift—still held to Calvinist formulae on the central doctrines of the faith. Moreover, throughout Elizabeth's reign the great majority of those we label Puritans refrained from separatism.

Nevertheless, under Whitgift the struggle to hold Puritanism at bay extended across the whole field of church government and culminated in the 1590s with the *Treatise on the Laws of Ecclesiastical Polity* by Richard Hooker (c. 1554–1600), which attained widespread and lasting acceptance as an ideological pillar of the Church of England.[33] The grandeur of its scale, the logic of its structure, and the broad erudition of its author elevate this work above its Elizabethan forerunners. It contains constructive, as opposed to critical, elements. For all that, it remains in essence a *livre de circonstance* and openly shapes many phases of the argument to attack contemporary Puritanism.[34] The *Laws* also seem less original than Anglican opinion has tended to assume; many of the points were anticipated by Jewel, Whitgift, Bancroft, and other contemporaries.[35] The volume does not fit readily into any genre. It is hardly a work of theology or a treatise on the principles of government, although it frequently enters both fields.[36] Least of all can it be called a church history, but it does contain certain historical passages, some of them rather vulnerable.

To put the matter briefly and somewhat crudely, the treatise seeks to establish the existence among mankind of a Law of Reason emanating from the mind of God and thoroughly in harmony with religion as revealed in the Scriptures. This law, claims Hooker, is faithfully mirrored in the beliefs and usages of the Anglican Church. Moreover, using language very similar to that of Bishop Gardiner half a century earlier, the author regards the Church and the Commonwealth of England as essentially identical, the Commonwealth, like the Church, being a Christian institution that serves souls as well as bodies.[37] Through much of the book this defense of the *via media* is specifically addressed to the criticisms of the Puritan minority headed by Thomas Cartwright (1535–1603). Cartwright was an exile under Queen Mary who in 1569 became Lady Margaret Professor at Cambridge, was deprived of his position the following year, visited Beza in Geneva, and returned to England, but again fled abroad in 1573 for several years to escape arrest because of his *Second Admonition to Parliament* and his campaign for a Presbyterian system of church government.[38] Cartwright's arguments for a scriptural remodeling of Anglicanism are the ones most frequently attacked by Hooker.

Although the positions he adopted in defense of the Establishment were often based on practical utility and secular philosophy, Hooker seldom accords much space to historical arguments or historical analyses of the Reformation itself, and, in general, cites few proper names. He devotes substantial passages of Book 7 to demonstrating that bishops played important roles in the Church from very early times, even though it remains uncertain whether he regarded them as essential on strictly theological grounds. In considering the contemporary functions of English bishops, he avoids any concrete examination of their actual performance, preferring to discuss the ideal models set forth by the Church.[39]

Indeed, Hooker takes greater interest in laws and models than in hard historical evidence and real people. In Book 7 and elsewhere, he does fruitfully utilize the fathers, whose works were richly represented in the library of Corpus Christi, his Oxford college. Hooker also sometimes exploited the resources of the scholastic philosophers, particularly Aquinas, who had long been unfashionable in Tudor England. He understood their uses far better than did his English contemporaries and, like Melanchthon, was a leader in reviving scholasticism from the contempt into which it had fallen since Erasmus.[40] He made himself an expert on the common law of England; not least because his arguments led to the claim that Parliament could legislate for the national Church as well as for the State and so involved some major legal and historical considerations. Furthermore, Hooker acknowledged that the national Church was a Church of the Reformation as well as a continuation of the *Ecclesia Anglicana* of earlier centuries. In no way did he resemble the medievalizing romantics of more recent times.

These affinities, wide as they were, left no room for Cartwright or his Calvinist progenitors. Hooker's surface moderation and avoidance of mere invective do not conceal a distinct bias concerning both facts and deductions, which should be apparent even to those who feel general sympathy with his aims and applaud his adversaries' failure to presbyterianize the Anglican Church. Although he abandoned the old legends and time schemes, Hooker scarcely attained objectivity regarding recent history. Not without justice, his account of Calvin in the second chapter of the preface has been described as misrepresentation, a subtle but deliberate attempt to undermine. While professing great respect for Calvin as a person and a theologian, Hooker accuses him of a pious but pragmatic fraud, aimed at imposing his novel discipline on the citizens of Geneva.[41]

This criticism leads naturally enough into a general attack on the English Puritans, in which Hooker astutely seeks to drive a wedge between their clergy and laity, suggesting that the laity wished to draw the wealth of the Church toward themselves and impose a so-called apostolic poverty on the clergy. The Puritan discipline, he urges, would not only destroy the Royal Supremacy but overthrow learning, especially in the universities, and replace the common law with a scriptural law. Well aware of the vital differences between the Anabaptists and the Calvinist Puritans, Hooker nevertheless raises the old Anabaptist bogey, which since the horrors of Münster had terrified middle-class society throughout Europe.[42] This tactic had already proved a superb means of suppressing claims to private judgment in interpreting the Scriptures.

By the same token, Hooker gravely exaggerates the biblicist rigor of most Puritans when he suggests that they sought not only to regulate religion but also to impose upon civil society a universal Law of the Bible, thereby making "the bare mandate of sacred Scripture the only rule of all good and evil in the actions of mortal men." In all justice, although Cartwright sometimes wrote incautiously, and did want to apply an absolute rule of the Scriptures to the Church and the whole way of salvation, he did not desire to impose secular bonds of this severity. Like Luther before him, Cartwright recognized a plane of salvation quite distinct from that of everyday human life and subject to different laws.[43] Less fanatical than Hooker supposed, he was willing to leave the definition of *adiaphora* to the Church.

Despite these half-hidden prejudices, Hooker remained a man of high principle, a victim of overanxiety rather than an eager persecutor or dangerous authoritarian. He knew more and wrote better than the other Elizabethan contestants, remaining highly conscious of the practical problems and manifold tensions which were bound to survive the Reformation in this relatively free and highly argumentative society. He advocated neither despotic monarchy nor harsh ecclesiastical discipline. On the other hand, those who have exalted him as the forerunner of Locke's contractual theories have overstrained the evidence and created superficial parallels.[44]

Charged to consider the historical analyses of the Reformation by its English contemporaries, one is relieved to find that state documents and the controversialists, official and unofficial, contain so much relevant material. Had we needed to rely on formal histories and chroniclers, there would have been little to report. Despite the earlier introduction of humanist historical ideas by the Italian sojourner Polydore Vergil,[45] the Tudor chroniclers such as Hall, Holinshed, Grafton, and Stow continued in a medieval tradition, providing a mass of useful if uncoordinated facts but hardly any analyses or original opinions concerning the Reformation. They sometimes added trite thoughts on the mutability of human fortune, the justice of God's verdicts on the wicked, and the appearance of comets and other portents. We may respect Hall's surprisingly wide reading, together with no little panache and color in his writing; similarly, we can acknowledge Stow's indefatigable pursuit of records and his desire to be accurate.[46] Yet even if some of the chroniclers had developed far stronger and more independent personalities, they could not have published in serious contention with the government. A chronicle acceptable to the middle class needed a long gestation and incurred heavy capital expense: it could not be produced and sold by elusive or underground publishers. Fortunately for their own peace of mind, these chroniclers all typified their class and period. They were patriotic, still clinging to national legends; more important, they were loyal subjects of the dynasty. Except for Foxe, there were no large-scale analytical historians until in 1615 Camden published his *Annals*—a Jacobean rather than an Elizabethan event, which we shall discuss in Chapter 5.

We cannot leave the British contemporaries without mentioning a Scotsman, the greatest of his nation and period, although by no means the most attractive. John Knox (c. 1514–1572), the leading figure in the politicoreligious victory of the Scottish Reformation, also became its chief contemporary historian.[47] To most modern Christian eyes he appears the least acceptable of all European Reformation personalities. By nature inflexible, dedicated, and tenacious, he became during exile in England and in various Reformed cities on the Continent a Calvinist fanatic who never doubted his divine commission, never overlooked the shortcomings of a follower, never had a generous word for his Catholic enemies.

Knox wrote his substantial *History of the Reformation in Scotland* almost wholly between 1659 and 1667, the harshest period of the troubles, when at all times his life was in danger.[48] In every sense the book encapsulates the man and the harsh tenor of that crisis in the northern kingdom. In 1560, when Mary, Queen of Scots, seemed to have triumphed over the Protestant lords, Knox penned a passage of chilling hatred. Her reign, he tells us, should be seen as "God's hand in his displeasure punishing our former ingratitude. Let men patiently abide, and turn unto their God, and then shall he either destroy that whore in her whoredom, or else he shall put it in the hearts of the multitude to take the same vengeance upon her that has been taken of Jezebel and Athaliah . . . for greater abomination was never in the nature of any woman than is in her, whereof we have but seen the buds; but we will after taste of the ripe fruit of her impiety, if God cut not her days short."[49] These words should not be dismissed as the mere accents of a man who had for a time suffered as a galley slave at the hands of his enemies, for Knox accounted his discomfort trivial in comparison with the insults he supposed the Papists to be heaping on God. He had indeed the virtues of his faults, for he was utterly fearless, sincere, and even—in terms of material ambitions—selfless.

In the context of his day Knox must also be judged an outstanding writer, with a fine sense for the dramatic and an ability to depict a scene in a few graphic sentences. Here and there comes a grim touch of humor, and still more occasionally a passage of stately prose or, for example, a moving paragraph on prayer. Knox exceeds all his contemporaries in conveying local atmosphere; he was well attuned to the gloomy, chaotic Scotland of his day. Considering its author's prejudices and the circumstances of its composition amid this hurly-burly of intrigue and warfare, the factual accuracy of Knox's *History* has stood the tests of modern research rather well. He did not write merely from his visual impressions or from oral reports, but consulted and incorporated documents when, under these adverse conditions, he could secure them.[50] Essentially a prophet and a pattern setter for Calvinist activism, he wrote with total conviction, certain that all action would prove vain unless dictated by religious inspiration and controlled by an authentic and responsible belief in the divine purpose. The *History of the Reformation* was written by a veritable agent of destiny, effectually if unknowingly initiating the complex processes which in the end made backward Scotland one of the most creative of Europe's smaller nations.

4

A Sense of Distance:
French Historians in the
Age of Religious Wars

As seen in the textbooks, the period 1560–1600 appears to have been a uniformly tragic phase of French history, a succession of civil wars, massacres, assassinations, feuding noble houses, and religious hatreds. We observe a nation weakly led and still dangerously threatened by its old foes the Hapsburgs, almost as it had been endangered two centuries earlier by the English crown. Yet even today a journey across that majestic and fruitful land restores a certain sense of proportion: here disaster could never have become total. Exquisite châteaus were still rising and great cities expanding. Countless writers labored in many areas of literature, while in the teeming faculties of law young men were reading far outside the prescribed books and learning to think creatively about sovereignty and power, Church, State, and civilization.[1] Even before the outbreak of the wars, France was displacing Italy as the powerhouse of European thought and culture.

From our present viewpoint, France appears perhaps the most historically minded European nation.[2] During the period 1550–1610 at least 657 historical works were published in France, more than half in the exceptionally troubled years from 1560 to 1588.[3] Historians, biographers, memoirists—although almost all concerned with near-contemporary events—were seldom rigidly exclusive in their religious allegiances. Despite the emotions aroused by the Saint Bartholomew massacre and

72

other horrors, the men of iron—the black Calvinists and pitiless inquis-itors—far from dominated the scene; French realism and patriotism cre-ated more subtle and varied situations.

Glancing at some "typical" writers, we may well be astonished by their differences, complexities, compromises, and many shades of belief and unbelief.[4] We meet in François de La Noue an author whose rigorous Reformed principles do not warp a most tolerant disposition, in Michel de Castelnau a scholarly moderate, convinced that physical violence does not change opinion, in Pierre de Brantôme an entertaining but uncritical and antifeminist scandalmonger. Pierre de l'Estoile, a Catholic politique, denounced hypocrites of both confessions for cloaking worldly ambitions in religious pretenses. Claude Haton, a parish priest, took the perspective of the suffering populace and blamed Catholic kings and nobles for the national predicament. Etienne Pasquet, the advocate whose valuable let-ters document Parisian life, was a patriot who adhered to Henry of Navarre and a tolerant Catholic who detested the Jesuits more than the Protestants. Even Pierre Matthieu, having started his career under the Guises, joined the tolerant king of Navarre, whose cause he defended from a secular, moderate, and patriotic viewpoint.

The few Catholic writers with ferocious aspects, such as Blaise de Montluc and Gaspard de Tavannes, were too incompetent as historians to argue convincingly. More revealing is that eminent Catholic moderate Jacques Auguste de Thou (1553–1617), who in 1593 began writing his monumental *Historia sui temporis,* which ultimately filled some ten thou-sand pages.[5] Rich, well traveled, almost uniquely acquainted with the notabilities of the day and librarian to Henry IV, he collected a splendid archive for his grand project. His first part, covering the years 1545–1560, appeared in 1604. The Guises and other Ultramontanes combed it for heresies and then attacked the second part in 1608 because, among other affronts, de Thou failed to praise the Saint Bartholomew massacre, by which he had been horrified. De Thou's enemies appealed to Rome, and, despite the opposition of two French cardinals, the book appeared in the papal Index in 1609.[6]

Thus, within the Catholic body, the usual chasm grew between the ultras and the moderates. Similarly, while Huguenots like Régnier de la Planche and Pierre de la Place wrote as partisans, Philippe de Mornay, a scholar and gentleman, produced the sanest of the Huguenot sources and urged that the "true Church" be seen as comprising all the Christian churches. As a poet capable of prophetic grandeur and an individual who had suffered terribly in the cause, Théodore d'Aubigné in *Les Tragiques* was a special case; even in his *Histoire Universelle* (1616–1620) he strove for historical values. It has been said that the Catholics tended to write more readable memoirs; the Huguenots seemed constrained, as a minority of "innovators," to argue in more intellectual and searching terms. A favorable example is Jean de Serres, a pastor trained in Geneva yet dreaming of genuine reconciliation and achieving remarkable accuracy even as he defended his party against the charge of sedition and placed chief blame for the divisions on the Guises, a faction equally disliked by moderate and patriotic Catholics.[7]

Our attention will shortly be claimed by the astonishing case of La Popelinière, a Huguenot historian attacked by powerful coreligionists for carrying objectivity to the point of giving a generous benefit of the doubt to their Catholic opponents. Equally curious is Nicholas Vignier, not a "contemporary historian" but a learned medievalist who had been converted to Calvinism by fellow students and was forced to flee to Germany. Nevertheless, his patriotic studies eventually convinced him of his error; he returned to France and reentered the Catholic communion, leaving his defiant wife in Germany. It seems appropriate that, of his three intelligent sons, one became a militant Calvinist theologian, another an Oratorian, and the third a peaceable numismatist![8]

In France the Reformation had thus aroused problems and concepts different from those east of the Rhine. Unlike the Holy Roman Empire, France boasted an effective monarchy, which could stage a widespread persecution of heretics. France's new urban citadels of Protestantism were more vulnerable than their German equivalents; and even the powerful city of Lyons, having in 1562 turned Protestant as a result of a rebellion, was forcibly restored to Catholicism a year later. Although a few territorial nobles with extensive clientages among the squirearchy and civic leaders could organize armed resistance, neither their legal independence nor their military forces could compare with those of major German Protestant princes such as the elector of Saxony and the landgrave of Hesse.

On the other hand, both the geographic situation and intellectual leaders of Geneva were excellently adapted to a coordinated attack on Catholicism in France, primarily on distant provinces notoriously hard to control from Paris. The Protestants had every inducement to reexamine relations between Church and State and the tensions between religious toleration and social stability. To these problems Luther and Melanchthon had provided no clear answers. Even Calvin had hesitated to encourage armed resistance, although from 1552 he did claim that rulers who resisted the commands of God were forfeiting their authority.[9]

There developed among the Huguenots a powerful group of youngish men who were no mere pious fighting squires but political thinkers conversant with Christian humanism and the new political researches into Roman and Germanic law, men distinctly capable of well-argued convictions and even novel ideas. It would be a mistake to suppose that the demand for toleration arose solely from the dangers the Huguenots faced. Guillaume Postel and Sebastian Castellio, writing respectively in 1544 and 1554, were liberals who fully believed in toleration as a high principle and gave their reasons.[10] In retrospect we may see them (and Rabelais) as the French introducers of freewheeling philosophical and religious opinions which had originated mainly in Italy and were taken up not long after by Bodin and other rationalists.

Initially, almost alongside these Protestant liberals, stood many liberal Catholics whose intellectual foundations were in Gallican humanism, which the patronage of Francis I had done so much to develop. With its aid they sought the salvation of France through sober and secular thinking which rejected identification of their government with clerical heresy hunting. In 1518 Claude de Seyssel's *La Monarchie de France* had argued that the structure of French government did not depend on the sanctions of divine law or the teachings of churchmen in general, but on tradition, reason, and necessity.[11] More recently, this attitude had been strengthened by the lively researches of civil lawyers in Toulouse, Bourges, and Paris. During the years 1560–1562 a politique party developed with striking rapidity. Appointed chancellor in May 1560, Michel de l'Hôpital still pleaded in December for "one faith, one law, one King," urging people to stop using the very words *Lutherans, Huguenots,* and *Papists.* Yet during 1561, perhaps influenced by Etienne Pasquier's tract, *Exhortation aux Princes,* he changed his emphasis, as indicated by his influential speech to the representatives of the Parlements in January 1562 in St.-Germain.[12] L'Hôpital now urged that, however desirable uniformity of belief might be, its enforcement would gravely endanger France. Maintenance of internal tranquillity must therefore take precedence over duty to support the established religion. This policy should not lead to catastrophe. Church and State need not be precisely coincident, and people could be citizens who were not even Christians. As it was, many Catholic families lived amicably with others of the new faith. The task ahead was to settle the bases of the body politic under a paternal monarchy standing high above the religious contests of the day.

Unfortunately, the rulers of France failed to maintain this posture. Endangered by the intolerance of the Spanish-educated Henry II, the royal minorities under the Italian queen mother, the intolerable pressures of ambitious noblemen, and finally the slaughter of 1572, the ideals of a paternalist Gallicanism survived by only a narrow margin. Persistent oppression forced the Huguenots to envisage an alternative philosophy of the State, based on "free" Germanic institutions as opposed to Roman law and enlivened by another ancient heritage: the concepts of tyrannicide and republicanism. Nevertheless, the resultant "monarchomach" books and pamphlets also stood as identifiable progeny of the Reformation. They did not ignore Luther's theology—on which most of Calvin's was so closely modeled—but they did reject what Luther had supposed to be its political concomitant: a submissive dynasticism brought about by "the good old German loyalty." True, the winds of protest did not blow from the same quarter as those at the time of Luther's revolt. Order was no longer threatened by fanatical peasants, but by "godly" nobles and magistrates. Or, to put it more bluntly, neither the Reformation nor improved counterinsurgency weapons had wholly banished neofeudalism, clientage, and family vendetta from politics.

This monarchomach ideology produced its most characteristic expression in the *Franco-Gallia* (Geneva, 1573) of the eminent jurist François Hotman (1524–1590).[13] With little to say on religion as such, this informed historical treatise was useful to the radical Protestant parties. Nevertheless, it misinterpreted history from early Frankish times to prove that the Estates had always been recognized as expressing the people's sovereignty and that royal despotism, bureaucracy, and the Parlements had been recent innovations. Thus, it remained lawful for the Estates to depose evil kings. Civic autonomy also received Hotman's recognition as a pillar of ancient freedom, a claim blatantly supporting the recent demand for independence by groups of Protestant cities in Languedoc and Guienne. Similar views partially based on history soon emerged in the tract attributed to Calvin's successor at Geneva, Théodore de Bèze (Beza), *Du droit des magistrats* (1576).

Even more widely read than these works—and destined to be translated and used by English seventeenth-century republicans—was the *Vindiciae contra tyrannos,* published in 1579 under the pseudonym "Junius Brutus," but probably written by Philippe de Mornay and Hubert Languet.[14] Concisely and frankly, it absolves subjects from obedience to rulers who issue commands against the law of God. If led by the Estates and the magistrates, the people could rightfully rise against such rulers and against civil oppression too. Monarchy was originally instituted by the people; kings—born without crowns—were not proprietors but administrators. Applauding the assassination of Julius Caesar, the *Vindiciae* also maintains that the longer tyrants are tolerated, the more intolerable they become. The officers of a kingdom have not merely the right but the duty to remove them, and neighboring princes are obligated to help the insurgent subjects of such tyrants. Here and elsewhere, the book clearly reflects current situations. It has much to say about those "tyrants without title" who take advantage of feeble or dissolute kings to gain royal authority: a transparent reference to the Guises. The obligation of neighboring princes to assist oppressed peoples refers to William the Silent: de Mornay was a leading French confidant of that ruler when the Huguenots' cause became merged with that of the Netherlanders rebelling against Philip II. Thus, the *Vindiciae* forthrightly declares the remedies Calvin had cautiously adumbrated, with the clear understanding that the Reformation had attained not merely a political but a revolutionary phase, championing both political and religious victims. The primary claim to resist the enemies of God had spilled over into the secular world, legitimizing the overthrow of any alleged tyrant.

The second generation of Protestants had hence—at least in Calvinist, if not Lutheran, lands—extended the whole concept of the Reformation. The newcomers had set the movement in the context of not merely apostolic Christianity but also Roman republicanism and Frankish constitutional law. Of course, Luther's social vision of 1520 had embraced a thoroughgoing princely reform of education and mores,[15] but half a century later the more advanced French Reformers provided this aspiration with executive machinery and a magistrature armed with legal rights against monarchy itself. These demands contained something more concrete than a philosophical apotheosis of toleration; they had become desperate remedies for a minority church, faced with extermination yet large enough to avoid this fate through self-reliant propaganda and action.

These Frenchmen were not the first Europeans to use history and Scripture to broaden the functions of Reformed churches. A century and a half earlier the Hussites had successfully resisted papal and monarchical "crusades," and only a couple of decades earlier certain English fugitives from the Marian persecution had claimed substantially similar rights. These were John Ponet in his *Short Treatise of Politique Power* (Frankfurt, 1556) and Christopher Goodman, author of *How Superior Powers ought to be obeyed of their Subjects* (Geneva, 1558).[16] Also in 1558 John Knox's *Letter to the Commonalty of Scotland* announced that lawful kings are not made by birth alone and that rulers or magistrates who are idolaters or persecutors may be deposed.[17] However, the long duration and the rising European significance of the French crisis made it inevitable that general refinement of such ideas would come through French writers and from them enter the stream of modern European thought. The monarchomachs were the ancestors of John Locke and the Protestant Revolution of 1688, not to mention the more radical aspects of the Enlightenment and their outcome in the French Revolution.[18]

Despite first appearances, the new political activism did not mean that Geneva had a serious chance of snatching Rome's scepter, or that some Gallic-Helvetian ghost of the Roman Empire had arisen to restore religious uniformity in western and central Europe. As the years passed, it became increasingly obvious that recruitment to Calvinism was declining, leaving the Huguenots a small if still dynamic portion of French society. The very bases of controversy began to shift. Political opportunism had grown so intensely that the ultra-Catholics themselves began to clutch at defensive theories of resistance similar to those of the Protestant monarchomachs.

Their calculations became painfully obvious. In 1584 the death of the duke of Anjou made Henry of Navarre legal heir to the throne of France should Henry III die childless, which he did when assassinated in July 1589. The Huguenots were automatically transformed into legitimists, while the strict Catholics unified their regional associations under the Catholic League and issued from Paris a spate of radical propaganda against the new heretical "tyrant." This vigorous attempt to tarnish the Reformation in France is exemplified by the pamphlets of lawyer Louis d'Orléans, the sermons of curé Jean Boucher, the treatises by Guillaume Rose (Rossaeus),[19] and eventually by the work of Spanish Jesuit Juan de Mariana, notorious as an advocate of political assassination.[20] To a marked extent these writers borrowed and inverted populist arguments from Hotman and the *Vindiciae*. With the rise of the great Catholic League no unusual originality was required to confer the sovereignty of the people on the hungry, priest-ridden mob of blockaded Paris. Even though this new sovereignty might not emerge convincingly from Scripture and early constitutional history, in the last resort the Leaguers could base it on the cause of salvation: *salus animarum, suprema lex.*

Meanwhile, during the series of civil wars waged from 1572 to 1580, a "third force" of politiques, or peaceable Catholics, developed and regarded the problem of the Reformation from the viewpoint of State and society. True heirs of paternal monarchy as envisaged by Claude de Seyssel and Michel de l'Hôpital, these men specifically resembled the Huguenots in their plea for mutual forbearance, yet they lacked positive enthusiasm for religious toleration, save as a means of escaping material ruin. They are represented by such works as the influential *Six Books of the Republic* by Jean Bodin,[21] the *Apologie Catholique* of Pierre de Belloy,[22] and a much later work by one of several gallicized Scotsmen involved in the struggle: William Barclay's *On the Kingdom and Royal Power.*[23]

Deploring the prevalent anarchy, Barclay denounced the *Vindiciae* and the whole basis of the claim that malcontent subjects could legally dethrone kings. Such writers, who glorified the State as omnicompetent in the secular sphere and towering above religious disputation, saw disaster in the appeal to arms by champions of either Reformation or Counter-Reformation. They moved on to a positive belief in the divine right of kings. Whereas Rossaeus announced that the supreme law lies in the salvation of souls, Bodin placed it in *salus reipublicae,* and propounded exactly the right metaphor:

> If there is such an agreement of princes and peoples in the new religion that it cannot be suppressed without the ruin of the State, all the wisest rulers of states should imitate in that capacity the helmsman, who, when he cannot proceed in the course he desires, directs his course in whatever direction he can, and by frequently changing his sails, gives way to storms and tempests, lest he should suffer shipwreck in holding directly for port. Therefore that religion should be tolerated when you cannot abolish it without the destruction of the State. For the safety of the State is the supreme law.[24]

These were indeed the patriots and men of good sense, who were being heeded as never before: their version of the Reformation should not be regarded as more cynical or less honest than those of the strict Calvinists or the Catholic League. After all, had not both these "religious" parties unblushingly concocted general theories from Scripture, history, and law to meet political and military exigencies? In any event, the disasters of the age had strongly suggested that wise men should no longer contemplate the Reformation without strict regard to its social, military, and political context.

Such a cool reaction to the rival claims of Protestants and Catholics became widespread among the thinkers of this generation. On the whole, they adjusted to a new age with commendable speed and insight, even though the replacement of confessional ardor by skepticism or an apotheosis of the nation-state was not destined to deliver Europe from the rigors of warfare. Yet in France the new ideas worked after a fashion, especially after 1593, when Henry IV renounced Protestantism to capture Paris. Almost alone among the great figures of his day, he united in his person the three major parties. By upbringing he had been a Huguenot, but for the sake of his crown and his people he professed to have become a Catholic. Yet by temperament he had always been a sensualist and a politique.

These changing attitudes toward the Reformation soon registered in discussions concerning religion, society, and historiography. To a certain extent they arose from the discovery of new cultures overseas, cultures far stranger and less assimilable than the familiar Turks on the Bosporus or at the gates of Vienna. Still more important was the mighty flow of rationalist beliefs into France from Italy, not least from the Paduan skeptics headed by Pomponazzi. Mere study of the ancient classics resulted in a readier acceptance of certain pagan ideas, such as the atheism of Cicero's *De natura deorum* and Pliny's rejection of the soul's immortality. The many Frenchmen who did not wait for these ideas but rushed to study them in Italy, developed numerous sorts of skepticism and non-Christian Deism. In its various forms Platonism also stemmed from Italian sources and proved capable of infiltrating and subtly transforming Christian spirituality by a rival magic. Along with these impulses came Antitrinitarianism, which Michael Servetus successfully taught to many Frenchmen before he was caught and executed in their compatriot's city of Geneva.

Noting the incursion of such heresies from the time he first published the *Institutes*, Calvin soon started to answer back, combating the Paduans on the immortality of the soul, and, in his edition of 1550, specifically attacking Pantheists and Platonists. So did humbler Protestants like La Noue and de Mornay. Indeed, many clues to the history of free thought come from the counterattacks on it by both Catholic and Protestant champions of orthodoxy, for here was a new competitor, offensive to Reformation and Counter-Reformation alike. A simple religious dualism no longer suffices to describe the French mind in the second half of the century. The non-Christian aspects of intellectual history were for the first time adequately covered by Henri Busson's major work on rationalism in sixteenth-century French literature, which reveals unorthodox trends not merely in the great figures—such as Rabelais, Bodin, and Montaigne—but also in scores of lesser intellectuals.[25]

Jean Bodin (1530–1596) illustrates these developments on several fronts and his proverb of the helmsman by no means fully characterizes a complex mind full of bizarre erudition and unresolved tensions.[26] Like so many of the more adventurous thinkers of his day, Bodin entertained sweeping doubts about the traditional world picture based on Aristotle and scholastic dogma, although he lived in a cloud of esoteric mysteries and prescientific beliefs, including witchcraft and demonology. Nevertheless, many of the learned cranks who inhabited Shakespeare's hybrid age were granted flashes of genuine illumination, even as their minds ranged imaginatively across frontiers forbidden to the pedestrian pietists of the earlier Reformation.

Bodin was nothing if not versatile. A teacher of law at Toulouse, and for a time drawn to Calvinism, he remained essentially a free spirit and an avid reader in many fields, although he never achieved his ambition to unite them in an encyclopedic synthesis. He must stand among the ancestors of modern economic thought because he analyzed the causes of monetary inflation with greater intelligence than his contemporaries. Probably moved by professional ambition, he went to Paris about 1560 and soon after published his *Method for the Easy Comprehension of History,* a thoughtful inquiry into the practical lessons to be learned from history, as exemplified by case studies of Sparta, Rome, Germany, Italy, and France.[27]

But from our viewpoint Bodin stands out among those who saw the Reformation as an opportunity for discovering a natural religion, which should appeal to men of all faiths and cultural backgrounds and so unite the human race in harmony and happiness. The broad concept was by no means novel, although ecclesiastical pressures still tended to drive it underground. It can, nevertheless, be traced to the Nominalists of the fourteenth century and the Platonists of the fifteenth, even to Nicholas of Cusa, who saw some such bond as an escape from the schism between the Roman and Greek churches, and from the struggles against the Hussites or even the Turks. Bodin appears to have been attracted by the vision of Pico della Mirandola, who had wanted to synthesize Christianity with Platonism and the ancient Jewish wisdom of the Cabala. Amid the problems and opportunities of the Reformation, various sorts of liberals from Erasmus to Sebastian Franck had shown similar leanings.[28]

Bodin speculated in terms so bold that he dared not publish his *Heptaplomeres (Colloquy of the Seven)*, commonly dated 1593 but now known from a recently discovered manuscript to have been written in 1588.[29] Surviving also in several other manuscripts, it was not printed until 1857. Although influenced by various currents of Renaissance and Reformation thought, it offended even the most liberal ecclesiastical standards of the sixteenth century. It recounts a lengthy discussion—suitably placed in cosmopolitan Venice—among a Catholic, a Lutheran, a Zwinglian, a Muhammadan, a Jew, a philosopher seeking the natural religion, and a skeptic looking indifferently at all forms of religion. Bodin has ostensibly least in common with the Catholic, who is given little to say except that the Church cannot err. Both Protestants are more forceful but hardly more convincing champions, each dogmatically confident in his own beliefs and showing more enmity to the Catholic than to the Jew or the Muhammadan. None of the Christians shines in reasoned argument; all three appeal to blind faith, whether in the Church or in the Bible, and so are unlikely to impress people not raised in their respective traditions. By contrast, the Islamic spokesman defends a straightforward monotheism, free of miracles and approximating more closely the desired natural religion. Bodin suggests that the Turks may enjoy certain advantages through being more tolerant than Christians. In other places he regards the Jew most warmly, as custodian of the earliest and most primitive form of divine revelation.

It would, however, be hazardous to identify any of these characters with Bodin himself, for he pretends to welcome every contribution, although he is primarily concerned with advancing the claims of reason against authority while admitting that sacred books have their uses. He is not attempting to establish any one impregnable position, because he trusts that Nature will eventually bring forth that hidden mystery, that magical formula known only to the greatest sages of history, but perhaps still attainable. Armed with optimism, Bodin does not seek to throw off all tradition or construct a wholly new system on rationalist principles. Even when those revelations come, they will serve the needs of an elite rather than create a new religion for all.

In general, Bodin's response to Reformation Europe falls outside Christian dogma, whether "magisterial" or sectarian. Brought up a Catholic, he had become a Huguenot by the age of thirty; yet at sixty-three his skepticism extended to all religions and was applied more critically to the forms of Christianity than to Islamic and Jewish beliefs. If he retained enthusiasm for any one authority, it was the Old Testament, because that book had achieved recognition as holy by Jews, Christians, and Muhammadans.

Although Bodin typifies some limited groups of intellectuals, many other innovating minds in France rejected the monolithic habits of both Rome and Geneva. Tensions had become multilateral, and nowhere more than in France. To say this is not to repeat the familiar charge that Protestantism proved uniquely divisible, because pagan-humanist influences could also produce many mutations. Moreover, when it came to formulating practical plans, even Catholic nations and groups showed serious divisions, while at the other extreme innumerable sects diverged from all the major churches. And if Europe contained relatively few close intellectual relatives of Bodin, Servetus, and the Sozzini, a certain waywardness, a skeptical individualism, is often observable even in those who desired neither to shock the world nor to disqualify themselves from public life.[30] When one recalls the Italian parallels of the High Renaissance, half a century earlier, one dare not claim that French intellectuals had been the first to learn the art of living simultaneously on two or more planes.

Of this art a prime and familiar example is Michel de Montaigne (1533–1592), whose famous *Essais* appeared by installments in 1580, 1582, and 1587–1588.[31] Concerning his actual religious beliefs, a number of intimate modern studies have revealed patterns even more complex and curious than those in Bodin's writings. Outwardly, and sometimes inwardly, Montaigne was a devout Catholic, an exemplary mayor of Bordeaux like his father before him, a pilgrim to Loreto, and occupant of an edifying deathbed. Biographers no longer crudely dismiss his official persona as the smoke screen of an atheist, agnostic, or crypto-Protestant. On the other hand, many positions in the *Essais* seem plainly inconsistent with Montaigne's shining Catholic image, and even with one another. A number of his personal friends—such as La Boétie, the Jesuit Maldonado, and Florimond de Raemond—were strict Catholics. One does not fundamentally change the picture by remarking that in his later years Montaigne leaned toward the politiques and criticized the Guises (as well as Henry of Navarre) for using religion as a means to political ends.

Nevertheless, having made every effort to trace a consistent system of thought, we are still entitled to doubt whether Montaigne should be regarded as essentially Christian. His chosen intellectual milieu is the world of pagan Greek thought, and he hardly ever cites or mentions the historic Christ. His mockery of scholastic arguments for the existence of God tends to reflect adversely on Christian theology in general. He grants that we adopt Christianity through custom and tradition, that we are Christians in much the same way we are Périgordins or Germans. Remarking that the hallmark of a true religion is its members' conduct, he confesses that Muhammadans and pagans live up to their beliefs more successfully than do Christians. Like Bodin, Montaigne entertained an overmastering curiosity about the non-Christian religions; an extensive reading of his *Essais* would surely tend to weaken a simple thinker's belief in Christianity's uniqueness. In fact, Montaigne found it acceptable to cultivate ignorance in order to believe by faith alone.

Cynical as it may at first appear, all this relativism may claim some advantages. Tactfully but persistently Montaigne manifests his hatred of superstition and fanaticism. Despite his gestures of assent to orthodox belief, he substantially favors religious toleration, although he treats—or affects to treat—it as a matter of political expediency. Certainly he resents the Protestant Reformation as a disturber of what should be a largely aesthetic life, which at least the chosen few ought to be permitted to enjoy. While the ignorant masses practice custom-ridden Catholic observance, the educated should be left free to believe what they desire without extraneous constraint or public avowal. The civilized scholar's study is private, the place where thought is free.

One's thoughts about Montaigne are inevitably impressionistic; he is hard to pin down to any coherent system of ideas. Even more than Erasmus—whom Luther considered "as slippery as an eel"—Montaigne is multilateral to the point of self-contradiction. In the enthusiasm of the moment he can introduce a fresh idea which runs well outside what one has taken to be the orbit of his argument. To encapsulate "this truth of the moment," the essay—or still better this large collection of essays—provides an ideal vehicle. Not only genius but good fortune attended Montaigne, for he escaped retribution in his own day, and from the seventeenth century on became a most influential writer. Like Erasmus again, the companionable Montaigne was a great creator and purveyor of intellectual atmospheres, in which precise theology and institutionalized religion found it hard to breathe. In this negative sense Montaigne's personality forms a lurid comment on changing attitudes about the Reformation.

Beside Bodin and Montaigne, we must now place a third prophetic figure: Lancelot du Voisin, sieur de la Popelinière (1541–1608).[32] He demands recognition not merely as one of the ablest contemporary historians of the Wars of Religion, but also as an original thinker on the basic aims of historical research and composition. A Protestant gentleman of Poitou, he aspired to a life of study but was plunged into both family and public affairs by his elder brother's death. He served gallantly in the Huguenot armies and also as a diplomat, until in 1577 a severe wound relegated him to private life. During the 1570s he anonymously published two brief works on the period, but these were eclipsed in 1581 by his massive and well-documented *Histoire de France,* which began in 1550 and came almost up to date.

In its remarkable objectivity this book outdid even the work of Sleidan, and with a similar result, because it attracted the abuse of Catholics and Protestants alike. Odet de Nort, a forceful Calvinist minister at La Rochelle, accused the author of lies, impiety, and defamation, the last against the princes of Condé and Henry of Navarre. Henry himself believed these charges, perhaps because the national synod at La Rochelle already had. Although La Popelinière strove to get the case transferred to the Huguenot congregation in Paris, he failed and in 1585 had to sign a confession of error. Several passages were expunged from later editions by Huguenot censors.

Although in modern eyes this story reflects no credit on a cause which claimed tolerance from others, it must be acknowledged that La Popelinière asked for trouble. Dedicating his work to Catherine de Médicis and her unpleasant son Henry III, he scarcely blamed either the queen or the Guises for the massacre of 1572. Correctly enough, he exonerated the government from the charge of planning the deed far in advance, and he avoided tributes to the Huguenot magnates. His general critique of the Reformation still seems strangely uncommitted. Observing its advent across the Channel, he gives an important role to the English gentry's greed for monastic lands. The rise of Dutch Protestantism is depicted as owing much to discontent over the decline of trade. La Popelinière does not hesitate to denounce the impatience and arrogance visible in the French movement, or to offend its supporters by sometimes calling them Lutherans, a term greatly disliked by the Huguenots. Huguenot prejudices were also aroused when he referred to earlier-sixteenth-century Catholicism as "the Faith." La Popelinière took similar attitudes toward many debatable events. He relates how the Huguenot congregation had taunted the Catholics and so provoked the notorious massacre of Vassy. He describes in detail Protestant acts of violence and retails the abuse each side hurled at its opponents.

Why did La Popelinière go to such extremes in his quest for even-handedness? He protests that such attitudes are neither irresponsible nor based on exalted scruples, but that they reflect the absolute need to attain credibility. He warns his critics that if the Protestants fail to produce totally reliable histories, future historians will have to accept Catholic interpretations. He adds that he has dedicated his work to the queen mother and Henry III in order to attract Catholic readers, and claims that he is being persecuted because he differs from the partisan historians, whose work will not be believed. Not unnaturally, he recalls his own devoted services to the Protestant cause. Above all, he insists that he has avoided entanglement in theological issues: his trade is history, a broad, secular discipline based on factual truth. Albeit prematurely, he imagines that history has outrun clerical controls and reached the end of its career as a mere weapon of religious propagandists.

Unlike Sleidan, La Popelinière survived for many years after publication to face the poverty and neglect his courageous impartiality had invited. Yet he did not waste those years in bitterness; he wrote his most original book, the *Histoire des histoires,* published in 1599 and in part dealing with "The idea of Perfect History" (*Idée de l'histoire accomplie*).[33] In this late work La Popelinière announces that historiographic method had made no progress since Herodotus until recent years, when a few historians attempted a new sort of "general history." By this he did not mean a "universal history," as then envisaged in religious terms by both Catholics and Lutherans, because he did not believe that historians could elucidate human history shaped by God, or indeed by any "hidden laws" operating from outside the observable world. In his terminology, "general history" involves a new vision of the past in all its dimensions: as we should say, "in depth." War and politics in Xenophon or Thucydides did not in his opinion provide an understanding of the Greek way of life or of the bases of the Greek State—its structure, religion, laws, and manners. Likewise, he felt that the current narratives of the Wars of Religion merely continued the old-style tradition of "simple" history, which was no more than a rehash of annals, diaries, journals, memoirs, and other unprocessed narrative materials. What one really needed was a deeper synthesis, comprising *moeurs, coutumes, façons de faire,* and indeed every aspect of life which could be investigated, understood, and restructured into a new totality. This "representation of everything" is La Popelinière's "idea of perfect history," an objective historians can approach yet never wholly attain. It would at least enable them to acquire "period-sense" and avoid anachronism. For example, they would understand how the *early* Greeks or the *early* Romans actually thought and behaved, instead of depicting them in the deceptive images of later classical times. The present lively interest in La Popelinière arises from the fact that in the late twentieth century we are recovering something resembling his multilateral vision of societies and their driving forces.

La Popelinière would have done well to rewrite his earlier account of the Reformation and its French sequels in the light of his general theory. Doubtless in his day the feat remained impossible, if only because so many of the necessary source materials had not yet been assembled. In fact, La Popelinière shows himself well aware of the special problems besetting contemporary history, hitherto the commonest—although perhaps the shallowest—assignment of historians, and one from which he sought liberation. Renouncing the old "universal" history's aspirations to decipher God's plan, he directed his successors to a far more modest but more feasible task: to demonstrate exactly how particular triumphs, problems, and tragedies of men have emerged from an ever-shifting, highly complex, and all-too-human past.

A modest man, La Popelinière avoided regarding himself as a solitary genius and recognized similar ideals in such contemporaries as Hotman, Etienne Pasquier, and, above all, Nicholas Vignier, who as an erudite, inquiring medievalist was also demonstrating the freedom from contemporary obsessions for which La Popelinière appealed. Nevertheless, despite his earlier work on the Reformation and the Wars of Religion in France, neither La Popelinière nor any of his contemporaries fully realized the possibilities he was envisaging. The period thus concluded by proposing innovative approaches, methodologies, and critical parameters rather than by exploiting them in a new and consummate history of the age.

Despite the forward-looking sophistication of several French historians, the problems set by the advent of the Reformation in France demanded urgent decisions, for they were no exalted theological dilemmas which could await enlightenment: they involved the survival of millions of Christians. The major question had political and historical as well as religious implications. When the Reformation produced a stalemate likely to become lethal, and when two or more religions were joined in combat within one state, where did the highest duties of rulers, individuals, churchmen, and corporate bodies lie? Must there not come a breaking point, when irreconcilable religious principles should be ceded for the sake of survival? And could one cede such principles without reducing one or even both religions to spiritual destruction? Clearly, religious revolutions could not be carried through as if secular society did not matter.

In France contemporary historians thus sought to handle a Reformation crisis more acute than its predecessor in the empire and all the more disastrous because it could not be confined to the theological sphere. Confronted by a choice between incommensurate values, the French nation postponed it to a more favorable age by choosing Henry IV, and with him that "third force" already represented by the politiques. This decision, made by a large majority, was based in part on simpler forces: patriotism and fear of anarchy. Yet a subtler change of mental atmosphere—a complex latitudinarianism, often rationalist in tone but seldom atheistic or crudely anti-Christian—made the choice easier.

It remains to note some important French contributions to historiography of the Reformation which fell outside the parameters marked by Bodin, Montaigne, and La Popelinière. Chief among these was the *Histoire ecclésiastique des églises reformées au royaume de France*, published in Antwerp in 1580—a work of enduring utility despite its polemical character.[34] In three volumes comprising nearly three thousand pages, it covers the "primitive" Huguenot churches from 1521 to 1577. The simple attribution of the work to Calvin's successor, Beza, was rightly rejected a century ago. All clues indicate that it is closely based on reports sent to Beza by a considerable number of congregations throughout France, and then arranged, but not too radically revised, for collective publication. One of Beza's own letters in fact grumbles that such reports were not being promptly dispatched to him. Much of the editing seems to have been done under Beza's supervision by his assistants Nicolas des Gallars and Simon Goulart. (Goulart survived for almost another half-century to become a voluminous author in his own right.)[35]

By general agreement the reports and hence the book were composed in a deliberately subdued style. Yet the lack of literary refinement is compensated by an authenticity which no single author could have achieved.

At first sight, the texture of the *Histoire ecclésiastique* seems all too similar to that of the French narrative histories we have been discussing; the book contains a surprising amount of straightforward political and even military history. But its value lies in its unique and detailed survey of actual Protestant communities still in their formative stages. We observe a rather unsophisticated "Church under the Cross," from which detached history could not be expected. For example, these impatient Huguenots could not grasp the deep problems of the French monarchy and its genuine inability to follow Protestant designs directly opposed to both the Catholic opinion of the great majority of Frenchmen and the balance of power in the ruling classes. Yet the compilers and editors are by no means devoid of self-criticism. They describe rivalries and doctrinal quarrels among their ministers, hesitation and cowardice among the faithful, and the "ignorance and insolence" of their own soldiery, who on occasion destroyed monuments and libraries. Passages written soon after the massacre of 1572 exonerate the king and discuss the event with touching calmness. Beza himself was recognized by a generous Catholic opponent as one whose "partisanship is tempered by the breadth and elevation of his spirit."[36] One particular characteristic of the *Histoire ecclésiastique* gratifies modern interest in the regional history of religious movements: constructed in terms of local congregations, it helps us understand the grass roots of French Protestantism, countering the assumptions that its supporters thought and behaved uniformly or that circumstances in and around Paris typified all of France.

The biographical interest which we have already noted in German circles (Chapter 1) found an echo among French writers. In 1564, the year of Calvin's death, Beza rushed out a rather perfunctory life of his great predecessor, a conventional tribute which was not followed up by the substantial and authoritative biography that circumstances demanded.[37] Much more common were biographies of leading Reformers penned by their opponents. During the 1560s adversaries like François Baudouin (1562) and Gabriel Dupréau (1569) were making harsh attacks on Calvin's personal character as well as his supposed tyranny over Geneva; the delicate balance of forces there was little understood outside the city. In such writings we find already the stories of Calvin's "debauched" youth and his alleged death from the loathsome disease of Herod.[38] The second notion in particular remained effective propaganda when it was all too generally held that a man's death indicated God's judgment on his life.

In 1577 a more skilled biography, which stamped these unpleasant pictures on popular Catholic opinion, came from the pen of Jérôme Bolsec, a former Carmelite and doctor of theology in Paris.[39] Renouncing his vows, Bolsec had fled to Italy about 1545 and married. After serving as physician to a nobleman in Chablais, he had appeared in Geneva in 1551 and publicly attacked the dogma of predestination in the presence of Calvin, who had confuted him face to face. Banished from the city, Bolsec had sought Protestant appointments elsewhere, until his reputation caught up with him. Soon after he reconverted to Catholicism. While practicing medicine at Lyons he seems to have been encouraged by the archbishop to write and publish his *Histoire de la vie, moeurs, actes, doctrine, constance et mort de Jean Calvin*. This work of an enemy with a strong personal grudge repeats the allegations about the Reformer's youth and deathbed, where he is represented as frenziedly invoking devils to his aid. Furthermore, Bolsec attacks the severity of Calvin's rule over Geneva and his innovating doctrines, especially those concerning the Mass. His criticisms do not substantially extend to the already notorious trial and execution of Servetus, whom he calls "a filthy and monstrous heretic," regretting merely that Servetus had been arrested on a Sunday, in contravention of Geneva's laws! Bolsec died in 1585, having three years earlier produced an almost equally bitter account of Beza. Biographies by Reformed scholars amounted to a Protestant counterpart to the "lives of the saints," and Catholic biographies of heresiarchs were an inverted form of the same genre. This genre flourished in succeeding decades, yet did little to advance historical understanding; it functioned at best as an indication of contemporary religious attitudes and a repository of often questionable "facts."

Part Two

REASSESSING THE INHERITANCE

1600–1840

5

An Age of Crisis:
The Seventeenth Century

To intellectual historians, the age between the sixteenth-century Reformation and the eighteenth-century Enlightenment is the "century of genius," which ushered in modern times.[1] From a broader perspective, however, the period resists such straightforward definition. Designations such as *age of reason* or *age of absolutism* offer partial perspectives but are contradicted as much as confirmed by the phenomena they seek to embrace. In truth no descriptive term can fully comprehend the rich diversity of this complex age. Nevertheless, one characterization, used by social and political historians in particular, has remarkably wide applicability to the age as a whole yet retains sufficient flexibility to avoid doing violence to the subject matter—it is the notion of *crisis*.[2] Used with caution, this term can illuminate many features of this "age between the ages," especially its relation to the past and future.

The Reformation's legacy of unresolved problems in religious allegiance and political organization provided much of the seventeenth century's agenda. But ultimately more significant, perhaps, was what Paul Hazard called the *crise de conscience* near the end of the century—a radical questioning of tradition on an unprecedented scale, not generally addressing directly the issues of the Reformation, yet inevitably entailing a total reexamination of the Reformation heritage.[3] The concept of crisis, understood in this way, provides useful insight into the historiographic reassessment of the Reformation in the years leading to the Enlightenment.

Politically, Europe in the early seventeenth century presented a pattern of power relations different from that of the sixteenth. After dominating much of the political history of the previous two centuries, Italy and Spain had declined. France, the German states, England, and the United Provinces made most of the running, while Sweden experienced a brief efflorescence as a major European power. Among the German states a period of comparative stability following the Peace of Augsburg gave way in 1618 to three decades of war waged across Germany largely by outside forces: Sweden was locked in a conflict with the empire, and France intervened on the Swedish side. These wars were fought on religious pretexts and sapped religious life, yet nothing could more clearly indicate the thorough politicization of the struggle in this late phase of the Reformation.

In the part of Germany which owed allegiance to the Augsburg Confession this was a time not for making fresh initiatives but for guarding the inheritance of sacred dogma. That task naturally required some reference to Luther, but it was formal rather than material. What mattered was not Luther himself, but legitimizing his divine appointment to reform the Church. This was the burden of the disputation conducted in 1617, on the hundredth anniversary of the Ninety-five Theses, by Johann Gerhard (1582–1637). Gerhard was the dominant intellectual figure in early-seventeenth-century Lutheranism, a leader in the revival of Aristotelian metaphysics in German universities, but more widely known for his devotional work, *Sacred Meditations,* which was translated into most European languages and achieved a circulation exceeded only by those of the Bible and Thomas a Kempis's *Imitation of Christ.*[4] In the face of objections from leading Catholic theologians Robert Bellarmine and Martin Becanus,[5] Gerhard concluded that Luther had, in addition to his ordinary appointment within the Church, an extraordinary commission to carry out its reform.[6]

The desire to "revive [Luther's] blessed memory which has almost faded away due to the inauspiciousness of the times" was not entirely absent among orthodox theologians, but they achieved nothing significant along these lines.[7] The historical Luther remained almost totally hidden behind his "pure doctrine," and his writings were scarcely read at all. Indeed, in the foreword to his spirited defense of Luther in 1634, Johann Müller (1598–1672)—scholar, polemicist, and pastor of Saint Peter's, Hamburg—explicitly excused Lutherans from answering accusations against their founder, because such matters had no bearing on the fundamental truth of his doctrine.[8] To the orthodox, Luther was not a subject for historical investigation, but an object of faith. For them the Reformation was not so much a historical movement as a supernatural act in the history of salvation, to which they traced their religious roots, but which they viewed in a way that can only be described as profoundly ahistorical.

As the new century unfolded and Germany's tenuous peace again gave way to renewed warfare, France experienced a time of rebuilding and consolidation following the religious wars of the late sixteenth century. The Edict of Nantes (1598) had not solved the religious issue, but to Richelieu, who dominated French political life during the minority of Louis XIV, the Huguenots presented an internal political problem to be solved by statecraft. His policy was to depoliticize the difficulty by depriving the Huguenots of their fortresses and cities without inflaming passions by attempting to coerce consciences. On the other hand, certain measures of the Counter-Reformation, long delayed by the Wars of Religion, were implemented. This was in many respects a peaceful movement—in details strikingly reminiscent of early Protestantism—concerned with education, individual salvation, and deeper personal commitment. It was led by men like Francis of Sales and Vincent de Paul, to whom the earlier bitter confessional struggles were a distraction from the tasks of practical Christianity.[9]

A decidedly polemical spirit, however, was expressed by men like the Bordeaux magistrate Florimond de Raemond (c. 1540–1602), whose account of the heresies of his time, written in 1595–1600, first appeared posthumously in 1605 and was reissued so frequently that it became the leading French polemical work against the Reformation.[10] Like Jérôme Bolsec a generation earlier (see Chapter 4) and Jean Haren more recently, Florimond converted to Calvinism only to revert to enthusiastic support of Rome. As a Frenchman he was predominantly concerned with Calvin, although he did compare Calvin's heresy with that of Luther, whose personal life and doctrines he found far grosser. Florimond had a few fresh things to say about Calvin's career, notably concerning the early influence of Melchior Wolmar, who had persuaded Calvin to abandon legal studies in favor of theology. More perceptively than many modern writers, he refused to consider Calvin's biography simply in terms of Geneva and assessed the great influence Calvin exercised from an early date throughout France. With less reason, yet equally in tune with the spirit of his age, Florimond noted that the sum of the letters of Luther's and Calvin's names in Hebrew is 666, the Mark of the Beast in Revelation 13:18.

Notwithstanding the declining importance of Italy and Spain, the leading spokesmen of the Church of Rome in those countries displayed a renewed spirit of confidence, not only in determined onslaughts on Protestantism but in celebration of the Counter-Reformation's positive fruits. Among these onslaughts, the most weighty was the official Catholic counterblast to the Magdeburg Centuries (see Chapter 1), furnished by the Oratorian Caesar Baronius (1538–1607), who began as an over-worked protégé of Saint Philip Neri and ended as a reluctant cardinal. His twelve volumes of *Ecclesiastical Annals* (Rome, 1598–1607) reached only to the year 1198; after an interval they were continued in a further ten volumes (1647–1677) by another Oratorian, Oderico Rinaldi, who brought the story to 1565.[11] These considerable scholars pioneered in many fields and discovered some "new" documentary sources, yet almost by definition they remained selective partisans; Baronius in particular focused church history too heavily on the Roman primacy. Like the Magdeburg Centuriators, Baronius and Rinaldi contributed far more to polemics than to the historiography of the Reformation, which in any case they did not reach until after 1650.

In a more positive spirit, the native Catholic tradition of the "lives of the saints" received a new lease on life as writers followed the footsteps of the new saints of the Catholic Reformation. No organization did this to better effect than the Society of Jesus, which then stood at the height of its prestige and confidence. In 1569 Pedro de Ribadeneira had finished his life of Saint Ignatius of Loyola, which on every count surpasses the other contemporary narrative, by the miracle-seeking Italian Maffei.[12] Ribadeneira, who published his work in 1572 after much discussion and correction within the society, described exactly the right episodes to impress on the world Loyola's intense convictions and force of character. In addition, his narrative produces some unexpected and revealing touches, as, for example, when Loyola studied the *Enchiridion* of Erasmus only to reject it as a spiritual guide upon finding that it caused his devotions to grow cold. This verdict we may regard as instinctive rather than rational, yet it seems singularly in character, because the *Enchiridion* was after all an essay in biblical theology, later manipulated by Protestants.

One chapter of Ribadeneira's work is devoted to that other great Basque member of the society, Saint Francis Xavier, whose heroic missionary travels in the Far East had ended in 1552 with his lonely death on the island of Saint John, at the gateway to his last objective: China. The Jesuits were in general aware that outsiders—and not least members of other missionary orders—would remain alert for inordinate claims. Ribadeneira credits to Xavier certain spectacular episodes of spiritual healing which some of his colleagues regarded as inadequately docu-

mented, calling them *"muy grande hiperbole."* Although he was not by
the standards of the day a flamboyant biographer, in the words of a
modern Jesuit historian, Ribadeneira "dropped a few seeds which grew
into a substantial tree of legend."[13] At the same time such writings,
inspired by the direct evidence in the circulating autobiographies of Ignatius of Loyola, Saint Theresa of Ávila, and other mystics, can claim
an honorable place in the rise of biographies which seek to depict the
interior life, an approach implicitly discouraged by Protestant doctrine.

Regarding the general history of the Jesuits, we have in the *Historiae
Societatis Jesu* a major cooperative work begun by Niccolo Orlandini,
who by his death in 1606 had written up to the death of Loyola.[14] His
successor, Francesco Sacchini (1570–1625), continued to the year 1580
in several installments. Important problems of moderation and verisi-
militude involved Sacchini much as they had Ribadeneira and his colleagues.[15] Certainly Sacchini sometimes used dramatic phraseology, as
when he claimed to be describing "wars by the human race against the
monsters and the powers of hell, wars embracing not only single provinces, but every land and sea, wars in which no earthly power but the
kingdom of heaven itself is the prize." On the other hand, he well understood the perils besetting the loyal historian of a successful missionary
order with competitors. For the Jesuits this overwhelming esprit de corps
was further complicated by incipient national rivalries within their society.

When the Portuguese members claimed that the *History* did injustice
to Simón Rodriguez, Loyola's early companion, Sacchini sent one of the
complainants a noble letter denouncing all concealment of historical facts,
however unpalatable: "Should anyone be unwilling to set down aught
save the good, then let him call his book, not History, but Select History . . . To wish to persuade the world that our Society never was touched
by a breath of scandal, would be . . . extravagance and pride, seeing that
there were scandals among the Apostles and first deacons . . . All history,
sacred or secular, has the same tale of imperfection to tell, so why should
we want our history to be something special?"[16]

Likewise, Sacchini mentioned the Jewish lineage of Loyola's successor, Diego Laynez. In the more racialist communities of Spain, especially Toledo, this was taken as a poisonous libel, and the general of the
society received hectic demands that the page be torn out and replaced
by an assertion of the "purity" of Laynez's descent. Again Sacchini protested, pointing out that the facts had been confirmed by Laynez himself,
who was by no means the only man of Jewish extraction Loyola had
admitted. Denouncing "vulgar and prejudiced minds," Sacchini cited
Saint Paul (Romans 11), who had encountered a similar problem.[17] We

must acknowledge that some sixteenth-century historians, whom we readily dismiss as strong partisans, did have distinct if limited ideals of historical truth even though they found it hard to penetrate beyond mere "true facts" and attain a just understanding of their opponents' broad arguments.

More profoundly controversial than any of these writers was the most technically accomplished historian of the period, Paolo Sarpi (1552–1623).[18] The son of a Venetian merchant, he showed prodigious intelligence from childhood, and, although he entered the Servite order, he continued to live—albeit amid great personal austerity—in the higher circles of public life. After four years as court theologian to the duke of Mantua, he worked in the Roman Curia under three popes before returning to Venice in 1588. Sarpi's studies in magnetism, optics, mineralogy, and physiology, not to mention canon and civil law, and Hebrew and classical studies, were truly encyclopedic and might qualify him as the most genuine "universal man of the Renaissance." His opportunity to participate in politics arose in 1606, when Paul V placed Venice under an interdict and Sarpi was named chief theologian and canonist to the republic. Now detested by the Curia, in 1607 he escaped with severe wounds a murder attempt by its supposed emissaries, causing him to remark when shown the dagger (*stylus*), "I recognize the style of the Roman Curia."

It has often been said that Sarpi was never in doctrine a Protestant, and that his harsh criticisms of the papacy were impelled by the papal attack on the proud and ancient traditions of ecclesiastical independence long upheld by the republic. When he thought politically, Sarpi believed that the liberties of Venice and all Italy were ominously threatened by an unholy alliance between the papacy and Spain, backed by the Jesuits. Yet here some writers seem inclined to simplify, for Sarpi also thought on another plane, where he approved some characteristically Protestant ideas as well as the powerful antipapal tradition in Italy from Dante to Guicciardini. His scientific treatises have been lost, but he was clearly a man of tolerant and rational outlook who denounced superstition as even more dangerous than impiety.

In 1611 Sarpi announced that he would be delighted "to witness the advance of the Reformation, for it would tend to advance the interests of mankind." Like any Protestant, he believed that priests should not monopolize control of the Church, which was the body of the faithful. For him, as for many Anglicans and Lutherans of the Reformation, State and Church comprised the same body of men, performing different functions, each avoiding interference with the other. Sarpi thus attracted immense admiration in the Protestant world of his day, most especially from King James I, who gave his work what amounted to protective patronage.

Although he wrote other historical pieces, Sarpi's fame has arisen from his weighty and often brilliant *History of the Council of Trent* (1619), which was based not only on documentary studies and on the Protestant Sleidan—from whom he takes his initial account of the Reformation—but also on the recollections of actual participants, some of them Protestant.[19] The tenor of the work runs directly against that of the Counter-Reformation as organized by the victorious faction at Trent and supported by Rome and the Jesuits. On the first page Sarpi asks three questions which provide the key to his whole standpoint. How did it happen that the council, longed for as a means of restoring the Church's unity, actually consolidated the schism and so embittered the parties that it made reconciliation impossible? How had the princes' plans to reform the clergy through the council been frustrated and the bishops' attempt to recover their authority ended in complete submission to the pope? Finally, how did the Roman Curia, which had at first feared the curtailment of its powers by the council, emerge more deeply entrenched than ever before? Sarpi seeks to answer these questions by a detailed exposure of the clever intrigues through which the council, instead of being a synod open to both Catholics and Protestants, was made a closely packed *conciliabulum,* which excluded Protestants and submitted Catholics to control by Italian representatives of the Curia.

Of course, objections of some weight have been raised against this admirably written but slanted interpretation.[20] Like any Venetian, indeed like any Frenchman of Gallican sympathies, Sarpi believed in the unique effectiveness of State-Church reforms. He also assumed that a genuine accord between Rome and the Protestants was still attainable around the midcentury, whereas powerful opinion in Rome and at Trent tended to write Germany off as hopeless and concentrate on preserving Catholicism where orthodox belief still predominated. To allow a strong and vocal German presence at Trent would have imperiled what the council did achieve—an unambiguous restatement of the Roman positions without subtle arguments and qualifications. In another sense also the outcome supported these criticisms: by 1600 the papacy's credit stood far higher throughout Europe than it had in 1550.

The controversy over the council continued through somewhat more ecumenical periods. Meanwhile, Sarpi had his book published in London with a dedication to King James, and he prudently gave the author's name as Pietro Soave Polano, an ingenious but by no means impenetrable anagram of Paolo Sarpio Veneto. One need scarcely add that the papacy and the Jesuits soon planned a counterblast to this damaging attack. It came in the form of the *History of the Council of Trent* (1656–1657) by Sforza Pallavicino, who was selected by the general of the society to refute Sarpi point by point.[21] Cardinal Pallavicino compiled 361 accusations of error in a conscientious but by no means always convincing performance, which was doomed through its very plan to be altogether less entertaining than that of Sarpi. Sarpi's remained a living book, in tune with the skeptical Enlightenment. He was for Macaulay "my favourite modern historian"; Ranke, though recognizing his bias, praised his unrivaled critical powers. Not until our own time has scholarship dispensed with the need to consult Sarpi, and even today, despite Hubert Jedin's achievement, no history of the epoch-making council is so free from bias that it is totally satisfying. However, in this thorny field, are we not fated to go on demanding the impossible?

While the forces of Catholic reaction were consolidating their influence in Italy and Spain, notwithstanding Sarpi's impact in Italy, the United Provinces and England were moving just as clearly in other directions, although not without a continuing legacy of internal problems. The United Provinces, whose independence became secure in 1609, were deeply preoccupied with Holland's political struggle for hegemony over the other provinces and with the complex tensions—religious, political, social, and economic—between the strict Calvinist Orangists and the more liberal, Arminian-influenced burgher party. This period was more notable for the expression of fierce party loyalties than for considered historical reflection. Seventeenth-century England, by contrast, saw a rich and varied development in historical writing about the Reformation. England's peculiar lot was to be not so much wrestling with the Reformation legacy as still undergoing the Reformation process, whose results were by no means assured. The conflict was not merely Rome versus Reform but more particularly Anglican versus Puritan, and even that struggle was complicated by inroads of Arminian thought into English religious life through Peter Baro and his successors.

Still experiencing the second phase of their Reformation, seventeenth-century Englishmen were in no state to take a detached view of its first phase; they referred back to it to substantiate their own varied positions. Despite the intellectual range of their theologians, the English retreated into insularity. Concentrating on their native history, they failed to realize the English Reformation's heavy debt to Continental movements. Although their own roots had been in Geneva, even the Presbyterian Puritans tended to share this insularity; likewise, the radical sects preserved little sense of their numerous Continental affinities. As for the

Anglicans, their belief in an autonomous and self-explaining English Reformation has notoriously lingered into our day. Moreover, the gradual merging of religious controversy into political conflict caused most historians of the Stuart period to see the whole Reformation in political rather than social or religious terms: they were encouraged by their own background to accept all the more readily the historiographic tradition of Sleidan and his followers.

On the other hand, Stuart historians' outlook and methodology were not slavish, static, or for that matter monothematic. In John Milton they included a fundamental reinterpreter of the Reformation who attained a truly prophetic dimension. With more immediate significance, the English produced in this period a most scholarly group of antiquaries marked by a common passion for documented history. Here emerged a healthy factor which prompted genuine factual research and gradually tended to modify religious partisanships. Although this stiffening of narrative through documents had already occurred in Foxe, it culminated a century later in Burnet and Strype, and it has made the works of such scholars desirable resources for their modern successors.

In Burnet, with his liberal Anglicanism and informal yet sophisticated presentation, we find one of those transitional figures—a true contemporary of Locke and Bayle—who advanced into the foothills of the Enlightenment. After the revolution of 1688, the mob continued to shout "No Popery," but the intellectuals found such emotions irrelevant for an age which had outgrown the triangular clash of Roman, Laudian, and Puritan. In brief, early Stuart historiography made meaningful progress, and even on the religious-ecclesiastical front it had begun by 1700 to adapt itself to the changes that would mark the new century in Europe.

As their mingled constitutional and religious differences drew them into the whirlpool of civil war, Englishmen looked back on Elizabeth I as that "bright occidental star,"[22] and most of them saw in her reign statesmanlike wisdom and a stability which they longed to recover. Thomas Cartwright (1535–1603), leader of the moderate Presbyterians, had defended the Reformation against opponents on both sides, identifying a continuous succession of reformers from Wycliffe to Luther, praising Henry VIII for disseminating the Bible, and reiterating Foxe's view of Elizabeth as a providential instrument to bring the gospel back to England.[23]

A more political interpretation of Elizabeth's role was expressed by the classicist antiquarian William Camden (1551–1623). A versatile scholar who became master of Westminster School, Camden acquired a deep knowledge of England's antiquities and also of her current politics and mode of government. In 1586 he dedicated his regional and topographical history *Britannia* to his hero and patron Lord Burghley, Elizabeth's first minister,[24] but he did not begin his famous history of Elizabeth's reign until the accession of James I.

The *Annals,* first published in Latin in 1615, appeared in a succession of English translations, but only after the author's death.[25] They showed the pervasive influence of Sleidan, who furnished almost word by word the ideals Camden announces in his preface to the reader. In particular, Camden insists on his objectivity, his vigorous adherence to the documents, and his refusal to enter by mere imagination into "the hidden meaning of princes."[26] Even more intriguing are Camden's connections with his contemporary, the already famous Jacques Auguste de Thou (see Chapter 4), for initially Camden intended to send his manuscript to help de Thou, who needed assistance with Anglo-Scottish affairs in the time of Elizabeth and Mary Stuart. In this project King James supported Camden, because he feared that de Thou would succumb to the rival influence of his former tutor and present enemy, George Buchanan. In the event, de Thou did not follow Camden's guidance in these still delicate matters.

Nevertheless, a close affinity remained between the two historians. In regard to the Reformation and the political struggles arising from it, both were politiques in the Bodin tradition, having read his *Method for the Easy Comprehension of History* (see Chapter 4). They detested fanaticism as corrupting true history, whether by a Catholic or a Protestant. Their common aim was helping to create political stability rather than finalizing religious truth. De Thou and Camden both rejected not only the Melanchthonian vision of history as divine Providence, but also the older humanist historiography, with its speeches invented by the author, moralizing conclusions, and heroic exemplars (see Chapter 1). Not for them were the "Four Empires" or the astrological prophecies still accepted by many ecclesiastically minded writers. Although willing to describe war, diplomacy, and the intrigues of rulers, both writers found more significance in the totality, the organic continuity of nations and societies. In several passages Camden figures as a pioneering socioeconomic historian. Nevertheless, he was at least as much a Protestant as Bodin and de Thou were Catholics. Delving deeper than any contemporary, he used the papers of Burghley and Sir Robert Cotton to trace the making of the Elizabethan settlement in Church and State, admiring the queen's *via media* and praising her above her due for a consistent and rational policy. What Camden most admired was the prudent moderation of Burghley and Archbishop Parker. What he hated most was fanatical Puritanism, together with the political attempts by Leicester and his son-in-law Essex to exploit it.

In his professional capacity as a historian, Camden seems to regard religion as a prop of sound civil government and, in the grave classical temple which he fashioned, religious history as such has no central place. He tells the reader that he cannot omit ecclesiastical matters because "Religion and Commonwealth cannot be parted asunder." Yet, because such matters have their own specialists, "I for my part have not touched them but with a light and chary hand."[27] Thenceforth, although his sympathies and duties obviously lie with the Reformation, he adopts a cool approach to the original clash between Catholics and Protestants and regards no party as holding a monopoly of truth.

An important key to Camden's inquiring but "no-nonsense" approach—which came to be called *civil history* in England—lies in his study of Polybius, from whom he quotes with approbation the sentence "Take away from History Why, How and To what end things have been done, and whether the thing done hath succeeded according to reason, and all that remains will rather be idle sport and foolery than a profitable instruction."[28] Yet while regarding the *Annals* as the most "modern" historiography practiced in England at the time, we should not conclude that they dominated the field during their century. For example, the contemporary *History of the World* by Sir Walter Raleigh continued to exalt divine Providence, including the scheme of the "Four Empires." [29] Readers may be surprised to find an analysis as sophisticated as Camden's framed within a narrative ordered under regnal years. But this backward-looking form does not prevent Camden's mind from ranging freely, or from explaining the "Why, How and To what end" in a manner wholly unattempted by the popular annalists such as Holinshed, who refer to the Reformation and the Elizabethan settlement in patriotic yet uncritical terms.

In contrast to Camden, who firmly upheld the Elizabethan *via media* as the proper solution, Puritans interpreted the English Reformation as an aborted movement, brutally cut off before it could come to full fruition. Henry Jacob took the view that only Henry VIII's death had prevented him from completing the wholesale abolition of popery.[30] In *The Pope's Deadly Wound* (1635), Thomas Clark outlined a scheme of church history—presumably derived from Foxe—which considered that some form of Protestantism had always been present in England among men as diverse as Grosseteste, Langland, and Wycliffe and had even influenced the episcopate until the decline of religion set in.[31]

The most original Puritan perspective on the Reformation came, however, from the pen of John Milton (1608–1674) under the title *Of Reformation touching Church discipline in England and the causes that hitherto have hindered it* (1641).[32] Milton may be regarded as the greatest

Puritan spokesman, yet from another point of view he was not a Puritan at all. Certainly he was not a typical figure in Puritan circles, but a man whose highly individual—and at times clearly heretical—perspectives on religion and social life were matched by an unparalleled gift for imaginative Christian writing.[33] Milton believed that England from the time of Wycliffe had played a leading role in the restoration of the Gospel but, through the actions of "halting and time-serving prelates" —among whom he included Cranmer and Latimer—had fallen behind. Purity of doctrine had not followed through into purity of discipline. The obstacle was not so much particular bishops as episcopacy itself, and without its destruction liberty of conscience would come to nothing. Had it not been for the perverseness of prelates, he declared in *Areopagitica* (1644), Wycliffe's reformation would have led the way for the whole of Europe, which then might never have heard of Huss and Jerome of Prague, of Luther and Calvin.[34] Yet, although Wycliffe's voice had been stifled, a new age of the Reformation was opening, which would make possible "the reforming of the Reformation itself" through the abandonment of the "prelatical tradition of crowding free consciences or Christian liberties into canons and precepts of men."[35]

In this view, Rome was the foe of all liberty and could not be tolerated, yet Geneva offered an unacceptable yoke of conformity. Toleration of all Protestant sects, Milton believed, would advance true knowledge and thence a decline in schismatic sectarianism. Fifteen years later, in his *Treatise of Civil Power in Ecclesiastical Causes* (1659), he attacked the stifling menace of Presbyterian hegemony and identified Protestantism with the individual's freedom to seek his own way to God.[36] Milton's discussion of the Reformation was the most original English contribution of his time, because it avoided a narrowly English perspective and conceived of the Reformation as a continuous, unending process opposed to the mere erection of a new orthodoxy to replace the old. In this, Milton provided the Enlightenment with the germ of one of its great historiographic issues.

The restoration of the English monarchy in 1660 brought no immediate resolution of the religious issues of previous decades, although the large exodus from the Church of England in the Great Ejectment of 1662 signified permanent institutionalization of dissent and effectively closed off some future options for the Anglican Church. Nevertheless, conflict continued unabated, still tied inextricably to political issues. Lord Clarendon's *History of the Rebellion and Civil War in England*, begun in the 1640s but completed only after his fall from power in 1667, presented a view contrary to Milton's on liberty and religion.[37] Clarendon regarded the Civil War as plain insurrection, and to no small extent class warfare. He underestimated religious factors, although he had no doubt that the mania for preaching was crucial in undermining authority. This royalist standpoint was developed with more specific reference to the Reformation in Peter Heylyn's *Ecclesia Restaurata,* begun as early as 1637 but published in 1661.[38] A sincere Laudian who found the Church of England's inheritance in the Church of Rome rather than in the Wycliffite, Waldensian, and Hussite traditions, Heylyn produced a work of considerable erudition based on a wide variety of sources, including convocation registers, parliamentary acts, and privy council papers and manuscripts. Like other High Churchmen, he viewed Protestantism's development in the light of his hatred for Puritanism and dwelled on the losses rather than the gains. For him, as for so many, the true Reformation came under Elizabeth and was directed against that Puritan extremism which also threatened government and property.[39]

Another leading historian of the Civil War era was Thomas Fuller (1608–1661), a moderate royalist and Laudian who had suffered some reverses during the hostilities but was restored to his benefices in 1660 and became a chaplain of Charles II. He is best remembered for his collection of pithy and readable biographical studies, *The History of the Worthies of England* (1662), in which he applauded the English Reformation for its gradual and nonviolent nature but found many to praise who did not follow the Reformation and many to criticize who did.[40] Standing essentially for an ideal of moderation, he found extreme forms of Protestantism unpalatable, yet his basic fairness to the Puritans earned him Heylyn's criticism. Almost one-third of Fuller's *Church History of Britain* (1656) is allotted to the Reformation, and he acknowledges Foxe as a source, although he was not unaware of the martyrologist's defects.[41] His history is notable for anticipating Burnet and Strype by the extensive use of original documents.

The advent in 1685 of a determined Catholic monarch, James II, exacerbated many of the political and religious conflicts in English society, and his overthrow in the Glorious Revolution of 1688–1689 brought a resolution of some issues. The throne was now securely and permanently Protestant, and Protestant dissent from the Church of England was tacitly tolerated. In the post-Restoration years, and especially in the wake of 1689, the urgent issue for the Church of England was comprehension. By what means could the Church tolerate and even include Protestant dissenters? Latitudinarians may have defined the Reformation as the common heritage of all Protestants, but their High Church opponents anticipated their own nineteenth-century descendants by trying to isolate the English Reformation from European Protestantism, even to the point of denying the legitimacy of the Lutheran and Calvinist churches.

During this period two major histories of the Reformation appeared in England—those of John Strype and Gilbert Burnet, who were both born in the same year. Strype (1643–1737) has with some justice been placed with the annalists rather than the historians.[42] In the last forty years of his long life, he produced a whole library of volumes on Reformation England, including the *Annals of the Reformation* (1708–1709), covering the reign of Elizabeth, and the *Ecclesiastical Memorials* (1721), extending across the reigns of Henry VIII, Edward VI, and Mary.[43] As a Low Churchman and a Whig, Strype welcomed the 1688 revolution as a divine deliverance from popery, yet, as a complacent Anglican, he detested Puritanism as much as Romanism. In general, he defended Henrician ecclesiastical policy and saw the reign of Edward VI as a time when learning and the arts flourished. During these two reigns the constant element of spiritual progress was provided by Cranmer, "the greatest instrument under God of the happy Reformation of the Church of England."[44] The supreme threats to her survival had come in the reign of Elizabeth, whose religion still stood firm against the twin challenges of Papists and Puritans, thanks largely to the character of Elizabethan prelates like Grindal, Parker, and Whitgift, whose biographies Strype also compiled.[45] In all these volumes the history of the Church is presented as the story of a constantly changing institution.

Taking pride in his objectivity and accuracy, Strype constantly stressed the variety of his original sources. He possessed a major collection of documents relating to the Reformation period and had personally seen all the papers he had used, and in so many cases reprinted. He also acknowledged the assistance of many correspondents. The *Memorials* were intended to rectify errors and omissions in earlier accounts, and the *Annals* sought to provide what had been previously lacking: a full-scale and documented church history of Elizabeth's reign. When new materials came to light, the *Annals* were reissued in a revised version. Among earlier writers Strype looked especially to Foxe, whom he admired for his extensive use of original records, although he was aware of Foxe's imperfections. Inevitably, modern scholarship regards Strype's immense labors with a growing reserve. Not infrequently his transcriptions show inaccuracies of detail or omit substantial passages without warning; on occasion he misunderstood a whole document.[46] Nevertheless, until these vast documentary collections are properly edited, Strype will remain an indispensable source.

Strype's contemporary Gilbert Burnet (1643–1715) occupied a far more exalted political and social station. The son of a prosperous Edinburgh lawyer, he became a courtier, politician, and Whig bishop and mixed freely with the leading figures of the day. Unlike Strype, he was also a consummate literary artist, and his *History of My Own Time,* published posthumously, is not merely a prime historical source but a highly readable memoir distinguished by marvelous skill in the concise delineation of character.[47] Burnet became entangled in the political disputes between the court and the Scottish Presbyterians and was forced into exile in 1685, only to return in triumph with William of Orange and be made bishop of Salisbury in 1689. Here was a career bound to influence a man's perspective of the Reformation: an Anglican of Scottish origins, who spent some years with Continental Protestants, could be expected to take a broader view of that movement than did his insular contemporaries. His *History of the Reformation* was strongly influenced by his conviction that the true principles of the movement were being endangered not merely by Romanism and dissent but also by High Church Toryism, and he called for the Church's reinvigoration on the basis of Reformation principles.[48] Burnet had been stimulated to write Reformation history by Nicholas Sander's work on the Anglican schism, which appeared in French translation in 1676 and exercised considerable influence in High Church Anglican circles.[49] The first volume of Burnet's history appeared in 1679 during the Popish plot, the second in 1681— by which time he was increasingly identified with opposition groups— and the third in 1714.

Burnet considered most earlier historians superficial and aimed to write a critical narrative tracing the Reformation in relation to political history. He dedicated his first volume to Charles II, urging him to continue Elizabeth's work in restoring Christianity to its primitive state by purging it of accumulated corruptions. In defending the English Reformation he accepted the need to be critical and objective, especially concerning the earlier phases. He did not defend Henry VIII's "great enormities," but recognized him as a providential instrument who had enabled a truly religious Reformation to follow.[50] Anxious to concede nothing to the hostile Romanist interpretation of Sander, Burnet strongly defended Cranmer and Cromwell and at times distorted his account of the Henrician martyrs. On the other hand, he praised the Marian martyrs in somewhat conventional tones, stressing the horrors that Romanism might once again bring to England. He saw the Church as still threatened by sectarianism and Catholicism, but regarded Catholicism—in its Roman and Anglican forms—as the more dangerous. Burnet lost no opportunity of pointing out the relevance of Reformation history to contemporary affairs, using it to instruct ecclesiastical politicians.

Burnet's sense of the Reformation as a developing historical movement has rightly been seen as "a major contribution to the emancipation of English history from the annalistic method,"[51] and it seems just to add that he was aware of the Continental historians who had thus liberated themselves. His history derives strength from its use of documentary sources and its discriminating analysis of the varied elements in the movement—for example, his distinction between the history of the royal divorce and that of the religious Reformation, a point all too often overlooked in subsequent work. Despite his aspiration to write a fully documented and objective history, Burnet's partisanship is easily discerned, yet he had discarded not a little of the narrowness and virulence which had persisted into his time. Aware of Anglicanism's connection with Continental Protestantism, he was also convinced of its peculiar strength: it combined unity with comprehensiveness and latitude—ideals which remained strong in the Anglican Church through the eighteenth century, although they would come under attack in the nineteenth.

Continental Europe in the second half of the seventeenth century presented a picture sharply distinct from the situation around 1600. The political organisms, especially the nation-states, were differently aligned; Louis XIV had become the protector rather than the adversary of Hapsburg Spain, and England had eventually been linked by dynastic ties with its former rival, Holland.

France's domination of European affairs in the latter half of the seventeenth century was a function not merely of Louis XIV's personal influence but of Germany's exhaustion after the Thirty Years' War. Within France, Louis pursued a policy against the Huguenots which in some respects was an aspect of royal absolutism, but passed well beyond Richelieu's strictly political motivation. Louis was sentimental over religious issues; his persecution of the Huguenots culminated in the 1685 revocation of the Edict of Nantes, which led to large-scale emigration, especially to the Netherlands.

The two great internal issues in France at the time were Gallicanism—which brought conflict between royal and papal authority—and Jansenism—a revival of Augustinian thought originating in the Low Countries but domesticated in France and deeply influencing some of the country's finest thinkers, notably Pascal. Superficially these two issues evoke the political and theological themes of the Reformation, yet they in no way represent the emergence of "Protestant" concerns in France. The Gallicans had no quarrel with Rome on Tridentine dogma, and Jansenism was as anti-Protestant as it was anti-Jesuit. The Reformation legacy became a matter of public debate, though mainly in reference to the internal problems of French society, as the exchanges between Bossuet and Pastor Claude make clear.[52]

Nevertheless, in other ways these issues increasingly came to transcend national boundaries, and the late seventeenth century saw a great deal of interaction among France, Germany, and the Netherlands. Three aspects stand out: the emergence of the great journals, especially those emanating from the Huguenot refuge in Holland; international discussions about reunion of the separated churches; and the continuance of confessional controversy at an international level. All three provided significant opportunities for a reexamination of the Reformation heritage.

The advent of the journals was an important development in European intellectual history and a major step toward the modern specialized journal. Pierre Bayle participated in their growth between 1684 and 1687, after which he withdrew to concentrate on his critical dictionary. His literary activities on behalf of toleration represent a wrestling with his Calvinist inheritance in the context of late-seventeenth-century culture, as much as a foretaste of Enlightenment attitudes.[53] Jean Le Clerc (1657–1736), although he was the grandson of a Huguenot refugee, had been won over to Arminian views. He became especially active between 1686 and 1693, when his journal helped disseminate the views of Locke, Burnet, and Newton.[54] Bayle and Le Clerc distrusted each other, yet had much in common; each looked to reason rather than authority as a path to understanding. Both evaluated the Reformation in a positive light: for Bayle, its ambiguity and contradictions did not remove its liberating quality. In Le Clerc's eyes its very turbulence and disorder formed part of the onward movement of history; without it Europe would still have been in darkness.

The controversial writings of the late seventeenth century show signs of increasing distance from the heat of the original battles. Many early themes were perpetuated, but harsh invective gave way to more sophisticated presentation of the issues. The most notable products of this discussion were French, but they were addressed to an international readership. The writings of the Jesuit scholar Louis Maimbourg (1610–1686) on Lutheranism and Calvinism showed a balance by no means characteristic of earlier writings in this genre.[55] Where others had used Luther's actual works sparingly and usually in distorted form, Maimbourg took care to present both sides of the picture and to outline Luther's own views. The passage of a century and a half had clearly provided the possibility for a more objective assessment of events, and Rome came in for its share of criticism. Maimbourg freely acknowledged that Leo X was more prince than pope, possessing few of the qualities demanded by the occasion, and he sharply criticized the gross abuses which had corrupted the preaching of indulgences and thereby given rise to the Lutheran movement. [56]

As for Luther himself, Maimbourg reasserted many of the standard accusations, but he accorded due recognition to the Reformer's outstanding personal gifts and early academic achievements. In the grand mélange of Luther's personal qualities, there were some good traits, although they were outweighed by defects. His pride and presumption tipped the scales against him, for in them lay the ultimate roots of that hostility to authority from which, in no small measure, the chaos, disorder, and warfare of the Reformation period had sprung.[57] For Maimbourg, the Peasants' War represented both the logical consequence of Luther's ideas on authority and the turning point of his influence in the movement. After it, Luther receded into the wings as Melanchthon and the Swiss Reformers assumed center stage. Yet Maimbourg regarded these later phases of the Reformation not as new movements but as the continuing ripples from those early Reformation years.

More widely influential than Maimbourg's writing was Jacques Bénigne Bossuet's study of Protestantism. Bossuet (1627–1704) was a popular preacher and a skillful controversialist whose first published work had been a refutation of a Protestant catechism. In his maturity he combined the roles of bishop of Meaux, tutor to the dauphin, and trusted adviser to the king, showing himself in the last capacity as a staunch defender of the Gallican Church's rights against papal interference. His *History of the Variations of the Protestant Churches* (1688) argues that Protestantism's inherent tendency was toward creation of a multiplicity of sects.[58] For Bossuet variation was intrinsically "a mark of falseness and inconsistency," whereas true faith spoke with a clear and simple voice and taught a truth that was uniform, constant, and unchangeable. Rather than isolating the Reformation as a sixteenth-century tragedy attributable to the actions of Luther and his followers, Bossuet sees it as a chapter in the history of heresy, which was almost as old as the Church itself. He notes that the roots of the Reformation may be seen in the reform movements and reformers of the Middle Ages: the Waldensians, the Albigensians, Wycliffe, and Huss. Yet we search in vain for any genuinely historical analysis of the connections between these movements and the Reformation. Rather Bossuet seems to have seen them as recurring manifestations of the heretical spirit, rooted ultimately in that fundamental human predilection for the "deceptive sweetness" of novelty.[59]

Of the fifteen chapters of the *Variations* which cover the history of Protestantism to the seventeenth century, the first six deal with the three decades from 1517 to Luther's death in 1546; this gives some indication of the vital importance Bossuet accorded Luther as leader of the Reformation. The support the Reformer received is attributed not to his doctrines but to his great personal qualities: eloquence, passionate conviction, and extraordinary toughness. On the other hand, he is sternly criticized for the tone of his writings, his abusive language, and above all for the fact that "he set himself above all mankind, not only his contemporaries, but the most illustrious of past ages."[60]

Much of Bossuet's attention is directed to the irony inherent in the Reformation from the beginning: that Luther, who presided over this heresy, was unable to enforce his authority over it because, like all heresies, its fundamental trend was toward further "variation." In exploring this divisive process, Bossuet pays particular attention to the Swiss Reformers and differences concerning the Eucharist. Melanchthon is especially fascinating to the bishop, who employs his progressive turning away from Luther's views as a telling internal witness to a false and inconsistent foundation.[61] Bossuet does not hesitate to exploit as fully as possible issues such as the bigamy of Philip of Hesse to discredit Luther,[62] yet he avoids the libelous legends and scurrilous muckraking of earlier controversialists, and is animated throughout by a desire to bring erring Protestants back to the truth rather than vilify them for their progenitors' errors. He carefully concedes the necessity of a true Reformation to advance the general hypothesis that the so-called Reformation was not a reformation at all, but a destructive and negative revolution.[63] True Reformation would come, Bossuet believed, only through a correction of faults from within; Luther's way had threatened not only the unity of the Church but the whole order of society.

That Bossuet's writings against Protestantism had a fundamentally positive purpose is shown by his leading role in the wide-ranging debate on ecclesiastical reunion and reconciliation which became popular in the last decades of the seventeenth century.[64] This debate arose out of a growing recognition that religious unity would not be achieved by coercion. Bossuet used François Véron's distinction between objective dogma and subjective interpretation[65] to argue that a wide variety of opinion was possible in matters not defined by the magisterium of the Church, and that the substance of the dispute with the Protestants could be narrowed to the decrees of Trent, setting aside the whole paraphernalia of scholastic theology. He entered discussions about reunion already taking place in Germany between the Austrian bishop Spinola and the Lutheran Molanus, translating Molanus's plan into French and approving most of its suggestions.[66] Molanus was able to envisage the Catholic Church eventually sanctioning communion in both kinds, clerical marriage, and the vernacular Bible.

Even more significant in the long run was Bossuet's series of exchanges with the Hanoverian statesman, mathematician, and philosopher Gottfried Wilhelm von Leibniz (1646–1716), which were aimed at clarifying the issues between the churches. Leibniz's letters to Bossuet project a genuinely historical understanding of the Reformation in the framework of Europe's and Germany's concrete problems in the preceding centuries. Rejecting the apocalyptic imagery and abusive tactics of both sides, Leibniz accepted some key doctrines of Trent, such as free will and transubstantiation. In many ways he seems much closer to Rome than to Wittenberg, and his attraction to the notion of a universal institution under Roman authority was clearly very strong. Yet he continued to hold the Catholic Church at arm's length and firmly denied that Luther was a heretic. Underlying the course Leibniz steered between opposing camps were his convictions that differences were theoretical rather than practical and that piety and free conscience rather than dogma represent the true foundation for unity. In Leibniz the two Reformation principles of free conscience and justification by faith alone became separated, and the triumph of the former over the latter indicated an important direction for the eighteenth century.[67]

Toward the end of the seventeenth century, and into the early eighteenth, there were signs of major change in historical writing in Germany; they found their clearest expression in the work of the historians Seckendorff and Arnold. These changes were not unrelated to the conflicts and issues already outlined—Seckendorff's work was a specific answer to Maimbourg and Bossuet—but they can be properly understood only against the background of radical intellectual reorientation.

Our exposition so far has depicted a Europe living out of the past, settling in various ways and with varying degrees of success the issues inherited from the Reformation. Yet these processes form only part of the story. The seventeenth century witnessed not merely an adjustment of traditional concepts, but a radical questioning of all tradition, in the course of which preoccupation with the past yielded increasingly to concern with the present and, by implication, the future.

Paul Hazard has brilliantly illuminated the many facets of this dramatic expansion of the European consciousness. Not the least important factor conspiring to unsettle traditional values was travel, together with the vast literature which widely disseminated its lessons. "As one pondered on these warring dogmas, every one of which claimed to be the vehicle of the one and only Truth; on these divers civilizations, each one of which boasted that it, and it alone, was perfect—what a School for Sceptics was there!"[68] What had been assumed to be transcendent truth was now seen as circumstantial cultural variation; what had appeared a universal archetype was revealed as a particular manifestation. Even the existence of God was not a matter of universal consensus, and it became clear also that morality could function without theological foundation. The result, in short, was a radical relativizing of the European religious experience.

Not many of those who participated in this revolution of consciousness were concerned with the Reformation as such, and this in itself is notable. But their collective impact on the interpretation of the Reformation became substantial. In philosophy the giant was Descartes (1596–1650), whose influence reached its height near the end of the century.[69] His dethronement of Aristotle was almost as much of a threat to Protestant theologians as to Catholics, for Aristotle had been banished by Luther only to be restored by Lutheran orthodoxy. Responses to Descartes varied widely, from Malebranche's attempt to harmonize Cartesian and Christian principles to Pascal's radical attack on the new philosophy based on a tragic vision recalling the dimensions of biblical faith. Among those influenced by Descartes, some attempted a constructive theological response, but small comfort remained for traditional religion in Spinoza's pantheistic vision or even Leibniz's "monadology."

Political thought was dominated by the creative genius of two Englishmen, Thomas Hobbes (1588–1679) and John Locke (1632–1704), the one evoking a pessimistic vision of human corruption, the other enunciating the positive and optimistic principles which were to influence English Whigs and American revolutionary ideologues.[70] In the period from Bacon to Newton, scientific knowledge underwent a most dramatic advance: not until the present century has so radical a change in consciousness occurred.[71] The universe was stripped of a number of its mysteries, while many new problems—unanswerable by traditional theology or scholastic philosophy—were posed.

Few if any of these men were conscious foes of the Christian religion. Indeed, Descartes's intention was to provide solid proof of God's reality; Hobbes and Locke had by no means excluded religion from their vision of the human commonwealth; and Newton aimed to provide a better understanding of God's universe. But we must distinguish sharply between intention and effect. Cartesian philosophy and Newtonian science contained the seeds of destruction for traditional theology. Hobbes's *Leviathan,* although it reads at times like a work of theology, was notable not only for its stern attack on the papacy, that "Ghost of the deceased Roman Empire, sitting crowned upon the grave thereof,"[72] but also for its sharp restriction of the religious sphere. Locke's religion undermined rather than supported traditional Christianity, for he saw evil not as innate but as injected into men by society, and therefore largely the result of the ideological systems on which they had based their thought, especially Christianity as taught by the churches.

Telling evidence of the impact of this reorientation in Christian circles is provided by Richard Simon (1638–1712) and Pierre Bayle (1647–1706)—the one a Catholic, the other a Protestant—both expressing the spirit of radical criticism. Richard Simon's pioneering work on biblical exegesis attempted to establish the supremacy of the critical principle over a priori dogmatic considerations.[73] It was his aim to undermine the source of Protestantism's authority by showing that Protestants were relying solely on writings which had been altered and mutilated over time. He also alienated many of his coreligionists and was eventually condemned by the Church, although he sincerely regarded himself as a defender of Catholic truth.

Ultimately more significant in this context is Pierre Bayle, a writer of immense influence whom Gibbon characterized as "a calm and lofty spectator of the religious tempest."[74] Bayle was born in southwestern France in 1647, the son of a Protestant minister but educated by the Jesuits and briefly converted to Catholicism. From 1680 he was part of the community of exiled Huguenots in Holland, where his first major work, on the comet of 1680, appeared two years later.[75] This book moved swiftly from an explanation of the comet as a natural phenomenon (rather than a manifestation of divine purpose) to a broad attack on superstitions and a call for greater freedom for the exercise of man's natural qualities. In a series of works from 1682 to 1686, Bayle developed his views on toleration and freedom of conscience, going beyond Locke in extending these principles even to Catholics and Moslems, while defending man's basic goodness and the natural light of reason as sure and infallible rules of judgment.[76]

In 1697 Bayle's great *Historical and Critical Dictionary* was published: a work destined to become one of the vital books of the Enlightenment, although it deserves consideration first of all on its own terms.[77] Essentially a biographical collection with some geographic additions, the dictionary derived its massive influence not from its factual content but from what its author called "a miscellany of proofs and discussions" in the form of footnotes far more substantial than the text itself. These contained the controversial material which led Voltaire to describe Bayle as "advocate-general of the philosophes"[78] and created a demand for nine French editions before 1750. The notes also clearly show the author's concern to establish a proper basis for discussion by using sound and reliable evidence and analyzing it impartially, neither selecting arbitrarily to suit preconceived ideas nor relying on others who had already, consciously or unconsciously, distorted the facts.

The *Dictionary* salvaged many a reputation from inaccurate and prejudiced vilification, including that of Martin Luther, whom Bayle considered the object of two centuries of lies and misplaced censures.[79] Luther had indeed been rash and ill-advised in some respects, for instance in his view of the Epistle of James. But despite his faults—which in many ways were those of his age—he had shown eminent qualities and was especially to be admired for the rude shock he had administered to the Roman Church. Far from contributing to the growth of disbelief, the new faith had challenged Rome to break free from its corrupt and barbaric state and conceive a new ardor for religion. Bayle's attitude toward schism is essentially cool and pragmatic: "Zeal cools when we are not taken notice of, nor surrounded by another sect, and rekindles when we are."[80]

In view of Bayle's staunch advocacy of toleration, his judgments on Erasmus are especially interesting. An undogmatic Protestant living in an era of continuing persecution, Bayle was impressed by Erasmus's irenic and inclusive teachings insofar as they represented the position of a free man who rejects established creeds.[81] Given Bayle's distaste for religious controversy and hatred of partisan strife, it is not surprising to find his staunch approval of Philipp Melanchthon, "one of the wisest and greatest men of his age."[82] Less expected, however, is his defense of Calvin, "a man on whom God had conferred extraordinary talents, a great deal of wit, an exquisite judgement, a faithful memory, an able, indefatigable and elegant pen, an extensive knowledge and a great zeal for truth."[83] The significance of this approbation is heightened, for our day at least, by the important role of Geneva and other Calvinist cities in the eighteenth-century Enlightenment.

Bayle's moderation and his judicious treatment of Reformation controversies make his treatment of the Anabaptists all the more intriguing.[84] His chief point against them is that they endangered the Reformation by associating it with revolt and civil disorder. Yet, despite his obvious disapproval of what is often called the Radical Reformation, he avoids blind prejudice, deplores many of the actions against the radicals, and attributes the faults of pacifist groups to mistaken zeal rather than evil disposition.

The same balance illumines Bayle's article on the skeptical philosopher Pyrrho and led to unjustified accusations from orthodox Protestants that he was a defender of atheism.[85] In fact, he was neither an atheist nor a Deist, yet he did much to form skeptical eighteenth-century attitudes toward superstition and intolerance. This contribution lay behind Ferdinand Brunetière's judgment: "To forget Bayle or to omit him is to mutilate and falsify the whole history of ideas in the eighteenth century."[86]

The period which witnessed these major intellectual revolutions also saw notable developments in historical writing about the Reformation, emanating especially from Germany. For most of the century, Germany had remained so much under the spell of orthodoxy that even Lutheran and Reformed parties could not reach any consensus about the Reformation. But the late seventeenth century brought signs of new life, at first through the movement we know as Pietism. Like the somewhat parallel movement of Quietism in Catholic countries, German Pietism assumed the character of a protest against rationalistic and authoritarian religion.[87] Its leading spokesman, Philip Jakob Spener (1635–1705), although doctrinally orthodox in Lutheran terms, shifted the balance decisively from dogma toward ethics. He was able to do this because, unlike his orthodox opponents, he conceived of the Reformation in dynamic terms. Luther, he believed, was not God's final word, but simply a faithful messenger who could only be truly followed by a Church prepared to push the Reformation forward in new directions. Spener believed his age needed a moral reformation, to be achieved not through state coercion but through the exercise of the free conscience. Paradoxically for a Lutheran, he believed that the Reformation heritage could only be properly preserved by a fresh emphasis on works. Here he saw no contradiction of the original Reformation, but simply a recognition of new needs for a new age.[88]

The most significant church historian of the late seventeenth century had no formal connection with Pietist circles, but was profoundly influenced by the values and attitudes they fostered. Veit Ludwig von Seckendorff (1626–1692) was an official at the court of Duke Ernest the Pious at Gotha and later chancellor of the new University of Halle. Unlike Leibniz, he retained a deep personal commitment to Lutheran doctrine, and his prince commissioned the massive *History of Lutheranism* (1692) as a defense of the Reformation against criticisms by Maimbourg and Bossuet.[89] Seckendorff's declared aim was "to bring to light, from material in the archives of the principalities and cities, and those in private ownership, why the reformation of religion took place and with what success, and how from small beginnings it achieved its present state, at which the world never ceases to wonder."[90] He had a deep emotional commitment to the Lutheran Reformation, but not a blind one. There is never any doubt where the author's allegiance lies, yet his partisanship is consistently measured and restrained. Moreover, although he is clearly as keen to provide a word for the present as to reconstruct the past, his determination to rely on genuine historical sources remains unequivocal and bears comparison with Ranke's. This resolve was backed by solid achievements in editing contemporary documents, always aimed at the composition of a universal history free of confessional bias.

Seckendorff differed from many of his forebears in having a close and intimate acquaintance with Luther's writings; he was, therefore, not dependent on any ecclesiastical distillation of "pure doctrine." This knowledge helped him discover the man behind the image projected by orthodox Lutheran tradition. Seckendorff's distance from that tradition is nowhere more evident than in the detailed biographical sections of his work, which evince a powerful desire to apprehend Luther the man. A genuinely human figure emerges: a wonderfully creative and talented man, but a man nevertheless. Seckendorff provides a "warts-and-all" picture of Luther without thereby diminishing his subject's stature: indeed, Luther's personal defects are turned to positive advantage, for God's choice of a flawed human being to lead the reformation of the Church is seen as a positive testimony to divine Providence.[91]

An implicit—and at times explicit—contrast is drawn between the early creative years of the Reformation and the later years of State-Church consolidation. In terms to be echoed by subsequent writers, Seckendorff saw those early years as a time when the creative impulses of reform flowed naturally, without political manipulation, social confusion, or the divisive wrangling of theologians. The essence of the Reformation lay in its liberating spiritual quality, and the core of that achievement was bringing the scriptural message to the common people.[92] Looking beyond Lutheranism, Seckendorff was unusually open in his attitude toward Rome, acknowledged the manifest improvements in the Church of Rome since the sixteenth century, and showed genuine distress at the persistence of disunity.[93] His work continued the tendency of Leibniz and Spener: to emphasize ethics over dogma. Seckendorff, however, achieved a balanced outlook not because doctrinal considerations lacked importance for him, but because they were not all-important.

In 1699, when Seckendorff's history was attaining considerable popularity, another large-scale work emerged from Pietist circles, echoing a number of his key ideas but greatly extending the attack on authoritarian religion. Gottfried Arnold (1666–1714) was forty years Seckendorff's junior and had pursued a somewhat checkered career, briefly occupying a chair in church history at Giessen and then undergoing a phase of religious enthusiasm before settling down to parish work. Arnold's *"Non-*

partisan" History of Churches and Heresies (1699) stirred great controversy in Lutheran circles because it amounted to a celebration of heresy.[94] The quality of "variation" which Bossuet considered a sufficient condemnation of Protestantism Arnold regarded as cause for rejoicing. Yet he carried no banner for Protestantism against the Catholic Church: that kind of confessional opposition was totally superseded by a contrast between living, vital piety and dogmatically regulated religion. From this viewpoint, official Lutheranism had no more to recommend it than Romanism, for it had violated free conscience, subjected piety to dogmatic control, and persecuted the true spirit of the Gospel. Orthodoxy was not faith but blind belief in authority; true Christianity was more likely to be found among those generally called heretics.

Arnold showed a warm regard for Luther himself and appealed to him against institutionalized Lutheranism. Like Seckendorff, he exalted the young Luther, the liberator, in contrast to the conservative, middle-aged statesman and church builder.[95] He valued Luther's great gifts of piety, yet avoided uncritical reverence, noting his faults and idiosyncrasies and making clear that truth and righteousness were not his peculiar preserve but existed in abundance elsewhere. In Arnold's eyes the Reformation was an act of God, but that was because it represented a revival of mystical and practical religion. Orthodoxy was a betrayal of that original impulse, yet one could grasp and reexpress the religious spirit in defiance of the deadening hand of authority, and here lay Arnold's principal aim.

Pietism was at least in part a positive response to the crisis of authority which characterized European intellectual life toward the end of the seventeenth century. Its deepest impulse was rejection of the link between religion and authority. In Seckendorff and Arnold it was associated with an appeal to aspects of the Reformation inheritance which had been shut out of the imposing edifices of orthodoxy. In particular, the appeal was to the spiritual values expressed by the young Luther and in some of the sectarian movements. In breaking once and for all the power of orthodoxy, Pietism gave fresh life to these neglected religious impulses. Yet, powerful though it was as a religious force, it proved somewhat sterile theologically and thus paved the way not for a creative revival of authentic Reformation perspectives but for the disintegrating tendencies of the Enlightenment.

6

An Age of Optimism:
The Eighteenth Century

"An age of faith as well as reason": so, half a century ago, Carl Becker repudiated the simplistic view of the Enlightenment as an age of reason, pure and simple.[1] That view forgot that Newton's new physical world revolved around an acknowledgment that God existed and that, in Alexander Pope's words,

> All are but parts of one stupendous whole
> Whose body nature is, and God the soul.[2]

Becker's four essays proved a masterpiece of persuasion, and few books have exercised such power over opinion about a past age, even though scholars have long since exposed the deep flaws in his argument.[3] Not the least of these was Becker's failure to discern—in his enthusiasm to bridge the gulf between the thirteenth and eighteenth centuries—the sharp differences between them in the scope and goal of reason, and the nature and object of faith.[4]

The details of this scholarly controversy need not long detain us, but it is worth noting that the "faith" Becker observed—faith in a man-centered paradise on earth—had no resemblance to the faith of Martin Luther and the Reformers and indeed struck somewhat indiscriminately at all forms of Christianity. Did not Baron d'Holbach declare that the world "cannot have an object, for outside itself there is nothing towards which it can tend"?[5] Did not David Hume conclude that Christianity "not only was at first attended by miracles but even at this day cannot be believed by any reasonable person without one"?[6] And did not Voltaire contemptuously dismiss the eucharistic beliefs of the Churches, telling his readers that "the Papists eat God without bread, the Lutherans eat bread and God, while the Calvinists, who came soon after, eat bread without eating God"?[7] On the other hand, d'Holbach and other skeptics were adamant that their atheistic ideas were for the educated elite alone, not for the masses, for whom religion remained a mindless consolation and an aid to civil peace.

If speaking of Enlightenment thought in terms of "faith" ultimately creates more problems than it solves, we can perhaps discern a pervasive confidence and optimism which embraced the works not only of the age's atheists and skeptics but of those who retained traditional religious sympathies. The writers of the Enlightenment, like none of their predecessors except perhaps the scholars of the fifteenth-century Renaissance, were acutely aware of their distinctiveness, their radical break from the past, their crucial importance for the future direction of European thought. Here the religious paradigm may help rather than hinder understanding, for were they not in their own eyes an elect band charged with a historic mission—to dispel ignorance and spread knowledge? And did not some of them at least bring to that commitment a fervor more characteristic of religious causes?[8]

The notion that there was a body of truths—which could be rationally perceived, by whatever method, universally agreed on, and applied in various ways to the welfare of mankind—found its quintessential representation in the encyclopedia, a genre which embodied both aspects of this surpassing confidence: on the one hand, the view that it was possible to give a complete and certain account of what is known and, on the other, the expectation that this expert knowledge could be effectively diffused to a wider public.[9] The encyclopedic treatment of knowledge found its counterpart in an approach to history which was "universal" in a way totally different from Bossuet's *histoire universelle* (see Chapter 5). Bossuet's history had in practice been narrowly biblical and European; the men of the Enlightenment set Christian European history in a worldwide context and thus relativized every aspect of it, not least its religious experience.

Gibbon's magnum opus on the Roman Empire not only implicitly denied that civilization had begun with Christ, but identified Christianity as a prime cause in the collapse of that greatest constructive achievement of ancient times. Condorcet insisted that his contemporaries look beyond the Christian centuries for the origins of their age's mental climate and identified ancient Greece as the true fount of wisdom for modern man. Looking even further afield, Montesquieu in his *Persian Letters* used imaginary accounts of a very different culture to criticize European prejudices.[10] And Voltaire sought to de-Christianize world history by beginning his essay on European history with the ancient Eastern civilizations—China, India, and Persia—which had reached their heights centuries before Christ, when the Jews were still primitive nomads.[11]

Voltaire (1694–1778) is one writer whose work demands closer inspection, if only because his reputation has made him an archetypal symbol of the Enlightenment. Born François Marie Arouet and educated for a time by Jesuits, he became a strong promoter of Deism and an enemy of every form of Christianity—a stance immortalized in his famous slogan *Ecrasez l'infâme.* His reputation, it has to be said, was based not on any profound originality or depth of thought but on a brilliant literary style which remains immensely attractive in comparison with some of the more sober and reliable literary products of his age. As a historian, however, Voltaire was more than a superb stylist. He undertook a genuinely comprehensive history of society and strove to ground his observations in genuine evidence. Far more than a chronicler or a polemicist, he selected evidence carefully, and his analyses of past ages and the history of other cultures to understand better his own society reveal a highly sophisticated mind at work.

Voltaire's *Essai sur les moeurs* (1756), although replete with information about Eastern and Islamic civilization, is focused on European history from Charlemagne to Louis XIII, and a good deal of his factual material comes from Bossuet. At the same time, the work is notable for its avoidance of narrow political chronicling and its preference for a broad view of human society. The sixteenth century, for example, is set firmly in the context of the expansion of Europe's horizons, both physically and intellectually, the discoveries in the New World, the effects of Islamic civilization on Europe both through the Moors in Spain and more recently through the Turks. Although figures of heroic stature—Charles V, Francis I, Henry VIII, and Leo X—strut across Voltaire's stage in a *grand spectacle,* they are far from dominating the drama.[12] Especially interesting, for example, is a short chapter on the sixteenth century in which the author leaves aside the great personalities to speak of the religious crisis in Germany and concurrently in the Islamic world—all this when European horizons were being expanded, industry and the economy flourishing, and artistic and intellectual life in full flower.[13]

A central figure in his account is Leo X, whose election signified to Voltaire a veritable Roman rebirth, a recovery from the excesses of the pontificate of Alexander VI, and the promise of a new age of cultural richness. Leo is portrayed as a man at home in the world of high culture, and the papacy is hailed as a civilizing force in European society. Although there is no hint of irony in this description, Voltaire is clearly aware of the negative impact of the papal court's opulence on the Church at large, and of abuses which brought the Church and its leaders into question.[14] But nowhere does he indicate that he sees these problems as grave and fundamental. Rather, he portrays the higher clergy as legitimately enjoying their temporal status and wealth, while the general public remained in a state of happy ignorance.

It is precisely here that the serious limitations of Voltaire's perspective become clear. If his strength lay in the breadth of his view of human society and culture, his weakness was his total inability to recognize the spiritual dimensions of the Reformation conflict, either in the crisis of the Catholic Church or in the Reformers' response. He can, for example, perceive no spiritual issue in the indulgences dispute, simply an economic conflict between Dominicans and Augustinians, a petty "monk's squabble" which "produced more than a hundred years of discord, fury and misfortune for thirty nations."[15] And if he notes in passing that all heresies have had their basis in theological disputes, this is in no way to grapple with the issues at stake, but only to scoff them out of court for their stupidity and irrelevance.[16]

Even when he discusses intellectual points, Voltaire lacks any sense of their spiritual ramifications. Proud of his own intellectual capabilities, and convinced of reason's ability to unravel every problem, he shows no interest in looking beyond arguments over dogma and protests against corruption. This inadequacy was perhaps less one of ability than one of motivation. Voltaire simply did not bother to become conversant with the basic Reformation texts or to grasp the essence of Luther's biblical theology, where he might well have found a more "reasonable" alternative to dogma and superstition.

There is, at the same time, in Voltaire more than a hint of the elitist's scorn for the unlearned who dare to debate with their betters on issues essentially beyond their comprehension; this aspect of his stance lends a highly equivocal character to many of his judgments. He applauds the questioning of dogma, yet is clearly dubious about challenging established authority. He approves of the Bible's greater accessibility, but shows contempt for the pretensions of the unlearned to interpret it. Moreover, although he identifies Erasmus's skepticism and irony as more damaging to the Church than Luther's assault, Voltaire saves his greatest derision for Luther's attack on the papacy and interprets it as a triumph of rude barbarism over Roman civility.[17] This elitism, moreover, has overtly political dimensions, and Voltaire's general observation that requests for change and statements of grievances ultimately overturn the throne is an especially poignant statement from a Frenchman of the ancien régime.[18]

Voltaire treats in some detail the Reformation's progress beyond Germany, dealing in turn with Zwingli, Scandinavia, the Anabaptists, Calvinism, England, and Scotland. All are seen as a widening of the conflagration ignited by Luther, although Voltaire clearly believes that the Anabaptists rather than the Lutherans were chiefly responsible for the disasters which overtook Germany.[19] In this recounting of the Reformation's spread, the figure of Luther pales beside the vast social and political turmoil he ushered in. It becomes increasingly clear that, despite the importance of Luther's protest, it was in the end only a catalyst for much larger historical forces, by whose results the Reformation has ultimately to be judged. In Voltaire's mind, although he was no friend of the Roman Church, the unleashing of religious war and civil strife was clearly too high a price for the marginal improvements the Catholic Church undertook in response to the Protestant movement.[20]

Voltaire's judgments on the Reformation are, in the end, more memorable for witty aphorisms and bons mots than for any sustained historical argument. By contrast, his fellow countryman Condorcet (1743–1794), born fifty years later, a disciple of Voltaire and a devotee of constitutional and educational reform, was before all else a philosopher of history. He articulated more clearly than any other writer the doctrine of progress which has become so closely associated with Enlightenment attitudes.

Although his first major writing on the Reformation, *Receuil des pièces sur l'état des Protestants en France* (1781), was essentially practical and contemporary, dealing with Protestantism in France and state policy toward it, Condorcet used the occasion to make some general observations about the Reformation.[21] He clearly shared his contemporaries' almost universal contempt for that persistent feature of Christian history—religious persecution—and accordingly condemns the brutality and inhumanity with which the French state pursued the impossible goal of religious conformity. There was, however, no question of his accepting Protestant views. "We do not suggest that the dogmas of the Reformed religion should be accepted but that the oppression of those who profess them should cease."[22] He could perceive no fundamental difference between the Protestants and their Catholic opponents, neither of whom could stand comparison with the ancient Greeks.

The final section of the *Receuil* discusses the Reformation itself in some detail. Condorcet indicates no more interest than Voltaire did in dogmatic issues. The causes of the Reformation are clearly identified as papal and priestly ambition, which drowned Europe in blood. Papal power, wealth, intolerance, pride, and corruption came to disgust all manner of men, from nobles in their castles to peasants in the fields, first in Germany, but soon after in France, which had always nourished a tradition of independence from Rome.[23]

The more ambitious dimensions of Condorcet's historical thought were revealed in his *Esquisse d'un tableau historique des progrès de l'esprit humain*, written shortly before his condemnation and suicide in 1794.[24] Here, as the title hints, his theme is mankind's general progress toward perfection, in which superstition and corruption are vanquished by the steady advance of reason. But this philosophy of history is also a work of psychology. The author explores the effects of sensations on the inner man, who is born with certain faculties which are then acted on by external forces, compelling him to enlarge his vision of the world.

Although it has some superficial similarities to Marx's historical dialectic, Condorcet's thought is fundamentally idealist, even mystical. In his eyes the stuff of history is not class conflict but a clash of ideas. History falls into ten epochs, in the last of which (the millennium?) men are destined to become perfect under the rule of reason, while tyranny, oppression, slavery, poverty, disease, famine, and ignorance cease. It follows that for Condorcet, past history is to be understood as the gradual advance of reason, despite many setbacks, the slow victory of enlightened philosophers over priestly apostles of darkness and ignorance.

Technological advances represent major milestones along the way toward man's ultimate goal. Accordingly, Condorcet's eighth period of history commences with the invention of printing and is associated with the geographic discoveries which opened up a world of new possibilities to sixteenth-century man. For Condorcet, printing was the handmaid of reason, the means by which humanity's forward march might be quickened; it held out the promise that tyrants and priests could no longer stifle philosophers' criticism.[25] But this revolution had not lived up to its potential, and the papal tyranny had continued in force until Luther rose to denounce it.

Luther therefore performed a crucial historical function. He "taught an astonished people that those revolting institutions were certainly not Christianity, but in fact depravity and infamy, that in order to be faithful to the religion of Jesus Christ they must renounce that of the priests."[26] Through printed books Luther's teachings were quickly made accessible to all Europe, which became involved in a profound debate on the basics of Christianity.

Luther's reform, moreover, would have spread even more widely "had not the false statecraft of certain princes raised anew that same priestly sceptre which had so often pressed down on the heads of kings"[27]—

a reference to French and imperial support for the papacy. Condorcet believed that the original raison d'être of the Reformation had been forgotten as its doctrines became enmeshed with the political ambitions of the secular rulers. He shows a penetrating understanding of the political motives behind various rulers' attitudes toward the religious schism: Francis I's balancing act, crushing the Protestants at home and supporting their leaders in Germany; Charles V's desire for victory against the princes, which would destroy their independent power; Henry VIII's embracing of his own brand of reform simultaneous with his continuing suppression of Protestants; Edward's and Elizabeth's need to oppose Rome for political reasons; the Scandinavian monarchs' adoption of Lutheranism to exclude Catholic autocracy.[28] Further, rulers soon realized how easily attacks on legitimate religious authority could lead to questioning of secular authority. But missing from this account is any recognition that kings might entertain genuine religious sympathies—that Charles V might also have opposed the Protestants because of his devout Catholicism and desire to fulfill his imperial obligations, or that English monarchs might have had genuine Protestant sympathies. For Condorcet, reasons of state provided their sole motivations.

Toward the end Condorcet returns to the theme of intolerance and provides some intriguing observations on its long-term effects. Mutual persecution served the papacy well and proved essential to the survival of religion. Here, in the author's view, was the rock on which the Reformation ultimately foundered. Those in ecclesiastical and civil authority united to suppress that small minority which regarded religion as a man-made invention, and so provided them with more ammunition in their fight to have natural law recognized as the basis of human society. A number of truly enlightened men (those whom Condorcet saw as forerunners of his own school of thought) had optimistically embraced the principles of the Reformation and were revolted at their betrayal. There was no point in changing from the old faith only to find themselves under the same constraint, no point in simply reducing the number of absurdities they pretended to believe. So they remained true to the old religion, strengthening its authority by their renown. The philosophers, therefore, were obliged to keep their own counsel, and their healthy influence was denied to society as a whole.[29]

Condorcet concludes that the Reformation did not contribute to freedom of thought, at least not directly. Each religious group forbade particular opinions in areas under its control, yet a certain freedom arose almost by accident from the very variety of opinions prevailing in different parts of Europe. The Reformers did not want to give free rein to reason, yet they found it convenient "to make her prison less confined: the chain was not broken but became longer and less weighty."[30] Liberty flourished best where one faith had been unable to triumph totally, although that liberty was not extended to atheists and Deists. It was, therefore, no more than intolerance tempered by raison d'état, and this caused thoughtful men to take up seriously the issue of liberty and the rights of man.

The sixteenth century thus seems an authoritarian age which produced some movement toward freedom of thought, but more by accident than design. In destroying confession, indulgences, religious orders, and priestly celibacy, it diminished moral corruption: here Condorcet had in mind the sexual offenses of celibate clergy, a frequent target of Protestants and anticlericals alike. But against this moral belief had to be set the horrors of religious warfare. "Hypocrisy covered Europe with butchers and assassins. The monster of fanaticism, irritated by these wounds, seemed to redouble his efforts in ferocity and the desire to heap up more victims."[31] On the whole, Condorcet saw no direct advantage for humanity and no progress for the human spirit in its own terms. Perverted from the start by political considerations, the Reformation soon came to represent an intolerance as bad as that of Rome, an oppression just as strict; but at least the winter of scholasticism and orthodoxy had ended forever, and people could hold different religious beliefs. More significant, some men had been enabled to see through the whole sham of religion and understand that mankind's best future lay in a total repudiation of its teachings. Momentous forces had been unleashed.

It was characteristic of the philosophes to unite a strong sense of their originality with an ardent quest for intellectual ancestry, in both the recent and the remote past. This duality was particularly embodied in Denis Diderot (1713–1784), whom Peter Gay has aptly characterized as "a partisan of empiricism and scientific method, a skeptic, a tireless experimenter and innovator . . . possessed by the restlessness of modern man," but at the same time a man for whom identification with the ancients was a "sustained fantasy."[32] Born in Champagne and educated at the Sorbonne, Diderot was a versatile and prolific writer on philosophy, science, religion, education, and literature. Though a confidant of rulers, he was an avowed atheist and not averse to attempting to shock his readers. His *Pensées philosophiques* (1746) set out to deny the validity of revealed religion and was duly condemned by the Parlement of Paris. Another work, *Lettre sur les aveugles,* led to his imprisonment; and a psychological novel, *La Religieuse*—which ruthlessly exposed convent life as revolving around sadism and lesbianism—avoided further trouble only because its publication was delayed until after the author's death.[33]

Diderot's major contribution to Enlightenment thought came through his editorship of the famous *Encyclopédie,* a product of several hands representing a conspectus of philosophers' attitudes concerning the issues it covered. The reactions of the European Establishment varied. The first volume's appearance in 1751 resulted in Diderot's election to the Berlin Academy, but in France it ran into difficulties; some volumes were banned, and in 1759 the entire work was suppressed as clerics attempted to stem its influence. Such tactics, however, only drove it underground, and the work continued without serious interruption.

It is difficult to assess how much of the *Encyclopédie* can be attributed to Diderot; although his name appears under many articles on a wide variety of subjects, much of their content was clearly plagiarized. Whole pages from works such as Bayle's *Dictionary* (see Chapter 5) and Johann Jakob Brucker's *Critical History of Philosophy* appear in the *Encyclopédie* under Diderot's name, although at times he took issue with his borrowed material.[34] A further difficulty in assessing how closely the articles reflect their authors' views lies in the fact that much of the content is basic information and definition rather than opinion. However, our concern here is not so much with Diderot himself as with the *Encyclopédie* and its perspective on the Reformation.

Given Diderot's reputation as a radical skeptic and atheist, relevant *Encyclopédie* articles are at times surprisingly bland and traditional. The one on religion is mostly confined to objective description and definition, although the role of superstition in revealed religion is noted in passing.[35] The article on Christianity favorably compares it with various earlier philosophical sects and views it as the only revealed religion which could be considered worth embracing.[36] Founded on the ruins of idolatry, Christianity reestablished the rule of natural law and revealed to mankind a moral system based on that law. In comparison with the cruelties and uncertainties of ancient paganism, it was essentially conservative of social custom, and this made it, of all religions, the most desirable.[37]

This observation is quite astonishing in view of Diderot's known attitudes to Christianity. There are just as many surprises in the article on the Reformation, a prudent, even timid survey which at times conveys the impression that it might have been written by Bossuet; indeed, the good bishop's name appears as a reference more than once.[38] Nowhere is the Reformation identified as a step from superstition toward more rational belief, and therefore a step forward for humanity. In fact, the whole issue is presented very much from the viewpoint of the Catholic Church. "Reformation" is defined first as something belonging solely to the Church, and only secondarily as "the name which the so-called Reformers or Protestants give to the novelties which they have introduced into religion and the pretext with which they dress up their separation from the Roman Church."

As Diderot saw it, the Reformation was begun by Frederick the Wise at Luther's behest and spread rapidly, not least because of Henry VIII's illicit passion for Anne Boleyn. Having listed the most notable Reformers, Diderot analyzes the movement through a series of rhetorical questions. "What abuses," he asks, "have they claimed to correct? Faith in the real presence, transubstantiation, the merit of good works, prayer for the dead, fasting, monastic vows, priestly celibacy, and so forth. But it is only necessary to open a history of the Church to realise that all these things were believed or practised from earliest antiquity."[39] From such a perspective, to change is not to reform but to destroy. Furthermore, the author cites as a basic weakness of Protestantism that freedom of thought and individual interpretation which others had identified as a positive legacy to the Enlightenment. Here, free interpretation of the Bible is seen to lead to a multiplicity of sects based on the arrogance of ignorant men with no legitimate authority to judge matters of faith. It could be Bossuet speaking.

It is hardly surprising, then, that the *Encyclopédie* provides an unattractive view of Luther. Described as a "violent and passionate man and also excessively vain and full of himself," Luther is also said to have seduced and debauched an ex-nun before marrying her.[40] This approach does not, however, prevent Diderot from giving a relatively unbiased account of Luther's early career or recognizing that of all Protestants, the Lutherans were least removed from the Catholic Church. The indulgences dispute is once again presented in terms of monkish rivalries, and there is virtually no attempt to explain the Reformation's detailed progress apart from the observation that Luther led all Germany toward his own views, and a list of regions and cities which accepted the Reformation. Luther himself is seen as a divisive figure, playing on the thirst for novelties, the progenitor of a movement which caused great trouble for France. His theological views, especially his denial of human free will and its consequences, identify him as an obscurantist.

The article on Calvinism is understandably concerned primarily with the rise of the Calvinist party in France and its threat to both Church and State.[41] Tolerated after the Wars of Religion, the Calvinists had deliberately stirred up trouble under Louis XIII, which had led to their expulsion by his successor. Again, Protestantism is identified as a divisive and anarchic influence, while the right of the French State to suppress it is staunchly defended.

The *Encyclopédie* throughout takes a stance on behalf of Catholicity, which is understood as the quality of universality in time and place that separates the Roman Catholic Church from the sects which have grown up since the "so-called Reformation." That Church authenticates itself by still comprehending more people and lands than all the other churches together. Its comparative respect for Catholicism and intolerance toward Protestantism remain striking features of the *Encyclopédie* in view of Diderot's broader conception of Christianity as a savage, persecuting faith. It is astonishing that no intellectual parallels are discerned between the Reformers and the eighteenth-century philosophes. Did fear of suppression or commercial disaster inhibit the editors of this expensive and ambitious work?

To move from eighteenth-century France to Germany is to enter a world in which new influences had to come to terms with a continuing legacy from the Lutheran Reformation.[42] There was no uniformity, however, in how this tension between old and new found its resolution. Although orthodoxy had been under sustained attack from the Pietists, it had by no means been vanquished. Scholars like Valentin Ernst Löscher (1673–1749) defiantly rejected the spirit of the age to maintain, in the tradition of Flacius Illyricus and Johann Gerhard, that Luther's doctrine was unequivocally identifiable with Christian truth and was therefore the sole criterion for judging history. [43]

An altogether different spirit is evident in the writings of Johann Georg Walch (1693–1775), the author of works on the theological controversies in the Lutheran Church since the Reformation, but better known as the editor of a major compilation of Luther's writings, to which he attached a substantial biographical sketch.[44] A convinced although not strictly orthodox Lutheran, influenced by Pietism but not totally identifiable with it, Walch was an exponent of the so-called pragmatic history.[45] This approach eschewed overt theologizing of history in the style of Bossuet's *Histoire universelle*[46] in favor of a more "objective" concern for setting facts in order, understanding origins, explaining past events and their links with the present, and drawing beneficial lessons for contemporaries and posterity.

In a man of Walch's religious convictions, such an outlook was entirely consonant with a providential understanding of history, and his biography of Luther abounds with acknowledgments of the operations of divine Providence.[47] On the other hand, he avoids the apocalyptic and supernatural interpretation of Luther characteristic of orthodoxy, identifying his subject as a man possessed of ordinary gifts—albeit in rich abundance—a great orator, a courageous opponent of tyranny, but nevertheless human. The movement Luther led, although recognizable with hindsight as the working out of a wise Providence, was to be understood in natural terms against the background of centuries of preparation by earlier reformers, together with the revival of learning and the invention of printing. In Walch's account, the essence of the Reformation was not the doctrine of justification by faith, but elimination of Roman tyranny, and high among the benefits of its success was the advancement of princely authority over religion. Walch betrays no consciousness of how far this political result was from Luther's intentions: he welcomes it unreservedly as the basis of a fruitful union in which the faith validates itself through its civic utility.[48]

Some of the tendencies which appeared in Walch were given a much clearer statement in the work of the Halle theologian Johann Salomo Semler (1725–1791), best known as the father of modern historical biblical criticism. Semler devoted considerable attention to evaluating the Reformation inheritance, and like Walch he portrayed the Reformation as the end result of a century or more of preparation, stressing both the low state of the papacy and the beneficial effects of education and printing.[49] He also bypassed the central theological issue of justification altogether, concentrating on the papacy's despotism and moral corruption and interpreting Luther's role as a leader of the new forces against tyranny, rather than an articulator of true doctrine. Viewed as an intellectual event, the essential achievement of the Reformation was proclaiming every man's freedom to think for himself. Thus, the "variations" which Bossuet had regarded as a damning indictment of Protestantism, Semler welcomed as evidence of its positive, enduring achievement for both outward and inward freedom.[50]

Semler's stress on inwardness and liberation from dogma shows how deeply the emphases of Pietism had influenced the early Enlightenment in Germany. But his critique of dogma went further, and his emphasis on freedom of conscience placed virtually no limits on individual subjectivity and relativism in religious thought. Luther's doctrinal formulations were to be understood as his private views—his exercise of freedom—but certainly not to be imposed on others. Indeed, part of Luther's legacy was precisely the freedom to dissent from his formulation of doctrine, and, in the absence of the bonds of uniform doctrine, the focus of Lutheran self-consciousness shifted to the Church, which was understood to be held together externally by the civic community and internally by a common religious purpose of genuine inwardness rather than mere outward conformity.[51]

The later years of the eighteenth century were to see these various tendencies working themselves out in even more extreme ways. Gotthold

Ephraim Lessing (1729–1781) showed how a genuine enthusiasm for Luther's person could be combined, by appeal to the spirit instead of to the letter, with a religious understanding utterly remote from the Reformer's own: a deistic or even pantheistic faith verging on disbelief, a perspective in which faith in human improvement had commandeered the ground of faith in salvation.[52] Johann Gottfried von Herder (1744–1803) followed a similar line of thought and added to the picture of Luther as herald of the Enlightenment and individual freedom the vision of a German hero who "roused a whole nation to think and feel."[53] Others—the most significant example being the Osnabrück historian and civic secretary Justus Möser (1720–1794), who wrote the famous letter to Voltaire—stressed the civic and political aspects of the Lutheran inheritance, closely identifying it with social and moral unity and radically separating it from personal belief, which remained a matter of private conscience.[54]

Few of the men of letters who dominated eighteenth-century German intellectual life were primarily historians, although most of them held decided historical opinions, which they were not reluctant to express. From among those German Lutherans who were primarily historians, the most comprehensive historical account of the Reformation was the *Ecclesiastical Institutes* (1737–1741) of Johann Lorenz von Mosheim (1693–1755), chancellor of the University of Göttingen.[55] In the third volume of this work, which is wholly devoted to the Reformation and its fifteenth-century antecedents, Mosheim sets the scene with the usual references to the expansive possibilities of the great discoveries and the invention of printing, but he proceeds swiftly to a more negative stance.[56] Few historians have painted such a black picture of the pre-Reformation Church, notable for the vicious propensities of the popes, the luxurious and jovial lives of priests and monks, the ignorance of scholastic philosophers who resisted the new learning, and the gross superstitions of popular religion. Mosheim stresses the sound basis of these judgments, claiming that his picture of the monastic orders as containing "herds of ignorant, lazy, dishonest and debauched people" is "evinced by numerous documents and the testimony of all the best historians" and that this low esteem of the Latin religion is "a fact so well attested that even those who have the strongest inclination dare not deny it."[57]

Line by line, Mosheim draws a picture of decay, corrupt arrogance, and indolent acceptance of the status quo barely concealing the continuing ferment of incipient revolt. Yet, despite all this—as well as the assaults of the Waldensians, the Wycliffites, and the Hussites and the positive influence of movements like the Brethren of the Common Life—

Mosheim sees the early-sixteenth-century papacy as confidently ignoring the clamor for reform, apparently secure in the strength derived from its careful preservation of the notion of supreme papal power in matters of religion. As long as the pope was considered the vice-regent of Christ, he was safe enough, but once the foundations of his authority were seriously questioned, he stood to lose all his powers.

Mosheim makes much of the character of particular popes: Alexander VI, a "monster of a man"; Julius II, arrogant, vain, and warlike, pope by fraud and bribery; and Leo X, a man "of a milder disposition, but no better guardian of religion and piety," learned but no administrator, more concerned with his own comforts than with the well-being of his flock. What all popes had in common was "an insatiable thirst for money"; they robbed the faithful to finance their own pleasures. Among their chief artifices of deceit were the indulgences, which were sold by men of base and profligate character.[58]

Although Mosheim refers in passing to disputed points of doctrine, his overwhelming concentration on the deep corruption of the Roman system virtually dictates a presentation of Luther in terms other than doctrine. There is little reference to Luther's piety and none to his deep spiritual anguish. Rather, the Reformation is presented as an onslaught on the corrupt ecclesiastical system which Mosheim has so graphically detailed. He does recognize that the Church's evils could not be overcome "without first extirpating various absurd and impious opinions which gave birth to these evils,"[59] but, characteristically, he treats the doctrinal issues as instrumental for the desired church reform rather than as matters of concern in their own right.

At stake in the Reformation, according to Mosheim, was not doctrine but the tyrannical Romish authority. Given that emphasis, a dominant role is accorded to the "little obscure monk [who] . . . with astonishing intrepidity opposed himself alone to the whole Romish power." Mosheim's portrait is a heroic one: "That Luther was possessed of extraordinary talents, uncommon genius, a copious memory, astonishing industry and perseverance, superior eloquence, a greatness of soul that rose above all human weaknesses and consummate erudition for the age in which he lived, even those among his enemies who possess some candour, do not deny." The defects Mosheim acknowledges in his hero are considered intelligible in the context of the time and religion in which he was trained.[60] When Mosheim deals with the Reformation's early progress—from the indulgences affair and various interviews with representatives of Rome to the Diet of Worms—there is again no recognition of Luther's emotional and spiritual turmoil, and consequently no hint of Seckendorff's understanding that Luther's trials resembled those of a vast number of other men in the early sixteenth century.

Mosheim sees two major threats to the progress of Luther's reform: the controversy with "the discerning and erudite Ulrich Zwingli" concerning the Real Presence, and the Peasants' War. He clearly thinks highly of Zwingli and is aware of his distinctive emphases, even of his claim to have "discovered some points of the truth before Luther openly contended with the pontiff."[61] The Peasants' War he sees as a "sudden tornado" brought about by "an innumerable multitude of seditious and delirious fanatics," which began as a civil affair but under Münzer's influence developed into a religious struggle. Mosheim acknowledges the influence of Luther's doctrine of Christian liberty but absolves the Reformer of any blame for the obvious misunderstanding of his views.[62]

It is entirely consistent with his slight concern for theological issues and his concentration on ecclesiastical power that Mosheim's interpretation of the Reformation becomes ultimately political. The role of Frederick the Wise is clearly recognized, and even more those of his successors, among whom John Frederick might be considered "the second parent and founder of the Lutheran church."[63] The Augsburg Confession is seen less as a theological declaration than a political document presenting a case to the emperor. And Mosheim's detailed treatment of key political turning points—Speyer, Augsburg, Nuremberg—contrasts with the paucity of his references to Luther's writings and their spiritual impact. For Mosheim, the Reformation was essentially a series of political events leading to the establishment of a state Church, and Luther was instrumental to that end. Although he was a convinced Lutheran, Mosheim in this work presents a Luther almost totally divorced from the great theological issues with which he was concerned—justification and the bondage of the will. In so restricting his awareness of Luther, Mosheim trivialized and diminished the true power of the Reformer's revolution against Rome. Extraordinary as this may seem from the standpoint of current scholarship on the Reformation, it was typical of an age that was peculiarly blind to the fundamental theological concerns which activated the Reformers.

This feature of Mosheim's history represents an unfortunate narrowing of perspective, but from another point of view his work is highly comprehensive, tracing in considerable detail the history of all major groups—from the Roman and Greek churches to the Anabaptists and Socinians—and his judgments are on the whole reasonable and fair-minded. His view of Melanchthon as a man of great personal gifts held back by a timidity of spirit is close to more modern assessments.[64] The usual conventional condemnation of the Anabaptists does not prevent Mosheim from acknowledging Menno Simons as "a man of integrity, mild, accommodating, laborious, patient of injuries and so ardent in his piety as to exemplify in his own life the precepts which he gave to others."[65]

Similar moderation marks Mosheim's judgment of Rome; he denies that the Roman religion has been altogether corrected since Trent, but he is willing to acknowledge elements of improvement, and, although he underestimates Loyola, he does not deny the greatness of Francis Xavier.[66] He has nothing good to say of Henry VIII and dates the real commencement of the Reformation in England from 1547, thereby ignoring Tyndale and the other early English reformers.[67]

Mosheim cannot, however, be judged totally uncritical about the Reformation. The Reformers, in his view, evaded many important issues and resorted at times to their opponents' coarse and ferocious manners, yet these faults appear slighter when estimated by the customs of the times and their opponents' cruelty.[68] In his mind, despite all its defects, the Reformation was the greatest of all events affecting the Christian world since its foundation; and in contributing to better knowledge of doctrine and duty, it deserves an honored place with the Enlightenment as one of the great forward movements in human history.

Mosheim's work first appeared in English in 1764 and became a major sourcebook on church history for English historians, including Edward Gibbon (1737–1794), who recommended it to his readers, although he observed that when Mosheim dealt with the Reformation, "the balance which he has held with so clear an eye and so steady a hand, begins to incline in favour of his Lutheran brethren."[69] That Gibbon's own treatment of the Reformation is confined to about six pages should occasion no surprise.[70] His purpose was not to write a history of Europe but to chronicle and explain the slow decline of Rome, and, because his narrative concludes in the fifteenth century, the surprise is that the Reformation appears at all. It does so in Gibbon's discussion of the seventh-century Paulicians—one of the recurring manifestations of the ancient Manichean heresy—and Gibbon's clear intention is to place the Reformers, along with the Cathars of the eleventh and twelfth centuries, in this tradition. This detachment of the Reformation from its natural historical setting makes it difficult to assess Gibbon's understanding of its significance in European history. On the other hand, he was one of few historians of his age prepared to take doctrine seriously in forming his judgment of the Reformation, and for that reason alone his views are worth exploring.

Gibbon suggests that the Paulician heresy derived its coherent features and its name from the writings of Saint Paul. He catalogs the Paulician rejection of relics, the veneration of Mary, mediation of the saints, and much of the ecclesiastical hierarchy, together with the identification of the words of the Gospel as the "baptism and communion of the faithful."[71] All these features could be readily associated with Protestantism. Furthermore, Gibbon attributes the success of the eleventh- and twelfth-century heretics in France and Italy to "the strong, though secret, discontent which armed the most pious Christians against the Church of Rome," her oppressive avarice and odious despotism, her scandalous innovations, her corrupt clergy—all factors traditionally used to account for the Reformation's success.

After the thoroughgoing extirpation of these heretical movements, "the invincible spirit which they had kindled still lived and breathed in the Western world," and subsequent disciples of Saint Paul "protested against the tyranny of Rome, embraced the Bible and the rule of faith and purified their creed from all the visions of the Gnostic theology."[72] Gibbon includes in this "latent succession" the "premature" reforms of Wycliffe and Huss, as well as those of Zwingli, Luther, and Calvin. At no time does Gibbon betray any uncertainty about his identification of the Reformers as heirs of the Manichees, or any recognition that, despite some superficial similarities with earlier movements of protest and reform, the Reformers could not have been clearer in their rejection of fundamental Manichean dualist tenets. Had Gibbon known more about the Reformers and their theology, he might have apprehended that their denial of transubstantiation had nothing to do with the Paulician rejection of the physical reality of Christ's body. Moreover, although he recognizes later the Reformers' wholehearted embrace of the Hebrew Scriptures, this does not lead him to question their alleged Manichean-Paulician connections.[73] His grand scheme of a persistent Manichean tradition remains undisturbed by the disclosure of uncomfortable facts.

More interesting is Gibbon's evaluation of the sixteenth-century reform from the standpoint of reason, which is the primary topic of his brief direct exposition. His conclusion is not unexpected: that "we shall rather be surprised by the timidity than scandalised by the freedom, of our first Reformers." He notes their adoption of all the Hebrew Scriptures and their orthodoxy concerning the Trinity and the Incarnation. Gibbon attributes some of the Reformers' initial conservatism on the Eucharist to a failure to consult the evidence of their senses, although he alleges that Zwingli's view has gradually come to prevail. However, "the loss of one mystery was amply compensated by the stupendous doctrines of original sin, redemption, faith, grace and predestination, which have been strained from the epistles of St Paul," and although other thinkers had prepared for those doctrines, the Reformers enforced them "as the absolute and essential terms of salvation."[74]

Gibbon is unusual among his contemporaries in considering these theological issues central to the Reformation, but he counts them as points against the movement. Unlike the Paulicians, the Reformers did nothing to free Christianity of belief; they merely exchanged one burden for another. And Gibbon wryly observes that "many a sober Christian would rather admit that a wafer is God than that God is a cruel and capricious tyrant."

On the other hand, Gibbon does acknowledge a philosopher's debt to those "fearless enthusiasts" the Reformers, because they demolished superstition and broke the chains of authority. They restored former monks and nuns to a useful social life and brought a purer form of worship, although Gibbon has his doubts about its consistency with the needs of popular devotion. The Reformers advanced individual freedom of conscience; however, this must be considered "the consequence rather than the design of the Reformation," because the Reformers were as tyrannical as those they replaced and imposed their creeds and confessions with equal rigor, punishing heresy by death. "The pious or personal animosity of Calvin proscribed in Servetus the guilt of his own rebellion: and the flames of Smithfield, in which he was afterwards consumed, had been kindled for the Anabaptists by the zeal of Cranmer."[75]

But "if the nature of the tyger was the same . . . he was gradually deprived of his teeth and fangs." The Reformation in Gibbon's opinion achieved a result other than it intended because the Reformers' appeal to private judgment was accepted well beyond their wishes.[76] A "secret Reformation"—in which Gibbon discerns the influence of Erasmian views—diffused a spirit of freedom and moderation which advanced liberty and toleration, bringing the Protestantism he observed to a condition far removed from its origins: "The volumes of controversy are overspread with cobwebs: the doctrine of a protestant church is far removed from the knowledge or belief of its private members; and the forms of orthodoxy, the articles of faith, are subscribed with a sigh or a smile by the modern clergy. Yet the friends of Christianity are alarmed at the boundless impulse of enquiry and scepticism . . . and the pillars of revelation are shaken by those men who preserve the name without the substance of religion, who indulge the licence without the temper of philosophy."[77]

Gibbon was one of a number of British historians designated in their day as "philosophical historians" because their style of historical writing was opposed on the one hand to antiquarianism—the indiscriminate accumulation of historical fact and detail[78]—and on the other to party history of a political or ecclesiastical kind. In its desire to be impartial and instruct in a practical way, "philosophical history" embraced concerns not unlike those of the German "pragmatic" historians and of Bodin, La Popelinière, and Camden. It is easier to see what this concept brought to interpretation of the Reformation if we turn to two of Gibbon's Scottish contemporaries, Hume and Robertson—one an archskeptic, the other a Presbyterian churchman—both of whom provided more direct and substantial accounts of the Reformation.[79]

David Hume (1711–1776) was first and foremost a philosopher—perhaps the greatest British philosopher—and his observations on the Reformation can only be understood in the context of his philosophical outlook, particularly of his fundamental hostility to religion. His views on religion are best described as radically skeptical. Indeed, Hume's unwillingness to accept the atheistic outlook of d'Holbach and his circle was not because he found their views too skeptical but because they seemed not skeptical enough—they seemed to assume knowledge outside man's capacities.[80]

But although Hume retained a notion of "true religion," this appears on closer examination to be no more than an abstraction to set against the twin corruptions of "superstition" and "enthusiasm," which are in a broad sense identifiable respectively with Catholicism and Protestantism.[81] In a 1739–1740 essay on this subject, he developed at some length the contrast between the two false forms of religion, identifying superstition with priestly power and tyranny and enthusiasm with rejection of the ecclesiastical yoke and of any human mediation with the divine. He observed that enthusiastic religions are more violent in their beginnings but become more moderate and that "superstition is an enemy to civil liberty and enthusiasm a friend to it."[82]

These observations, particularly the last, might suggest Hume's decided preference for Protestantism over Catholicism, but the issue remains much more complex. Hume's major connected observations on the Reformation are in a "Digression concerning the ecclesiastical state," at the beginning of Chapter 29 of his *History of England* (1754–1762).[83] The digression occurs partway through his discussion of the reign of Henry VIII: having reached the point when Henry became embroiled in the religious quarrel, Hume finds it necessary to explain these disputes, and "to trace from their origins those abuses which so generally diffused the opinion that a reformation of the Church or ecclesiastical order was becoming highly expedient, if not absolutely necessary." At the same time, he declares his intention of looking beyond the actual controversy, to "take the matter a little higher, and reflect a moment on the reasons why there must be an ecclesiastical order and a public establishment of religion in every civilised community."[84]

Religion might be assumed a matter to be left to individuals, but Hume felt this would result only in anarchy, "because in every religion except the true it is highly pernicious, and it has even a natural tendency to pervert the true by infusing into it a strong mixture of superstition, folly and delusion. Each ghostly practitioner, in order to render himself more precious and sacred in the eyes of his retainers, will inspire them with the most violent abhorrence of all other sects and continually endeavour, by some novelty to excite the languid devotion of his audience." To avoid such a situation, the State should take responsibility for the Church's maintenance and upkeep—"and in this manner ecclesiastical establishments, though commonly they arose at first from religious views, prove in the end advantageous to the political interests of society."[85] Thus, although religion is in effect a confidence trick practiced by priests on gullible people, it is useful to temporal rulers in regulating society.

Hume is almost totally negative about the Church of Rome, which he considers to have been built on the worst of foundations and to act in a manner "hurtful to the peace and happiness of mankind," using its financial and economic power to guard itself against the intrusion of secular authority, hiding in its monasteries lazy and indolent men who might otherwise have been gainfully employed to the betterment of society, and always headed by a "foreign potentate." On the other hand, he allows that the Roman Church checked royal despotism and provided a degree of unity in Europe, together with artistic advances, even though all these were "small compensation for its inconveniences."[86]

In Hume's view, however, Rome's deficiencies were not alone responsible for the Reformation. Rather, a concurrence of incidents produced that "great revolution," and among these indulgences ranked high. Hume assumes that Leo X was totally cynical and fully aware of the falsity of the doctrine he was supposed to uphold, yet he evinces no sympathy for Lutheran opposition to the traffic in indulgences. As so many others had before him, Hume sets the issue in the context of intense rivalry between Augustinians and Dominicans over profits. Less expected is his judgment that the morality behind the Catholic practice of indulgences is superior to that of their opponents. Even after obtaining an indulgence, the sinner remained subject to civil punishment, public infamy, and inward remorse, "the great motives that operate on mankind," whereas the Protestant position amounted to replacing a partial indulgence with a general and unconditional one. Accordingly, indulgences were to be understood as "no more criminal than any other cheat of the church of Rome, or of any other church."[87]

In transforming an incident into a revolution, Luther's role was absolutely crucial, for he was "a man qualified to take advantage of the incident." He began by objecting to the slight against his order, but, "being naturally of a fiery temper and provoked by opposition," he pushed the matter and objected to indulgences themselves, until he finally came to question the authority of the pope. The process fed on itself, for as Luther read more widely and deeply, he discovered more abuses to attack, and as his attack broadened his followers increased until all Europe was listening to this "daring innovator." Hume perceives Luther to have been motivated above all by glory. A man "naturally inflexible, vehement, opinionative," he became "incapable, either from promise of advancement or terrors of severity, to relinquish a sect of which he himself was the founder, and which brought him a glory superior to all others, the glory of dictating the religious faith and principles of multitudes."[88]

Possibly by reference to certain passages in Foxe, Hume anticipates modern research in regarding Lollardy as fertile soil for Luther's ideas. Henry VIII's defense of the Roman Church against Luther is described as a "performance which does no discredit to his capacity"; Luther, in his reply, is depicted as reacting almost blindly to the stimulus of dissension. Nevertheless, Hume admits that Luther had the best of the argument, partly because he benefited from popular sympathy for the underdog, partly because of the great publicity, which spread his message more and more widely. In this, the invention of printing as well as the revival of learning played a vital role.[89]

Hume is adamant that the Reformation's success was in no way a result of reason and reflection, although well-supported historical facts were influential. Nevertheless, the Reformers in the end relied more on violent denunciations of the Roman Church as "abominable, detestable, damnable; foretold by sacred writ itself as the source of all wickedness and pollution"; and these methods had a far more telling effect on the masses. Hume sees the twofold stimulus of "contest and persecution" on the one hand and "success and applause" on the other as driving the situation beyond mere conflict within the Roman Church to the emergence of Protestantism as a new religion of a different character. In opposition to the "multiplied superstitions" with which Rome was burdened, the Protestants "adopted an enthusiastic strain of devotion which admitted of no observances, rites or ceremonies, but placed all merit in a mysterious species of faith, inward vision, rapture and ecstasy."[90]

Notwithstanding his earlier observation that enthusiasm was more of a friend to civil liberty than was superstition, Hume can find nothing positive to say about Protestantism's influence in the civil sphere. The

Lutherans supported civil authority against ecclesiastical power to gain protection, and the dissolution of the monasteries merely released into society those licentious monks and nuns who were tired of their vows and made their wealth available as "lawful spoil to the first invader." Although in Hume's view the Reformers had all the advantages of the quarrel, the Reformation's progress was assisted by the death of Leo X— whose sound judgment and moderation might have stemmed the tide— and by his successor, Adrian VI, playing into the Reformers' hands by acknowledging too readily the sins of Rome and forging a fateful alliance with the empire.[91]

At this point Hume ends his digression and returns to the more congenial topic of European politics. But he reverts to the subject of religious controversy in the following chapter while discussing the royal marriage. He is sympathetic with Henry and seems to accept without question the sincerity of his scruples about the marriage to Catherine of Aragon. This question, combined with long-standing opposition to Roman avarice and usurpation, "paved the way for the Lutheran tenets and reconciled the people in some measure to the frightful ideas of heresy and innovation." Hume sees the progress of the English Reformation in highly political terms and concentrates on the parliamentary debates, but he is not blind to the economic gains Henry stood to make from the dissolution of the monasteries, or to the influence of Henry's personality. The king is seen as impelled by circumstances into the break from Rome, although his impetuous and obstinate nature made it plain that "having proceeded so far in throwing off the papal yoke, he never could again have been brought tamely to bend his neck to it."[92]

Hume shows an unexpected interest in the common people's re-actions to the revolutionary change, and he is sensitive to their confusion, their wavering between the old and the new, their tendency to acquiesce blindly in innovations in doctrine and worship ordered by the State and in the disturbing and potentially destructive appeals to the open Bible and the right of private judgment.[93] But although he is interested in the people's response, at no point does he recognize popular religious initia-tive as an active force in the movement, which remains, in his view, the single-handed act of the king.

In the end Hume is far more generous in his judgment of the English Reformation than of its Continental counterpart, and he seems to regard the English movement as the nearest approach to "true religion."[94] Al-though in its course party zeal often triumphed over reason, it nevertheless resulted in "a greater simplicity in the government by uniting the spiritual with the civil power" and thereby prevented disputes between contending jurisdictions. Furthermore, it prepared the way "for checking the exorbitances of superstition, and breaking the shackles by which all human reason, policy and industry had so long been encumbered." Accordingly, "there followed from this revolution many beneficial consequences; though perhaps neither foreseen nor intended by the persons who had a chief hand in conducting it."[95]

Hume's assessment of the Reformation's very limited achievement in its own time is most poignantly illustrated in his description of Thomas More: "at once an object deserving our compassion and an instance of the usual progress of man's sentiments during that age." Here was a man whose "elegant genius and familiar acquaintance with the noble spirit of antiquity had given him very enlarged sentiments," who in his youth advanced principles far ahead of his time, yet who had been "so irritated by polemics and thrown into such superstitious attachment to the old faith that few inquisitors have been guilty of greater violence in the prosecution of heresy."[96] To Hume, the triumph of passion and violent attachment to doctrine over More's better instincts typified the age of the Reformation.

If Hume remained much less enthusiastic than most of his contemporaries about the progress of the Reformation, this was perhaps because he was less optimistic about the progress of human reason. In his *Treatise of Human Nature* (1739–1740), he had specifically sought to show the limited powers of reason in human actions, asserting that it was "the slave of the passions and can never pretend to any other office than to serve and obey them." His *Natural History of Religion* (1757) insisted that religion, faith, and the supernatural remained impenetrable mysteries.[97] Religion, in Hume's view, consisted of socially useful metaphysics detached from a world where true morality was discoverable by natural means. A more moral world implied for him a less religious one, and in a sense the Reformation, despite itself, had represented a move in this direction. Only in this very limited sense—and certainly not because of its aims—could the Reformation be acknowledged as "one of the greatest events in history."[98]

Hume's Scottish contemporary William Robertson (1721–1793), when not altogether neglected, has generally been regarded as puzzling. As an active and committed Presbyterian leader, he may seem oddly related to most other Enlightenment historians, although he was attached to Hume and greatly admired by Gibbon. But later church historians tended to regard his writings as unfriendly to the Reformation or at least insensitive to its theological dimensions.[99] Along with most of his contemporaries, he has been linked to the tradition of Montesquieu (1689–1755), which was especially influential in eighteenth-century Scotland.

Montesquieu's much read and reprinted work *The Spirit of Laws*—a pioneering essay in political science and sociology—had comparatively examined states and societies, seeking to show how objective conditions such as geography, climate, and size of population had shaped constitutions and customs.[100] His great contribution to the debate on religion and morality had been a relativist perspective, in which systems of morals were seen as the products of varying elements influencing the inhabitants of different lands; therefore, no one system could claim universal applicability.

Robertson clearly shared this fresh interest in the history, culture, and customs of distant countries, of which his *History of America* (1777) was to be a distinguished product.[101] This work entailed extensive archival research and interviews with officials in the colonial administration, and in the preface the author declares a commitment to "scrupulous accuracy" very much in the tradition of Sleidan.[102] When Robertson dealt with historical subjects closer to home, he expressed the same concern for accuracy and became particularly critical of religious historians who advanced partisan opinions and "wrote an apology for a faction rather than the history of their country."[103]

If we are to understand Robertson's account of the Reformation in the two major works in which he discussed it, however, we need to look further than the traditions of Montesquieu and Sleidan. We must also examine the peculiar character of the Scottish Enlightenment and the role of the Presbyterian Church in relation to its intellectual milieu. It has been convincingly demonstrated that the Scottish Enlightenment, although certainly influenced by contemporary French thought, had a highly distinctive character, much of which derived from the central role played by the Presbyterian Church.[104] Although Puritanism was increasingly out of favor, there was in Scotland no counterpart to the virulent anticlericalism which characterized the Enlightenment in France: indeed, most of the significant literary products of the age were by clerics, and Hume rather than Robertson is the exception in this context.

Robertson was for many years the leader and dominant intellectual influence of the Moderate party in the Church of Scotland, and, far from holding an attenuated rationalist version of Christian belief, he struggled for thirty years to reinvigorate the Church by appealing to its best and most "enlightened" historical traditions. How adequately in so doing he interpreted the Reformation tradition can only be assessed through a closer look at his works.

Robertson's *History of Scotland* (1759) may be regarded not only as the first reasonably objective account of the Scottish Reformation, but also as a truly international rather than parochial work set in the wider framework of Reformation Europe. The author's attention focuses first on Henry VIII's indecisive commitment to reform, which satisfied none of the contending parties in England.[105] In Scotland a new climate of controversy and questioning of long-held beliefs had emerged in the early sixteenth century, and the stage seemed set for the victory of truth. Even barbarous persecution did not stop the spread of new ideas there; indeed, "the discovery of one error opened the way to others; the downfall of one impostor drew many after it; the whole fabric, which ignorance and superstition had erected in times of darkness, began to totter; and nothing was wanting to complete its ruin but a daring and active leader to direct the attack."[106]

Robertson identifies a strong positive relationship between the Reformation and the revival of letters, thereby clearly aligning Protestant opinion with the Renaissance's new views of the world and mankind. The reawakening of learning had "roused the world from that lethargy in which it had sunk for many ages. The human mind felt its own strength, broke the fetters of authority by which it had been so long restrained and, venturing to move in a larger sphere, pushed its enquiries into every subject with great boldness and surprising success." Martin Luther had held aloft the standard of truth, yet his voice had scarcely been heard in southern Europe. It was "the fierce spirit of the north"—here we detect the influence of Montesquieu—which warmed to the new teachings most readily; Mediterranean Europeans were susceptible to "the deepest impressions of superstitious terror and credulity."[107]

Robertson saw his native land as the victim of an extremely bigoted and intolerant form of Catholicism, which required a man of Knox's heroic stature to overcome. His portrait of the Scottish Reformer is at once subtly critical and profoundly fair. Knox was zealous, intrepid, learned, and eloquent, but also severe, impetuous, and rigid, inclined to utter his admonitions "with an acrimony and vehemence more apt to irritate than to reclaim." Nevertheless, "those very qualities . . . which now render his character less amiable, fitted him to be the instrument of Providence for advancing the Reformation among a fierce people, and enabled him to face dangers and to surmount opposition, from which a person of a more gentle spirit would have been apt to shrink back."[108]

The *History of the Reign of the Emperor Charles V* (1769), as its name suggests, is essentially a comprehensive political history of which the Reformation forms only a part, albeit an important one. Greatly admired by Voltaire, it might well be judged the best work in the field until Ranke. Robertson, too, approaches the Reformation by depicting papal tyranny, claiming as his source the authentic memorials of the imperial diets. Against this background Luther's success may be readily understood: "To men thus prepared for shaking off the yoke, Luther addressed himself with certainty of success . . . Hence proceeded the fond and eager reception that his doctrines met with and the rapidity with which they spread over all the provinces of Germany. Even the impetuosity and fierceness of Luther's spirit, his confidence in asserting his own opinions, and the arrogance and contempt wherewith he treated all who differed from him . . . did not appear excessive to his contemporaries . . . who had themselves endured the rigours of papal tyranny."[109]

Luther is set in the context of a long line of reformers and would-be reformers—including Peter Waldo, Wycliffe, Huss—all of whom failed because their times had not been propitious. But Luther appeared "at the critical and mature juncture" when "circumstances of every kind concurred in rendering each step he took successful."[110] There had been the papal schism, the pontificates of Alexander VI and Julius II, lower down the hierarchy the many and varied abuses of position, the *gravamina* of the German nation—and, on the positive side, the invention of printing and the revival of learning through which mankind seemed to have "recovered the powers of inquiring and of thinking."[111]

Among the factors contributing to Luther's success was the activity of Erasmus; Robertson declares that "there was scarce any opinion or practice of the Roman Church which Luther endeavoured to reform, but what had previously been animadverted upon by Erasmus and had afforded him subject either of censure or of raillery." Erasmus stood with Luther in attacking scholasticism and turning attention to Scripture as the standard of religious truth—although he was finally prevented from following his course by natural timidity, deference for persons of high station, dread of losing financial support, and love of peace. Nevertheless, Erasmus scattered the seeds which Luther brought to maturity.[112]

Notwithstanding this contrast between the "timid" Erasmus and the bold and impetuous Luther, Robertson is keenly sensitive to the facts that Luther's opposition to Rome developed only gradually and that when he opposed Tetzel "he was far from intending that Reformation which he afterwards effected; and would have trembled with horror at the thought of what at last he gloried in accomplishing."[113] Occasional critical comments on Luther, however, do not significantly modify an overwhelmingly positive portrait. Many common traditional criticisms of the Reformer's style and manners are either excused by reference to the standards of the age or, by a subtle shift of wording or context, turned into compliments. Robertson is occasionally inclined to attribute unworthy motives to Luther's opponents where the evidence does not necessarily require such a view,[114] yet his description of improvements in the Roman Church since the Reformation is for its day a model of fairness.[115]

Given Robertson's demonstrable commitment to both Enlightenment ideals and institutional Christianity, the chief interest in his works finally lies in how they reconcile these impulses. We have already suggested that in Scotland there was no need to consider them necessarily contradictory. It remains to discuss to what extent, if at all, Robertson's "Enlightenment" ideals influenced his depiction of the Reformation. Clearly, he is unequivocal in his support of the Reformation, seeing it as a manifestation of the divine Providence which attended the beginnings of Christianity, although it was not accompanied by the same supernatural signs. Its achievement was to have "rescued one part of Europe from the papal yoke, mitigated its rigour in another, and produced a revolution in the sentiments of mankind, the greatest as well as the most beneficial that has happened since the publication of Christianity."[116] This description unites the notion of a revolution against tyranny with that of a revolution in "sentiments"; but what seems to be lacking is any reference to basic doctrinal issues, and this omission would arouse most criticism from Robertson's nineteenth-century Protestant successors.[117] Was this criticism justified?

Certainly Robertson shows no sensitivity to Luther's profound spiritual anguish and no awareness of the significance of this aspect of sixteenth-century religious life—a characteristic blind spot he shared with virtually all his scholarly contemporaries. Close examination of his argument reveals, however, that he was not unaware of the specific doctrinal issues at stake and at times draws explicit attention to them. He notes, for example, that during the attack on indulgences Luther "was obliged to inquire into the true cause of our justification and acceptance with God" and that it was *this* knowledge which led him to his rejection of pilgrimages, penances, the intercession of the saints, and Purgatory, and ultimately to his questioning of papal power.[118]

However, Robertson does show a certain reticence about discussing doctrinal issues in detail, and he partially explains this when he declares that such discussion is the province of ecclesiastical historians.[119] Although this "division of labour" clearly raises many problems, there is no doubt that Robertson recognized the joint operation of religious and political factors in the Reformation's success. Given that he was writing a predominantly political work for a nonsectarian public, it is not surprising that he chose to commend the Reformation in the terms most likely to win general acceptance; and, however much we may regret his unwillingness to examine doctrinal issues more consistently, we do not need to explain his failure to do so by positing a profound rationalist bias, especially because Robertson makes clear that the emancipation the Reformation brought to mankind was not an unintended result (as many of his contemporaries alleged) but was directly connected with the Reformation's fundamental religious concerns. The strong link Robertson establishes between the revival of letters and the Reformation, far from making the Reformation superfluous, adds luster to it as a movement which transformed a slow, limited, and tentative rebirth into a universal cause through resolute proclamation of the standard of truth.[120]

The views explored thus far by no means exhaust the variety of eighteenth-century scholarly opinion on the Reformation. A number of scholars chiefly notable in fields other than history provided interesting historical perspectives. Adam Smith (1723–1790), best known for his contributions to economic theory, explored church history especially in terms of its functional and practical relationship to civil government and social and material progress. In so doing he anticipated Ernst Troeltsch's distinction between "Church" and "sect" (see Chapter 11). Placing a high value on moderation and the avoidance of fanaticism, Smith registered his strong suspicion that congregational church government contained the seeds of disorder and expressed a corresponding preference for the Anglican and more particularly the Scottish Presbyterian form of government.[121]

Joseph Priestley (1733–1804), the English natural scientist who emigrated to Pennsylvania, produced in later life the first comprehensive church history originating in the New World.[122] Written from a Unitarian point of view, it identified the Reformation as a stage in Christianity's purification. In it Luther is regarded as an agent of Providence, "an extraordinary man raised up by God to be a principal instrument in promoting this great and necessary work of Reformation."[123] That work is understood to include not only morality and institutions but dogma, and at this point Priestley's reservations become apparent. Although he could identify with some of Luther's doctrinal views, especially with the "sleep of the soul," he believed that the Reformers had prematurely limited doctrinal reform by imposing basically Augustinian views. At the same time, he was open-minded enough to allow that what he regarded as an overemphasis on continuity with traditional Catholicism may have been the only way at that time of freeing the Church from papal tyranny.[124]

We have already noted that the characteristic intellectual postures of the Enlightenment—in particular optimistic notions of progress and emancipation—tended to inhibit a sound historical grasp of the Reformation's religious and doctrinal dimensions. Among those who stood somewhat apart from these assumptions and pursued a more direct and sympathetic encounter with the Reformation tradition were Johann Georg Hamann (1730–1788) and John Wesley (1703–1791). Hamann, at one time a teacher of Herder, underwent a personal conversion to vital religion which led him to a deeper encounter with Luther as interpreter par excellence of the Christian Gospel and theologian of the human heart. He thence proceeded to a clear-cut rejection of Enlightenment notions of reason and natural religion.[125] Wesley, who, with his brother Charles, is chiefly identified with the Evangelical Revival in Britain and the development of Methodism, experienced a similar conversion, which was directly associated with a public reading of Luther's preface to the Epistle to the Romans.[126] Wesley had previously been profoundly influenced by contacts with the Moravian brethren, pietist descendants of the fifteenth-century Hussites, but he later distanced himself from their passive outlook.

The Evangelical Revival, of which the Wesleys were the center but by no means the totality, brought back to light a number of forgotten themes of Reformation Christianity and expressed them in a variety of ways. George Whitefield (1714–1770), a close associate of the Wesleys, was a firm Calvinist; the Wesleys themselves were deeply committed to an Arminian understanding of Grace.[127] Through preachers the revival spread to America, which was swept by the "Great Awakening." Although in some manifestations this movement appealed chiefly to raw popular emotion, in Jonathan Edwards (1703–1758) it united religious fervor with intellectual power and scholarly depth. His efforts revitalized a Calvinist tradition into which rationalistic thought had made deep inroads and enabled it to speak once more in authentic Reformation accents.[128]

In its eighteenth-century context, the Evangelical Revival gives the superficial appearance of a thoroughgoing reaction against Enlightenment values and a rejection of the assumptions of those scholars, both skeptic and Christian, whose work we considered earlier. In some respects this was undoubtedly the case, and the movement's influence in the Church of England was deep and lasting. Yet surprising positive correspondences, seen perhaps most clearly in John Wesley himself, also existed. Although his preaching often produced among his hearers dramatic and at times bizarre religious behavior, Wesley remained, like a true man of his age, profoundly suspicious of "enthusiasm," and he warned repeatedly of its dangers.[129] Notwithstanding his emphasis on religious experience, he had no hesitation in affirming that "to renounce reason is to renounce religion, that religion and reason go hand in hand, and that all irrational religion is false religion."[130] Moreover, for all his obvious dependence on the

Reformation traditions of Luther and Calvin, Wesley distanced himself from them in a number of respects and articulated a markedly different doctrinal emphasis, which focused more on sanctification than on justification; indeed, he proclaimed a doctrine of "entire sanctification" or "Christian perfection."[131] Can we not see here that same spirit of confidence which had a profoundly secular expression in other writers—an "optimism of grace" rather than of nature?

The immense persuasiveness of Enlightenment attitudes so readily detectable in Wesley's transformation of the Reformation theological tradition is equally evident in the survival of broad Enlightenment concepts of the Reformation among the Romantic historians, such as Jules Michelet (1798–1874). In his famous *History of France* (1833–1867), that fervid patriot and anticlerical devoted a volume each to the Renaissance and the Reformation, ranging well outside French history.[132] He nevertheless glorified the Reformation in traditional terms as a victory over clerical autocracy and a forerunner of the French Enlightenment.

An earlier example appears in Madame de Staël's observant work on Germany (1813), with which she became well acquainted during her exile from the France of Napoleon.[133] To no small extent her assessment of German religions represents a survival from Jean Jacques Rousseau, the apostle of sentiment and sensibility she idolized. Perhaps this celebrated woman (1766–1817) enjoyed a more substantial advantage as the Geneva-born daughter of Louis XVI's minister Jacques Necker, or even as the granddaughter of a Swiss pastor. De Staël had much to say on Lutheranism, sects, Moravians, and Protestantism in general. She regarded the whole movement as one of several phases of Christianity, which had been "founded, then altered, then [at the Reformation] examined, then understood." These phases had been necessary to Christianity's development; some had lasted for a century, others for a thousand years: "the Supreme Being who draws upon eternity does not economise in time, as we do."

In de Staël's opinion neither Protestantism nor the Counter-Reformation arose essentially from the clash between the popes and Luther. It is "a poor way of considering history" to attribute it to personalities, because "Protestantism and Catholicism exist in the human heart; they are moral powers which develop within nations because they are inherent in every individual." The inward peace of mankind depends on reconciling imagination and reason. Such revolutions as the Reformation do not proceed from mere reasoning, but from the march of the human spirit, of which individual men are not the causes but the consequences. Luther, a man who uniquely combined abstract study and courageous action, placed the Bible in everyone's hands, thus putting Christianity into the twin contexts of humanism and printing. De Staël also attributed to the Reformation's liberating power the marked superiority of northern over southern German universities.[134]

These rather cloudy yet interesting opinions later found a sympathetic reader in Lucien Febvre, who badly wanted to demonstrate that the Reformation was "operated by ideas," not politics or reaction against abuses in the Church.[135] Nevertheless, de Staël herself did not simplify along these lines: she gave full weight to the political intervention of Charles V, and she certainly believed that abuses were also to be reckoned among the causes of the Reformation. Although the Enlightenment displayed a strong ideological tendency, it did not in that respect rival Febvre!

A comprehensive judgment on eighteenth-century historiography would oblige us to say that historians of the period rarely matched their intellectual verve and literary skill with profound insight into the idioms of Reformation thought. Their intellectual postures made it extraordinarily difficult for them to enter a world so different from their own. Dominated by an understanding of history which tended to regard "enlightenment" as diametrically opposed to traditional belief, they were hardly in a position to evaluate the Reformation dispassionately, even when they sought to approve it by detaching it from its "superstitious" Catholic origins. Their widening sympathy with far cultures found its counterpart in a total lack of empathy for a large part of their own direct intellectual inheritance, and their moral and intellectual assumptions— every bit as dogmatic as those they denounced—severely restricted their ability to evaluate the sixteenth century soundly.

In defense of these historians, however, Peter Gay has noted that their work, like other products of Enlightenment thought, was "part of an effort to secure rational control of the world, reliable knowledge of the past, and freedom from the pervasive domination of myth. In the midst of the struggle for objectivity, they could not themselves be objective: myth could by sympathetically understood only after it had been fully conquered, but in the course of its conquest it had to be faced as the enemy . . . Scholars could see the Christian millennium fairly only after polemicists had freed themselves from it by seeing it unfairly." Thus, the Enlightenment historians "freed history from the parochialism of Christian scholars and from theological presuppositions, secularised the idea of causation and opened vast new territories for historical enquiry."[136] In that sense, their work—for all its limitations—was integrally related to the solid and durable achievements of nineteenth-century historical scholarship.

7

New Directions: Ranke and Some Contemporaries

This chapter has a certain unity of purpose, even though it depicts some historians who seem to have few characteristics in common. They have been chosen precisely because they illustrate that phase of diversification which preceded the rise of the new social sciences. Although the eighteenth century had enlarged the historical content of the Reformation, the nineteenth extended it even more dramatically. To display this process before the middle of the nineteenth century, we now take five famous authors, all publishing in the field between 1828 and 1847. They arose from varied national and social backgrounds. Though a Protestant, Guizot seems here more closely related to his countrymen of the Enlightenment than to his coreligionists and contemporaries. Macaulay and Carlyle, both outstanding and widely read historical writers, differed immensely in temperament, native background, and philosophical approach; Macaulay was a major public servant and a complacent Whig; Carlyle a free-lance writer and protosocialist, yet also a "dangerous" admirer of historical heroes. From these two Froude inherited the characteristics which attracted so much admiration—and not a little obloquy—from late Victorian readers of Tudor history. Meanwhile, in Ranke there had emerged the best-equipped and most productive historian of the century, much influenced yet not engulfed by his conservative Prussian-Lutheran context. All aware of one another, and of their contemporaries in general, these five authors followed their own instincts with an almost primitive individualism impossible to emulate in our professionalized world of learning. Yet together they provide a panorama of Reformation historiography during the early stages of a period of ever-accelerating change.

In François Pierre Guillaume Guizot (1787–1874) we encounter an academic of the highest ability, one as truly French as Ranke was German, whose thought and writing must be seen in light of the fact that he also became one of the most respected and eminent politicians of nineteenth-century Europe.[1] Following the execution in the Terror of his father, a Protestant lawyer of Nîmes, the young Guizot grew up in the Geneva of the Enlightenment, where he fully assimilated the broad literary, historical, and philosophical instruction there available while naturally retaining his family's long religious tradition. Returning to the law schools of Paris, he found himself still detesting radical democracy while feeling no attraction toward either the Napoleonic Empire or the hard-line monarchists surrounding the exiled Louis XVIII. Even so, his striking abilities attracted influential friends, who in 1812 brought him to a chair of modern history at the Sorbonne. Within two years he went as a representative of the liberal monarchists to Ghent, where he took a prominent part in persuading the king to return on the basis of the charter and the dismissal of his ultraroyalist ministers. Marrying Pauline Meulan, a notable journalist, Guizot combined academic life with political appointments of rising importance. His Protestant devotion did not greatly distance him from the Catholic mainstream of French culture. In 1827 he consoled his wife, on her deathbed, in a manner then acceptable: by reading aloud Bossuet's famous funeral oration on the queen of England!

In 1833, as minister of public instruction, Guizot organized passage of the epoch-making law which established universal education in France. Nevertheless, two years later he revealed his strong and basic conservatism by approving legislation restricting freedom of the press. During these years he followed his influential lecture courses on European and French civilization with the exacting research later set forth in his classic volumes on the history of seventeenth-century England.[2] With the advent of bourgeois monarchy under Louis Philippe (1840–1848), Guizot returned from a brief but highly successful tenure in the French embassy in London to head the new government in Paris. Exiled to England by the revolution of 1848, he returned three years later to live on his estate in Calvados, writing his history of Oliver Cromwell and *Meditations on Christianity*. Yet, despite his political isolation, he remained influential in the consistory of the Reformed French Church.[3]

In historical scholarship, Guizot was a man of the seventeenth as opposed to the sixteenth century, and to obtain his concise and balanced view of the Reformation we must turn not to his major works but to his Sorbonne lectures, *The History of Civilization in Europe*. First published in 1828 and long popular in the English-speaking world through the able translation by William Hazlitt, this is no dead book.[4] Even today any thoughtful reader could benefit from its range, its limpidity, and its searching intelligence. Amid the crabbed learning which marks so much writing on the Reformation, Guizot's twelfth lecture forms a refreshing interlude.

Although in the previous lecture Guizot has sketched the ominous events of the fifteenth century, in neither does he closely examine the Reformation's causes. Instead he analyzes its effects, reading backward to arrive at the movement's most essential characteristics. By this debatable test he criticizes the Protestant view that the Reformation was basically aimed at purification of the Church. He observes instead a campaign for enfranchisement of the human mind, based on the recent multiplication of schools and universities and the rise of classical learning, with all its new intellectual values. But this "insurrection" of the European mind collided with a Church weakened by spiritual indolence although maintaining all its former pretensions. In Guizot's view, the Church of 1500 suffered attack not because it was tyrannical or morally worse than it had ever been, but because, in the new mental climate, it *could* be attacked. Suppose the Church of Rome had swiftly undertaken the specific disciplinary reforms its critics demanded, would the Reformation have ceased? Obviously not, because revolution and not mere reform lay at its heart. It had arisen directly from various causes, yet its ultimate objective was to disarm the spiritual power, the systematic and formidable "government of thought" by pope and clergy.

Despite its enunciation by a convinced Protestant, this concept retains the emphases of the Enlightenment, refined and deepened by a maturer sense of intellectual history. In addition, we recognize the creed and values of an inspired educational reformer, which Guizot was then about to become. As this review develops, we meet a politician by no means insensitive to the problems of those holding power; Guizot remained in spirit a man of government rather than of opposition. With remarkable restraint, he says little concerning the positive religious beliefs held by the makers of the Reformation. Although as a pillar of "enlightened" Calvinism Guizot officially shared most of these beliefs, he refused to allow them a commanding place in his ostensibly historical and philosophical system. In this behavior he resembles Ranke, who refused the help of a clerical busybody by declaring that he himself was a historian first and a Christian second.

Moving away from the iron age of Luther and Calvin, Guizot concentrates on the Reformation's political and social effects in a later, and to him more familiar, period. He acknowledges that in Germany the Reformation's earlier stages had strengthened princely power. Nevertheless, the liberalizing of thought had become even more conspicuous in Germany than elsewhere, while it had occurred more simply in "progressive" countries like England, the Netherlands, and Denmark.

Even in France the Reformation had penetrated more deeply than was generally understood; until the revocation of the Edict of Nantes in 1685, Protestantism had legally existed there. Thus, throughout most of the seventeenth century relatively free debate had marked French intellectual life, while outside the religious sphere philosophy and natural science had flourished. Even the revocation had marked a reaction of limited extent and duration, because the Enlightenment had begun to attain significance about forty years later. French Protestantism had generally been satisfied with the degree of liberation it had done so much to foster: it had even become more pliant, because in the more favored areas it had largely realized its spiritual objectives. As for his contemporaries among historians, Guizot thought they would understand more by examining these eventually liberating results instead of the Reformers' original intentions.

Guizot then deals with a formidable reproach against the Reformation: that the main Protestant church had first spawned a multiplicity of extremist sects and then destroyed them with no little cruelty. This charge he seeks to soften by admitting what he calls the Reformation's defective self-consciousness, which did not fully understand its own essential character. In strong contrast, the Roman Church remained consistent, fully aware of its actions and objectives. Even as they ultimately failed, Rome's most powerful agents, the Jesuits, preserved this clarity of outlook.

Refusing to lose himself in dogmatic disputes, Guizot continues to insist that the Reformation's concrete achievement was overthrowing the Catholic clergy's monopoly of spiritual power. This empowerment of the laity meant the rescue of the European states from clerical controls. As the people began to exercise influence over organized religion the clerical hierarchies gave up their attempt to govern politics and society. In other words, the Reformation destroyed those authoritarian bonds which the Church had been steadily tightening since the early Middle Ages, when religion had put itself in the hands of a spiritual aristocracy even as civil society submitted to the government of a lay aristocracy. Insurrections finally occurred in both fields, but they came first in religion, and Guizot regarded this sequence as a historical norm.

It would not prove difficult to criticize this type of interpretation. That it is so boldly philosophical and contains so few proper names and so little social history may not be in themselves lethal objections; although clearly based on considerable factual knowledge, the lecture was not intended to discuss detailed problems. It is not an illustrated guide but an aerial photograph. Yet this very attempt to discover the "essentials" or the "essential nature" of so complex a movement arouses suspicion, for even the most objective historian is likely to select some components and ignore others, according to his personal values and his desire to present a consistent image suited to the needs of his day. In any event, to discuss so complex a phenomenon in twenty pages involves a violent exercise in selectivity, and the result can only be placed alongside rival exercises as one of many partial answers. In this case the almost total preoccupation with effects does not allow Guizot to address some of the primary problems. Why had the Reformation gained so much momentum when its originators were still consciously involved in promoting certain specific religious values, not in a general liberation of the human mind? If the movement was at length diverted into broader and less dogmatic channels, when and how did this occur?

On the other hand, had Protestantism changed so radically by the nineteenth century for the great mass of its adherents? French Calvinism, it is true, had greatly cooled since its early days. Nevertheless, one cannot reasonably suppose that the Reformed ministers, whose sermons Guizot heard from week to week, conceived of the Reformation in the terms of his lecture. They and their flocks still regarded the movement as first and foremost one of religious principle or dogma; even in 1828 it must have been unrealistic to cancel these terms in favor of a high-minded, aseptic, nondenominational historiography befitting an eminent French politician of the mid-nineteenth century. Was not Guizot consciously living in two worlds and thereby producing a neutered survey of the Reformation? He has been rightly praised for his avoidance of antipathies, yet even this virtue can entail problems.[5]

In many respects Thomas Babington Macaulay (1800–1859) can be regarded as a British parallel to Guizot. A leading politician who sponsored important legislation at the ministerial level; one who saw himself as liberal but remained essentially conservative; one who pursued politics and historical writing with equal seriousness—in all these respects he resembled the *père des modernes*.[6] Each derived basic ideas from eighteenth-century philosophical rationalism, yet each wrote his greatest work on seventeenth-century England.[7] Throughout his life, far shorter than Guizot's, Macaulay worked even more intensively, and, perhaps above all his contemporaries, he enjoyed the advantage of an almost supernatural memory.[8] An eloquent champion of reformist legislation in the House of Commons, he projected his oratorical performances into his writing, which for that reason alone became "dated" long ago. Nevertheless, once habituated, many readers still accept his spectacular literary presence, his energy and irony, his polished if unduly numerous antitheses, his far-ranging and original comparisons.

With even greater ease we recall the less attractive features. Too often Macaulay judged men by their politics, condemning them if they lacked his Whig partisanship, which in turn rested on his conviction that modern history itself had passed judgment on men and nations in strict accordance with Whig principles. Leslie Stephen observed of his historical characters that, when not wholly black or white, they are bundles of violently contrasting qualities. Nobody escapes dramatization. Macaulay's lack of cultural and religious sensibility has also been reproved, yet he cannot fairly be dismissed as a one-dimensional historian of politics. For who, before or since, has written a more attractive essay on English social history than Macaulay's famous third chapter of the *History of England?*

Likewise, Macaulay's harsh pronouncements and brazen literary persona have tended to obscure his loyal friendships and warm family affections. He had left the slave-abolitionist world of his father, Zachary, hating its "negrophile" cant; yet he too detested slavery and felt a responsibility toward the non-British populations of the empire. Striving to repair the broken family fortunes, he spent the years 1834–1837 as a hard-working member of the Supreme Council of India, although he learned little of the indigenous culture, assuming that this vast Asiatic society would be best understood by Britons traditionally raised on the Greek and Roman classics.

Whatever his motives, Macaulay gave value and strove to excel. Although by then his essays had already adorned the *Edinburgh Review* for over a decade, he wrote better and more mature essays after his return from India.[9] The one relevant to the Reformation is on Ranke's *History of the Popes,* published in October 1840; compared with Macaulay's earlier work it shows more than a merely technical development. Among all his forty or more essays and biographies only about half a dozen deal with Continental European subjects, and here we encounter the grandest of these, however flawed by unrelenting prejudices. Without it we should never have appreciated the breadth of Macaulay's European reading or his capacity to investigate the most momentous and long-term problems of Western history.

Although the essay concerns the Renaissance popes and their successors, it soon encounters Reformation issues, and along paths by no means commonplace in his day. Characteristically, Macaulay says little about theology, which he regards as an unprogressive science, in which little can be proved or disproved by reason. After all, had not theology been carried to its limits by men scarcely emerged from barbarism? When one so eminent as Thomas More was willing to die for transubstantiation, such "absurd" doctrines must all too easily in lesser minds triumph over reason. According to Macaulay, man does not advance far in the sphere of the supernatural: even Samuel Johnson retained a mass of trivial superstitions.

The history of the papacy itself shows that reason does not necessarily prevail over superstition. Since the authority of the Roman Church had become established in Western Christendom, its yoke had been threatened by four major revolts, yet from two of them the Church had emerged entirely victorious. Unlike so many English scholars of his day, Macaulay was commendably aware that the Reformation had a long prehistory. He notes that in early medieval Languedoc by far the most refined civilization of the period arose, yet the Albigensians became heretics and the papacy erased their high culture along with their heresy by a simple stratagem. It called in the raw, land-greedy warriors of northern France, whose victory was consolidated by establishment of the Inquisition and the new religious orders.

The second great threat came when the emissaries of Philip IV of France brought about Boniface VIII's death and removed the papacy to Avignon. Eventually, its very survival was gravely menaced as rival claimants disputed the Holy See. Scarcely had the papacy extracted itself and returned to Rome when the voice of Wycliffe aroused the Hussite movement in Bohemia, a land already made dangerous by native heresy. Perhaps mistakenly, Macaulay also gives weight to Bohemian economic connections with the Lower Danube, where the Paulician sect had flourished. But, despite the formidable Hussite Wars, a measure of papal authority and discipline was recreated by loyal European powers and conciliar reforms, even though the popes themselves feared and obstructed those reforms.

Hence, the revolt of Martin Luther initiated "the third and most memorable struggle for spiritual freedom."[10] This arose when the renaissance of letters and the invention of printing had already wrenched away the ecclesiastical monopoly on learning. Throughout northern Europe, and especially in the Teutonic world, men saw the popes as alien gatherers of tribute. Both good and bad men, rich and poor, had their motives for backing the Protestant Reformers. Ireland, its hatred directed against English rather than Roman overlords, provided the sole exception. In southern Europe, however, very different considerations affected the issue. Among Italians pride and profit combined to support the papacy. The desire to regulate morals prevailed over the dangerous urge toward doctrinal reform; already Savonarola's protest had failed, having shown little resemblance to Luther's. The Spanish monarchy now belonged to the Hapsburg emperor, whose established military power in Italy allowed him to use the papacy as a political tool. More important still, the Reformation found Spain in a mood of Catholic and nationalist euphoria. Victory over the Moorish infidels of Andalusia had been succeeded by a spectacular phase of empire building in Central and South America. Liberation, glory, divine favor, and world power all bade Spain eradicate unorthodox beliefs: "In the very year in which the Saxons, maddened by the exactions of Rome, broke loose from her yoke, the Spaniards, under the authority of Rome, made themselves masters of the empire and of the treasures of Montezuma."[11]

Launching into the disciplinary reforms of the Council of Trent, Macaulay pays a handsome tribute to Rome's methods of control, which so clearly surpassed those of the Protestants. The fanatical enthusiasts—from Ignatius Loyola down to the most ignorant begging friars—Rome put into her own uniform, thus gaining countless unpaid agents. If Ignatius had attended Protestant Oxford, his sheer enthusiasm would speedily have carried him outside the Anglican fold. Conversely, under Roman management the countess of Huntingdon, instead of founding a sect, would have been given a place in the calendar as Saint Selina, and John Wesley would have been appointed the first general of a new order devoted to church expansion. Nowadays this amusing passage may well seem overclever because the author, concentrating unduly on England, overlooks the enthusiastic but well-ordered Lutheran missionary enterprises, which in Luther's lifetime had firmly established outposts as far afield as Finland, Transylvania, and Slovenia. The Calvinist expansion had been equally organized through great areas of France, the Netherlands, Scotland, Hungary, and elsewhere. Yet if Macaulay ever entertained second thoughts on the matter, he must have swept them aside as weakening his main argument!

He drives on into the Thirty Years' War, which had brought Wallenstein and the Imperialists to the Baltic, and later propelled the Swedish counterthrust led by Gustavus Adolphus into the heart of the empire. Equally significant was the alliance between the Swedes and Richelieu, that supposed prince of the Catholic Church who nevertheless put France first. The cooling of religious fanaticism followed, and in 1648 the Peace of Westphalia, since which "there has been no religious war between Catholics and Protestants as such."[12] This remains broadly true, although

Macaulay would have done well to temper his transition in view of the continuing religious hatreds which marked both the exploits of Louis XIV and the Glorious Revolution of 1688, episodes he treated with more realism in his *History of England.*

Meanwhile, in this essay Macaulay hastens into the eighteenth century, that triumphal age when wealth and intelligence alike deserted the Mediterranean for the Protestant North. Countries little favored by nature, such as Prussia and Scotland, became the most flourishing and best governed in the world. They did so in clear contrast with those southern countries where reactionary religion had held down both social and scientific advances. The Spaniard, once in no way inferior to the Englishman, now yielded to him in arms, science, letters, and commerce. Likewise, the achievements of Portugal, hitherto indisputably superior to those of Denmark, became in all respects markedly second rate. In short, Macaulay believed that the "decay" of southern Europe had arisen largely from the social and political doctrines of the Roman Catholic revival which followed the Reformation. Characteristically, he selected examples to suit his thesis; one could counter by citing the more important case of France, which retained a heavily predominant Catholicism while dominating the Continent both militarily and culturally for two centuries.

Here one might add with confidence that Macaulay would have been little impressed by the argument that Spanish mysticism, together with the art of Velázquez and Murillo and the picaresque novel of Cervantes, had flowered with rare splendor on the dunghill of Spain's economic decline. With the exception of Cervantes, such cultural forms did not appeal to Macaulay. Moreover, if asked to elaborate on the issue, he would probably have retorted that in Spain these fragile survivors from a brief Indian summer had died away before the end of the seventeenth century. Likewise, in celebrating the industrial triumphs of England and Scotland, this complacent observer does not consider how far the common people of these "successful" countries had benefited. As an active politician, Macaulay should have been aware in 1840 that the Industrial Revolution had if anything diminished the living standards of large occupational groups. Yet, given Macaulay's values, however controversial, some solid substance usually remains in his contentions. The Church *had* become a mental and material incubus in some Catholic countries: economic and scientific leadership *had* gone over to the Protestant countries and to France, where ecclesiastical pressures had been significantly moderated by the power of the State and by Gallican opinion. Those who have written about Macaulay do not seem to have realized that he and his like advanced more than halfway toward the subsequent

"Weber thesis," which refused to ascribe material success solely to economic factors (see Chapter 11). In effect Macaulay was already making claims for a psychoreligious factor in the countries of the Reformation, a quality resembling the now familiar "Protestant work ethic."

At this point Macaulay introduces "the fourth great peril of the Church of Rome," by which he means the corrosive rationalism of the eighteenth century. Thinking mainly of Voltaire and other French anticlericals, he contends that —far from consciously accepting the Protestant Reformers as ancestors—these polemicists rejected or disregarded Albigenses, Lollards, Lutherans, and Calvinists alike. Thus, they tended to equate Christianity with its familiar French Catholic forms, even as they utilized old Protestant arguments to demolish the irrational elements in Catholicism. This said, Macaulay also praises their humanity, for had Voltaire and his friends been mere scoffers they could never have moved European opinion. Despite their injustice toward Christianity, these champions of the Enlightenment had shown the same charity toward men of all classes and races which Christianity enjoins. And, in the last resort, Macaulay seems to allow for a real link between Reformation and Enlightenment. He regards Voltaire's mordant but humane attacks on brutal miscarriages of justice (with dubious accuracy) as borrowed from a merciful and tolerant Evangelical morality. The ostensible opposition had slackened, because the Church, intellectually debilitated since the days of Bossuet, no longer sought to defend itself by reasoned argument. Nevertheless, its surviving powers irritated but did not silence its critics. While the Society of Jesus, assailed by philosophers and politicians alike, suffered abolition, the secular Parisian culture dominated all Europe, so that even arbitrary governments sought to practice the reforms it advocated.

During these years of influence, claims Macaulay, the radical followers of Voltaire loosened their relationship with their leader as had the Anabaptists with Luther, or the Fifth Monarchy Men with Pym. Extremism triumphed with the escalating Revolution, which carried away the old Church of France. Some of its priests were butchered; others joined the Revolution as its most ferocious minions. The bust of Marat replaced the statues of martyrs, and a prostitute impersonating the Goddess of Reason sat enthroned in the church of Notre Dame to receive the adoration of thousands, who "exclaimed that at length, for the first time, those ancient Gothic arches had resounded with the accents of truth."[13]

Nevertheless, "the new unbelief was as tolerant as the old superstition,"[14] and it was not long before French armies occupied Rome itself, bearing off the pope, pillaging the ancient shrines, and erecting new republics throughout Italy. As if by a miracle the papacy survived, defying the floods like some ancient pyramid. Once again polarization developed on the Continent, where all too many men became either thoroughgoing Papists or rabid atheists, instead of sensibly adopting a peaceable intermediate position where, during the Reformation itself, so many wiser spirits had found resting places. Here Macaulay reaches a pragmatic and truly English conclusion!

Only at the beginning and end of this essay, and then briefly, does Macaulay mention Ranke, for this is in no sense a genuine review and still less an attempt to outline Ranke's arguments or think in his categories. Though admirably versed in classical and French literature, Macaulay knew little about German scholarship. He praises Ranke in astonishingly vague terms and could well have written his essay without troubling to read extensively in *The Popes*. In effect, Macaulay is retailing his own meditations on papal history, drawing from his well-stocked and orderly mind rather than more highly specialized studies.

Macaulay's essay displays not a few controversial judgments, although its historical merits seem striking enough when we reflect either on the jejune character of so much contemporary writing on these themes or on the paucity of the author's other contributions to papal or even European history. His often acute insights and ability to generalize operate within a by no means congenial field. Even his praise of papal methods is meant to reflect a deep albeit controlled distrust of their ultimate motives: indeed, he has less praise for either Catholics or Protestants than for Voltaire. But there remain both the familiar literary virtues—the nervous, unflagging, and lucid prose together with that supreme ability to engage and hold the reader's attention—and the equally familiar vices—the overemphasis on materialist values and the urge to pronounce final and peremptory judgments on every person and situation in this Miltonic combat between good and evil.

Macaulay's general suspicion of Romanism inhibited him from praising adequately some positive achievements, which he must have witnessed on his recent visit to Italy and could readily have grasped: for example, Sixtus V's re-creation of Rome as not merely a monument but a living city, and the patronage of glorious baroque architecture and sculpture by eminent Roman ecclesiastical families. All in all, although he handles large-scale political events with masterly proportion and skill, he refrains from discussing the strictly religious problems and characteristics of the papacy or its opponents. His most serious failure derives from his lack of any sense of proximity to those religious debates of the age, which, because they engaged men of all social classes, can claim a central place in early modern history. In an essay mainly concerned with the Reformation and Counter-Reformation, must not this omission be accounted grave, even disastrous? And, rather surprisingly, this restraint did not enable Macaulay to avoid—as Guizot had so ably—the acquisition of strong personal antipathies.

Unlike the other four historians considered in this chapter, Thomas Carlyle (1795–1881) earned his living by his pen, working as a full-time professional writer almost throughout his career.[15] The son of a Scottish stonemason, he pursued desultory studies at the University of Edinburgh, gave up the idea of entering the ministry, did a little teaching, visited Coleridge in London, became known in Edinburgh society, and married a cultivated wife. The young Carlyle soon acquired a deep knowledge of modern German literature and Idealist philosophy; his first achievements were a translation of *Wilhelm Meister* (1824) and a biography of Schiller (1825).

In 1834, the year of his permanent emigration to London, Carlyle published a book distinctly relevant to his thought on religion and the Reformation. *Sartor Resartus*, a broad philosophical treatise, purports to set forth the views of Herr Diogenes Teufelsdröckh, professor of Allerley Wissenschaft in the University of Weissnichtwo, whom some insular readers imagined to be a real person![16] It contains the actual author's spiritual biography to date, showing how as a reader of Voltaire and Hume he had descended into "a howling desert" of infidelity, skepticism, and despair. About 1821 this impasse had been broken by a sudden psychological experience or "conversion," which broke the spell of the "Everlasting No."

Affirmative as it had been, this experience did not lead Carlyle back to any denominational code of faith but rather to a broad and dynamic Christianity. He saw that men had gone astray because they had accepted self-regarding happiness as their chief object. The way back to inner peace lay through self-renunciation, not through mystical speculation or scholastic theology, still less through any belief in the physical sciences or the salvation of society by industrialization. In short, Macaulay's cheerful interpretation of the human predicament seemed to Carlyle shallow and materialist in the extreme. According to Carlyle, God reveals himself only in symbols, "idols," "vestures," which men perversely esteem as independent values. But all these visible things are no more than the disposable clothing of God, who alone is the underlying, unchanging reality.

Moreover, according to Carlyle, culture, modes of government, social machinery, even creeds and rituals, are no more than transient symbols, needed to prevent anarchy, but due to be broken and renewed as they outlive their significance. Past dogmas once expressed man's hunger for God, yet they betray the ignorance of the times when they were constructed. Catholic Christianity sufficed for Dante, but its forms and spirit are no longer viable for nineteenth-century minds. In such a situation men too often respond by extremist gestures. They either ignore modern extensions of knowledge and cling to a dead formalism or throw out all belief and lapse into spiritual anarchy. The latter process represents a prime error: even as we change the outlook of our age, we should move forward with caution, showing a measure of respect for the outworn forms of religion and culture, which did good service in their day. Carlyle thought of himself as a radical, yet here and elsewhere he preserved a strong instinctive element of gradualism. In 1837 he published his *French Revolution*, a prose epic distinguished by graphic writing rather than "scientific" research. Even before completing it he had lost all enthusiasm for what he called *sansculottism:* the barbarity of mob revolution, which had rendered Napoleon a desperate necessity as well as a hero of sorts.

Carlyle enshrined his direct references to the Reformation in the book *On Heroes, Hero-Worship and the Heroic in History* (1841), which was based on a cash-raising course of lectures delivered the previous year amid the neurotic agonies with which Carlyle confronted the public. Despite his noble facade and deep, incorruptible devotion to spiritual values, he remained a dyspeptic valetudinarian rather than a hero. In the words of Edmund Gosse, "what was a swelled finger in other men was nothing less than elephantiasis in Carlyle."[17] All the same, Carlyle became at least an adulator of the Hero, brashly proclaiming that "the History of the World is but the Biography of Great Men."

How did he reach this vulnerable position? *Heroes and Hero-Worship* is in effect an extension of *Sartor Resartus,* a suggested remedy for the problem set forth in that book.[18] It asks how and under what leadership we can break the shells of dead cultures to recover a living moral and spiritual life. To find an answer, Carlyle consults history and learns that the masses have always proved far too ignorant to produce anything better than anarchy. They desperately need the guidance of exceptional men, the stern call of prophets, the governance of the wise. These giant figures are not the creatures but the creators of historical periods. Rejecting the current urge to "level down" mankind, we should seek to discover and revere men of destiny, because our one hope lies in the strength and wisdom of the few, not in the organized unwisdom of the many.

The extent to which Carlyle swam against the tide of his century and ours could not have become instantly apparent. But before long historians like Buckle and Taine would subordinate even great leaders to the "spirit of the age" and propound "scientific" laws governing the development of human societies. Whatever we may think of this alternative approach, our century has quite intelligibly turned against the notion of hero-leaders. We find it impossible to ignore the dangers presented by this solution or to understand the motivations of Carlyle and the many civilized people who both inspired and followed him.

In his day Carlyle was far from standing alone on this point. The plea for government by the *best* men, the preference for aristocracy as opposed to democracy, had flourished among the ancient Greeks and been further inflated by Romantic poets such as Shelley and Byron. More important, they appealed to several of the German philosophers and literary men Carlyle was purveying to the British public. A recent close investigation of Carlyle's intellectual development has indicated that Johann Gottlieb Fichte (1762–1814) stood paramount in this regard among Carlyle's direct forerunners.[19] Of course, when Carlyle wrote these books Friedrich Nietzsche (1844–1900) was not yet born, and in any event the amoral Nietzschean superman has little in common with Carlyle's intensely moral purposes. Although it would seem both unjust and anachronistic to place Carlyle among the ancestors of twentieth-century tyrannies, even an observant reader of his day might well have detected ambivalence in those passages of *Heroes and Hero-Worship* which seem to assign Napoleon and Frederick the Great places within the heroic circle. Even as Carlyle wrote, he realized that a chasm separated such militarist politicians from those others whom he found wholly credible: the giant prophets like Mahomet and Luther. Certainly he ranked religious men of action—those who most conspicuously broke the "idols" of the past—above the passively spiritual guides such as his contemporaries Coleridge and Wordsworth, whom he regarded as ineffective almost to the point of being contemptible.

In his fourth lecture, "The Hero as Priest," Carlyle devotes some twenty pages to a biographical sketch of Martin Luther, worth reading for its apocalyptic enthusiasm, although not for any balanced analysis of Luther's theology or the spiritual needs of the German nation in his time. In accordance with the principles already observed, Carlyle does not regard Reformers like Luther and Knox as representing a total break from the medieval past: men needed to have been "priests" of firm faith before they could become Protestant Reformers. Yet Carlyle greets Luther's affirmation at Worms—"Here stand I; I can do no other: God assist me"—as the deliverance of the whole European world from "stagnant putrescence": "It is, as we say, the greatest moment in the Modern History of Men. English Puritanism, England and its Parliaments, Americas, and vast work these two centuries: French Revolution, Europe and its work everywhere at present: the germ of it all lay there: had Luther at that moment done other, it had all been otherwise!"[20]

Here the author acknowledges that wars and contentions followed the Reformation, but why, he asks, blame Luther? When Hercules turned the river into the Augean stables, he must have caused confusion all around, yet we do not blame Hercules for this result! Luther and his beliefs are not guilty, but "the false Simulacra that forced him to protest, they are responsible." Carlyle recalls that the bloodshed was prevented while Luther lived, and "a man to do this must have a kingly factor." So Luther continued "Sovereign of this greatest revolution," being at once a man of peace and a sincere, rugged writer. At the same time, he fulfilled that essential function demanded in *Sartor Resartus:* "I find Luther to have been a Breaker of Idols, no less than any other Prophet: the wooden Gods of the Koreish, made of timber or bees wax, were not more hateful to Mahomet than Tetzel's pardons of sin, made of sheepskin and ink, were to Luther."[21]

One need scarcely add that Carlyle's idea of liberation went much further than that of the Lutheran Church. For example, he held private judgment in matters of religion to be indispensable to human development; his standpoint was not Lutheran, Anglican, or Presbyterian, but far closer to that of the Puritan Independents of seventeenth-century England, who were tolerationists except in regard to Catholicism. Concerning Catholicism, Carlyle's tolerance seems to spring less from his general principles than from his mistaken supposition that English Catholicism had fallen into gradual but irreversible decline. Denouncing as shallow and stupid the rabble's "No popery" slogan, he also castigates those inane Britons who apprehensively counted the growing number of Catholic chapels and proclaimed that mortal blows were being struck against Protestantism. He bids the nation leave Catholicism alone "while good work is still capable of being led by it . . . It lasts here for a purpose. Let it last as long as it can."

For the rest of the chapter Carlyle wears a British face; he holds that it was not amid the jangling theological debates in Germany that the Reformation attained its climax. Instead, he finds what he calls "the genuine thing" in English and Scottish Puritanism. Apart from its epoch-making character in these two centuries, he also sees Puritanism in the context of the Pilgrim fathers and contemporary America. Likewise, he is far from limiting attention merely to spiritual achievements. Despite its weak beginnings, Puritanism "has got weapons and sinews: it has fire-arms, war-navies: it has cunning in its ten fingers, strength in its right arm; it can steer ships, fell forests, remove mountains;—it is one of the strongest things under this sun at present!"[22]

To no small extent these emotions had been aroused in Carlyle by the spectacle of Puritan-led progress in his native Scotland. "The history of Scotland . . . contains nothing of world-interest at all but this Reformation by Knox. A poor barren country, full of continual broils . . . little better perhaps than Ireland at this day . . . And now at the Reformation the internal life is kindled, as it were, under the ribs of this outward material death. A cause, the noblest of causes, kindles itself, like a beacon set on high . . . whereby the meanest man becomes not a Citizen only, but a member of Christ's visible Church; a veritable Hero, if he prove a true man!"[23] Even the great Scotsmen of the Enlightenment seem to Carlyle the direct offspring of Knox, although he admits "the unforgivable offence" of Knox was that he wished "to make the Government of Scotland a Theocracy." But Carlyle soon forgives his hero!

The power of Scottish Puritanism having been "handed back" to England, the Civil War led on to the Glorious Revolution. The earlier generations of fighters—John Knox, Oliver Cromwell, and the Covenanters who under the Restoration so heroically maintained Scottish Presbyterianism—had to struggle and suffer in the mud "before a beautiful Revolution of Eighty-eight [could] step over them in official pumps and silk stockings." Nevertheless, these founding fathers of British Protestantism obviously lacked the supreme stature of Mahomet and Luther. Knox had "a good honest intellectual talent, no transcendent one: a narrow, inconsiderable man, as compared with Luther." Yet in sheer sincerity Knox had no superior, being a prophet cast in the authentic Old Testament mold, armed with the same inflexibility and intolerance, narrow and rigid adherence to revealed religion, and zeal to administer stern rebukes in the name of God to all who forsake truth. Predictably, Carlyle ends these powerful biographical paragraphs at Knox's grave, with the valediction of the earl of Morton: "He lies there, who never feared the face of men."

There remains an English Protestant hero whose full Carlylean portrait is found in both the sixth lecture of *Heroes and Hero-Worship* and *The Letters and Speeches of Oliver Cromwell* (1845), the texts of which are permeated by Carlyle's own spirited interpretations. In the *Letters and Speeches* Carlyle attempted something fresh and creative, however unconventional his methods and wholesale his admiration for Cromwell, whose oratory (or lack of it) presented an ideal opportunity for editorial amplification. In some universities at least, this book has survived as a superb item of teaching equipment. Dull indeed would be the reader who

failed to catch the mental reverberations provided by this daring interpreter. The first and perhaps last of his type, Carlyle admittedly claims
the privileges of genius; his editorial stratagems could not be recommended to successors with less instinctive power and charisma. For example, he often breaks the flow of a speech by interpolations in square
brackets, which take two forms. In the first the editor conjectures what
the hearers in Parliament were thinking. In the second Carlyle comments
as an emotional partisan. He regarded Cromwell as a true hero, a patient
and earnest Christian, whose more ruthless acts sprang from a series of
terrible necessities. This highly subjective approach, often shrewd, always
lively, tends to become too obtrusive during the Protector's last years,
when we see him striving to heal the divisions and educate his pettifogging
followers, all to balance the constitutional wig on the point of the sword.

Readers of our day, trained by the entertainment industry to detect
or even invent bathos, may well find these interjections too close to the
edge of the precipice. In his speech of 25 January 1658 to the second
Protectorate Parliament, Cromwell is recorded as saying "And while I
live, and am able, I shall be ready to stand or fall with you." Here Carlyle
exclaims: "Courage my brave one! Thou hast but some seven months
more of it, and then the ugly coil is all over: and thy part in it manfully
done: manfully and fruitfully to all Eternity!"[24]

This sort of editing caters to the cult members of a Protestant saint,
and those who dislike cults are entitled to question the method even when
exercised by an editor not only well informed but armed with remarkable
insight. Here, as in all his writings, Carlyle scorns caution as fearlessly
as his heroes had during their great religious and political crises. His
exaggerations also represent a counterblow—even a preemptive strike—
against those who transgressed in the opposite direction: the overrefined,
the pedants, the "Dryasdusts" and philistines, in short all those who did
not want to be made to *feel* historical situations. Thus, a unique historian,
using methods which would soon seem bizarre to his increasingly professionalized colleagues, made a positive contribution to Reformation
history because he sought to reveal its inherently emotional dimension.
The broad objective would seem legitimate enough: yet can anyone accomplish such a feat without the gravest risk to his objectivity?

We need not examine in detail the writers who immediately succeeded Macaulay and Carlyle, except for James Anthony Froude (1818–
1894), chief disciple, literary executor, and controversial biographer of
Carlyle.[25] In addition, Froude's vivid antitheses and dramatic presentation
owe much to Macaulay. As an Oxford don in the 1840s, Froude broke
from Newman and the High Church movement, in which his brother

Hurrell (d. 1836) had figured so prominently. In 1849 he became a close personal friend of Carlyle and began to write his twelve-volume *History of England from the Fall of Wolsey to the Defeat of the Spanish Armada.*

From a stylistic viewpoint, and as a political history of the Reformation, this extensive work might well be regarded as the best of its time, yet as a history of the Reformation it has obvious shortcomings. The author's antipathy to Catholicism and Catholics is remarkably consistent: he portrays the English Reformation as a victory over the powers of darkness, personified by Philip II and the popes. Catholic Christianity had reshaped human values in accordance with its own mistaken image of God as the merciless Judge. The Reformation at least initiated a new order, having "untwisted slowly the grasp of the theological fingers from the human throat." Despite the rival fanaticism represented by Calvin, men gradually learned that "religion does not consist in an assent to propositions."[26] On the other hand, Froude distrusted, even resented, the participation of the common people—both Catholic and Protestant—in the religious life of the period. He shows little sense of regional differences in religious opinion, and his few genuflections toward economic and social forces now seem perfunctory. Except when popular rebellions occur, the story seldom leaves eminent figures, high politics, and international diplomacy.

A hero-worshiper in the Carlylean tradition, Froude admired Henry VIII and recognized the political genius of Thomas Cromwell when such opinions were unfashionable.[27] He showed pity for the "insane" Mary Tudor,[28] but profoundly admired Queen Elizabeth—or rather her minister William Cecil. A passage of overwhelming force describes the execution of that "bold, restless, unscrupulous, ambitious woman" Mary Stuart.[29] On the other hand, though handicapped by a lack of calendars and other guides to study which we now take for granted, Froude made a hitherto unparalleled use of manuscript state papers in London, Simancas, and Vienna. His occasional errors must hence be regarded with sympathy, even though his urge to be readable occasionally caused him to follow unreliable sources if they yielded good stories. Although his literary genius has always evoked praise, almost everything Froude wrote became the object of bitter attacks, mainly from writers even more prejudiced. Like Michelet before him, he still deserves to be restored to readers of a generation increasingly incapable of appreciating the grand manner.

The career of Leopold von Ranke (1795–1886) seems more attuned to our day than do those of the other historians discussed in this chapter.[30] Apart from his early, brief experiences of schoolmastering and political journalism, he lived the life of an academic professional historian, enjoying tenure and emoluments in a major university. He held a chair of history at the University of Berlin for sixty years, during which he did more than any other man to make its history school the best in Europe.[31] Meanwhile, displaying remarkable industry and thoroughness, he acquired a range of specialities scarcely rivaled by any historian before or since. His center of gravity lay in sixteenth- and seventeenth-century Europe, yet he could and did transcend these boundaries in many directions and sometimes on a large scale.

Ranke published major works on war and politics in the High Renaissance, Spain and the Moslem world, the popes, Germany during the Reformation, and the national histories of France and England. In addition, his other writings would have created a significant personal reputation. His *Nine Books of Prussian History* (1847–1848) caused Carlyle—as biographer of Frederick the Great—to place him among the "Dryasdusts." It is indeed not one of Ranke's most attractive creations, but such criticism did not prevent him from expanding the nine books to twelve. In his eighty-first year, Ranke started on a *World History,* which had reached the fifteenth century in nine volumes by the time of his death. Within our present scope Ranke's chief work is the *German History in the Age of the Reformation,* but we shall be better able to examine it after some broad consideration of his characteristics as a historical thinker.[32]

Despite Ranke's worldwide influence, many of these characteristics derived from somewhat narrow Lutheran traditions. Springing from a long succession of Evangelical clergy and spending his youth in theological and classical studies, Ranke regarded the discovery of historical truth as a species of religious obligation. Yet, being a seeker rather than an ecclesiast, he synthesized Lutheranism with Platonism and the humanism of Goethe and Herder. He was later on cordial terms with liberal Catholics like Acton and Döllinger, who thought of him as "plainly touched by healthy Catholic ideas."[33] He did, however, retain not a little of the spirit of Melanchthon, who had seen God's hand in all human history. Ranke was also familiar with Sleidan, who had said a number of things often regarded as Rankean. As we have observed, Sleidan proclaimed the interdependence of religious and secular history: he also urged historians to avoid excitement and rancor, think tentatively, and refrain from passing judgment on all and sundry.

This last principle, ignored so totally by Macaulay and some other English "hanging judges," relates quite closely to Ranke's view "that every epoch is immediate to God and its value does not rest upon what derives from it but upon its very existence in its individuality."[34] As Carlyle also said, human objectives, values, and modes of expression undergo constant change; each era is meaningful in itself. On the other hand, Ranke was not an ax grinder. He did not, like Carlyle or Engels, use history to attack the errors of his day. Nevertheless, he continued to distrust the worship of Progress, which Guizot respected, Macaulay apotheosized, and Carlyle loudly condemned. In effect, Ranke warns us against taking dead men and women as mere stepping-stones toward our noble selves, against using them as the white rats of modern political and social theory. For example, he sensed the special ethos of the Reformation and would certainly have held that historians create misunderstanding when they discuss it as a mere staging post on the way to the heavenly city of the eighteenth-century philosophes.

Politically, Ranke was a German conservative whose world had been overrun by Napoleon.[35] With Carlyle, he detested the mad bloodshed and conquest which had arisen from the French rabble and its militarist offspring. As an associate of the kings of Prussia and Bavaria, and the onetime editor of a journal sponsored by the Prussian government, he viewed Prussia—not without reason—as both constitutional and reformist. He even stood in a cordial relationship with the archconservative Metternich, who had opened important archives for his inspection. (Metternich could not, however, gain him access to those of the Vatican, which until the advent of Ludwig von Pastor did not encourage even Catholic scholars.) Nevertheless, Ranke should not be grouped with his younger contemporaries, the chauvinists such as Droysen, Leo, and Treitschke.[36] He remained a universalist with a generous respect for all civilization and a positive reverence not merely for the State in general but for the advanced national cultures of Christian Europe. Beside Church and State he placed Culture, in its widest aspects, as the third great force in human affairs.

Ranke did not achieve all these convictions without some struggle; he needed first to accomplish a series of withdrawals from the fashionable trends of his youth. He extricated himself not merely from religious and patriotic prejudices and revolutionary liberalism, but also from Idealist philosophy and its volatile relative, literary Romanticism. At the time of his appointment as a supernumerary professor at Berlin, the dominant thinker on the faculty was G. W. F. Hegel, no mere harmless metaphysician but an impassioned Protestant who saw the Reformation as inaugurating a "third phase" of German history: the triumph of the secular State, which would lead to the hegemony of Prussia, as opposed to that of indecisive Catholic Austria, over central Europe. In this Hegelian scenario, particular nations were charged with world missions. In the real world, some of them (like Great Britain) did not need encouragement from absolutist philosophers to launch such missions! Yet, in addition,

Hegelian metaphysics concluded that the individual can realize his spiritual and moral potential only through the State: "The Divine idea as it exists on earth . . . the embodiment of rational freedom, realising and recognising itself in an objective form."[37]

Despite his abiding respect for Prussia, Ranke eluded the control of this half-mystical creed to attempt objective historical inquiries, which he felt should operate in terms of fact, evidence, and documentation.[38] Thus, he outgrew his adherence to the subjective and pantheist notions of Herder and Fichte. Yet, while still unliberated, he wrote in 1817 a characteristically Romantic *Luther Fragment*, which has little in common with his sober assessment of the Reformer twenty years later. Eventually, Ranke would ascribe his development to three diverse influences: Thucydides, Niebuhr, and Luther himself, "the three spirits to whom I owe the basic elements upon which my later historical studies have been built."[39] He had completed this transformation by 1824, when his *Critique of Modern Historians,* a hard-headed examination of the main sources of early modern European history, appeared.[40]

As we have already implied, Ranke's first great work, the *History of the Popes* (1834–1839), has obvious relevance to Reformation studies, although it naturally throws far more light on the Counter-Reformation, a term Ranke invented. (He used it in the plural [*Gegenreformationen*] and regarded the phenomenon as a series of interlocked developments.)[41] Here also is a memorable passage, depicting Reformation and Counter-Reformation as two springs arising close together on a mountaintop and then flowing down by different paths.[42] Another striking page presents the contrast between the biblicist Luther and the vision-seeing Loyola, a contrast to the disadvantage of Loyola, whom Ranke nevertheless understood surprisingly well.[43] Despite his general lack of chauvinism, Ranke allows himself a patriotic reference to the Reformation as an essentially German triumph, crediting Germany "with the immortal merit of having restored Christianity to a purer form than it had worn since the first ages of the Church."[44]

For the rest, our assessment of Ranke as a historian of the Reformation must largely depend on his *German History in the Age of the Reformation,* a versatile and substantial work published in Berlin in six volumes from 1839 to 1847. Its English translation proved unfortunate, although it was undertaken by Sarah Austin, who had dealt so admirably with *The Popes.* Her edition omitted four of Ranke's ten books; it contained the narrative from 1535 to 1555, together with cultural chapters. Moreover, it altered the title to *History of the Reformation in Germany,* so mistaking Ranke's intention.[45]

Often regarded in Germany as Ranke's finest and most readable work, the whole book has a somewhat variable quality best appreciated by reading the portion most original for its time and still acceptable as a "standard" account, despite weighty additions by more recent research. This portion (books 2 and 3) contains an elaborate analysis of the causes and early progress of the Reformation in Germany. Ranke misses very few of the numerous factors we are still debating. He describes the tensions in both cities and universities; the disruptive influences of Nominalist theology and philosophy; the "Reformers before the Reformation" at work in the mid-fifteenth century; the pressures on Luther from Lorenzo Valla, John Huss, and Greek Orthodox traditions.

Above all, Ranke already employs both educated and popular sources to illustrate public opinion before and after Luther's initial protest. He pioneers the use of the *Flugschriften,* the popular pamphlet literature which today we are still cataloging and studying to great advantage.[46] Needless to add, Ranke was familiar with the works of both pietists and humanists; the *Theologia Germanica;* Luther's religious counselor Staupitz; the *Letters of Obscure Men;* and the writings of moralists such as Geiler von Kaysersberg, Sebastian Brant, and Erasmus. He illuminates religious themes by allusions to medieval architecture as well as to contemporary partisans like Dürer and Cranach. With the bibliographical aids that then existed, he counts up the *Flugschriften* published year by year, proving not merely their swift multiplication, but also the immense preponderance of Lutheran over Catholic pamphlets. Such contents demolish the widespread but misguided impression that Ranke took little interest in anything except high politics, rulers, diets, courts, and diplomatic missions.

On the side of theology Ranke proved less a leader, partly because the foundations of the so-called Luther renaissance had not yet been laid by theologians like Karl Hoffman (d. 1877) and Albrecht Ritschl (d. 1889). A fuller exposition of the doctrinal issues would certainly have improved the *German History.* Ranke prevents Luther's personality from dominating the whole picture by introducing him gradually into the narrative. He treats Luther's declarations of belief with discernment and even originality, making him essentially a reforming Catholic who detested the notion of founding a new Church, an antipapal Catholic who believed himself called to restore early Christian doctrine, an "early" Catholic opposed to both the innovating scholastic theology of the Middle Ages and the vulgar externalized superstitions of his day. Neither of these last aberrations could claim descent from New Testament or patristic Christianity. That monument of Lutheranism the Augsburg Confession

Ranke regards as "a product of the vital spirit of the Latin Church," an identification supported by Luther's instant attack on the extremists who had spawned in his shadow as well as in Zwingli's.

Ranke then proceeds to the years of social protest, during which the sectarians' religious enthusiasms became fused with the peasants' economic woes, evoking the great revolt of 1524–1525. Although he lacked modern research on Thomas Münzer and other radical leaders, he fully understood that the German Reformation was "a thing of the people," on whose receptivity its character and eventual fate depended. Ranke's chapter can reasonably be called the first "modern" account of the crisis, and again he uses the printed sources and local histories then available to investigate issues which are still active.[47] He explores regional variations, the rebellious roles of the townsmen, the influences of the ideological leaders who elevated material grievances into visionary blueprints for a new society. He describes the new financial exactions by ecclesiastical landlords which are today occasioning a heavy emphasis on anticlericalism as a major cause of the rising. In this chapter the just and measured interpretation is Ranke's own. The idiosyncratic but informed account of Münzer by Wilhelm Zimmermann was still being written; Friedrich Engels's short but gripping book on the Peasants' War was first published in 1850 in the *Neue Rheinische Zeitung*.[48] In their historical verdicts Ranke the conservative and Engels the socialist do not differ basically, both possessing an adequate fund of political realism.

Ranke viewed the revolt as a revival of old tensions brought about by four main factors: the vacillation of German government at all levels; the loss of public confidence in both Church and State; the influence of visionary preachers, who lacked Luther's sense of the possible; and the predictable loss of moderation among peasant leaders, who began with reasonable grievances, but on gaining a measure of success wanted "to reconstitute the Empire from the groundwork of society upwards." Yet Ranke freely acknowledges the absence of revolutionary intent in their initial Twelve Articles. He stresses the landlords' new exactions and observes with compassion the barbarity of the final slaughter. Noting the revival of infantry throughout Europe, he regards peasant successes as a distinct possibility had an abler leadership emerged. Yet he cannot envisage a triumphant peasantry administering the empire and erecting new social and governmental structures.

Engels wrote similarly, showing that Münzer rushed too far ahead of the ideas of his followers, who—hampered by their own localism and arrogance—rapidly became demoralized. Engels did not think that the rebels either could or should have won, because conditions were not ripe for their seizure of power and the effective domination of society by their class. In comparison, Ranke shows a personal sympathy with the peasant-victims, which is more remarkable because his mild and optimistic outlook so often prompted him to omit the blood and tears.

All in all, Ranke rebuffs his critics by writing not a staid, old-style politicoreligious book, but one singularly versatile and aware of the social issues. On the other hand, his views on the Reformation in England, mainly expressed in his immense volumes covering the Tudor and Stuart periods (*Englische Geschichte, 1859–1869*) fail to anticipate the advances of our century.[49] He announces that in Germany the movement was theological and popular, while in England it was juridicocanonical, not connected with appeals to the people or with free preaching but based on the unit of the nation.[50] For this simplification Ranke can hardly be castigated; even his English contemporaries, ignoring the clear evidence given by John Foxe and others, had failed to discover the popular Reformation running alongside the state reformation of Henry VIII and soon producing psychological forces more powerful than those attainable by a mere structural change.

Ranke understood the Reformation in Switzerland more deeply, yet his sympathies were not warmly engaged by it.[51] His partial alienation doubtless sprang from many factors: special admiration for Luther, dislike of Swiss iconoclasm, rejection of the Zwinglian fusion of Church and State, possibly even monarchist convictions which were opposed to the stark republicanism of so many Swiss cities and cantons. With Luther's spiritual struggles and passionately dogmatic zeal Ranke contrasts the plodding, unemotional character of Zwingli, whose original views seemed to him of a merely "moral and political nature." On the other hand, in describing the breakdown of talks between Luther and the Swiss at Marburg, Ranke is fair to the Swiss and does justice to the mediating theologian Martin Bucer, who was too often regarded as an opportunist by Lutheran zealots. Yet the Swiss had created their separate nationality, and with engaging frankness Ranke admits that his own primary concern is with the politicoreligious energies of the German nation.

Ranke regards Germany with a most critical eye. While declaring that it had given birth to a religious movement with deeper significance for the progress of mankind than that of the Italian Renaissance, he frankly deplores the Germans' failure to build a functioning nation-state of their own. The inconclusive reign of Charles V was far from rivaling those great political "climaxes" which Ranke discovered in the histories of other nations: in France the reign of Louis XIV, in England the Glorious Revolution of 1688.[52] By contrast, Germany saw the Hapsburg dynasty and the old empire split apart and the territorial princes become residuary legatees, too small and mutually jealous to supply effective national leadership until the nineteenth century.

Our account should not conclude without an updated view of Ranke's techniques and sources, because he has deservedly been placed among the exemplars of modern professional historiography. How far did Ranke deserve his formidable reputation as researcher, as discoverer and user of source materials, including those hitherto unprinted?[53] He clearly wanted to figure in this ambitious role, and in 1828–1831 had in fact conducted those prolonged researches into Italian and Austrian archives which had so enlivened his *Popes*. A decade later, in his preface to the *German History*, he supplied a significant account of the researches which had preceded it. In the autumn of 1836 he had discovered at Frankfurt am Main ninety-six volumes containing the acts of the imperial diets from 1414 to 1613. He claims that he had rapidly assimilated the first sixty-four of these volumes, reaching the year 1551. Realizing that this single city could not have preserved the whole documentation, he had obtained permission at the beginning of 1837 to investigate the Prussian royal archives in Berlin and then moved on to those of Saxony in April and to the Ernestine collection at Weimar in August. "The walls and the whole interior space," he relates, "are covered with the rolls of documents" relating to the Reformation crisis. Nevertheless, no scholar who has conducted researches in such major repositories will believe that Ranke could have inspected more than a small proportion of this manuscript material in a total of little more than one year.

We are not the first to entertain doubts regarding Ranke's purely archival achievements; as early as 1861 the distinguished Czech historian Anton Gindely attacked them with respect to Ranke's work on papal and French history, alleging in addition that, despite his repeated reference to the Simancas archives, Ranke could not have seen more than a dozen volumes in that collection. "His citations," concluded Gindely, "are mere crumbs stuck together in a chance fashion to produce the appearance of being the results of systematic study."[54] Even his admirer Acton wrote ironically that Ranke had started without manuscripts, then lightly skimmed them, and ended by holding "that it is not science to extract modern history from anything less than the entire body of written evidence."[55]

All the same, Gindely's near-implication that Ranke deliberately hoodwinked his readers by exaggerating the scope of his archival researches would be hard to sustain. Had Ranke intended, he could easily have manipulated the preface to conceal the relative brevity of his visits to Frankfurt, Berlin, Dresden, and Weimar. Instead, he actually mentioned the months. It remains true, however, that his preface, taken in isolation, seriously understresses his debt to the printed works of earlier German historians and archivists. Admittedly, he expresses gratitude to ten important scholars, yet a recent examination of some sixty books cited in the footnotes of the *German History* has revealed a mountain of printed material—for the most part published during the period 1700–1830—used for the *German History* and then largely forgotten. Many of the items are multivolume historical treatises on particular states or regions of Germany; several are weighty collections of documents relevant to both the political and religious aspects of the period under review.

From one perspective, Ranke's work on Reformation Germany forms a sepulchral monument to the laborious German writers of former generations: the real "Dryasdusts," on whom Ranke's synthesis depended. He used the work of these predecessors with outstanding intelligence, raising their bald facts and documents to a higher plane of creative scholarship. In this sense, rather than in a narrowly archival one, his effort is well supported. Whether he relied mainly on these printed documents or personally discovered vital sources in manuscript cannot greatly affect Ranke's reputation. The claims on his intelligence and industry remained immense, and he duly met them. As for Acton, he was not ridiculing Ranke: rather he was questioning those overambitious assumptions widely current among the earlier generations of "scientific" historians. In effect, Acton asked whether operations on the grand scale of Ranke's are really compatible with a sustained attempt to rewrite history by recourse to detailed archival research. For most would-be historians, does this not remain the most searching question of all?

Part Three

A STUDY IN CONTRASTS
The Modern Era

8

Polemics Transcended:
The Church Historians

Long-standing traditions reinforced by strong religious commitments limited the vulnerability of most Catholic and Protestant scholars to passing whims and even more significant shifts in European scholarly opinion in the centuries following the Reformation. Yet cultural influences which developed in Europe in the seventeenth and eighteenth centuries inevitably left a mark on the work of church historians and theologians. Only a superficial observer would fail to discern beneath the polemical thrust of much Catholic and Protestant writing clear signs of change extending beyond style and language to basic approaches and even fundamental scholarly aims.

Among the influences to which Catholic scholarship in Germany clearly responded, three deserve special note: the impact of Enlightenment thought, the influences of Hegelian philosophy, and the heritage of Rankean historiographic principles. The Enlightenment had been more positively appropriated by Catholic scholars in Germany than in France, particularly in university circles, where the abolition of the Jesuit order in 1773 had opened wide possibilities for new academic directions. Catholic intellectuals' tendency during this period to stress the inward voice of reason over external dogmatic revelation loosened rigid confessional structures, and the clearly irenic implications of this stance were mirrored concretely in common participation by Catholics and Protestants in the nation's cultural life. Hegelian dialectical philosophy, inherently inimical

179

to notions of truth as monolithic and unchangeable, profoundly influenced leading Catholic intellectuals, such as Franz Xaver von Baader (1765–1841), a social philosopher, lay theologian, and leader of the Munich circle of "Romantic" Catholics working for renewal of the Church.[1] A pioneer of ecumenism, Baader argued that confessional differences were a stage on the road by which Papist and Protestant would ultimately find a renewal of unity greater than both. Finally, and most significantly for the future, leading Catholic historians enthusiastically embraced the methodology of Ranke.

The first two factors go a long way to explain the significance of Catholic scholar Johann Adam Möhler (1796–1838), theologian and church historian at Tübingen and later Munich. Möhler was strongly influenced by Hegelian idealism, and his remarkably irenic disposition led him to seek out and maintain contacts with leading Protestant scholars and pursue a lifelong preoccupation with the question of unity and division in the Church. His first work on that subject, *Die Einheit in der Kirche,* written in 1825, demonstrates a deep sympathy with Reformation ideas about the Church's mystical and invisible character.[2] Möhler never entirely lost these ideas, although in response to accusations of modernism and heterodoxy he later stressed the divine institution of the Catholic Church and the objective truth of its faith.

Möhler's investigations of early and medieval Christianity led him to a study of the Reformation and, in particular, the doctrinal differences between Protestantism and Catholicism: he publicly acknowledged the need for a Reformation in the sixteenth century, although he argued that it had been unnecessarily revolutionary and destructive. He became increasingly preoccupied with close study of doctrinal differences, as evidenced in creeds or "symbols," and was the first Catholic scholar to develop the hitherto exclusively Protestant science of "symbolics": the comparative study of creeds and confessions.

In his major work *Symbolics* (1832), Möhler used a detailed study of the sources, especially Lutheran confessional writings, and presented the differences between Catholic and Protestant theology in an essentially calm and dispassionate manner, even when he sharply criticized the Protestant position.[3] Even more significant is the fact that Protestant doctrine appears as a reasonably coherent and self-consistent whole rather than a series of isolated propositions. Möhler genuinely attempted to understand not only its individual features but also its fundamental structure and the relationship among its parts. In this respect his work could scarcely be further from that of his sixteenth-century forebears.

As a theologian studying confessional documents, Möhler was not particularly interested in biographical comment on Luther's personal life and theological development. Yet his analysis of Reformation doctrine clearly implies a view of Luther as a man whose motivation was genuinely religious, despite the one-sidedness of his ideas and the perverse way he applied them. (This view is remarkably similar to Joseph Lortz's a century later.) Although Möhler's writings are by no means free of religious bias, they form a significant landmark in Catholic historiography, and not merely because of their pervasive conciliatory spirit. Committed to work from genuine historical sources, Möhler was also sensitive in his use of them. Earlier scholars had treated the doctrinal confessions as an arsenal of polemical ammunition; Möhler sought to understand their inner logic and the relationship of each part to the whole.

The historical seriousness in Möhler's work was symptomatic of an increasingly evident development in both Protestant and Catholic scholarship. For the Catholic Church the Romantic era became a time of profound renewal and some notable conversions to the cause. Intellectually, it was marked by the revival of a sense of history, which at times manifested itself in a naive and idealized recovery of the Middle Ages but among more profound thinkers emerged in a more highly developed historical sensitivity. Although the Protestant scholar Leopold von Ranke provided the most obvious stimulus to channel these intentions into a more "scientific" form of historical writing, some Catholics eagerly embraced his principles, not least because they disputed Ranke's success in following those principles and saw his work as an implicit apologia for the Protestant Reformation. Accordingly, the nineteenth century witnessed a new flowering of Catholic historical writing which was intended, at least in part, as a corrective to Ranke. This was, for instance, the explicit purpose behind the massive three-volume study of the Reformation by Ignaz von Döllinger (1799–1890),[4] and even if Döllinger seems in the end more obviously biased than Ranke, there is no need to doubt his sincere commitment to historical accuracy.

Catholic historiography of the Reformation from Döllinger in the middle of the nineteenth century to Grisar in the early twentieth is often interpreted as a grand finale to a tradition of confessional polemic extending back to the sixteenth century.[5] But such a view, although plausible, can only be admitted if one recognizes a concurrent development of serious and painstaking historical scholarship, sometimes mitigating the power of polemics, sometimes reinforcing it. Döllinger's long and stormy academic career had its center in Munich, where he served as professor of church history from 1826 to 1873, but his influence extended through correspondence and personal contacts across Europe. His writings reveal a fascinating interplay between polemical and historical interests. In his history of the Reformation and his 1851 "sketch" of Luther, we can see the beginnings of the intense psychobiographical preoccupation with Luther which became such a prominent part of modern Roman Catholic research on the Reformation.[6]

Döllinger differed radically from the early polemicists in his concern with Luther's inward dispositions and motives rather than with merely external factors and in his use of biographical investigation as the key to Luther's thought. He highlighted Luther's pride as the source of his problems and noted a propensity to distort and pervert true ideas, an innate tendency to violence, and a morbid preoccupation with evil, all of which influenced not only Luther's doctrine but his conduct as a theologian.[7] Notwithstanding his scathing criticism of the Reformer and his ponderous moral judgments, Döllinger's writings are a far cry from the superficial abuse and demonological fantasies of the early polemicists. His analysis at least derives from the Reformer's self-analysis and is plausibly related to the major tenets of his thought, such as the omnipotence of God, the doctrine of imputed righteousness, and man's inability to cooperate with God's grace.[8]

Döllinger remained intensely fascinated by Luther, and his understanding of the Reformation underwent significant change, not only because of the great length of his academic career—he died at age ninety-one—but because of his changing relationship with the papacy. A stern Ultramontane in his early period, he became increasingly opposed to the notion of papal infallibility in the years leading up to the Vatican Council and was finally excommunicated when he refused to subscribe to the newly proclaimed dogma.

In his later writings, Döllinger increasingly stressed Luther's Germanic qualities and portrayed him as the leader who personified the yearnings of the German people and was able to manipulate them to his purposes. Concurrently, Döllinger moved away from his intense preoccupation with psychobiography and no longer saw the Reformation as the product of Luther's tortured spirit. Instead, he delineated with some care the historical situation into which Luther came: the long German tradition of devotion to the Catholic faith and the prevalence of clerical abuses and justifiable hostility to Rome.[9]

Döllinger's Luther, it should be stressed, does not shrink in stature through this broadening and deepening of historical perspective. He remains a towering individual. But if he moves history, it is because he is the spokesman of his people and the man of the moment. In his 1871 lectures on church reunion, Döllinger offered the most mature statement of his new perspective, stressing the fundamental crisis among the German Church and people, which would have drawn them away from Rome even without the "Titan of the world of mind."[10] In elaborating on the

Curia's heavy responsibility for the Reformation schism, Döllinger emphasized the decades of papal silence in the face of manifest abuses and doctrinal confusion, and a refusal to confront the question of reform because of the threat to papal power and profits. No longer is the Reformation understood as the product of Luther's diseased and violent mind. Rather Luther is seen as the catalyst of reform in a Church which had been unable to bring about the changes it desperately needed.[11]

This alteration of outlook is symptomatic of a more fundamental process in Döllinger's maturing as a historian. His early writings, although intended as history based on sources, remain basically polemical, whereas his later work, despite the continued rejection of Luther as the "great heresiarch and seducer of the German nation,"[12] is historical writing with a high degree of objectivity. His discussion of the relative significance of Luther's personal influence and the deeper forces in German society is an admirable piece of sensitive, balanced judgment, and his identification of the Church's doctrinal confusion anticipates the position developed more substantially by Lortz. Döllinger's ability to realize so impressively in his later writings his early commitment to historical accuracy was undoubtedly assisted by his personal alienation from the ideological assumptions of the papacy, which gave him the freedom to be more open-minded about Luther and more critical of Rome. Nevertheless, his estrangement from the papacy made it highly unlikely that Döllinger's mature views would exercise any normative influence in Catholic scholarship.

More influential in the long run was the Frankfurt church historian Johannes Janssen (1829–1891), whose life and career were marked by intellectual consistency and a uniformly harmonious relationship with ecclesiastical authority. Perhaps for this very reason, advances in historical objectivity are harder to discern in his massive *History of the German People since the Close of the Middle Ages* (1876–1894), which was to provide a dominant historical framework for Catholic interpretation of the Reformation during subsequent generations.[13]

Despite his deep dependence on the early writings of Döllinger, Janssen did not lack originality. His use of archival sources was more extensive,[14] and he was less intensely preoccupied with the person of Luther. As his title indicates, Janssen's subject was the German people, not just towering individuals. He was, therefore, less interested in political history than in what he called *Kulturgeschichte*. His purpose, he declared later, was "not to give marked preference to so-called leading state events, campaigns and battles, but to depict the German national life in all its varying conditions and stages and phases of destiny."[15] When Janssen did attend to Luther's person, echoes of the early Döllinger are unmistakable. But he was more preoccupied with Luther's impact on the Church, and the image of the Reformer which dominates his history and unifies all his statements about Luther is that of the destroyer.

Such a judgment depends very much on a prior verdict about the condition of the Church into which Luther came. It is one of Janssen's most distinctive features that he attempted to refute the notion, derived especially from Protestant writings, that the fifteenth and early sixteenth centuries were a period of degeneration in the Church. He argued that evidence depicted the late medieval Church as fundamentally healthy and flourishing, and that the mid-fifteenth century in Germany witnessed the beginnings of a great period of reform in all levels of society—expressed in a prodigious output of sermons, scriptural translations, and devotional writings and a great blossoming of religious art.[16]

On the negative side, Janssen pointed to the empire's political weakness, which threatened its fundamentally harmonious relationship with the papacy, the source of Germany's strength during the Middle Ages; the introduction of alien Roman law, which fostered princely despotism; and the pernicious effects of capitalist commerce. Nor did Janssen, as is commonly thought, gloss over altogether serious clerical abuses and the pervasiveness of confusion and unrest that preceded Luther's emergence. Rather, he asserted that the Church's fundamental health and vitality provided the resources for cleansing from within, and that many of the Church's leaders were already utilizing those resources.

Luther's error was not that he saw the need for reform, but that he failed to see that all the necessary means were at hand and already at work. He therefore undid past achievements and nipped new reform in the bud.[17] Accordingly, Janssen heavily stressed the profound arrogance which, he believed, motivated all Luther's thought and action and the reckless violence with which Luther attacked church traditions— violence born of his attempts at self-justification in the face of a disquieted conscience. Yet at times Janssen freely recognized Luther's profound religious gifts, the sublimity of his language, the depth of his religious grasp, which recalled the heyday of German mysticism. Janssen naturally attributed these positive qualities to the "rich stream of influence from the Catholic past,"[18] and used them not so much to balance his portrait as to highlight his central image of Luther as the sledgehammer which destroyed everything hitherto held sacred and venerable.

Janssen's charges were ably rebutted from the Protestant side by Julius Köstlin (1826–1902), professor of church history at the University of Halle/Wittenberg, whose writings on Luther were widely influential not only in Germany but especially in Britain and the United States.[19]

Köstlin had followed up a major study of Luther's theology with a substantial two-volume work on Luther's life and writings, which he subsequently rewrote as a popular one-volume biography.[20] In the course of an essentially fair and balanced narrative account of the Reformation, Köstlin paid tribute to Luther as the one who "has united in his own person the true German nature with the deepest Christian piety," yet also recognized his personal failings and the divisive results of his work, noting that "even the highest aims and noblest principles are liable to suffer from human weakness and the human conditions by which they are surrounded."[21] Apart from his substantial personal contribution to studies of the Reformation, Köstlin was instrumental in forming the *Verein für Reformationsgeschichte* and publishing the early volumes of the Weimar edition of Luther's works. Through his many-sided work, German Protestantism remained closely in touch with its founder and original basis.

Another dimension to the nineteenth-century Protestant encounter with the Reformation developed, however—one more complex and perhaps ultimately more significant—the thoroughgoing reexamination of the Reformation heritage in light of the major philosophical changes stemming from the Enlightenment. Ironically, most of the key figures in nineteenth-century German philosophy emerged from Lutheran backgrounds, yet the overall effect of their recasting of philosophical ideas was to undermine the accepted basis of most theological work since the Reformation and radically question the relationship of contemporary Protestantism to its historical roots.

The refutation of rationalistic epistemology by Immanuel Kant (1724–1804), although specifically directed against the philosophical trends of his day, proved equally destructive of orthodox theology. Some Protestant scholars defiantly adhered to traditional patterns of thought, but the more flexible among them searched for a fresh nonrationalist basis for theology. The German idealist philosophers—Fichte, Schelling, and above all Hegel—developed the implications of Kantian epistemology into a comprehensive metaphysical system which, although it affirmed the primacy of spirit (*Geist*) in human existence and was thereby open to religious perspectives, essentially undermined the basis of most key Christian doctrines.[22]

Fichte's development of Kant's definition of religion into ethical pantheism, Schelling's doctrine of God as the "world-spirit" (*Weltgeist*), and Hegel's generalization of the doctrines of the Incarnation, Crucifixion, and Resurrection into a universal pattern of nature and history left theology with the alternative of adapting its concepts to the Hegelian system or striking out in new directions.[23] The first response came from F. C. Baur, D. F. Strauss, and the Tübingen school.[24] The second was evident, in radically different ways, in the German Protestant theologian Friedrich Schleiermacher (1768–1834) and the Danish philosopher Sören Kierkegaard (1813–1855).

Schleiermacher, profoundly influenced by Romanticism, defined religion as the feeling of unconditional dependence, and he restructured theology on that basis.[25] Kierkegaard rejected Schleiermacher's aestheticism along with Hegelian intellectualism and Kantian moralism in favor of the absolute "leap of faith."[26] Schleiermacher appealed to the experiential dimension of Luther's thought and Kierkegaard, more plausibly, to Luther's notion of faith, yet each had a highly ambivalent attitude toward the Reformation, and their obvious subordination of historical analysis to the philosophical-theological task places their work more clearly in the history of theology than of historical scholarship.

The most significant contribution of Protestant scholarship to historical understanding of the Reformation came from Albrecht Ritschl (1822–1889) and the "Ritschlian school," whose most direct intellectual dependence was on Kant.[27] The Ritschlians tended to interpret Kant as the philosopher of Protestantism because he rejected the identity of divine and human and insisted on human finitude. Hostile to all forms of mysticism, and indeed to any theology based on "experience," their scholarly program had a twofold basis— theology based on Kant's moral imperative and commitment to genuinely historical research opposing dogmatism of all kinds. The narrowness of their theological perspective has tended to preclude adequate recognition of their historical scholarship. Yet it was this very restriction of theology, and the consequent abandonment of any total intellectual system, which freed them to pursue historical inquiry with genuine openness.

Ritschl and those who followed him were avowedly Protestant but stood firmly for fair historical scholarship as the pathway to intellectual understanding. Accordingly, Ritschl's major work on the doctrine of justification and reconciliation was conceived in two parts, with historical study forming the basis of a dogmatic construction.[28] He thereby reversed the almost universal tendency of Protestant scholarship to examine the Reformers' thought through their creeds and confessions and chose to approach dogmatics through history. This led him, for example, to question on strictly historical grounds the basis of Möhler's comparative symbolics by indicating the fundamentally different purpose of doctrinal statements in Protestant and Catholic theology.[29]

In his theological analysis of the Reformation, Ritschl's strictly historical approach enabled him to anticipate by many years some insights of recent research. At a time when faith tended to be seen in subjective terms and the Reformation seen as an expression of individualism, Ritschl identified the essence of Lutheran faith as a conjunction of two elements—justifying faith, a frame of mind essentially determined by the historical appearance of Christ, and an objective conception of the Church as a divinely founded community of believers.[30] Ritschl's stress on Luther's catholicity, commonplace today, was remarkable in his time. On the other hand, the major historical weakness of Ritschl's analysis was his tendency to treat Luther without reference to his inheritance from late medieval thought. Nevertheless, Ritschl showed a fine sense of the similarities and differences among Luther, Calvin, and Zwingli and of the modifications in their traditions since the Reformation.[31] Moreover, his insight into the nature and origins of Anabaptism led him to articulate clearly views often thought to have originated in the 1930s.[32]

More influential than Ritschl in the long run was his pupil, Adolf von Harnack (1851–1930) who, although primarily a patristic scholar, wrote extensively on the Reformation.[33] Harnack's father, Theodosius, was the most significant representative of traditional Lutheranism, which had stayed aloof from the disturbing currents of nineteenth-century thought. He wrote the most influential book on Luther's theology published in the nineteenth century,[34] and his son remained influenced by this tradition, despite his clear rejection of it. The younger Harnack's distinguished academic career took him from Leipzig to Giessen, Marburg, and finally Berlin. His lectures on the nature of Christianity, which articulated his view of Protestantism as a reduction of religion to the essentials of the Word of God and faith, were widely read and extraordinarily influential.[35]

Yet Harnack's most imposing work was his massive *History of Dogma* (1886), which analyzed the development of Christian dogma from the New Testament to the Reformation.[36] The study of Luther with which this work concludes is especially impressive and derives much of its power from the way it relates Luther to the entire tradition of Christian thought. To Harnack, the rise of dogma evidenced the triumph of the Greek spirit in Christianity, and his judgment on Luther was highly ambivalent. On the one hand, the Reformer had liberated religion from ecclesiasticism and moralism; on the other, he had strengthened the structures of Catholic dogma in which it was cast. Harnack's task, as he conceived it, was to apply to dogma the same liberating critique which Luther had applied to religion; and although this implied that Luther's Reformation had not gone far enough, Harnack also asserted that Luther had gone too far in rejecting some abidingly valid aspects of the Catholic tradition, such as the doctrine of sacrifice and monasticism.[37]

The ability of some Protestant scholars to criticize their own tradition was even more clearly displayed in the work of Ernst Troeltsch (1865–1923), who belongs to the history of nineteenth-century theological scholarship as much as to the beginnings of sociology. Despite an early interest in jurisprudence and classical philology, Troeltsch had turned to theology because of its unique ability to unite metaphysical and historical questions. He served as professor of theology at the University of Heidelberg from 1894 to 1915 and subsequently as professor of philosophy in Berlin until his death. Never an "ivory-tower" academic, he held political office concurrently with his academic post during the early years of the Weimar republic, a testimony to his conviction about the close relationship of theory and practice, knowledge and ethics, past and present.

Troeltsch's views were expressed most directly in a major essay on Protestantism,[38] although they also informed his massive and influential study *The Social Teachings of the Christian Churches* (1912).[39] Unlike Ritschl and Harnack, he made no independent study of the primary sources and was content to reflect on others' findings, which made him vulnerable to scholarly attack. His mind was as committed to the present as Ranke's was to the past, and accordingly he approached the Reformation as a means to understanding his own time.

This posture led Troeltsch to challenge the widely held assumption that Protestantism represented the dawn of the modern era and that modern Protestantism was an authentic development of Reformation principles. To him, the Reformation was essentially a reshaping of the medieval idea and proposed new solutions to essentially medieval problems. In offering new solutions it was a genuine reshaping, yet it kept intact the basic features of the medieval system: the preoccupation with individual salvation, the ideal of a total Christian culture, the notion of the Church as a divine institution, and acknowledgment of an absolute authority. The result of the Reformation, therefore, was a second blossoming of medieval life for two centuries and a devitalization of the secular culture which had begun so tentatively to emerge.[40]

Troeltsch, to be sure, recognized that Luther's key ideas were essentially destructive of the medieval system, but he insisted that their impact remained limited to the religious sphere and brought no basic change in social life. Change, in his view, was made possible by the Enlightenment, with its assertion of human autonomy carried forward by the alliance of the secular state with the secular study of science.[41] Further, unlike other liberals, who argued that nineteenth-century neo-Protestantism was a legitimate development of the Reformation, Troeltsch could see only complete contradiction between the two. The neoorthodox Protestants of the next generation would share this view, although they would draw from it opposite conclusions.

In Continental Europe during the nineteenth century, no country rivaled Germany in vigor and vitality of scholarship on the Reformation. Scandinavian research had as yet made no substantial impact outside the region. France, which had exercised such a pivotal role in the age of Bossuet and Bayle, had produced no successor of their stature, and French scholars who considered the Reformation at all remained largely preoccupied with local or national issues. However, a history in the French language by a Swiss Evangelical, J. H. Merle D'Aubigné (1794–1872), who had worked in Germany and the Low Countries, was translated into many languages and became more widely influential than any other single Evangelical contribution, especially in Scottish Calvinist circles, where its unstinting support of Reformation doctrine found a ready response.[42]

If German preeminence was challenged anywhere, it was in Britain, where a vigorous scholarly debate on the Reformation continued throughout the nineteenth century.[43] This debate was less insular than has often been assumed, for its links with German scholarship—particularly through books, translations, and personal scholarly contacts—were both extensive and profound. Nevertheless, British scholarship on the Reformation preserved distinctive characteristics and preoccupations arising out of its unique inheritance from the Reformation period. Spokesmen of the established Church of England were confronted by opponents in the Roman and dissenting traditions, powerful and articulate despite their continuing social and political disabilities. More significantly, these spokesmen could not even agree among themselves on whether the Church of England was a legitimate child of the Reformation, and whether the reformation it had undergone was a renewal or a perversion of the true faith. Consequently, the interweaving of historical judgments and contemporary preoccupations—never absent from scholarly debates—was in nineteenth-century British studies of the Reformation particularly acute.

The Tractarian movement in the Anglican Church preserved its estimate of Anglicanism's integrity by driving a wedge between the English and Continental Reformations, holding up the Anglican Church as a *via media* between the superstition of Rome and the sectarian divisiveness of Geneva. It saw the Church of England seeking to unite true interpretation of Scripture with preservation of the apostolic succession. The Anglican Church, as Walter Farquhar Hook (1798–1875) put it, was "one and the same Church before and after the Reformation," which was "not a beginning but a turning-point."[44] Tractarians were generally willing to recognize the sincerity of Luther's reforming intentions, but had no doubt about their lamentable outcome, not only in religious disintegration but in their supposed social and political fruits in the English and French revolutions. They were not, however, all of one mind on the details. E. B. Pusey (1800–1882) had originally asserted that error had been introduced not by Luther but by his successors, who had progressively lost his Christian inspiration and debased his doctrine of Christian freedom. Later Pusey argued that the crucial error lay in the schism and the Lutheran churches' loss of the apostolic succession.[45]

John Henry Newman (1801–1890), however, was already convinced during his Anglican phase of Luther's fundamental theological errors. In his *Lectures on Justification* (1838, 1840), he attacked the heart of Luther's theology, accusing him of denying the unity of Scripture and treating faith as an end in itself, thereby leaving Christians in bondage to their feelings.[46] Luther's problem was not so much what he taught as what he left out or denied, for a partial and unbalanced view of truth was to Newman the very essence of heresy. Newman, it must be said, had little direct knowledge of Luther or the Reformation, but centered his reflections on the history of the early Church, which he used as his measure.

At the opposite extreme of the spectrum, the Evangelicals saw themselves as spiritual heirs of the Reformers, although that consensus guaranteed neither the uniformity nor the reliability of their interpretation. Evangelicals were divided in two ways: ecclesiastically between adherents of the established Church and those of various dissenting traditions; and theologically between Calvinists, who identified Reformation theology with scriptural truth, and Arminians, who believed that the early Reformers had remained under the spell of Augustinian scholasticism. Yet all Evangelicals were at one in their anti-Romanism and their vision of an "evangelical succession" of true faith through the Christian Era derived from the traditions of the *Magdeburg Centuries* (see Chapter 1) and John Foxe (see Chapter 2).

This notion received its clearest statement in the work of Joseph Milner (1744–1799), his brother Isaac (1750–1820), and John Scott (1777–1834). Joseph Milner's *History of the Church of Christ* (1794–1797) traced the story to the eve of the Reformation; Isaac Milner dealt with the first half of Luther's life, depicting the Reformer as God's instrument to reestablish the true basis of Christian faith. Scott continued their work, and at the time of his death had reached the death of Calvin, although a planned volume on the English Reformation never eventuated. Together, these works formed the standard Evangelical account until superseded by the translation of D'Aubigné's book.[47]

Universal conviction among Evangelicals about Luther's divine mission in no way preserved the Reformer from criticism. Henry Stebbing (1799–1887), an Anglican, condemned Luther for his intolerance of Karlstadt;[48] the Baptist Augustus Cox (1783–1853) regarded his sacramental theology as a superstitious remnant of Romanism.[49] Luther's defects of character and personal behavior were widely and clearly indicated, though generally excused in view of his divine mission. Other common Evangelical themes included stern criticism of Erasmus for offenses ranging from weakness to apostasy and emphasis on pre-Reformation figures such as the Waldensians, Wycliffe, and Huss as Luther's spiritual forerunners in the "evangelical succession."[50]

Involvement of scholarship on the Reformation in the ecclesiastical controversies of the day resulted paradoxically in some major scholarly achievements, including the Parker Society's edition of the English Reformers' works and the Calvin Translation Society's fifty-two volumes of Calvin in English.[51] Neither was a labor of disinterested scholarship: the first reflects the Evangelicals' determination to remind an English Church which appeared to be heading pell-mell for Rome of its Protestant origins; the second reflects the Scottish Free Church's confidence "that the days of latitudinarian belief and ecclesiastical subordination to the temporal power were over."[52] In the second half of the century, the Scottish Free Church provided the most notable writers on Reformation theology, James Buchanan and William Cunningham, whose uncompromising Calvinist orthodoxy embodied the triumph of dogmatic tradition over genuinely historical analysis. In England, by contrast, Evangelicalism tended to decline into narrow fundamentalism and antiintellectualism in the face of challenges from both Rome and secularism.

The 1883 celebration of the 400th anniversary of Luther's birth provided some redirection of Evangelical energies in the face of these challenges, although Anglicans were divided about whether or not to observe the event.[53] More significant than the celebrations was the stimulus they provided to informed and critical analysis of the Reformation, of which the outstanding products were Henry Wace and C. A. Buchheim's *First Principles of the Reformation* (1883)—a translation of the Ninety-five Theses and the Reformation treatises—and the translation of Köstlin's great biography of Luther.[54]

Between the Tractarians on the one hand and the Evangelicals on the other, English liberal Protestants were broadly committed to a scriptural religion in which ethical concern took precedence over narrow dogmatism. Among the large group of broad churchmen, this standard tended to govern attitudes about the Reformers. Not surprisingly, Erasmus was accorded a better reception; and Zwingli, as the disciple of Erasmus and the Reformer most free from the scholastic inheritance, seemed more in line with the critical spirit of the times than either Luther or Calvin.[55] Isaac Taylor (1787–1865) and John Tulloch (1823–1886) both criticized the Reformers for having compromised scriptural religion by their continued adherence to metaphysical dogma. They saw in this failure to transcend the dogmatic spirit seeds of the Reformers' ultimate inability to carry the movement through to its proper conclusion.[56]

The most comprehensive attempt to set this perspective in the full context of church history was provided by Henry Hart Milman (1791–1868) in his *History of Latin Christianity* (1855).[57] Milman accepted unequivocally the notion of progress and regarded Christian history as an incomplete historical development. The Reformers were in his view men of destiny who set the Church on its future course although they remained burdened by past legacies. The Reformation needed a Luther rather than an Erasmus to carry it out, although in the long run Erasmus's ideas were closer to the Christianity of the future.

Another circle of liberal Protestants owed much to the influence of the Anglican cleric and Christian socialist leader F. D. Maurice (1805–1872), whose reaction against narrow dogmatism was directed as much toward recovery of a deeper sense of the infinite as toward concrete social reform. For Maurice and his circle, contemporary liberal rationalism was no better than its scholastic ancestor; both made man the measure of religion and morality instead of aspiring to the absolute. Accordingly, Maurice responded warmly to Luther's passion for God, his great spiritual depth, his ability to lift man outside himself, and the hatred of formalism and definition which distinguished him from the other Reformers.[58] In striving for the infinite, Luther had captured one half of Christianity admirably, although he had neglected the other half, the message of social renewal.

From Maurice's circle emerged probably the most substantial and impressive work on Luther in nineteenth-century British scholarship, Julius Charles Hare's *Vindication of Luther against his recent English assailants* (1852).[59] Hare (1795–1855), who was archdeacon of Lewes and brother-in-law of Maurice, attacked a variety of opponents from the liberal critics William Hamilton and Henry Hallam to the Catholics Newman and W. G. Ward. All, he believed, were guilty of prejudice, selective quotation out of context, and reliance on secondhand information. Moreover, they showed themselves unable to grasp Luther's spirituality because of their coldly rational attitude toward religion. Hare's point-by-point refutation of his opponents owes its strength to his direct and intimate acquaintance with Luther's writings in the original language, rare in Victorian English scholarship. But his criticism attained a deeper level. A great admirer of Ranke, Hare pleaded consistently for broad historical thinking about the

Reformation as an alternative to submission to the exigencies of nine-teenth-century Anglican polemics. In this respect, he had no more time for the Evangelicals' support of Luther than for the attacks of his detractors, because the Luther they had created in their own image—the individualistic proto-Evangelical—was equally a falsification of history. In his positive treatment, Hare showed an unerring sense of Luther's priorities. He insisted on the centrality of the doctrine of justification, and much of his defense of Luther focuses on proper interpretation of that doctrine.[60] He also insisted on Luther's positive and complementary relationship to the Anglican Reformation, which had added to Luther's concern for fundamental theology a gift for practical application.[61]

English Roman Catholic scholarship in the eighteenth century had manifested virtually no interest in the Continental Reformation, and the first substantial treatment of it for some time appeared in the fourth volume of John Lingard's *History of England* (1819–1830), as an extended aside to the main theme.[62] Writing a balanced Catholic account of the Reformation in the years leading up to Catholic emancipation was a sensitive and delicate assignment. Lingard (1771–1851), trained at Douai and influenced by its Gallican tendencies, eschewed the obvious distortions of the polemical tradition and wrote in such a spirit of fairness that some Catholics considered his work unduly conciliatory. He freely admitted the prevalence of corruption in the late medieval Church and attributed much of it to the apostasy of the papacy. Although Lingard acknowledged some admirable qualities in Luther, the Reformer emerges from his work essentially as a self-seeking opportunist, grossly intemperate and subservient to princely interests, one who in destroying regard for authority had become the father of sectarian division despite his bitter opposition to the sects his movement spawned.[63] Lingard's account of the English Reformation is notable for its heavy emphasis on the impact of the Henrician divorce, its assessment of the reign of Edward as a time of confusion and anarchy, and its gross misjudgment of Cranmer as despicable.

Toward the middle of the century, in an essay attached to the English translation of the Tridentine decrees, James Waterworth gave a picture—similar to Lingard's and anticipating Janssen's—of Luther as a learned but undisciplined scholar launching a reckless attack on a Church which, despite its problems and abuses, remained fundamentally peaceful.[64] The predictable recurrence of traditional Catholic perspectives did not indicate, however, a uniformity of view about the Reformation's place in the development of Christianity from medieval times. Some Catholics expressed a naive and romantic idealization of the Middle Ages and identified Protestantism with the evils which had borne fruit in the nineteenth century.[65] On the other hand, scholars like Charles Butler and Sylvester Mahony, each of whom attempted to rehabilitate Erasmus as the proponent of wisdom and enlightenment, explicity rejected the medieval scholastic tradition as barbaric, anticipating Newman's stance on the side of Renaissance classicism against a Gothic barbarism which he saw extended in the Reformation.[66] Lord Acton gave further proof that being a Catholic and rejecting the Reformation did not necessarily mean attachment to an idealized Middle Age or opposition to the contemporary world.

John Emerich Edward Dalberg-Acton (1834–1902) brought to his historical studies an unusual background and training. Born in Italy of an aristocratic Catholic family, he grew up in a cosmopolitan environment, studying in Paris, Edinburgh, and Munich (where he was a pupil of Döllinger); acquiring a sound knowledge of major European languages; traveling widely through Europe and to America. He knew nothing of the political and social restrictions under which many of his coreligionists had labored in England, and his remoteness from them was only accentuated by his friendship with Gladstone and acquisition of a peerage, on Gladstone's recommendation, in 1869.

Acton remained, nevertheless, highly conscious of his Catholicism and deeply preoccupied with the relationship of Catholicism to the contemporary world, which became an important concern in the third quarter of the century and culminated—despite the best efforts of scholars like Acton and Döllinger—in the Church's resolute stance against modernity. From 1858, when he began his close association with the *Rambler*, Acton popularized a conception of the Catholic Church as the natural ally of freedom through its role as liberator of humanity from the tyranny of the antique state. Unafraid of historical truth and critical scholarship, Catholicism in this view contrasted sharply with Protestantism, which was naturally illiberal, fearful of critical scholarship, theologically barbarous, and tied to current creeds of political tyranny. The Reformation represented a narrowing of the European spirit after the freedom of medieval civilization.[67] Yet this liberal and optimistic vision of Catholicism was shattered by promulgation of the doctrine of infallibility. From that point Acton's role in Catholic intellectual life diminished, although his commitment to unbiased historical scholarship as an expression of his Catholic faith only became firmer.

From around 1875 to 1900, British scholarship among Catholics and Protestants alike exhibited signs of increasing specialization. Apologetic motives often lay behind this trend, as was clearly the case with Abbot F. A. Gasquet's work on the dissolution of the English monasteries, an impassioned defense of English monastic life on the eve of the Reformation as healthy, vigorous, popular, and beneficent, and an account of its destruction through the greed of Cromwell and his supporters.[68] Gasquet (1846–1929) also republished William Cobbett's *History of the Protestant Reformation* and was much influenced by its romantic conception of monastic estates as the "patrimony of the poor."[69] In Gasquet's eyes the Reformation was a revolution of the strong against the weak, and—here he echoed Janssen—a blight on a society in which religion was "the bloom upon the choicest fruit." Far from being quintessentially English, as Froude had claimed, the movement had been a foreign import of "false and poisonous teachings."[70] Gasquet's strength and originality lay in his setting of institutional history in a rich social and intellectual context, and this was certainly a healthy corrective to biased Protestant views of the dissolution. On the other hand, he was flagrantly inaccurate in his transcription and citation of sources, too much inclined to fill gaps with unsubstantiated conjecture, and, despite his foreign ancestry, stubbornly insular.[71]

Scarcely less insular was the Anglo-Catholic version of Reformation history published by Canon Richard Watson Dixon of Carlisle (1833–1900), who triumphed over his remote situation by short, intensive visits to the library of the British Museum.[72] Dixon severely criticized the Reformation's achievements, especially the dissolution of the monasteries, which he regarded as vulgar profiteering. He insisted, nevertheless, that there had been no break in the continuity of the English Church during the Reformation. Although corrupted, robbed, and seized by alien influences, it had remained the true Church of the realm. In line with this perspective, Dixon began the history of the English Reformation with the 1529 parliament, and saw the religious revolution as the result of a tragic combination of circumstances (including the king's divorce) without which the Church would have beaten off the Protestant challenge while absorbing healthy new influences from humanism.[73] In his neglect of Lollardy and the earliest manifestations of Protestantism, Dixon reflected the characteristic attitudes of late Victorian High Churchmen. His prejudice mingled with chauvinism, leading him to attribute most evils to sinister foreign influences, which had their way for a time until the firm actions of churchmen like Gardiner managed to preserve the Catholic principle and save the old religion from heresy while dispensing with the Roman tyranny. Notwithstanding its prejudices, Dixon's conscientious six-volume *History of the Church of England* (1878–1902) retains a distinct value, especially in its close analysis of the Henrician statutes and its aspiration to describe the Reformation's social and economic consequences.[74]

The upsurge of Protestant fervor in the celebrations of 1883 met a predictable response from Catholic circles in the form of a series of pamphlets rekindling the old fires of confessional prejudice. Yet the maturing of historical scholarship could not but affect church historians writing at this time. Although most scholars' personal religious stances remained abundantly clear, the trend toward historical realism and objectivity was no less apparent.

Henry Wace (1836–1924), dean of Canterbury and formerly professor of ecclesiastical history at King's College, London, complemented his joint work on Reformation documents with some significant interpretive writings which, despite their moralizing tendency, are valuable for their stress on the positive relationship between the Continental and English Reformations and their placement of the Reformation in the context of late medieval spirituality and scholastic theology.[75]

With his multivolume *History of the Papacy* (1897), Mandell Creighton (1843–1901), professor of ecclesiastical history at Cambridge and later bishop of London, demonstrated a clear commitment to Rankean principles of scrupulous objectivity and provided a most informative survey.[76] On the other hand, his fifth volume, which deals with the Reformation, affords a somewhat superficial view of the German movement and scant understanding of its major ideas.

Charles Beard (1827–1888) was a Unitarian scholar, personally committed to evolutionary science and empirical reasoning, and this profoundly shaped his distinctive—some would say perverse—view of the Reformation as a movement for free rational inquiry which had broken the authoritarian system but arbitrarily stopped short of its goal.[77] Yet this rather narrow perspective did not prevent him from demonstrating a remarkably broad understanding of historical variety. Sympathy with the more radical trends of Reformation thought and a conviction that the path of the future lay with Erasmus rather than Luther in no way prevented Beard from recognizing Luther's profound spirituality and indispensable contribution. Meanwhile, Lord Acton, in his maturity as Regius Professor of Modern History at Cambridge, continued to be preoccupied with notions of liberty. Most of his work appeared posthumously as collected essays and lectures, but he did enunciate some genuine insights, among which his recognition of Luther's essential conservatism deserves particular mention.[78]

The outstanding British historian of the Reformation in this period was undoubtedly the Scotsman T. M. Lindsay (1843–1914), who not only summed up much of the best of nineteenth-century church historical scholarship but in a number of ways broke genuinely new ground. A minister of the Free Church of Scotland, he was professor of church history from 1872 and from 1902 principal at a theological college in Glasgow; he wrote extensively on the Reformation for more than thirty years.

Lindsay's first major contribution was an article on Luther for the ninth edition of the *Encyclopaedia Britannica,* in which he united a firm grasp of Luther's central religious insight of justification by faith and spiritual freedom with a critical judgment about its inadequate social and political realization in Germany, for which Lindsay held Luther in part responsible.[79] The Swiss Reformers were seen as having more fully put into practice the implications of Reformation doctrine, although there is no doubt that Lindsay regarded Luther's forceful enunciation of the Reformation's spiritual basis as the linchpin of the whole movement. In *Luther and the German Reformation* (1900) and in his chapter for the second volume of the *Cambridge Modern History,* Lindsay broke free of the narrow confines of ecclesiastical history and academic theology, setting Luther squarely in his social context and arguing that the Reformer's central insight sprang from the religious understanding of the common people from whom he had come.[80] Luther thus became spokesman of the popular spirit against a sterile and lifeless theology.

In Lindsay's last major work, the comprehensive two-volume *History of the Reformation in Europe* (1906–1907), he maintained his interest in popular religion and argued that Luther's teaching succeeded because it presented no startling novelties to the people, but "something which they had always at heart believed, though they might not have been able to formulate it."[81] The first volume gains much of its strength from detailed study of social, economic, and religious background, which forms the basis for Lindsay's account of the German Reformation up to the Peace of Augsburg. The second volume, treating the Reformation outside Germany, is especially notable for its demonstration of the author's sympathy for movements as diverse as Calvinism and Anabaptism. Particularly significant is his recognition—some decades before the revival of Anabaptist studies—that these sectarians had been unfairly treated by historians. Lindsay paid tribute to their high moral qualities, the learning of many of their leaders, and their pioneering commitment to religious toleration.[82] In short, Lindsay provided the clearest indication that sincere confessional commitment need not preclude historical writing which transcends party allegiances. The thoroughness and professionalism of his works make them not only definitive for their day but enduringly valuable to students of the Reformation.

The trend toward greater professionalism in British studies of the Reformation, of which Lindsay's work is the outstanding example, was not yet so evident on the other side of the Atlantic, although there were significant exceptions. The academic environments of the two major English-speaking nations in the late nineteenth century had little in common, and a comparison is instructive.

Despite its geographic remoteness, the United States had maintained a more intimate connection with the European Continent than had Britain through a continuing stream of European immigrants and their descendants, who generally retained their linguistic and religious traditions. In particular, the strong complement of German and Scandinavian Lutherans in the United States had no counterpart in Britain. On the other hand, American religious life had as yet done little to foster scholarship on the Reformation. Nineteenth-century American Protestantism was characterized by either a narrow, inward-looking confessionalism or a proliferation of new denominations which owed more to contemporary American ideals than to an awareness of religious traditions. The Luther jubilee of 1883 brought to America, as to Britain, a heightened consciousness of the Reformation heritage, but most of its expressions were anything but scholarly. Celebrated as a folk hero and champion of American ideals of civic and religious freedom, Luther also became a focus for Protestant suspicion of a Catholic Church which was not only advancing theoretical claims but making its presence felt through large-scale immigration to major urban centers.[83]

The celebrations, however, also bore positive fruits. Köstlin's activities as a writer, organizer, and editor were even more influential in America than in Britain, aided by a strong Lutheran confessional tradition and persistence of a large German-language reading public. These initiatives stimulated significant academic enterprises in America, including the first critical edition of the Lutheran confessions in English and the large St. Louis edition of Luther's works.[84]

Moreover, when most American scholars remained bound by their confessional horizons, there was one who made a distinctive and enduring contribution to international scholarship of the Reformation. Philip Schaff (1819–1893) was anything but typical of American Protestantism and perhaps for that reason personified the best of its intellectual traditions. Born in Switzerland and educated in Germany, where he was deeply influenced by August Neander and the Tübingen school of Hegelian historians, he developed an intense commitment to his adopted country. A supporter of the Prussian Union Church, which had united Lutheran and Reformed traditions in Germany, he maintained wide contacts across denominational boundaries in his new homeland and progressively sought a less restricted constituency for his academic work.

After two decades in a Reformed denominational seminary in Mercersburg, Pennsylvania, Schaff moved to cosmopolitan New York and the ecumenical setting of the Union Theological Seminary, where he became affiliated with the Presbyterian Church, a body predominantly British in origin. His career embraced New Testament studies, chairmanship of the American committee for revision of the English Bible (which involved close contact with the parent committee in England), editorship of a major religious encyclopedia, coeditorship with Henry Wace of an edition of the church fathers, and a leading role in founding the American Society for Church History.[85]

Schaff's reputation, however, was based chiefly on his historical work, which displayed an unusual blend of confessional and ecumenical concerns. As early as 1845, in *The Principles of Protestantism*, he claimed that catholicity belongs to the Reformation rather than the Roman Church. That church had exchanged true catholicity for Roman particularity; by contrast, the Reformation was "the legitimate offspring, the great act of the Catholic Church," and hence truly catholic.[86] The same preoccupation informs Schaff's *History of the Christian Church*, which covers from the Apostles to the Reformation era and was completed in six volumes in 1892.[87] It is an antisectarian but by no means anticonfessional work. Schaff's ecumenical aspirations enabled him to appreciate and give full weight to the strengths of various confessional traditions without regarding any of them as final. This work remained for some time the most substantial account of the Reformation in English, and much of it is still valuable, although in some respects dated by its strong emphasis on Hegelian notions of development.

Schaff's vision of church history is embodied concretely in the substantial book *Creeds of Christendom* (1877), which assembles the bulk of the confessional writings of both Catholic and Evangelical churches with a massive and detailed analytical study. In thus introducing Americans to comparative symbolics, Schaff was highlighting confessional differences, but he made clear in the preface that this was an integral part of the ecumenical and historical process. In what amounts to a statement of his philosophy as a church historian, he declared that "honest and earnest controversy conducted in a Christian and catholic spirit promotes true and lasting union. Polemics looks to Irenics—the aim of war is peace."[88]

Fitting though this may be as an epitaph for Schaff's work, early-twentieth-century developments in the Roman Church would show that polemics might be used for a purpose far removed from irenics. The manifest progress of Catholic and Protestant historians of the late nineteenth century toward a more critical and historical approach was not likely to be permanently reversed. Yet the work of two scholars whose writings dominated Roman Catholic research on the Reformation in the first two decades of the 1900s underlines the unpredictability of historical scholarship and the complex relationship between polemical and historical interests. Heinrich Denifle and, to a lesser extent, Hartmann Grisar manifested a spirit of bitterness difficult to parallel in the history of Catholic thought; yet, paradoxically, much of the power of their attack derived from the wealth of genuine sources on which their writings were based.

Heinrich Denifle (1844–1905) was a distinguished medievalist whose lifetime study of the problems of the late medieval Church ultimately led him to Luther. After five years' painstaking research in German, Austrian, and papal archives, he published *Luther and Lutheranism* (1904), which burst through the confines of the learned world to become a subject of debate in press and government circles.[89] The work's staggering impact was a result not merely of the author's ferocious style, but of his claim that its only sources were Luther's own writings. This was no idle claim; he had made extensive use of sources previously available and unearthed in the Vatican library a copy of Luther's early *Lectures on Romans,* previously inaccessible to historians.[90] These provided an arsenal with which Denifle attempted to discredit Luther as a creature thoroughly corrupted by his sensual nature and an ignoramus, incompetent to handle theological issues.

Several aspects of Denifle's historical outlook deserve note, specifically his implicit rejection of Janssen's idyllic picture of the fifteenth-century Church and his recognition of its deep and unresolved crisis. Yet the real importance of Denifle's work lies not in any specific historical judgments but in its attempt—virtually unparalleled at the time—to place Luther squarely in his historical context: ecclesiastically, by relating him to patterns of church life in the fifteenth century, and intellectually, by showing his dependence on a particular stream of medieval theology.[91] Its inadequate analysis by no means negates the importance of this development in historiography. Denifle's failure to capitalize on the possibilities of this approach is attributable not merely to a passionate hatred of Luther, which overwhelmed all objectivity, but to his ultimately greater interest in philosophical patterns of history than in particular phenomena. Luther the man, the theologian, the reformer, was lost in the delineation of Luther the decadent type, the incarnation of that evil current running through the late medieval Church.

This fundamentally unhistorical aspect of Denifle's treatment did not escape the more astute Protestant critics, who were thrown on the defensive by such a savage indictment.[92] The distinguished medievalist had exposed, if nothing else, the appalling ignorance of many of Luther's admirers about the medieval world from which the Reformer had emerged. If the immediate effect of Denifle's attack was a mixture of outrage and panic, in the long run it forced Protestant scholars to reexamine their approach to Luther. The seminal work of scholars like Karl Holl and Otto Scheel originated largely from the challenge Denifle posed. By a strange irony, therefore, this archenemy of Luther became, indirectly and unconsciously, one of the major impetuses for the "Luther renaissance" of the early twentieth century.

That Denifle also substantially influenced contemporary Catholic scholars was to be expected. Yet it is remarkable how severely he was criticized by his fellow Catholics and how swiftly his most distinctive emphases were drastically modified or discarded. Such changes were facilitated by the appearance of another major Catholic work on Luther with a recognizably different perspective. Hartmann Grisar's three-volume study, published in 1911–1912, was also the product of years of scholarly research and centrally concerned with Luther's inward life as the key to the Reformation.[93] Yet Grisar (1845–1932) openly rejected some of Denifle's basic conclusions, especially the notion of Luther's submission to sensuality, and traced the Reformer's intellectual and moral decline to profound pride and egoism, rooted in a deep-seated psychopathic illness.

Grisar's work displays an impressive erudition. He was profoundly influenced by the school of Ranke, and he consciously aimed at an objectivity which he believed Denifle lacked. In many parts of his work, where he analyzed specific issues of historical interpretation in close detail, his talents are shown to good advantage. Yet few scholars could credit his work as a whole with that basic fairness he sincerely believed it to have. This was because Grisar's achievements were invariably balanced by failures. If he boldly refuted a number of palpable fables and groundless calumnies against Luther, he revivified just as many and left standing by innuendo others, which he acknowledged in the telling as unproven. He exhibited throughout a deep hostility and partiality, which led most scholars—both Catholic and Protestant—to conclude that his differences from Denifle were, in the last analysis, marginal.[94]

It is true that Grisar's analysis permitted a certain softening of the picture of Luther. He dwelled on the Reformer's favorable personality traits, credited him with the best of motives, and showered him with the sympathy appropriate to a diseased soul where Denifle could manage only scorn and contempt for a degenerate wallowing in his bestiality. Yet many Protestants found Grisar's condescending pity more offensive than Denifle's open hostility.[95] Nevertheless, Grisar's work, based on such solid if selective research, continued to force scholars back to the sources to question unexamined assumptions and poorly founded conclusions.

Revolutions in scholarship can rarely be dated with precision, yet the four hundredth anniversary of the posting of the Ninety-five Theses, in 1917, saw the appearance of two major essays—one Protestant, one Catholic—each signaling something of great importance in the history of research on the Reformation. Karl Holl's essay on Luther's understanding of religion has long been regarded as central to the Luther renaissance of the twentieth century. Franz Xaver Kiefl's shorter and less known essay on Luther's "religious psyche" has more recently been recognized for its pioneering significance in Catholic scholarship.[96] Yet more than mere scholarly caution warns against ascribing too much significance to particular dates. Seminal essays generally derive their power as much from favorable conditions as from their inherent qualities, and such was certainly the case with these two. Holl's work, for all its originality, is arguably the descendant of nineteenth-century scholarship, inconceivable apart from the historical traditions of the Ritschlian school and the textual research which from 1883 bore fruit in the monumental Weimar edition of Luther's works. Yet Holl's significance is equally illuminated by comparison with another group of Protestant scholars who began, from the second decade of the century, to reappropriate the Reformers' theological insights.

The theological revival led by the Swiss pastor and theologian Karl Barth (1886–1968) and somewhat misleadingly known as *neoorthodoxy* arose in opposition to the anthropocentric and humanistic theology of the Ritschlians and sought to reestablish theology as an authentic discipline in its own right, not dependent on changing patterns of philosophy or the spirit of the times. Although he was a product of the Reformed tradition, Barth pursued no narrow confessional bias, but used both Luther and Calvin, and indeed the whole tradition of historical Christianity, in a creative manner. Over a long career—as professor of theology at Göttingen, Münster, Bonn, and finally, when expelled from Nazi Germany, at Basel—Barth never wavered from his original goals. His thinking was oriented, above all, to a rediscovered biblical theology, yet it could equally well be regarded as a repristination of Reformation thought, stressing revelation over reason, the righteousness of God over religious experience, and divine grace over human works.[97]

There can be little doubt that Barth and his circle recaptured authentic accents of the Reformers' thought which the liberals had lost by refracting Christian doctrine through the prism of Kantian moralism. Moreover, as Barth moved beyond the prophetic criticism of his earlier writings to the positive reconstructive task, the Reformers' thought continued to play a decisive role in his dogmatic reformulations.[98] Such was the power of the reorientation Barth offered that he dominated Protestant thinking for decades, and even theologians who took widely divergent pathways, such as Dietrich Bonhoeffer, Paul Tillich, and Rudolf Bultmann, were demonstrably dependent on him and shared some of his orientation to the Reformation.[99] Yet if the Barthian movement of the early twentieth century helped revive interest in the Reformation, it was not without its threat to historical study. Barth's work could scarcely be regarded as a return to traditional orthodoxy, because he accepted the principles of critical biblical and historical study. Yet he did in effect reestablish the priority of dogmatics over history and reduce church history to a lesser role than it had exercised under the Ritschlian school.

The scholarly work of Karl Holl (1866–1926) can be seen as an important alternative to Ritschlian liberalism on the one hand and Barthian theology on the other. Holl's research was impeccably historical in the best Ritschlian traditions, based on exact historical and philological scrutiny of sources. But, precisely through his historical study of Luther, Holl brought to attention those profound religious themes which Barth had appropriated dogmatically, but which the Ritschlians had tended to ignore. In particular, he demonstrated the significance of the doctrine of conscience and its essentially theocentric character.[100]

Holl therefore made possible a genuine rediscovery of forgotten dimensions in Luther's thought, yet without any sacrifice of a scrupulously historical method. This was especially important because Denifle's and Grisar's attack on Luther, based on historical sources, required something more effective than a dogmatic counterblast. Holl's studies of Luther address the kinds of questions the Catholic polemicists had raised. He had the breadth of historical knowledge to answer Denifle's charges about Luther's ignorance of the medieval tradition, and he also took up the question of ethics, showing in a major essay how Luther's doctrine of justification—far from ignoring ethical considerations—involved precise moral principles capable of wide application in social life.[101]

Holl's pioneering work on Luther was significantly complemented by other scholars. The exhaustive documentary studies by Otto Scheel (1876–1954) provided the basis for much interpretive discussion of the Reformer's thought. Heinrich Bornkamm (1869–1927) produced a major—and still valuable—biographical study of the young Luther.[102] Through scholars like Walter Koehler (1870–1946), the Luther renaissance soon spread its influence beyond studies of Luther to work on Calvin and the other Reformers, and even into some important preliminary investigation of Reformation radicalism. Its results became accessible to English-speaking readers through the substantial works of James Mackinnon (1860–1945).[103] As a scholarly movement, it has been as much concerned with the edition and publication of texts as with issues of interpretation, and, if its early provenance was chiefly theological, its implications for historical scholarship have been far-reaching.

The essay published in 1917 by German Catholic scholar and churchman Franz Xaver Kiefl (1869–1928) bears scant comparison with Holl's in scope, depth, or impact, yet it was, in its restricted circle, an important contribution.[104] Kiefl brought no new sources to light and offered no original insights, yet his attempt to understand Luther's religious stance not only provided an interesting parallel to Holl's approach, but opened new possibilities for a Catholic scholarship still closely attuned to the harsh accents of Denifle and Grisar. Kiefl's willingness to take a fresh look at Luther was influenced, as he freely acknowledged, by the German war experience, which had forced the nation as a whole to come to terms with its deep religious cleavage, and forced Catholics in particular to reconsider their views of the man who, although a religious enemy, was a national hero. Yet Kiefl also pointed to an influence which was less obvious but ultimately more enduring: the advances in research which Catholic scholars could not afford to ignore and which provided an environment favorable to informed discussion and inhospitable to attitudes based merely on prejudice.[105]

Kiefl differed from Catholic writers of the previous century not so much in his basic method as in the context of his interpretation. Döllinger, Janssen, Denifle, and Grisar had, after all, tried to interpret the Reformation through an understanding of Luther's inner life. Kiefl thought along similar lines, but found his subject fundamentally motivated not by violence, lust, or psychic illness, but by genuine and profound religious interests.[106] His recognition of Luther's integrity and sincerity, however, in no way eroded his conviction about the Reformer's heresy. Indeed, basic doctrinal differences were stressed precisely because they were acknowledged to be rooted in fundamental divergences of religious perspective rather than trivial or external circumstances. To take Luther seriously as *homo religiosus* one could not dismiss his doctrine as the ignorant or misguided aberrations of a sensualist or psychotic. Like Möhler a century earlier, Kiefl provided the basis for a reasonable discussion across the lines of religious division, while highlighting the breadth and depth of that division.

Recognition of Luther's fundamentally religious motivation remained the keynote of much subsequent Catholic scholarship in Germany; in 1931 Hubert Jedin was able to report the end of Denifle's influence.[107] But the newer approach made no substantial inroads into non-German scholarship. British and American Catholic writers perpetuated Denifle's and Grisar's ideas decades after their German counterparts had abandoned them.[108] French scholars like Jacques Maritain, Jacques Paquier, M. J. Lagrange, and Leon Cristiani added a dimension of xenophobia.[109] One who stood out from the rest was Pierre Imbart de la Tour (1860–1925), who, though influenced by Grisar in his view of Luther, provided a more sympathetic portrait of his compatriot Calvin. In ways only fully recognized in recent years, he broke genuinely new ground, especially with his rich and subtle analysis of *évangelisme*—the world of Lefèvre and Marguerite of Navarre—in the early decades of the sixteenth century.[110]

The new direction of German Catholic scholarship on the Reformation found further expression in 1929 in a book of essays by both Protestant and Catholic authors, edited by Alfred von Martin. Scholars such as Sebastian Merkle, Johannes Albani, and Anton Fischer combined an exploration of Luther's religious piety and churchmanship with a critical discussion of the problems of the Church which made a Reformation necessary yet inhibited a positive Catholic response.[111] If any Catholic writer summed up the state of Catholic work on the Reformation in the mid-1930s, it was Konrad Algermissen, whose massive study of Christian denominations, published in 1935, attributes to the Reformation the stuff of tragedy because of its juxtaposition of noble religious motives with dire theological error.[112] But the views of scholars from Kiefl to Algermissen had no apparent influence outside Germany and limited impact within, because they were usually expressed in occasional essays or a few paragraphs of larger works. To this point, no Catholic scholar had provided a full-length, comprehensive, coherent statement of the revisionist view comparable in scope with the works of Denifle and Grisar.

That deficiency was remedied by Joseph Lortz (1887–1975), who shared Kiefl's general approach but went much further in providing a comprehensive history of the German Reformation (1939–1940), which attained as definitive a status in Catholic scholarly circles as Janssen's had earlier.[113] The extent to which Lortz's work represented a revolutionary change in Catholic historiography has at times been exaggerated. His raw judgment that "Luther *was* the Reformation,"[114] although qualified in actual exposition, was symptomatic of a tendency, shared with writers like Denifle and Grisar, to exaggerate the undeniably crucial personal role of Luther in the outbreak and early development of the movement. Likewise, Lortz's theological assessment of Luther's heresy loomed large and similarly discredited the Reformation.

Nevertheless, Lortz's differences from these polemicists were more than variations of emphasis. His judgment of Luther's heresy was clear and unequivocal, but he understood it as the product not of base motives, moral depravity, or psychic collapse, but of a one-sidedness born of an earnest and godly spirit. According to Lortz, Luther had distorted a crucial and neglected part of the Catholic tradition by isolating it from the whole.[115] Moreover, this error was no mere personal failure; it reflected a basic lack of clarity in the late medieval Church about the Church's teachings. Here was a far more serious problem than the alleged moral corruption emphasized by earlier Protestant writers.[116]

An especially interesting aspect of Lortz's approach is his attribution of a large share of blame for the Church's intellectual confusion to the disintegrating effects of Erasmian humanism.[117] Essentially a restatement of a view first voiced by the sixteenth-century papal nuncio Aleander, this judgment places Lortz in line with Janssen, but sharply at variance with other contemporary Catholic historians, such as Imbart de la Tour and Gasquet.[118] Underestimating Erasmus's constructive demand for a theology closely based on the New Testament, Lortz considered him a "half-Catholic," a born relativist and individualist. By contrast, he paradoxically viewed the rebel Luther as a contender for Catholic truth against the corrosive tendencies of Renaissance humanism. Luther's error arose not from false doctrines but from an unbalanced emphasis on true doctrines. Lortz's assessment of Luther's one-sidedness and subjectivism was influential with a generation of Catholic scholars, but his delineation of the intellectual uncertainty of the pre-Reformation Church achieved far more general acceptance and helped direct attention away from the barren process of moral charge and countercharge, characteristic of many Protestant and Catholic writers, to a more fruitful study of the bewildering intellectual ferment in the early sixteenth century.

No less important than Lortz's constructive synthesis was the devastating critique of Catholic historiography pursued concurrently by Adolf Herte (b. 1887). Herte's subject was not Luther himself but Catholic interpreters of the Reformation, and his major work demonstrates that virtually all Catholic interpretation of Luther from the sixteenth century to the early decades of the twentieth, was dominated by the baneful influence of Cochlaeus's *Commentaries*.[119] He argued that, with few exceptions, Catholic scholars, even those like Denifle and Grisar, who worked to a large extent with genuine historical sources, had derived their understanding of Luther directly or indirectly from Cochlaeus. Herte's critique was motivated by a positive desire to clear away centuries of interpretation based on malice and prejudice, as much for the sake of historical truth as for confessional harmony.

Although Lortz's work has rightly been recognized as an important turning point in Catholic scholarship, developments since 1940 moved far beyond his vision. Some significant work was done on other aspects of the Reformation, but the focus remained primarily on Luther and the German Reformation. Notwithstanding the continued influence of Grisar in some circles, Lortz's view of Luther as *homo religiosus* has been the fundamental starting point for most Catholic scholars' attempts to interpret the significance of the Reformation. Johannes Hessen provoked considerable controversy when in 1947 he published a small book which cast Luther in the role of a prophet, on the pattern of the Old Testament prophets.[120] Erwin Iserloh, a pupil of Lortz, initiated a lengthy debate by denying the historical basis for the posting of the Ninety-five Theses on All Saints Eve, 1517.[121] Iserloh, like Lortz, interpreted Luther as at that moment essentially conservative in his aims, a self-consciously loyal son of the Church who sought only a proper redress of errors by appeal to the duly constituted authorities. Most Protestant scholars remained unconvinced by Iserloh's arguments and saw in them a form of special pleading, but his painstaking dissection of the evidence stimulated close study of the events of 1517, which undoubtedly enlarged knowledge of the immediate circumstances and their broader implications. As in earlier generations, confessional concerns proved capable of advancing historical understanding.

Nowhere was the subtle interconnection of confessional and historical interests more clearly demonstrated than in the study of Luther's theology, which took over from historical biography as the main focus of Catholic research and in which the most significant advances beyond Lortz were made. In his major work on the Reformation, Lortz had characterized Luther's thought as an "inchoate flood" and denied that he could be properly described as a theologian.[122] Although he later modified this view somewhat, the most he expected from the study of Luther's thought was confirmation of the judgment that Luther had rejected a Catholicism that was not fully Catholic.[123] Scholars since Lortz have expected, and obtained, far more.

A number of studies published in the 1960s demonstrate that Luther had considerable familiarity with Thomist thought through passages quoted in the writings of Gabriel Biel.[124] Otto Pesch asserted, on the basis of a comparative study of Aquinas and Luther, that there was a surprising degree of basic agreement, obscured chiefly by sharply contrasting but potentially complementary styles of doing theology—Aquinas was a "sapiental" and Luther an "existential" thinker.[125] Parallel works by other scholars examine the influence of Augustine, Gregory of Rimini, and Saint Bernard on Luther's thought.[126] Harry McSorley's exhaustive study of the controversy with Erasmus on freedom of the will asserts the fundamentally Catholic content of Luther's theology of salvation.[127]

The ecumenical spirit which pervaded the writings of this generation of Catholic scholars was strikingly evident, especially in the years following the Second Vatican Council, yet their confessional orientation was no less clear. They sought, on the one hand, genuinely Catholic elements in Luther's thought and action and, on the other, explanations for his deviations from Catholic orthodoxy by reference to the confused state of Catholic thought at the time. Yet in many Catholic writings on Luther these confessional limitations were increasingly abandoned, and his thought was considered on its own terms and subjected to the scriptural test Luther himself acknowledged rather than to rigid dogmatic criteria emanating from the magisterium.[128]

The result of this trend has been not only to blur the formerly clear boundaries of Roman Catholic research on the Reformation, but also to add to the debate a dimension of internal Catholic argument. Scholars accustomed to assessing "the Catholic view" must now reckon with a range of widely divergent perspectives.[129] Frido Mann, Jan Aarts, and Wolfgang Schwab, for example, offered highly positive assessments of particular aspects of Luther's theology.[130] Daniel Olivier, in a work on Luther's faith, presented the Reformer to Catholic readers as a "teacher of the Gospel" par excellence.[131] On the other hand, Riccardo Garcia-Villoslada's biography of Luther in Spanish, subsequently translated into Italian, breathes again the spirit of Grisar.[132] Theobald Beer's weighty study of Luther's theology is so comprehensive in its negative judgments that it aroused much critical comment in Catholic circles.[133]

Works of this character have been rare, however, and in the years leading to the Luther quincentenary in 1983 a variety of books from Catholic scholars notable for their balanced assessment appeared. These included biographies by Peter Manns and John Todd, a study of Luther and Erasmus by the Belgian scholar Georges Chantraine, a comprehensive guide to Luther's thought by Otto Pesch, a collection of essays by Yves Congar, and a biographical and theological assessment by the American Jesuit Jared Wicks.[134] All in different ways present Luther from a perspective still recognizably Catholic, at times judiciously critical, but always fundamentally appreciative.

Scholarship on the Reformation in Protestant circles since the Second World War exhibited, as earlier, a close interaction with Catholic research and many parallel developments. Germany never abandoned its role as the originator of new trends and interests, but scholars in other countries increasingly made genuinely original contributions. Scandinavians in particular pursued a style of scholarship on the Reformation which has become very much their own. Nathan Söderblom and Einar Billing, both of the University of Uppsala, were among the pioneers of a fresh approach to Luther in the early years of this century,[135] and their work was followed by a continuous tradition of research on Luther closely tied to a particular method of theological inquiry yet rigorously historical in its approach to the sources. The "Lundensian" theologians Anders Nygren and Gustav Aulen used study of the Reformation as an auxiliary aspect of a more fundamental interest in systematic theology.[136] Regin Prenter, Lennart Pinomaa, and Gustav Wingren, working respectively in Denmark, Finland, and Sweden, were principally concerned with the historical exposition and contemporary relevance of Luther's doctrinal and ethical positions.[137]

Continued preoccupation with Luther in the Scandinavian countries was virtually guaranteed by the presence of large national churches bearing his name. In England, where no significant Lutheran Church existed and Luther had been overshadowed since the sixteenth century by the more pervasive presences of Calvin and Zwingli, Methodist scholars like Gordon Rupp, Philip Watson, and Rupert Davies did most to revive interest in studies on Luther from the 1950s.[138] Yet, notwithstanding some excellent work on the Continental Reformers,[139] English scholarship has understandably maintained its preoccupation with the complex history of its own Reformation tradition, both at home and overseas.

French writers on the Reformation characteristically showed a special interest in the peculiarly French dimensions of the movement, and in their native son John Calvin. Protestant scholars in particular explored the movement exhaustively, aided by the industry of the long-standing Société de l'Histoire du Protestantisme Français. In postwar writings the balance has been redressed, and a number of notable studies of Luther have been made by scholars such as Richard Stauffer and Marc Lienhard.[140] In the same period general works on the Reformation moved away from narrow "church historical" interests. Emile Leonard's *History of Protestantism* (1961), for example, although in many ways a traditionalist work, presents Protestantism as a complex, living reality embodying not only ecclesiastical structures but social groups and individual responses.[141]

Scholarship in Germany continued to show a propensity for exhaustive and extended debates about precise historical issues, such as the controversy about the posting of the Ninety-five Theses and the vexed question of dating Luther's evangelical "breakthrough,"[142] but such exchanges took place in an increasingly broad and diverse range of historical and doctrinal investigations, made possible by the wealth of source material now open to scholarly investigation. Of particular significance was the inquiry undertaken at Tübingen by Heiko Oberman (1930–) into the complex intellectual background of the Reformation: a fresh approach to questions which had been on the agenda since Carl Ullmann's publication in the 1840s of *Reformers Before the Reformation*.[143] Ullmann had dealt in particular with the mid-fifteenth-century reformists, sometimes called Augustinizers, cited and edited by Luther—John of Wesel, John Pupper of Goch, and Wessel Gansfort—and with John Huss, who had assumed a parallel role, at least from the year 1520—when Luther read his *De Ecclesia* and had it printed, urging Germans and Bohemians to drop their old feuds and work together to further the Gospel. On the same general theme, Gerhard Ritter had contributed an article in 1927 entitled "Romantic and Revolutionary Elements in German Theology on the Eve of the Reformation," showing that the so-called Augustinizers derived their views directly from Scripture, which they sometimes cited to contradict Augustine.[144]

Oberman's specific concern was the Nominalist tradition, which Catholic controversialists like Denifle had used to discredit Luther. In a major study of Gabriel Biel, intended as the first part of a trilogy linking the later Middle Ages and the Reformation, Oberman employed the image of a "harvest-time" to argue for the health and vigor of the Nominalist tradition.[145] In the second volume of the trilogy he studied late-fifteenth-century theological development through focus on the University of Tübingen; the third is intended to discuss Calvinism. Meanwhile, in a biography marking the quincentenary of Luther's birth, Oberman focused on the Reformer "not as a desk-bound research scholar but rather as a man besieged by and responsive to the conditions and convictions of his day and age."[146]

Although we will refer in Chapter 12 to Oberman's professed desire to develop a "social history of ideas," his major contribution to studies of the Reformation is undoubtedly on the theme of intellectual continuity. In this respect his immensely learned and detailed trilogy should not obscure the more straightforward contribution of his *Forerunners of the Reformation* (1967), a superb collection of pre-Reformation texts with illuminating comments and an incisive essay on the "problem of the forerunner."[147] Oberman was also instrumental in the publication by others of many detailed studies of late medieval scholars, theologians, and preachers, which has continued to enrich our understanding of the early Reformation intellectual environment.[148] These range from highly specialized monographs to the useful collection edited by Steven Ozment *The Reformation in Medieval Perspective* (1971), which brought together European and American contributions on the general theme of continuity.[149]

The emergence of American scholarship to a prominence rivaling that of Germany was signaled as early as 1946 with the foundation of the American Society for Reformation Research, and that society's collaboration with its German counterpart to revive the journal *Archiv für Reformationsgeschichte*.[150] The United States had been well served for a generation or more by scholars in theological seminaries and universities, many of whom explored the traditions of their respective religious confessions. But more often, in a country as ecumenically minded as it is confessionally diverse, narrow denominational barriers were ignored. J. T. McNeill's studies of the Calvinist tradition characteristically look outward.[151] Roland Bainton showed himself equally at home interpreting Luther, Erasmus, and the radical sectarians.[152] Wilhelm Pauck set his primary study of Luther in the context of the Protestant movement as a whole.[153] One needs only to place the articles in the American-edited *New Catholic Encyclopedia* (1967) beside their counterparts in the original *Catholic Encyclopedia* (1907–1914) to see how deeply these expansive attitudes influenced Catholic scholars.[154]

The establishment in 1957 of the Foundation for Reformation Research in St. Louis, with its ambitious program of archival acquisitions, was only the most obvious example of using modern technology to expand the resources available to scholars. Research on the Reformation not only was a lively interest in the theological seminaries but found an equal welcome in the graduate schools of American private and state universities. The mobility of faculty and students at that time and the flourishing of professional societies combined to stimulate wide overlapping of scholarly interests and creative application of historical research in contexts as diverse as arcane points of theological interpretation and the study of sixteenth-century urban society.[155]

Protestant and Catholic scholarship has clearly traveled a long way since the first insults were exchanged. Once partisan and myopic, it has become ecumenical and genuinely international; once limited to theological and ecclesiastical concerns, it has, without losing this primary focus, become increasingly interdisciplinary and concerned with the fullness of historical experience. Once preoccupied exclusively with great leaders and broad sweeps of history, it has come to share the fascination of general historical scholarship with lesser-known figures and the largely anonymous multitude who brought the Reformation what success it achieved in the towns and countryside of Europe. Discovery of a large neutral territory in social history has been as important as ecumenical sentiment in enabling Protestant and Catholic scholars to find common ground.

The religious commitment so many of these scholars brought to the study of the Reformation over four and a half centuries has been both a strength and a problem. At its best, it has engendered the enthusiasm without which historical study readily becomes lifeless; at its worst, it has falsified the past. The historian can only be thankful, in retrospect, that the cruder forms of bias by which devout scholars reinforced self-righteous prejudices have been eradicated. Yet it is difficult to escape the conclusion that the involvement of deeply committed partisans produced much of the tangible progress in historical research in this field. They may have been hell-bent on some private or group theological triumph, but in the process they uncovered lost sources and provoked inquiry into neglected subjects. Leopold von Ranke's supposedly objective history stimulated Döllinger to bring forth materials Ranke had passed over. Denifle's violent attack on Luther proved a major motivation for Protestant scholarship to abandon its complacent hagiography and seriously explore the Reformation's intellectual roots. Even since the Second Vatican Council, when Catholic scholars have chaired seminars and delivered papers to international congresses of research on Luther with ecclesiastical blessing, some of the more productive historical work has originated in confessional commitment. Religious interests can raise genuine historical questions which might not otherwise be investigated, and even unhistorical questions need not be antihistorical.[156]

Where Catholic and Protestant scholarship failed to advance understanding, that failure was not so much the result of confessional commitment as of the unnecessary tyranny such commitment exercised over historical judgment. The problem, which has its parallel in political affairs, is exacerbated when any group of scholars is obliged by overt, covert, or self-imposed restraint to work in a narrow intellectual environment. A solution is, however, less likely to lie in the pursuit of a chimerical ideal of pure objectivity than in the breaking down of situations in which bias runs rampant because it is unchecked by counterbias. The clearest evidence of the historical maturity of Protestant and Catholic study of the Reformation is the distance it has already traveled along that road.

9

Rediscovered Dimensions: The Reformation Radicals

During recent decades it has been generally accepted that the Anabaptists and other radicals of Luther's day exercised highly important influences not only on the Reformation but throughout the development of modern Christianity. The tardiness of this acknowledgment derived from the intolerant prejudices long current in the major churches; yet it also sprang from a widespread ignorance of the sources: voluminous, difficult, scattered, and in many cases only recently printed by agencies such as the Mennonite Society. In fact, although so much has been written about the sects since Luther denounced them, the first comprehensive survey in modern historical scholarship appeared only in 1962: George Huntston Williams's *The Radical Reformation*. Williams (1914–) rightly stressed that no branch of sixteenth-century research is so dependent on recently discovered materials, which "have almost the same significance for the interpretation of modern church history as the discoveries in the Dead Sea caves and in Upper Egypt are having for New Testament studies and early church history."[1]

Yet the remaining problems are by no means limited to details. The radicals have been rehabilitated as a continuous and valid Christian tradition, but too many gaps persist when we seek to establish continuities between the earlier sects and their more familiar seventeenth- and eighteenth-century successors, many of which still survive in both Europe and the United States. Another problem, by no means merely semantic, relates to the realities behind the very concept of a Radical Reformation. With

213

the radicals we find at most a tumultuous, multipointed, often inconsistent series of trends, certainly not a phenomenon so integrated as those we denote by terms such as *Evangelical Reformation, Reformed Christianity,* and *Anglican Church.* In the third place, it is hard to anticipate any agreed value judgment between sympathetic historians of religion and unsympathetic political historians, who have remained acutely conscious of the threats radicalism presented to the social and political cohesion of sixteenth-century Europe. Here we still observe something like a dialogue of the deaf!

For over two centuries the term *Anabaptist,* often used quite indiscriminately to label all sorts of radicals, was almost universally one of abuse. Leading Protestant Reformers had been unsparing in their condemnation of these heretics, whom they considered subversive in Church and State: Luther found the ideal one-word weapon when he called them *Schwärmer*—enthusiasts, dreamers, visionary fanatics. In Switzerland, the chief hub of early Anabaptism, both Zwingli and Bullinger wrote lengthy attacks, although we observed in Chapter 1 that Bullinger took great trouble to analyze Anabaptists' beliefs and had some regard for their virtues. On all sides bitter words were reinforced by fierce persecution, especially in the Catholic Netherlands, where radicalism abounded, but also in several other states where Lutherans, Calvinists, and Anglicans desperately wanted to display their essential "moderation" and retain the traditional links between ecclesiastical and secular authority. As late as 1575 Queen Elizabeth executed a few Dutch Anabaptists, chiefly perhaps to display to Philip II and other sovereigns the fact that Anglican England was no cesspit of heretical extremism. The alleged inconsistencies, absurdities, and indecencies of Anabaptists were still ridiculed in the mid-seventeenth century, by which time few believed that they seriously threatened the social fabric of Europe.

During the first half of that century—but very gradually—new attitudes began to emerge. In Germany the rise of the Pietist movement in Lutheranism brought a sharp awareness of the failings in the rigid faith which had succeeded Luther's revolt. Some of the qualities which had made the *Schwärmer* so hateful to Luther appeared less despicable to his critical heirs. A cooling of the old hatred was evident in Meshovius's *Anabaptist History* of 1617—one of the earliest objective treatments— and then, late in the century, in the writings of Gottfried Arnold (see Chapter 5).[2] In the Netherlands martyr books like *The Bloody Theatre* (1685), replete with pathetic illustrations of Anabaptist sufferings, were published and widely read.[3]

That forerunner of the Enlightenment Pierre Bayle could not totally abandon traditional hatred of the Anabaptists: he censured their lack of regard for society's demands. In his eyes their most serious offense lay in the fact that their extremism had hindered progress of the Reformation in general. Nevertheless, Bayle was still more critical of the persecutions, which had been motivated partly by hostility to the admirable pacifism of the radicals; and he argued that the meekness of Menno Simons (c. 1492–c. 1559) was more characteristic than the violence in 1535 at Münster (see Chapter 5). Bayle's toleration typified the coming revolution in European thought, for only a few decades previously even the English Nonconformist Richard Baxter (1615–1691) had condemned the Quakers and compared them with the sixteenth-century radicals, "the ignorant, proud, giddy sort of professors."[4] Thereafter, the Enlightenment's general distaste for persecution—so evident in the writings of Voltaire and Condorcet—combined with a notion that a multiplicity of beliefs, albeit so unpalatable to Bossuet, could be beneficial. Variety in religion ensured freedom of choice and weakened the grip of dogma. However ludicrous their views, the early dissenters were believed to have struck a powerful blow for freedom of conscience by their very rejection of a majority faith. This was the view of Condorcet, who believed that the Reformation had most benefited humanity where no creed had been able to attain total dominance (see Chapter 6).[5] Less extreme views prevailed in most historical works of the period.

Johann Lorenz von Mosheim, whose widely read *Institutes of Ecclesiastical History* (1755) presents the Reformation as the fount of the Enlightenment and the beginning of modern history, devoted a significant portion of the book to the radicals, whom he discovered to be from many viewpoints descendants of medieval heretical movements (see Chapter 6). His condemnation of the violent spirits who "raved and howled rather than instructed" in no way prevented him from acknowledging the integrity and piety of a man like Menno Simons.[6] Yet perhaps the significance of Mosheim's contribution lies less in its sympathies than in the sheer amount of space it allots to the radicals in a general history of the Reformation. At that time the attentions of so influential a historian had greater weight than the increasing number of specialist studies, for example those by J. A. Starck in Germany (1780) and Herman Schijn in the Netherlands (1743–1745), many of which were Mennonite hagiography.[7]

Modern historiography of the radicals might be regarded as beginning in the mid-nineteenth century. In Germany pioneering work on the still emotive issue of the Münster affair was done by Carl Adolf Cornelius (1819–1903). Derived in part from contemporary manuscript materials, his *History of the Münster Rising* (1855–1860) ventures a moderate defense of the rebels' motives.[8] The work is generally favorable toward radicalism, although like some others in this field Cornelius was a liberal Roman Catholic, a friend of Lord Acton.

One reason for Catholic interest in the Anabaptists remains clear. As Acton himself explained, "The only subversive portion of their doctrine was that they held, with the Catholics, that the state is not responsible for religion."[9] Not content even with this bold generalization, Acton described the rise of the sects as "one of the great generative factors in modern history—a turning-point in the epic of modern history." He followed the philosophers of the Enlightenment in accepting the growth of sectarianism as an aspect of the slow development of freedom, and he regretted that the extremism of some radicals had provoked the lengthy intolerance of the Protestant establishment of northern Europe.

From the Protestant side, Albrecht Ritschl's massive *History of Pietism* (1880–1886)—completed near the end of his scholarly life, after his major dogmatic studies—signaled an important change of approach toward Reformation radicalism.[10] This was not merely because Ritschl thoroughly studied original sources, but because of the context in which he placed the movements. His approach not only invited consideration of the radicals' relationship to Reformation Protestantism, but set the entire issue in the context of the wider history of Western Catholic Christianity. He insisted that the medieval Church should not be approached in terms of its having prepared the way for the Reformation but in terms of its intrinsic issues. Ritschl identified a continuing tradition of religious reform, from Gregory VII to Francis of Assisi, as one of the most distinctive features of Western medieval Christianity, in sharp contrast with the placid history of the Eastern Church.[11] He did this not with any confessional purpose of identifying a succession of "forerunners" or "proto-Evangelicals," a trend in research which he explicitly criticized,[12] but with the more genuinely historical purpose of setting all the religious movements of the Reformation period in their true context.

In accord with this approach, Ritschl came to understand the radical movements of the Reformation, despite some similarities with Luther and Zwingli, as essentially distinct and even opposite in character. Moreover, he identified some intriguing positive relationships between the radicals and the ascetic, ceremonial, and legal tendencies of medieval Catholicism, from which Luther and Zwingli remained far removed.[13] Early associations between the radicals and the mainline reformers Ritschl explained as arising out of a common acceptance of the scriptural norm, which at first hid the major and irreconcilable differences in religious substance, differences in kind and not merely in degree.[14] Ritschl's boldest suggestion, which he prudently described as no more than a hypothesis, was that the radical groups had their origin among the Franciscan tertiaries.

He supported this notion by reference not only to shared concerns and intentions but to a common clientele among the urban lower classes.[15]

Other German historians pioneered the local and regional researches which attained a special importance in this field. Joseph von Beck (1815–1887) and Johann Loserth (1846–1936) studied Anabaptism in Hungary, Tyrol, and Moravia.[16] Ludwig Keller (1849–1915) shared Ritschl's interest in the survival of heretical traditions from the Middle Ages into the Reformation period and in their classification. His *Reformation and the older parties of Reform* (1885) argues for a continuous tradition of "evangelical brotherhood."[17] Keller had made a close study of Hans Denck and others in the wing of the radicals later characterized as "Spiritualists." He postulated the existence of an alternative mystical reform tradition, carried through the Reformation in the writings of Johann von Staupitz and others and still existing as a lively force. The actual term *Spiritualist,* now so commonly used in studies of the Radical Reformation, seems to have been coined by Alfred Hegler, who in 1892 published a life of Sebastian Franck.[18]

Local research advanced also in Switzerland. The liberal Catholic Father Emil Egli (1848–1908) published works on the spread of Anabaptism in the cantons of Zurich and Saint Gall; in 1879 he edited a major collection of Zurich court records.[19] A pioneering and broadly sympathetic historian of Swiss Anabaptism, Egli inspired many useful local studies. In the Netherlands, where Schijn's *History of the Mennonites* had been published in the 1740s, a Mennonite-sponsored scholarly journal, *Doopsgezinde Bijdrahen,* was established in 1861. Samuel Cramer, himself a Mennonite and professor at the University of Amsterdam, edited four large volumes of Anabaptist records for the *Bibliotheca Reformatoria Neerlandica,* a collection of source materials issued between 1903 and 1913. Dutch local studies also included Jules Frederichs's work on the "Libertine" Loists of Antwerp (1891).[20]

In the Netherlands, a permanent religious tradition rooted in sixteenth-century sectarianism had survived, so keen interest in its origins naturally arose. In contrast, English historians, whatever their religious sympathies, remained for the most part ignorant of Anabaptism, which did not appear to them to have continuity into more recent times. To Anglicans, all the extremist sects of the sixteenth century seemed a murky backwater of religious history. Even Nonconformists lacked much interest in their spiritual ancestry before the seventeenth century. The harshly Protestant Victorian historian J. A. Froude made a characteristic defense of the English Anabaptists, whom he presented as martyrs for religious liberty who died for their beliefs as surely as did More and Fisher. Yet, because they had been enemies to established society, Froude disapproved of them as protosocialists.[21] R. W. Dixon, James Gairdner, and other Anglo-Catholic historians felt a deep hostility to Anabaptism, a sinister foreign infection which they associated with Lollardy and the popular disorders of the mid-Tudor period.

Unusually objective in the context of nineteenth-century England was the treatment of radicalism in Charles Beard's Hibbert Lectures of 1883, subsequently published as *The Reformation of the Sixteenth Century in Its Relation to Modern Thought and Knowledge.*[22] Beard sought to integrate the radicals into Reformation history and thought their achievement had been to emphasize truths which Protestantism had neglected to its great loss. These "individualists of the Reformation" represented to him the true voice of a democratic reform movement, and he pointed out that many of their ideas had later been generally adopted by European society. Beard's views have an added interest in light of later attempts to portray the radicals as pioneers of various forms of social advance: they "were half-blindly reaching forward to something better and more stable than they knew or could firmly grasp."

Another Englishman, Richard Heath, produced a reasonably informative survey entitled *Anabaptism: From Its Rise at Zwickau to Its Fall at Münster, 1521–1536* (1895). More important was the work of the Marxist E. Belfort Bax, who published his *Rise and Fall of the Anabaptists* in 1903 as part of a three-volume social history of Reformation Germany. He regarded the sixteenth-century religious radicals as primitive yet unconscious forerunners of modern socialism, people whose doctrines were nevertheless "retrograde" and "foredoomed to failure."[23] Bax's interest in the period had been inspired by the work of Friedrich Engels and Karl Kautsky on sixteenth-century popular movements, including the German Peasants' War. The Marxist tendency to abstract Münzer and other radicals from their spiritual context has been rightly criticized, yet the perilous association of religious radicalism with social and political radicalism has been equally emphasized by many Western historians, both liberal and conservative.

Writing over half a century ago, Preserved Smith in *The Age of the Reformation* claimed that the religious radicals primarily represented the confused cause of the poor: "The party of extreme measures is always chiefly constituted from the proletariat"; such men "have not usually the education to judge the feasibility of the plans, many of them quack nostrums, presented as panaceas for all their woes."[24] Earlier still G. P. Fisher of Yale had condemned "the wild and disorganizing theories of the Anabaptists," which were based on "licentious and revolutionary principles."[25] By no means wholly unsympathetic toward "enthusiast" movements in religion, Father Ronald Knox more recently took Anabaptism as akin to "Tolstoyan anarchy." Its tenets—rejection of capital punishment, war, and private property—"appear to the modern mind as an anticipation of many disruptive tendencies in our own day."[26] Specialists with sensitivity to the fragility of early modern society and its limited capacity to absorb violent and fundamental changes almost inevitably took a stern view of the radical wing of Anabaptism. For example, G. R. Elton dismissed Münzer as "an unrestrained fanatic" and "a dangerous lunatic"; he condemned Anabaptism because it led to terror and its appeal "rested on the claim to bring power and glory to the poor, the weak and the resentful."[27]

On the other side, many modern scholars have been anxious to be more understanding of Anabaptism; some have gone to the point of blandly overlooking dangers which were far from fictitious. Yet they did realize that the movement had a large nonviolent wing, and they were shocked by the indiscriminate cruelty of the persecutions against all sorts of Anabaptists by both Catholic and "orthodox" Protestant authorities.

Not all these sympathetic historians were members of later denominations related to early sectarianism. One was T. M. Lindsay, whom we saw in Chapter 8 in the early years of this century publishing a remarkably lucid and well-informed general history of the Reformation. In his second volume (1906) he devoted over sixty pages to the Anabaptists, who in his view had been treated in a glib and partisan fashion by historians uninterested in their social milieus or heritages from both mysticism and peasant radicalism. The radicals should not, Lindsay argued, be regarded as a part of the Protestant Reformation, even though "their main thought was to reproduce in their own lives what seemed to them to be the beliefs, usages, and social practices of the primitive Christians." In this aim Lindsay found them "medieval to the core."[28] Insofar as there was an Anabaptist theology, it was medieval in tenor and little related to the salvation-oriented theology of the magisterial reformers. Lindsay also sensed that the ossified and stagnant Protestant establishment of the later sixteenth century had presented a broad target for radical attack. Here he had been anticipated by others, even A. F. Pollard, who in the *Cambridge Modern History* had commented on the "rigid, respectable" tone assumed by Lutheranism as early as 1530. At first Luther had been borne along by the revolutionary enthusiasm of many who later were bitterly disappointed by the "meagre results" of the Reformation.[29]

The diversity of the religious scene in the United States, where the Mennonites and other sects had taken refuge and flourished, provided both stimuli and problems for historians of religious radicalism. Toward the end of the nineteenth century, the American historical profession became increasingly aware of these. Among the more competent writers in this field was Williston Walker, author of a major study of Calvin (1898) and a general survey of the Reformation (1897). Walker's sympathy for the sufferings of sixteenth-century Anabaptists arose from a recognition that Calvin and other Reformers had pursued an intolerant policy indefensible in any modern liberal society: "When one recalls their patient endurance of persecution, their devotion to truth as they understood it, and their courageous faith, one is often tempted to query whether they did not exhibit more of the spirit of Christ than did the more conservative reformers who persecuted them."[30]

The admission that history of the Reformation has to include the radicals became less grudging as monographs on the radical wing of the Reformation became available. A. H. Newman's *History of Anti-Pedobaptism* (1897) is a painstaking survey of its theme, but the author remained little interested in the social and historical setting of the early Baptists.[31] H. C. Vedder's *The Reformation in Germany* (1914) boldly presents the Anabaptists as "the real reformers, and indeed the only real reformers, of the sixteenth century."[32] H. E. Dosker's *The Dutch Anabaptists* (1921) is a major study by a professor of church history at the Presbyterian Theological Seminary in Louisville, Kentucky.[33] He stressed the importance of primary sources, basing his work on Cramer's volumes in the *Bibliotheca Reformatoria Neerlandica*. He set the rise of Netherlandish Anabaptism in various contexts: medieval Pietism, heresies like that of the Waldenses, social tensions, anticlericalism, and popular unrest. Dosker made a serious attempt to classify the various strands of radical religion. Condemning the violence of Münzer and Hoffmann, he focused new attention on the proponents of spiritual religion, including David Joris and Sebastian Franck.

More influential than the work of these historians was the scholarly, lucid, and readable corpus of Rufus M. Jones (1863–1948), a Quaker who taught at Haverford College from 1893 to 1934. The links between pacifist types of Anabaptism and Quakerism had been often remarked, and W. C. Braithwaite's *Beginnings of Quakerism* (1912) had outlined a long tradition of quietist religion. Jones's conviction that "religion is primarily and at heart the personal meeting of the soul with God and conscious communion with him" led to an early interest in medieval mysticism. Indeed, mysticism became intellectually fashionable during these years, which saw publication of a number of studies of it, among which those by William Ralph Inge, Friedrich von Hügel's *Mystical Element of Religion* (1908), and Evelyn Underhill's *Mysticism* (1911) are noteworthy.

The mystical element in non-Catholic religion had been all but ignored for centuries. Luther's rejection of those "false brethren" who looked to the spirit alone for guidance had established a pattern of neglect, but Jones sought the revival of a spiritual Protestantism which would revitalize Christian life in the new century. He identified two fundamental tendencies through religious history—one stressing permanence and the other revivification through spontaneous experiences.[34] Both seemed to Jones essential aspects of Christianity, and he considered the Church most vital and healthy when they achieved a proper balance. Religious institutions sunk in habit and custom needed the fresh and spontaneous experiences of original minds to restore their vigor. Figures like Saint Francis, Meister Eckhart, and John Wycliffe typified this approach; the Anabaptists—in contrast to the politic, cautious, and temporizing Lutheran and Calvinist Reformers—stood for a new type of free and independent Christian society which the modern world had been slowly realizing.[35]

In *Spiritual Reformers in the Sixteenth and Seventeenth Centuries* (1914), Jones argued that this creative tendency had received a massive boost from Luther's revolt, but that he had soon abandoned spiritual religion for the compromise of a state Church, "deeply marred with residual superstition and mysteries and heavily laden with the inheritance of dark and medieval ages." Luther, indeed, had "staved off and postponed for nearly four hundred years the truly liberating and thoroughly adequate reformation."[36] The true reformers of the sixteenth century were, in Jones's view, products of both the medieval mystical tradition and the humanist revival, who produced a new expression of spirituality, of which Hans Denck was among the earliest exponents. Whereas Catholics insisted on grace and works, Lutherans on justification by faith alone, and the mystics on union with God, adherents of this new Spiritualism, at once humanistic and mystical, stressed the transformation of man by Christ. As early as 1530 Franck had spoken of such a new spiritual faith beside the Lutheran, Zwinglian, and Anabaptist creeds, and he and Schwenkfeld pioneered it among small, scattered groups of believers guided by their vision of a divine inner light. A line of descent from these pioneers led via Sebastian Castellio and Hans Boehme to seventeenth-century Quakerism, the original center of Jones's interest. By contrast, the Protestant Reformers had ruthlessly suppressed this fertile tradition, which had been a vital element in Luther's own spiritual milieu.[37]

The work of American—mostly Mennonite—historians reflects that group's dominant position in modern historiography of the radicals. Nevertheless, the basic conceptual apparatus of their work was largely created by Continental European scholars, notably Max Weber (1864–1920) and Ernst Troeltsch (1865–1923), both of whom we shall examine in detail in Chapter 11. Weber's best-known but most vulnerable work, *The Protestant Ethic and the Spirit of Capitalism* (1904–1905), analyzes the interconnections between Protestantism, especially Calvinism, and the growth of a secular, "ascetic," capitalist spirit.[38] As for the radical sects of the Reformation, Weber observed that they possessed the Calvinists' self-imposed discipline in an intensified form.

Weber's visit to the United States in 1904 stimulated his already growing interest in the dynamics of sectarianism, but the basic work on sects was to be done by the Berlin polymath Troeltsch, friend of Weber, Meinecke, and Harnack. In *The Social Teaching of the Christian Churches* (1912), Troeltsch also sought the origins of the modern capitalist world in the Reformation period, particularly the conservative nature of the Protestant Reformation, which evidenced a compromise with the world. Following Weber, he based his analysis of religious groupings on the ideal "types" of Church and Sect. The Reformation largely confirmed the dominance of the inclusive Church, coterminous with the State, which had existed through the medieval period. On the other hand, the Sect was characterized by rejection of the secular, although most sects eventually compromised with the world. The Sect idea stemmed from the early Church and had survived secretly beside the majority Catholic faith, to be given a new impetus by the Reformation.[39]

Troeltsch articulated a major distinction between the sects proper, typified by Anabaptism, and the spiritualist impulse deriving from the medieval mystical tradition and personified in leaders like Denck, Franck, and Schwenkfeld. Herein lay his most important contribution to the study of Reformation radicalism, for the mystical strain had previously been largely ignored. In *The Varieties of Religious Experience* (1902), for example, William James had dismissed Protestant mystical experience as "almost exclusively sporadic."[40] As Troeltsch saw it, the mystics dwelled on the inward experience of Christ and were far less concerned than the Anabaptists with a scriptural reconstitution of Christianity. Their separation from the world was marked not by ethical severity and close discipline but by a concentration on inward religion pursued among casual groups of believers, generally free of sacrament and dogma.[41] Sociologically, sectarian and mystical religion differed as much from Protestantism as from Catholicism, yet both were, in a sense, the logical outcome of Protestantism, one deriving from the Protestant idea of the "calling" and the other from the tendency toward "autonomous individualism."[42]

The influence of European sociology on the historiography of the radicals has been considerable. One of Weber's pupils, Ernst Correll, produced in 1925 an interesting sociological investigation of the Swiss

Mennonites.[43] Soon after, Correll went to the United States, where he began to work with American Mennonite scholars. Mennonites, Hutterites, and other refugees from European religious persecution had established self-contained communities in America in which from the first they constituted the majority. In remoter parts of the continent, religious fundamentalism could ignore the pressures of an increasingly skeptical society. By the early twentieth century, technology had reduced these communities' isolation, and new values threatened their traditional ways of life. Their first reaction was to tighten their old codes of behavior, to place a much stricter emphasis, for instance, on forms of dress which distinguished sect members. A more fruitful reaction was the desire, especially among Mennonites, to learn more about the history and background of their faith and thus place it in its historical and religious context.

In 1924 Correll joined Harold S. Bender (1897–1962), of Goshen College, Indiana, to found the Mennonite Historical Society. Three years later the *Mennonite Quarterly Review* began to publish scholarly articles on sectarian faith and history. Bender was for a long time editor of the journal and the central figure among Mennonite historians: his many learned articles formed a major contribution to knowledge of the radicals, and his biography of Conrad Grebel (1950) is a basic work. He was convinced that the radicals provided the inspiration for a renewal of modern Christianity in believing "that Jesus intended that the Kingdom of God should be set in the midst of earth here and now, and this they proposed to do forthwith."[44] Bender's interpretation of "the Anabaptist Vision" was to inspire much of the work produced by historians of his school. John Horsch was another important early contributor to the *Mennonite Quarterly Review,* and Cornelius Krahn, author of a major book on Menno Simons, also came to the Unites States.[45]

By the 1930s a number of historians outside these denominational circles had acquired a strong interest in radicalism. Prominent among them was Roland H. Bainton (1894–1984), a historian of the Reformation with wide interests and incisive scholarship. Bainton's close and fruitful interest in Luther did not lead him to follow Holl and the other historians of the Luther renaissance in defending Luther's criticism of Anabaptism as seditious and destructive of social bonds. In a 1936 article Bainton stressed as especially characteristic of radicalism its concern for the restitution of early Christianity.[46] His biography of David Joris (1937) presents its hero as a "fighter for toleration."[47] Bainton's later researches on the growth of religious liberty produced a life of Michael Servetus (1953) and a major article (1964) on Sebastian Castellio, "champion of religious liberty."[48] He presented the Anabaptists as pioneers, character-ized their achievement as "comparable to that of the Norsemen who visited America prior to Columbus," and described them as "the left wing" of the Reformation.[49]

The essential line of division, which made the radicals "left" and the Protestants "right," could be drawn on the issue of Church and State. From this angle Bainton saw the left wing as "those who separated Church and State and rejected the civil arm in matters of religion."[50] The distinguishing characteristics of the radical sects came from their ethical, primitivist view of the Church. They were often antiintellectual, and some stressed community of possessions. An understanding of the radical sects could help modern historians view Lutheranism and Calvinism in per-spective and in the context of these opposing movements.

Bainton's classification was accepted, even anticipated, by the no-table historian of Calvinism J. T. McNeill in a 1940 article.[51] In surveying recent interpretations of Anabaptism in 1955, Robert Friedmann argued that most historians of the Reformation were still failing to understand its true nature. They had not realized its importance in the Christian tradition or the fact that it was a "new type of Christianity," "existential Christianity" based on fellowship and love.[52] The left-wing metaphor did not, however, appeal to every observer of early radicalism. A 1953 article by Bender sought to explain the nature of the "third choice," the "middle way" open to the men and women of the sixteenth century. According to him, the radical view of religious liberty, for example, derived "not from any merely prudential, rationalistic, or ethical considerations, but from its central understanding of the nature of Christianity."[53] This cen-trality of Anabaptism to the Christian tradition was again claimed in 1952 in an important article by Robert Kreider examining its relationship with sixteenth-century humanism.[54]

The American Methodist Franklin H. Littell (1917–) wrote one of the most penetrating works on the radicals published during the 1950s: *The Anabaptist View of the Church,* later reissued as *The Origins of Sectarian Protestantism.* He pushed forward the categorizing process pioneered by Bainton, McNeill, and others, insisting that the nature of the Christian community, of the Church, was the key issue among six-teenth-century sects. The Anabaptists proper, he argued, "were those in the radical Reformation who gathered and disciplined a 'true church' (*rechte Kirche*) upon the apostolic pattern as they understood it."[55] They wanted a vigorous voluntary association contrary to that of the Spiri-tualists. Littell classified the ideas of the Zwickau prophets and Münster as "Maccabean" and distinct from both Anabaptism and Spiritualism.

Littell characterized Anabaptism by its ecclesiology, based on two principles. The first asserted that the Church was a voluntary body of true believers. The second was the desire to restore the Church of the New Testament: the principle of "restitution." He thought of the Anabaptists as "primitive heroes," rebels against a corrupt world, looking back to a golden age before the Church's fall from grace. For them the rottenness of state churches was compounded by the practice of universal infant baptism. The marks of the new "alternative" church, of which the Anabaptists saw themselves as forerunners, were rebaptism, spiritual government by believers—not by secular potentates—and fellowship. Primitivism, restitution, discipleship: all had been presented as characteristics of the great "third way" of the Reformation period. The "whole religious style" of this movement, wrote Littell, was "of a different order and era from that of the old 'Christendom.' "[56]

Commenting on the terms *radical* and *left-wing* in the context of the Reformation, Hans J. Hillerbrand balanced the common belief among sectarians that they were carrying the Reformation to its true conclusion against the recognition that the sects were medieval and even reactionary, as Ritschl and Harnack had long since suggested. In general, Hillerbrand accepted the claim that the sectarians should be recognized as a religious force distinct from Protestantism. Examining the key Reformation issues of grace and free will, he demonstrated the weight of anti-Lutheran beliefs among sectarians. The Anabaptists accepted the existence of free will—men could *choose* the path of discipleship—and they maintained that men could do good despite the existence of original sin. To them, sin appeared external rather than internal, and they assigned importance to ethical behavior. Quite intelligibly, the Anabaptist vision of mankind proved hateful to the Protestants, who often branded sectarianism as akin to Catholicism. Nevertheless, Anabaptism had arisen historically out of the Reformation, even if it contained doctrinal reactions against the movement. It was "a child of the Reformation, though perhaps not . . . an altogether legitimate one."[57]

The final result of these massive researches over more than half a century was a revolution in the historiography of the radicals. The "Radical Reformation" became an accepted concept, enshrined in George Huntston Williams's book by that title.[58] Williams (1914–), who had already edited (with Angel M. Mergal) a selection called *Spiritual and Anabaptist Writers* (1957), presented the Radical Reformation as a phenomenon of great significance even for modern Christians, whose sense of living in a basically hostile or alienated environment draws them "closer to the despised sectaries of the Reformation than to the classical defenders of a reformed *corpus Christianum*."[59] In this herculean work of over 860 pages, Williams often moved outside the familiar central

European and Netherlandish backgrounds: he sought to recategorize the many radical movements, inventing new labels for some and making an ambitious attempt to trace the course of each. Like Troeltsch, Williams freely recognized the absence of rigid frontiers and the flow of individuals among groups. He described the Radical Reformation as "a loosely interrelated congeries of reformations and restitutions which, besides the Anabaptists of various types, included Spiritualists and spiritualizers of varying tendencies, and the Evangelical Rationalists, largely Italian in origin."[60] All these disparate groups shared a "dissatisfaction with the Lutheran-Zwinglian-Calvinist forensic formulation of justification and with any doctrines of original sin and predestination that seemed to them to undercut the significance of their personal religious experience."[61]

There was indeed a wide range of "experience" among the radicals, some of it closer to the spirit of the Catholic reformation than to that of "magisterial Protestantism." Constitutionally, the radicals rejected the Reformation of the Protestants—based on the concept of a true but invisible church—in favor of an attempt to restore the primitive Church, but in effect to create numerous "gathered churches" or congregations. Those who aimed at an inwardly disciplined but externally free "apostolic" Church differed on how that Church should be organized. The various "Evangelical Rationalists" reacted strongly against a rigid church structure; the Anabaptists confidently believed they could construct an ideal church. Sixteenth-century Protestants had grouped all their radical critics together under various pejorative terms, irrespective of the immense differences which Williams sought to disentangle. His aspiration to describe each trend exactly led him not only to coin new titles but sometimes to reject existing ones: for example, he preferred *anti-Nicene* to *Anti-Trinitarian*. Yet behind all these intricacies and inconsistencies, Williams saw at the heart of the Radical Reformation a profound sense of hope, "the over-riding conviction that they were living at the opening of a new age."[62]

The massive erudition and immense horizons of Williams's survey have not deterred basic criticism of its conceptual basis. How useful is the idea of "The Radical Reformation"? The question is far from merely semantic. Williams himself has written of "reformations" and "restitutions," encouraging one to argue that he gave an unreal unity to a vast gamut of movements differing all too widely in origin and beliefs. Could any general label be meaningfully applied to this staggering cross section of the diverse heresies of Europe?

Soon after the publication of Williams's survey, A. G. Dickens insisted that there was no effective "third choice" for the people of the sixteenth century. Even setting aside all the other sectarian and spiritualist movements, there still remains no Anabaptist Reformation: "The Anabaptists had no great spiritual leader, no generally accepted epitome of doctrine, no central directive organs. They did not guide governments, shape national societies or control for any considerable period a functioning polity." Although he recognized the admirable idealism of many radicals, Dickens argued that in general they "had in fact by no means that near-monopoly of tolerationist sentiment attributed to them by some of their less cautious admirers."[63] A "gathered church" which consigned the rest of humanity to perdition was not basically tolerant. An ecumenical age was trying hard to do justice to the once-persecuted sectarians, but the idea of a Radical Reformation was being "canonized" in the United States, leading to a great "danger of over-estimating both the achievement and the potential of the radicals."[64] Furthermore, despite the immensity of its vision of the sixteenth century, *The Radical Reformation* did not go far toward relating the radical groups of that age to their predecessors: the wide range of heresies which had existed in medieval Europe. Even Joachimism got less than adequate treatment, and the survey of English developments showed the author's readiness to claim as "Anabaptist" beliefs which could more credibly have been attributed to late Lollardy, a flourishing phenomenon even after 1500, which Williams did not examine.

A distinctive radical background had already been explored in Norman Cohn's *The Pursuit of the Millennium* (1957), a survey of the recurring tradition of popular revolutionary millenarianism in medieval and early modern Europe. Cohn regarded Anabaptism as related to this tradition and described it in general as "a successor to the medieval sects . . . not a homogeneous movement." His main interest lay in the violent Münsterite wing of Anabaptism, but the pacific wing "continued the tradition of peaceful and austere dissent which in earlier centuries had been represented by the Waldensians."[65] Cohn's view of all such dissent was critical to the point of hostility. The radicals had been praised as pioneers of religious toleration, political democracy, and other Western values, but they could just as readily be taken as forerunners of left-wing extremism in modern Europe and the United States.

Contemporary parallels have appealed to a number of writers: William Klaassen saw the radical view of Church and State as "much more suited to today's situation than that of sixteenth century Catholic or Protestant. And we even see the development of similar consequences. The names of Daniel and Philip Berrigan and William Sloane Coffin Jr., Martin Niemöller and Dietrich Bonhoeffer, Dom Helder Camara and Father Antonio Henrique of Brazil make the point clear enough."[66] Klaassen, whose principal concern seems to have been the failure of the traditionally pacifist Mennonites to support resistance to the Vietnam War, described Anabaptism as "a socio-religious movement."

A more detailed social analysis of early Anabaptism may represent a fruitful direction for future research. Paul Peachey's study of the social setting of Swiss Anabaptism (1954) rightly remarks that the sect was by "no means entirely drawn from the lowest social classes."[67] A. L. E. Verheyden's *Anabaptism in Flanders, 1530–1650* (1961) makes a notable regional contribution to the distinguished series of Studies in Anabaptist and Mennonite History, and J. S. Oyer produced significant articles on the movement in central Germany.[68]

A new breadth of vision is evident in the work of Claus-Peter Clasen (1931–), a wide-ranging and nonpartisan historian who produced *The Palatinate in European History, 1559–1660* (1963). In 1963 Clasen also published two significant essays which showed his ruthlessly critical approach to sources and the accepted interpretation of Anabaptist history.[69] In "Medieval Heresies in the Reformation" he examined the survival of the heresy of the Free Spirit into the Reformation period and the influence of its doctrines of sexual license in Anabaptist circles. This was a theme Mennonite historians had shown no enthusiasm for exploring! Clasen concluded that the influence of medieval heresies in general on Anabaptism had been underestimated, presumably by those who wanted to stress Anabaptism's novel and progressive nature.

In an article on the sociology of Swabian Anabaptism, Clasen called for abandonment of all doctrinaire approaches, Marxist or Mennonite.[70] Despite all the recent research, he noted, too little was still known about the motivation of those who became Anabaptists. Clasen took a large sample of Swabian Anabaptists (539 individuals, perhaps up to 30 percent of the sect in that region) and attempted to determine their social position. At first, he revealed, Anabaptism drew on a wide social spectrum, including a number of wealthy burghers in addition to tradesmen, scholars, and clerics. Urban craftsmen also showed strong interest. The intellectual element soon defected, however, which probably aided the movement, for it was basically antiintellectual. Not only the educated but the rich and officeholders were quickly alienated by Anabaptist tenets. Yet the fact that Anabaptism lost ground in the towns cannot be explained in these terms alone. Its rival, Lutheranism, was genuinely popular and gradually won over the artisan class with the aid of incessant propaganda from press and pulpit.

Anabaptism retreated in the towns but advanced in the country, where social control—both physical and via propaganda—was less strict and Lutheran preachers thinly spread. There was "a certain connection between Anabaptism and poverty."[71] The lower classes, the peasantry, took to Anabaptism because of its specific appeal to the poor, which was bound up with its emotionalism, sense of community, and rejection of theology. Most important was the fact that commitment to radical sectarianism offered a new start to the disgruntled: landless and indebted laborers "had nothing to lose by joining a communistic society"; those condemned to privation and social stigma were "psychologically most prepared to start life again on a new basis."[72]

Why, then, did Anabaptism fail to become a mass movement? The danger of persecution was an obvious deterrent and perhaps explained why family-minded women were less susceptible to conversion than men. Fear of betrayal to an increasingly rigorous authority meant that membership in the sect was based not only on kinship but also on close occupational ties.

Clasen subsequently published articles on the social background of Anabaptism in other areas, including Bavaria and the city of Nuremberg. Most of his researches were synthesized in his *Anabaptism: A Social History, 1525–1618* (1972), a study of the sect in Switzerland, Austria, Moravia, and south and central Germany. This account, claimed its author, was "based on fact," whereas previous studies had either been simplistic or motivated by strong religious, moral, or political feelings. The most obvious characteristic of Anabaptism in these areas was its divisiveness: no fewer than twenty distinct groupings could be identified. This fact alone suggests that the control of religion in the sixteenth century by governments and educated theologians was firmly grounded in common sense. Anabaptism created its own alternative system of social and political mores which, had they been practically applied, would have resulted in social chaos but which in fact brought disaster on the Anabaptists themselves.[73]

Clasen's detailed regional analysis displayed beyond doubt that Anabaptism was led and supported by craftsmen in the areas he studied.[74] On the other hand, it remained impossible to deny the religious motivation of most adherents. The relationship between orthodox Protestantism and Anabaptism proved especially interesting; many individuals moved on from Protestantism to Anabaptism, but some returned to orthodoxy. Sectarianism seemed to be a safety valve for the more extreme reaches of Protestantism. Clasen regarded it as little more, in the last resort, than "a minor episode in the history of sixteenth-century German society." The Anabaptists had no marked effect on political, economic, social, or cultural institutions and exhibited "a cultural primitivism that has characterised some Anabaptist groups down to our own day." This remark seems clearly directed against American admirers of the sects, one of whom, Paul Miller, reviewed Clasen's book and ventured a moderate defense of the Anabaptists as a progressive force in Christianity.[75] Others felt that the author had usefully brought fresh treatment to a field of historical investigation where piety, not to say hagiography, had at times threatened to distort the picture.

The apotheosis of the sixteenth-century radicals, mainly by latter-day sectarians, as the true forerunners of modern religious and social thought, inevitably encountered the closest scrutiny. Growing rejection of partisan approaches to history of the Reformation was in the end reflected even in the *Mennonite Quarterly Review*. Meanwhile, in Europe political rather than religious partisanship had made its appearance. Engels, Kautsky, Bax, and other Marxists presented Anabaptists as the representatives of a true people's reformation. Their hero was Thomas Münzer, regarded as the people's Luther, and in recent years this interpretation has been reiterated by Max Steinmetz, M. M. Smirin, Alfred Meusel, and other East European historians (see Chapter 10).

On the other hand, British and American historians of the Continental Reformation have largely ignored Münzer or dismissed him as a fanatic, following the lead of Holl and other champions of the Lutheran Reformation.[76] The American Mennonite historians found Münzer an uncomfortable bedfellow. Lutheran scholars presented him as the founder of Anabaptism, but the Mennonites countered that he never rebaptized adults, never broke totally with the concept of an inclusive state Church, and labored for reformation rather than *restitutio*. No leading Anabaptist had ever followed Münzer, apart from Melchior Rinck, who survived the slaughter of the peasants at Frankenhausen to become the prophet of Anabaptism in Hesse.[77] Münzer's role as a Spiritualist was stressed in 1963 by E. W. Gritsch, who called him "the first theologian of the Reformation who opposed the Lutheran doctrine of Biblical authority by attempting to substitute the authority of the 'inner word' for that of the outer."[78]

G. H. Williams characterized Münzer as "the principal spokesman of Revolutionary Spiritualism." He was prepared to admit the participation of a number of Anabaptists in Münzer's movement. Johann Hut alone provided good material for the Lutheran view that Münzer was the founder of Anabaptism.[79] Williams placed Münzer firmly within the Radical Reformation, as a representative of one small arm of that vast and complex phenomenon; Gritsch proceeded to a sympathetic study of Münzer's ideas in *Reformer without a Church: The Life and Thought of Thomas Müntzer, 1488(?)–1525* (1967).[80]

These American historians' efforts to attain a new view of Münzer were paralleled by those of a number of European, mainly German, scholars. A work by Annemarie Lohmann, published as early as 1931, had argued for a "spiritual" understanding of Münzer; Carl Hinrichs's *Luther and Müntzer* (1952) had examined the political and social implications of theological differences between the two leaders.[81] Walter Elliger's important biography of 1960 demonstrates how Münzer's revolutionary activities were dictated by his theology, which revived the ancient Christian defense of the oppressed classes, and traces Münzer's defection from allegiance to Luther. Münzer's "gospel of all creatures" has been emphasized by a number of writers.[82] Williams described how this doctrine "took the *whole* creation of nature as filled with divine emblems, instructing man as to the universality, the solidarity in, and the purposefulness of suffering, the whole of creation groaning in travail."[83] The complex nature of Münzer's revolutionary thought was further dissected by Thomas Nipperdey in a 1963 article partly deriving from Elliger's work but placing more emphasis on Münzer's independence from Luther.[84]

Münzer also attracted the attention of the distinguished British historian of the Reformation E. G. Rupp, who elucidated the Reformer's espousal of the gospel of all creatures.[85] In his stimulating essay "Word and Spirit in the First Years of the Reformation" (1958), Rupp examined the emergence of the divide between rigid Protestant biblicism and the spiritualist emphasis on individual experience of the divine. Even before the Reformation, he claimed, "we find the wholeness of Christianity splitting into strands of mysticism, rationalism and churchly piety . . . The Protestant left was the heir of the medieval underworld."[86] Rupp criticized many historians' confidence in imposing a typology on the religious situation of the early Reformation, when there was no clear division between Lutherans and Anabaptists. The rift came only gradually: "The bitter controversies of the 1520s and 30s provoked both sides to extremes, while there was a whole 'No man's land' of misunderstanding, with Lutherans and radicals making precisely the same theological charges against one another, until on the one hand an orthodoxy arose which over-stressed pure doctrine, and to it an extreme and one-sided spiritualism remained truculently and abusively opposed."[87]

Rupp's approach is that of the historian of religious ideas, who rejects attempts at classification based on simplifying the issues. By this stage it had become widely accepted that the ideas of sixteenth-century radicals could be advantageously studied in the context of medieval unorthodoxy, a tangled field where research is still suggesting new approaches to Reformation sectarianism. Marjorie Reeves's work on the survival of Joachimism (1969) has obvious relevance for studies of the Reformation.[88] In mid-Tudor England, however, Anabaptism supervened in kindred elements in Lollardy, which from about 1520 had themselves been merging with Lutheranism.

Irvin B. Horst's *The Radical Brethren* (1972) concerns a wide spectrum of religious dissent which had been partitioned, largely by publicists like John Foxe, into Protestant pioneers and hated Anabaptists. Horst showed that "the brethren," as they called themselves, were influenced by both homegrown and imported ideas and that the term *Anabaptist* was a pejorative used by their enemies and a convenient means of spreading terror among the propertied classes, especially after Münster. According to this view, the so-called English Anabaptists were not separatists and did not believe in rebaptism: theirs was a specifically insular sect.[89] It could, of course, be asked whether the "composite heresy" Horst described should be termed Anabaptist at all, because it possessed so few accepted distinguishing marks of that sect.

Research and publication on this area continue, and the coming decades will surely produce fresh insights into the complex phenomena of radicalism. The committed "internal group" of historians, chiefly American Mennonites, will go on interpreting their ancestry in their attractive but somewhat detached and socially unpractical spirit. The interest of East European Marxist historians in the radicals shows no sign of decreasing.[90] The importance of the radical groups in Italy and elsewhere in Catholic Europe is becoming more widely recognized, as the work of Domenico Caccamo, Antonio Rotondo, and others proves.[91] Meanwhile, more detailed sociological investigations of the radical sects are constantly appearing, such as K. H. Kirchoff's study of the specific structure of Münster in 1534–1535.[92]

Among the more comprehensive recent studies of Reformation radicalism, two American contributions are notable for their revisionism. James M. Stayer's *Anabaptism and the Sword* (1972) rejects the unqualified stereotypes of "revolution" and "non-resistance" and suggests that Anabaptism included a broad spectrum of political thought, predominantly pacifist, to be sure, but marked by inherent illegitimacy and radicalism, in some cases compatible with violence.[93] In *Mysticism and Dissent* (1973) Steven Ozment, one of the most incisive and independent American historians, argued from theological and social bases for a broader ideological understanding of the radicals. They were dissenters whose revolt from established society was based on absolute spiritual values: "For our dissenters final authority lay in principle with the individual, the invisible, the ethically ideal, the perfect community—things no earthly society could ever be. When the values and goals of mystical theology were gathered into the arsenal of dissent, the institutional links with truth were severely weakened, if not severed altogether. A *translatio imperii* from institutional to anthropological structures, from official to experiential criteria, from traditional to ethical norms of authority was undertaken."[94]

In short, the phenomenon of radicalism has become less and less peripheral: it stands nearer than ever to the center of that highly complicated turmoil we call the Reformation. The radicals were the "host of free spirits . . . unable to shut their dreams within the limits strictly defined by theologians" of whom Lucien Febvre wrote. Their lives constituted "that drama, which for thousands of consciences tormented with scruples and divided between contradictory obligations, set the need for social discipline against the free aspirations of individual conscience."[95]

10

Materialist Perspectives:
The Marxists

Ernst Troeltsch speculated in 1911 that the Marxists' attempts "to make Christianity into a changeful reflection of economic and social history" might prove in the end a "foolish fashion."[1] A century after Marx's death, it is abundantly clear that his perspective on history, far from being a mere "fashion," has inspired a continuing and highly influential historiographic tradition. No other line of historical writing has been responsible for such a radical reassessment of the European past, and few aspects of that past have been more profoundly influenced than study of the sixteenth-century Reformation. This is not because of anything specific Marx had to say about the Reformation, but because of the far-reaching impact of his methodological presuppositions, which radically questioned virtually all previous assessments of the relation between religion and social change.

Troeltsch was by no means opposed to drawing causal connections between religion and social reality, but only to a representation of Christianity as no more than "an ideological reflection of economic reality"; he accused the Marxists of concealing "under cover of the most recent science . . . a hidden attack on the religious value of Christianity."[2] Yet there was certainly nothing hidden about Marx's assault on Christianity, and the very concept of "religious value" was meaningful to him only in terms of its social function. He made his views clear in an early essay, where he defined religion as "the self-consciousness and self-feeling of man who has either not yet found himself or has already lost himself again." Seen in broader social perspective, religion was a "reversed world-consciousness" produced by State and society: "the general theory of that world, its encyclopaedic compendium, its logic in popular form, its spiritualistic *point d'honneur*, its enthusiasm, its moral sanction, its solemn completion, its universal ground for consolation and justification."[3] The struggle against religion was therefore "the fight against the other world of which religion is the spiritual aroma" and the criticism of religion was "the premise of all criticism."[4]

These passages appear in Marx's introduction, written in Paris in 1843, to his slightly earlier critique of Hegel's *Philosophy of Right*. Two years earlier, he had planned to found a review titled *Atheistic Archives* with a close friend, Bruno Bauer, whose critique of the synoptic Gospels had denied that Christ existed and suggested that the Gospels were a clever invention.[5] Yet five years before, when he entered the University of Berlin in 1836, Marx had been a self-confessed Romantic and a disciple of Kant and Fichte. The son of a Jewish lawyer who adopted Protestantism to satisfy the discriminatory law of the Prussian State, he never held any strong religious views beyond the ethical Deism of Kant.

In Berlin Marx entered an intellectual milieu dominated by the thought of G. W. F. Hegel, who had died in 1831 after thirteen years as professor of philosophy. Marx had already read Hegel, but his conversion to Hegelianism, a crucial event in his intellectual life, was sudden. Jettisoning the abstractions of Kant and Fichte, he gave allegiance to a systematic philosophy which linked constant historical movement with the development of the human spirit in history. According to this line of thought, the human spirit progresses through knowledge, the highest form of which is religious, and knowledge is gained through not only reason but imagination. Hegel specifically rejected rationalism as inadequate and insisted that religion was necessary to man's self-understanding. But Marx was later to complain that Hegel's view of human history, although soundly based on a process of change and progress, was anchored in the lofty realm of ideas, concerned with spirit not with society, the true world of man.[6] Moreover, Hegel's political philosophy, despite his lifelong admiration of the French Revolution, tended strongly to support the bureaucratic, centralizing Prussian State. To many Germans, including Rhinelanders like Marx, who had been born shortly after the comparatively liberal French rule ended, the rise of Prussia represented a threat to all freedom.

The Hegelians' revolt against their master was first in the realm of religion. In Prussia the established religion, deemed by Hegel the highest flight of the human spirit, was a very conservative and rigid Lutheranism. If attacks on the State itself seemed too dangerous, the state Church presented a safer and very relevant target. Influenced by the controversy over the mythical character of the Gospels sparked by D. F. Strauss's *Life of Jesus* (1835),[7] Marx and his friends went much further and began to argue that all religion was a mythical human construct. Having already, in his doctoral thesis, proclaimed man's self-consciousness as "the highest divinity,"[8] Marx argued in his critique of Hegel that religion and the State were manmade entities which deprived human beings of an essential part of their humanity—the right to be themselves and create their own destinies. In separating man from the world, his fellows, and his real self, religion was the prototype of all ideology,[9] and it followed that the criticism of religion was "the premise of all criticism."[10]

Whereas Hegel had conceived of alienation (*Entfremdung*) in terms of the spirit's conception of the world, Marx saw it as man's realization that he was not in control of his own destiny, his proper powers having been alienated to other agencies: God, the State, capitalism. Marx drew also on Ludwig Feuerbach's *Essence of Christianity* (1841), although he criticized Feuerbach's failure to recognize religious sentiment as a social product. To Marx, alienation was a social phenomenon stemming from economic alienation of the worker, and religion was its ideological "sacred cloak." But there was more at stake than a different way of understanding the problem, for Marx's views were associated with a theory of revolutionary change which saw religion and the State as destined to be swept away,[11] and his distinctiveness is suggested in his terse judgment that "the philosophers have only interpreted the world in various ways; the point, however, is to change it."[12]

It was precisely in the context of changing the world—and specifically Germany—that Marx took up the question of the Reformation, as part of his critique of Hegel. The Reformation as a failed revolution is contrasted with the coming revolution. The one began in the brain of the monk, the other begins in the mind of the philosopher. In his brief comment, Marx captured better than most the highly paradoxical character of Luther's achievement. The Reformer "overcame bondage out of devotion by replacing it with bondage out of conviction. He shattered faith in authority because he restored the authority of faith. He turned priests into laymen because he turned laymen into priests. He freed man from outer religiosity because he made religiosity the inner man. He freed the body from chains because he enchained the heart."[13]

Marx could not regard the Protestant Reformation as the true solution of Germany's problems, but he did allow that it provided their "true setting." "It was no longer a case of the layman's struggle against the priest outside himself but of his struggle against his own priest inside himself, his priestly nature."[14] Protestantism resulted in the emancipation of the princes, the "lay popes" with the whole of their priestly clique, but the true emancipation of the future would see the transformation of the priestly Germans into men.

By no means insensitive to the power of religious forces in history, Marx allowed that "the Peasants' War, the most radical fact of German history, came to grief because of theology."[15] Yet it is difficult to escape the conclusion that his interest in the Reformation was limited to its function as a foil for the "true" revolution to come. Caught up in the sharply drawn contrasts between Germany's theoretical revolutionary past and her actual revolutionary future, her former enslavement to Rome and her present enslavement to Prussia and Austria, the crippling burden of theology and the liberating potential of philosophy, the Reformation appears in Marx's presentation as a cluster of symbols rather than a slice of history. His bold and pithy epigrammatic assessments of its character, although at times powerful and suggestive, lack any basis in sustained historical analysis.

That basis was furnished by Marx's collaborator, Friedrich Engels (1820–1895). The son of a Prussian industrialist, Engels had been brought up in a family setting dominated by a narrow and doctrinaire Lutheranism, but he moved toward a radical Hegelianism through reading Strauss's *Life of Jesus*. Although the two men had previously met—Engels wrote for the *Neue Rheinische Zeitung,* which Marx edited—their serious collaboration began in 1844 while Engels was working for his father's firm in Manchester. An active revolutionary in 1848, Engels returned to Manchester in 1850, staying for twenty years and completing a classic sociological study of the English working class, which is often considered his finest achievement.[16] The last twenty-five years of his life were spent in London working with Marx and, after Marx's death, acting as his literary executor.

Engels was a tireless organizer and agitator throughout his life and made important contributions to the development of Marxist thought, especially in *Anti-Dühring* (1878) and *The Origins of the Family, Private Property, and the State* (1884).[17] An original thinker, Engels was important too as a codifier of Marxism, applying Marxist techniques to fields unexplored by Marx. Engels's study of the Peasants' War in Germany made him the first Marxist historian of the Reformation, indeed, the first Marxist historian.

Leonard Krieger stressed Engels's empiricism as important in both the general development of Marxism and the rise of Marxist historiography. Inheriting from Marx a philosophy of history formed in the logical system of the historical dialectic—the means whereby history "progressed"—Engels was faced by the problem of reconciling this philosophy with the apparently random and illogical events of history. His work greatly widened the scope of Marxist philosophy of history by enabling it to take proper account of political history and the history of ideas, both of which could be interpreted in Marxist terms. By the end of his life, Engels had openly recognized that noneconomic forces play a large role in historical causation, that historical dialectic is based on "interaction" and not simply causation, that necessity is complemented by "accident"—in short, that historical materialism is less an inexorable logic than "a guide to the study of history."[18]

Commenting on the different theoretical approaches of the two "founding fathers" of Marxism, Krieger observed that Marx's history has "the texture of a plait, in which theory and fact, social structure and political events, are braided together in continuing contact"; Engels's has "the sound of factual nuggets jostling against one another inside a theory-ribbed receptacle."[19] But such methodological differences were not clearly evident in the middle of the century, when Engels first published his two major historical works, *The Peasant War in Germany* and *Germany: Revolution and Counter-Revolution,* complementary studies of Germany's two unsuccessful revolutions, written in the aftermath of the failure of 1848.[20] The latter work, first printed in the *New York Tribune* in 1851–1852, is a specific study of the 1848 revolution. The former focuses on the revolutionary dimension of the Reformation period and first appeared in the *Neue Rheinische Zeitung* in 1850.

In a preface to the second edition of *The Peasant War in Germany,* published some twenty years later, Engels wrote that it had been produced "under the vivid impression of the counter-revolution that had just been completed."[21] Engels's passionate feelings as a German and a revolutionary in the aftermath of 1848, when he believed that the bourgeoisie had betrayed the revolution, have to be borne in mind when reading this work. He did not claim that his study of the events of 1525 was based on original research. He had freely borrowed from Wilhelm Zimmermann's *History of the Great Peasant War in Germany* (1841–1843),[22] a massive work which Engels declared "the best presentation of the facts," despite its simplistic quality. A radical Hegelian and an old friend of Engels and Marx, Zimmermann (1807–1878) possessed a "revolutionary instinct" which made him a champion of the oppressed.[23] Yet his ideas had developed in a very different direction from those of Marx and Engels, for he had radicalized Hegel's philosophy without discarding its mystical elements. Thus, he was able to see the approaching revolution in Germany in terms of the coming of the kingdom, the realization of the "idea" in Hegelian terms. He sympathized instinctively with Münzer and read with approval G. C. Treitschke's conclusion that Münzer was not, as generally supposed, an irrational fanatic but a precursor of modern democratic movements in Germany. So the Peasants' War became in Zimmermann's estimation the central event of the Reformation epoch, the beginning of the age of bourgeois revolution which was to reach its climax in 1848.

Zimmermann's book was unfortunately based on free plagiarism of Treitschke and other historians.[24] Yet it provided the raw material for a work which, despite its weaknesses, represents an interesting experiment in Engels's attempt to write an empirically based Marxist history. The subject was obviously apposite. Marx had written with approval of Münzer's passionate denunciation of the way living creatures were "transformed into property" and saw this as suggesting his theory of alienation.[25] Engels, always more interested in specifically German affairs than Marx, was determined to prove that the German people had a sturdy revolutionary tradition beginning even before the sixteenth century, which shamed the "traitors" of 1848.

Surveying the social divisions of Germany in the early sixteenth century, Engels drew more parallels with his own age. In both periods economic changes brought about the rise and decline of classes. In political terms, an increasingly affluent middle class, based in the great towns, wanted moderate reforms but pursued only its own narrow ends, as had the "constitutional" reformers of 1848. There was also an urban *Lumpenproletariat*—a rabble, largely reactionary in the few demands it voiced—and a peasantry, at the base of the social pile, oppressed and ripe for revolt. Before that revolt could come, however, they needed a theory of revolution, and this was provided by religion, which had formed the context of revolutionary theory throughout the medieval period.

Engels had no difficulty explaining the theological character of sixteenth-century revolutionary thought. Given the central place of the Church and theology in medieval civilization, any attack on the hated system had to take the outward form of a theological heresy. The struggles involved class interests, but these were naturally clothed in religious shibboleths. Medieval heresies, Engels explained, were partly middle class—the demand for a "cheap Church" which would cease to hinder property interests.[26] But there was also a lower-class heresy rooted in ideas of primitive Christian equality, which was the force behind Wat Tyler in England and the Taborites in Bohemia. Artisans and peasants facing a rootless existence were able to look beyond existing property relations and anticipate in their fantasies a society based on the abolition of property.

In the Reformation conflict, Engels perceived three groups. A conservative Catholic camp embraced all those interested in maintaining existing conditions. A Lutheran bourgeois reformist camp comprised the propertied elements of opposition, including some lay princes who desired greater independence. A revolutionary party, led by Thomas Münzer, embodied the desire for radical change.[27] Engels perceived in Luther a process of change similar to that undergone by the "constitutionalists" of 1846–1849. Luther's revolutionary ardor of 1517 was a focal point for all existing heresies against Catholic orthodoxy, yet it proved short-lived. Once these diverse forces were set in motion, Luther had to choose between competing interests, and he aligned himself with the burghers and princes rather than the popular movement. A process of haggling over institutions and dogmas to be retained or reformed and the "ugly, diplomatizing, conceding, intriguing and compromising the result of which was the Augsburg Confession, the final draft of the constitution of the reformed middle-class Church" followed. This process involved steering a pathway "between the Scylla of revolution and the Charybdis of restoration," for which Engels had no difficulty finding further parallels in the bourgeoisie of 1848.[28]

When the lower classes rose in arms, Luther hesitated until Protestant areas were threatened and then sanctioned a merciless extermination of the rebels in "the same language that was used by our late socialist and philanthropic bourgeoisie, when, after the March days [of 1848] the proletariat also demanded its share of the fruits of victory." In using the Bible to excuse oppression and serfdom, Luther "not only betrayed the popular movement to the princes, but the middle-class movement as well."[29] Münzer, on the other hand, gradually abandoned theology and became a political agitator, preaching his ideas "under the cloak of Christian phraseology which the new philosophy was compelled to utilise for some time": a cloak Engels believed Münzer took much less seriously than many a Hegelian of Engels's time. Münzer's program was "a genius's anticipation of the conditions for the emancipation of the proletarian element that had just begun to develop among the plebeians."[30] It was, in short, communism. His revolutionary energy and resolution appealed to an advanced faction of peasants and plebeians. But although Luther won a cheap popularity by expressing the conceptions and wishes of the majority of his class, Münzer's ideals remained those of a small minority of the insurgent masses.[31]

The revolutionary demands of the popular movement in Germany had become apparent long before the Peasants' War, and Engels sketched in considerable detail the history of various popular movements of the preceding two decades. None of these came near the realization of its aims, and even Münzer's movement was faced with an unbridgeable gap between revolutionary theory and actual practice. Indeed, Münzer's early success in Mühlhausen, where he became the dominant influence in the "eternal Council," illustrated to Engels the unfortunate fate which befalls the revolutionary leader in a position of power during an epoch not ripe for domination by the class he represents.[32] What he can do contradicts his principles and previous actions, and what he ought to do cannot be done. "In the interests of the movement itself he is compelled to defend the interests of an alien class, and to feed his own class with phrases and promises, with the assertion that the interests of that alien class are their own interests. Whoever puts himself in this awkward position is irrevocably lost."[33] Nevertheless, Münzer's failure was, to Engels, heroic. He "went to his death with the same courage with which he had lived," and the movement he headed was no less magnificent because it ended in ignominious defeat.[34]

Those who gained from the bloody suppression of the peasant forces were the princes, who had benefited from Luther's "cowardly servility" and increased their domination over an undeveloped country incapable of true nationhood.[35] The bulk of the nation, small bourgeois artisans and peasants, was "left in the lurch by their nearest and natural allies, the bourgeoisie, because they were too revolutionary, and partly by the proletariat because they were not sufficiently advanced."[36]

Engels's study of the Peasants' War, although brief and open to profound criticism in light of more recent research, still calls for attention from historians of the Reformation. It is certainly not, as some critics have claimed, a deterministic or narrowly economic view of its subject. Its exploration of the relations between religion and politics is original and stimulating. But it poses as many questions as it answers, especially relating to the position of a supposed protoproletarian movement in what Engels had admitted to be an underdeveloped economy. There is evidence that Engels later had doubts about his conclusions on this issue.[37] The problems inherent in the theme of economic development in sixteenth-century Germany have, as we shall see, proved controversial in later Marxist treatments of the period. Engels's admiration for Münzer was essentially that of one revolutionary for another; it was a strong moral approval which overrode dialectically based objections. In more recent Marxist writing, Münzer has acquired an increasingly bourgeois character.

Although Engels's *Peasant War* has understandably remained central to the discussion of his thought, some of his later writings shed important light on his understanding of the Reformation. In his *Dialectics of Nature*, written between 1873 and 1886, he stressed the prophetic character of the Peasants' War: behind the peasants stood "the beginning of the modern proletariat with the red flag in their hands and the demand for common ownership of goods on their lips."[38]

A new emphasis, however, appears in his curious judgment that "modern research into nature" dates from that mighty epoch which the French call the Renaissance, the Italians the Cinquecento, and the Germans the Reformation, "from the national misfortune that overtook us at this time." This was an age of giants, among whom Engels mentioned Leonardo, Dürer, Machiavelli, and, not least, Luther, who "not only cleansed the Augean stable of the Church but also that of the German language," creating modern German prose and composing the text and melody of "that triumphal hymn which became the Marseillaise of the sixteenth century."[39] It was a time also when the Church's dictatorship over men's minds was shattered; it was directly cast off by the majority of Germans and overtaken among the Latin people by the growing influence of free thought. Among new intellectual developments, Copernicus's astronomical discoveries, though timidly advanced, represented a throwing down of the gauntlet to ecclesiastical authority parallel to Luther's burning of the papal bull and signaled the coming emancipation of science from theology. Yet this positive trend owed nothing to Protestants, who outdid Catholics in persecuting a new race of martyrs— who died not for religion but for free investigtion of nature. One was Servetus, whose death in Geneva Engels absurdly attributed not to the Trinitarian heterodoxy for which he was hounded by Catholics and Protestants alike, but to the fact that he was "on the point of discovering the circulation of the blood."[40]

In *Ludwig Feuerbach and the End of Classical German Philosophy* (1886), many of Engels's familiar themes reappear with interesting variations. The contrast between "feudal Catholicism" and "bourgeois Protestantism" led him to identify the Albigensian heresy in the cities of southern France as the first manifestation of Protestantism.[41] More significant is his interpretation of Calvin's role as the one who "republicanised and democratised" the Church, thereby providing "the ideal costume for the second act of the bourgeois revolution which was taking place in England" and which culminated in the compromise of 1689.[42] In France the situation was entirely different because suppression of the Protestant minority from 1685 made it easier for the bourgeoisie to carry through their revolution in an irreligious and exclusively political form, as free thinkers rather than Protestants.[43]

In the introduction to the English edition of *Socialism: Utopian and Scientific* (1892), Engels reiterated the intimate connection between Catholicism and feudalism which made it necessary for every struggle against feudalism to be directed first against the Church.[44] History had seen three great battles between feudalism and the bourgeoisie: the original Protestant Reformation, where the defeat of popular movements through bourgeois indecision led to the victory of princely absolutism and adaptation of the Lutheran creed to it; the Great Rebellion in England, which made the bourgeoisie a recognized component of the ruling classes with a vested interest in keeping down the lower orders; and finally the French Revolution, which saw the bourgeoisie's political triumph and the clearing away of feudalism's last vestiges.[45]

In assessing Engels's influence on subsequent Marxist historical writing, fundamental questions of methodology have ultimately proved more significant than specific historical data. For this reason, a letter Engels wrote to Josef Bloch in September 1890, in which he clarified his views on historical causation, is particularly important. Although he yielded nothing on the ultimately decisive character of economic factors in history, Engels freely allowed the importance of other factors, especially political ones. Historical events are to be recognized as the product of "innumerable intersecting forces," arising out of a conflict between wills, each "made what it is by a host of particular conditions of life." Engels commented that younger Marxists had sometimes stressed the eonomic factor more than was appropriate and had consequently produced "the most amazing rubbish" because they had assimilated the major Marxist principles without fully understanding them. This was regrettable, but entirely explicable; the urgent need to emphasize the main principle against strenuous opposition had made it difficult to give other elements their due, and for this Engels accepted a measure of blame.[46] Sensitive and subtle in its treatment of historical causation, this letter remains a valuable reference point for correcting overenthusiastic epigoni as well as over-eager detractors.[47]

Engels's book was to make the German Peasants' War a popular subject for socialist historians. August Bebel published his version, an elaboration of Engels's account, in 1876.[48] Engels's secretary Karl Kautsky (1854–1938) made the Peasants' War the subject of one chapter in a broader study on the theme of religious and social revolt, translated as *Communism in Central Europe in the Time of the Reformation* (1894). Kautsky was long a leading figure among the German Social Democrats, the founder of *Die Neue Zeit*, and the man behind the "Erfurt program," through which the Social Democratic Party adopted Marxist goals. When he wrote his study of the ancestry of German communism, Kautsky was an orthodox Marxist, although he later advocated a "revisionist" line and opposed both Bolshevism and the revolutionary tactics of Rosa Luxemburg and the German Communist Party.[49]

Kautsky was genuinely interested in Christianity in a way that Marx and Engels were not, and he composed a number of works on early Christian history. His study *The Foundations of Christianity* (1908) asserts that "Communism dominated the philosophy of primitive Christianity" and traces the decline of communism in the early Church and the rise of a clerical elite who transformed Christianity into a religion of domination. Jesus himself had been a rebel, but when Christianity had been absorbed into the Roman state he acquired a new identity as the preacher of passive suffering. "The crucified Messiah," Kautsky lamented, "became the firmest prop of that debased and infamous society whose complete destruction the messianic congregation had expected him to accomplish."[50] Yet the Gospels remained a source of communist doctrine and, insofar as they had not been falsified, continued to provide inspiration for the plebeian radicals cataloged by Kautsky in *Communism in Central Europe,* offering "an arsenal full of weapons to all those who . . . might wish to confiscate the wealth of the Church." These heretical movements had a genuine class character, although it was "effectually concealed by a veil of religion."

Kautsky analyzed the Hussite movement and the revolutionary Taborites to highlight the transitional character of communism during this period. It was distinguished from the passive and unpolitical communism of early Christianity by its revolutionary spirit and from modern communism by being "based on the needs of the poor and not on those of production." Because production demanded private proprietorship, "communism could never become the universal form of society in those days, as the necessity for it among the poor must have ceased the moment they had established it, i.e., as soon as they had ceased to be poor." The fate of the Taborites, who earned the bitter antagonism of the masses because they were the sole obstacle to peace for a war-weary society, was to Kautsky "of the greatest interest," because it showed "what would have been the outcome of the Müntzer movement in Mühlhausen and of the Anabaptist movement in Münster if they had remained unconquered by military force."[51]

Kautsky's close study of the pre-Reformation radical movements strongly influenced his estimation of Münzer's movement, in particular of its novelty. Among all the historians whose writings on this period he examined critically, Kautsky declared that only Zimmermann had correctly analyzed the historical importance of Münzer and his personality.[52] But it was precisely on Münzer's relationship to his past that Kautsky differed most sharply from Zimmermann, who had portrayed his hero as far ahead of his time. Kautsky, by contrast, saw Münzer as operating entirely in the sphere of earlier thinkers and declared that he had "not succeeded in discerning a single new idea in him." Moreover, Kautsky considered Münzer "much overrated" as an organizer and propagandist. Where he surpassed all his communistic confederates was in his "revolutionary energy" and "statesmanlike discernment." Münzer's failure was caused by circumstances beyond his control. He did what he could with the means at his disposal, and the fact that an insurrection of unarmed peasants could for a time threaten the very foundations of existing society was in no small degree a result of his "extravagant communistic enthusiasm, combined with an iron determination, passionate impetuosity and sagacity."[53]

Unlike Engels, Kautsky had firsthand acquaintance with many of Münzer's writings and perhaps for that reason showed none of his mentor's inclination to dismiss Münzer's theological views as pretense. Rather, he freely recognized his subject's genuine interest in religion, church organization, and liturgy, and he was careful to guard against mistaken and oversimplified judgments of Münzer's views.[54] Kautsky's knowledge of Luther was both less extensive and less direct, hence the initiator of the Reformation plays a secondary, although by no means unimportant, role in Kautsky's drama. A protégé of the prince-elector and a spokesman for the University of Wittenberg, Luther was judged to have been carried further than he at first intended. That a "monks' quarrel" was eventually transformed into the rebellion of a whole nation was less a result of Luther's undoubted gifts as an agitator and unifier of dissent than of the sheer movement of events, which determined that Saxony should become the intellectual center of both aristocratic opposition to Rome and democratic revolt. Luther was initially uncertain about where to throw his support and "allowed himself to be borne along on the tide of popularity, stirring up the expectation of all classes." In the end, he resisted all attempts of the lower classes to gain material benefit from the Reformation and favored the princes. By 1524 it had become clear that the lower classes could expect nothing from Luther's Reformation, and that if anything more was to be gained it would be through their own efforts.[55]

Kautsky's analysis of the progress of the Peasants' War is careful and judicious. Among the errors he corrected is that concerning Münzer's role in Mühlhausen; whereas Engels had taken Münzer to be president of the eternal council, Kautsky insisted that he had no official position and no decisive influence as a preacher because the town's policy was "entirely out of harmony with his own."[56] The descriptions of the decisive battle of Frankenhausen and Münzer's demise are chiefly notable for Kautsky's sharply critical attitude toward the sources, in particular Melanchthon's accepted account. The revolutionaries, Kautsky declared, were not such utter fools as they were depicted, and the alleged battle speeches of Münzer and the landgrave Philip of Hesse were simply devised by learned schoolmasters on the pattern of Livy and Thucydides. Equally worthless was Melanchthon's testimony on Münzer's last moments, about which nothing certain could be known.[57] Attacks on Münzer by the advocates of reaction, Kautsky concluded, have only kept his memory green among the German working classes as "the most brilliant embodiment of heretical communism."[58]

Kautsky's longest chapter is devoted to the Anabaptists, on whom he had carried out substantial original research. He followed the view of Leipzig church historian Ludwig Keller, who distinguished clearly between the radical centers of Zwickau and Zurich and saw the origins of Anabaptism in the medieval heretical sects, which had emerged from their secrecy early in the Reformation. But whereas Keller had argued that Münzer was no Anabaptist, Kautsky seemed anxious to maintain some positive connection—despite the Zurich Anabaptists' rejection of Münzer's violence—and he preserved the story, probably derived from Bullinger, of a meeting between Münzer and the Swiss brethren.[59]

Kautsky's account of Anabaptism comes to a climax in its description of the Münster uprising. What is perhaps the most openly partisan section of the entire work, graphically describes the tortures inflicted on the rebellious leaders and excoriates historians who portrayed the debacle as "merited punishment for their misdeeds," ignored the "bloodcurdling cruelties" carried out by the prince-bishop of Münster six months later, and "exult[ed] over the triumph of the priestly bloodhounds while they drag[ged] his victims through the mire as infamous criminals."[60]

After the debacle of Münster, the "proletarian cause . . . lay helpless in the dust," and the movement rapidly succumbed to political submissiveness under Menno Simons, who "did not hesitate to stab his grievously afflicted Münster associates in the back by initiating an agitation against them." Eventually, these heirs of revolutionary Anabaptism became no more than a small middle-class community "of no importance either to the proletarian struggle for emancipation or to the development of socialistic ideas." Regrettable though this failure of Christian communism was to Kautsky, it was only to be expected, because the movement had never been based solidly on economic changes in society, which still lay ahead. The century that saw the death of Christian communism likewise saw "the birth of a new system of production, the modern state and the modern proletariat; and it also saw the birth of modern socialism."[61]

British socialism in the later nineteenth century had been less influenced by a vital Marxist tradition than by the social criticism of the moralizing school of Carlyle and Ruskin. But the Marxist influence was strengthened, especially by the artist and poet William Morris and his circle. Deeply influenced in his earlier years by Ruskin's ideas on aestheticism and social progress, Morris later took up Marxist ideas with enthusiasm, joined the socialist Democratic Federation in 1883, and founded the Socialist League in 1884. A notable speaker and agitator, he also produced two significant political works, *A Dream of John Ball* (1888) and the utopian *News from Nowhere* (1891), in which he contrasted the ugliness of the machine world with the poetry and beauty of the Middle Ages and set forth his conviction that art provides the only real salvation for mankind—a somewhat unexpected and unorthodox development of Marxist perspectives.[62]

Among Morris's circle was the socialist philosopher Ernest Belfort Bax (1854–1926) who, unlike Morris, addressed in some detail the Reformation. Bax had been brought up in a strict Evangelical household and grew to hate the "repulsive Calvinistic theology" of his parents. Educated on the Continent, he came to socialism through the Positivism of Comte, joined the Democratic Federation in 1882, and became friendly with Morris and Engels. With Morris he wrote a series of articles in *The Commonweal* based on a reading of Marx's *Capital* and entitled "Socialism from the Root Up" (1886–1887). Bax's works, especially *The Religion of Socialism* (1887) and *The Ethics of Socialism* (1889),[63] have been described by Morris's biographer E. P. Thompson as "the first serious critique by an English Marxist of a score of problems in religion, ethics and social morality." Thompson applauded Bax's "flexible understanding of the historical method of Marxism in its relevance to all branches of human behaviour," although he noted the author's odd preoccupations with bourgeois values and the dangers of feminism.[64]

Bax's three works on the Reformation period were *German Society at the Close of the Middle Ages* (1894), *The Peasants' War in Germany, 1525–1526* (1899), and *The Rise and Fall of the Anabaptists* (1903).[65] The author claimed that they contained "an exhaustive history of certain sides of the Reformation period in Central Europe such as is not to be found otherwise, I may venture to say, in the whole range of English historical literature."[66] This was no idle boast; Bax's work will undoubtedly continue to be widely used by English-language readers until an English translation of Günther Franz's *Der deutsche Bauernkrieg* appears.[67]

At the beginning of *German Society,* Bax announced his aim: to give "a general view of the social condition and the popular movements during the period known as the Reformation."[68] This was to be true social history, not preoccupied with the massive personalities who, he imagined, had provided the major themes of Ranke's historical work. Bax was unjustly critical of Ranke's "bourgeois Philistinism" and of the "great man theory of history," which had led Ranke to see the Reformation almost "as the purely personal work of the Augustine monk who was its central figure."[69] Bax did not want to belittle the achievement of Luther, but to set it in its social, political, and religious context. The book performs this task with great effectiveness, and its chapters on popular literature, the folklore of the Reformation, and the German towns, as well as its discussion of issues such as humanism and the significance of printing, make it advanced for its date.

Bax's work on the Peasants' War is inevitably dependent on Engels and possesses a more Marxist tone than *German Society*, yet it is notable for its freedom from narrow dogma. The Reformation, wrote Bax, was the "ideological side" of a process of economic and social transformation "from a basis mainly cooperative to one individualistic in its essential character."[70] Bax avoided a narrow, "class-oriented" approach and did not attempt to portray the peasants as a progressive force, seeing most of their ideas as based on a reactionary conception of a past golden age. The Peasants' War was complex in its causation; in it political, economic, and religious factors were freely and confusingly intermixed. So too was the spread of Protestantism; the German people had turned to Luther for many reasons, not all strictly religious. Bax condemned Luther's betrayal of the popular cause as strongly as did other socialists; in particularly scathing terms he attacked Protestant historians' efforts to palliate Luther's crime and "shield him against the charge of time-serving and cowardice in adopting an attitude of benevolent neutrality to the peasants' cause at a time when it bade fair to be successful, whilst hounding on its executioners to hideous barbarities when its prospects were obviously desperate."[71] In his moral repugnance for Luther's actions, it never occurred to Bax to ask how far Luther had actually ever supported the peasant cause.

Nevertheless, its rich narrative and elevation of fact over theory make Bax's book on the Peasants' War in some ways a considerable improvement on that of Engels. One of its particular strengths lies in Bax's freedom from a sense of obligation to fit the revolt into the general line of progress—indeed, he specifically declared that it was "out of the line of natural social progress."[72] He followed Kautsky in segregating the heretical communism of the sixteenth century—the last efflorescence of a medieval tradition—from modern communism—which was dependent on the rise of a capitalist economy and an industrial proletariat. He also went further than Kautsky in modifying Engels's conception of Münzer as a social revolutionary. Münzer, he said, remained "before all else a theologian," and Bax found in him "no evidence of any constructive theory beyond the most casual expression."[73]

In *The Rise and Fall of the Anabaptists,* Bax recognized the legitimacy of the aspirations of sixteenth-century working classes, but judged them historically retrograde in their form, "both as regards the end conceived, and the means by which it was believed that end would come to pass." However, although they were for this reason doomed to failure, Bax could not suppress his admiration for them; with all their follies and shortcomings they were, in a sense, the forerunners of modern socialism and as such deserved "a passing tribute of recognition."[74]

The apparent absence in the English Reformation of great popular upheavals closely resembling the German pattern made it a far less attractive subject for Marxist historians.[75] But this was curiously compensated for by the enigmatic author of *Utopia,* who powerfully appealed to some writers as a forerunner of socialism. Max Beer, whose *History of British Socialism* appeared in 1919–1920, accounted the highly conservative Thomas More "one of the greatest figures in the history of communism" and for good measure reckoned Erasmus a communist too. He followed Engels's and Kautsky's views on the communism of the early Christians and saw the Reformation as a major turning point, for "with the rise of Protestantism the clear Scriptural text of the Ten Commandments prevailed over the communistic traditions of Primitive Christianity."[76] As a result, communism remained a force only among the sectarians, while society as a whole developed toward individualism. Beer did not attempt to explain how More and his bitterest religious opponents shared the same ideological tradition.

More's *Utopia* had, of course, already been identified as a work of idealistic communism by Kautsky and other earlier socialists. Kautsky in *Thomas More and His Utopia* (1890) had elevated the supposed communism of *Utopia* to a central place in More's thought and unwisely claimed More as a forerunner of nineteenth-century scientific socialism.[77] Such judgments appear strange today, but we must remember that little research had been done on More's life and thought; he was judged solely on the basis of *Utopia,* because most of his writings were unknown. Frederic Seebohm was among the first to highlight, in *The Oxford Reformers* (1896), *Utopia*'s significance as a deliberate contrast to the disordered and corrupt state of early modern Europe. R. W. Chambers, whose major biography of More was published in 1935, similarly stressed that the book was a product of its age, but took an extreme view in emphasizing More's "reactionary" stance as "rather the last of the old than the first of the new." He did admit that *Utopia* had been an inspiration to many radical critics of society, although it was a very faint echo of modern socialist doctrines.[78]

In the 1930s A. L. Morton had produced an immensely popular *People's History of England*, which first appeared under the imprint of the Left Book Club in 1938 and was subsequently reprinted many times. It displays a rather crude Marxist approach to the English Reformation, portraying it as "part of the long struggle of the European monied classes for power," a political movement in religious guise. Yet the Reformation released forces that it could not control and in many lands took on a broad popular character and democratic forms. In England the Reformation was first imposed from above, but it soon inspired a popular reform movement which turned to the radical criticism of existing society, and the Bible became "a veritable revolutionist's handbook."[79]

Although Morton's book contains some stimulating ideas about the origins of radical politics in England and is particularly informative about the Civil War period, it is marred by a lack of historical understanding which led its author to isolate personalities from their age. Thus Morton, conveniently ignoring Hugh Latimer's strictures on disobedience, was able to portray this "yeoman's son become bishop" as the representative of the revolutionary tradition of sixteenth-century England because he "carried the radicalism of More into the Protestant Reformation and remains as the true voice of the nameless weavers and peasants who formed its genuinely revolutionary wing."[80] Returning to the subject of More himself some years later, Morton described *Utopia* as "one of the great works in which the classless society is visualised and mapped out" and the essential link between the primitive communism of the Middle Ages and modern scientific socialism.[81]

A number of Marxist writings of the 1930s emphasized the Reformation's character as the triumph of individualism; of these Maurice Dobb's much-reprinted *Outline of European History* (1925) is typical. In it, Protestantism is seen as "the religion of the individual" and the Reformation as "a revolt in favour of the individual and of the individual conscience as against the authority of the feudal superior and of the Church to say what was right and wrong."[82] Dobb's major work *Studies in the Development of Capitalism* (1946) contains a much more sophisticated analysis of Protestantism's social impact and urges that the new economic system did not originate in a "spirit" or set of ideas but in the hard facts of production and the resulting class relations.[83] An increasingly rigid schematic view of history dictated that the sixteenth century be deemed the period of modern capitalism's emergence, but the problem remained, When did communism originate as a political force, and how?

One of the most widely read interwar British intellectuals, Harold J. Laski, followed his Marxist predecessors in assigning to the idea of communism a long ancestry. Laski, professor of politics at the London School of Economics from 1926 until his death and for several years chairman of the Labour Party, published a series of highly influential books, among them *A Grammar of Politics* (1925) and *The State in Theory and Practice* (1935). In *Communism* (1927) Laski duly identified the Reformation as a period when economic individualism prevailed. Although a medieval communistic tradition survived, its basis was more "a sense that a rich man cannot enter the kingdom of heaven, a *cri de coeur* against the rigidity of feudal structures, than a genuine social philosophy." Laski, moreover, was not receptive to the idea that Thomas More was a protocommunist, and with greater realism considered the views expressed in *Utopia* no more than "an attractive fancy."[84]

Most of these English writers had touched on the Reformation only marginally, in terms of other concerns. The first substantial and comprehensive English Marxist study of the Reformation since Bax's was Roy Pascal's *The Social Basis of the German Reformation,* published in 1933, which set out to place Luther in the context of the social and political history of sixteenth-century Germany. Unlike earlier Marxist historians, Pascal (1904–1980) gave Luther a central role: indeed, it is subtitled "Martin Luther and His Times." Pascal's declared aim, to "find the principle guiding Luther's thought and the political developments attendant on it," already indicates the nature of his interest in the Reformer. If Luther's age was unthinkable without him, the reverse was equally true.[85] In a time of rapid social change and incipient class conflict, in which every sphere of human endeavor from metaphysics to practical life was in flux and various groups were competing for social hegemony, the Reformation was clearly no chance occurrence and no mere product of great personalities. It was the corollary of comprehensive change: political (the decline of the empire and the rise of the great German cities), intellectual (the new critical humanism), and economic (the growth of capitalism).

E. G. Rupp spoke for many critics of Pascal when he accused him of bypassing the theological issues and insisted that the "sociological element" in the Reformation "does not account for nearly half the story of sixteenth-century Europe, let alone Martin Luther."[86] Yet it is important to see that Pascal's intention was not to bypass the theological issues so much as to set them in their social context, and he freely recognized the centrality of theological concerns and the secondary character of everything else in Luther's frame of reference.[87] His point was that

Luther, despite himself and perhaps quite unconsciously, occupied as large a role in social history as in theological and ecclesiastical history and that his true theological and ecclesiastical significance could be measured only by recognition of his place in social history.

According to Pascal, Luther's historical role had been to define the moral and spiritual principles of the newly emerging individualistic society. His central doctrine of justification was imbued with this spirit; his social outlook, far from seeking a society ordered according to scriptural principles, looked toward domination of the Church by the State.[88] Although unconscious of the fact, Luther was representative and leader of the rising bourgeoisie, and it was "the logic of a social class" which finally made sense of the inconsistencies in his activity. The Reformer's moral doctrine was "consistently that of the settled middle-class who, while striving for a greater measure of freedom in economic affairs, still depended for their prosperity on the continuance of the social order." Having enjoyed some status before the Reformation, the class for whom Luther spoke "needed to sustain some authority in order to maintain its privileges against the claims of other classes." Hence, Luther worked within the traditional framework of ideas and even preserved the traditional concept of dogma.[89]

Although Luther achieved a compromise between the interests of the middle class and the princes—where there was a great deal of common ground—Pascal thought it inevitable that the oppressed lower classes should have taken Luther's teachings to their logical conclusion, deriving from them a gospel of social revolt. And it was equally inevitable that Luther's class policies and hatred of disorder would lead him to condemn the rebels. His acceptance of the distinction between "the rich man in his castle and the poor man at his gate" and his subordination of Christian love to his reverence for social order were expressions of "the attitude of extreme conservatism" for which he basically stood.

Writing against the background of the rise of Nazism in Germany, Pascal fell into the temptation of blaming later German history on the Reformation, asserting that Lutheranism had always been a weapon of the ruling classes and that "Bismarck's oppression of the Social Democrats was the logical continuation of Luther's oppression of the peasants."[90] Absolutism had provided an appropriate political setting for the advance of the class interests Luther championed, in particular maintenance of private property and the family.

Pascal's views are likely to be misunderstood unless we note two important qualifications he made concerning historical method. First, he made clear that he was willing to recognize the place of the dominant personality in historical causation, although he considered that individuals could make history only within the bounds of historical possibilities laid down in the past. Second, he was careful to distinguish "the materialistic conception of history" from "the crude theory that historical events are determined by economic conditions." Hence, he was not arguing that the Lutheran Reformation was "simply and solely the rationalisation of the economic needs of the contemporaries of Luther." The metaphysical system and particular concepts of such a class might well have taken a different form. Nevertheless, "economic moments" were responsible for creating social and political forms, and class; the understanding of class was "a presupposition for the understanding of history." Warring classes have created competitive systems, and individual idealism has contributed to the self-preservation and self-assertion of the class. It is, therefore, "a complex task to penetrate the heart of so elaborate a structure."[91]

Such refinements and qualifications of the Marxist perspective were unable to satisfy critics like Rupp, who saw theology forced into the straitjacket of a preconceived ideological construct which ultimately did not allow it to be itself and was, therefore, historically false. Granting the strength of this objection, it could also be argued that Pascal and other Marxists provided a valuable corrective to studies of the Reformation which focused too narrowly on theological issues and great personalities and so gave insufficient recognition to the social elements in historical change.

The vitality in the British Marxist historical tradition from Bax to Pascal was less obvious among Continental writers, and if there was no overwhelming evidence of a hard-line orthodoxy, there were also few signs of a creative reinterpretation of the tradition. Jean Jaurès saw Luther's fight against Roman tyranny, and in particular his doctrine of Christian equality, as paving the way for social equality. But these views came not so much from Marx as from an extravagant doctrine of progress which led Jaurès to see every valid human achievement as a forerunner of socialism.[92] Franz Mehring incorporated many of Kautsky's perspectives in his study of German history.[93] However, although he showed a greater preoccupation with the cultural impact of the Reformation, he presented virtually nothing new in specifically Marxist terms.

One exception to this trend was Ernst Bloch (1885–1977), who emphasized the strong connection between Münzer and the chiliastic tradition. What earlier writers like Engels and Kautsky had noted in passing, Bloch regarded as central to Münzer's revolutionary drive. His success with the peasants from July 1523 came in no small part from his ability to inspire a people living under worsening conditions with a vision of justice drawn from primitive Christian sources. Even more significant than this judgment was the methodological implication Bloch was prepared to draw—the denial that economics necessarily forms the ultimate motive force in history.[94]

The period of about a century from Marx's first observations on the Reformation to the end of the Second World War produced a considerable body of historical literature, identifiable as a cohesive tradition. If some of it tended to be highly dogmatic, it was no more so than much church history of the same period, and it evidenced considerable flexibility and adaptation of original perspectives. Engels's discussions with Kautsky provide a prime example of how Marxists could differ from one another on significant points within a framework of mutual respect and could modify their views in the light of discussion.[95] For most of this period Marxists wrote as self-conscious outsiders, at odds with the mainstream of European intellectual and political life. Although the Russian Revolution had yielded a major state committed to revolutionary Marxist goals, hopes among European Marxists that these goals would be more widely realized were at best intermittent, and they were swept away altogether when Europe was once more engulfed by war and the struggle for national survival.

The connections between Marxist scholarship on the Reformation and Marxist political fortunes, tenuous and remote during this first century, acquired a new significance with the advent of Communist regimes in Eastern Europe. This was especially true in the Saxon-Thuringian heartland of the Reformation, which was incorporated into the German Democratic Republic. Scholarship and politics intersected in a direct way as the new regime—anxious to sever itself from the recent political past and chart a radically different course—reached back to recapture the revolutionary inheritance which Engels had first clearly articulated in his study of the Peasants' War and link it with their recent triumph as Engels had linked it with the failure of 1848. In this endeavor scholars willingly cooperated with politicians and party leaders, and it is easy enough to portray their work as a submission of the academic enterprise to political control. Such judgments ought to be tempered, however, by the recognition that the scholarly traditions being overturned were by no means free of political ideology. Yet it is difficult to deny that the swift accomplishment of this historiographic revolution led to a hard-line orthodoxy sanctioned and reinforced by political power and patronage.

Russian scholarship in the twentieth century had no particular reason to be interested in the Reformation, yet it was a Russian historian who first gave substantial form to the new postwar Marxist orthodoxy.

M. M. Smirin's (1895–1975) study of Münzer and the Peasants' War, published in the USSR in 1947 and translated into German in 1952, was essentially a defense and restatement of Engels's views.[96] Indeed, it is characteristic of the new style of Marxist writing Smirin represented that he turned out to be more "orthodox" than Engels himself, for whereas Engels had approved of Kautsky's work and implicitly accepted his revised view of Münzer, Smirin denounced Kautsky for his deviations from Engels[97] and reaffirmed the image of Münzer as an inspired and advanced leader of the oppressed masses, a man for whom religion was not a matter of genuine personal commitment but a necessary means of communicating his real message to a people who knew no other language.[98]

In one important respect Smirin was obliged to modify, or perhaps clarify, Engels's position. Engels had written on the Peasants' War some time before formulating his concept of the "early bourgeois revolution," and this concept sat rather uneasily with the notion of Münzer as a protocommunist. Accordingly, Smirin toned down Münzer's communistic tendencies and distinguished between his ultimate commitment to a classless society and his realistic immediate goals of redistributing property and political power to the common people.[99] In another work, *Germany before the Reformation* (1955), Smirin focused in detail on conditions of the peasantry and again offered what amounted to a restatement of Engels's views. Engels had explained the apparent nonparticipation of the bourgeoisie in this bourgeois revolution by observing that this class had failed to recognize its true interests. Smirin argued that, despite a common interest with the peasantry in opposing the feudal system, the bourgeois class was weak and finally betrayed the common interests of the masses.[100]

Smirin's views were not, however, universally accepted, and a vigorous debate transpired in Soviet historical circles about the early bourgeois revolution and its connections with the Reformation. The most radical criticism came from O. G. Chaikovskaia; A. D. Epstein and Josef Macek generally supported Smirin's views, though with significant modifications.[101] Common commitment to Marxist presuppositions did not preclude a variety of views on particular issues.

The close relationship between state policy and historical interpretation in the German Democratic Republic was signaled in 1952 by a joint call for revision of German history by East German party leader Walther Ulbricht and historian Leo Stern. Stern sought a decisive rejection of traditional German historicism and idealism in favor of a "progressive" and "polemical" historiography focused on the German revolutionary tradition, and he unashamedly supported conformity to the official policy line.[102] In an address in 1967 on the 450th anniversary of the Reformation, he reaffirmed the derivative character of religious controversy by insisting that it was "not the cause but the result of that stage of development which was reached on the verge between the feudal and the early capitalist ways of production."[103]

Stern's mantle as unofficial leader of the historians of the German Democratic Republic was assumed by Max Steinmetz (1912–), director of the Institute for German History at the Karl Marx University of Leipzig, whose numerous writings on German history display impeccable Marxist orthodoxy. Like that of Stern, Steinmetz's approach to the Reformation's theological dimension was not to ignore it but to accord it a significance in strict conformity with Marxist attitudes. Hence, he described Luther's thought as "the theological expression of the economic and political struggle between the bourgeoisie and the masses of people against the Church of the Pope which was governed by Rome and which hampered any social progress."[104] These words appear in a textbook on German history from 1476 to 1648, the third volume in a comprehensive series on German history. The subtitle indicates the explicit intention to interpret the Reformation in the context of the early bourgeois revolution; 1476 was chosen as the starting point because it witnessed publication of the famous *Reformatio Sigismundi* aimed at reform in Church and empire and also the anticlerical movement initiated by Hans Böhm, the "drummer of Niklashausen," which Steinmetz saw as inaugurating a period of "class struggle" in German society, leading to the early bourgeois revolution of 1517–1526.

The role Steinmetz assigned to Luther depended on a close identification between medieval Catholicism and the feudal order on the one hand and between Luther and the new economic forces on the other. Steinmetz argued that the advance of the capitalist mode of production had rendered the feudal mode, and with it the Catholic ideology, anachronistic. Luther's struggle against that ideology, following his unsuccessful attempt to identify with it, was the intellectual expression of the economic and political struggle of the bourgeoisie and the masses against the old Church, and his reformulation of theology represented the new ideology of a bourgeois church. The doctrine of free grace was the theological counterpart of the bourgeois desire for a "cheap" Church.[105] Luther is presented, therefore, not as a free agent so much as an unconscious instrument of the secularizing dialectical process, which had pushed him, despite himself, toward a total break with the Roman Catholic Church. This accounted for the contradictory "Catholic" impulses in his thought and for his eventual unpreparedness for the radical social consequences of his attack on clerically sanctioned feudalism.[106]

In a later writing Steinmetz summed up his thoughts on the period by restating the view that the Reformation and the Peasants' War were parts of a single revolutionary process which played itself out from 1517 to 1526. The first stage—inaugurated by the Ninety-five Theses—was Luther's attack on the feudal Catholic order, which unified all the forces opposing the Church. The second stage was Münzer's independent "people's reformation," based on a revolutionary rather than moderate bourgeois ideology, and the third stage and climax of the early bourgeois revolution was the Peasants' War itself. The Anabaptist experiment at Münster represented an epilogue to the drama.[107]

Non-Marxist Western historians have been quick to point out the problems raised by this kind of interpretation, especially by its tendency to reduce a complex social crisis to a single explanation relating to changes in productive forces—an explanation seemingly based not so much on hard evidence as on deductive application of an ideological presupposition. Yet there has been no shortage of critics in the Marxist community, who, without rejecting basic Marxist presuppositions, have questioned aspects of this identification between Reformation and early bourgeois revolution.

A book of essays published in the German Democratic Republic in 1961, far from establishing any broad consensus, reveals the problems inherent in this concept—not the least of which was the difficulty of locating any significant bourgeois participation in the alleged revolution—and historians responded to these problems in a variety of ways.[108] The Czech historians Josef Macek and Robert Kalivoda in different ways asserted the fifteenth-century Hussite revolution's claims to stand with the Peasants' War as part of the early bourgeois revolution. Kalivoda's interesting argument stresses the disintegrating effects on the feudal order of commercial capitalism from the fourteenth to the sixteenth centuries, a variation from the more common emphasis on changes in production, although by no means a unique view among Marxists.[109] The archideologue Leo Stern managed to write a book on Luther and Melanchthon without using the phrase *early bourgeois revolution* at all.[110] Bernard Töpfer, from his standpoint as a medieval historian, argued that it was arbitrary to isolate those of 1476 from expressions of lower-class revolt in fourteenth-century England and fifteenth-century Bohemia and denied that the Reformation and Peasants' War had to be related in terms of an early bourgeois revolution at all.[111] More recently, Gerhard Brendler insisted that the Reformation and the early bourgeois revolution are only partially identifiable and that the ideological aspect of the Reformation should be recognized as relatively independent.[112]

The problematic nature of the concept of the early bourgeois revolution is likely to be an ongoing factor in Marxist discussion of the

Reformation. But it would be false to assume that Marxist interpretation is wholly concerned with it or finally dependent on its viability. In a number of studies on Luther which have appeared in the German Democratic Republic, the concept surfaces only marginally or not at all, and detailed attention is given to Luther's ideas and their historical significance, although still within a Marxist framework.

The first major contribution of this kind was Karl Kleinschmidt's *Martin Luther*, which appeared in 1953. Kleinschmidt (1902–) interpreted Luther's spiritual struggles as an unconscious attempt to identify with a superseded ideology, the failure of which led him to the Bible, where he discovered the doctrine of imputed righteousness. In proclaiming this new doctrine in opposition to Catholicism, Luther undermined the ideology which supported the feudal system and thereby prepared for transition to the new order. Kleinschmidt projected Luther as a national hero by resorting to the traditional Marxist distinction between the revolutionary early years and the later reactionary period. He also stressed, as Engels had, Luther's key role in unifying the German people by giving them a language.[113] Stern's work on Luther and Melanchthon, published the same year, similarly accented the doctrine of justification by faith, which undermined the Catholic Church but also brought together Reformation thought and humanism as variant expressions of bourgeois ideology.[114]

The 1960s saw a continuing Marxist preoccupation with Luther and some new accents in interpretation. Günther Fabiunke concerned himself specifically with Luther's economic views and, building on the scattered references to usury and other economic issues which had interested Marx, tried to reconstruct the Reformer's economic outlook as a whole and portray him as the first German economist.[115] Apart from the intrinsic dubiousness of such an enterprise, the author's overt hostility to Luther's evangelical doctrine was hardly conducive to understanding dimensions of his thought which other Marxists had freely acknowledged to be bound up with his economic outlook. Rosemarie Müller-Streisand's study of Luther, published in 1964, is a more traditional presentation, based on the familiar contrast between early revolutionary and later reactionary.[116] She interpreted Luther's return to a more Catholic theology as his conservative reaction to the social upheavals of the mid-1520s.

Other scholars, however, cast Luther in a more consistently bourgeois role, most notably Gerhard Zschäbitz (d. 1971), whose biography strongly argues for the consistency of Luther's social attitudes over the years 1517–1526.[117] As Zschäbitz saw them, Luther's views were from the beginning, and unconsciously, those of the moderate bourgeoisie, but because his sole target in those years was the papacy, he was able to unite all the forces of opposition to Rome. When the more radical social goals of Münzer, Karlstadt, and the peasants became clear, a definite parting of the ways occurred, not because Luther had changed his position but because the radicals had clarified their more extreme goals. Accordingly, Luther did not "betray" the peasants: he had never supported the objectives they now made clear.[118] In a similar vein, Manfred Bensing argued that Luther's actions were those of a man defending his own Reformation and not those of a political opportunist.[119]

The capacity to modify received tradition has shown itself equally clearly in approaches to Münzer. Two issues in particular proved difficult to resolve: how Münzer's religious views are to be understood, and how—if he were indeed a sixteenth-century communist—he could have exercised a key role in a bourgeois revolution. On both these issues Zschäbitz pointed in a new direction, although he had been to some extent anticipated by Kautsky. Engels had interpreted Münzer's religious views as a facade maintained to communicate with his followers. Although he later implicitly accepted Kautsky's modification of this stance, Smirin had reinforced the original view in opposition to Kautsky. Zschäbitz argued, on the basis of Engels's later writings, that religion, albeit certainly illusory, was an important historical force, and he insisted that Münzer was at heart a theologian and deeply religious man whose chiliastic views united mystical and social revolutionary elements.[120] Recognition of the religious dimension of Münzer's views—the hope for a divine order in which God's will would find fulfillment—had implications also for the second issue, the bourgeois revolution. Münzer's status as a revolutionary was not undermined, for his ideas had been a catalyst to insurrection. But his revolutionary qualities increasingly assumed a more bourgeois appearance.

Zschäbitz's placement of Münzer in his sixteenth-century context and his criticism of attempts to modernize Münzer were widely accepted, but not without a desire to maintain his significance for future events.[121] Ernst Werner offered a solution to this problem by stressing Münzer's prophetic anticipation of an idea whose time had not come: that the new order would arise from the revolutionary initiative of the poor. Münzer's significance for future history was thereby retained without wrenching him from his period context. Bensing went so far as to assert that Münzer consciously set aside those future goals because the time was not ripe for their realization.[122]

Changes in the Marxist interpretation of Anabaptism are harder to plot because of the generally peripheral function of Anabaptist studies in the Marxist tradition.[123] Among the early Marxists, only Kautsky dealt with the Anabaptists at length and on the basis of original research. After his work, Zschäbitz's study of the Anabaptists in central Germany, published in 1958, was the first major treatment. Zschäbitz strongly attacked the growing consensus of Western historians in sharply differentiating the Anabaptists of Zurich from Münzer's revolutionary radical tradition—a tendency which he interpreted as a church historians' conspiracy against the Marxists.[124] Although Kautsky had recognized the distinction between the revolutionary tradition of Zwickau and the pacifist tradition of Zurich, he had retained the notion of a relationship between the two, and subsequent Marxist writers increasingly stressed Münzer's influence on Swiss Anabaptism. Even Bensing, who admitted in 1966 that Engels had been wrong in seeing the Anabaptists as Münzer's disciples, did not deny his influence.[125] Zschäbitz reaffirmed that this influence was decisive, arguing that differences on the superficial issue of baptism were far less significant than the strong common social and economic bonds. The movement brought together those who had suffered from the recession induced by the price revolution, and its basis was hatred of governmental authority in Church and State. In line with this view, and in apparent defiance of clear evidence about the early origins of Swiss Anabaptist pacifism, Zschäbitz maintained that pacifism had resulted from defeat in the Peasants' War and the Münster debacle and that the severity of persecution and the expulsion of revolutionaries from the movement had hastened Anabaptism's development into a petit bourgeois sect.

It was ironic that Zschäbitz, who accused Western church historians of ideological distortion in their assessment of Anabaptism—and perhaps not without justice—in the end maintained his Marxist assessment of the movement by ignoring evidence which contradicted it. Similarly, A. N. Tschistoswonow brushed aside all evidence of involvement of the wealthy in Anabaptism to maintain its class-based character by appealing to an understanding of the movement's "essence" rather than its "superficial analysis."[126] But not all Marxist analysis of the Anabaptists was of this kind, and the most impressive results have come when scholars abandoned grand perspectives for a close study of local and regional manifestations of the movement. Of these the best example is Macek's study of Michael Gaismair, leader of the peasant movement in the Tirol, which was based on solid and detailed archival research.[127]

That Marxist scholars were able to produce impressive empirical studies free of obvious dogmatic bias had already been demonstrated by Johannes Schildhauer in his study of three Hanseatic towns—Stralsund, Rostock, and Wismar—published in 1959.[128] Schildhauer explored the undercurrent of class feeling on the eve of the Reformation, which prepared people for total revolt against the ecclesiastical establishment. The

poor and underprivileged urban masses took up Lutheranism with enthusiasm, and the new faith became entwined in a long-standing battle
against hierarchical town government. The Lutheran preachers were
themselves outside the ruling classes, and Lutheranism and the demand
for radical governmental change became almost synonymous. The triumph
of Lutheranism was aided by partial victory of this reform movement
when the city government was opened to a wider section of the burgher
class and by its subsequent betrayal of the proletarian majority, which
prompted groups of the lower classes to move toward complete social
revolution in Church and State. The coincidence of Schildhauer's broad
social analysis with that attempted recently by Western European and
American historians of other urban Reformation movements suggests the
possibility of a genuine meeting on the broad common ground of social
history.

When Schildhauer wrote this work such a possibility seemed remote
in the extreme, and so it remained until the early 1970s. Indeed, Marxist
scholarship was in many ways as isolated as Roman Catholic scholarship
on the Reformation had been in the heyday of Denifle and Grisar. This
was not only for reasons of its own making. Strong ideological commitment to the notion of fundamental economic causation and the primacy of class interest, and the prevalence of broad historical generalizations
based on inadequate empirical evidence were not likely to engage the
sympathies of most historians outside the Marxist ideological orbit. But
by the same token, as R. W. Scribner pointed out, West German historical
writing was hardly "value-free" itself and was dominated by a politically
conservative historical establishment molded by the heritage of idealism
and historicism.[129] From whichever side one looked there was little common ground to be seen and a very limited possibility of dialogue.

Accordingly, the publication in 1972 of the volume *Reformation or
Early Bourgeois Revolution?* represented an important landmark.[130] Edited by Rainer Wohlfeil, a professor at Hamburg, it brought together
major Marxist contributions to this theme and so challenged Western
scholars to evaluate the arguments on their academic merits. But if this
was its aim, it achieved little success, and Wohlfeil's subsequent collection
of essays, published in 1975 on the 450th anniversary of the Peasants'
War, although it brought together the work of scholars from both sides
of the ideological divide, seemed only to reveal the absence of any common ground.[131]

The anniversary of the Peasants' War understandably led to a preponderance of Marxist emphasis on Peasants' War studies over the subsequent decade and to a massive increase in the volume of work on this
aspect of sixteenth-century history. Indeed, Tom Scott, who reviewed the

field in 1979, argued that despite the prominence of the Peasants' War in historical debate for more than a century, serious analytical study of the movement was just beginning.[132] Not all the work he reviewed is precisely relevant to study of the Reformation, yet in another sense none is irrelevant, given the Marxists' abiding conception of the Reformation and the Peasants' War as a single process. Although the tendency of much of this work to annex the Reformation to the Peasants' War as its ideological expression is narrow and limiting, it is no more so than the tendency of some other historians of the Reformation to divorce the two entirely.[133] Further, close study of the popular movements of the Reformation period has at least provided a healthy corrective to narrowly confessional approaches to the sixteenth century.

The studies of the Peasants' War emanating from the 1975 celebrations were of uneven quality, as one would expect. Among those from Marxist circles in Eastern Europe, a collection edited by Steinmetz and originating in a conference at Leipzig is disappointing in its almost unrelieved hard-line statement of Marxist orthodoxy,[134] in contrast to a number of local and regional studies in which Marxist scholars, setting aside their dependence on deduction from ideological premises, undertook the same kind of close analytical studies as some of their Western counterparts.[135] The possibility that this sort of work might lead to genuine dialogue was demonstrated from the Western side by Peter Blickle's volume *The Revolution of 1525* (1982), in which he developed the theme of the revolution of the "common man."[136] Although clearly diverging from Marxist economic perspectives, Blickle showed himself willing to approach openly the problems posed by German Democratic Republic historians, in particular the connections between Reformation doctrine and social discontent.

The creative possibilities of dialogue were most clearly shown, however, in two volumes published in English in the wake of the anniversary. In 1976 Janos Bak of the University of British Columbia edited a collection of essays by Eastern and Western scholars which, without rejecting broader questions, emphasizes the close study of archival sources and includes a symposium on Engels's *Peasant War in Germany* 125 years after its first publication.[137] Marxist contributions to this volume, although they concede nothing on the unique validity of the materialist conception of history, are notable for the absence of simplistic Marxist dogma.

The other volume, edited by R. W. Scribner and Gerhard Benecke— *The German Peasant War 1525: New Viewpoints* (1979)—is, as its title suggests, an attempt to look as much forward as backward. Its essays provide an excellent sample of Marxist and non-Marxist views, of close regional studies and general perspectives, but the book is chiefly notable for its attempt to define the broader historiographic issues with which Marxist and non-Marxist scholars alike need to deal: the relation between precise empirical studies and the application of analytical concepts, the correspondence between particular historical events and long-term historical developments, the problem of "monocausal" and "pluralistic" interpretations, and the applicability of interdisciplinary approaches.[138]

Such an agenda suggests that "Marxist historiography" could progressively overcome the academic isolation which has marked most of its history and become more clearly a part of the broad area of study comprehended by social history and the social sciences (see Chapters 11 and 12), just as Roman Catholic historiography has shed its former isolation and become part of a broader tradition of church historical writing (see Chapter 8). It is far too early to say, though, whether this will be anything more than a theoretical possibility, for such a development depends not only on a willingness among Marxist scholars to question hard-line orthodoxy but on an equal willingness on the part of non-Marxists to look at issues, questions, and relationships too often ignored and to open themselves to the challenges which Marxist writing at its best has presented.[139]

II

Models and Patterns:
The Social Scientists

Among the methodological issues confronting historians in the twentieth century, the challenge posed by the sophisticated development of the social sciences has been most pressing and controversial—pressing because these disciplines represent alternative approaches to the study of human society, and controversial because historians by no means agree on the appropriate response to these initiatives. Social science methods, enthusiastically embraced by some historians as a pathway to deeper historical understanding, have been vigorously rejected by others as either irrelevant or counterproductive. This is especially true of sociology, which historians widely regard as a fundamentally ahistorical method that imposes on the particularity and complexity of historical phenomena alien methods and patterns.

The founding fathers of sociology in the modern sense were Emile Durkheim (1858–1917) and Max Weber (1864–1920), although its roots are commonly traced back as far as Montesquieu and Auguste Comte.[1] Of more immediate importance in this context is the tendency to include Marx and Engels as pioneers of sociological analysis. Without denying this, we must note that Marxism's most distinctive features—its synthetic, deterministic, and progressive nature—distinguish it rather sharply from the more analytical and empirical character of general sociology. Having already discussed the Marxist tradition in Chapter 10, we will include it here only where it suggests fruitful comparisons.

Inquiry into the nature and origin of the social organism was no

Marxist monopoly; it equally engaged the attention of liberal intellectuals seeking to understand their social milieu. The last decades of the nineteenth century—the age of imperialism—saw the apotheosis of capitalism in Europe, despite periods of recession and doubt. Paradoxically, the success of European capitalism nurtured the forces pursuing a new economic and political order. In Britain the 1880s and 1890s saw the rise of mass trade unionism and the rebirth of the dormant socialist tradition. In Germany the Social Democratic Party—an avowedly Marxist organization working through liberal democracy but officially committed to revolutionary action—made steady gains and became, before 1914, the largest party in the Reichstag. The debacle of 1914–1920 all but destroyed the German socialist movement, but in Britain the First World War opened the way to the advance of the Labour movement in the 1920s.

This political background is of some importance for understanding the work of two key scholars, the German sociologist Max Weber and the English historian and social reformer R. H. Tawney. Although both made more significant contributions to their respective fields, they are best known to historians through the so-called Weber-Tawney thesis, a highly dubious conjunction of two divergent, if not wholly incompatible, views of the relationship between modern capitalism and the Protestant Reformation.[2] Both Weber and Tawney were deeply imbued with Christian ideals and profoundly interested in the impact of Christianity on modern industrial society. Such concerns were not in themselves new. In England William Cobbett had popularized a conspiracy theory of the Reformation in which the wealthy and the clergy had collaborated to cheat the British people; Romantics like A. W. N. Pugin had seen the Reformation as the triumph of a new class of grasping parvenus who destroyed abbeys and robbed altars.[3] But such writers had little in common with those whose approach was scholarly rather than propagandist.

Certainly Max Weber's scholarly credentials were impressive. By training a jurist and historian, he grew up in a stimulating family environment, which introduced him to many leading intellectuals of late-nineteenth-century Germany. He taught political economy in Freiburg and later in Heidelberg and Munich, yet he was also active in political life as a consultant to government agencies and the German Armistice Commission at Versailles. His considerable literary output included strictly economic-historical studies of the ancient and modern worlds, works of epistemological and philosophical criticism, and an epoch-making work in general sociology entitled *Economy and Society* (1922).[4] His essay *The Protestant Ethic and the Spirit of Capitalism,* which is our immediate concern, was not one of his major writings, but only the first in a series of comparative monographs on the sociology of religion, ranging from Confucianism and Hinduism to ancient Judaism.[5] Yet it was to become the best known and most widely debated of all his works.

Weber's essay was first published in 1904–1905 as a series of articles in a learned journal and did not appear in English until 1930. His concern, as he declared in the introduction, was with the phenomenon of modern Europe. The person who wanted to comprehend European civilization was bound to ask "to what combination of circumstances the fact should be attributed that in Western civilisation, and in Western civilisation only, cultural phenomena have appeared which (as we like to think) lie in a line of development having *universal* significance and value."[6] Like Marx before him, Weber sought to understand the historical foundations of European capitalism. But although Weber used and reworked many Marxist concepts, he considered that dialectical materialism overstressed material factors and simplified a complex causal process. A massive historical transition such as the development of capitalism could not, according to Weber, be attributed merely to changes in class structure or models of production; its explanation needed the force of ideas and ideology.

Weber's work has been aptly described as "a long and intense dialogue with the ghost of Karl Marx,"[7] but the notion that his views represent a straightforward inversion of historical materialism, which he specifically denied, is certainly too simplistic. He recognized the crucial importance of technology and economic organization in social change and never asserted an exclusively religious causality. Instead, he argued the more modest case that economic attitudes can be governed by systems of belief and that economic developments can be shaped by religious motivation. Weber's specific aim in this study was to "chart Protestant asceticism as the foundation of modern vocational civilisation—a sort of spiritualist construction of the modern economy."[8] So capitalism derived from Protestantism, even if unconsciously, attitudes and ideology which assisted in its victory over a decayed feudal order. The "Protestant spirit" was at the most an essential for this victory, at the least an accelerating factor.

What was new in the sixteenth century, according to Weber, was not capitalism as such, but rational, impersonal capitalism as a routine social factor.[9] The rationalization of ideas into the capitalist economic system was spearheaded by Protestantism. For whatever doctrines it preached, Protestantism gave prominence to a particular mode of conduct: "a certain methodical, rational way of life which—given certain conditions—paved the way for the 'spirit' of modern capitalism. The premiums were placed upon 'proving' oneself before God in the sense of attaining salvation . . . and proving oneself before men in the sense of socially holding one's own within the Puritan sects. Both aspects were mutually supplementary and operated in the same direction; they helped to deliver the 'spirit' of modern capitalism, its specific ethos: the ethos of the modern *bourgeois* middle classes."[10]

Weber attributed to the Protestant era, therefore, not the economic, material data of capitalism, but its "spirit."[11] His study of the German capitalist class led him to conclude that among the owners and managerial elite, even among the skilled artisans, Protestants seemed far more numerous than adherents of other faiths. The Protestant ethos motivating such men was no mere superstructure on a material basis; it had to be fought for against traditionalist opposition, the habit of mind which had clung to ideas of just rates of profit and established ways of working. The capitalist system needed a new devotion to maximizing profits. It is "one of the fundamental characteristics of an individualistic capitalistic economy that it is rationalised on the basis of rigorous calculating, directed with foresight and caution toward the economic success which is sought in sharp contrast to the hand-to-mouth existence of the peasant, and to the privileged traditionalism of the guild craftsman and of the adventurer's capitalism, oriented to the exploitation of political opportunities and irrational speculation."[12]

Weber identified the notion of calling (*Beruf*) as the origin of the Protestant ethic, but noted a clear distinction between Luther's conservative articulation of this concept—with his repudiation of the profit motive and of the practice of usury—and the Calvinist doctrine based on predestination. The Calvinist led a systematically ordered and rational existence, his ethical notions methodically integrated into his total view of life. Calvinism represented a psychological revolution of the most profound importance. Its spirit of worldly asceticism—so distinct from the asceticism of the medieval monk—influenced German Pietism and English Nonconformity and had in common with the more radical sects "the conception of a state of grace which marks off its possessor from the degradation of the flesh, from the world."[13]

The unhistorical nature of many of Weber's more controversial conclusions left his work wide open to attack. Lacking knowledge of Reformation religious literature, he had turned to later writers, whose works provided fruitful quarries for his subjective analysis of Protestantism. The most extreme source was Benjamin Franklin, whose connections with Reformation Protestantism could scarcely have been more tenuous.[14] H. M. Robertson, writing in 1933, was especially critical of Weber's insistence on the role of the calling, a doctrine which he showed to be as prevalent in Catholic circles as among Puritan ideologues.[15] More telling was Weber's insistence that the new industrial entrepreneurs' creed was basically secular and owed little to Puritan teachings, which were highly critical of it. A similar line of argument was followed by M. M. Knappen[16] and more recently Charles and Katherine George, whose study of Puritan literature largely unknown to Weber emphasized the profound Calvinist criticism of "capitalist" methods and the importance Puritan writers placed on the organic nature of society. They concluded that Weber was "less anti-Marxist than anti-empirical."[17]

Historians working on specific situations where Protestant ideology interacted with capitalist development have been reluctant to derive general conclusions. A. E. Sayous, in a pioneering article, was unable to discover any especially religious perspective on trade and profit in Calvin's Geneva.[18] Rather, the increasing casuistry of the Calvinist ideologies sought to reconcile religious conscience to the basically earthy appetites of most Genevans. André Biéler's study of Calvin's social ethics similarly offered no support for Weber's views.[19] Norman Birnbaum concluded that in Zurich capitalism did develop concurrently with Zwinglianism, but he saw no evidence of any causal link.[20] Notions of an intimate connection between Protestantism and capitalism were further undermined by evidence that the capitalist spirit was thriving long before the Reformation in medieval Italy.[21] Little wonder, then, that historians like G. R. Elton and A. G. Dickens found virtually nothing to say in support of the Weber thesis.[22]

Weber, however, was not without his defenders. The English historian Christopher Hill, writing from a predominantly Marxist standpoint, maintained that, although some of Weber's examples were not apposite, other evidence he used did demonstrate some link between Protestantism and capitalism, whatever their causal relationship.[23] Hugh Trevor-Roper allowed that there was a "solid, if elusive core of truth in Weber's thesis,"[24] yet his own analysis of the interwoven strands of religion and socioeconomic change in early modern Europe only underlined specific doubts about the alleged relationship. Of the Calvinist entrepreneurs of the age, few were religious zealots and fewer still given to an ascetic style of life; Catholic Italians and Flemings contributed equally to the acceleration of economic activity. Furthermore, he argued, notions that Weber supposedly derived from Luther stemmed in fact from Erasmus, whose ideas were distinctly favorable to business enterprise. Trevor-Roper did allow, however, that in the restrictive environment of the Catholic Reformation, Calvinism was associated with freedom and revolt.[25]

Critical investigations into the actual conditions in European societies of the sixteenth century and detailed analysis of the Protestant ideology have inevitably dented theories grounded essentially in hypothetical models. Yet the weakness of Weber's central theoretical concept and his presentation of evidence should not obscure the significance of his pioneering work. In a Germany where historical writing was dominated by the conservative influence of the Rankean school, sociologists carved out their own view of the past with courage.

Weber's *Sociology of Religion* (1922), part of his massive and unfinished *Economy and Society,* shares a basis in evolutionary theory with the work of Durkheim and seeks to disentangle the religious phenomena common to all societies.[26] A study of this work suggests some reasons for Weber's break with the historical approach and his emphasis on the need for a close analytical method founded on "the ubiquity of conceptions of the supernatural." His interest was less in the Reformation than in reformations and reforms in general. In his work on the Protestant ethic, Weber was laying conceptual foundations for a possible future study of the phenomena he had isolated, set in an empirical framework of social investigation. His essay "The Protestant Sects and the Spirit of Capitalism" (1906) was a move in this direction.[27] Weber had visited the United States in 1904 and made observations on the rich and varied life of American Protestant churches. He became increasingly interested in the dynamics of sectarianism and noted the tendency "in the direction of breeding that ascetic occupational ethic which was adequate to modern capitalism during the period of its origin."[28]

Weber's study of sects scratched the surface of ground more profoundly explored by Ernst Troeltsch, and it was Troeltsch's work which led Weber to abandon his detailed study of Protestantism in favor of a broader examination of religion and society and the interaction of community and State. His work on the second theme produced *The City,* which was written in 1911–1913 and published in 1921 and contains material on the place of religion in urban life directly relevant to research on the Reformation.[29] Weber's studies of religion in non-Christian societies further developed the theme of conflict between spiritual aspiration and material acquisitiveness and underlined religion's role as a reflection of more mundane concerns and an aspect of social groups' competition. A study of these later works demonstrates the breadth of Weber's historical perspective and sets the argument of his work on Protestantism in the context of several thousand years of European historical development.

Among those who responded to Weber's writings on Protestantism, the historian R. H. Tawney (1880–1962) merits special attention, as much for the distinctiveness of his view as for the importance of the intellectual tradition he represented. Tawney was profoundly influenced by Weber and introduced him to English readers, yet he was careful to identify some fundamental differences in outlook. In his foreword to the English translation of Weber's work, Tawney argued that capitalism and Calvinism could both be seen as results of one process and, although he allowed that Weber's views were "illuminating," he observed that Weber had ascribed too much to the influence of ideas and neglected the extent to which those ideas were molded by social and economic realities.[30]

Tawney's views suggest a return to a Marxist perspective, with religious ideas understood as superstructure. Yet he was not a conventional Marxist, but a reformer in the tradition of Christian socialism, a movement which had flowered briefly but significantly in late Victorian and early-twentieth-century Britain. Among those who influenced this tradition were Thomas Carlyle, who had seen in the inspiration of heroes like Luther and Knox a hope for the rescue of society from the abyss into which it had sunk;[31] the theologian F. D. Maurice, who saw the doctrine of the Incarnation as a wellspring for the renewal of society through Christian influence;[32] and Charles Gore, bishop of Oxford and a close friend of Tawney, who argued that the nation's ills were soluble only by a renewal of the spirit of the Christian Gospel.[33]

Tawney's approach was therefore, from the start, that of a committed, compassionate reformer rather than a disinterested critic, but he argued for the most part on historical grounds. In an introduction to Max Beer's *History of British Socialism* (1919–1920), he denied that British radicalism needed Marx and looked to an ideal of social cooperation and solidarity rather than class war as a means of social change.[34] Capitalism, to Marxists an inevitable development, was in Tawney's eyes an imposition on humanity which could be replaced by a more humane system, and it was the role of religion, which had abdicated its responsibilities, to lead the revolt against a decadent system.

Tawney's famous lectures *Religion and the Rise of Capitalism*, first published in 1926, were given in a series founded in memory of the Christian socialist Henry Scott Holland;[35] the prescribed theme was "the religion of the Incarnation and its bearing on the social and economic life of man." Tawney began with the premise that there is a "moral and religious, as well as material environment, which sets its stamp on the individual even when he is least conscious of it."[36] So from the first, Tawney's debt to Weber's pioneering work was clear. In fact, he claimed in a preface to the 1937 edition of *Religion and the Rise of Capitalism* that a restatement of the problems Weber raised was urgently needed.[37]

Tawney declared that his own studies were about "attitudes," by which he meant attitudes to the reality of economic change, and he worked from a sustained comparison between the Middle Ages and the Reformation. In the Middle Ages, the Church had constituted a state apart. It had provided a system of social ethics which underpinned the laws of nations. The Church elevated labor to a place of honor, but found the world of business anathema, at least in principle. Papal Rome might practice usury while Florentine and Flemish capitalists flourished there, yet the social code was unchallenged, and its hostility to materialism and money-making was central and unshakable. The medieval social code was anticapitalistic and hence akin, in the totality of its condemnation, to modern Marxism. Marx was therefore "the last of the schoolmen."[38] Medieval Europe was, in economic terms, a somewhat static entity, even its nascent industry being bridled with monopolies and assorted restrictions preventing forceful competition and vigorous expansion. Medieval society was deeply conservative, and its Christian ideology reinforced its conservatism, protecting the poor, prohibiting usury, sanctioning serfdom, and stressing the rights of those in authority.

This conservative creed, bequeathed by the Middle Ages to the age of the Reformation, came under attack in the sixteenth century from an economic revolution threatening all the foundations of accepted social ethics. But the response of Luther and other Reformers to the changing economic climate was hostile. Luther himself condemned usury and economic exploitation, desired not freedom but more rigorous control of economic life, and possessed an "organic" rather than an "individualistic" view of society. His mentality, wrote Tawney, was that of a peasant and a monk; he was at heart an unswerving defender of the hierarchic principle, even censuring the concessions of certain canonists.

It was not Luther but Calvin who came to terms with the new society and gave the commercial classes a creed of their own. Where Lutheranism had been introspective and personal, Calvin created a radical and active faith. Tawney's assessment of the reasons underlying Calvin's new approach to social ethics owed much to Weber and his analysis of the calling. The Calvinist equated profitable labor with a form of worship and worldly success with evidence of salvation. The powerful discipline and asceticism present in Calvinism tended toward an intense individualism of the kind which prevailed in seventeenth-century England. In Geneva, where it was the established religion, Calvinism came to stand for a close state regulation of all aspects of life. In England it was the faith of a militant minority who saw themselves engaged in a struggle against an ungodly and restrictive Establishment. Calvinists acknowledged that all human activities, including those of the exchange and the marketplace, were the business of the Church. They demanded not an end to the direction of society but its direction according to the Calvinist interpretation of the law of God. "The Church became the ecclesiastical department of the State, and religion was used to lend a normal sanction to secular social policy."[39]

The conflict between traditional social ethics and Calvinist individualism was resolved by an adjustment of religious theory to economic reality, and Puritanism emerged as the religion of the new commercial classes, the "true English Reformation" from whose struggle against the old order "an England which is unmistakeably modern emerges."[40] Here was no mere change in economic life but a change in human consciousness, as a broad mercantile religion emerged in England, hostile alike to conservative Puritanism and the extreme radicalism of the sects. From this separation of economics and morals flowed three centuries of social policy. But was there no evidence that Puritan writers had, in the tradition of Latimer and Crowley, lashed the increasing commercialization of society and the abandonment of old values? Tawney was forced to admit that such evidence did exist, yet he asserted that it came from "that part of the Puritan mind which looked backward."[41] The forward-looking aspect of Puritanism sanctified the increasingly ruthless methods of businessmen. The device which enabled Puritan theologians to make appropriate adjustments to Calvin's thought was the notion of the calling: a creed which "transformed the acquisition of wealth from a drudgery or a temptation into a moral duty" and saw success as indicating a state of salvation.[42]

Tawney's reputation as an economic historian rests firmly on his studies of sixteenth-century agrarian and political history.[43] But his book on religion and capitalism, like some of his other writings,[44] was at base a moral tract in the form of a historical study, and his historical analysis was directed toward criticism of contemporary English society and the Christian Church's failure to prevent the rise of the capitalistic social order.

Moral conviction, however, is no substitute for historical evidence, and Tawney's evidence must be judged unimpressive in bulk, weak in pertinence and quality, and outweighed by data to the contrary. He supported his judgments with the views of a number of late-seventeenth- and eighteenth-century economic writers whom he optimistically took to represent "later Puritanism." And although he did not wholly ignore the embarrassing fact that Puritans up to 1660 consistently argued against the profit motive, he effectively dismissed such evidence by appeal to the notion of a latent urge toward the capitalist spirit which later came to the fore.[45] At the very best, Tawney's late evidence might indicate a connection between capitalist business and the distant heirs of Calvinist

Puritanism, but because these heirs had for the most part thrown off the faith of Luther and Calvin in favor of a moralistic belief in self-help tinctured by the new rationalism, even this residuum of truth cannot be said to contribute to an understanding of the Reformation.

If Weber's writings on Protestantism have stimulated the most comment, the views of his friend and colleague Ernst Troeltsch (1856–1923) have been of more solid and enduring significance, especially for historians. Troeltsch was by training neither a socialist nor a historian but a theologian, and we have already noted his significance in the theological development of the late nineteenth and early twentieth centuries, in particular his argument that the Reformation should be understood as a conservative reshaping of the medieval idea rather than the beginning of modernity (see Chapter 8).

This fundamental perspective also informed Troeltsch's major work, *The Social Teaching of the Christian Churches* (1911),[46] which grew out of a book review into a series of separately published studies on the ancient Church, medieval Catholicism, and Lutheranism and was eventually expanded—with sections on Calvinism, sectarianism, and mysticism—into a comprehensive sociological study of historical Christianity. For all its massive erudition, this work makes little sense unless related to its contemporary European political context and its author's intensely practical moral concern.

That concern is indicated in the opening pages, where he identified his aim: "to pave the way for the understanding of the social doctrines of the Gospel, of the early Church, of the Middle Ages, of the post-Reformation confessions, right down to the formation of the new situation in the modern world, in which the old theories no longer suffice, and where, therefore, new theories must be constructed, composed of old and new elements, consciously or unconsciously, whether so avowed or not."[47] But individual moral concern cannot be isolated from its historical and contemporary setting. Troeltsch, noted his American follower H. Richard Niebuhr, lived and thought "in the presence of the confusions and alarms, the hopes and threats that issue from class and party conflict, church and state tensions, international wars remembered and impending, from colonial imperialisms and rising nationalisms, from industrialism growing in extent and in power over the common life, from the spectacular development of the natural and social sciences, from the radical criticism of modern civilisation by Marx and Nietzsche."[48] Troeltsch realized that scientific and moral reasoning are necessarily interdependent, that "no amount of study could relieve the responsible person from the necessity and risk of decision," but also "that decisions could be made responsibly only in the light of the fullest understanding possible."[49]

Troeltsch's acute awareness of the flux of history had already been given philosophical formulation in a work entitled *Historicity and Its Problems* (1923).[50] He knew of two dogmatic approaches to the problem of historical change: the Marxist—which interpreted man's social and spiritual life as functions of economic conditions—and the orthodox Christian—which understood faith as the basic element in human life. Conscious of the appeal of each approach, Troeltsch nevertheless felt that both had narrowed the infinite variety and complexity of human life. Against Marx, he insisted that religion is a primal force in the human spirit, but that the actualization of this power in the great historical religions can no more be explained in purely religious than in purely economic terms. In a complex way, religious life interacts with political structures, social institutions like the family, and ethical and cultural concerns, each of which has its own roots. Faced with this recognition, Troeltsch sought a synthesis which would provide understanding without destroying the manifold and dynamic variety of human social life. In this search, he relied heavily on Weber's distinction between Church and sect, to which he added a third category: mysticism. The threefold pattern was not so much a framework from which he started as a conclusion he reached, and it is not surprising that its clearest statement comes in the closing pages of *Social Teaching*. Yet it certainly forms the core of his analysis of the Reformation period and beyond.

Troeltsch understood the Gospel of Jesus as a message of personal piety and spiritual fellowship, but "without any tendency towards the organisation of a cult or towards the creation of a religious community."[51] When a new religious community is formed on the basis of faith in the risen and exalted Lord, therefore, the ethos of the Gospel undergoes the beginnings of a compromise with the world, which remains a basic feature of its historical development. None of the three main types of "sociological development" is inherent in the Gospel of Jesus, but all three have been present in Christian history from the beginning.

Troeltsch defined the Church as "an institution which has been endowed with grace and salvation as the result of the work of redemption"; the sect is "a voluntary society, composed of strict and definite Christian believers bound to each other by the fact that all have experienced the 'new birth.' " It is, therefore, more selective than the Church, which is open to the masses and preoccupied with subjective holiness rather than the objective treasures of grace. In contrast to both these forms, mysticism is characterized by a "purely personal and inward experience" and a weakening of the significance of forms of worship and doctrine. Troeltsch clearly did not think of these types as utterly discrete or as sequential developments. Rather, "from the beginning these three forms were foreshadowed and all down the centuries to the present day whenever religion is dominant they still appear alongside of one another, . . . strangely and various interwoven and interconnected."[52]

To Troeltsch, the character of the Reformation became clear only when related to the whole history of medieval Catholicism. The medieval Church was inclusive and universal, totally involved in society, with whose values it first came into conflict but later assimilated. The Church evolved a sociological theory—based on an organic, patriarchal view of society which recognized and incorporated the life of the world. Christian influences helped civilize the medieval world, but the Church had to abandon its scrupulous morality for the casuistry of natural law theory. The medieval heresies propagated by the Waldensians, Lollards, and Hussites arose as a reaction to the conservative church system which had developed in medieval Europe. These were the first sects, and they rejected the objective, institutional character of the Catholic Church in favor of separation and exclusiveness. Christianity in its primitive form contained both universal and individualistic elements, and the sects emphasized individualism to the exclusion of the universal. The sectarian tendency could only develop as a reaction against and development from the hegemony of the universal Church; it was closely related to the social development of medieval Europe, especially to the rise of independent and rich urban communities.[53]

The Reformation was compelled by circumstances to maintain the unity of Church and State—but sectarianism grew and was responsible for most of Protestantism's internal tensions. These tensions form the pervading theme of the remainder of Troeltsch's book, which deals in detail with the development of Protestantism and its division into Church-types and sect-types of organization. Lutheranism was very soon pushed into a backwater by the new radical and activist forces of Calvinism, which imprinted its ideas permanently on later Protestantism, of which it was the dominant form.[54] Calvinism was marked by a "combination of practical sense and cool utilitarianism with an other-worldly aim, of systematic conscious effort united with an utter absence of interest in the results of effort." It tended to encourage political activism, industry, and social concern—all conceived of as expressions of the glory of God— but its social ideas were conservative.[55] Neo-Calvinism, however, such as evolved in seventeenth-century England, was of a very different stamp from the "aristocratic" Calvinism of Geneva. Although it retained the basic idea of the Church, it accepted individualism and social reform and came close to fusion with sectarianism, which had always had affinities with Calvinist notions of a Church of the elect.

Since the Reformation, the sects had operated on the fringes of the Protestant churches. These "small groups of earnest souls" based their ethics on the pure Gospel: "Their sociological expression naturally took the form of a society of persons united by a deep common personal conviction, who were entirely opposed to the ecclesiastical system, with its inclusive character, and its claim to be the sole depository of grace. This development took place within all the Christian Churches, because in them all, along with the Bible, and the endowment of grace, the germ of the sect-type was latent."[56] Sectarian developments could occur on the fringe of the churches, but the sects had also become "free Churches" along the lines of the heirs of Calvin and had abandoned their radicalism for a bourgeois creed which accepted the world. The union of sectarianism and Calvinism was the progenitor of "ascetic Protestantism," which in turn was the formative basis of Protestant civilization.[57] The crisis of this civilization, which had first stimulated Troeltsch's inquiry, was the point to which he ultimately returned.

Yet despite the immediacy of Troeltsch's preoccupation with the theological and ethical problem of the Protestant churches in his time, his work has exercised a profound and enduring influence on subsequent study of the Reformation. His ideas were taken up most directly by the American theologian and religious sociologist H. Richard Niebuhr (1894–1962), whose lectures *Christ and Culture* (1952) acknowledge a fundamental debt to Troeltsch while undertaking "to supplement, and in part to correct" his work.[58] Niebuhr declared that Troeltsch had taught him to respect the multiformity and individuality of men and movements in Christian history, to be loath to force this rich variety into prefashioned, conceptual molds, and yet "to seek *logos* in *mythos,* reason in history, essence in existence."[59]

Like Troeltsch, Niebuhr saw the relationship of Christianity and civilization—or Christ and culture—as an enduring problem in Western history, and he modified Troeltsch by identifying five fundamental types of response to it. At one extreme were those who saw Christ and culture in opposition, at the other those who understood them to be in fundamental agreement. Between these extremes, he identified three distinct (but at times overlapping) responses: the synthetic type, in which culture is fulfilled and perfected by Christ; the dualist type, in which the claims of culture and Christ are both acknowledged but held in tension; and the conversionist type, which recognizes opposition between Christ and all human institutions but expects culture to be transformed through

Christ.[60] Niebuhr drew his examples for each type from every period of Christian history. Within the Reformation, he identified the radical sects as expressions of the first type (Christ against culture), Luther as archetypal exponent of the dualist attitude, and Calvin (like Augustine) as an exponent of the conversionist ethos.

Niebuhr's work strongly stimulated religious sociology in the United States, although most of this academic activity was directed not toward study of the Reformation as such, but toward exploring the extraordinarily complex structure of American Protestantism.[61]

Another interesting sociological perspective on the Reformation was provided by the American sociologist Werner Stark (b. 1909), whose massive five-volume study of Christendom matched Troeltsch's work in scope, although not in depth.[62] Stark shared Troeltsch's dissatisfaction with the simple Weberian Church-sect model and replaced it with a threefold model, although not that of Troeltsch.[63] Stark's categories were Established Religion, Sectarian Religion, and Universal Church. The second corresponds fairly closely to the perspective of Weber and Troeltsch, although Stark placed considerable stress on its essentially revolutionary character.

The particular interest of Stark's work lies, however, in his distinction between the other two categories, which is directly relevant to his understanding of the Reformation. An Established Religion is a religious body coinciding or closely associated with the inclusive society which contains it and is therefore as essentially conservative as sectarian religion is essentially revolutionary. A Universal Church, by contrast, lacks that close identity with a particular society and in principle embraces the whole world. Yet the nature of that embrace differs from that of Established Religion; in the tradition of Augustine, it is indifferent to the State, but, unlike the sect, it is willing to establish a modus vivendi with particular states. Further, although Established Religion comprehends the upper levels of society and sects appeal to the lower, the Universal Church is in principle socially comprehensive.

This pattern led Stark to identify Lutheranism and Anglicanism as Established Religions and Catholicism and Calvinism as Universal Churches, thereby overcoming some of the rigidities of Protestant-Catholic and Church-sect dichotomies and recognizing the infinite complexities of Reformation Christianity's social manifestations.[64] Strong contrasts could be identified between Protestant ecclesiastical traditions normally placed together, and unexpected and interesting parallels emerged between apparent ideological opposites. The complexities deepen in the last two volumes of Stark's work, in which he explored the contrasts between "individualist" and "collectivist" thought and between patterns of religious culture based on "community" and "association," once again avoiding simplistic identification with the sides of the religious divide.

The integrated perspective Stark offered was a significant challenge to old sociological orthodoxies, although few of his detailed judgments were entirely new and some had been anticipated by Troeltsch. We in no sense negate Stark's work as an essay in religious sociology if we observe that it is seriously hampered, as was Weber's, by a lack of primary research. It may have been helpful to rescue Reformation leaders and their communities from superficial and oversimplified categorization, but in the end Stark simply assigned them new roles on the basis of an equally partial and distorted vision. To identify Luther as enslaved to princely authority, to contrast Luther and Calvin in terms of mystical piety and militant activism and their respective reformations in terms of "private" and "public" phases, is to betray an approach to the history of the Reformation no less selective and superficial than the views Stark was trying to overcome. Ultimately, he surrendered the particularities of history to the tyranny of the sociological model.[65]

Recent decades have seen a burgeoning study of radical and sectarian movements, emanating from both the Continental Radical Reformation (see Chapter 9) and the tradition of English Dissent. Among studies of the English movements, Michael Walzer's substantial *Revolution of the Saints* (1966), although it ignores Troeltsch and criticizes Weber, owes much to their basic methodology. Walzer's concern was the "spirit" of Puritanism, which he related to a general theory of radical politics. He saw Puritanism, with its emphasis on discipline and order, as a reaction to disorder and confusion—spiritual, material, and, above all, psychological—and much of his study is a searching analysis of the mentality of the individual Puritan "saint."[66]

Another work which relies heavily on a sociopsychological approach is Norman Cohn's richly detailed and wide-ranging study of revolutionary millenarianism, *The Pursuit of the Millennium* (1957), which sets the sectarian movements of the Reformation into a long tradition of apocalyptic and millenarian mass movements.[67] Guenther Lewy's *Religion and Revolution* (1974) includes a chapter on the German Reformation in a cross-cultural study of the relationship between religion and revolutionary activity. Profoundly critical of Marxist class-struggle analysis, Lewy stressed the genuineness of religious dissent as a revolutionary force and identified the revolutionary movements of the Reformation era as "revolutions within a revolution," exploiting the more limited aims of a great historical movement in the struggle for a radically new world.[68]

Keith Thomas's important *Religion and the Decline of Magic* (1971) illuminates another aspect of the relationship between religion and society by drawing parallels between early modern England and the undeveloped countries of the modern world.[69]

The sociopsychological approach is likely to be a continuing, if relatively minor, aspect of studies on the Reformation. Less clear is the future of another area of psychology—psychoanalysis—whose results historians have received rather skeptically. Psychoanalysis is, by its nature, concerned with individuals, and it is no surprise that in terms of the Reformation almost all its attention has been focused on Martin Luther, who provided the most substantial and plausible body of data concerning his inner life. Analyses of Luther in the light of modern psychology originated in a decidedly unscientific way, with Catholic writers like Döllinger, Denifle, and Grisar attempting to discredit the Reformer and his work by exposing his personal depravity or psychic illness (see Chapter 8), as well as with the American historian Preserved Smith, who offered an amateurish and highly superficial Freudian perspective, attributing the origins of Luther's key doctrines to his subjective states rather than to biblical and theological sources.[70]

A more substantial and plausible approach was made by the Danish psychiatrist Paul Reiter (1895–1973), whose massive study of Luther (1937–1941) exhaustively dissects the psychological evidence and concludes that Luther demonstrated all the signs of a "manic-depressive psychosis."[71] Reiter was a Catholic and accepted without question some of Denifle's and Grisar's conclusions; however, he claimed that his intention was not to undermine Luther's significance in world history or to downgrade the greatness of his personality, but simply to explain the workings of his psyche, leaving each reader to draw his own conclusions about Luther's religious importance. Reiter attempted to counter the problem inherent in all pathological explanations of Luther—his prodigiously creative literary and intellectual achievements—by explaining that Luther's psychosis was of the kind which fostered his creative genius rather than occasioning a disintegration of personality.[72] But although he avoided some of the pitfalls of his polemical predecessors, questions remain about Reiter's selective use of evidence and the adequacy of his narrow focus on Luther's physical and personal problems.

An alternative perspective was offered by the Swiss psychoanalyst Oscar Pfister (1873–1956), who concentrated on religious fear and its resolution.[73] Pfister, a Protestant pastor and a pioneer in the use of psychoanalytic methods in pastoral work, was a correspondent of Sigmund Freud, who wrote an introduction to Pfister's earlier book on psychoanalytic method.[74] With the precision possible at that early stage of psy-choanalytic theory, Pfister analyzed Luther's religious fear, showing sensitivity toward the intricate balance between healthy and unhealthy factors and relating his study to the development of Luther's mature theological understanding.

The potentialities and problems of the psychoanalytic approach were most fully realized by the American neo-Freudian psychoanalyst Erik Erikson (1902–1982), whose study of the young Luther (1962) has remained under the spotlight for over two decades, both as a specific study of Luther and as a test case for the psychoanalytic approach to history.[75] Erikson, though deeply influenced by Freudian ideas, had articulated his own understanding of human development in terms of critical stages in the individual's life.[76] His study of Luther focuses on one of those stages, the identity crisis, which in Luther took the form of an attempt to achieve personal independence from parental domination and was inextricably related to his resolution of the theological problem of the angry and vengeful God, whom he had created in the image of his earthly father.

Although Erikson professed, with some justice, to be adopting a strictly scientific and clinical approach, his work is inevitably a provocative challenge to accepted methods of explaining Luther's development, and its very audacity makes it vulnerable to attack. Critics had little difficulty establishing that many of Erikson's individual assertions are not only baseless but contradicted by the available evidence—for instance, the Reformer's alleged dethronement of the Virgin Mary because of disappointment with his mother and his volubility in the German language, an alleged reaction to being punished at school for not using Latin. In fact, it proved easy to demonstrate that Luther had maintained a lifelong reverence for Mary and was scarcely less voluble in Latin than in German.[77]

But larger questions were also raised about the kind of evidence on which any psychoanalytic view necessarily depends: evidence which in Luther's case was almost entirely late, fragmentary, and unreliable. Some historians were anxious to outlaw the approach in principle; others, more sympathetic, still felt obliged to insist on a stricter use of evidence and in particular on the acknowledgment of contrary evidence where available.[78] Many of Erikson's basic assertions about Luther's allegedly difficult relationships with his parents, reliant on a few snippets of gossip, have foundered on the substantial evidence of the exceptionally warm relationships he maintained with them over many years. Even historians who have no wish to discourage psychoanalysts' entry into the historical field maintained grave doubts about whether such inquiries will significantly explain Luther the writer, preacher, and agent of history, a man too large and creative to fit into any routine psychological mold.[79]

That Erikson's book has continued to play a pivotal role in this area of study on the Reformation is attributable not merely to the popularization of his views in drama[80] and the lack of any more recent work of sounder historical quality, but to an element of genuine strength in the work. Notwithstanding the manifest defects in his use of historical evidence, Erikson demonstrated impressive empathy with a subject remote from him in time and outlook: he displayed a keen awareness of the complexity of human motivation and the intimate relationship between an individual's development and social processes. Works of this genre since Erikson have been either slight and unimpressive, such as Norman O. Brown's brief analysis,[81] or highly derivative, such as Roland Dalbiez's study of Luther's anxiety which, although more recent, is too dependent on Grisar to represent anything fresh.[82]

The fundamental issues posed by application of the social sciences to history of the Reformation were highlighted by the appearance in 1967 of Guy Swanson's book *Religion and Regime*.[83] Swanson (1922–), who had earlier produced a study of the origins of primitive religion,[84] subtitled his work *A Sociological Account of the Reformation*. Although he made a brief reference to the issue of "Protestantism and Capitalism,"[85] Swanson was influenced largely by Weber's general sociological theories, and still more by those of Durkheim. The model he brought to the Reformation was essentially political rather than economic, and his purpose was to establish why certain regimes were susceptible to the Protestant message.

Swanson identified as the major difference between Protestantism and Catholicism their attitudes about immanence—that is, the direct, palpable presence of the divine—and transcendence, and he asserted that a continuum could be established between Calvinism and Zwinglianism—the least committed to immanence—and Catholicism—the most committed—with Lutheranism and Anglicanism holding intermediate positions. Further, he argued that these attitudes could be closely correlated with political structures. In Catholic areas strong centralist regimes reaching into their subjects' daily lives conditioned them to accept an immanentist view of the divine; in Protestant states the penetration into government of special interest and power groups outside the ruling circle accorded with Protestant views of divine transcendence.

To test this assumption Swanson analyzed forty-one regimes from before the Reformation until their definitive response to reform, and he classified these into five types, according to their nature of participation in central government—centralist, limited centralist, balanced, commensal, and heterarchic.[86] On this basis he established that centralist and commensal regimes remained Catholic, that limited centralist regimes which turned Protestant did so in Lutheran or Anglican form, and that the more decentralized balanced or heterarchic regimes adopted a Zwinglian or Calvinist version of reform.

Swanson's thesis was very critically received by a wide range of historians.[87] His classification was judged faulty or artificial: was not a limited monarchy like England, for example, as effectively centralist as an absolutist state?[88] His definition of the theological issues was described as everything from oversimplified to positively erroneous,[89] and situations he had analyzed with ostensible success were given more straightforward explanations.[90] Nowhere did he seem to recognize that the establishment of Protestant communities owed at least as much to popular enthusiasm as to government action. Unfavorable comparisons were drawn with the close analytical studies of Bernd Moeller on the German cities, which Swanson appeared to have ignored, despite their obvious relevance.[91]

But beyond these specific criticisms, historians' responses also indicated a striking divergence between those who rejected the sociological approach as inherently defective because it sacrifices the individual and particular to its search for the typical and universal,[92] and those who believed Swanson's book was an important step toward interdisciplinary collaboration. These reviewers concluded from its defects in detail and approach not that sociologists ought to leave the Reformation alone, but that they should work more closely with historians in their investigations of particular societies, so that their analytical models might take more account of historical change and variety.[93] Such collaboration has proceeded apace across a broad range of subject matter, and although some historians have remained deeply skeptical about both the practical results and the suitability of social sciences methodology in historical inquiry, the past decade suggests that these approaches have become a genuine part of the broad enterprise of social history. For this reason, we will treat the more recent contributions of this character at the conclusion of Chapter 12.

12

The Secular Setting:
The Social Historians

Our "study in contrasts," exploring the rich diversity of modern research on the Reformation, has brought us finally to social history, not by an arbitrary process of elimination but by persuasive logic and conscious choice. Social history in its multifarious expressions has had an overwhelming impact on history of the Reformation in recent decades and arguably now represents the most prominent "cutting edge" of contemporary research, providing many of its more interesting developments and most of its new directions.

When an area of historical research becomes as fashionable as social history has lately, it is especially important to be aware of its deeper, and often unrecognized, roots. Despite the popular tendency to hail it as a modern discovery, social history boasts a long and distinguished pedigree, going back virtually to the Reformation itself. In earlier chapters we have drawn attention to some of its clear signposts, erected at times in unexpected locations; perhaps the most notable were Ranke's consciously planned social history in the *Deutsche Geschichte* and the long English tradition from Macaulay's famous third chapter to the more recent work of J. R. Green and G. M. Trevelyan. Indeed, the origins of social history of the Reformation could arguably be traced back as far as Crespin and, even more clearly, Foxe, whose graphic depiction of the daily life, physical facts, and social backgrounds of the martyrs would have made possible a social history of the Tudor period even if all other evidence had vanished. Here, then, is a distinguished tradition which not only provided materials for social history but consciously exploited them for historical purposes (see Chapters 2 and 7).

On the other hand, modern research has certainly taken up social history in a more sustained and systematic way and pursued it in fresh directions. This highly distinctive development demands detailed analysis in its own right. In view of the decidedly "international" character of recent sociohistorical debate on the Reformation, it is perhaps surprising to observe how early-twentieth-century contributions to social history reflected diverse national traditions operating apart from one another and with differing methods and perspectives. Indeed, an assessment of the peculiar contributions of French, English, and German social history provides an indispensable background to understanding the more open and interactive debates now in progress.

In France, a lively though now somewhat overestimated influence on social history of the Reformation derived from Lucien Febvre (1878–1956),[1] whose doctoral thesis on Philip II and Franche-Comté (1911) was largely concerned with the social history of that important province. It deals with not only the local effects of the Reformation but also the conflict between the declining nobility and the rising bourgeoisie, which was buying up its lands. Already Febvre's interest in social psychology is indicated by passages describing the distinctive attitudes, literary interests, and life styles of the middle classes. After his war service, he completed a work on geography and history (1922), attacking the deterministic geohistory of Friedrich Ratzel and stressing mankind's assertive—as opposed to passive—responses toward its environment:[2] a stance already adopted by Vidal de la Blache and other French scholars. In close association with the medievalist Marc Bloch, Febvre founded in 1929 the periodical *Annales d'histoire économique et sociale,* which later assumed its present title, *Annales: Economies, sociétés, civilisations.* This journal required some decades to attain international influence, but it takes a broad view of social history and has long accepted work differing from Febvre's initial approaches.

Meanwhile, Febvre developed a strong interest in problems of the Reformation, especially the mental attitudes of societies traversing that crisis, which he emphasized more than the Church's institutional problems. He regarded the Reformation as primarily a campaign to satisfy the spiritual demands of the rising middle class. His chief manifesto along these lines was the seventy-page essay "A Badly-put Question: The Origins of the French Reformation and the Problem of the Causes of the Reformation" (1928).[3] In the same year appeared *A Destiny: Martin Luther,* a spirited counterattack on Denifle's black portrait of the Reformer, which develops into an account of the adaptation of Luther's message—largely by Melanchthon—into forms acceptable to German burghers.[4] Of these declarations, the more original and controversial is the essay, although it owes no small debt to earlier historians like Augustin Renaudet and Henri Hauser,[5] as well as to the many scholarly articles published over the preceding thirty years in the *Bulletin de la société de l'histoire du protestantisme français*. As Febvre acknowledged, such authors were no mere old-style church historians: they had also begun to analyze society's spiritual aspirations and had set the Reformation beside the social and economic backgrounds of France and Europe.

All too absolutely, Febvre denied that the Reformation arose from ecclesiastical abuses, and he attacked the favorite conundrums of French historians about their own early Reformer, Lefèvre d'Etaples. Did he precede Luther as originator of the French Reformation, or was early French Protestantism really Lutheran? In Febvre's mind these were the wrong questions to ask. The history of religion is not the history of churches, but the mental history of individuals and communities, which are in turn affected by the intellectual, social, and economic factors of the outer world. In the sixteenth century people were swayed by religious sentiments, not institutions: they wanted to break through ecclesiastical frameworks and build a range of free religions on the ruins. Along with Erasmus, the antiecclesiastical, pacifist bourgeoisie dreamed of a single Christian fatherland. In the end, the Erasmian dream faded and the period of "magnificent religious anarchy" was followed by renewed ecclesiastical servitude. Unfortunately, the first historians of the Reformation had been propagandist clergymen defending their rival churches rather than examining the people's spiritual needs and hopes.

Following Sleidan, continued Febvre, three centuries passed during which the Reformation was never put into the right historical context; between the partisans and the mere annalists a great and rich movement "was reduced to two very dry elements, the one ecclesiastical, the other political." Catholic culture gleefully answered anti-Catholic reproaches by pointing out the endless quarrels among the Protestant churches: both sides became too preoccupied by Luther and abuses. Erasmus was numbered among Luther's precursors, the Anabaptists were made his followers, and even the Catholic recovery was dismissed as a rival "Reformation." Historians argued ceaselessly about personal priorities and relationships, between not only Lefèvre and Luther, but Zwingli and Luther, and Luther and Calvin. Patriotic writers like Merle d'Aubigné "nationalized" the French Reformation. With the rise of modern historical attitudes, this habit of asking nonsignificant questions continued. Many scholars took on the hoary old controversies, injecting little more than their own national prejudices.

Even in his day, thought the agnostic Febvre, history of the Reformation continued to be written on an ecclesiastical, not a religious basis. Yet had not the Reformation been "the outward sign . . . of a profound revolution in religious sentiment"? Surely it was the work of men seeking not to set up new churches, but rather to find a version of Christianity suited to their new needs, more in harmony with the changing conditions of their social lives, more able "to find a remedy for the disturbed consciences of a good number of Christians." Far from being eroded by unbelief, French religion around 1500 was increasing in fervor, as evidenced by the new devotions to the rosary and the stations of the cross, fresh directions in Christian art, and dissemination of printed materials to stimulate devotion.

Wandering preachers spread crude superstitions, cynical lawyers exploited religion, and theologians—indeed, the clergy in general—closed their eyes to the spiritual aspirations of laypeople. Both successful businessmen and humanist intellectuals were resenting the clergy's claim to mediate between them and God. The Reformation's task was "to appease such troubled states of mind"; and it overcame anticlericalism by restoring the Bible to the laity. Believing in its literal inspiration, Protestants thought that God spoke directly to men, that every believer could be his own priest, and that salvation depended solely on faith. The intellectual and theological revolution "was nothing compared with the accompanying revolution in sentiments."

Febvre accounted for the ensuing variations among Protestants by stressing their inevitability, given the marked variance of national and regional outlooks, which still demanded further research. The complexity of the sects, the "frantic desire for freedom," could not be satisfied by the major Reformers. The vision of Europe being split between two religions was thus woefully inadequate: the rich diversity of attitudes made nonsense of attempts to decide whether someone like Lefèvre was "Catholic" or "Protestant." Catholicism itself was shifting, and the positions of a man who passed for respectable in 1520 might well have been dubbed heretical in the harder world of 1570.

Above all, the Reformation could not be dated from the constitution of the first Lutheran congregations: it originated in a vast moral crisis, and its effects transcended the petty regulations and trivial observances of rival churches. The tiresome old problems dictated by "specificity, dating and nationality" had to be struck off the list in favor of a broader and more methodical analysis, starting with the situation at the beginning of the sixteenth century. Febvre ended by prophesying that no single generation of historians would complete these assignments. No one was likely to dispute this conclusion!

Few social historians nowadays lack sympathy with these claims, urged as they were with the writer's tense, oratorical enthusiasm and broad horizons. Is this not an eloquent plea for something like the grassroots history we are still, half a century later, trying to write? Nevertheless, some vulnerable points in the structure remain, which critics have not failed to indicate. One of the more sustained counterattacks is that by Dermot Fenlon in a shorter but still widely ranging paper, *"Encore Une Question:* Lucien Febvre, the Reformation and the School of *Annales"* (1974).[6] Disputing the detail and suspecting anachronism, Fenlon maintained that the men of the sixteenth century did not share Febvre's distinction between "religious" and "ecclesiastical" problems. Almost universally, they still saw spiritual needs in the context of organized churches and defined doctrines. Despite the adoption of so-called Erasmian ideas during the abortive reunion conference in 1541 at Regensburg, their sponsors consisted of a very few liberals like Contarini, who did not base his thoughts on Erasmus, but directly on Saint Paul's teachings on justification. In any event, the ecumenical bid failed because Protestants were not prepared to accept either transubstantiation or papal primacy in return for a Catholic adoption of justification by faith.

Febvre's picture of an Erasmian Europe clamoring for freedom from ecclesiastical management remained quite unrealistic. Many of the so-called Spanish Erasmians, discussed by Marcel Bataillon in a work which Febvre ecstatically applauded,[7] turned out to be Lutherans and in some cases Calvinists. Likewise, the famous *Beneficio di Cristo* was not an Erasmian book, but Protestantism transplanted to Italy. Even Cardinal Pole's group at Viterbo, deeply suspected of heresy by stiff conservatives like Carafa, in fact contained Lutheran moderates who hoped to convert the Council of Trent to their own concepts of faith. Such examples indicate the overriding importance of those confessional and ecclesiastical allegiances which Febvre so contemptuously dismissed.

By the same token, abuses within the Church, also discounted by Febvre, proved crucial, first by driving Luther into rebellion and then by forcing the Council of Trent to undertake practical reforms. This, added Fenlon, was not a theme which could be orchestrated by a posthumous conductor into separate religious and ecclesiastical movements. Fenlon further doubted whether Febvre's essay should be regarded as a landmark in studies of the Reformation, especially because the sounder features of his theory had been anticipated by another French historian, whose achievement Febvre had most curiously and somewhat tragically ignored.

Already in 1914 Pierre Imbart de la Tour had revealed these more solid realities in the masterly third volume, subtitled *Evangelism,* of his *Origins of the Reformation.*[8] Febvre had read and attacked Imbart's first two volumes (1905, 1909), but after the war he showed no sign of having read the third, the very volume which should have formed the heart of the case he argued in 1928. For example, Imbart anticipated Febvre by contending that historians made a cardinal error when they assumed that after Luther's revolt only two major forces confronted each other: Protestantism and Counter-Reformation. Since the early years of the century, in France, Italy, and elsewhere, there had arisen that third zone of faith which Imbart christened *Evangelisme* and which was represented in France by Lefèvre and Briçonnet. Not unlike Luther, these people had adumbrated a spiritual reform based on Bible study, especially on the Pauline Epistles. Although related to Christian humanism, they cannot accurately be dubbed disciples of Erasmus. With the rise of Lutheranism, the champions of *Evangelisme* sought for many years to mediate, but they too became divided and polarized before falling—however reluctantly—into one of the two hard lines: Protestantism and Tridentine Catholicism.

As Fenlon also remarked, a number of recent scholars found the concept of *Evangelisme* useful and sought to define the corresponding realities further.[9] In particular, they explored the Pauline movements in Italy represented by Valdés and the circle around Pole. Imbart de la Tour rather than Febvre caused historians to treat Italian movements more seriously in a Reformation context.[10] They became interesting because—like Erasmianism in Spain—they either drifted northward into Protestant allegiances or were eradicated by Tridentine orthodoxy.

Thinking independently of Fenlon, and taking Febvre's message most seriously, do we not need to reject doctrinaire notions of "wrong" and "right" questions? Alongside the new approaches, must we not continue the old ones? We cannot afford to cease studying the churches and sects, if only because their contemporaries obstinately exalted them as essential in a Christendom threatened by civil and religious chaos. By the same token, we cannot abandon the specificity which Febvre scorned in theory but adopted in practice when he later wrote a book which purported to analyze unbelief in the sixteenth century, yet in fact heavily centered on Rabelais (1942).[11]

Fenlon's criticisms of Febvre have undeniable weight, and they appear in some respects to be strengthened by recent practical experience. Social history demands detailed attention to local affairs, specific persons, and small groups: almost always the fragmentary nature of the evidence forces us to assemble regional and national pictures by a patient, cumulative process. The solid achievements seem to be arising from collaborative rather than Promethean attitudes, from modest enterprises resembling Febvre's first work on Franche-Comté rather than the grandiose theories he later propounded but failed to fulfill. We shall soon observe that in England and Germany modern social history arose humbly from old traditions of local research, from "natural" fascination with our ancestors and the land and communities into which they and we were born. Such studies have been successfully professionalized and are now being weaned of mere antiquarianism, lifted where possible into the mental sphere, and redirected and broadened as contributions to national and even international history.

Social historians need diligence and discipline rather than theoretical dogmas: they develop their intellectual muscles by crawling on the earth rather than entering philosophical satellites capable of instant global investigations. Yet here we are thinking in terms of experience gained since Febvre's initial proclamation, and it cannot be denied that, in France at least, his lively preaching encouraged scholars to think more freely and envisage new categories, even though these had already been adumbrated by others less eloquent. Furthermore, Febvre's manifestos proclaimed changes of emphasis by no means limited to France. In Germany, America, and Britain—countries where his influence was not immediately felt—similar but less vehement approaches to social history of the Reformation were developing independently.

Before leaving France we must observe that for more than a century highly specific studies have increasingly dominated the scene and provided some firm foundations for modern social history. In regard to studies of the Reformation, Beza's primary history of the early congregations has been greatly augmented by detailed articles in the *Bulletin de la société de l'histoire du protestantisme français* and elsewhere.[12] Extensive regional histories of the Wars of Religion[13] and the Catholic League[14] have been emerging since the mid–nineteenth century and have been extensively used in the national histories of France. Since 1940 these histories have been deepened by a grasp of social dimensions, a sense of regional variations, and an abandonment of denominational and clerical prejudices. While Henri Hauser, E. G. Léonard, and Samuel Mours displayed these advances,[15] other Frenchmen began to exhibit interest in the European Reformation as a whole. Few concise surveys embracing modern scholarship can rival that of Jean Delumeau on the "birth and affirmation" of the Reformation, which begins somewhat in the spirit of Febvre with an extremely broad survey of the social and spiritual landscapes of Europe on the eve of the movement.[16]

A good many scholars have even defied Febvre's ban on further reflections on Lefèvre d'Etaples and other familiar individuals, even though they may have benefited from his strictures against nationalist attitudes. Nevertheless, his positive enthusiasms, reinforced by the contributions of several early followers in the *Annales,* can be traced in the work of recent social historians. His discipleship has, however, perhaps been too widely attributed. For example, despite Fernand Braudel's cordial dedication to Febvre, we can scarcely regard his great work on the Mediterranean in such terms: its scope and dominantly geographic concepts remain very different from those of Febvre.[17]

Whatever the case, in history of the Reformation Febvre's true executors are surely scholars like Janine Garrisson-Estèbe and Natalie Zemon Davis, who explored in detail the *mentalités*—in particular the concerted violence of Catholic and Protestant crowds in Paris, Lyons, and other urban societies, most notably during the Saint Bartholomew massacre.[18] The pioneer work was that of Garrisson-Estèbe, who stressed both rising grain prices and primitive group emotions directed in 1572 against Protestants in general and rich Huguenots in particular. Reexamining the evidence, Davis refined this analysis, showing that the Catholics hated the heretics for their "polluting" and divisive actions, but not as a separate class or "race." Although some instances of pillage were inspired by social resentment, in general both Catholic and Protestant movements in the French cities cut vertically through the social structure: both the mobs and their victims were classless.

In such works, the lurid events of the Reformation contribute to the large and growing literature on crowds and violence in various countries throughout medieval and earlier modern history. To do it justice, however, we must note that the collected volume by Davis is by no means limited to what she called "the rites of violence": it also contains illuminating essays on the very real feminist trends in the cities of Reformation France, the influence of printing and publishing among the people, and the role of festivals, "misrule," and youth groups in popular movements of the day. We shall encounter parallel investigations in England and Germany, because recent movements of social history are highly international, led as much by Americans as by Europeans, and therefore tending to lift Europeans out of their nationalist attitudes.

Among the chief ancestors of modern English social history is an exceptionally old and powerful tradition of topographic history. Since the time of John Leland (d. 1552), such studies were compiled in the countryside as well as in libraries. The first genuine county history appeared as early as 1570, William Lambarde's *Perambulation of Kent.*[19]

Soon after came Richard Carew's *Survey of Cornwall* (1602) and Sampson Erdeswicke's *Survey of Staffordshire* (1593–1603). John Stow's *Survey of London* (1598–1603) applied historical recording to a city undergoing phenomenal expansion. Through the next three centuries numerous volumes were subsidized by local nobility and gentry, who often achieved minimal immortality by ensuring that the publishers inserted their names in a prefatory list of subscribers.

By the end of the eighteenth century, most of the southern and midland counties of England were represented by more or less competent works, although—with some rare exceptions such as Francis Drake's *Eboracum* (1736)—neither the major cities nor the northern counties were adequately covered until after the rise of the Industrial Revolution. The old county histories dwell far longer on genealogies and manorial descents than on religious and cultural history, yet they remain valuable aids to local research. By 1900 many useful urban histories were in existence, and nearly all English counties boasted historical societies publishing journals and volumes of records. Nevertheless, from our viewpoint serious shortcomings lingered well into the twentieth century. Too few professional historians reinforced the gallant amateur contributors, many of whom were antiquarians lacking the broad concepts to balance their technical skills. Even in our day the archaeology of Roman Britain and the ecclesiology of the Middle Ages are widely regarded as more appropriate focuses of local history than are great movements such as early Protestantism.

The foundation in 1901 of the epoch-making *Victoria History of the Counties of England* did not at first dramatically improve the field, partly because ecclesiastical history was dominated by clerically minded Anglicans, many of whom felt little spontaneous interest in the Reformation heritage of their own Church, let alone in Puritanism or Nonconformity.[20] This factor apart, however, the tenor of local history remained materialist, and seldom, before the mid-twentieth century, did matters such as the progress of elementary education or the religion of the middle and poorer classes enter its purview.

Fifty years ago English readers met the Tudor populace in the plays of Shakespeare rather than the pages of historians digging around the roots of Tudor society. Well-established economic historians could hardly rectify this situation beyond the limited extent suggested by their specialty, but social history did tend to emerge from their margins. Likewise, historians of government began to see that administrative machines were only narrowly significant unless examined with the social phenomena they purported to regulate. A good example is Rachel R. Reid's *The*

King's Council in the North (1921), an important institutional monograph which provides the best account to date of northern English society
in Tudor and early Stuart times.[21]

The rebellions of the period, especially the extensive and richly
recorded Pilgrimage of Grace (1536–1537), also left much evidence concerning the opinions of the common people, and they often revealed
something far livelier than the brutish rustics and boring craftsmen who
had filled the austere pages of economic history.[22] Through such records,
and by reading wills, deeds, letters, court books, corporation minutes,
parish registers, ballads, miracle plays, local chronicles, sermons, and
devotional manuscripts, English social historians of the 1930s began to
reconstruct the human background in a manner which Febvre—unknown
to most of them—would have approved.

Against this miscellaneous background, state papers and diocesan
records, both ceaselessly reflecting on local conditions, could be exploited
to create a close-knit social history of the Reformation in any given area.
Moreover, from this earthy level it was possible to build regional surveys
illustrating and explaining the Reformation's very uneven impacts on
various provinces. A. L. Rowse's *Tudor Cornwall: Portrait of a Society*
(1947) provides at least one first-rate study, which, although not written
chiefly as a survey of the Reformation, yields much vivid detail about
religion and culture in a highly conservative and still half-Celtic county.[23]
Otherwise, apart from articles on particular themes, full-scale surveys
occupying sizable books took some decades to evolve.

Among the earliest was that by A. G. Dickens, *Lollards and Protestants in the Diocese of York,* published in 1959 but partly based on
work written (and in some cases published) many years earlier.[24] The
area involved—Nottinghamshire and nearly all Yorkshire—was known
to be conservative in religious matters; it contained the heartland of the
Pilgrimage of Grace. It proved less simple than expected, however, boast-
ing a few Lollard groups and some direct contacts with Germany, together
with a small but growing Protestant minority under Henry VIII and
Edward VI. There also coexisted in Yorkshire parish priests who rev-
erently studied the fourteenth-century mystics while reviling as lecherous
their numerous up-to-date colleagues who married as soon as the Reformation permitted.

In due course Dickens's study was followed by others of similar
scope, such as Christopher Haigh's able *Reformation and Resistance in
Tudor Lancashire* (1975), which displays the more isolated communities
west of the Pennines.[25] The localized cloth trade of south Lancashire did
not encourage integration of that area with the rest of England. Manchester apart, the towns remained small and uninfluential, with Liverpool

as yet a minor port. And although Yorkshire was governed by the powerful council in the north, one trusted family—the Stanleys, earls of Derby—dominated the official life of Lancashire. This immobile area was disturbed by Protestantism only when a new generation of natives brought back advanced ideas from Oxford and Cambridge, but even they made little impact until the reign of Elizabeth.

Other regional surveys reflecting on the English Reformation have been published, for example in 1965 that of Essex by J. E. Oxley, and more recently Peter Clark's capacious work on Kent and Margaret Bowker's volumes based on the diocesan records of Lincoln.[26] Also notable are the articles by K. G. Powell on early Protestants in Bristol and Gloucestershire.[27] At present the coverage remains highly incomplete, yet the outlines of a national pattern can be deciphered. A great body of pre-Elizabethan evidence attests to the gradual but substantial growth of Lutheranism duly transmuted into Edwardian Anglicanism in London, Essex, Suffolk, Kent, Sussex, and westward in the Bristol area. The presence of some convinced Protestants in most other counties can also be proved, but extant evidence suggests that, even throughout so large an area as the diocese of Lincoln—which embraced most of the East Midlands —Protestants with strong convictions were still thinly spread at midcentury.

Nevertheless, this likelihood is far from proving that these slow-moving areas were replete with satisfied, let alone ardent, Catholics. Apart from the brief reign of Edward VI, open Protestants might at any time have incurred a long sojourn in a lethal prison or the swifter agonies of the stake. It seems obvious that the unheroic majority of sympathizers would have striven to keep out of these troubles. Such people cannot be counted, however, because they do not occur in the records, which are demonstrably incomplete.[28] Ralph Allerton, one of the martyrs under the Marian persecution, observed rightly that a large class of Englishmen were "neuters," "i.e. observing all things that are commanded . . . his heart being wholly against the same."[29] Elizabeth I and her minister William Cecil judged it safe to revert to Edwardian Protestantism within a few months of Elizabeth's accession. And were they not proved right by the peaceful outcome?

The geographic pattern just outlined is well confirmed by John Fines's recent *Register of Early English Protestants,* which contains biographies of nearly 3,000 Protestants mentioned from 1525 to 1558 not only in Foxe but in numerous other sources now available.[30] A list of this size lends more precision to the topographic distribution: it also broadly indicates the social composition of that bolder Protestant element which did get itself into the records. In fact, something like 80 percent of those in Fines's *Register* were working-class men and women: textile operatives, tailors, shoemakers, and other craftsmen rather than farming people, although farmers are by no means unrepresented. Needless to add, these congregations followed clerical leaders, mostly graduates of Oxford and Cambridge, who figure prominently in both the *Register* and the far smaller list of Protestant martyrs. On the other hand, several hundred gentry and others of substance, who provided so few martyrs, appear in the *Register* because so many fled Mary's persecution, joining the well-documented communities of English exiles in Switzerland and Germany.[31] The *Register* also lists a considerable proportion of people whose ages are recorded, and these prompt us to envisage the majority of Protestants as young or youngish, those who, especially during the six years of Edwardian Protestant rule, found it easier than their elders did to embrace the "new" beliefs. As Susan Brigden has recently shown, much circumstantial evidence also supports this probable religious "age gap."[32]

The social dimension now dominates research in England, and centers of interest have shifted considerably since 1940. In particular, the growth and character of Protestantism have tended to push aside that favorite topic of the 1930s, the functions and dissolution of English monasteries. The two most recent books on this theme, by G. W. O. Woodward and Joyce Youings, deliberately contribute less to monasticism than to social history, which was indeed deeply influenced by so vast a transfer of landed properties.[33] The rising attraction to religion observed in a broad social context has also extended the story of Elizabethan Puritanism, the social and spiritual dimensions of which have been illuminated by Patrick Collinson and other distinguished specialists, mostly Americans.[34] Among the most significant books of our time concerning the Elizabethan Church is that by Christopher Hill, which is almost purely social and economic.[35] Yet the term *social history* remains highly elastic. In a very different idiom John Bossy has in effect refounded the social history of the English Catholics.[36] Our summary account of these major achievements should be accompanied by caveats, because the tenor of modern research on the Reformation, in both England and Britain as a whole, does not closely correspond to either Febvre's manifesto or the overintellectualized perspective of so much modern writing on the German Reformation.

This national differentiation springs from many circumstances. First, the English Protestant movement, unlike its central European equivalent, was not involved with peasant revolts and participated little in city politics. London apart, English towns were still relatively small, and under a powerful monarchy none enjoyed anything resembling the freedom of action assumed by municipal governments in the Holy Roman Empire or the Swiss Confederation. A great deal of the recent publication about religion in Tudor England is still concerned with long-familiar institutional, biographical, and clerical themes, to which current documentary research so readily contributes. With her work on the consolidation of the clerical profession, Rosemary O'Day has in large measure continued Peter Heath's older standard study of the early Tudor clergy.[37] Felicity Heal has brightly illuminated the social and economic status of the Tudor episcopate.[38] Margaret Bowker and others have examined particular dioceses in depth.[39] Numerous young scholars have cooperated on several enterprising yet methodologically conservative volumes.[40]

All these valuable additions to knowledge are not, and do not pretend to be, "a new kind of history." Virtually no one has thought to fit the English Reformation into the procrustean beds of Marxism or transatlantic sociology. Yet no reasonable historian of English Protestantism could so concentrate on the grass roots as to ignore Tudor central government. After all, even in the earlier stages of the Reformation, that government did far more than merely exclude papal jurisdiction and abolish monasticism: it put English Bibles into the churches and promulgated a Protestant liturgy. Although primarily a social historian, A. G. Dickens found himself compelled to devote to governmental activities a large part of his general monograph *The English Reformation* (1964), a book which should be regarded as an agenda, not as a summa.[41] Similar considerations apply to the substantial contributions of Claire Cross and D. M. Loades.[42] Conversely, G. R. Elton, the leading historian of the Tudor state, became extremely informative on the activities of both Catholics and Protestants across the English landscape when in his masterly *Policy and Police* (1972) he described in detail enforcement of the Henrician Reformation.[43] To think in terms of Reformation from above versus Reformation from below would thus take us into an unreal world.

In Scotland and Wales the social history of the Reformation has lately developed along similar lines. Michael Lynch, who began by studying German city histories, ended by producing for Edinburgh one of the most advanced and effective works in the urban studies genre.[44] His documentation is elaborate and has enabled a detailed display of the interrelations of civil authorities, citizens, national government, and Reformers in Edinburgh. As one would anticipate, Scotland could already boast a strong tradition of research on the Reformation, represented, for example, by the many publications of Gordon Donaldson.[45] On the other hand, Wales, although long distinguished in medieval scholarship, has only recently begun to produce work on the social history of the Reformation. Glanmor Williams showed with erudition and objectivity that the Welsh Reformation was not—as romantic nationalism had tended to suppose—a mere incursion of English influence.[46] Along with the advent of humanist literary and educational ideas, the Reformation, and in particular the Welsh Bible, marked a crucial stage in Welsh national culture and the origins of its major religious component: Nonconformity.

The social historiography of the German Reformation seems to have arisen from more complex influences. Yet, somewhat like its English equivalent, it includes a huge output of local and regional works from the seventeenth century on, a phenomenon linked with the great number of German states, from which sprang the pride and patronage of ruling houses. The outlook of these works—many of them erudite, immense, and factually informative—does not much resemble that of modern social history. Yet, as we observed in Chapter 7, Ranke made good use of such materials in both the political and social passages of his *German History in the Age of the Reformation*. The next stage came in 1875–1891, with the eight volumes of Johannes Janssen's *History of the German People,* which, despite its polemical selectivity, contained a mine of unfamiliar detail on the social and religious life of all classes from the early fifteenth century to the Thirty Years' War (see Chapter 8). [47] By this time the work of Engels on the Peasants' War was already influencing social historians, and it has continued to do so, especially in the German Democratic Republic (see Chapter 10).

Likewise, recent social historiography relates closely to the outlook of the founders of the sociology of religion, Weber and Troeltsch, who prepared the way for a hybrid standpoint that acknowledged powerful religious and intellectual factors without neglecting the material environment (see Chapter 11). Troeltsch in particular regarded the social teachings of the Christian churches as changing in response to mental and material development in the surrounding world. This was not the detached, otherworldly stance of a religious philosopher: it came from a thinker alert to the class conflict and international tensions of the early twentieth century. Troeltsch showed himself equally aware of the historic tensions of the sixteenth and seventeenth centuries, not only among the sects but within and around Calvinism, which he took to be the most socially and intellectually dynamic bequeathal from the Reformation to modern times. Troeltsch did not regard the eventual blessings of tolerance, spontaneity, and release from the grip of the State as springing solely from intellectual leadership; he saw the Reformation linked with the rise of the bourgeoisie, and he credited even the common people with a creative role. He stood abreast of recent thinking when he recognized

urban life as the main social focus of the permanent changes wrought
by the Reformation, although he had chiefly in mind the west European
cities, which fostered Calvinism and Puritanism and thus derived their
benefits.

Present emphasis on the role of the German cities should not be
considered a novelty of our day. With some satisfaction Ranke noted
that the Reformation could have strengthened the urban communal spirit
as episcopal controls were eroded and municipal assumption of church
administration and property gave all classes a new common interest. He
rightly observed that in some places "very violent political tendencies
mingled themselves with the attempt to reform the church; and it was a
question how far the former could be guided in the channel of established
institutions, or how far they would assume a revolutionary character."[48]
Ranke had to acknowledge that the Reformation also brought conflict
with urban society: "a vehement and continual ferment" spread through
towns where religion divided council from commune. He presented a
vivid picture of a society in change, and parts of his work—for example,
his description of the Reformation in Westphalia—anticipate modern
demands. Ranke's synthesis of the German Reformation paved the way
for a period of historical discovery, when "new" sources were opened
and put to use in religious and social history. The vast archives of German
towns had lain almost unexplored for many centuries, but from 1862 a
series of town chronicles, dating from the fourteenth to the sixteenth
centuries, was printed in Leipzig in thirty-six volumes.[49] Selections from
the archives of particular cities appeared in learned editions. Ferdinand
Frensdorff's edition of the town ordinances of Dortmund and G. F. von
der Ropp's corresponding collection for Göttingen are typical examples.[50]

In nineteenth-century Germany urban life entered a period of revival, and inevitable parallels were drawn with that other great age of
towns, the sixteenth century. One consequence was the appearance of
massive town histories, most of which gave detailed coverage to the
Reformation. J. D. W. von Winterbach's history of the wonderfully preserved Rothenburg ob der Tauber appeared in 1826–1827, and Leonard
Ennen's extensive works on the city and archdiocese of Cologne were
published between 1849 and 1880.[51] F. Roth, who published an account
of the Reformation in Nuremberg in 1885, was also the author of a very
full study of Augsburg, which came out in four volumes between 1901
and 1911.[52] Axel Vorberg's work on Rostock (1897) and E. Nübling's
history of Ulm from 1378 to 1556 (1904–1907) are other examples.[53]
Major city histories and other works on local and regional affairs have
steadily appeared during this century: they figure prominently in Karl
Schottenloher's great bibliography of German history (1933–1939) and

Erich Keyser's bibliography of German city history (1969).[54] Goslar was investigated by Uvo Hölscher (1902), Hamburg by Kurt Beckey (1929), and Regensburg by Leonhard Theobald (1936).[55] Hans von Schubert published a study of Lazarus Spengler and the Nuremberg Reformation in 1934, some years after his general survey of the movement in that city.[56]

The resultant information did not escape the notice of historians of religion. Over forty years ago Joseph Lortz, a leading modern Catholic historian of the Reformation, declared that "the German cities were nothing less than the determining factor in the development of the collective life of Germany in this period. They created the models, the roots and the stimuli for that which later became the function of the modern state in war, finance, civil service and the planned concern of governments for the rights of the community and the individual." Accordingly, Lortz saw much of the constructive energy in the Reformation as stemming from the urban middle classes: "a ruling, self-assured and self-contained power, conscious of its own worth in trade, commerce, art and ecclesiastical policy."[57]

Still more pointedly, the unifying strand in recent German research on the Reformation has been detailed analysis of the urban background to religious change, the social causation of that change, and the interaction of social classes and power groups in the cities. In a pioneering article of 1937, "Religion and Politics in the German Imperial Cities during the Reformation," Hans Baron stressed the diversity of problems and attitudes arising in three places which superficially seem comparable: Nuremberg, Strasbourg, and Augsburg.[58] Concisely he displayed their striking differences, especially in internal and external economic systems and the varying political necessities imposed by their neighbors and historical traditions.

Although this article pointed the way for comparative studies on a larger scale, they were not forthcoming until the publication in 1962 of Bernd Moeller's brief but striking synthesis, *Imperial Cities and the Reformation*.[59] Observing the limited but all-important group of sixty-five imperial cities, Moeller confirmed that, during the late fifteenth and early sixteenth centuries, their councils already exercised powerful control over local churches and clergy: "Exaggerating a bit, one could assert that the German town of the late Middle Ages tended to view itself as a miniature *corpus christianum*."[60] This was an age of decline for ancient municipal ideals of solidarity. The councils became in truth "governments," drawn from a narrow ruling elite or patriciate; the mass of the citizenry became their "subjects." Yet the humanist clerics who adhered to Luther favored broader-based and more democratic tendencies. In general, religious conflicts became deeply entangled with long-standing social tensions. Moeller supported the claim that in most cases the Reformation was forced on civic authorities by popular pressure: to some extent he echoed Franz Lau's vigorous reassertion of the popular character of Protestantism after 1525.[61] Those in power believed that the unity and security of their cities was in grave danger; their first reaction was to resist what they saw as divisive trends, and the Reformation made swiftest progress in the less oligarchic municipalities. In some places council and commune agreed to move toward religious reform: the occasion was often a communal assembly or public debate to decide the city's future policy. Once the decision was taken, all citizens were bound to observe it. Moeller cited as an example the church ordinances of Brunswick: "Whoever wants to rise above the law would fight with God himself and would cause the ruin of bodies and souls by disturbing the peace of the community."[62]

Over fifty of the sixty-five imperial cities accepted the Reformation; more than half remained fully Protestant, the others tolerated both religions. In a mere handful, Protestantism won early successes but later underwent suppression. Of the total, only fourteen never tolerated Protestantism, but most of them had to struggle hard to avoid its onset.

A cooperative Reformation could thus preserve civic unity and, by increasing the element of popular participation in civic life, move toward a more democratic regime. In Moeller's view, the attraction of Protestantism for German city dwellers bore a direct relation to its theology, most particularly to Luther's doctrine concerning the priesthood of all believers. Luther openly sought to free secular life from its sense of inferiority and divest the priesthood of its claim to authority and special privilege. Here was another element which promoted a willing civic cohesion. On the other hand, some features of Luther's thought pointed in an opposite direction. His concept of the relationship between Church and State supposed a separation of powers between secular and ecclesiastical. Believers were distinguished by their faith, not by mere church membership: they constituted only part of the commune but formed the true Church.

Moeller saw Luther as less sensitive to the needs of the city community than were the Reformed theologians. Luther was the product of a small Saxon town under princely domination, but Zwingli and Bucer came from great free cities. They were more deeply imbued with the humanists' view of the *respublica* and keenly interested in political life; and this was important to understanding their theology. Even the Anabaptist agitation which affected both Zurich and Strasbourg tried to reaffirm the ancient identification of citizen with Christian.

In Moeller's view—which might be taken as a bold generalization

—the cities of southern Germany and Switzerland, where the Reformed faith soon took root, were more advanced economically, socially, and culturally than those of the Lutherans in the north. They were also more liberal, displaying greater popular involvement in politics. Moeller concluded: "The victory of the 'Reformed' Reformation in the Upper German imperial cities is finally explained by the encounter of the peculiarly 'urban' theology of Zwingli and Bucer with the particularly vital communal spirit in Upper Germany."[63] But this spirit was disturbed by the emperor's victory over the Schmalkaldic League in 1546–1547, and the spread of Reformed religion was checked through the decline of that distinctive "urban mentality" common to townsmen irrespective of class: "Gradually city dwellers changed from participating citizens, responsible for the vigor of the commonwealth, into mere subjects, owing obedience to the city government, and the city governments in turn no longer saw themselves as instruments of the urban community. A rampant nepotism often seized control and men worked only to fill their own pockets."[64] Where Protestantism of either variety survived, it did so by bowing to the changed climate. In the south German cities the Reformed faith eventually withered, yet it found new life in Switzerland, Scotland, Holland, and elsewhere.

Moeller's thinking proved a catalyst in studies of the Reformation, stimulating both comparisons between cities and closer analysis of their internal tensions. He encouraged deeper and wider researches into the relation of the various religious forms to urban social and political structures. Yet Moeller's view of the Reformation as a period of consolidation which strengthened ancient urban ideals has not gone unquestioned, and it has also been said that "he finally deems the Reformation most successful where it changed religious thought and practice the least."[65]

Of course, the most famous cities, like Nuremberg and Strasbourg, have been subjected individually to many detailed investigations. Following Roth and Schubert, Paul Kalkoff (1926) and Adolf Engelhardt (1936–1937) wrote important accounts of the Reformation in Nuremberg,[66] which has since been well served by both German and American historians. Gerald Strauss's *Nuremberg in the Sixteenth Century* (1966) contains a concise and lucid treatment of the religious movement; in a separate article he explored the motives which led some of the city's leaders to adopt Protestant beliefs.[67] He regarded these men as hard realists who believed in a rigidly controlled society and suppression of lower-class insurgency. They found their views of mankind echoed in Luther's teaching on the essential sinfulness of unredeemed humanity. Protestantism could thus be embraced because it rationalized the prevailing ideology of a ruling group, confident in the necessity of oligarchic powers. In a more recent analysis of the situation in Nuremberg, Gottfried Seebass confirmed Strauss's view: in this case the Reformation invigorated the existent power structure.[68]

Nevertheless, forces existed outside the ruling patriciate strong enough to ensure the prevalence of Lutheranism, and this change had been simplified by the city council when it assumed management of the churches. Even before Luther's revolt, the city had been visited by his former teacher Johannes Staupitz, whose Pauline-Augustinian emphases were accepted by a group of prominent citizens, including Lazarus Spengler, Albrecht Dürer, and Christoph Scheurl.[69] In 1518 the Augustinian friar Wenzeslaus Linck preached Lutheranism to appreciative congregations;[70] in the same year the Reformation cause was furthered, even among conservative rulers, by Luther's visit.

Pressure on the Nuremberg council from various directions led to admission of Protestant preachers and growth of a genuinely popular movement. Once that movement existed, maintenance of civil peace seemed to demand at least the toleration of Lutheranism. When in 1524 thousands of Nurembergers took communion in both kinds, the council organized a great public debate concerning religion, and as a consequence abolished the Mass and erected a territorial church. Thus, the urge to maintain internal unity prevailed over religious conservatism, although Nuremberg never became a center for vigorous Lutheran missionizing.[71] Probably its leaders did not forget their city's traditional loyalty toward empire and emperor, which had prompted them to such caution at the onset of the Reformation.

To modern liberal opinion, Strasbourg presents a spectacle more attractive if more complicated, as progressively revealed by recent researches. One senses in comparison with Nuremberg more independence among the guilds and lower orders; the educated citizenry evidenced a notable liveliness of spirit. Strasbourg had not only an early humanist tradition but a remarkable proto-Reformer, Geiler von Kaysersberg, who from 1478 to 1510 thundered from the city's pulpits, announcing the supremacy of the Scriptures and arousing strong emotions against not merely sin in general but the shortcomings of the clergy in particular. After his death, his printed sermons continued to prepare the way for Matthäus Zell, whose preaching in defense of Luther divided Strasbourg in the early 1520s.[72]

On this situation the earliest substantial treatment by a modern historian occurred in 1830–1832 with T. W. Röhrich's history of the Reformation in Alsace.[73] Over forty years later, Charles Schmidt's *Literary History of Alsace* provided well-informed accounts of humanism and Protestant propaganda, which are still useful.[74] More recently, Strasbourg has been even better served than Nuremberg. In 1942 François Wendel published a major work on the contribution and organization of the Church in Strasbourg during the 1530s.[75]

Two significant studies have since come from the American scholar Miriam Usher Chrisman. Her *Strasbourg and the Reform* (1967) begins by surveying the economy on the eve of the Reformation and confirming Baron's view that this was a regional market and manufacturing center rather than an international emporium like Nuremberg.[76] Yet, standing on the western frontier of Germany and the empire, Strasbourg had long resisted imperial demands and was inclined to temporize with the French monarchy. Before 1520 the ruling oligarchy encountered little demand for social or religious change, although the old quarrel between cathedral canons and the bishop revived when the canons backed Zell against the bishop. The intellectual atmosphere was pervaded by a critical humanism, this being the city of Wimpfeling, Jakob Sturm, and Sebastian Brant as well as Geiler. Nevertheless, preaching even more than printing swiftly furthered the Reformation's earliest phases, and it inspired enthusiastic support among the unprivileged.[77]

The council in Strasbourg, anxious to preserve order and hierarchy, was subjected to sustained popular pressure and eventually persuaded that political stability would be best guaranteed by religious change, especially because it seemed to offer a better bulwark against the Anabaptists and other sectarians who were flooding into the city in terrifying numbers.[78] Thus, Strasbourg does not in all respects support Moeller's broad proposition that the Reformation was a reassertion of the communal spirit. Reform came not so much from close cooperation between preachers and magistrates as from the zealous efforts of a minority, and its official adoption was the tactical move of a patriciate bent on preserving its own power.[79]

The position of the Strasbourg patriciate was further illuminated when Thomas A. Brady published in 1977 a close structural examination of the city's ruling class based on biographies of 105 of its members between 1520 and 1555.[80] They are revealed as a far from purely urban group; in fact they were an alliance between nobleman-rentiers and rich merchants, both enjoying financial and feudal support from outside the city. Having long manipulated the guilds, and in 1525 having retained control by concessions to popular pressure, this elite suffered heavily in 1548, when the emperor's recent victory over the Protestants combined with a local outburst of hatred to drive many rich families into exile, thus producing what the onset of the Reformation had failed to: a substantial modification of the patriciate. Further dimensions, however, remain to be investigated in this historiographically favored city.

In her second major work, *Lay Culture, Learned Culture* (1982), Chrisman penetrated further into the intellectual history of Strasbourg across the whole Reformation, utilizing the changing character of the numerous books which emerged from the city's presses.[81] She asked, Who communicated what to whom?

During the period 1480–1520 her picture is still dominated by clerical books in Latin, although illustrated books for laymen and some scientific treatises were already in view. Two intellectual worlds coexisted and were catered to by separate groups of printer-publishers. From about 1515 to 1548, biblical humanism and Protestantism claimed priority, as justification by faith and the priesthood of all believers replaced Catholic penitential theology. Biblical knowledge seems to have been generally disseminated, but humanist values remained the perquisite of an educated minority. In addition, these interests came to be accompanied by a larger number of scientific works and other works necessitated by the expansion of classical education. After 1549 the internal crisis of the Reformation passed, and publishing chiefly represented a lay world of vernacular literature and popular science. Finally, the last thirty years of the century saw a new wave of doctrinal books arising from the attempt to fend off both Catholicism and Calvinism, establish a Protestant orthodoxy, and place the new religious establishment firmly in the context of urban life.

All in all, this mental dimension makes for a sounder concept of the social history of the Reformation. We can observe the Reformers becoming the true spokesmen for ordinary people, yet we overcome the mistaken notion that religion swamped all other mental activities. Although the developments in Strasbourg do not necessarily represent the experience of other cities, and although the citizens doubtless also read books published elsewhere, future historians would be well advised to respect and extend Chrisman's methodology, which brings us nearer to the complex world of the Reformation.

Meanwhile, in several Hanseatic cities Lutheranism certainly revived rather than pacified the long-standing divisions between ruling classes and people. This theme has naturally attracted Marxist historians, one of whom, Johannes Schildhauer, wrote an important account of the developments at Stralsund, Rostock, and Wismar (1959).[82] None was an imperial city, and, although all enjoyed internal self-government, all paid heavy taxes to princely rulers. Schildhauer's documents show a similar sequence in all three cities. The lower and middle classes had little power over municipal policies and especially resented the misuse of taxes for warfare. According to this account, the Church itself tended to be identified with the hated secular establishment. Indulgences, church taxes, clerical affluence, and abuse of excommunication were all considered parts of the unpopular system. In the early 1520s Lutheran preaching provided the catalyst for revolt, and a reform movement appeared in all three cities under the leadership of middle-rank merchants and rising craftsmen. Under this impulse Lutheranism was accepted by the ruling councils, which were enlarged to give seats to the main oppositionists. In addition, there emerged a "left wing," favoring something like social revolution and infected by sectarian religious ideas. Nevertheless, the remodeled councils collaborated with the Lutheran establishment to suppress this radical element, and thereafter they used Lutheran religion as a prop for the new—but not greatly democratized—regime.

Further westward along the Baltic stood the prestigious imperial city of Lübeck, and its notable archives have yielded somewhat similar patterns through the researches of Wilhelm Jannasch and others.[83] A rigid and ultraconservative oligarchy confronted a series of popular councils backed by the many ambitious merchants hitherto excluded from government. This opposition also pressed for church reforms and provided the first lay recruits to Lutheranism. The famous Jürgen Wullenwever led an almost simultaneous politicoreligious rebellion and seized power, but on his tragic fall the patrician council regained political control. Nevertheless, Lutheranism could not be eradicated: having achieved victory in partnership with secular forces, it adapted itself to changed circumstances and coexisted with the revived oligarchy.

In central and southern Germany such dramatic exchanges proved uncommon; as observed in Nuremberg and Strasbourg, the larger cities had controlled the administration of their churches long before Luther. Rolf Kiessling's work on Augsburg (1971) shows that in this international center of finance a similar integration of the Church with secular government began well before 1500.[84] So did the assault on clerical immunities, while the more gradual rise of humanist schooling eventually diminished churchmen's hold over education and culture in general. On the other hand, Augsburg's heavy concentration of bankers—especially the Fugger family—were the financiers of the emperor, and they naturally remained Catholic. The interests of the Establishment thus clashed with the people's spontaneous preference for the Reformation. When the emperor defeated the Protestants in 1546–1547, the Fuggers besought him to spare the city, yet he forced on it a council of Catholic patricians, under whom Lutheranism survived only amid hardship and on a reduced scale. Although other southern cities also stood exposed to the emperor's wrath, his triumph was short-lived, and most escaped the penalties Augsburg incurred. Not far away—in Ulm and its exceptionally large dependent territory—the Protestant revolution, so smoothly accomplished in 1531–1532, did not suffer reversal.

Certain other cities displayed patterns even more involved and curious. One of these was Erfurt in Thuringia, which despite its size and the fame of its university was no imperial city but an outlying dependency of the archbishop-elector of Mainz, surrounded by the lands of the electors of Saxony, who also claimed a measure of overlordship. Here, amid a declining economy, the multilateral party struggle had already in the "mad year" 1509 disgusted one of its academic witnesses, the young Luther. While the council played off the Mainz and Saxon interests against each other, the unprivileged, students, and younger teachers welcomed Luther's emissaries, and in 1521 a mob tore apart the cathedral canons' houses.

Three years later the unscrupulous councillors, also embroiled with the churchmen, admitted a crowd of rebellious peasants and encouraged them to destroy the archbishop-elector's headquarters. As the peasant revolt collapsed, the council kept face by executing a few ringleaders and allowing Catholic services in several churches. Finally, in 1530, the archbishop-elector, fearing that Erfurt might fall under Saxon rule, agreed to a compromise giving ten churches to the Lutherans while the cathedral and three others remained Catholic. The involved and cynical struggle thus ended in a pragmatic solution.

This extraordinary story has been told best by R. W. Scribner,[85] who later found an almost equally unusual theme at Cologne, the largest city in Germany and one of the few which at no stage became Protestant. In a significant 1976 article, based in part on the researches of several German scholars, Scribner examined and summarized the causes of this important phenomenon.[86] The most basic factor was Cologne's dependence on good relations with the Hapsburg rulers of the Netherlands, because all the main channels of the city's commerce passed through Antwerp. Second, the security of Cologne had long relied on friendship with its close neighbors, the princes and prince-bishops of the Rhineland, who had not accepted Lutheranism.

Internal influences also pointed to a Catholic destiny for a city with romantic Christian traditions and a huge ecclesiastical establishment. After the city council, the leading corporate body was the civic university, a powerful interest group dominated by a theological faculty which firmly adhered to Rome and competed successfully against both liberal humanists and Lutherans. The populace of Cologne lay under unusually firm control. In the past, the council had often clashed with the guilds and had evolved a system of corporate discipline through a militia, managed by a series of district committees. Thus, incipient movements of Protestant sympathizers were discouraged from the first and failed to develop on any dangerous scale: the one serious rising occurred in May–June 1525 and was connected with popular anticlericalism and the Peasants' Revolt rather than the Reformation.[87]

Thirteen years after Moeller published his valuable synthesis on the urban contribution, some important revisions were suggested in *The Reformation in the Cities* by Steven Ozment, a historian who approached the subject from a somewhat different angle.[88] Well versed in late medieval spirituality, he paid more regard to personal religion than to social institutions—or to salvation as a collective facility provided by civic authorities. His basic aim was to explain why Reformation doctrines attracted German and Swiss townsmen; in short, he wanted to restore religious ideas and sentiments to center stage.

Ozment extensively analyzed the popular religious literature, both Catholic and Protestant, of the pre- and early Reformation periods. He ended by reacting forcibly against Weber's notion that Protestantism proved excessively burdensome to the individual. On the contrary, his study indicated that resentment against the truly onerous beliefs and practices of the medieval church—fear of Purgatory, the "tyranny" of the confessional, and rigorous control by penances—characterized the pre-Reformation period. Of course, behind these factors remained the familiar causes of anticlericalism: clerical privilege and ill-disciplined ecclesiastics, especially those who rebelled against celibate living.

By contrast, Ozment's evidence shows that Luther's teaching lightened the townsmen's burdens; it bade them through faith to transfer the task of salvation to Christ. The "new" Pauline emphasis thus became a message of simplification, liberation, and enlightenment. It also removed the caste status of the priesthood; Protestant ministers—with legitimate wives and families—became in a real sense the fellow citizens of laymen. Ozment referred in the main to the early stages of the Lutheran movement, when the cities were being evangelized and still marched in the vanguard of the Reformation. He was by no means unaware that, later in the century, the princes enlarged their ecclesiastical powers, while Lutheranism hardened into a somewhat restrictive orthodoxy. Yet on balance he regarded Luther as a liberator of the human spirit, not one who glorified or sacralized urban communities.

Inevitably, Ozment's sources related for the most part to the more literate and thoughtful city dwellers, who presumably carried heavier spiritual burdens. In a 1980 work he maintained that "the religious beliefs and practices that reshaped sixteenth-century towns and territories were the work of generations of intellectuals and reformers, trained theologians and educated laymen." Unlike the most recent generation of social historians, he did not take very seriously the lower reaches of popular religion, which "clung more naively to traditional religious practices and to much pagan folklore and magic." These elements he relegated to "the realm of fancy and emotion."[89]

Ozment's more recent contributions to study of the Reformation, focusing on the abundant pamphlet literature of the early sixteenth century, signal an attempt to overcome the potential abstraction of intellectual history by moving toward a "social history of ideas." A similar aim was embraced by Heiko Oberman in his capacious and erudite volume *Masters of the Reformation,* to which we referred in Chapter 8. In that work the fifteenth-century struggle between the *via antiqua* (Thomism) and the *via moderna* (Nominalism) is used imaginatively to explain why the south German Reformers destroyed images while Luther refused to do so and why the southern cities allegedly exceeded those of the north in their zeal to integrate the popular drive for emancipation with struggle for the Gospel.[90] Much of the detail is fascinating to specialist scholars: for example, the passages on the *devotio moderna,* German capitalism, and witchcraft. So too is the *pietas,* which seeks to tell the story from the curious viewpoint of the then recently founded University of Tübingen. Nevertheless, the effect could be to exaggerate the more esoteric and tenuous intellectual continuities behind the Reformation at the expense of more obvious and mundane considerations, such as the popular attraction to the "new" biblicism and the force of German nationalist antipapalism.[91] Here and elsewhere is a danger that history of ideas developed along such academic and intellectual lines may end by removing itself from social history, where Febvre rightly wanted to see it develop.

Study of the cities has not excluded all other problems from the minds of those who since the mid-1960s have investigated the social history of the Reformation in central Europe. In Chrisman's analysis of Strasbourg we already encountered another highly important theme: the impact of printing on religious and cultural history. This theme goes back to the beginning, because both Luther and Foxe regarded printing as a John the Baptist, a providential forerunner of the rediscovery of true Christian doctrine.[92] Using G. W. Panzer's annals of the press, Ranke analyzed the output of popular pamphlets (*Flugschriften*).[93] Oscar Schade in the 1850s and O. C. Clemen soon after 1900 reprinted multivolume selections.[94] In the late 1940s Henri Gravier and others wrote intelligently on this aspect of Luther's mission.[95] Since then Elizabeth L. Eisenstein surveyed, on a wide basis, the whole range of the printing press as an agency which "reset the stage" for the Renaissance, Reformation, and scientific revolution.[96]

From the viewpoint of printing and publication, the Reformation may well be the most difficult to study of these great changes. Confronted by the huge mass of "hard" evidence in print, we hardly need to be devout Marxists to experience that supreme temptation—to make the Reformation wholly or largely dependent on a technological revolution. Yet even this factor operated within a web of social limitations which should modify our urge toward simplification. In fact, cities were decisively converted to Protestantism by the arrival of preachers and personalities, even though their mental climates had been affected by printed books and pamphlets. We cannot effectively disentangle the press from the pulpit. The pulpit remained what it had been for centuries: the primary influence on a still largely illiterate public. The printers, who had published best-selling collections of sermons before Luther, were still in no small measure intent to reproduce what had already been delivered from the pulpit, or was at least in tune with fashionable preaching. Furthermore, in Bohemia a smaller-scale national Reformation had been accomplished before the invention of printing.

If historians of the Reformation have been consistently attentive to the social importance of printing, they have tended to ignore until very recently the role and influence of women in the movement. Although this topic was raised in the English context by Keith Thomas and Patrick Collinson,[97] it was not until the 1970s—during wider movements in the historical profession—that this neglected aspect of social history began to receive the attention it deserves.

The scarcity of information about women in the standard historical works was remedied to some extent by Roland Bainton's three volumes of studies of individual women of different nations and various religious persuasions (1971, 1973, 1977).[98] Although he concentrated on women who had inherited, or acquired through marriage, positions of social prominence, Bainton also gave some attention to the lower orders of society by using Foxe, whose 358 Henrician and Marian Protestant martyrs included forty-eight women, of whom only two were gentlewomen. Bainton's work is invaluable as a sourcebook of biographical data, but it makes no attempt at the kind of systematic social analysis which characterizes more recent essays on the subject, such as Miriam Chrisman's work on the women of Strasbourg, Charmarie Blaisdell's study of Renée of France, and Nancy Roelker's essays on French noblewomen.[99]

A more ambitious attempt at systematic analysis is Natalie Zemon Davis's "City Women and Religious Change" (1975), which offers some generalizations, on the basis of her study of Calvinism in the French cities, about the Reformation's appeal to women, the part of women in religious change, and the Reformation's effect on women's status and roles. Concluding that Protestant religious commitment was not a desperate reaction to a sense of futility and restriction but "seems to have complemented in a new sphere the scope and independence that the women's lives already had," Davis provided a sensitive and balanced assessment of the genuine gains and opportunities Protestantism brought to women, the real limitations which remained on their roles and activities, and the losses it caused—including disappearance of the celibate alternative.[100] Her illuminating comments on the influence of factors such as learning and literacy, widowhood, and independent employment, underline the urgent need for comparable studies of other sectors and regions of reform.

A most welcome addition to the debate is Steven Ozment's *When Fathers Ruled* (1983)—a study of the patriarchal family in German and Swiss Protestantism—which challenges some of the prevalent orthodoxies about male domination and female subservience.[101] A comprehensive analysis of women and the Reformation, however, remains a desideratum, and it is likely to be some years before it becomes genuinely possible. Among the reasons for optimism about the future of such studies is the realization that available data are not limited, as in some other areas of history, to social elites. Especially significant in this respect is the wealth of material provided by Foxe and the other martyrologists about the responses of ordinary women—a source as yet barely tapped.

Recent years have witnessed a prolific growth of studies in social history of the Reformation focused on the rich area of popular culture and folk religion. Here especially there has been a welcome interaction between scholars of different national traditions and an increasingly fruitful interchange between social history and the social sciences. This area has been illuminated by major research into magic, witchcraft, and popular superstition, such as Keith Thomas's *Religion and the Decline of Magic* (1971),[102] a remarkable work which recreates in detail the folk religion of a population still largely rural. It outlines the attack of the Lollards on exorcism and consecration of physical objects, which these pre-Reformation critics compared with magic spells and condemned as ineffective. This denunciation foreshadowed to a surprising degree the Protestant assault on quasi-sacramental magic, which led to the abolition by the Edwardian government of extreme unction, acts of penance, holy water, the sign of the cross, and similar rites. Eventually the Elizabethan Puritans came to assert the uselessness of ceremonies in general. Coupling

Catholic ritual with magic, the Reformation thus became also a destroyer of folk religion. By 1971 this theme was by no means novel, yet its revival by Thomas encouraged others to reexamine the whole complex of ideas on a European basis, and during the 1970s a number of books and articles appeared on French and German parallels.[103]

It became increasingly desirable to evaluate a subculture which, on the level of everyday life in villages and small towns, seemed often to have overshadowed Christian belief. The subject cannot be confined to actual witch cults: more generally a beneficent "white magic" made a powerful appeal in an era of notable epidemics and agricultural catastrophes. Whereas medieval persecutors burned many witches in spasmodic campaigns, both Reformation and Counter-Reformation gave rise to forceful reeducation calculated to expunge non-Christian beliefs from the popular mind.

Regarding folk religion, a sensational contribution came from Gerald Strauss in 1978, *Luther's House of Learning*.[104] Most of this volume is devoted to Lutheran pedagogy and will attract our attention later. But its last three chapters study in depth the efforts of German Lutheran governments and clergy to indoctrinate their populations as a whole. This they attempted by ceaseless preaching and catechizing, followed by periodic visitations to examine the results in both schools and parishes.

The voluminous reports on these visitations still remain almost entirely in manuscript and had not before Strauss's work been presented on such a scale. Covering most of the Lutheran principalities at fairly frequent intervals from the mid-sixteenth to the mid-seventeenth centuries, they provide a most consistent impression of failure. A singularly impartial interpreter, Strauss attributed much of this failure to the direct, harsh, and overhasty means by which the Lutheran propaganda drive sought to eradicate the comforting if superstitious folk religion. The visitation reports themselves provide a wealth of information on this world of "cunning women," crystal gazers, casters of spells, operators of the evil eye, distributors of potions and herbs, ringers of bells to ward off storms: all such practices had met with easy tolerance from the medieval parish clergy. On the side of the peasants and inhabitants of small towns, there is ample evidence of sullen resistance, bored apathy toward preachers who talked over their heads, and refusal to learn the Lutheran catechism. Conversely, the pastors, somewhat bureaucratized as servants of the princely states and progressively distanced from their flocks by rising standards of education, failed to comprehend the popular mind and showed total contempt for the manifest superstition, ignorance, and loose living of their parishioners.

The picture Strauss derived from the visitation records is emphatically not motivated by anti-Protestant prejudices. Indeed, he demonstrated that the governments and clergy of Catholic states such as Bavaria and Austria encountered the same problems when, under the impetus of the Counter-Reformation, they applied methods of indoctrination strikingly similar to those of the Lutherans.[105] Here Strauss had been to some extent forestalled by John Bossy's researches into Catholic life at the parish level elsewhere.[106] Strauss was also aware that the complexities of the German Lutheran world went beyond a mere clash between godly ministers and the old, underground religion. To suppose, for example, that German peasants, overworked for six days a week, would voluntarily spend their Sunday afternoons undergoing instruction on the catechism betrayed a fund of clerical optimism at great variance with Lutheran theology. Doubtless we should spare some pity for both sides. Do modern admirers of the popular religion expect educated clergymen of that day to have baptized witch doctoring as good Christianity? Must they not see something in the eighteenth-century view that the Reformation represented an early phase of the Enlightenment? We find it difficult to envisage the actual situation as quite so uniformly dark as the visitation reports at first seem to suggest. Strauss pointed out that the major cities exempted themselves from these visitations and might somewhat have lightened the darkness had they been included. He also remarked that there must have been at least some sincere, practicing Lutherans, perhaps implying that they must have been very few.[107]

Yet, does the written record tell everything? Despite these consistent clerical condemnations of the laity, we can never know, even approximately, what percentage of the population deserved this treatment. Were the Germans so much more degraded than other people, whose reputations were not adversely affected by spotlights? Certainly we may not laugh off such a graphic mass of evidence, yet we are entitled to reflect that later Lutheranism improved greatly on this performance, and thence we may ask the real key questions. When did things start changing for the better? Was the Enlightenment needed to enforce the Reformation?

Inquiry into popular culture and folk religion is concerned with both proletarian and middle-class outlooks, popular observances and magic in relation to official Christianity, the exercise and effects of church discipline, and localized cults, confraternities, and sects. Though preoccupied by tensions between clergy and laity, and still more by those between "higher" and "lower" cultures, it has little interest in Marxist materialism, because it is so deeply attracted to the "mentalities" of the people which, at least until recently, most Marxist historians regarded as superstitious irrelevances.

It has now become clear that the ancestry of these studies is not restricted to modern investigations into witchcraft but dates back to the folklorists, who provided data from the mid–eighteenth century on. During the 1930s numerous works appeared on the popular religion of the Middle Ages, together with studies of peasant belief like that of Max Rumpf (1933), who described the German rural concept of a *Bauerngott*, the divinity who looked after peasants, as opposed to the "standard" medieval image of God as feudal king.[108] By appropriate rites peasants could enlist the aid of the *Bauerngott* in their ceaseless struggle against crop failures, animal diseases, pestilence, and famine. In addition to their obvious need for material insurance, the agrarian classes felt themselves standing between supernatural forces, evil as well as good, so their malaise became also spiritual.

Both folklorists and liturgists have looked at that sector of popular religion which impinged on—and was partly derived from—the liturgical religion of the Catholic Church. Here stretches a picturesque jungle of observances, ranging from one locality to another, and from near-conformity to boisterous sub-Christian performances initiated by the laity and already in danger of condemnation by medieval reformists such as Nicholas of Cusa.[109] This "folklorized ritual" became especially prominent during Holy Week and at Easter, when a variety of realistic theatrical representations occurred in church, though not in any official liturgy. In parts of Germany Christ rose on Ascension Day in the form of a statue passing through a hole in the church roof, through which a puppet Devil subsequently crashed down to the inferno amid the noise of rattles. On Whitsunday a wooden dove representing the Holy Spirit was lowered through the same aperture to commemorate his descent on the Apostles, accompanied by tongues of fire in the form of burning paper, or small wafers representing Christ's presence in the Eucharist. Though equally allowed and shared by the clergy, there were rites even more remote, such as the ecclesiastically sanctioned children's game of the Boy Bishop, who, having undergone a mock election, was duly robed, preached a mock sermon, and bestowed episcopal blessing.

Beneficent magic arose in such forms as the crucifix raised from the holy sepulcher on Easter morning, which was believed to heal the sick. Likewise, the palms of the Palm Sunday liturgy, having been duly blessed, developed a protective magic to guard houses against summer storms; and water, blessed in church on the feast of Saint Blasius, was believed to cure throat infections and cattle diseases because this saint was the special patron of horses and cattle. Exorcism and ritual blessings were also in order. Yet certain superstitious usages crossed even the tolerant boundaries drawn by the medieval Church when they involved the sacrilegious use of consecrated hosts as charms to secure love or make a fortune. Sacramentals, as opposed to sacraments, were recommended by the popular preacher Geiler von Kaysersberg as a form of counter-magic; and although others doubted whether sacramentals worked *ex opere operato,* Cardinal Bellarmine later thought it probable that they did.

All these and many other beliefs constituted a vast penumbra around the ministrations of the Church, and, following the medieval critics, the Protestant Reformers naturally sought to modify or expunge them, although apparently with doubtful success. As various scholars are likewise asking of the equally "repressive" Counter-Reformation, did these "cleansing" events of the sixteenth and seventeenth centuries create a new and more pious sort of Christian? Did that age of policing by clerics and magistrates for the first time Christianize the masses? Here is the ultimate query of the "new" social history, one far from irrelevant in regard to our subject, although unlikely to find answers inspiring general satisfaction.

A book which helped revive interest in these aspects during the early 1960s was Jacques Toussaert's *Le Sentiment religieux en Flandre à la fin du Moyen Age,* which argues that during the fifteenth century the Flemish population adhered in large part to pagan and pre-Christian beliefs.[110] The crucial year 1971 saw not only the work of Keith Thomas but the equally seminal contribution by Jean Delumeau, *Le Catholicisme entre Luther et Voltaire.*[111] In parallel, John Bossy stimulated further interest in such problems by a series of original articles on the Counter-Reformation, published from 1970 to 1975, suggesting that Tridentine parochial discipline weakened the bonds of natural kinship as well as those of the religious fraternities.[112]

Delumeau and Pierre Chaunu developed the thesis most relevant to historians of the Reformation, that both Protestantism and Tridentine Catholicism were essentially efforts by "orthodox" Christianity to suppress the primitive folk religion.[113] This substantial episode seemed to justify the recent revival of that venerable American term *acculturation,* defined as early as 1904 by the *Century Dictionary* as "the process of adoption and assimilation of foreign cultural elements."[114] Rescued from mere colonial situations, *acculturation* is nowadays also applied to the interaction between learned and popular elements or classes in the same culture. There has also developed a clearer understanding that such confrontations can involve a two-way process, whereby—as with the medieval "penumbra"—the popular culture also penetrates and permeates official religion.

During the late 1970s further publications drew attention to this range of problems. In his *Popular Culture in Early Modern Europe,* Peter Burke provided a vivacious survey based on immensely wide reading across most of the national cultures, stressing their varieties of structure and experience.[115] He described the withdrawal of the upper classes from popular culture, a process occurring much earlier in western than in eastern Europe. It occurred along with deliberate campaigns to banish popular superstitions and festivities, conducted first by both Catholic and Protestant clergy, and then from around 1650 mainly by lay action.

This topic was more closely investigated by Robert Muchembled in his *Culture populaire et culture des élites dans la France moderne* (1978), a work which ranges widely from the fifteenth to the eighteenth centuries, but draws its historical examples from a limited area of northeastern France and the neighboring border of Flanders.[116] Muchembled argued that the rural religion—with its magical rites arising from the need to insure against calamity and propitiate natural powers—reached its greatest height during the century 1450–1550. Thereafter, both Catholic and Protestant reformations sought its destruction, partly by associating it with witchcraft. In France the judicature and other organs of the State joined the attack.[117] These hostile forces also furthered acculturation in France by a general campaign against both popular festivities and sexual offenses. In addition, an orthodoxy based on fear and patriarchal rule resulted in misogyny and the devaluation of women, many of whom had been the chief transmitters of rural magic. The full effects of this assault became manifest during the seventeenth and eighteenth centuries, when, in Muchembled's view, they dwarfed the clash between Catholics and Protestants. They also resulted in a dull "mass culture," which, although marked by an improvement in popular literacy, nevertheless was only a thin parody of the old learned culture.

The time has not yet come to attempt definitive judgments on theories of acculturation as applied to early modern social history, and we feel unqualified to venture far into this unfinished project. Muchembled's thesis cannot without further research be presumed to apply closely to the whole of France, a country with endless regional variations. He depicted the collision of the two class-cultures in terms too dramatic to apply to countries such as England and those of Scandinavia, where authority enforced acculturation less violently and a relatively mild and slow process of public education rather than persecution reduced a picturesque mental world to boring nonentity. Moreover, the acceptance of so tragic a theory even for France must involve value judgments unlikely to command anything like general acceptance. Are not social historians in danger of falling into sentimentality, idealizing rural magic, and banishing any talk of "popular superstition" as obscene?

On the relationship of acculturation to our subject, some historical criticisms appear almost inevitable. Considering the enormous social and political effects of the struggle between Catholics and Protestants, especially those which continued through the seventeenth century, it would seem irrational to banish the Reformation to a lower status than that bestowed on acculturation, so many aspects of which remain disputable and which still demands more plentiful facts and reevaluation of much unfamiliar or half-explored evidence. As R. W. Scribner suggested in a recent review, the alleged timing of the process seems unduly restricted, because acculturation had been operating in the Middle Ages.[118] Witches had long been extensively if intermittently burned, and that highbrow reformist Nicholas of Cusa had busily campaigned against the popular "religion" a century before the Reformation. Nevertheless, the problems posed by the confrontation of class-cultures cannot be ignored: here are probabilities and possibilities demanding sober investigation over much larger areas than those so far covered.

Concerning the popular cult itself, findings vary so much from place to place that they force observers back to regional conclusions, especially because certain beliefs seem to have been shared by all or several classes in a given area. This discovery has led to studies on the localization of particular cults, especially those of shrines, relics, pilgrimages, and apparitions. Although reminiscent of aboriginal "holy" areas—like those legally recognized in Australia—such cults persisted throughout medieval and modern times and often in sophisticated communities which thus discovered and apotheosized their own identities. In 1980 R. C. Trexler investigated the phenomenon in his *Public Life in Renaissance Florence,* and W. A. Christian considered it in his *Local Religion in Sixteenth Century Spain* (1981).[119] Far more controversial than either is Lionel Rothkrug's *Religious Practices and Collective Perceptions: Hidden Homologies in the Renaissance and Reformation* (1980).[120]

Rothkrug's chain of events begins with the Franks, who on their conversion to Christianity ceased to bury grave goods in their own tombs and transferred their offerings to the sepulchers of sainted abbots, bishops, and kings. These shrines, eventually enclosed in churches, attracted increasing flows of devotees, and, because Germany notoriously lacked indigenous saints, they received many relics of foreign saints, commonly brought from Rome.

The resultant popular multiplication of shrines based on these imports ensured that the vast majority were founded in the settled south, whereas in north Germany, which was colonized later, shrine religion never came to dominate the rural areas. In fact, the amassing of relics was long discouraged by the Cistercian and Premonstratensian monks,

who converted and civilized the northern territories. This regional differentiation produced in the religion of the people two radically different
emphases, which persisted through the medieval centuries. Strengthened
by a crusading aristocracy and firmly professing loyalty to the concept
of Holy Roman Empire, the ancient relic worship of the south developed
a strongly communal spirit. By contrast, the north, especially when exposed to the influence of the numerous Beguines, the Rhineland mystics,
and the *Devotio Moderna,* cultivated a more individualist type of spirituality and brought forth new idioms of devotion, such as the rosary
confraternities of the fifteenth century.[121] Long before Luther, the northern process of salvation had become detached from terrestrial controls:
it was regarded as a relationship between God and the individual, and
one which owed far less than the religion of the shrines to the participation
of whole communities in the divine plan.

Apart from one or two areas where special factors existed, this broad
division persisted into the sixteenth century and, in Rothkrug's view,
created the map of the Reformation. The northern areas accepted Protestantism with its congenial accent on personal piety, while in the south
the shrine mentality of the countryside, dominated by a conservative
aristocracy, naturally tended to reject the new religion. Nevertheless, most
southern cities at first welcomed the Reformation, because their interests
and outlook differed from those of their rural neighbors. Proud of the
freedoms they had won and swollen by generations of "democratic"
refugees from the country, the southern cities resisted aristocracy and
episcopal power. They also rejected the romantic appeal of the empire.
Within them developed that familiar city Reformation which soon felt
affinities with the Reformation of the Swiss towns led by Zwingli and
Calvin. Penetrating deeply into secular affairs, the Reformation thus divided the south and linked itself with the urban opposition to aristocracy
and empire.

This scenario is apt to sound farfetched when thus baldly summarized; yet, presented with lively if undisciplined erudition and accompanied by an intensively researched catalog and map of shrines and by
an imaginative re-creation of regional mentalities, it assumes a certain
compulsive fascination—at all events until we test the weak links and
review the counterarguments. In addition to the north-versus-south division, Rothkrug similarly established further frontiers, in particular those
separating German from French religion. In France, the monarch played
a crucial role in the popular religion. Each king derived sacred powers
from his long line of royal ancestors, who had been exalted to a quasi-
prophetic eminence by both learned writers and popular believers. Until
the French Revolution, these *rois thaumaturges* continued to be legiti-

mized by religion. By contrast, despite the alleged sanctity of the Holy Roman Empire, its medieval emperors, merely elected from various ducal families, lacked this hereditary magic. Meanwhile, France's unique royal inheritance was augmented by French leadership in the Crusades and still more by the nation's apotheosis of the Virgin as coredeemer.[122] Possessing this centralized, communal type of Christianity, the French masses felt relatively little attraction toward the personal, individualist modes of Lutheranism. All these considerations lead Rothkrug to insist that medieval and premedieval patterns of observance and belief determined the expansion or failure of the Reformation across Europe.

The difficulties with Rothkrug's theory may be described under two headings: some different factual evidence concerning German religion, and some problems of presentation and methodology.[123] In regard to the first, one might well question the sharpness of Rothkrug's division between north and south Germany. Rothkrug himself noticed that Westphalia in the north remained largely Catholic, and Württemberg in the south went Protestant. More important, although pilgrimage shrines were indeed far more numerous in the south, many of the most famous were in the north and the lower Rhineland: Wilsnack in Brandenburg, Kevelaer in Gelderland, Roermond in Limburg, Echternach in the duchy of Luxembourg; together, of course, with the venerable Christian centers of Trier and Cologne. Few southern shrines equaled the fame and mass attendance commanded by any of these, which were admittedly not rural shrines, yet presumably nonetheless influential. Moreover, the sacralizing of local politics extended to cities in the north as much as the south. This has been recently demonstrated by Heinz Schilling's researches on northern towns and Scribner's on places in central Germany.[124] Concern for the city as a sacred community, and the frequency with which secular conflict went into partnership with Protestant movements, seem at least as obvious in the north as in the south.

On another factual issue, did Rothkrug accurately characterize Lutheranism itself when he insisted on a "subjective individualism" linking it to the northern piety of the fifteenth century? If any component of the early Reformation inherited such characteristics, it was surely not Luther's movement but the "spiritualist" wing of radicalism, springing from Karlstadt, Münzer, and a host of lesser enthusiasts. This sort of popular religion spread successfully even as Lutheranism came to appear unduly magisterial, depersonalized, and "communal." After all, Luther spent a great part of his energies not creating but combating subjective individualism, and the Lutheran churches flourished on a positive urban and collectivist spirit which amounted to far more than a revolt against relic worship. Then, in regard to the ultimately Catholic stance of southern

Germany, must we not attach infinitely more importance to the brilliant missions of Peter Canisius and his colleagues in 1556–1569 than to the ancient stereotype of a shrine religion?[125] Canisius presented a truly "modern" force, recreating and not merely recalling old traditions. All in all, a rigorous application of Rothkrug's arguments succeeds only in betraying serious weaknesses in factual substructure.

Rigor is the keyword, because Rothkrug appears to have dispensed with all proximate, commonsense causes and governing factors of the Reformation in favor of a unitary, overriding pattern emerging from the medieval and still earlier past. His "right" answer seems to rise up on a conveyor belt from the deepest basement of the historical factory! Here indeed is a determinist plan akin to those envisaged by Joachim of Floris and Marx, but in another sense this plan is revealed as Hegelian: it represents the domination of ideas over the secular world. Even the commonplace political motivations recognized by Sleidan disappear or are subordinated to ideological (but usually sub-Christian) forms of devotion. Indeed, the rational elements of religion, whether Catholic or Protestant, are crushed by a series of cults, most of them irrational and overimaginative. These doubtless did flourish in many medieval minds, but they may well prove far too weak to sustain the crucial sixteenth-century role allotted to them, far too lacking in credibility and relevance to the recorded teachings of Christ, the Apostles, and the major saints and doctors of the Church. To explain the Reformation climax, Rothkrug seemed to need neither the great missionary personalities and systematizers—such as Luther, Calvin, and Canisius—nor the rulers with their *cuius regio eius religio.*

Though extremely difficult to verify beyond doubt, the basic theory concerning shrines and relic worship may well have some substance, yet it cannot reasonably be accepted as the sole leitmotiv of this complicated symphony, wherein so many better-documented themes compete for our attention. And concerning countries other than Germany—and in a limited measure France—this theory is even further from explaining the course of the Reformation, although it may confirm another approach to the problem, which many English and French historians have been strenuously pursuing over several decades. This approach examines not only national forces but regional mutations. Although outside Germany it has little concern for the shrine cults and discovers situations far more complex than Rothkrug's north-versus-south division of Germany, this regionalist inquiry is necessary to explain the evidence arising in both France and England.

In short, to read Rothkrug is to have some stimulating but vertiginous experiences in historical literature, because his ideas are presented more in the manner of a poetic exercise than in terms of a historical structure based on solid pillars of evidence. Corners are cut, seemingly outrageous generalizations made, esoteric explanations preferred to more obvious ones, affinities between very different elements "discovered" with remarkable ingenuity and versatile learning.

Such avant-garde studies have naturally attracted more immediate attention, but it would be misleading to suppose that they now dominate the field. Having examined numerous books and articles which appeared since 1979, we conclude that the great majority still attack traditional problems and would have startled nobody had they appeared twenty or thirty years ago. This impression of a basic conservatism is modified but by no means destroyed by a perusal of two up-to-date guides to the present state of research, both of which pay special regard to modish problems and seek to indicate the ways ahead. One of these, compiled by Rainer Wohlfeil, concerns the Reformation in Germany: its successive episodes, terminology and concepts, problems and controversies.[126] The other, edited by Steven Ozment, is strongly American in flavor but broad in coverage.[127] It divides historiography of the Reformation into sixteen topics, each with a specialized discussion culminating in a select bibliography of recent books and articles. Yet even in this guide a majority of items refine long-established themes, much as historians have been doing throughout the first six or seven decades of our century. We continue to learn more about the political and social ideas of the leading Reformers, the spread of Anabaptism, the social and intellectual development of various Continental cities, the Zwinglian Reformation in the context of European church history, Staupitz's influence on Luther, the Peasants' Revolt.

Compared with the immense breadth of American writing, especially in social history, the present scene in Britain appears solid and industrious, but for the most part restricted to the old national interests. Notable exceptions do occur, for example, in the broad yet deep researches of R. W. Scribner in German urban history and more recently in the social iconography of Reformation pamphlets and the relationship between official and popular religion.[128] Other scholars have done significant work on the Reformation in France and the Netherlands.[129] Nevertheless, many British scholars are still finding more urgent tasks in their own rich archives than in broad Continental themes or European intellectual history. And surely, when fresh and perhaps crucial data can still be discovered and integrated, archival demands may legitimately be preferred.

During recent years, international conferences and cooperative enterprises have usually strengthened our grasp of familiar subjects rather than encouraged radical changes of outlook. The valuable discussions held in 1980 at Tübingen concerned pamphlets as a mass medium of the Reformation period, yet this subject has occupied many historians and bibliographers over the last twenty years or more.[130] Much the same can be said of the London conference of 1978, which attracted leading scholars from Germany and America and produced the substantial volume called *The Urban Classes, the Nobility and the Reformation*.[131] On the other hand, the continued vitality of avant-garde research is indicated in an international collection of innovating papers edited by Kaspar von Greyerz.[132]

The likelihood that these studies will continue to flourish along with more traditional pursuits suggests the need for a balanced and judicious response from historians of the Reformation. We should certainly lose by rejecting alliances with the developing social sciences, if only because the writing of history has always advanced by discovering new questions as well as new facts. Nevertheless, there are reasons for caution. In the last resort, historians should uphold the realistic methods they properly understand and not, like Melanchthon, try to force their discipline to undertake problems it cannot solve. Historians of the Reformation can afford less than any others to set aside the prosaic routines of investigation and proof so laboriously evolved over the last four centuries. Sociologists and anthropologists have given us many valuable concepts, but their objectives and methods still tend to differ from ours.

So long as it remains our aim to provide such documented truths and probabilities as our integrity and talents allow, the demands for sober evidence, just balance, and sensitivity to pluralist rather than simplistic ideological explanations must remain constant and unremitting. "Bright ideas," hypotheses of all sorts, must not without powerful verification be promoted to the realm of objective realities. Our world is not that of the film industry's special effects: we cannot escape into a surrealist wonderland where the old laws no longer operate. We need to explain without gross simplifying and generalize without amputating the stubborn facts to fit them into procrustean beds. Ours is a rigorous yet earthy discipline, and on its power to imbue the social sciences with these same tough attributes the future of a subject like the Reformation will in part depend.

In the final analysis, the anthropological approach's claims to represent a new age for studies of the Reformation seem by no means overwhelming. This fresh approach examines in depth only one of many sequences in the story: the popular cults and their involved relationships with ecclesiastical religion and authority. These features demand continuing research, but we are not obliged to regard them as deposing the higher cultures and more intellectual activities of the sixteenth century. All the same, this latest enlargement of our field forms yet one more illustration of the undiminished fecundity and perennial fascination shown by the mighty theme of this book.

Epilogue:
A Living Tradition

In beginning our work we thought this book most likely to interest students of the Reformation and its most direct results. We felt like historians of the Reformation who had already written on the sixteenth-century movement and wanted to enlarge our scope by appending an account of its historiography. Yet, as we progressed we saw our subject in another and more important role: as a window on the West, a major point of access to the developing Western mind through the last five centuries. We embraced the Reformation as something greater than a complex of events with related sequels. Broadly and deeply understood, its historiography could become one of the brighter searchlights exploring all subsequent periods. By any reckoning, the Reformation has proved a giant among the great international movements of modern times. We had been examining no mere ideology excogitated by a few individuals but a surviving, pervasive, and seemingly immortal force. As a complex of ideals, the Reformation has triumphantly survived the so-called Reformation period without fading into a mere academic ghost. So long as people look back on the Western tradition, they will be compelled to study both the movement and its historiography with purposes and methods far transcending those of the historical textbook.

Why did the Reformation attain this stature? Not so much because it arose with a great man, but rather for the reverse reason: that it was never swallowed by a single personality, or even a personally conceived ideology. Luther never would have become a Protestant Pope: he specifically denounced the idea of a "Lutheran" cult, such as some of his modern worshipers have threatened to create. Never limited to saints or intellectuals, the Reformation has been a historical experience shared— although in greatly varied degrees—by millions of men and women. For good or ill, it induced countless humble people to think for themselves and make decisions which, as they supposed, would determine their future in this world and the life to come. In the end many let others think for them, but the experience nevertheless passed into popular as well as educated minds of the Western world, so that in each succeeding age it has proved an ingredient, a catalyst. Although the movement started as a dispute over doctrine and authority in Western Catholicism, each generation sought to enlarge and diversify its issues according to developing needs of their day. Eluding the "pure" philosophers, it has yielded more of its inwardness to historians, most of all to those who investigated with mingled sympathy and detachment its multifarious and perplexing legacies. This is the slowly revolving kaleidoscope through which we have peered through the preceding chapters.

In that undertaking we have observed that the issues the Reformation aroused have at no stage been solely religious, and that even the religious arguments never remained merely two-sided, because almost simultaneously with Luther's revolt the radical sectarians ensured that its very nature and legacies should be multilateral. Well within its first century the Protestant movement encountered numerous other reactions and tensions which both hampered and remodeled it: for example, Tridentine Catholicism, rival nationalisms, class conflicts, and cosmological speculations, together with the eventual recovery of those rationalist trends which derived from the Italian Renaissance.

The rationalist perspective assumed consciously historical form at the hands of men like Bodin and La Popelinière, observers who evolved concepts of history and historiography different from those of the early Protestant Reformers. These Frenchmen and their followers, such as Camden, perceived—as Sleidan had before them—the obvious limitations of a church history abstracted from its secular context. In addition, they abandoned Melanchthon's claim that the historian should seek to read the very purposes of God as revealed in human affairs and the tides of history. Armed with a fuller understanding of multiple causation, they secularized the task itself, making it once more a realistic analysis of the ways of men. Thus, from quite early days history of the Reformation started to lose its Catholic-versus-Protestant bilateralism and began a broadening that would be accelerated by the Enlightenment and still further by manifold intellectual developments of the nineteenth century.

In view of its sensational diversification since 1800, it is tempting for a modern historian to strip the movement of its strictly religious components and regard it as a time bomb, the major effects of which appeared long after the mechanism had been primed. Yet such an image would be simplistic; from the very beginning the Reformation also operated—as in education—through gradualist, organic processes unsuited to metaphors involving explosion and destruction. By the same token, its mass effects should not be judged by reference to the narrow fanatics who once loomed so large on its surfaces. Despite the frustrations and sufferings arising out of intolerance, division, and warfare, the Reformation did contribute creatively to the extension of Western mental horizons. By something resembling a miracle it did not, as Bossuet supposed, fly apart like an overheated machine into thousands of irresponsible sects. Amid our present enthusiasm for investigating the sects, we should not overlook the facts that they could not have suited all types of minds and that the more permanent and influential among them were those which came to value restraints and thus to match the social moderation of the major Protestant churches. Further, the Reformation's ultimate effect was not a general denial of traditional Christian values, even though its own early historians and ideologists openly denied some of the religious and philosophical values which had been imposed on Western Christians from Hildebrand to Aquinas, a period which Protestant thought regarded as beset by satanic but impermanent forces and by no means as part of a venerable Christian norm stretching back to apostolic times. It was left to the nineteenth century to idealize the Middle Ages.

At no time were the legatees of the Reformation swamped by Italianate rationalism, although some maintained a dialogue with its champions. On the contrary, Protestant intellectuals implanted some strong religious values within and on the frontiers of the eighteenth-century Enlightenment. We have criticized the philosophes who misinterpreted history by greeting the Reformation as the forerunner of their own movement while crassly ignoring or misinterpreting its religious content. Yet throughout much of Europe the mainstream Reformation which moderated the sects also tempered the political wing of the Enlightenment, helping it limit its head-on collision with clericalism to a rather brief phase of the French Revolution. In other words, throughout much of Europe the Reformation legacy acted as a peacekeeping force between these immoderate antagonists. It might reasonably be contended that in modern times the compartmentation of a diversified Christianity has afforded better protection against such disasters than any monolithic Christendom could possibly have provided.

Nevertheless, historians' critiques developed further as Protestantism adapted itself to its secular surroundings. Certainly it did absorb elements of that environment and so toned down the lurid images of its past. Despite the ferocious years of the French Revolution, the secular yoke of the Enlightenment proved in most places far from uniformly oppressive. In England, for example, it allowed John Wesley, an Anglican clergyman, a lifetime of independent preaching and church organizing amid an evangelical fervor derived largely from Luther yet equipped with Arminian views of grace. And this mingling of Protestant and Enlightenment influences was also observable in most former citadels of Calvinism, which in the eighteenth century assumed leadership of the Enlightenment: Amsterdam, Geneva, Edinburgh, and many towns of New England.

On the other hand, the Roman Church did not at this stage soften its historical attitudes toward the Reformation. Having within its reduced territories restored discipline under the papal monarchy, Rome set its face against this world of multilateral change. Still commanding a heartfelt devotion among peasantries, rural aristocracies, and reformed religious orders, it preserved its integrity, though at a high cost. Rejecting compromise even in the most debatable areas of doctrine, it countered doubts with defiant assertions against Protestantism and rationalism alike. The successes and failures of this modern Catholicism, which have so considerably modified the later stages of Reformation history, were themselves as deeply affected by national traditions and needs as those of Protestantism. Roman Catholicism successfully identified itself with Polish and Irish nationalisms. Having anesthetized Italy and stifled its hopes of regaining a lost intellectual supremacy, Catholicism lost what remained of its influence on the glittering urban culture of France. In time, along with its Anglican imitators, it won over some neo-Romantics in England, together with many other refugees from nineteenth-century individualism and industrialism. At the same time, it reinforced its strength in the Hispanic cultures on both sides of the Atlantic. However, Catholicism then lacked the mental and economic resources to inspire a rebirth of social reform or solve the intractable politicoeconomic problems of Latin America. Meanwhile, in the west European and North American intellectual worlds, expanding claims of the Catholic hierarchy, which culminated in 1870 with the declaration of papal infallibility, became self-defeating. Nevertheless, amid the decline of the Tridentine spirit there has arisen through the twentieth century a sincere if hesitant Catholic ecumenism, which has struck a responsive chord among the Reformation's heirs. These more charitable and percipient attitudes have not been limited to historians or even intellectuals. Nowadays to praise them seems banal, yet to undervalue them would be to overlook one of the more significant episodes in Christian history. All the same, the wisdom born of historical experience seems scarcely enough to solve the old problem of authority.

Having so long reflected these changing patterns of Christian opinion, the historiography of the Reformation has since about 1930 entered some methodological phases little related to current religious politics. It has tuned its instruments more finely to observe events and ideas in smaller social and geographic contexts. Whether within the German city, French province, or English county, this grass-roots history affords some experiences more pleasurable to writers and readers than any mere re-telling of the old politicoecclesiastical stories. It bids us walk beside the still waters of archival research, and sometimes it achieves definitive if limited conclusions and a sense of intimate contact with particular individuals and groups. Yet this local antiquarianism is not self-sufficient, and Lucien Febvre—however wrong in rejecting "specificity," was right in urging us to control particular fact by developing larger concepts of human society and culture. Normally conservative, historians are now inventing—or rather borrowing—concepts and terms to explore the mental processes of Luther's "common man" and the small communities which the old national and ecclesiastical histories tended to ignore. It was a major step forward when historians began recognizing that the ordinary people of the sixteenth century could boast a mental history, and that the mental life of a seemingly dull province could offer insights of no little significance.

At the other extreme, historians of the Reformation—especially those with an understanding of the Middle Ages—are finding it increasingly possible and desirable to collaborate with theologians, because theologians are increasingly adopting historical approaches and seeing religion, including doctrine itself, in a social as well as transcendental context. This relationship is of particular ongoing importance, for however gratefully we welcome the liberation of studies of the Reformation from narrow and partisan religious concerns and appreciate the broader human vistas which modern scholarship has opened up, we see no reason to alter our basic perception that the central element in the Protestant Reformation was a conscious, essentially religious, mission: to steer Christianity back in line with biblical sources after many centuries of hierarchical manipulation.

Whatever their disciplines and mental habits, it would seem that scholars will gain only superficial and fragmentary glimpses of the Reformation unless they can somehow enter imaginatively into the religious experiences of those who accepted and those who rejected its claims. In such a crucial venture, sensitivity to theological questions can be a decided advantage, yet scholars of Christian persuasion should not imagine that they are automatically guaranteed better access than their uncommitted colleagues, for they are no less likely to be hindered by youthful experiences and present loyalties from apprehending the peculiar quality of Reformation religion. History bears eloquent testimony to the fact that individuals and communities who prize the Christian label may be as far, or farther, removed from the historic traditions of that faith and the spirit of its founder than those who affirm no such allegiance. Historians of the Reformation, whatever their backgrounds and loyalties, ultimately face a common need for a supreme effort of controlled imagination if they are to inform the twentieth century about the men and women of the sixteenth: their hopes, their fears, their most pressing concerns.

To explore half a millennium of historiography of the Reformation is to apprehend a living tradition which in large ways and small continues to inform the present and to pose searching questions for the future. If this exploration has yielded more questions than answers, we may nevertheless on one point be emphatic: we have not written the epitaph of a defunct or even waning enterprise of Western intellectual history.

APPENDIX

NOTES

INDEX

Appendix:
Sins of Omission

In this appendix our first task must be to look back critically at some significant omissions of which the knowledgeable reader will be all too clearly aware and which reviewers will doubtless enumerate. These have resulted in part from the chapter structure which for various good reasons we adopted, but more fundamentally from the unpredictably vast explosion of writing on the Reformation since the Second World War, which has compelled us to avoid, or treat very lightly, a number of aspects and contributions which deserve fuller acknowledgment.

At the outset we should remind the reader of a principle which, with no small effort, we have continuously been seeking to remind ourselves: that we have been writing not a direct analysis of the Reformation itself or even of all forms of its interpretation, but an account of the *historical* writings and opinions which that movement inspired. We have mentioned a number of commentators whose instincts and training were primarily in other disciplines, notably theology. Yet in the study of a movement primarily concerned with religion, frequent reference to theological dimensions cannot be avoided; they often constitute an important sector of some distinctly historical analysis. We have also taken account of the increasing tendency for historical studies to be invaded by concepts from the social sciences, which historians cannot reject without betraying a narrow conservatism. Nevertheless, occasional forays beyond our self-imposed boundaries cannot disguise the fact that our own territory remains incompletely charted. This chapter provides an opportunity to mention some of our reluctant and controversial omissions.

Have we erred, for example, in not according a more important place to the Protestant like movements which preceded Luther, in particular the Hussite Revolution, which, although it did not directly help initiate Luther's movement, provided him with confirmatory arguments just when he needed the support of "modern" history? More significant, the Hussite left wing did much to create the central European sectarian movements which embarrassed Luther and, a century later, survived the collapse of the main Bohemian independence movement at the Battle of the White Mountain. Justifiably, this drama—extending across more than two centuries—has played an essential role in the self-consciousness of the Czech nation. Its historiography has evolved in close association with German scholarship, but it has by no means been subject to German opinion. It found some competent champions: František Palacký crushed Austrian propaganda history by sheer scholarship, and Anton Gindely, the historian of the Thirty Years' War, administered salutary reproofs of another sort to Ranke himself.[1] Although many important items of twentieth-century Czech history are not yet translated into the major languages, a number of the best works have been made available, while the outstanding contributions of Howard Kaminsky, Matthew Spinka, F. G. Heymann, R. R. Betts, Peter Brock, and others were composed in English-speaking countries.[2] In addition, a number of guides to both original and secondary sources enable us to follow the progress of a Bohemian historiography not much different in its techniques from that of the Reformation in the German lands and Western Europe.[3]

Regarding Protestantism in Poland and Hungary, not to mention its somewhat more esoteric forays into Slovenia and Rumania, materials are by no means so extensive. In Poland, always at heart ardently Catholic, the early history of Protestantism has long tended to recede or be pushed into the background. Its main interest lies in the advanced levels of religious toleration under the rule of the Polish nobility. Throughout the sixteenth century and far beyond, Italian Antitrinitarians, German Lutherans, Dutch Mennonites, English Quakers, French Huguenots, and Scottish Presbyterians emigrated to Poland, where in addition the Jewish population developed its influence. This wonderful experiment, already wearing thin by the later seventeenth century, prompted Janusz Tazbir to entitle his scholarly survey *A State without Stakes* (1967).[4] A number of Polish historians are now showing themselves well abreast of modern advances in the social history of religion.[5] The same is the case in Hungary, where Calvinism and its history still maintain a lively existence, especially in Calvinism's old citadel, Debrecen.[6] There the old seminary library contains a remarkable collection of Dutch and English "Puritan" books imported by the many westward-wandering Hungarian scholars of the seventeenth century.

All in all, a potentially great book on the Reformation would cover its history throughout all the lands to the east of Germany and Austria.

But such a work, embracing so many cultures, would surely require a team of scholars. Given a wholly free hand, the talent available in these countries could certainly accomplish the task with up-to-date approaches. Yet, despite the relative freedom of discussion in both Poland and Hungary, the history of religion remains at present neither fashionable nor greatly encouraged. In recent "official" histories, the subject still tends to receive less notice than it warrants.

The close attention we have given to theological questions needs no justification, yet it tends to highlight the fact that other significant intellectual issues have been all too lightly passed over. Have we, for example, too readily dismissed as superficial historians who have accorded the whole Protestant Reformation a subordinate role in the early modern history of the West? This notion does not come exclusively from the "dated" secularists of the last century. It also applies to the well-informed Dutch cultural historian H. A. Enno van Gelder, whose book *The Two Reformations in the Sixteenth Century* appeared twenty years ago.[7] In this broad assessment of the period, the Protestant Reformation becomes the "minor" phenomenon; the "major" transformation is the movement of literary rationalism, beginning in fifteenth-century Italy, developing through Erasmus, and culminating in Rabelais, Shakespeare, Marlowe, Montaigne, and Bodin. Enno van Gelder saw this portentous and multilateral phenomenon—which we encountered in the secularist French thinkers of the late sixteenth century (see Chapter 4)—as the true foundation of the modern Western outlook, represented by the gradual growth of "enlightened" and liberal values over the last three hundred years or more.

This reemphasis, by no means novel, may well command respect on one plane of generalization; yet in terms so unqualified as Enno van Gelder's it simplifies a situation of infinite complexity. One cannot reasonably compare two entities such as rationalism and Reformation in terms of major and minor, as if they were mere physical objects or forces. This alleged major factor arising from the Renaissance operates almost uniquely in the sphere of high culture, indeed of literary culture, taking no account of ordinary lives or popular cultures, to which great interest now attaches. Even on the higher levels, it devalues the immense social and cultural effects of Protestant religion and makes no mention of two other mighty trends: the Counter-Reformation, which soon damped down Italianate rationalism, and the scientific revolution, which was far from a mere outcome of secular humanism.

Enno van Gelder's so-called Major Reformation must surely be regarded as an inchoate, swiftly changing process, a Proteus which created outlooks as diverse and conflicting as those of the prim Christian Platonist Erasmus and that agnostic of the tavern and demimonde ennobled by his splendid flair for language, Christopher Marlowe. Enno van Gelder thus simplified the High Renaissance years as well as the following century, stressing the semipagan glorification of man and the individualism apparent in Machiavelli and Castiglione rather than textually minded scholarship, to which the term *humanist* was then, and should by right still be, applied. This scholarly tradition ran, although less conspicuously, from Valla to Erasmus, and then met Luther's warmest praises as the basis of his own biblical theology. Valla does indeed figure among the cult heroes of the rationalist Major Reformation, but without Enno van Gelder's realization that he stood among the most assured predecessors of both Erasmus and Luther.

Even if we follow Enno van Gelder in regarding a trend so different and shifting as a third "Reformation," we cannot make it into a specifically Christian force mediating between the other two: Catholicism and Protestantism. Few of its figures professed actual atheism, but it tended in the long run to produce a truncated Christianity, a facile moralism wherein Christ and his recorded teaching played but a small part, leaving the tragic aspects of humanity and the universe to its more distinctly Christian rivals. It seems to us no minor circumstance that the Protestant Reformers' efforts to recover the Christianity of Christ were concurrent with this gradual dilution and that accordingly the great mass of men and women continued to be organized in specific churches and sects, from which their "liberation" was neither desired nor, in our view, ostensibly desirable. Nevertheless, Enno van Gelder discussed a reality, and although we desire to abolish his *major* and *minor* terminology, we cannot disregard the fact that, as the sixteenth century advanced, a growing number of sophisticated minds ceased to adhere devoutly to any ecclesiastical version of Christianity. Several roots of the Enlightenment can be discovered in that century, although not all came from Italianate individualism, the reformist Christian Erasmus, or the ambivalent Montaigne.

Enno van Gelder pursued his theme no further than the sixteenth century and was therefore unable to include in his purview that far more comprehensive estrangement of European intellectuals from ecclesiastical culture which accompanied the development of modern science. This was a movement of truly revolutionary dimensions for Western civilization, which could hardly fail to influence and reshape views of Luther's other, very different revolution.

The coincidence in time of the Lutheran and Copernican "revolutions" has provided the focus for much discussion by modern historians of science, who have presented a nearly unanimous picture of the Protestant Reformers as bitter opponents of the new science. This uniformity now appears far less remarkable, because historians of the Reformation have conclusively demonstrated how this picture developed. As early as 1931 Werner Elert identified the German tradition of scientific historiography from Franz Beckmann and Franz Hipler to Leopold Prowe and Adolf Müller as a "house of cards" lacking any proper foundation in the sources.[8] A similar tradition in English-language historical writing from the early nineteenth century through Bertrand Russell to T. S. Kuhn was sharply questioned in 1961 by John Dillenberger and comprehensively exposed in 1968 by Brian Gerrish as a self-perpetuating tradition based on flimsy evidence taken out of context, outright fabrication, and anachronistic judgments which had been handed on without any proper examination of the sources.[9]

Gerrish outlined a "sacred tradition" among historians of science which alleged that the Reformers not only opposed the heliocentric theory and refuted Copernicus by quoting Scripture but were antagonistic in principle to scientific investigation and sought to suppress the Copernican viewpoint, although with less success than the Catholics. In 1960 Edward Rosen had exposed Calvin's celebrated and oft-repeated anti-Copernican judgment—"Who will venture to place the authority of Copernicus above that of the Holy Spirit?"—as a sheer invention of one writer's imagination faithfully passed on.[10] He concluded that Calvin's writings contain no evidence that he had ever heard of Copernicus. Gerrish pushed the issue further by demonstrating the baseless character of many fundamental assertions and anachronistic reasoning which presumed to hold the Reformers guilty of benighted dogmatism for failing to endorse a hypothesis which even the majority of scientists found no compelling reasons to accept. More significant, Gerrish demonstrated how Melanchthon's astronomical views derived from his humanistic philosophy and not his theology, and how Luther and Calvin had each established a sound theological basis for openness to scientific inquiry and accepting scientific conclusions that contradicted the written word of Scripture.[11]

Elert's description of this tradition as a "house of cards" was surely apposite, for only rarely does the history of scholarly writing in any field present such a clear example of a revered and long-standing tradition so unequivocally found wanting in the most elementary requirements of evidence. Here was the true stuff of irony—a "scientific" tradition so demonstrably lacking scientific rigor. Yet even the exposure of this false tradition has cleared the ground for more productive exploration of the intersection of science and the Reformation.

Much of the more promising analysis has focused on whether there might be some strong positive correlation between Protestant thought and the development of natural science. Max Weber's sociological theories about Protestantism (see Chapter 11) imply a connection between modern science and Puritan theology as two elements associated intimately with modern capitalist culture. Robert K. Merton applied this perspective to a detailed study of seventeenth-century England and affirmed a strong positive link between Puritan values and beliefs and the contemporary scientific dominance of England, although he recognized that science had also flourished in other historical contexts.[12] The Dutch historian of science Reijer Hooykaas has developed over many years an impressive case—based on evidence from England and the Continent and uniting statistical data and theological analysis—that the religious attitudes of "ascetic Protestantism" furthered scientific development.[13]

There now seems little doubt that "non–Roman Catholics exhibited a significantly greater predilection for the study of nature over the whole period from the early sixteenth to the mid-seventeenth centuries than did Roman Catholics,"[14] but there is far less agreement about what conclusions may reasonably be drawn from this evidence. Vigorous debate on these issues has continued with no sign that a last word is likely to be uttered.[15] Meanwhile, Dillenberger's *Protestant Thought and Natural Science* still remains the most useful and concise study of the relationship of Protestantism and science in the centuries following the Reformation.

Whenever the modern significance of the Reformation comes under discussion, Puritanism looms large, yet we have treated this important phenomenon only slightly so far. Indeed, this topic, given its importance in the English-speaking world, deserves a book rather than a chapter; yet here a few pages must suffice.

The term *Puritan* was at first satirical and derogatory: it lacked any philosophical exactitude.[16] Like *precisian* and other alternatives, it denoted a person who thought the Elizabethan religious settlement had not gone nearly far enough toward a Church based on the New Testament, which was already—in the eyes of many such people—exemplified by Geneva. But Puritanism never meant merely Calvinism with an English face, and several Anglican bishops who persecuted Puritans maintained a more systematic Genevan theology than that of their victims. Although their personal severity varied, the Puritans should not be dismissed as antiritualists who denounced ecclesiastical vestments as "Aaronic," or as killjoys who were shocked by the occasions for sin which maypole dancing offered.

To grasp the Puritans in terms of modern historiography, we must recognize that they were united less by doctrines than by a common social experience, a way of life. They belonged to groups which met in private houses to study the Scriptures, went about together singing psalms, and made excursions to hear their favorite "godly" preachers. They did not form any mere class phenomenon. They included many cloth workers and itinerant artisans, yet their cohesion depended on educated clerics, and they were often sheltered from the bishops by justices of the peace and other gentry. For much of Elizabeth's reign, their relative immunity owed not a little to great nobles like Leicester, Bedford, and Huntingdon, magnates close to the queen yet holding religious sympathies at variance with her masterful concept of a national Church under a monarchical supreme governor. Yet the vast majority of those who could be called Puritans wanted to change the Church of England from within; they were not rebels seeking liberation from some imaginary Anglo-Catholic norm. Until the Arminian Archbishop Laud harried the Puritans out of the Church, only an exiguous minority of Englishmen became Separatists. As Nicholas Tyacke argued, it was Arminianism which—arriving not long before 1600 as a theological attack on the whole Calvinist position—constituted the revolutionary element in the Church of England.[17] On the other hand, even during the civil wars and the Cromwellian years, the majority of the nation never accepted rigorous Puritan beliefs.

Modern research on Puritanism has made great progress beyond the censorious Anglican images still widespread half a century ago, when people naively identified the type with Shakespeare's Malvolio, and with cant and hypocrisy in general. Whatever the defects of their theology or sense of human practicalities, the Puritans included many of the most unselfish and socially benevolent men and women in England. They may have been hard to live with, if one did not share their views. But their great figures, such as Oliver Cromwell and John Milton, add a grand and impressive quality to a movement more often marked by excessive delicacy of conscience than by iron resolution and ruthless action.

Another aspect of Puritanism looming large in recent research is the mingling of its biblicism with a near-rationalist disbelief in ex opere operato theories: it rejected out of hand the automatic efficacy of holy words, relating not merely to the Catholic doctrine of the Eucharist but to all exorcisms and "hallowings" of physical objects—holy bread, holy water, holy oil—and many rites of medieval religion. In minds of this stamp, as to the Lollards, such claims to manipulate God's supernatural power were equated with necromancy. This aspect of the Reformation has been wonderfully documented by Keith Thomas in his *Religion and the Decline of Magic* (1971).[18]

Like Lutheranism, Puritanism has attracted many American historians of great ability. That it has attained so large a role in the American tradition arises not from some sentimental regard for the Pilgrim fathers, but from the fact that New England became the intellectual center of nineteenth-century America, amplified its old religious views, and diffused them along with its secular culture across the whole continent. Reinforced by sectarian immigrants from Germanic Europe, Puritan social and religious attitudes became an important ingredient in a fully assimilated American mentality, one which transcended ecclesiastical frontiers.

However, although a Puritan profile established itself so widely, it has not become the basis of a united church in America or Europe, a penalty paid for its lack of theological integration and its appalling ideological and political fragmentation in the mid–seventeenth century. Yet this outlook, which played so great a part in the English Revolution, the origins of liberal democracy, the tenor of American society, and the ancestry of international churches such as the Methodist and Congregationalist, had at least some marks of a world religion. It therefore earned its present impressive role in the historiography of the Reformation, which is by no means dependent on the controversial social and economic theories of Weber and Tawney (see Chapter 11).

The early historians of Puritanism assumed far more pedestrian and quasi-denominational attitudes than present views would lead one to suspect. The Tudor and early Stuart propagandists left a huge deposit of primary literature which we are still evaluating, but historical retrospection began with systematic hagiological biography, best exemplified by Samuel Clarke's collections of *Lives,* which mostly appeared between 1646 and 1662.[19] Between 1696 and 1729 that equally voluminous biographer Edmund Calamy was active in London; he was chiefly concerned with the sufferings of Puritanical ministers and academics ejected from their livings and silenced by the Restoration of 1660.[20] Then between 1732 and 1738 followed Daniel Neal's *History of the Puritans,* covering the period 1517 to 1603 in four volumes.[21] Neal, a distinguished and well-connected London dissenting minister, produced an informative but by no means impartial collection, the accuracy of which was systematically challenged by Zachary Grey and other contemporary historians. Yet another useful but partisan contribution came from Benjamin Brook, whose *Lives of the Puritans* (1813) extended from the Elizabethan settlement to 1662 and exerted considerable influence throughout the nineteenth century.[22]

One may still learn something about Puritanism from these recollections of a heroic age, yet a more strict and analytical critique did not emerge until scarcely before the end of that century. It is observable by

1911 in the first volume of H. W. Clark's *History of English Noncon-formity from Wiclif to the Close of the Nineteenth Century.*[23] Yet because the first requisite for progress was an immense expansion of factual and mental evidence, the rise of modern Puritan studies was marked by two capable pieces of editing. The volume *Puritan Manifestoes* by W. H. Frere and C. E. Douglas came out in 1907, and Albert Peel's *The Seconde Parte of a Register* appeared eight years later.[24] Peel's work is a scholarly calendar of a huge collection of documents formed about 1593 by Puritans themselves with a view to eventual publication. In 1915 they threw a broad shaft of light on Puritan grievances and objectives at this crucial stage of their campaign.

Since those years, research on Puritanism has developed so rapidly that it has exceeded in bulk, and even diversity, all other branches of research on the English Reformation. In 1983 Patrick Collinson, the leading British authority, provided his pamphlet *English Puritanism* with a working bibliography of more than 120 important books and articles, nine-tenths of them published during the preceding thirty years.[25] This represents little more than the routine background reading which would be demanded of doctoral students aspiring to make original contributions to the theme.

The accessibility of this list, and of others in various standard works, may help exonerate us from attempting a disproportionately large task in this context: a full bibliographic review of the main modern works on Puritanism. We will, nevertheless, indicate their chief purposes insofar as these can be classified. As represented by Leland H. Carlson, collaborator and then successor of Albert Peel, and by L. J. Trinterud and H. C. Porter,[26] a number of scholars published further source materials or made documents available to students. Others sought to explain the relations between Puritanism and the political figures of both Church and State; yet others investigated the personal, social, and intellectual links between the religious movement and the political revolution of 1640–1660. These groups are building on the broad foundations generally established since the 1930s by Christopher Hill in an impressive sequence of books and articles.[27] Meanwhile, a strong trend toward regional and local studies is lending more substance and realism to the national surveys: M. E. James on the Durham region, Peter Clark on Kent, W. J. Sheils on Northamptonshire, Christopher Haigh and R. C. Richardson on Lancashire and the Northwest, Margaret Spufford on Cambridgeshire, R. B. Manning on Sussex, R. B. Marchant on the York diocesan courts in relation to the Puritans, and H. C. Porter on their intellectual base in Cambridge.[28] In addition, and with some assistance from other social sciences, attempts are being made to dissect with greater precision the complexities of Puritanism as a religious culture in relation to the family. One of the authors on this topic, Alan Macfarlane, equipped his researches on the seventeenth-century cleric Ralph Josselin with the significant subtitle *An Essay in Historical Anthropology*.[29]

To return to our unfortunate doctoral students, if they gained too early an interest in these new dimensions, they might give prior attention to three works by masters of the whole field, all admirable, yet showing distinct progress over twenty-eight years: Marshall M. Knappen, *Tudor Puritanism* (1939); C. H. George and K. George, *The Protestant Mind of the English Reformation* (1961); and Patrick Collinson, *The Elizabethan Puritan Movement* (1967).[30] To these might well be added William Haller's somewhat dated classic *The Rise of Puritanism* (1938), Perry Miller's two main works on New England (1933, 1939), and a much more recent item, R. L. Greaves, *Society and Religion in Elizabethan England* (1981).[31] And then again, our aspirants might do worse than break out occasionally from the official lists to sample Louis B. Wright, *Middle Class Culture in Elizabethan England* (1935), which they would find surprisingly relevant.[32] In short, we have in Puritanism a Reformation theme certain to remain a major area of growth for the rest of the twentieth century and far beyond.

An equally broad omission from our story, although of a different kind, is the theme of *secularization,* a term with two distinct, albeit not entirely unrelated meanings. In its general sense, understood as a description of life-style and mental outlook, we have already encountered it: in the self-conscious distancing of earlier French writers from religious controversy and in the development of rationalistic and scientific thought (see Chapter 4). Readers interested in this aspect of the theme could find no better starting point than the perceptive essay contributed by Peter Burke to the *Companion Volume* of the *New Cambridge Modern History*.[33] Here, however, we shall discuss the historiography of secularization in the more restricted sense commonly used since the seventeenth century: the conversion of ecclesiastical lands and property to lay usage. This indeed is a significant and concrete aspect of the Reformation, although because it was at once ecclesiastical and political, economic and social, it did not readily fit into any of our previous chapters. Moreover, in the present state of scholarship, this subject will not definitively respond to summary treatment.

Historians and men of religion have often denounced the expropriation of church property which marked the Reformation, but only in recent years have they begun to observe such transactions in a long perspective and broad context.[34] During many periods of Christian history, ecclesiastical lands were returned to lay ownership, although this occurred to a lesser extent than usual during the High Middle Ages, when churchmen received immense gifts and in certain parts of Europe came to own about a third of all land. Important secularizations occurred under the Byzantine emperors of the eighth century, the Carolingians, and the medieval kings of France and England. Even the "Catholic Kings" Ferdinand and Isabella assumed the immense lands of the rich military orders and, excluding all effective papal power from Spain, drew heavily on the resources of the Spanish Church. Subsequently, the many great prince-bishops of the Holy Roman Empire stood to lose their temporal sovereignty as distinct from their spiritual functions. Even as he championed the Catholic cause, Charles V in 1528 annexed the great bishopric of Utrecht to the Netherlands. His strictly Catholic enemy Henry II of France, having in 1552 captured the bishoprics of Metz, Verdun, and Toul, annexed their religious foundations. Between 1524 and 1529 Cardinal Wolsey dissolved twenty-nine small religious houses to finance his personal foundations at Oxford and Ipswich.

Meanwhile, since the fourteenth century critical theory more than kept pace with orthodox practice. Marsilius of Padua declared the right of the State to take all properties not needed for support of the clergy; Wycliffe denied the right of the papacy and religious orders to hold worldly power or property. Even the Catholic reformers of the sixteenth century did not necessarily regard monastic properties as sacrosanct. In 1537 the famous *Consilium de emendanda ecclesia,* drawn up by a commission including four cardinals, suggested to Paul III the suppression of all the numerous houses of conventual (unreformed) friars. And, of course, for the greatest of all such actions we look ahead to the French Revolution, the wholesale depredations of which the Pope himself was forced to recognize as the price of his concordat with Napoleon.

Consequently, when in his *Christian Nobility* of 1520 Luther called for the sequestration of all surplus church holdings and their conversion to charitable uses, he was scarcely demanding a revolution. Among the first to follow his recommendation were a number of important German towns. On Luther's advice in 1523, Leisnig placed all church properties under a "common chest" administered by an elected board of ten laymen.[35] Before the end of 1526 Frankfurt am Main, Magdeburg, Ulm, Strasbourg, Bremen, and Nuremberg followed suit, as did Zurich under Zwingli. In the years immediately following, several north German princes, the Scandinavian kings, and the Germanized cities of the east Baltic all undertook extensive programs of secularization throughout their dominions. The most spectacular example was Albrecht of Brandenburg-Ansbach, grand master of the Teutonic order, who in 1525 took over the ample Prussian territories of the order and, avoiding allegiance to the empire, held them from the king of Poland. Understandably enough, German historians have described individual actions rather than attempted a synthesis of so many diverse and scattered cases. Scores of local books and articles have appeared since the early nineteenth century,[36] although they have been accompanied by very few regional surveys, such as those by W. H. Wolff for the monasteries of Hesse-Kassel (1913) and Alfred Hilpert for a large part of Saxony (1912).[37]

Concerning the broad social and political effects, some shifts of opinion have occurred during the last thirty years. Nevertheless, historians have in general agreed that in many Lutheran areas, especially Brandenburg and Pomerania, the hard-faced landlords prospered from their grants and purchases, while the status and conditions of their peasants underwent an inexorable decline.[38] It seems, however, certain that this trend had begun well before the end of the fifteenth century, and that the Reformation changes enlarged and speeded a development which would in some considerable measure have occurred anyway. The more basic causes lay elsewhere. The Church could no longer offer lucrative employment to the young noblemen who had hitherto monopolized its higher offices, and noble families had more inducement than ever to exploit the Church by actual dispossession. Moreover, the growth of demesne farming, together with the flight and expropriation of many peasants, created a vicious circle by rendering progressively heavier the burdens of those who remained on the land.

A second major question concerns the German princes. Were they, like the landowners, conspicuous beneficiaries from the material processes initiated or extended by the Reformation? Only recently it was generally maintained that the growth of princely power owed much to these events. Not only did the princes directly gain wealth from monastic dissolutions; they also became *summi episcopi* who left spiritual functions to the clergy, yet guided the administration and patronage of all church lands in their domains. It should be recalled that Luther's scheme for the Reformation was to be applied on two planes, spiritual and worldly. The Church's material possessions lay on the worldly plane, for Luther did not imply a Church versus State distinction.

Despite these considerations, it has lately been widely argued that most Protestant princes gained very little in wealth and power.[39] The best of the paternalist Lutheran princes—such as Augustus I of Saxony, William IV of Hesse-Kassel, John George of Brandenburg, and Christoph of Württemberg—devoted their enlarged resources to charity and education rather than political and military aggrandizement. In addition, the main shackles on princely power lay with the various estates, and it can be demonstrated that in most cases the estates, not the princely administrations, consolidated their power during the second half of the sixteenth century. Ironically enough, some Catholic princes enlarged their authority at this stage with greater success than their Protestant rivals. The dukes of Bavaria won decisive victories over their estates; they were immensely aided by the financial and political backing of the clergy, who badly needed princely power to execute the Counter-Reformation. Similarly, although half a century later, the Hapsburgs enjoyed heavy clerical support in curtailing the estates' influence in Austria, Bohemia, Moravia, and Silesia.[40]

To this revised impression, it should be added that a large number of ecclesiastical states and Catholic religious houses actually survived the Reformation, and that the ecclesiastical states became the most deeply conservative element in German public life.[41] In the first decade of the eighteenth century, some sixty-five ecclesiastical principalities remained; they occupied about 14 percent of the empire's land and contained 12 percent of its population, more than three times the population of all imperial cities.[42] Yet these problems concerning secularization in Germany and Scandinavia must still be seen beside the pressing need for further local and regional researches. The immense variety of circumstances and the parallel complexity of surviving records still make vulnerable most provisional generalizations.

This picture does not apply to England, where secularization, led by a single, centralized government, left much fuller and more intelligible documentation. Yet here, too, the demands on research remain weighty. In the face of soaring military costs, that able minister Thomas Cromwell saw the need to reendow the Crown, and it is primarily in light of this agenda that we should see the Henrician Acts of 1536 and 1539, which dissolved, respectively, the lesser and greater monasteries. They were followed by the Edwardian Act of 1547, which confiscated chantries, religious guilds, and many minor parish endowments, together with some of the outlying chapelries in large parishes. Although the collegiate churches, some of them major foundations run by secular priests and used for public worship, fell within the scope of this act, most of the important ones were preserved, often through local pressures.[43] Yet, within little more than a decade, both monasticism and the system of intercessory masses were swept away, to the great financial profit of a government acutely embarrassed by inflation and the rising expense of warfare. Despite our heavy documentation, a reasonably long-term assessment of the social and economic results of this process is proving more difficult than might be expected.

One might regard the historiography of secularization in England as passing through five stages. The sixteenth century commentators included many anticlericals who rejoiced in the overthrow of allegedly idle and immoral monks and friars. On the other side, that major northern rebellion the Pilgrimage of Grace was in part directed against the monastic dissolutions. A few writers in the second half of the century attacked the process as legalized robbery affecting the material and educational interests of the nation as a whole.[44]

During the second stage, the seventeenth century, there developed a romantic interest in monastic antiquities. Sir Henry Spelman wrote (c. 1633, published 1698) *The History and Fate of Sacrilege,* encouraging the superstition that a dire fate had followed the purchase or inheritance of former monastic lands. By contrast, Sir William Dugdale published in London between 1655 and 1673 his learned *Monasticon Anglicanum,* containing a history of each English and Welsh religious house and a large collection of documents.[45]

The third phase is occupied by William Cobbett, who propagated the notion that the poor had suffered grievously by the dissolutions, because benevolent monks had been succeeded by rack-renting and enclosing landlords.[46] Later, in the nineteenth century, this overdramatized economic version was converted by some enthusiastic Catholic writers to their own purposes, which they supposed to be favored by the same conventional figures—the "proverbially generous" monastics and the oppressive laymen, filching by royal favor what had been the "patrimony of the poor." The resultant inaccuracies and the special pleading of Cardinal Gasquet[47] have since been denounced by his far more scholarly successor David Knowles, like Gasquet a member of a Catholic religious order and author of the standard English work on English monasticism.[48]

What we consider the fifth stage gradually developed during the forty years after the First World War. It took the form of a more impartial approach to the huge body of documents which not only describe the course of visitation and dissolution, but also record the sales and gifts of church lands to new owners. Though still far from complete, this task is no longer controlled by denominational prejudices. In addition to the work of Knowles, some briefer accounts by A. G. Dickens, G. W. O. Woodward, and (most valuable of all) Joyce Youings are now available.[49] Nevertheless, the fact that none of these should be taken as definitive has been demonstrated in a brief but significant essay by Christopher Kitching, whose outstanding knowledge of the relevant classes in the Public Record Office has helped revive a number of flagging debates which now depend on highly technical issues.[50]

What broad significance should we attach to this gigantic transfer of land from ecclesiastical to lay ownership? Did it depress the condition of the English peasantry? Did it significantly alter the shape of English society or political forces in the nation? Who, in the long run, were the real beneficiaries? In these matters historians are now achieving a growing degree of consensus. The landlordism of monks does not seem to have differed much from that of laymen. Indeed, the monasteries could not afford to be exceptionally generous to their tenants and workers. Their financial problems, so often enhanced by overbuilding, and later by inflation, prompted them to charge full economic rents and sometimes even to create enclosures. In any event, their policies were to no small extent controlled by the laymen who acted as their stewards and protectors. Had the monasteries survived into the period of acute inflation, they would have been compelled to enhance their rents to match the price rise, from which their tenants, incidentally, were benefiting as sellers of produce.

One result can be stated with certainty. The transfers of monastic lands to new owners were, with very few exceptions, not gifts but sales at market price, because the motive of the dissolution was to enrich the Crown. After the death of its chief planner, Thomas Cromwell, the process of sale was accelerated to pay for the war of 1542–1546 against Scotland and France. It has been estimated that little more than a third of these lands remained with the Crown at the end of Henry VIII's reign; yet even if that is true, a huge increase in the Crown's total holdings had occurred. To assess the long-term changes, we need not merely to explore records hitherto unfamiliar, but to investigate intensively local history covering a long period after the dissolutions. In most areas it is easy to list the first grantees of the land, but because many of these men bought property for immediate resale, they do not necessarily typify the owners into whose hands the ex-monastic properties settled during the following century.

Approximate as our knowledge remains, however, there can be no reasonable doubt that the class which gained most was the landed gentry, though not always its existent members; they were throughout the century constantly reinforced by families whose capital came from commerce and younger sons who found enough money to buy land when so much became available. The successive visitations of the counties compiled by royal heralds accordingly show that the families classed as gentry grew far more numerous between 1530 and 1580. Obviously, the immense role of the English gentry amid the dramatic tensions of the seventeenth century owed much to the great secularization. On the other hand, this alteration in the balance of forces seems only partially relevant to the religious struggle. Many of the most notable Catholic families of the period did not hesitate to receive monastic lands, and although Mary

Tudor wanted to restore the monasteries and see them recover their estates, her failure to enforce this reversal became painfully obvious to everyone, even the papacy, before the end of her brief reign.

One further aspect of recent scholarship deserves mention in our brief glance at secularization in England. It relates to the already-mentioned disposal of chantry and collegiate lands under Edward VI, a transaction considered by recent investigators to have involved property worth about one-quarter of the monastic lands, even though so much of it consisted of small urban units.[51] If this estimate is tolerably accurate, this transfer provided no small windfall for the young king's government—which was too readily parting with former monastic lands—and also for more of the sort of buyers who had come forward a decade earlier. Yet, in addition, various municipal corporations—such as those of Lynn, Coventry, and Beverley—went to law, and even Parliament, to preserve and secure churches and other amenities which would otherwise have been demolished. Because some of the chantry priests also served as schoolmasters, inquiries have been made to assess the losses to education. When these priests had been pensioned off, what happened to their schools?

Probably less than a tenth of all chantry priests taught, but their learning is usually described in the chantry surveys as superior to that of the rest, and most taught Latin, so their establishments had the status of grammar schools. The government usually refounded these as "King Edward VI grammar schools," many of which survive to this day. Thus, the masters were not dismissed but assigned salaries payable by the Court of Augmentations, founded in the previous decade to take over the monastic lands. Even so, A. F. Leach, the distinguished pioneer of English educational history, criticized the procedure, mainly on the ground that these salaries, payable in fixed sums, must have become less and less adequate in a time of rising inflation.[52] Would it not have proved wiser to base the restored schools on the real property they formerly held? On further thought this view seemed debatable, because the chantry surveys themselves show that rents from urban houses—the most common endowment for such foundations—remained liable to sudden collapse.[53] In fact, however little Edward VI deserved his reputation as a great educational founder, the sources make it clear that the survival of such grammar schools was in general secured, and private benefactions usually followed.

Moreover, one thing remains certain: that in England the advance of the Reformation cannot be truly portrayed as a period of educational decline, because it coincided with a time of marked enthusiasm for humanist schooling, and there were strong historical links between the two.

It can be statistically demonstrated that the foundation of new schools continued throughout the Elizabethan and Stuart periods; the gain from the new immensely exceeded any conceivable loss of the old. For example, in Yorkshire, then not an especially rich or progressive area, the twenty grammar schools recorded before 1500 were reinforced by about fifty more, which appear in the records between 1500 and 1558. Nearly all the schools supposedly threatened by the Edwardian changes were re-founded. But the important sequel comes in the reign of Elizabeth, when, in addition to the foregoing, more than sixty new schools appeared.[54] These hard facts doubtless seem more impressive than mere declarations of educational idealism, yet a number of early English Protestant leaders did make such declarations in memorable terms, and some took personal roles in founding schools and colleges.[55] One of them, the somewhat rabid Protestant propagandist Thomas Becon, was among the first of his countrymen to follow Luther in demanding that schools for girls also be erected by public authority.[56]

At this point a few observations are in order concerning the Reformation's impact on the schools of Germany, but here we shall move beyond secularization, which was not so significant historiographically in Germany as in England. In Germany it was never sensible to maintain that the Reformation brought disasters to education, although around 1530 in some traditionalist universities, such as Erfurt, enrollment did decline.[57] The link between leading Reformers and schools is even more demonstrable in Germany than in England. Luther set the tone with his powerful pleas that city councils found Christian schools (1524) and that parents continue their children's schooling as long as reasonably possible (1530).[58] The notion that he was merely promoting literacy to foster Bible reading is, of course, wholly mistaken; both in these writings and elsewhere he stressed the basic relevance of education to the needs of the State and secular society. Even more important was Melanchthon, who composed so many textbooks stretching across the curriculum and trained a whole generation of humanist teachers. These tireless activities as *praeceptor Germaniae* should perhaps have been given greater notice by general historians than his theological leanings, despite the internal conflicts they helped extend. Along with his passion for religious education by catechizing, Melanchthon honestly sought a synthesis between religion proper and ethical-intellectual elements. This balance laid solid foundations for German schoolteaching and helped preserve its repute and effectiveness amid the power politics, confessional strife, and popular resistance to religion which followed Luther's death and culminated in the Thirty Years' War.

Basically we may attribute much of this success to the fact that most secondary schools had long been maintained by city councils, yet these bodies were not invariably angels of light. Some patrician groups appear to have resisted the creation of schools, perhaps because they had no desire to enlarge education amid the turbulent classes outside their magic circle, who were so often intent to wrest power from the patriciates.[59] By the later sixteenth century, the best schools in Lutheran Germany were not town schools (*Stadt-Schulen*) but state schools (*Staats-Schulen*) recently founded by the princes.[60]

Unlike city patricians, the territorial rulers did not need to hesitate. With increasing conviction they realized that their future power to conduct efficient government and foster economic advance depended intimately on training the ablest boys—those who would become their loyal bureaucrats and leading clergy—irrespective of private means. Indeed, the ultimate necessities and methods of the German Catholic princes, founders of schools and patrons of the Jesuits, did not greatly differ from those of the Protestant rulers. Both Catholic and Protestant princes accepted the need for a systematic religious education based on approved catechisms.

Although important works of synthesis date from the late nineteenth century, the body of studies concerning the history of individual schools and the development of education in particular regions is distinctly less impressive than that concerning German universities.[61] A pioneering but still valuable history of both schools and universities was published in 1885 by Friedrich Paulsen, a philosopher who wrote concrete, well-documented educational history without losing interest in the appropriate intellectual backgrounds.[62] Not long after, the work of Paul Barth more nearly approached the attitudes of the later twentieth century. Barth's chief book, which appeared in 1911, has thoughtful chapters on German educational advances during the Reformation, yet its scope is international and its sociological thinking better developed than Paulsen's.[63] Far less detailed on institutional history than on sociological thinking, Barth nevertheless anticipated a new era of sociological analysis when he assigned separate chapters to "learned" education and "popular" schooling.[64]

Still further progress in the same direction may be observed in recent research, as in *Luther's House of Learning* by Gerald Strauss, the disquieting revelations of which we discussed in Chapter 12.[65] Yet its cheerful earlier chapters are as important as its gloomy findings on the Lutheran visitations: they concern school ordinances, pedagogical principles, attitudes about childhood and the family, and, above all, techniques of indoctrination, which Strauss handled with a delicate sense of period and without the crude modern comparisons suggested by that word. Despite the failure of Lutheranism's earlier attempts to impose religious patterns on the popular mind, secular education advanced steadily in both municipal and state schools. By a striking yet intelligible anomaly, the German Reformation had its major success with general education rather than with religious propaganda.

Among the less obvious omissions from our account of historiography of the Reformation, several others deserve brief acknowledgment. Growing consciousness of the Reformation's social and intellectual background, characteristic of writing after the Second World War, has resulted in another category underrepresented in our earlier chapters. This consists of both monographs and collections of shorter pieces dedicated explicitly to the multitude of background factors without which religious and ecclesiastical action is generally recognized to be unintelligible in terms of modern historiography.

It would indeed seem inadvisable to undertake any general work on the German Reformation without some knowledge of the massive survey by Heinrich Otto Bürger, *Renaissance, Humanismus, Reformation: Deutsche Literatur in europäischen Kontext* (1969), which enlarges the old literary category of *Germanistik*,[66] or Frank I. Borchard's *German Antiquity in Renaissance Myth* (1971), which illuminates quasi-historical ideas then common to popular and learned minds.[67] A partial English parallel, although it is concerned more with primitive scholarship than pure myth, is May McKisack's *Medieval History in the Tudor Age* (1971).[68] Long available on very different aspects has been Frederick Hertz's *Development of the German Public Mind* (1957), a fine panorama of political ideas and aspirations.[69] More narrow in geographic focus yet broad in time span is Gerhard Benecke's *Society and Politics in Germany, 1500–1750* (1974), which researches some less familiar areas of Germany.[70] Among collections, the festschriften, like that for Hans Rückert, are necessarily less integrated than, for example, the well-selected German articles in English translation *Pre-Reformation Germany* (1966), edited by Gerald Strauss.[71]

In general we have not ranked modern biographies of individual Reformers as a high priority in our discussions. The many lives of Luther published during the period 1920–1940—such as those by Heinrich Boehmer, Otto Scheel, and James Mackinnon—were concisely surveyed by Wilhelm Pauck, whose deep insights into historical theology have greatly influenced young scholars.[72] To these we should add a number of later works on Luther and his thought, such as those by Gerhard Ritter, E. G. Rupp, James Atkinson, E. G. Schwiebert, Gerhard Ebeling, and above all the magisterial account of Luther's earlier career by Robert

Herndon Fife.[73] The wealth of material on Luther's early career contrasts strikingly with the absence of any satisfying account of his later years, although Heinrich Bornkamm's *Martin Luther in der Mitte seines Lebens* (1982) covers in detail the years 1521–1530 and Mark Edwards's *Luther's Last Battles* (1982) indicates that this need is at last beginning to be met.[74] On the other hand, Walter Koehler in his *Zwingli und Luther* supplied half a century ago the standard treatment of that encounter of mighty opposites.[75]

Concerning Zwingli, Oscar Farner's four-volume work of 1943–1960 remains indispensable, although it was recently superseded for general reading by George Richard Potter.[76] Of the modern lives of Calvin, the one in seven volumes published by Emile Doumergue (1899–1927) is more comprehensive than any single biography of Luther.[77] Nowadays one must presume that it serves mainly reference purposes, having been succeeded by several more concise yet competent accounts, such as those by R. N. C. Hunt and François Wendel.[78] Nevertheless, readers desiring to understand the achievement of Calvinism would be frustrated by overmuch reliance on mere biographies; they need the books with wider horizons, such as J. T. McNeill's *History and Character of Calvinism* (1954) and E. W. Monter's *Calvin's Geneva* (1967).[79] In fact, few biographies of leading Reformers extend to broad and original ideas on the Reformation, which is the main reason we have given them no prolonged attention.[80]

Finally, we should acknowledge that in our selection of items for extended discussion we have inevitably tended to favor those which made innovations: the angular writers with strongly delineated opinions, in some cases those who pushed their dogmas well beyond the point of moderation. Especially from the plethora of histories written during the present century, we have chosen all too few of the less controversial, those chiefly marked by good sense, charisma, sweetness and light. This being so, we have managed to reach this point with only a brief mention of Roland H. Bainton, that doyen of American historians of the Reformation, who has illuminated so many sides of the subject that our belated tribute can scarcely do justice to one whose sheer humanity has attracted a huge readership to this field. Although he often followed the favorite themes, Bainton in fact pioneered a number of hithero neglected ones, such as the contributions of women to the advance of the Reformation.[81] Above all, he wrote a life of Luther, *Here I Stand* (1950), sound in referenced detail yet unexcelled in conveying that offbeat vitality and humor which—until his last savage years—carried the Reformer through dark inner crises, stern doctrinal dilemmas, and political emergencies which would have broken a less resilient spirit.[82]

Writing of Luther in the Erfurt cloister, Bainton noted the young monk's problem, that "after six hours of confessing he could still go out and think of something else which had eluded his most conscientious scrutiny."[83] As we conclude this lengthy catalog of historiographic "sins of omission," this is a sentiment with which we can wholly identify, as with Luther's even more disconcerting discovery that "some of man's misdemeanours are not even recognised, let alone remembered."[84] Here the authors' dilemma, like that of Luther, admits of no adequate defense, yet the danger of not telling the whole story is surely an insufficient reason for not trying to tell it at all.

Notes

1. Views from Within

1. For sound guidance on this problem see E. Menke-Glückert, *Die Ge-schichtsschreibung der Reformation und Gegen-Reformation* (Leipzig, 1912), chaps. 2 and 3. Here the author also discusses the historical concepts of the Spiritualist Sebastian Franck, whose main work appeared in the same year, 1532.

2. See A. G. Dickens, *The German Nation and Martin Luther* (London, 1974), chaps. 1 and 2.

3. J. M. Headley, *Luther's View of Church History* (New Haven and London, 1963), esp. chap. 3.

4. *J. Sleidani de statu religionis et reipublicae Carolo Quinto Caesare com-mentarii* (Strasbourg, 1555). Translated by E. Bohun as *The General History of the Reformation of the Church* (London, 1689). Fuller references to Sleidan are in A. G. Dickens, "Johannes Sleidan and Reformation History," in R. Buick Knox, ed., *Reformation Conformity and Dissent, Essays in Honour of Geoffrey Nuttall* (London, 1977), pp. 17–43, which has references to several passages below. On the background see also D. R. Kelley, "Johann Sleidan and the Origins of History as a Profession," *Journal of Modern History*, 52 (1980), pp. 573–598. Basic works on German historiography are Menke-Glückert, *Geschichts-schreibung*, and E. C. Scherer, *Geschichte und Kirchengeschichte an den deutschen Universitäten* (Freiburg, 1927).

5. P. S. Allen, ed., *Opus epistolarum Des. Erasmi Roterodami* (Oxford, 12 vols., 1906–1947), III, 200; compare *Collected Works of Erasmus* (Toronto, 1969), V, 177. Erasmus is protecting the new Trilingual College at Louvain against old-fashioned opponents who are satisfied with the two languages already taught.

6. On Sleidan's French connections see V. L. Bourilly, "Jean Sleidan et le Cardinal du Bellay," *Bulletin de la société de l'histoire du protestantisme français*, 1 (1901), pp. 225–242. On the du Bellays see V. L. Bourilly and F. Vindry, eds., *Mémoires de Martin et Guillaume du Bellay* (Paris, 4 vols., 1908–1919).

7. E. Böhmer, ed., *Zwei Reden an Kaiser und Reich*, Bibliothek des literarischen Vereins in Stuttgart, 145 (Tübingen, 1879).

8. References in Dickens, "Johannes Sleidan," pp. 20–21.

9. Quotations from ibid., pp. 22n12, 24.

10. Johannes Sleidan, *De quatuor summis imperiis libri iii* (Strasbourg, 1556).

353

11. More extended quotations from the preface and the apologia are in Dickens, "Johannes Sleidan," pp. 26–27.

12. Johannes Sleidan, *In describendo autem religionis negocio, politicas causas omittere non mihi licuit, nam ut antea dixi, concurrunt fere semper, et nostra cumprimis aetate nimime potuerunt separari* (1785–1786), I, 15.

13. See J. N. King, "Protector Somerset, Patron of the English Renaissance," *Papers of the Bibliographical Society of America,* 70 (1976), pp. 307–331.

14. See Kelley, "Johann Sleidan."

15. For Bullinger's historical work see E. Fueter, *Histoire de l'historiographie moderne* (Paris, 1914), pp. 322–325; and P. Polman, *L'Elément historique dans la controverse religieuse du XVIᵉ siècle* (Gembloux, 1932), pp. 95–109. For guidance on his numerous writings see J. Staedtke, ed., *Heinrich Bullinger Bibliographie,* I (Zurich, 1972); and for the literature: E. Herkenrath, ed., ibid., II (Zurich, 1977).

16. *Historia oder Geschichten,* etc., edited by J. J. Hottinger and H. H. Vögeli as *Heinrich Bullingers Reformationsgeschichte* (Frauenfeld, vols. I–III, 1838–1840; vol. IV, 1913).

17. For a more extended comment by Zwingli on Luther see H. J. Hillerbrand, ed., *The Reformation in Its Own Words* (London, 1964), pp. 125–127.

18. On Bullinger's attacks on the Anabaptists see G. H. Williams, *The Radical Reformation* (Philadelphia, 1962), pp. 201–203, 848–852; based partly on H. Fast, *Heinrich Bullinger und die Täufer* (Weierhof, Palatinate, 1959).

19. *Commentaria Ioannis Cochlaei de actis et scriptis Martini Lutheri Saxonis* (Mainz, 1549). Guidance on the secondary literature concerning Cochlaeus is available in Remigius Bäumer, ed., "Johannes Cochlaeus und die Reform der Kirche," in *Reformatio Ecclesiae . . . Festgabe für Erwin Iserloh* (Paderborn, 1980), pp. 333–354. On the theological and philosophical background of his reformist ideas see Hubert Jedin, *Des Johannes Cochlaeus Streitschrift de libero arbitrio hominis, 1525* (Wroclaw, 1927). See also the biography by Martin Spahn (Berlin, 1898).

20. Cochlaeus, *Commentaria, praefatio* (unpaginated).

21. Ibid., pp. 21, 552.

22. Ibid., p. 315; see also pp. 73–74.

23. Ibid., pp. 55, 176.

24. Ibid., pp. 69, 93, 113, 165.

25. Ibid., *praefatio.*

26. Ibid., p. 190.

27. Adolf Herte, *Das katholische Lutherbild im Bann der Lutherkommentare des Cochlaeus* (Münster, 1943).

28. Cochlaeus, *Commentaria,* pp. 154, 168–169, 176.

29. Johannes Cochlaeus, *Historiae Hussitarum libri duodecim* (Mainz, 1549).

30. Cochlaeus, *Commentaria,* pp. 81, 291–292.

31. Jedin, *Cochlaeus,* p. 98.

32. Cochlaeus, *Commentaria,* p. 140. The humanist aspect of Cochlaeus is a far from recent theme: see Karl Otto, *Johannes Cochlaeus, der Humanist* (Wroclaw, 1874).

33. Bruce Mansfield, *Phoenix of His Age: Interpretations of Erasmus, c. 1550–1750* (Toronto, 1979), chap. 2, describes the Catholic reversal against Erasmus. See also n. 48.

34. Cochlaeus, *Commentaria*, pp. 56–72.

35. Ibid., p. 4.

36. Ibid., pp. 58, 132.

37. Bäumer, "Johannes Cochlaeus," p. 352.

38. R. H. Fife, *The Revolt of Martin Luther* (New York, 1957), p. 678.

39. Cochlaeus, *Commentaria*, p. 316.

40. Bäumer, "Johannes Cochlaeus," p. 342.

41. *Histoire catholique de nostre temps touchant l'estat de la religion chrestienne contre l'histoire de Jean Sleydan composée par S. Fontaine docteur en Theologie* (Paris, 1558). A dedication by Claude Frémy explains that the manuscript had fallen into his hands after the author's death. It must therefore have been written soon after the publication of Sleidan in 1555.

42. See Herte, *Katholische Lutherbild*, pp. 8–11, where his debt to Cochlaeus is also discussed.

43. Fontaine, *Histoire catholique*, pp. 28, 198–199.

44. Ibid., pp. 65–66; cf. Cochlaeus, *Commentaria*, p. 552.

45. Ibid., p. 66; cf. Cochlaeus, *Commentaria*, p. 56.

46. Fontaine, *Histoire catholique*, p. 69.

47. Ibid., pp. 69–70.

48. Ibid., pp. 20–21; 97–98; for attacks on Erasmus by Ruvio and others see Mansfield, *Phoenix*, pp. 29–64. Already in 1534 Alfonso de Castro thought vernacular Bible translation "the fount of heresies," but was still reverent in general toward Erasmus. His editions of 1539 and 1543 begin to harden the tone, but the "great divide" is not evident until the 1550s.

49. Short biography citing selected works in *Allgemeine deutsche Biographie*, XXXVII, 166.

50. *De probatis vitis Sanctorum ab Al. Lippomano olim [1550] conscriptis nunc primum emendatis et auctis* (Cologne, 6 vols., 1570–1576).

51. Laurentius Surius, *Commentarius brevis rerum in orbe gestarum ab anno 1500 ad annum 1564* (Cologne, 1566; but we use here the edition of 1568, which is said to cover the years 1500–1568).

52. Ibid., pp. 115, 120, 127, 130–131, 134.

53. See Herte, *Katholische Lutherbild*, pp. 22, 117–182.

54. Cochlaeus, *Commentarius*, pp. 168–171.

55. Ibid., p. 199. See Mansfield, *Phoenix*, pp. 28–29.

56. Cochlaeus, *Commentarius*, pp. 164–165.

57. *Ecclesiastica Historia* (Basel, 13 vols., 1559–1574).

58. *Allgemeine deutsche Biographie*, XXIII, 123–127, provides the essential facts on Myconius. Further details by Myconius and by his editor, Cyprian, appear in the *Historia Reformationis* (see n. 59).

59. *Friderici Myconii Historia Reformationis vom Jahr Christi 1517 bis 1542 aus des Autoris Autographo, mitgeteilt und in einer Vorrede erläutert von Ernst Salomon Cyprian*, etc. (Leipzig, 1718).

60. "Herodes ist nicht wider Christum und Nero wider die Apostel so tyrannisch gewesen. Dies Königreich ist wohl gefärbt und gedungt worden mit Christen Blut," cited in *Allgemeine deutsche Biographie*, XXIII, 125.

61. Myconius, *Historia Reformationis*, p. 42.

62. Ibid., pp. 14–16.

63. Ibid., p. 36.

64. Ibid.

65. Ibid., pp. 78–80.

66. Ibid., p. 87.

67. Ibid., pp. 45–69. Though in modest terms, Myconius gives himself the leading role in the Reformation at Gotha.

68. Ibid., p. 99.

69. Ibid., chap. 20, "Von Uneinikeit zwischen den Rath und der Gemein zu Gotha"; chap. 21, "Vom Pfaffen-Stuermen zu Gotha."

70. E. Götzinger, ed., *Chronik der Aebte des Kosters St. Gallen,* Joachim von Watt, Deutsche historische Schriften, I and II (St. Gall, 1895). See also Werner Näf, *Vadian und seine Stadt St Gallen* (St. Gall, 2 vols., 1944, 1957); and E. G. Rupp, *Patterns of Reformation* (London, 1969), pp. 357–378.

71. The article by Brecher in *Allgemeine deutsche Biographie*, XXVII, 372–374, is amplified by Neudecker's informative preface to the biography and his account of Ratzeberger's literary activities (see n. 72). These are in turn supported by Ratzeberger's friend and biographer, Andreas Poach, *Vom christlichen Abschied . . . des lieben thewren Mannes Matthei Ratzenbergers,* etc. (Jena, 1559).

72. *Die handschiftliche Geschichte Ratzebergers über Luther und seine Zeit mit literarischen, kritischen und historischen Anmerkungen zum ersten Male herausgegeben von D. Chr. Gotth. Neudecker* (Jena, 1850).

73. Respectively, pp. 141–142 and pp. 144–230 of Neudecker's edition.

74. "Living I was your plague, dying I shall be your death, O Pope." On the illness and death of Luther see ibid., pp. 134–142.

75. On Melanchthon's divergence see ibid., pp. 124, 201, 210.

76. Ibid., pp. 150–151.

77. On the treasons see ibid., pp. 151–156.

78. R. W. Scribner, *For the Sake of Simple Folk: Popular Propaganda for the German Reformation* (Cambridge, 1981), pp. 222–226.

79. Neudecker's edition, pp. 201 ff.

80. See, for instance, *The New Schaff-Herzog Encyclopedia of Religious Knowledge* (New York and London, 1908–1914), I, 41–44. The theme became a favorite with the early English Reformers, who drew on Erasmus and Melanchthon. See the full account by Father Bernard J. Vercamp, "The Indifferent Mean: Adiaphorism in the English Reformation to 1554" (Ph.D. dissertation, St. Louis University, 1972).

81. The succeeding passage on biographies is based on its equivalent in A. G. Dickens, *Contemporary Historians of the German Reformation* (University of London, Institute of Germanic Studies, 1979); reprinted in the author's *Reformation Studies* (London, 1982).

82. Philipp Melanchthon, *Historia de vita et actis M. Lutheri* (Latin editions from 1546; German from 1555), reprinted in *Corpus Reformatorum*, VI, 155–170; his *Leichenrede* on Luther in ibid., XI, 726–734; and his *Oratio de vita Bugenhagii* in ibid., XII, 295–305.

83. Joachim Camerarius, *De Philippi Melanchthonis ortu, totius vitae curriculo . . . narratio* (Leipzig, 1566; later editions with variant titles). It occupies 164 double-column pages in A. F. Neander, ed., *Vitae quatuor reformatorum* (Berlin, 1841). Compare *Neue deutsche Biographie* (Berlin, 1956), III, 104–105; J. E. Sandys, *Short History of Classical Scholarship*, 2nd ed. (Cambridge, 1921), II, 266–267. Another early memoir of Melanchthon is J. Heerbrand, *Oratio in obitum M.* (Tübingen, 1560).

84. In 1534–1536; see *British Museum General Catalogue of Printed Books to 1955*, Capito, W. F., and Grynacus, S. These together with Oswald Myconius on Zwingli (see n. 85) were translated into English and published in 1561 by Henry Bennet of Calais as *A famous and godly history*.

85. Oswald Myconius, *Vita Huldrici Zwinglii* (1532), reprinted in Neander, *Vitae*. Compare H. W. Pipkin, *A Zwingli Bibliography* (Pittsburgh, 1972); and G. R. Potter, *Zwingli* (Cambridge, 1976).

86. Text in Allen, *Opus Epistolarum*, I, 56–71; English translation in J. C. Olin, ed., *Christian Humanism and the Reformation* (New York, 1965), pp. 31–54.

87. C. C. Neudecker and L. Preller, eds., *Friedrichs des Weisen Leben und Zeitgeschichte von Georg Spalatin* (Jena, 1851). The scholarly life by Irmgard Höss, *Georg Spalatin, 1484–1545* (Weimar, 1956), gives limited attention to his work as historian, but refers to W. Flack, "Georg Spalatin als Geschichtschreiber," in Otto Kerne, ed., *Zur Geschichte und Kultur des Elb-Saale-Raumes: Festschrift für W. Möllenberg* (Burg, 1939), pp. 211–230. Note also A. Seelheim, *Georg Spalatin als sächsischer Historiograph* (Halle, 1876). Other references in *Biographisches Wörterbuch zur deutschen Geschichte*, 2nd ed. (Munich, 1975), III, 2690–91.

88. A. J. D. Rust, ed., *M. Johann Mathesius Leben Dr. Martin Luthers* (Berlin, 1841). The text is taken from the first edition (Wittenberg, 1565).

89. *Joannis Calvini vita a Theodoro Beza* (1575; many later editions).

90. Cyriacus Spangenberg, *Historia vom Leben, Lere und Tode Hieronymi Savonarole Anno 1498 zu Florenz verbrand* (Wittenberg, 1556). The text is preceded by a list of fourteen principal sources. For references to Spangenberg see *Biographisches Wörterbuch*, III, 2692.

91. Compare H. Buscher, *Heinrich Pantaleon und sein Heldenbuch* (Basel, 1946).

92. *Plutarchi . . . opuscula quaedam, D. Erasmo . . . P. Melanchthone interpretibus* (1518).

93. For example, Justus Menius, *Ein tröstliche Predigt über der Leich und Begrebnis der Erwirdigen Herrn F. Mecums* [Friedrich Myconius] (Wittenberg, 1546); *Oratio J. J. Grynaei de vita et morte . . . Friderici Widebrami Doctoris Theologi* (Heidelberg, 1580).

94. "Nec tantum illos vocat ad hanc militiam, qui tenent ordinariam potestatem, sed saepe illis ipsis bellum infert per Doctores ex aliis ordinibus delectos" (*Leichenrede* in the 1555 edition of Melanchthon's *Luther,* sigs. H3–H4).

95. Sandys, *Short History,* II, 258–259, cites Karl Pearson to this effect, yet the remainder of his chapter effectively destroys this pessimistic view.

2. Weapons of Propaganda

1. Cited by H. C. White, *Tudor Books of Saints and Martyrs* (Madison, Wis., 1963), pp. 37–38.

2. H. Gee and W. J. Hardy, eds., *Documents Illustrative of English Church History* (London, 1896), p. 271.

3. *Die recht warhafft und gründtlich Hystori oder geschicht von bruder Hainrich inn Diethmar verprent* (Augsburg, etc., 1525); see also *Weimarer Ausgabe* (*W.A.*), XVIII, 215–230. English translation in J. Pelikan and H. Lehmann, eds., *Luther's Works,* American ed. (Philadelphia, 1958), XXXII, 265–286.

4. Rainer Pineas, "William Tyndale's Influence on John Bale's Polemical Use of History," *Archiv für Reformationsgeschichte,* 53 (1962), pp. 79–96, gives the references. On William Tracy, see *Dictionary of National Biography* (hereafter *DNB*), LVII, 140.

5. The title varies among the numerous editions. That of 1555 begins *Recueil de plusieurs personnes* and includes the phrase *depuis Jean Wicleff & Jean Huss;* others begin *Actiones et Monimenta Martyrum* or *"L'Etat de l'Eglise."* The modern standard edition by D. Benoit (Toulouse, 3 vols., 1885–1889) follows the text of 1619 under the title *Histoire des Martyrs persecutés et mis à mort pour la vérité de l'Evangile, depuis le temps des Apostres iusques à présent.* The introduction to Benoit is useful, but its list of editions is incomplete. These should include a German translation of extracts by Nathane Chytraeus (c. 1587) and an English translation (1602) by Simon Patrike.

6. Introduction by Benoit (see n. 5); *Dictionnaire de Biographie Française,* IX, 1222–23.

7. D. R. Kelley, "Martyrs, Myths and the Massacre: The Background of St. Bartholomew," in A. Soman, ed., *The Massacre of St. Bartholomew: Reappraisals and Documents* (The Hague, 1974), pp. 181–202.

8. Edition by Benoit (see n. 5), I, introduction, p. xxxiii.

9. Ibid., p. xli.

10. Ibid., p. 272. See Theodorus Beza, *Histoire ecclésiastique des églises reformées,* ed. G. Baum and E. Cunitz (Paris, 1883), I, 15.

11. Ibid., I, 35–46; III, 345–347, 366–367, on the massacres at Mérindol and Cabrières; see n. 20.

12. For instance, it was the target of Jacques Sévart, *L'Anti-martyrologe; ou, Vérité manifestée contre les Histoires des Supposés Martyrs de la Religion prétendue Réformée imprimées à Genève onze fois,* etc. (Lyon, 1622).

13. The chief biography is A. Garnier, *Agrippa d'Aubigné et le Parti Protestant* (Paris, 3 vols., 1928).

14. Ibid., I, 225–227.

15. The standard edition, cited henceforth, is by A. Garnier and J. Plattard (Paris, 4 vols., 1932). Recent editions include that by J. Bailbe (Paris, 1968) and the well-edited selection by I. D. McFarlane (London, 1970).

16. Théodore d'Aubigné, *Les Tragiques,* IV, 11. 91–94. On Book 4 see especially the essay by J. Plattard in *Miscellany . . . presented to Leon E. Kastner* (Cambridge, 1942).

17. D'Aubigné, *Les Tragiques,* IV, 11. 603–606.

18. Ibid., 11. 1259–61.

19. See R. Regosin, "D'Aubigné's *Les Tragiques:* A Protestant Apocalypse," *Publications of the Modern Language Association of America,* 81 (1966), pp. 363–368.

20. John Foxe, *Acts and Monuments,* ed. G. Townsend and S. R. Cattley, (London, 8 vols., 1839–1841; hereafter Foxe, *A and M*), IV, 474, 507.

21. Printed in J. H. Smith, ed., *The Latin Comedies of John Foxe the Martyrologist: Titus et Gesippus, Christus Triumphans* (Ithaca, N.Y., and London, 1973).

22. See White, *Tudor Books,* p. 133; Patrick Collinson, *Archbishop Grindal, 1519–1583* (London, 1979), pp. 79–82.

23. Foxe, *A and M,* preface, I, viii.

24. Ibid., p. viii.

25. Ibid., p. xxvi.

26. Ibid., p. xiv.

27. White, *Tudor Books,* p. 135.

28. Thomas Brice, *Compendious Register in Metre . . . ,* 2nd ed. (London, 1599), sig. B 2. The poem is reprinted in A. F. Pollard, ed., *Tudor Tracts* (Westminster, 1903).

29. Foxe, *A and M,* VIII, 672.

30. Cited by Glanmor Williams, "Some Protestant Views of Early British Church History," in *Welsh Reformation Essays* (Cardiff, 1967), p. 211.

31. John Aylmer, *An Harborowe for faithfull and trewe subjects* (Strasbourg, 1559), sig. P. 4v, marginal note; see also W. Haller, *Foxe's "Book of Martyrs" and the Elect Nation* (London, 1963), p. 87.

32. Foxe, *A and M,* VIII, 600–625.

33. Ibid., p.628.

34. J. F. Mozley, *John Foxe and His Book* (London, 1940), pp. 86–91. In general, Foxe was a moderate in the manner of Grindal; he denounced "these factious Puritans" (ibid., p. 112).

35. Cited by V. N. Olsen, *John Foxe and the Elizabethan Church* (Berkeley and London, 1973), p. 206. See also A. G. Dickens, "The English Reformation and Religious Tolerance," *XIIᵉ Congrès International des Sciences Historiques, I. Grands Thèmes* (Paris, 1965), pp. 184–185. Important on this and other aspects is J. T. McNeill, "John Foxe: Historiographer, Disciplinarian, Tolerationist," *Church History,* 43 (1974), pp. 216–229. On his personal relationships see the lecture by N. J. Williams, *John Foxe the Martyrologist* (Dr. Williams's Trust, London, 1975).

36. Olsen, *John Foxe*, p. 210.

37. John Foxe, Preface to *The Whole Workes of W. Tyndall, John Frith and Doctor Barnes* (1572–1573), sigs. A ii r–A iii r.

38. See J. A. F. Thomson, *The Later Lollards, 1414–1520* (London, 1965), p. 245; M. Aston, "Lollardy and the Reformation: Survival or Revival?" *History*, 49 (1964), pp. 149–170.

39. Foxe, *A and M*, VI, 676, the martyrdom of Hooper. That of Ridley was no less prolonged.

40. James Brooks, *Sermon very notable, Fruictefull, and Godlie, made at Paule's crosse* (1553), sig. K iv.

41. J. G. Nichols, ed., "Sermon of the Child Bishop, pronownsyd by John Stubs, Querester, on Childermas Day at Gloceter, 1558," *Camden Miscellany*, 7 (1975), p. 172.

42. *DNB*, 581–590.

43. S. R. Maitland, *The Reformation in England* (London and New York, 1906), p. 187.

44. R. W. Dixon, *History of the Church of England* (London and Oxford, 6 vols., 1884–1902), V, 328–329.

45. Mozley, *John Foxe*, pp. 239–240.

46. Ibid., pp. 206–222.

47. Ibid., pp. 223–235. See J. E. Booty, *John Jewel as Apologist of the Church of England* (London, 1963), pp. 104–106.

48. For example, K. G. Powell, *The Marian Martyrs and the Reformation in Bristol* (Bristol, 1972).

49. For Haemstede's biography see A. J. Jelsma, *Adriaan van Haemstede en zijn Martelaarsboek* (The Hague, 1970); short but referenced accounts are in P. C. Molhuysen and P. J. Blok, eds., *Nieuw Nederlandsch Biografisch Woordenboek* (Leiden, 1911), I, cols. 1013–16; P. P. de Brie and J. Loosjes, eds., *Biografisch Woordenboek van Protestantsche Godgeleerden in Nederland* (The Hague, n.d. [c. 1920], III, 439–446; *Allgemeine deutsche Biographie*, X, 310–311; see also n. 50. On Haemstede in London, see Collinson, *Grindal*, pp. 134–140.

50. See especially Jelsma, *Haemstede*, pp. 234–244; Jelsma gives the evidence for his unusual beliefs in chaps. 3 and 9.

51. Adriaan van Haemstede, *De gheschiedenisse ende de doodt der vromer Martelaren die om het ghetuigenisse des Evangeliums haer bloedt ghestort hebben van de tyden Christi af totten Jare MDLIX toe, by een vergadert op het Kortste.* The place of printing is not quite certain: see arguments in J.-F. Gilmont's article (cited below), pp. 393 ff. Modern edition by A. Kuyper (Rotterdam, 1911). Of the recent commentaries see (in addition to Jelsma, chap. 6). J.-F. Gilmont, "La Genèse du martyrologe d'Adriaen van Haemstede," *Revue d'histoire ecclésiastique*, 63 (1968), pp. 379–414; A. L. E. Verheyen, *Le Martyrologe protestant des Pays-Bas du Sud au seizième siècle* (Brussels, 1960); the articles by L. E. Halkin in *Mélanges historiques offerts à M. Jean Meghoffer* (Lausanne, 1952) and *Analecta Bollandiana*, 68 (1950).

52. On martyrology among the Radicals see H. J. Hillerbrand, *A Bibliography of Anabaptism, 1520–1630* (Elkhart, Ind., 1962); H. S. Bender and C. H. Smith,

eds., *The Mennonite Encyclopedia* (Hillsboro, Kans., 4 vols., 1955–1959), III, 517–524; A. F. Mellink, ed., *Documenta Anabaptistica Neerlandica* (Leiden, 1975), I.

53. *Allgemeine deutsche Biographie*, XXVII, 97–99; works on Rabus are listed in Karl Schottenloher, *Bibliographie zur deutschen Geschichte im Zeitalter der Glaubenspaltung, 1517–1585* (Leipzig, 6 vols., 1933–1939), II, 158.

54. Ludwig Rabus, *Historien der Martyrer . . . Darinn das Erster und Ander Buch von den Heyligen Auserwölten Gottes Zeugen, Bekennern und Martyren* (Strasbourg, 1554–1558).

55. For the figures see G. F. Nuttall, "The English Martyrs, 1535–1680: A Statistical Review," *Journal of Ecclesiastical History*, 22 (1971), pp. 191–197.

56. *Historia aliquot . . . martyrum, maxime octodecim Cartusianorum* (Mainz, 1550; Brugge, 1583): there are two English translations (1890 and 1935, the latter edited by G. W. S. Curtis).

57. Fisher's *Treatis* is printed in *Early English Text Society, Extra Series*, 117 (1921); see White, *Tudor Books*, pp. 107–110.

58. *Hall's Chronicle* (London, 1809), p. 817.

59. William Roper, *The Life of Sir Thomas More*, ed. E. V. Hitchcock, in *Early English Text Society, Original Series*, 197 (1935), pp. 26–72.

60. Ibid., p. 55.

61. Nicholas Harpsfield, *The Life and Death of Sir Thomas Moore, knight*, ed. E. V. Hitchcock, in *Early English Text Society, Original* Series, 186 (1932).

62. Thomas Stapleton, *Tres Thomae*, in *Opera* (Paris, 1620), IV, 932–1065; translated in part by P. E. Hallett as *The Life and Illustrious Martyrdom of Sir Thomas More* (London, 1928).

63. Ibid., p. 145.

64. A. L. Rowse, "Nicholas Roscarrock and His Lives of the Saints," in J. H. Plumb, ed., *Studies in Social History: A Tribute to G. M. Trevelyan* (London, 1955), pp. 1–31.

65. Robert Parsons, *A Treatise of Three Conversions of England* (Saint-Omer, 3 vols., 1603–1604), sig. D 3.

66. Robert Parsons, *An Epistle of the Persecution of Catholickes in Englande* (Douai, 1582), in *English Recusant Literature, 1558–1640* (London, 1973), CXXV, 6.

67. Ibid., pp. 96–97.

68. See White, *Tudor Books*, pp. 206–223.

69. William Allen, *A Briefe Historie of the Glorious Martyrdom of xii Reverend Priestes*, reprinted as *Father Edmund Campion and His Companions*, ed. J. H. Pollen (London, 1908), introduction, p. ix.

70. Ibid., p. 25.

71. William Allen, *Atrue, sincere, and modest defence of the English Catholiques* (Ingolstadt, 1584); [Lord Burghley], *The Execution of Justice in England* (1583), ed. F. L. van Baumer (New York, 1939).

72. *Catholic Record Society Miscellany*, 1 (1905), p. 45.

73. John Bossy, "The Character of Elizabethan Catholicism," in T. Aston, ed., *Crisis in Europe, 1560–1660* (London, 1965), p. 235.

74. John Mush, "Life of Margaret Clitherow," in J. Morris, ed., *The Troubles of Our Catholic Forefathers* (1872–1879), III, 360.

75. White, *Tudor Books,* pp. 248–249.

76. Cited in ibid., p. 272.

77. Nearly all are listed in Conyers Read, *Bibliography of British History, Tudor Period,* 2nd ed. (Oxford, 1959).

78. For the broad background see John Bossy, *The English Catholic Community, 1570–1850* (London, 1975). On English Catholics throughout the Reformation see J. J. Scarisbrick, *The Reformation and the English People* (Oxford, 1984).

3. A Middle Way

1. A general account, now being revised, is in A. G. Dickens, *The English Reformation* (London, 1964). It is enlarged by more recent works, such as D. M. Loades, *The Reign of Mary Tudor* (London, 1979); and Claire Cross, *Church and People 1450–1660* (London, 1976).

2. The best guide to Tudor historical writers is F. J. Levy, *Tudor Historical Thought* (San Marino, Calif., 1967); chapter 3 concerns the Reformation writers. Glanmor Williams, *Reformation Views on Church History* (London, 1970), is brief but penetrating. Quentin Skinner, *The Foundations of Modern Political Thought,* vol. II: *The Reformation* (Cambridge, 1978), is frequently relevant.

3. J. R. Tanner, *Tudor Constitutional Documents,* 2nd ed. (Cambridge, 1951), pp. 40–46.

4. R. Koebner, "The Imperial Crown of This Realm," *Bulletin of the Institute of Historical Research,* 26 (1953), pp. 29–52.

5. Edmund Dudley's *The Tree of Commonwealth* was written c. 1509; modern edition by D. M. Brodie (Cambridge, 1948).

6. *Defensor Pacis* (1324); edition by C. W. Previté Orton (Cambridge, 1928), and translation by A. Gewirth (New York, 1956). For its Tudor influence, see Skinner, *Foundations,* pp. 37, 101, and other references in his index. See also G. H. Sabine, *A History of Political Theory,* 3rd ed., revised (London, 1951), pp. 252–263.

7. Stephen Gardiner, *De vera obedientia Oratio* (London, 1535, etc.). Contemporary English translation in P. Janelle, *Obedience in Church and State* (Cambridge, 1930); for this passage see p. 93.

8. On Cromwell's propagandists see F. L. van Baumer, *The Early Tudor Theory of Kingship* (New Haven, 1940); W. G. Zeeveld, *Foundations of Tudor Policy* (Cambridge, Mass., 1948), chaps. 4, 5, 6; G. R. Elton, *Policy and Police* (Cambridge, 1972), chap. 4; and the same author's *Reform and Renewal* (Cambridge, 1973), chap. 3.

9. Zeeveld, *Tudor Policy,* p. 139n30, lists the main texts.

10. On Starkey see ibid.; see also K. M. Burton, ed., *A Dialogue between Reginald Pole and Thomas Lupset* (London, 1948).

11. J. K. Yost, "Taverner's Use of Erasmus and the Protestantization of English Humanism," *Renaissance Quarterly,* 23 (1970), pp. 266–276; quotation on p. 274; J. K. Yost, "German Protestant Humanism and the Early English Reformation: Richard Taverner and Official Translation," *Bibliothèque d'humanisme et renaissance,* 32 (1970), pp. 613–625; E. J. Devereux, "Richard Taverner's Translations of Erasmus," *The Library,* 19 (1964), pp. 212–214. On Taverner in general see T. H. L. Parker, *English Reformers,* Library of Christian Classics, 26 (London, 1966), pp. 221–252.

12. C. H. Williams, ed., *English Historical Documents,* vol. V: *1485–1558* (London, 1967), pp. 795–805.

13. Dixon, *History of the Church of England,* II, 233–234, summarizes the Latin text in *Journals of the House of Lords, 1509–1547,* p. 129. See also J. A. Froude, *A History of England from the Fall of Wolsey to the Defeat of the Spanish Armada* (London, 12 vols., 1856–1870), III, 291–292.

14. Edward Hall, *The Union of the Two Noble Families of Lancaster and York* (London, 1550), fol. cclxi, verso.

15. From the Breviary of Cardinal Quiñones, published by Paul III in 1535; from the Lutheran Church orders; and from the *Consultatio* of Hermann von Wied, archbishop of Cologne, recently turned Protestant (see F. E. Brightman, *The English Rite* [London, 2 vols., 1915]).

16. Rainer Pineas, "William Tyndale's Use of History as a Weapon of Religious Controversy," *Harvard Theological Review,* 55 (1962); Pineas, "Tyndale's Influence on John Bale."

17. Rainer Pineas, "Robert Barnes's Polemical Use of History," *Bibliothèque d'humanisme et renaissance,* 26 (1964), pp. 55–69.

18. Robert Barnes, *Vitae Romanorum Pontificum* (Wittenberg, 1536; Basel, 1555); see also Charles S. Anderson, "Robert Barnes on Luther," in J. Pelikan, ed., *Interpreters of Luther* (Philadelphia, 1968), chap. 3.

19. Robert Barnes, *A Supplycacion unto the most gracyous prynce H. the viii* (London, 1534). See also Levy, *Tudor Historical Thought,* p. 88, citing *The Whole Works of W. Tindall, John Frith and Doct. Barnes* (London, 1573). This collection exemplifies the parallel methods of Tyndale (p. 366) and Barnes (pp. 193–194).

20. On Bale see the biographies by Jesse W. Harris (Urbana, 1940) and Honor McCusker (Bryn Mawr, 1942); Levy, *Tudor Historical Thought,* pp. 89–101; and Rainer Pineas, "John Bale's Nondramatic Works of Religious Controversy," *Studies in the Renaissance,* 9 (1962), pp. 218–233. On his historical scholarship see May McKisack, *Medieval History in the Tudor Age* (Oxford, 1971), pp. 11–23.

21. John Bale, *Acta Romanorum Pontificum . . . usque ad tempora Pauli IV* (Basel, 1558, etc.). Translated by J. Studley as *The Pageant of the Popes* (London, 1574).

22. *The vocacyon of Johan Bale to the bishopric of Ossorie in Ireland* (London, 1553); reprinted in *Harleian Miscellany,* 6 (1810), pp. 437–464.

23. *The image of bothe churches* (London, ?1548; 1550, etc.), reprinted in H.

Christmas, ed., *Select Works of John Bale* (Parker Society, 1849), pp. 249–640. *The actes of Englysh votaryes* ("Wesel," ?London, 1546; later editions 1550, 1551, 1560).

24. *A brefe chronycle concernynge the examinacyon of Syr J. Oldcastle* (?Antwerp, 1544; London, ?1548). Bale also published the examinations of Anne Askew at Wesel in 1546 and at Marburg in 1547 (A. W. Pollard and G. R. Redgrave, eds., *Short-Title Catalogue* [London, 1950], nos. 848–851).

25. Foxe, *A & M*, I [text of Foxe], 9.

26. See, for instance, articles 9, 10, 11, 12, 13, and esp. 17.

27. On Jewel we follow mainly Booty, *John Jewel as Apologist.* Jewel's Latin version, *Apologia Ecclesiae Anglicanae* (London, 1562), was immediately followed by an English translation, *An Apologie, or aunswer in defence of the Church of England* (London, 1562). The able translation of 1564 was by Lady Ann Bacon, mother of Francis; this is edited by J. E. Booty (Ithaca, N.Y., 1963) with a useful introduction. On Thomas Harding of Louvain see Booty, *John Jewel as Apologist,* pp. 58–79.

28. Booty, *John Jewel as Apologist,* pp. 171–173. See p. 198 for Martyr's influence on Jewel's view of monarchy.

29. Ibid., pp. 186–188.

30. Ibid., p. 190; see also pp. 177–185.

31. Ibid., pp. 192–194.

32. Ibid., p. 197; on the "godly prince" see pp. 189–203.

33. Hooker's *Laws* have a complicated history. The preface and first four books appeared in 1593, the fifth in 1597. Books 6 and 8 were published only in 1648, although 6 was probably not intended to belong to the *Laws.* Book 7 came out in 1662, but this and the important book 8 are thought by some scholars to be early drafts. On this topic and the general purposes of the work see J. W. Allen, *History of Political Thought in the Sixteenth Century,* 3rd ed. (London, 1951), pt. 2, chap. 6; and C. Morris, *Political Thought in England: Tyndale to Hooker* (London, 1953), chap. 9. W. D. J. Cargill Thompson's chapter "The Philosophy of the Politic Society," in his collection *Studies in the Reformation: Luther to Hooker* (London, 1980), pp. 131–191, reviews the findings of modern scholarship and proceeds to a moderate revisionist view, which we largely accept. A sizable abridged version of the *Laws* was edited by A. S. McGrade and B. Vickers (London, 1975), with further valuable criticism.

34. Cargill Thompson, *Studies,* p. 140, following Morris.

35. Ibid., p. 143.

36. Ibid., p. 140.

37. Allen, *Political Thought,* pp. 195–196.

38. A. F. Scott Pearson, *Thomas Cartwright and Elizabethan Puritanism, 1535–1603* (Cambridge, 1925); A. Peel and L. H. Carlson, eds., *Cartwrightiana* (London, 1951).

39. McGrade's introduction, pp. 18, 27–28, in the abridged edition, cited in n. 33.

40. Cargill Thompson, *Studies,* pp. 147–149; on Hooker's use of Aquinas see also Allen, *Political Thought,* pp. 186–189.

41. Cargill Thompson, *Studies*, pp. 141–142.

42. Ibid., p. 142.

43. Quotation from W. Speed Hill, ed., *The Folger Library Edition of the Works of Richard Hooker* (London, 4 vols., 1977–1982), I, 188–189; Cargill Thompson, *Studies*, 3, pp. 150–151.

44. Cargill Thompson, *Studies*, pp. 165–169.

45. See Levy, *Tudor Historical Thought*, pp. 53–68.

46. See ibid., chap. 52.

47. On John Knox as a historian see especially the editor's introduction in W. C. Dickinson, ed., *John Knox's History of the Reformation in Scotland* (Edinburgh, 2 vols., 1949). Biographies are numerous: see J. Ridley, *John Knox* (Oxford, 1968). For an earlier appreciation see A. Lang, "Knox as a Historian," *Scottish Historical Review*, 2 (1905), pp. 113–130.

48. Dickinson's edition is in modern English; for the original text see volumes I and II of D. Laing, ed., *The Works of John Knox*, Bannatyne Club (Edinburgh, 6 vols., 1846–1864).

49. Quoted by Dickinson in *John Knox's History*, I, lxxiii.

50. Ibid., p. lxxx. Among Knox's followers was the great humanist George Buchanan, whose *Rerum scoticarum historia* (Edinburgh, 1582) henceforth provided the main source of information on Scottish history throughout Europe.

4. A Sense of Distance

1. On the relations between legal studies and political thought see J. H. Franklin, *Jean Bodin and the Sixteenth-Century Revolution in the Methodology of Law and History* (New York and London, 1963); and three articles by D. R. Kelley: "Guillaume Budé and the First Historical School of Law," *American Historical Review*, 72 (1967), pp. 807–834; "Legal Humanism and the Sense of History," *Studies in the Renaissance*, 13 (1966), pp. 184–199; "Jean du Tillet, Archivist and Antiquary," *Journal of Modern History*, 38 (1966), pp. 337–354.

2. On the rise of historicism in France and elsewhere see D. R. Kelley, *Foundations of Modern Historical Scholarship* (New York and London, 1970); Polman, *L'Elément historique;* E. Cochrane, *Historians and Historiography in the Italian Renaissance* (Chicago and London, 1981), esp. chap. 16; G. W. Sypher, "Similarities between the Scientific and the Historical Revolutions at the End of the Renaissance," *Journal of the History of Ideas*, 26 (1965), pp. 353–368; F. S. Fussner, *The Historical Revolution: English Historical Writing and Thought, 1580–1640* (London, 1962).

3. C. Vivanti, "Paulus Aemilius Gallis condidit historias?" *Annales*, 19 (1964), pp. 1117–24.

4. On the political ideas of the French Wars of Religion see, for instance, P. Mesnard, *L'Essor de la philosophie politique au 16ᵉ siècle* (Paris, 1936); Allen, *Political Thought;* Sabine, *Political Theory;* Skinner, *Foundations.* J. N. Figgis, *Studies in Political Thought from Gerson to Grotius, 1414–1625* (Cambridge, 1907; new edition, New York, 1960), is still useful. J. H. M. Salmon, *Society in*

Crisis: France in the Sixteenth Century (London, 1975), gives excellent background. On the influence of Geneva see the two volumes by R. M. Kingdon, *Geneva and the Coming of the Wars of Religion in France, 1555–1563* (Geneva, 1956) and *Geneva and the Consolidation of the French Protestant Movement, 1564–1572* (Madison, Wis., 1967).

5. The fifth and final volume, which brought the narrative to 1607, appeared posthumously in 1620. The sixteen-volume edition in French (Paris, 1734) is commonly used by scholars. See J. W. Thompson, *A History of Historical Writing* (New York, 2 vols., 1942), I, 568–570; H. E. Barnes, *A History of Historical Writing*, 2nd ed. (New York, 1962), p. 118. The standard survey is S. Kinser, *The Works of Jacques-Auguste de Thou* (The Hague, 1966).

6. *New Catholic Encyclopedia*, XIV, 142. It need hardly be added that its vast length and Latin language must have narrowed the work's direct influence.

7. See *Nouvelle Biographie Générale*, XLIII, 795–797.

8. Ibid., XLVI, 144–152.

9. Skinner, *Foundations*, II, 189–358, mainly concerns Calvinism and the theory of revolution; see also J. T. McNeill, "The Democratic Element in Calvin's Thought," *Church History*, 18 (1949), pp. 153–171.

10. For the extensive recent bibliography on the tolerationists see H. Lutz, ed., *Zur Geschichte der Toleranz und Religionsfreiheit* (Darmstadt, 1977), pp. 483–490. General guidance in J. Lecler, *Toleration and the Reformation*, trans. T. L. Westow (London, 2 vols., 1960); W. K. Jordan, *The Development of Religious Toleration in England* (London, 1932); Skinner, *Foundations*, II, 244–254; Allen, *Political Thought*, pt. 2, chap. 5; F. E. Buisson, *Sébastien Castellion: Sa vie et son oeuvre* (Paris, 1892).

11. Claude de Seyssel, *The Monarchy of France*, trans. J. H. Hexter, ed. D. R. Kelley (New Haven and London, 1981). On the broad field see G. Weill, *Les Théories sur le pouvoir royal en France pendant les guerres de religion* (Paris, 1891); Mesnard, *Philosophie politique;* Allen, *Political Thought*, pt. 3, chaps. 2, 8.

12. On this speech see Lecler, *Toleration*, II, 68–69; and Skinner, *Foundations*, II, 250–251. Following an error by the editor of the *Oeuvres de Michel de L'Hôpital*, it has been commonly misdated.

13. Hotman is discussed in the general works cited in n. 4; see also Beatrice Reynolds, *Proponents of Limited Monarchy . . . François Hotman and Jean Bodin*, Columbia University Studies in History, 334 (New York, 1931); G. H. M. Posthumus Meyjes, "Jean Hotman's *Syllabus* of Eirenical Literature," in D. Baker, ed., *Studies in Church History, Subsidia 2* (Oxford, 1979), pp. 175–193. D. R. Kelley, *François Hotman: A Revolutionary Ordeal* (Princeton, N.J., 1973); and *François Hotman, Francogallia*, Latin text by R. E. Giesey, trans. J. H. M. Salmon (New York, 1972).

14. "Junius Brutus," *Vindiciae contra tyrannos, sive de principis in populum populique in principem legitima potestate* (Basel, 1578–1579; French translation, 1581); English translation: *A Defence of Liberty against Tyrants*, 1689; new edition with introduction by H. J. Laski (London, 1924). On Philippe de Mornay,

sieur du Plessis-Marly (1549–1623), see *Dictionnaire de Biographie Française,* XII, 415–417.

15. Particularly in Luther's appeals *To the Nobility of the German Nation* (1520) and *To the Councillors . . . that they should establish Christian Schools* (1524).

16. On Ponet see Zeeveld, *Foundations,* pp. 241–263. On Goodman, Ponet, and Knox see Allen, *Political Thought,* pt. 1, chap. 6; and Skinner, *Foundations,* II, 21–41.

17. *Works of John Knox,* IV, 523–540.

18. See Skinner, *Foundations,* II, 347–348.

19. Guillaume Rose, *De justa reipublicae christianae in reges impios authoritate* (Paris, 1590; Antwerp, 1592), sometimes attributed to the Scotsman William Raynolds, who also used the pseudonym Rossaeus.

20. The *De rege et regis institutione* (1559) of the distinguished historian Juan de Mariana attracted little attention until the assassination of Henry IV in 1610, after which the hostile outcry gravely embarrassed and divided the Society of Jesus. *New Catholic Encyclopedia,* IX, 213; and F. L. Cross, ed., *Oxford Dictionary of the Christian Church,* 2nd ed. (1974), p. 873, both give references.

21. Jean Bodin, *Les six livres de la République* (Lyon, 1576, 1579; Paris, 1580, etc.). English editions by R. Knolles (1606) and K. D. McRae (Cambridge, 1962); excerpts by M. J. Tooley (Oxford, 1967). On its influence see Skinner, *Foundations,* II, 300–301.

22. On de Belloy (d. 1613) see *Dictionnaire de Biographie Française,* V, 1373.

23. William Barclay, *De regno et regali potestate adversus Buchanan, Brutum, Boucherium et reliquos monarchomachos libri vi* (Paris, 1600). On Barclay see *Dictionnaire de Biographie Française,* V, 383, with useful bibliography.

24. The Latin is in Figgis, *Studies in Political Thought,* pp. 276–277, from Bodin, bk. 3.

25. Henri Busson, *Le Rationalisme dans la littérature française de la Renaissance, 1533–1601* (Paris, 1957).

26. On Bodin several of the older works are still serviceable, notably R. Chauviré, *Jean Bodin, auteur de la République* (Paris, 1914); also H. J. L. Baudrillart, *Jean Bodin et son temps* (Paris, 1853); and E. Fournol, *Bodin prédecesseur de Montesquieu* (Paris, 1896). On this theme see P. L. Rose, *Bodin and the Great God of Nature* (Geneva, 1980). Sabine, *Political Theory;* Allen, *Political Thought;* and Busson, *Rationalisme,* have relevant chapters on Bodin; H. Denzer, ed., *Bodin* (Munich, 1973), exemplifies recent scholarship. For some texts and introductions see the edition by P. Mesnard in the series Corpus Général des Philosophes Français, vol. III: *Oeuvres philosophiques de Jean Bodin* (Paris, 1951). Mesnard also wrote on Bodin's trenchant religious views: "La Pensée religieuse de Bodin," *Revue du XVIᵉ siècle,* 16 (1929), pp. 77–121.

27. On the *Methodus ad facilem historiarum cognitionem* (Paris, 1566) see Franklin, *Jean Bodin;* and J. L. Brown, *The Methodus . . . of Jean Bodin: A Critical Study* (Washington, D.C., 1939). The Latin and French texts are in Mesnard, *Oeuvres philosophiques;* and a French text in an earlier book by

Mesnard, *Jean Bodin: La Méthode de l'histoire* (Paris, 1941). In propounding the *Méthode,* Bodin had an important predecessor: see D. R. Kelley, "Historia Integra: François Baudouin and His Conception of History," *Journal of the History of Ideas,* 25 (1964), pp. 35–57.

28. On Erasmus as an inspirer of both "liberal" and sectarian ideas see Williams, *Radical Reformation,* pp. 8–16; on Sebastian Franck see ibid., pp. 264, 457–466; and bibliography in Schottenloher, *Bibliographie zur deutschen Geschichte,* I, 263–266.

29. The first printed edition is *Ioannis Bodin colloquium heptaplomeres de rerum sublimium arcanis abditis. E codicibus manuscriptis . . . curavit Ludovicus Noack Suerjini Megalaburgiensium* (1857). There is a French translation edited by R. Chauviré (Paris, 1914), and one in English: *Jean Bodin: Colloquium of the Seven about Secrets of the Sublime* (Princeton, N.J., 1975), with introduction by Marion L. D. Kuntz.

30. For Michael Servetus see Williams, *Radical Reformation,* pp. 195–200, 311–318, 605–614, and other references in the index. For Laelius and Faustus Socinus see ibid., pp. 746–763, and other references in the index. Useful selected bibliographies may be found in the *Oxford Dictionary of the Christian Church,* pp. 1263 and 1285.

31. On the complexities of Montaigne's religion see D. Dreano, *La Religion de Montaigne* (new edition, Paris, 1969); and R. A. Sayce, *The Essays of Montaigne: A Critical Exploration* (London, 1972), chap. 9. The following paragraphs are mainly based on Sayce's remarkably close documentation. These and other writers cite C. Sclafert, *L'Ame religieux de Montaigne* (Paris, 1951); Busson, *Rationalisme,* also has two important chapters (13 and 14) on this theme.

32. For La Popelinière as historian see G. W. Sypher, "La Popelinière's *Histoire de France:* A Case of Historical Objectivity and Religious Censorship," *Journal of the History of Ideas,* 24 (1963), pp. 41–54. Myriam Yardeni, "La Conception de l'histoire dans l'oeuvre de la Popelinière," *Revue d'histoire moderne et contemporaine,* 11 (1964), pp. 109–126; D. R. Kelley, "History as a Calling: The Case of La Popelinière," in A. Molho and J. A. Tedeschi, eds., *Renaissance Studies in Honor of Hans Baron* (De Kalb, Ill., 1971), pp. 771–789.

33. On the general theory of La Popelinière see G. Huppert, *The Idea of Perfect History* (London, 1970), chaps. 8 and 9; the same author's "The Renaissance Background of Historicism," *History and Theory,* 5 (1966), pp. 48–60; and Yardeni, "La Conception de l'histoire."

34. The scholarly edition of the *Histoire ecclésiastique* was edited, also in three volumes, by G. Baum and E. Cunitz (Paris, 1883–1889), with a still viable introduction covering authorship, composition, and historical value: see III, i–lxxvii.

35. See L. C. Jones, *Simon Goulart, 1543–1628* (Geneva, 1917).

36. Alphonse de Ruble, *Commentaires et lettres de Blaise de Monluc* (Paris, 5 vols., 1864–1872), II, 343.

37. Beza's *Life* was originally prefixed to Calvin's *Commentary on Joshua* (Geneva, 1564). Another favorable early biography, prefixed to the second edition

of that work (1565), was really by Nicolas Colladon (*Oxford Dictionary of the Christian Church*, p. 223, which also has a useful list of later biographies).

38. On these hostile lives see J. R. Armogathe, "Les Vies de Calvin au xvie et xviie siècles," in P. Joutard, ed., *Historiographie de la Réforme* (Paris, 1977).

39. On Bolsec see ibid., pp. 46–47, and the *Dictionnaire de Biographie Française*, VII, 872.

5. An Age of Crisis

1. See, for instance, R. T. Vann, ed., *Century of Genius: European Thought, 1600–1700* (Englewood Cliffs, N.J., 1967).

2. See Trevor Aston, *Crisis in Europe, 1560–1660* (London, 1965).

3. Paul Hazard, *La Crise de la conscience européenne* (Paris, 1935). Translated by J. Lewis May as *The European Mind, 1680–1715* (London, 1953). References in this chapter are to the Penguin University Books edition, 1973.

4. Gerhard's *Meditationes Sacrae* appeared in many Latin and in even more English editions from the seventeenth to the nineteenth centuries, including R. Winterton's translation, *The Meditations of J. Gerhard* (Cambridge, 1627).

5. Bellarmine's views were stated in his *De Notis Ecclesiae* (Rome, 1606), bk. 4, chap. 13. Becanus set forth his ideas in a disputation in Vienna in 1616, *De Vocatione Ministrorum*. Extracts of both appear in Ernst Zeeden, *Martin Luther und die Reformation im Urteil des deutschen Luthertums* (Freiburg, 2 vols., 1952), II, 79–81, 239.

6. Johann Gerhard, *Beati Lutheri ad Ministerium et Reformationem legitima vocatio* (Jena, 30 October 1617); see Zeeden, *Martin Luther*, II, 70–79.

7. Johann Conrad Dannhauer (1603–1666), *Memoria Thaumasiandri Lutheri* (Strasbourg, 1661), foreword. Zeeden, *Martin Luther*, II, 126.

8. Johann Müller, *Lutherus Defensus* (Arnstadt, 1645); see Zeeden, *Martin Luther*, II, 110. Müller draws a parallel between Luther and the early Apostles. Judas betrayed Christ, Peter denied him, Thomas doubted him, and Paul persecuted the Church. Yet none of these failures, he argues, affected the truth of the apostolic teaching.

9. G. R. Cragg, *The Church and the Age of Reason, 1648–1789* (Harmondsworth, 1960). Herte noted that Francis of Sales took a critical view of Cochlaeus's interpretation of Luther (*Katholische Lutherbild*, I, 138–140).

10. Florimond de Raemond, *Histoire de la naissance, progrès et décadence de l'hérésie de ce siècle* (Rouen, 1623). On Florimond see Joutard, *Historiographie*, p. 47. Pierre Bayle has a long entry in his *Dictionnaire* (see n. 77), which is translated in E. A. Beller and M. du P. Lee, *Selections from Bayle's Dictionary* (Princeton, N.J., 1952), pp. 225–241. Bayle regards Florimond as "the unfittest man in the world to succeed in such an undertaking, considering the hatred he had conceived against the party wherein he had been brought up."

11. Caesar Baronius, *Annales ecclesiastici* (Rome, 1598–1607 and several later editions). An edition including additons by Rinaldi was published in Rome be-

tween 1646 and 1677. The standard work on Baronius is C. R. Pullapilly, *Caesar Baronius, Counter-Reformation Historian* (Notre Dame, Ind., 1975). Concise account and references in *New Catholic Encyclopedia*, II, 105–106. See also Barnes, *Historical Writing*, pp. 126–128.

12. The Latin and Spanish texts of Ribadeneira's *Vita Ignatii Loyola* are printed in *Monumenta Historica Societatis Jesu*, XCIII, which forms volume IV of the *Monumenta Ignatiana* (Rome, 1965). For background and discussion see the works by J. Brodrick: *Saint Ignatius Loyola: The Pilgrim Years* (New York, 1956); *St. Francis Xavier, 1506–1552* (New York, 1952); *The Origin of the Jesuits* (New York, 1940); *The Progress of the Jesuits* (New York, 1946).

13. See Brodrick, *St. Francis Xavier*, p. 536.

14. On these editions see A. Carayon, *Bibliographie historique de la Compagnie de Jésus* (Paris, 1864; reprinted Geneva, 1970), p. 102. Orlandini was a capable writer, neither enthusiastic about miracle stories nor secretive about the political activities of the Jesuits. See Barnes, *Historical Writing*, p. 1320. For a still useful survey of the sources for the early history of the Jesuits see Ludwig von Pastor, *History of the Popes*, ed. R. F. Kerr, 3rd ed. (London, 1950), XII, 1–3.

15. On the problems of Sacchini as a historian see Brodrick, *Progress of the Jesuits*, pp. 305–316.

16. Ibid., pp. 306–310.

17. On the matter of Laynez see ibid., pp. 311–314.

18. The literature on Sarpi is extensive. Thompson, *Historical Writing*, I, 541–547, has useful references to about 1940. Of the more recent articles see Frances A. Yates, "Paolo Sarpi's *History of the Council of Trent*," *Journal of the Warburg and Courtauld Institutes*, 7 (1944), pp. 123–143; G. Cozzi, "Fra Paolo Sarpi, l'anglicanesimo e la Historia del Concilio Tridentino" [with documents], *Rivista Storica Italiana*, 68 (1956), pp. 559–619. *Enciclopedia Cattolica* (1963) X, 1928–29; *Dictionnaire de Théologie Catholique*, XIV, 1115–21; Barnes, *Historical Writing*, pp. 128–129.

19. Paolo Sarpi, *Istoria del Concilio Tridentino* (London, 1619). By 1660 it had attained at least five editions in Italian and one in Latin. English translations appeared in 1620, 1629, 1640, and 1676.

20. As background, the best general history of the council does valuable service: Hubert Jedin, *Geschichte des Konzils von Trient* (Freiburg im Breisgau, 1957); translated as *A History of the Council of Trent* (Edinburgh, 2 vols., 1961). For Sarpi's questions see ibid., II, 7–12, where moderate Roman Catholic criticism is offered.

21. Sforza Pallavicino, *Istoria del Concilio di Trento* (Rome, 1656–1657).

22. The phrase occurs in the preface to the Authorized Version of the Bible (1611).

23. Peel and Carlson, *Cartwrightiana*, pp. 123, 207, 220. See Chapter 2.

24. William Camden, *Britannia sive florentissimorum regnorum Angliae, Scotiae, Hiberniae chorigraphica descriptio* (London, 1586, and five later editions to 1607, plus two in Frankfurt and two in Amsterdam). The first English translation was by Philemon Holland (1610); it was soon followed by several others.

25. William Camden, *Annales rerum Anglicarum et Hibernicarum regnante Elizabetha* (London, 1615). The second part was added in the edition of 1625, when the first English translation (by Abraham Darcie) also appeared; it was, however, made from a French edition (London, 1624) of the first part, to be succeeded by another of the whole work (Paris, 1627). Several English versions by others followed.

26. Camden, *Annals*, preface, MacCaffrey ed., p. 5 (see below). On the basic criticisms we are much indebted to H. R. Trevor-Roper, *Queen Elizabeth's First Historian, William Camden and the Beginnings of English Civil History* (Neale Lecture, London, 1971). With a most informative introduction, Wallace T. MacCaffrey edited selected chapters of the *Annals* under the original English title, *The History of the Most Renowned and Victorious Princess Elizabeth, late Queen of England* (Chicago and London, 1970) in the series Classics of British Historical Literature.

27. Camden, *Annals*, preface, MacCaffrey ed., p. 6.

28. Ibid.

29. Sir Walter Raleigh, *History of the World* (London, 1614).

30. Cited by S. B. Babbage, *Puritanism and Richard Bancroft* (London, 1962), p. 142.

31. Thomas Clark, *The Pope's Deadly Wound: tending to resolve all men in the chief and principal points now in controversie between the Papists and us* (London, 1635), p. 251.

32. *The Complete Prose Works of John Milton*, Yale edition (New Haven, 8 vols., 1953–1980), I (1953), 517–617.

33. Milton not only rejected orthodox Calvinist predestinarian theology in favor of Arminian doctrines of freedom of choice, but espoused heretical Arian views of the Trinity and creation, taught that the soul dies with the body until revived at the Resurrection, and professed support for polygamy and what amounted to divorce by consent.

34. *Areopagitica: A Speech . . . for the liberty of unlicensed printing*, in *Complete Prose Works of Milton*, Yale edition, II (New Haven, 1959), 485–570.

35. Ibid., pp. 553–554.

36. *Complete Prose Works of Milton*, VII (rev. ed., 1980), 239–272.

37. Lord Clarendon, *History of the Rebellion and Civil War in England* (Oxford, 1702). See Christopher Hill, *Society and Puritanism in Pre-Revolutionary England* (London, 1969), pp. 76–78.

38. Peter Heylyn, *Ecclesia Restaurata* (London, 1661).

39. See the moderate defense of the Reformation by Roger Twysden (1597–1672), whose *Historical Vindication of the Church of England* (1657) contrasted Elizabeth's Church with the disturbed times which succeeded it.

40. Thomas Fuller, *The History of the Worthies of England*, ed. J. Nichols (London, 2 vols., 1811).

41. Thomas Fuller, *The Church History of Britain from the Birth of Jesus Christ until the year MDCXLVIII*, ed. J. Nichols (London, 3 vols., 1868).

42. Dixon, *History of the Church of England*, VI, 39. The best recent study of Strype is W. D. J. Cargill Thompson, "John Strype as a Source for the Study

of Sixteenth Century English Church History," in his *Studies in the Reformation*, pp. 192–201.

43. John Strype, *Annals of the Reformation and Establishment of Religion and other occurrences in the Church of England during the first twelve years of Queen Elizabeth's Reign* (London, 1708–1709) and *Ecclesiastical Memorials relating chiefly to Religion and the Reformation of it, and the emergencies of the Church of England under King Henry VIII, King Edward VI and Queen Mary the First* (London, 1721).

44. John Strype, *Memorials of the most reverend Father in God Thomas Cranmer* (London, 1694; Oxford, 1840 edition), I, 1.

45. John Strype, *The Life and Acts of the Most reverend Father in God Edmund Grindal* (London, 1710; Oxford, 1821 edition), p. v; *The Life and Acts of Matthew Parker* (London, 1711; Oxford, 1821 edition), I, xiv; *The Life and Acts of John Whitgift* (London, 1718; Oxford, 1822 edition), II, 177.

46. See Cargill Thompson, *Studies in the Reformation*, pp. 199–201.

47. Gilbert Burnet, *History of My Own Time* (London, 1723, 1734; editions by M. J. Routh [1823–1833] and O. Airy [1897–1900]; supplement by H. C. Foxcroft [1902]).

48. Gilbert Burnet, *A History of the Reformation of the Church of England* (London, 1679–1715).

49. Nicholas Sander (1530–1581), *De Origine et Progressu Schismatis Anglicani* (Cologne, 1585).

50. Gilbert Burnet, *History of the Reformation*, new ed. (Oxford, 3 vols., 1816), I, xvi.

51. R. J. Madden, "Bishop Gilbert Burnet as a Man of Letters" (Unpublished Ph.D. dissertation, University College, London, 1963), pp. 73–74.

52. See Hazard, *European Mind*, pp. 103–106.

53. See Mansfield, *Phoenix*, chap. 8.

54. Ibid., pp. 249–250.

55. Louis Maimbourg, *Histoire du Lutheranisme* (Paris, 1681) and *Histoire du Calvinisme* (Paris, 1682).

56. Maimbourg, *Histoire du Lutheranisme*, pp. 18, 22.

57. Ibid., pp. 25–27.

58. Jacques Bénigne Bossuet, *Histoire des variations des églises protestantes*, in *Oeuvres complètes de Bossuet*, 2nd ed. (Paris, 10 vols., 1885), III, 159–451.

59. Ibid., pp. 159a, 160a.

60. Ibid., pp. 166b–167b, 175a.

61. Bossuet breaks from his chronological pattern and devotes the entirety of Book 5 to Melanchthon's reflections on the Reformation; see especially ibid., pp. 221a–233b.

62. Ibid., bk. 6, pp. 233a–237b.

63. Ibid., bk. 1, pp. 165–166a.

64. Hazard, *European Mind*, pt. 2, chap. 5.

65. François Véron (Veronius, c. 1575–1649), *Règle Générale de la Foi Catholique séparée de toutes les opinions de la théologie scolastique, et de tous autres sentiments particuliers ou abus* (Lyon, 1674), esp. cols. 1243–57.

66. Hazard, *European Mind,* pt. 2, pp. 259, 266.

67. Ernst Zeeden, *The Legacy of Luther* (London, 1954), pt. 2, chap. 2.

68. Hazard, *European Mind,* pt. 1, pp. 44–45.

69. René Descartes, *Discourse on method, and other writings,* trans. Arthur Wollaston (Harmondsworth, 1960).

70. Thomas Hobbes, *On Man* and *The Citizen,* ed. B. Gert (Gloucester, Mass., 1978); *Leviathan,* ed. C. B. Macpherson (Harmondsworth, 1968). John Locke, *Two Treatises of Government,* ed. P. Laslett (Cambridge, 1970); *An Essay Concerning Human Understanding* (London, 1964).

71. A. R. Hall, *The Scientific Revolution, 1500–1800* (London, 1954); H. T. Pledge, *Science since 1500* (London, 1966).

72. Hobbes, *Leviathan,* pt. 4, chap. 47, p. 712.

73. Richard Simon, *Histoire critique du Vieux Testament* (Rotterdam, 1678); *Histoire critique du texte du Nouveau Testament* (Rotterdam, 1689); *Histoire critique des versions du Nouveau Testament* (Rotterdam, 1690); *Histoire critique des principaux commentaires du Nouveau Testament* (Rotterdam, 1693). See also Hazard, *European Mind,* pt. 2, chap. 3.

74. Edward Gibbon, *Memoirs of My Life and Writings* (London, 1889), p. 34.

75. Pierre Bayle, *Pensées diverses écrites à un Docteur de Sorbonne à l'occasion de la comète qui parut au mois de décembre 1680* (1683). An English translation appeared in London in 1708.

76. Pierre Bayle, *Critique générale de l'histoire du Calvinisme de M. Maimbourg* (1682); *Ce que c'est que La France toute catholique sous le règne de Louis le Grand* (1685); and *Commentaires philosophiques sur ces paroles de Jesus-Christ: Contrain-les d'entrer, ou Traité de la tolerance universelle* (1686). The last appeared in English translation in 1708, and the work on Maimbourg's history of Calvinism in 1714.

77. Pierre Bayle, *Dictionnaire historique et critique* (Rotterdam, 1697). The second edition was translated into English as *The Dictionary Historical and Critical of Mr. Peter Bayle* (London, 1734–1738). Quotations are from this edition. See also Mansfield, *Phoenix,* chap. 9.

78. Cited by E. A. Beller and M. Lee, *Selections from Bayle's Dictionary* (Princeton, N.J., 1952), p. xiii.

79. Bayle, *Dictionary,* III, 934–954.

80. Ibid., p. 949.

81. Ibid., II, 800–815. In the article on Luther, Bayle endorses Simon Fontaine's judgment that Erasmus was Luther's "John the Baptist," who picked the lock and half-opened the door which Luther subsequently opened wide. Ibid., III, 938.

82. Ibid., IV, 183–193.

83. Ibid., II, 260–275.

84. Ibid., I, 284–290.

85. Ibid., IV, 653–658.

86. Cited in Beller and Lee, *Selections,* p. xix.

87. Cragg, *Church,* chap. 7; Zeeden, *Legacy of Luther,* pt. 2, chap. 3.

88. P. J. Spener, *Theologische Bedenken* (Halle, 4 vols., 1701), I, 158–160; III, 179–180. Extracts in Zeeden, *Martin Luther,* II, 198–200.

89. Veit Ludwig Freiherr von Seckendorff, *Historia Lutheranismi Commentarius historicus et apologeticus deLutheranismo,* 2nd ed. (Leipzig, 1694).

90. Ibid., I *Praeloquium,* a3.

91. Ibid., pp. 643–645.

92. Ibid., d, d2, p. 205.

93. Ibid., d2, d4, p. 700.

94. Gottfried Arnold, *Unpartheyische Kirchen-und Ketzerhistorie: Vom Anfang des Neuen Testament bis auf das Jahr Christi 1688* (Frankfurt, 1699; rpt. ed., Hildesheim, 3 vols., 1967).

95. Ibid., I, bk. 16, chaps. 5–13.

6. An Age of Optimism

1. Carl Becker, *The Heavenly City of the Eighteenth-Century Philosophers* (New Haven, 1932), p. 8.

2. Alexander Pope, "An Essay on Man," l. 267, cited in Becker, *Heavenly City,* p. 66.

3. R. O. Rockwood, ed., *Carl Becker's Heavenly City Revisited* (Ithaca, N.Y., 1958).

4. Peter Gay, "Carl Becker's Heavenly City," in ibid., pp. 27–51.

5. Paul Henri Thiry, Baron d'Holbach (1723–1789), *Système de la Nature* (1770), cited in N. Hampson, *The Enlightenment* (Harmondsworth, 1968), p. 94.

6. David Hume, *An Enquiry Concerning Human Understanding* (London, 1748), in T. H. Green and T. H. Grose, eds., *Philosophical Works* (London, 4 vols., 1882), IV, 108; cited in Peter Gay, *The Enlightenment,* vol. I: *The Rise of Modern Paganism* (London, 2 vols., 1973), p. 206.

7. Voltaire (François Marie Arouet), *Essai sur les moeurs et l'esprit des nations et sur les principaux faits de l'histoire depuis Charlemagne jusqu'à Louis XIII* (Paris, 2 vols., 1963), II, 219, cited in Gay, *The Enlightenment,* I, 255.

8. On this point see J. Lively, ed., *The Enlightenment: Problems and Perspectives in History* (London, 1966), pp. xiii–xvi.

9. Ibid. The most notable example, of course, was Diderot's famous *Encyclopédie* of 1751–1780.

10. Charles Louis de Secondat, Baron de La Brède et de Montesquieu, *Lettres persanes* (1721). English translation by C. J. Betts, *Persian Letters* (Harmondsworth, 1973).

11. Voltaire, *Essai,* I, chaps. 1–7.

12. Ibid., II, 133.

13. Ibid., p. 136.

14. Ibid., pp. 209–214.

15. Ibid., p. 216.

16. Ibid., p. 217.

17. Ibid., p. 221.

18. Ibid., p. 218.

19. Ibid., p. 238.

20. Ibid., p. 218.

21. Marie Jean Antoine Nicholas de Caritat, Marquis de Condorcet, *Receuil des pièces sur l'état des Protestants en France*, in *Oeuvres complètes* (Brunswick, 21 vols., 1804), X, 293–553.

22. Ibid., p. 365.

23. Ibid., pp. 477–478.

24. Condorcet, *Esquisse d'un tableau historique des progrès de l'esprit humain* (Paris, 1795). Translated as *Outline of an Historical View of the Progress of the Human Mind* (London, 1795). All references here are to the French edition.

25. Ibid., pp. 185–190.

26. Ibid., p. 198.

27. Ibid., p.200.

28. Ibid., pp. 200–201.

29. Ibid., pp. 202–206.

30. Ibid., p. 207.

31. Ibid., pp. 213–214.

32. Gay, *The Enlightenment*, I, 47.

33. Denis Diderot, *Pensées philosophiques* (1746); critical edition by R. Niklaus (Geneva, 1957); *Lettre sur les aveugles* (1749), in *Oeuvres complètes* (Paris, 20 vols., 1875–1877), I, 279–342; and *La Religieuse* (1796), English translation by F. Birrell, *Memoirs of a Nun* (London, 1959).

34. Johann Jakob Brucker, *Historia critica philosophiae* (Leipzig, 1742–1767); see Gay, *The Enlightenment*, I, 364–365.

35. Denis Diderot, *Encyclopédie*, modern reprint ed. (Stuttgart, 35 vols., 1966), XIV, 78–88.

36. Ibid., III, 381.

37. Ibid., p. 386.

38. Ibid., XIII, 890–891.

39. Ibid., p. 891.

40. Ibid., IX, 756–757.

41. Ibid., II, 566.

42. See J. Whaley, "The Protestant Enlightenment in Germany," in R. Porter and M. Teich, eds., *The Enlightenment in National Context* (Cambridge, 1981), chap. 7.

43. V. E. Löscher, *Ausführliche Historia motuum zwischen Evangelischen Lutherischen und den Reformirten* (Leipzig and Frankfurt, 2 vols., 1723). On Löscher see Zeeden, *Legacy of Luther*, pp. 108–109.

44. J. G. Walch, *Historische und theologische Einleitung in die Religions-Streitigkeiten der Evangelischen-Lutherischen Kirchen, von der Reformation bis auf ietzige Zeiten* (Jena, 1733–1736) and *Dr. Martin Luthers sämtliche Schriften in 24 Theilen* (Halle, 1740–1752), including biographical study: "Ausführliche Nachricht von D. Martino Luthero" (1750).

45. On "pragmatic" history see Zeeden, *Legacy of Luther*, pp. 110–111; a

notable comprehensive work of this kind was J. M. Schröck's *Lebensbeschreibungen berühmter Gelehrten* (Leipzig, 1766).

46. J. B. Bossuet, *Discours sur l'histoire universelle* (Paris, 1681).

47. Walch, "Ausführliche Nachricht," chap. 1, paras. 20–21, 97. Zeeden, *Martin Luther*, II, 253–255.

48. Walch, "Ausführliche Nachricht," chap. 5, paras. 12–14; Zeeden, *Martin Luther*, II, 265–268.

49. J. S. Semler, *Lebesbeschreibung, von ihm selbst verfasst* (Halle, 2 vols., 1971), II, 178–181. See also his *Versuch eines fruchtbaren Auszugs der Kirchengeschichte* (Halle, 3 vols., 1773). On Semler's view of Luther and the Reformation see Zeeden, *Legacy of Luther*, chap. 4.

50. Semler, *Lebesbeschreibung*, II, 128–134; Zeeden, *Martin Luther*, II, 273.

51. J. S. Semler, *Versuch einer freien theologischen Lehrart* (Halle, 1777).

52. On Lessing's view of the Reformation see Zeeden, *Legacy of Luther*, chap. 5; H. Bornkamm, *Luther im Spiegel der deutschen Geistesgeschichte*, 2nd ed. (Göttingen, 1970), pp. 20–21, 199–202.

53. On Herder's view of the Reformation see Zeeden, *Legacy of Luther*, pp. 169–188, quotation on p. 171; Bornkamm, *Luther*, pp. 24–30.

54. Justus Möser, "Lettre à M. de Voltaire contenant un Essai sur le caractère du Dr. Martin Luther et sa Reformation," 5 September 1750. A German translation of the letter appears in Zeeden, *Martin Luther*, II, 340–351.

55. Johann Lorenz von Mosheim, *Institutiones historiae ecclesiasticae*, trans. James Murdock and ed. with additions by Henry Soames (London, 4 vols., 1841). Mosheim is a surprising omission from Zeeden's otherwise very comprehensive study of the German Lutheran tradition.

56. Ibid., III, 3–9.

57. Ibid., pp. 32, 57.

58. Ibid., pp. 83–87.

59. Ibid., p. 96.

60. Ibid., pp. 97–98.

61. Ibid., p. 110.

62. Ibid., pp. 124–126, 145.

63. Ibid., p. 128.

64. Ibid., p. 109.

65. Ibid., pp. 549–581; quotation on p. 561.

66. Ibid., pp. 256–302, 247.

67. Ibid., p. 181.

68. Ibid., p. 171; see also the introduction to volume IV of the Maclaine edition (London, 1811), p. 5.

69. Edward Gibbon, *The History of the Decline and Fall of the Roman Empire* (London, 12 vols., 1815), X, 188n1.

70. Ibid., pp. 188–193.

71. Ibid., pp. 169–172.

72. Ibid., pp. 185, 188.

73. Ibid., p.189.

74. Ibid., pp. 188–189.

75. Ibid., pp. 190–191.

76. Ibid., pp. 190–192.

77. Ibid., p. 193.

78. See Becker, *Heavenly City*, pp. 91–92; M. C. Fearnley-Sander, "The Emancipation of the Mind: A View of the Reformation in Four Eighteenth-Century Historians" (Unpublished Ph.D. dissertation, University of Western Australia, 1977). We are particularly indebted to this thesis for its insight into the significance of the eighteenth-century British historians' interpretation of the Reformation and the "Revival of Letters."

79. On the Enlightenment in Scotland see N. Phillipson, "The Scottish Enlightenment," in Porter and Teich, *Enlightenment*, chap. 2.

80. See Richard Wollheim, ed., *Hume on Religion* (New York, 1964), p. 28.

81. The identification is not, however, complete. Jansenism, for example, is defined as "enthusiastic" and only "half-Catholic." See "Of Superstition and Enthusiasm," in Wollheim, *Hume on Religion*, pp. 246–251.

82. Ibid., p. 250.

83. David Hume, *The History of England from the Invasion of Julius Caesar to the Revolution in 1688* (London, 1754–1762). All references here are to the London edition of 1829.

84. Ibid., p. 337.

85. Ibid.

86. Ibid., pp. 337–338.

87. Ibid.

88. Ibid.

89. Ibid.

90. Ibid., p. 339.

91. Ibid., pp. 338–339.

92. Ibid., pp. 352, 357.

93. Ibid., p. 360.

94. See Fearnley-Sander, "Emancipation," p. 682.

95. Hume, *History of England*, pp. 352, 358.

96. Ibid., p. 361.

97. David Hume, *A Treatise of Human Nature,* in T. H. Grose, ed., *Philosophical Works* (London, 4 vols., 1886), II, 195; *The Natural History of Religion,* in Wollheim, *Hume on Religion*, pp. 31–98.

98. Hume, *History of England*, p. 337.

99. This was the charge, for example, by Isaac Milner and Julius Hare. See Fearnley-Sander, "Emancipation," pp. 110–114.

100. Montesquieu, *L'Esprit des lois* (1748). The book was first translated into English in 1750; see *The Spirit of Laws*, critical edition by D. W. Carrithers (Berkeley, 1977).

101. *History of the Discovery and Settlement of America* (London, 2 vols., 1777), in *The Works of William Robertson* (Edinburgh, 2 vols., 1830), II.

102. See Gay, *The Enlightenment*, II, 374.

103. *History of Scotland During the Reigns of Queen Mary and of King James VI* (Edinburgh, 1759), in *Works of Robertson*, II, preface, p. iii.

104. See Fearnley-Sander, "Emancipation," pp. 92–95.

105. *History of Scotland,* in *Works of Robertson,* II, 26.

106. Ibid., p. 44.

107. Ibid., p. 47. Robertson claimed as further evidence of the association of Renaissance and Reformation Luther's, Calvin's, and Zwingli's favor toward liberal forms of government: "The most ardent love of liberty accompanied the protestant religion throughout all its progress and, wherever it was embraced, it roused an independent spirit which rendered men attentive to their privileges as subjects and jealous of the encroachments of their sovereigns" (p. 59).

108. Ibid., p. 164. To Robertson's credit, it should be added that in admiring Knox he did not feel it necessary to vilify Mary Stuart, who is presented as pathetic and misled rather than evil.

109. William Robertson, *The History of the Reign of the Emperor Charles V* (London, 3 vols., 1769), II, 114–115.

110. Ibid., p. 101.

111. Ibid., p. 116.

112. Ibid., pp. 118–119.

113. Ibid., p. 99.

114. Cajetan is a case in point. Ibid., p. 89.

115. Ibid., III, 449–451.

116. Ibid., II, 78.

117. See n. 99.

118. Robertson, *History of Charles V,* II, 99–100.

119. Ibid., p. 120.

120. Ibid., pp. 116–172.

121. Adam Smith, *An Inquiry into the Nature and Causes of the Wealth of Nations* (1776), ed. E. G. Wakefield (London, 4 vols., 1843), IV, 176, 185.

122. Joseph Priestley, *A General History of the Christian Church in Six Volumes* (Northumberland, Pa., 1802–1803), in J. T. Rutt, ed., *Works* (Hackney, 1831), VII–X. On Priestley's understanding of Luther and the Reformation see G. H. Williams, "Joseph Priestley on Luther," in Pelikan, *Interpreters of Luther,* chap. 6.

123. Priestley, *General History,* in *Works,* X, 192–193, cited in Williams, "Joseph Priestley," p. 149.

124. Joseph Priestley, *An Appeal to the Serious and Candid Professors of Christianity* (1770), in *Works,* II, 400–401; *An History of the Corruption of Christianity,* in *Works,* V, 146. See also Williams, "Joseph Priestley," pp. 145–148.

125. See Zeeden, *Legacy of Luther,* pp. 189–200.

126. John Wesley, *Journal,* ed. N. Curnock (London, 8 vols., 1938), I, 475–476.

127. Arminianism, so called after the Netherlander Jacobus Arminius (1560–1609), reacted strongly against Calvinist theology, arguing that divine sovereignty was compatible with human free will and that Christ died for all, not only for the elect.

128. On Edwards's life and thought see James P. Carse, *Jonathan Edwards and the Visibility of God* (New York, 1967). On Edwards and Calvin see especially ibid., pp. 115–120.

129. Wesley, *Journal*, VI, 202; J. Telford, ed., *Letters of John Wesley* (London, 8 vols., 1931), VII, 190; Franz Hildebrandt, *Christianity according to the Wesleys* (London, 1956), p. 12. See also Vilhelm Grønbech, *Religious Currents in the Nineteenth Century* (Carbondale, Ill., 1964), p. 22.

130. Telford, *Letters*, V, 364.

131. See C. W. Williams, *John Wesley's Theology Today* (London, 1960), pp. 167–190.

132. Jules Michelet, *Histoire de France* (Paris, 19 vols., 1833–1867), VII, VIII (1855); note the apotheosis of Luther in VIII, chaps. 5, 6.

133. Madame de Staël, *De l'Allemagne* (London, 3 vols., 1813); an English translation appeared there almost simultaneously.

134. All these points occur in ibid., pt. 4, chaps. 2, 3, 4; see especially III, 277–285, 303–305.

135. Lucien Febvre, "Une Question mal posée: Les origines de la Réforme française et le problème général des causes de la Réforme," *Revue historique*, 161 (1929), see pp. 14–15. This article is discussed in detail in Chapter 12.

136. Gay, *The Enlightenment*, I, 36–37, 372.

7. New Directions

1. On his earlier career see C. H. Pouthas, *Guizot pendant la Restauration: Préparation de l'homme d'état* (Paris, 1923). More broadly helpful is Pouthas's former pupil Douglas Johnson, whose *Guizot: Aspects of French History, 1787–1874* (London and Toronto, 1963) has a valuable chapter (chap. 7) on the historiographical methods and ideals of Guizot.

2. F. P. G. Guizot, *Histoire de la révolution d'Angleterre depuis Charles I à Charles II* (Paris, 2 vols., 1826–1827); *Histoire de la république d'Angleterre et de Cromwell* (Paris, 2 vols., 1854); *Histoire du protectorat de Cromwell et du rétablissement des Stuarts* (Paris, 2 vols., 1856). Unlike most contemporaries, Guizot perceived that the English Reformation was popular as well as royal, and that the Nonconformists, in attacking the Anglicans, had eventually been obliged to attack the monarchy and claim politicoreligious liberties. See Johnson, *Guizot*, p. 358.

3. On Guizot and French Protestantism see Johnson, *Guizot*, chap. 8.

4. F. P. G. Guizot, *Histoire de la civilisation en Europe* (Paris, 1828); translated as *The History of Civilisation in Europe* together with *The History of Civilisation in France* (London, 3 vols., 1846); also available in Bohn's Standard Library (London, 1846) and Bohn's Popular Library (London, 1924).

5. Johnson, *Guizot*, p. 327.

6. Sainte-Beuve's title for Guizot, cited in ibid., p. 320.

7. T. B. Macaulay, *History of England to the Death of William III* (vols. I

and II, 1848; vols. III and IV, 1855; vol. V, 1861). He had planned this work since 1838, intending it to reach the death of George IV. There are several modern editions.

8. On Macaulay as historian see, for instance, Pieter Geyl, *Debates with Historians* (Groningen and The Hague, 1955; Fontana edition, 1962), chap. 2; G. R. Potter, *Macaulay,* in the series Writers and Their Work, no. 119 (British Council, London, 1959); J. P. Kenyon, *The History Men* (London, 1982). H. R. Trevor-Roper contributed an incisive introduction to his selection of *Critical and Historical Essays* (Fontana, 1965).

9. Many of Macaulay's essays first appeared in the *Edinburgh Review,* to which he began contributing with his "Milton" in 1825. The *Essays* have been published in book form, collectively or in selections, in more than 250 editions. The earliest of these were *Critical and Miscellaneous Essays* (Philadelphia, 5 vols., 1841–1844); *Critical and Historical Essays contributed to the Edinburgh Review* (London, 1843); *Essays Critical and Miscellaneous* (London, 1848); *Critical and Historical Essays* (London, 1850).

10. Macaulay, *Critical and Historical Essays* (London, 2 vols., 1907), II, 47.

11. Ibid., p. 50.

12. Ibid., p. 64.

13. Ibid., p. 69.

14. Ibid.

15. The bibliography on Carlyle is very large. The following are critical items: Julian Symonds, *Thomas Carlyle: The Life and Ideas of a Prophet* (London, 1952); Geyl, *Debates,* chap. 3; Frederic Harrison, *Carlyle's Place in Literature* (London, 1894); H. J. C. Grierson, "Thomas Carlyle," *Proceedings of the British Academy,* 26 (1940), pp. 301–325; E. E. Neff, *Carlyle* (London, 1932) and *Carlyle and Mill: Mystic and Utilitarian* (New York, 1924, 1926); Basil Willey, *Nineteenth Century Studies* (London, 1949).

16. For a concise (and very welcome) summary of *Sartor Resartus,* see W. H. Hudson's introduction to the Everyman edition (London, 1908 on).

17. Thomas Carlyle, *On Heroes, Hero-Worship and the Heroic in History,* in *Works* (London, 18 vols., 1913), IV, quotation from introduction to 1896 edition (London), p. ix.

18. On the hero worship element see B. H. Lehman, *Carlyle's Theory of the Hero: Its Sources, Development, History, and Influence on Carlyle's Work* (Durham, N.C., 1928); E. C. Bentley, *A Century of Hero-Worship* (Philadelphia and New York, 1944).

19. Lehman, *Carlyle's Theory,* pp. 103–129.

20. Carlyle, *On Heroes,* lecture 4, p. 111.

21. Ibid., p. 101.

22. Ibid., p. 119.

23. Ibid.

24. Thomas Carlyle, *The Letters and Speeches of Oliver Cromwell,* ed. S. C. Lomas (London, 3 vols., 1904), III, 183–184.

25. There are biographies of Froude by Herbert Paul (London, 1905) and

Marshall Kelly (London, 1907). Still the best concise account is A. F. Pollard's in *DNB*, XXII, supplement (1909).

26. Froude, *History of England*, VIII, 412–415.

27. Ibid., IV, 237–243; III, 339–341.

28. Ibid., V, 96–102.

29. Ibid., XII, 249–259; see also 149–152, 225.

30. The Ranke bibliography is extensive. For some general ideas see, for example, H. F. Melmont, *Leopold Rankes Leben und Wirken* (Leipzig, 1921); T. H. von Laue, *Leopold Ranke: The Formative Years* (Princeton, N.J., 1950); and L. Krieger, *Ranke: The Meaning of History* (Chicago, 1977). On the historiographical background see F. Engel-Janosi, *The Growth of German Historicism*, Johns Hopkins University Studies (Baltimore, 1944); G. P. Gooch, *History and Historians in the Nineteenth Century* (London, 1913, 1952), chaps. 6, 7; G. G. Iggers, *The German Conception of History: The National Tradition of Historical Thought from Herder to the Present* (Middletown, Conn., 1968); and P. H. Reill, *The German Enlightenment and the Rise of Historicism* (Berkeley and Los Angeles, 1975).

31. On his personal role see Gunter Berg, *Leopold von Ranke als akademischer Lehrer* (Göttingen, 1968). His three greatest pupils—Waitz, Giesebrecht, and Sybel—were all medievalists.

32. Leopold von Ranke, *Deutsche Geschichte im Zeitalter der Reformation* (Berlin, 6 vols., 1839–1847). See n. 45.

33. "Seine Seele ist offenbar von der gesunden Catholischen Idee ergriffen"; J. J. Ignaz von Döllinger, *Briefwechsel, 1850–1890* (Munich, 3 vols., 1943–1971), I, 412. In the same letter Acton reports Ranke's bitter dissent from Macaulay and other Whig historians. Compare Ranke's claim (ibid., p. 180) to have written English history to refute Macaulay. On Acton and Döllinger see Chapter 8.

34. Leopold von Ranke, *Über die Epochen der neueren Geschichte*, in *Aus Werk und Nachlass*, ed. T. Schieder and H. Berding (Munich, 5 vols., 1971), II, 59–60.

35. On his politics see O. Diether, *Ranke als Politiker* (Leipzig, 1911).

36. See Gooch, *History and Historians*, chap. 8.

37. Quoted in Bertrand Russell, *History of Western Philosophy* (London, 1946), p. 767.

38. See E. Simon, *Ranke und Hegel, Historische Zeitschrift*, supplement 15 (Munich and Berlin, 1938).

39. Ilse Mayer-Kulenkampf, "Rankes Lutherverhaltnis, dargestellt nach dem Lutherfragment von 1817," *Historische Zeitschrift*, 72 (1951), pp. 65–99.

40. Leopold von Ranke, *Zur Kritik neuerer Geschichtsschreiber* (Berlin and Leipzig, 1824).

41. H. O. Evenett, *The Spirit of the Counter-Reformation*, ed. John Bossy (Cambridge, 1968), pp. 4–5.

42. Leopold von Ranke, *History of the Popes of Rome*, trans. S. Austin, 4th ed. (London, 3 vols., 1866), I, 160.

43. Ibid., pp. 125–126.

44. Ibid., p. 872.

45. The best introduction to Ranke's *Deutsche Geschichte* is by P. Joachimsen, prefixed to the work in the *Gesamt Ausgabe der deutschen Akademie* (Munich, 1925); see especially pp. viii–cxvii. Note also K. Brandi, *Die Entstehung von Leopold Rankes deutscher Geschichte im Zeitalter der Reformation* (Göttingen, 1947); and, on the religious attitudes, Heinrich Hauser, *Leopold von Rankes protestantisches Geschichtsbild* (Zurich, 1950). Influenced by Döllinger and Janssen, Gooch, *History and Historians*, pp. 89–90, seems to underestimate the work.

46. Ranke, *Deutsche Geschichte*, bk. 3, chap. 3, which covers the diffusion of the new doctrines, 1522–1524.

47. Ibid., chap. 6.

48. See Abraham Friesen, "Philipp Melanchthon, Wilhelm Zimmermann and the Dilemma of Müntzer Historiography," *Church History*, 43 (1974), pp. 164–182. Engels's *Die deutsche Bauernkrieg* had new editions in 1908 and 1920, with English translations from 1927 on. On the Zimmermann and Marxist traditions see Chapter 10.

49. Leopold von Ranke, *Englische Geschichte* (Berlin, 7 vols., 1859–1869); English translation by C. W. Boase and others (Oxford, 6 vols., 1875).

50. Ibid., English trans., I, 154.

51. Ranke, *Deutsche Geschichte*, bk. 5, chap. 3; bk. 6, chaps. 2, 4.

52. Joachimsen, *Gesamt Ausgabe*, pp. xxxvi–xxxvii.

53. A somewhat more detailed treatment of this theme is in A. G. Dickens, *Ranke as Reformation Historian*, Stenton Lecture no. 13 (University of Reading, 1980).

54. Cited in A. W. Ward, "Anton Gindely," *English Historical Review*, 8 (1893), pp. 500–514.

55. J.E.E.D. Acton, "German Schools of History," *English Historical Review*, 1 (1886), 16.

8. Polemics Transcended

1. See *New Catholic Encyclopedia*, II, 1.

2. J. A. Möhler, *Die Einheit in der Kirche* (Tübingen, 1825).

3. J. A. Möhler, *Symbolik oder Darstellung der dogmatischen Gegensätze der Katholiken und Protestanten nach ihren offentlichen Bekenntnisschriften* (Mainz, 1832). Translated by J. B. Robertson as *Symbolism: or Exposition of Doctrinal Differences between Catholics and Protestants as Evidenced by Their Symbolical Writings* (London, 1843).

4. J. J. Ignaz von Döllinger, *Die Reformation* (Regensburg, 1846–1848; rpt. ed., Frankfurt am Main, 1962).

5. E. Stauffer, *Le Catholicisme à la découverte de Luther* (Neuchâtel, 1966). Translated as *Luther as Seen by Catholics* (Richmond, Va., 1967).

6. J. J. Ignaz von Döllinger, *Luther: Eine Skizze* (Freiburg im Breisgau, 1851); also as article in H. J. Wetzer and B. Welte, eds., *Kirchenlexikon* (Freiburg, 1891), VII, cols. 308–347. Translated as *Luther: A Succinct View of His Life and Writings* (London, 1853).

7. Ibid., in *Kirchenlexikon,* cols. 313–315, 242–244; English translation, pp. 19–23, 93–97.

8. Ibid., cols. 310–311; English translation, pp. 10–13.

9. J. J. Ignaz von Döllinger, *Kirche und Kirchen: Papsttum und Kirchenstaat* (Munich, 1861), pp. 9–11, 386–387. Translated as *The Church and the Churches* (London, 1862), pp. 26–27, 267–268.

10. J. J. Ignaz von Döllinger, *Über die Wiedervereinigung der christlichen Kirchen* (Munich, 1872). Translated by H. N. Oxenham as *Lectures on the Reunion of the Churches* (London, 1872).

11. Ibid., p. 53; English translation, p. 62.

12. Ibid.

13. Johannes Janssen, *Geschichte des deutschen Volkes seit dem Ausgang des Mittelalters* (Freiburg im Breisgau, 8 vols., 1876–1894). Translated by M. A. Mitchell and A. M. Christie as *History of the German People at the Close of the Middle Ages* (London, 17 vols., 1896–1910).

14. See Janssen's account of his archival research in the preface to the fifteenth German edition, translated in the English edition, I, vii–ix.

15. Ibid., p. ix.

16. Ibid., II, 285.

17. Ibid., chap. 5, and III, 364–365.

18. Ibid., III, 240.

19. Julius Köstlin, *Luther und Johannes Janssen: Der deutsche Reformator und ein ultramontaner Historiker* (Halle, 1883).

20. Julius Köstlin, *Luthers Theologie in ihrer geschichtlichen Entwicklung und ihrem inneren Zusammenhänge* (Stuttgart, 1863); *Martin Luther: Sein Leben und Seine Schriften* (Elberfeld, 1875); *Luthers Leben* (Leipzig, 1882), translated as *Life of Luther* (New York, 1883, and other editions). See also his festschrift piece *Martin Luther: Der deutsche Reformator* (Halle, 1883); translated by Elizabeth P. Weir as *Martin Luther: The Reformer,* 3rd ed. (London and New York, 1883).

21. Köstlin, *Martin Luther: The Reformer,* pp. vii–viii.

22. On the influence of German idealism on Christian doctrine see especially Karl Barth, *Protestant Theology in the Nineteenth Century,* trans. Brian Cozens and John Bowden (London, 1972), chaps. 7, 10; and Paul Tillich, *Perspectives on Nineteenth and Twentieth Century Protestant Theology,* ed. Carl E. Braaten (New York, 1967), chaps. 2, 3.

23. Johann Gottlieb Fichte (1762–1814), *Versuch einer Kritik aller Offenbarung* (Königsberg, 1793); translated by G. Green as *Attempt at a Critique of All Revelation* (Cambridge, 1978); see also Green's introduction, pp. 1–31. Friedrich Wilhelm Joseph von Schelling (1775–1854), *The Ages of the World,* trans. F. de W. Bolman (New York, 1942). Georg Wilhelm Friedrich Hegel (1770–1831), *On Christianity: Early Theological Writings,* trans. T. M. Knox and R. Kroner (New York, 1948). On Hegel's influence on theology see Barth, *Protestant Theology,* chap. 10; Tillich, *Perspectives,* pp. 114–135.

24. On this aspect of the work of Baur and Strauss see Barth, *Protestant Theology,* chaps. 15, 19; and Tillich, *Perspectives,* pp. 137–139.

25. Friedrich Schleiermacher, *On Religion: Speeches to Its Cultured Despisers,* trans. John Oman (New York, 1958). On Schleiermacher's understanding of the Reformation see B. Gerrish, "Schleiermacher and the Reformation: A Question of Doctrinal Development," *Church History,* 49 (June 1980), pp. 147–159.

26. Søren Kierkegaard, *Journals,* ed. A. Dru (New York, 1938); and *The Last Years: Journals, 1853–1855,* ed. R. Gregor Smith (New York, 1965). On Kierkegaard's highly complex intellectual relationship to Luther see Ernest B. Koenker, "Søren Kierkegaard on Luther," in Pelikan, *Interpreters of Luther,* chap. 9.

27. On Ritschl and his school see P. Hefner, ed., *Albrecht Ritschl: Three Essays* (Philadelphia, 1972), introduction; and Barth *Protestant Theology,* chap. 29. On Ritschl's historical scholarship see P. Hefner, *Faith and the Vitalities of History: A Theological Study Based on the Work of Albrecht Ritschl,* in J. Pelikan, ed., Makers of Modern Theology (New York, 1966); and Michael Ryan, "The Role of the Discipline of History in the Theological Interpretation of Albrecht Ritschl" (Unpublished Ph.D. dissertation, Drew University, 1967).

28. Albrecht Ritschl, *Die Christliche Lehre von der Rechtfertigung und Versöhnung* (Bonn, 1870–1874). The part dealing with the historical development of the doctrine, as distinct from its dogmatic presentation and biblical basis, was translated by John S. Black as *A Critical History of the Doctrine of Justification and Reconciliation* (Edinburgh, 1872).

29. Ritschl therefore regarded Möhler's entire project as "mistaken, fruitless, misleading"; see *Doctrine of Justification,* pp. 121–122.

30. Ibid., chap. 4, esp. pp. 157–158.

31. Ibid., chaps. 4–10.

32. Ibid., pp. 289–298; "Prolegomena to the History of Pietism," in Ritschl, *Three Essays,* pp. 70–83; see Chapter 9.

33. See J. Pelikan, "Adolf von Harnack on Luther," in *Interpreters of Luther,* chap. 10.

34. Theodosius Harnack, *Luthers Theologie mit besonderer Beziehung auf seine Versöhnungs und Erlösungslehre* (Erlangen, 1862).

35. Adolf von Harnack, *Das Wesen des Christentums* (Leipzig, 1900). Translated by J. B. Saunders as *What Is Christianity?* (London, 1901; rpt. New York, 1957).

36. Adolf von Harnack, *Grundriss der Dogmengeschichte,* 2nd ed. (Freiburg, 1889–1891). An English translation was made from the third German edition (1898) by N. Buchanan (London, 1900) in seven volumes and reprinted in four volumes (New York, 1961).

37. Adolf von Harnack, "Was wir von der römischem Kirche lernen und nicht lernen solten," *Reden und Aufsätze* (Giessen, 3 vols., 1904), II, 255. See also *What Is Christianity?* p. 288.

38. Ernst Troeltsch, *Die Bedeutung des Protestantismus für die Entstehung der modernen Welt* (Munich and Berlin, 1906). The enlarged second edition (1911) was translated by W. Montgomery as *Protestantism and Progress: A Historical Study of the Relationship of Protestantism to the Modern World* (Boston, 1958). On Troeltsch's attitude to Luther see K. Penzel, "Ernst Troeltsch on Luther," in Pelikan, *Interpreters of Luther,* chap. 11.

39. Ernst Troeltsch, *Die Soziallehren der christlichen Kirchen und Gruppen,* Gesammelte Schriften, 6 (Tübingen, 1912). Translated by Olive Wyon as *The Social Teaching of the Christian Churches* (London, 1931; rpts., New York, 1970, and Chicago, 1976).

40. Troeltsch, *Social Teaching,* pp. 511–515.

41. Ibid., II, p. 991.

42. J. H. Merle d'Aubigné, *Histoire de la Réformation du seizième siècle* (Paris, 5 vols., 1835–1853). The early volumes were translated by D. Walther as *History of the Great Reformation in the Sixteenth Century* (London, 1838–1841).

43. In this section we are particularly indebted to the excellent comprehensive study of Leighton Frappell, "Interpretations of the Continental Reformation in Great Britain during the Nineteenth Century" (Unpublished Ph.D. dissertation, Macquarie University, 1972).

44. W. F. Hook, *Lives of the Archbishops of Canterbury,* New Series (London, 12 vols., 1868), I, 41. See also his *The Church and Its Ordinances* (London, 2 vols., 1876) and *The Three Reformations: Lutheran-Roman-Anglican,* 3rd ed. (London, 1847). The *via media* was, of course, a sixteenth-century idea (see Chapter 3).

45. E. B. Pusey, *An Historical Enquiry into the Probable Causes of the rationalist character lately predominant in the theology of Germany* (London, 1828, 1830), pp. 21, 51. In Pusey's view this crucial difference from the Anglican Church bore its ultimate fruit in the decline of Lutheranism and Calvinism into rationalism. See H. P. Liddon, *Life of Edward Bouverie Pusey* (London, 4 vols., 1893–1894), I, 177; II, 224. Pusey's changed attitude became clear in a subsequent work, *The Doctrine of the Real Presence* (Oxford, 1855). See also Frappell, "Interpretations," pp. 90–96.

46. John Henry Newman, *Lectures on Justification* (London, 1838, 1840).

47. Joseph and Isaac Milner, *The History of the Church of Christ* (London, 1794–1797; new ed., London, 5 vols., 1824); John Scott, *The History of the Church of Christ: intended as a Continuation of the work of the Rev. Joseph Milner and the Very Rev. Isaac Milner* (London, 1826–1831). For a more detailed discussion of Evangelical views see Frappell, "Interpretations," chap. 6.

48. Henry Stebbing, *History of the Reformation* (London, 2 vols., 1836), p. 153.

49. Augustus Cox, *The Life of Philip Melancthon,* 2nd ed. (London and Edinburgh, 1827), p. 204.

50. For example, ibid., pp. 34–35 and 567–569. See also Frappell, "Interpretations," pp. 217–222.

51. The translations included Henry Beveridge's versions of *Tracts Relating the Reformation* (Edinburgh, 1844–1851) and *Institutes of the Christian Religion* (Edinburgh, 1845–1846), as well as a large number of Calvin's biblical commentaries.

52. Frappell, "Interpretations," p. 204.

53. W. Ince, *The Luther-Commemoration and the Church of England,* Sermon, 11 November 1883 (London, 1883).

54. Henry Wace and C. A. Buchheim, *First Principles of the Reformation* (London, 1883). For Köstlin see his *Luther und Johannes Janssen.*

55. See, for instance, the anonymous essays "Erasmus as a Satirist," *North British Review,* 32 (February 1860), pp. 49–67; and "Zwingli the Reformer," *North British Review,* 49 (September 1868), pp. 101–124; also Dean Stanley, *Christian Institutions: Essays on Ecclesiastical Subjects,* 4th ed. (London, 1884), pp. 121–122.

56. Isaac Taylor, introductory essay to Gustavus Pfizer's *Life of Luther,* trans. T. S. Williams (London, Edinburgh, and Dublin, 1840); John Tulloch, *Leaders of the Reformation* (London and Edinburgh, 1860).

57. Henry Hart Milman, *History of Latin Christianity* (London, 1855; 4th ed. London, 9 vols., 1883).

58. F. D. Maurice, *Moral and Metaphysical Philosophy* (London, 2 vols., 1886).

59. J. C. Hare, *Vindication of Luther against his recent English assailants,* 2nd ed. (London, 1855). On Hare's view of the Reformation see also William J. Baker, "Julius Charles Hare: A Victorian Interpreter of Luther," *South Atlantic Quarterly,* 70 (Winter 1971), pp. 88–101.

60. Ibid., p. 85.

61. J. C. Hare, *Miscellaneous Pamphlets on Some of the Leading Questions Agitated in the Church during the Last Ten Years* (Cambridge, 1855), p. 54; and *The Contest with Rome: A Charge to the Archdeaconry of Lewes* (London, 1852), p. 20.

62. John Lingard, *A History of England,* 6th ed. (Dublin and London, 10 vols., 1878), IV, chap. 7; V, chaps. 1–4.

63. Ibid., IV, 230.

64. James Waterworth, *The Canons and Decrees of the Sacred and Oecumenical Council of Trent* (London, 1848), pt. 1, pp. ii–iv.

65. For example, Kenelm Digby, *Mores Catholici, or Ages of Faith* (London, 3 vols., 1845); and Augustus Pugin, *An Apology for the Revival of Christian Architecture in England* (London, 1843).

66. Charles Butler, *The Life of Erasmus* (London, 1825); Sylvester Mahony, "The Days of Erasmus," in C. Kent, ed., *The Works of Father Prout* (London, n.d.).

67. For instance, John Henry Newman, "Political Thoughts on the Church" (1858), in J. N. Figgis and R. V. Laurence, eds., *The History of Freedom and Other Essays* (London, 1909), pp. 203, 210–211.

68. F. A. Gasquet, *Henry VIII and the English Monasteries* (London, 2 vols., 1888–1889 and 1906); see also *The Eve of the Reformation* (London, 1900).

69. William Cobbett (1762–1835), *A History of the Protestant Reformation in England and Ireland* (London, 2 vols., 1829).

70. Gasquet, *Henry VIII,* pp. 400–401; *Eve of the Reformation,* pp. 285, 313; *England under the Old Religion* (London, 1912), pp. 96–97.

71. For a sensitive but critical account of Gasquet's strengths and weaknesses as a historian see David Knowles, "Cardinal Gasquet as Historian," Creighton Lecture in History (University of London, 1956), reprinted in *The Historian and Character* (Cambridge, 1964), pp. 240–263.

72. R. W. Dixon, *History of the Church of England from the Abolition of the Roman Jurisdiction* (Oxford, 6 vols., 1878–1902).

73. Ibid., I, 2–7.

74. For an interesting evaluation of Dixon as a church historian see E. G. Rupp, "The Victorian Churchman as Historian: A Reconsideration of R. W. Dixon's History of the Church of England," G. V. Bennett and J. D. Walsh, eds., *Essays in Modern English Church History, In Memory of Norman Sykes* (London, 1966), pp. 206–216.

75. Henry Wace, *Principles of the Reformation, Practical and Historical* (London, 1911); *The Foundation of Faith*, Bampton Lectures, 1879 (London, 1886).

76. Mandell Creighton, *A History of the Papacy from the Great Schism to the Sack of Rome* (London, 6 vols., 1897); first edition entitled *A History of the Papacy during the period of the Reformation* (London, 5 vols., 1882–1894). On Creighton's interpretation of Luther see Owen Chadwick, "Creighton on Luther," inaugural lecture (Cambridge, 1959).

77. Charles Beard, *The Reformation of the Sixteenth Century in Its Relation to Modern Thought and Knowledge*, Hibbert Lectures, 1883, 5th ed. (London, 1907); *Martin Luther and the Reformation in Germany*, ed. J. F. Smith (London, 1889).

78. J. E. E. D. Acton, *Lectures in Modern History* (London, 1906, and later eds., including paperback, 1960), chap. 4.

79. *Encyclopaedia Britannica*, 9th ed. (Edinburgh, 24 vols., 1875–1888), XV, 71–86. For a thorough analysis of Lindsay's work see Frappell, "Interpretations," pp. 379–392.

80. T. M. Lindsay, *Luther and the German Reformation* (Edinburgh, 1900); *Cambridge Modern History* (Cambridge, 13 vols., 1903), II, chap. 4.

81. T. M. Lindsay, *A History of the Reformation in Europe* (Edinburgh, 2 vols., 1906–1907; rpt. ed., 1959), I, ix.

82. Ibid., II, 442. On these points see Chapter 9.

83. See E. Theodore Bachman, "Walther, Schaff and Krauth on Luther," in Pelikan, *Interpreters of Luther*, chap. 8.

84. Martin Luther, *The Book of Concord: Or The Symbolical Books of the Evangelical Lutheran Church*, trans. and ed. Henry Jacobs (Philadelphia, 2 vols., 1882–1883); *Dr. Martin Luthers Sämtliche Schriften* (St. Louis, 1881; republication of the Walch edition of 1740–1753).

85. Bachman, "Walter, Schaff and Krauth," esp. pp. 214–221.

86. Philip Schaff, *The Principle of Protestantism*, trans. J. W. Nevin (Chambersburg, Pa., 1845); new edition by Bard Thompson and George Bucher (Philadelphia, 1964), pp. 73–74.

87. Philip Schaff, *History of the Christian Church*, rev. ed. (New York, 6 vols., 1882–1892; rpt. Grand Rapids, Mich., 1950).

88. Philip Schaff, *Creeds of Christendom* (New York, 3 vols., 1877); 6th ed., ed. D. Schaff (New York, 3 vols., 1931), I, v.

89. Heinrich Denifle, *Luther und Luthertum in der ersten Entwicklung quellenmässig dargestellt* (Mainz, 1904).

90. On the discovery of Luther's *Lectures on Romans* see Wilhelm Pauck, ed., *Luther: Lectures on Romans,* Library of Christian Classics, 15 (Philadelphia, 1961), pp. xxi–xxiv.

91. Pauck, *Luther,* pp. 500–508; see also *Die Abendländische Schriftausleger bis Luther über Iustitia Dei (Rom. 1.17) und Justificatio* (Mainz, 1905).

92. Heinrich Boehmer, *Luther im Lichte der neueren Forschung: Ein kritischer Bericht* (Leipzig, 1906). Translated by E. S. G. Potter as *Luther in the Light of Modern Research* (London, 1930), p. 24.

93. Hartmann Grisar, *Luther* (Freiburg and St. Louis, 3 vols., 1911–1912). Translated by E. M. Lamond as *Luther* (London, 6 vols., 1913–1917). Grisar also published a one-volume work, *Martin Luthers Leben und seine Werke* (Freiburg, 1926); translated by F. J. Elbe as *Martin Luther: His Life and Work* (St. Louis and London, 1930).

94. See Stauffer, *Luther,* pp. 15–16.

95. For example, W. Köhler, *Das katholische Lutherbild der Gegenwart* (Bern, 1922), pp. 18–19; see also Heinrich Bornkamm, "Luther zwischen der Konfessionen: Vierhundert Jahre katholischer Forschung," in *Festschrift für Gerhard Ritter* (Tübingen, 1950), p. 221; W. Von Loewenich, *Modern Catholicism* (London, 1959), pp. 230–232.

96. Karl Holl, "Was verstand Luther unter Religion?" in his *Gesammelte Aufsätze zur Kirchengeschichte,* vol. I: *Luther* (Tübingen, 1921), pp. 1–110; F. X. Kiefl, "Martin Luthers Religiöse Psyche: Zum 400 jährigen Reformationsjubiläum," in *Hochland* (Munich, 1917), pp. 7–17.

97. Karl Barth, *Das Wort Gottes und die Theologie* (Munich, 1924). Translated by D. Horton as *The Word of God and the Word of Man* (London, 1928; new ed., New York, 1957).

98. Karl Barth, *Die christliche Dogmatik* (Munich, 1927) and *Die kirchliche Dogmatik* (Munich, 1932; Zurich, 1947); English translation *Church Dogmatics* (Edinburgh, 1936–1962); *Lutherfeier* (Munich, 1933).

99. Dietrich Bonhoeffer, *Ethics,* ed. E. Bethge, trans. N. H. Smith (London, 1955); *The Cost of Discipleship,* trans. R. H. Fuller (London, 1948); *Letters and Papers from Prison,* ed. E. Bethge, trans. R. H. Fuller (London, 1953); Paul Tillich, *The Protestant Era,* trans. J. L. Adams (Chicago, 1947); *The Recovery of the Prophetic Tradition in the Reformation* (Washington, D.C., 1950); Rudolf Bultmann, *Existence and Faith: Shorter Writings* (London, 1961).

100. Holl, "Was verstand Luther unter Religion?"

101. Karl Holl, "Der Neubau der Sittlichkeit," in *Gesammelte Aufsatze zur Kirchengeschichte,* I, 155–287.

102. Otto Scheel, *Martin Luther: Vom Katholizismus zur Reformation* (Tübingen, 1916) and *Dokumente zur Luthers Entwicklung* (Tübingen, 1911). Heinrich Bornkamm, *Luther* and *Der junge Luther* (Gotha, 1925); translated by J. W. Doberstein as *Martin Luther: Road to Reformation* (Philadelphia, 1946).

103. Walther Köhler, *Brüderlich Vereinigung etzlichen Kinder Gottes sieben Artikel betreffend* (Leipzig, 1908); James Mackinnon, *Luther and the Reformation* (New York, 4 vols., 1925–1930) and *The Origins of the Reformation* (London and New York, 1939).

104. Kiefl, "Martin Luthers Religiöse Psyche."

105. Ibid., p. 7.

106. Ibid., esp. pp. 8–9.

107. Hubert Jedin, *Die Erforschungen der kirchlichen Reformationsgeschichte seit 1876* (Münster, 1931), pp. 23–24.

108. For instance, Joseph Clayton, *Luther and His Work* (Milwaukee, 1937); Philip Hughes, *History of the Church* vol. III: *The Revolt against the Church, Aquinas to Luther* (London, 1947); Patrick O'Hare, *The Facts about Luther* (New York and Cincinnati, 1916); *Catholic Encyclopedia* (New York, 1910), IX, 438–458; H. O. Evenett, *The Reformation*, Studies in Comparative Religion (London, 1937).

109. Jacques Maritain, *Three Reformers* (London, 1928); Jacques Paquier, "Luther," in *Dictionnaire de Théologie Catholique* (Paris, 1926), IX, cols. 1146–1335; M. J. Lagrange, *The Meaning of Christianity according to Luther and His Followers in Germany* (London, 1920); Leon Cristiani, "Réforme," *Dictionnaire Apologetique de la Foi Catholique* (Paris, 1922), IV, pp. 590–613; and "Luther au Couvent," in *Revue des Questions Historiques* (Paris, 1913), pp. 590–613; (Paris, 1914), pp. 5–34, 356–378.

110. Pierre Imbart de la Tour, *Les Origines de la Réforme* (Paris, 4 vols., 1905–1944; rpt. ed., Geneva, 1978). For a sympathetic reappraisal of Imbart's work and a stern critique of Lucien Febvre's attack on it see Dermot Fenlon, "Encore Une Question: Lucien Febvre, the Reformation, and the School of *Annales*," *Historical Studies*, 9 (1974), pp. 65–81.

111. Sebastian Merkle, "Gutes an Luther und Ubles in seinen Tadlern"; Johannes Albani, "Hat Luther mit der Kirche gebrochen? Brach die Kirche mit ihm?"; Anton Fischer, "Was der betende Luther der ganzen Christenheit zu sagen hat," all in Alfred von Martin, ed., *Luther in ökumenischer Sicht* (Stuttgart, 1929).

112. Konrad Algermissen, *Konfessionskunde* (Hannover, 1930). Translated by J. W. Grundner as *Christian Denominations* (St. Louis and London, 1945); see esp. pp. 758–763.

113. Joseph Lortz, *Die Reformation in Deutschland* (Freiburg, 1939–1940). Translated by Ronald Walls as *The Reformation in Germany* (New York and London, 2 vols., 1968).

114. Lortz, *The Reformation in Germany*, I, 167; see also ibid., pp. 21, 388.

115. Ibid., pp.198–201.

116. Ibid., pp. 156–157, 233–239.

117. Ibid., pp. 144–157. On nineteenth- and twentieth-century Catholic views of Erasmus see Bruce Mansfield, "Erasmus, Luther, and the Problem of Church History," *Australian Journal of Politics and History*, 8 (1962), pp. 41–56.

118. Imbart de la Tour, *Origines*, III, 58–108. Gasquet, *The Eve of the Reformation*, chap. 6, esp. pp. 199–200.

119. Adolf Herte, *Das katholische Lutherbild im Bann der Lutherkommentare des Cochlaeus* (Münster, 3 vols., 1943). On Cochlaeus see Chapter 1.

120. Johannes Hessen, *Luther in katholischer Sicht* (Bonn, 1947; 2nd ed., 1949).

121. Erwin Iserloh, *Luthers Thesenanschlag: Tatsache oder Legende?* (Wiesbaden, 1962). Translated as *The Theses Were Not Posted* (London, 1968).

122. On this point see especially Lortz, *The Reformation in Germany*, I, 170–173.

123. Joseph Lortz, *Die Reformation als religiöses Anliegen heute* (Trier, 1948), translated by J. C. Dwyer as *The Reformation: A Problem for Today* (Westminster, 1964); and *Wie kam es zur Reformation?* (Einsiedeln, 1950), translated by O. M. Knab as *How the Reformation Came* (New York, 1964).

124. For example, Gerhard Hennig, *Cajetan und Luther: Ein historischer Beitrag zur Begegnung von Thomismus und Reformation* (Stuttgart, 1966).

125. Otto Pesch, *Theologie der Rechtfertigung bei M. Luther und Thomas von Aquin* (Mainz, 1967). See also Stephan Pfürtner, *Luther und Thomas in Gespräch* (Heidelberg, 1961); H. Vorster, *Das Freiheitsverständnis bei Thomas von Aquin und Martin Luther* (Göttingen, 1965).

126. See, for instance, Hayo Gerdes, "Luther und Augustin," *Lutherjahrbuch*, 1962, pp. 9–24; Bernard Löhse, "Die Bedeutung Augustins für den jungen Luther," *Kerygma und Dogma*, 11 (1965), pp. 116–135; Roland Mousnier, "Saint Bernard and Martin Luther," *American Benedictine Review*, 14 (1963), pp. 448–462; Paul Vignaux, *De Saint Anselme à Luther* (Paris, 1976).

127. Harry McSorley, *Luther: Right or Wrong?* (New York and Minneapolis, 1969).

128. Jared Wicks, ed., *Catholic Scholars Dialogue with Luther* (Chicago, 1970).

129. On this point we acknowledge our indebtedness to Father Jared Wicks, S.J., for drawing our attention, through personal conversation and his writings, to recent Catholic studies of Luther. His *Luther and His Spiritual Legacy* (Wilmington, Del., 1983) includes substantial accounts of recent Catholic scholarship.

130. Frido Mann, *Das Abendmahl beim jungen Luther* (Munich, 1971); Jan Aarts, *Die Lehre Martin Luthers über das Amt in der Kirche* (Helsinki, 1972); Wolfgang Schwab, *Entwicklung und Gestalt der Sakramententheologie bei Martin Luther* (Frankfurt and Bern, 1977).

131. Daniel Olivier, *La Foi de Luther: La cause de l'évangile dans l'église* (Paris, 1978); Translated by John Tonkin as *Luther's Faith* (St. Louis, 1972).

132. Riccardo Garcia-Villoslada, *Martin Lutero* (Madrid, 2 vols., 1973).

133. Theobald Beer, *Der fröhliche Wechsel und Streit: Grundzüge der Theologie Martin Luthers* (Einsiedeln, 1980); see also the reviews: Jared Wicks, *Theologische Revue*, 78 (1982), pp. 1–12; and Erwin Iserloh, *Catholica*, 36 (1982), pp. 101–114.

134. Peter Manns, *Martin Luther: An Illustrated Biography* (New York, 1982); John Todd, *Luther: A Life* (New York, 1982); Georges Chantraine, *Erasme et Luther, libre et serf arbitre* (Paris, 1981); Otto Pesch, *Hinführung zur Luther* (Mainz, 1982); Yves Congar, *Martin Luther: Sa foi, sa réforme* (Paris, 1983); Wicks, *Luther and His Spiritual Legacy*.

135. Nathan Söderblom, *Den Lutherska reformationens uppkomst*, vol. II: *Luthers religion* (Stockholm, 1893); Einar Billing, *Luthers lara om staten i dess samband med hans reformatoriska grundtankar och med tidigare kyrkila lärer* (Uppsala, 1900).

136. Anders Nygren, *Agape and Eros* (London, 1932–1939); Gustav Aulen, *The Faith of the Christian Church* (Philadelphia, 1948); *Christus Victor* (London, 1941).

137. Regin Prenter, *Spiritus Creator,* trans. J. M. Jensen (Philadelphia, 1953); Lennart Pinomaa, *Der Zorn Gottes in der Theologie Luthers* (Helsinki, 1940); Gustav Wingren, *Luther on Vocation,* trans. C. C. Rasmussen (Philadelphia, 1957).

138. E. G. Rupp, *The Righteousness of God: Luther Studies* (London, 1953); Philip Watson, *Let God Be God* (London, 1947); Rupert Davies, *The Problem of Authority in the Continental Reformers* (London, 1946).

139. In addition to the works cited in n. 138, see, for example, James Atkinson, *Martin Luther and the Birth of Protestantism* (Harmondsworth, 1968); G. R. Potter, *Zwingli* (Cambridge, 1976); T. H. L. Parker, *John Calvin: A Biography* (Philadelphia, 1975).

140. Richard Stauffer, *La Réforme,* 2nd ed. (Paris, 1974); Marc Lienhard, *Luther: Témoin de Jesus Christ* (Paris, 1973).

141. Emile G. Léonard, *Histoire générale du protestantisme* (Paris, 1961); translated by J. H. M. Reid as *A History of Protestantism* (London, 1965).

142. A substantial bibliography concerning the debate on the Ninety-five Theses may be found in Iserloh, *Theses Were Not Posted,* pp. 111–112; on the question of Luther's breakthrough see B. Lohse, ed., *Der Durchbruch der Reformatorischen Erkenntnis* (Darmstadt, 1968).

143. Carl Ullmann, *Reformatoren vor der Reformation* (Hamburg, 2 vols., 1841–1842); translated by R. Menzies as *Reformers before the Reformation* (Edinburgh, 2 vols., 1885).

144. Gerhard Ritter, "Romantische und revolutionäre Elemente in der deutschen Theologie am Vorabend der Reformation," *Deutsche Vierteljahrsschrift für Literaturwissenschaft und Geistesgeschichte,* 5 (1927), pp. 342–380; revised version in English edited by Steven Ozment, *The Reformation in Medieval Perspective* (Chicago, 1971).

145. H. A. Oberman, *The Harvest of Medieval Theology: Gabriel Biel and Late Medieval Nominalism* (Cambridge, Mass., 1963).

146. H. A. Oberman, *Werden und Wertung der Reformation: Vom Wegestreit zum Glaubenskampf* (Tübingen, 1979); translated by Dennis Martin as *Masters of the Reformation* (Cambridge, 1981), p. x. *Luther: Mensch zwischen Gott und Teufel* (Berlin, 1982).

147. H. A. Oberman, ed., *Forerunners of the Reformation* (London, 1967).

148. See, for example, the series *Studies in Medieval and Reformation Thought,* edited by H. A. Oberman and published by E. J. Brill (Leiden).

149. Ozment, *Reformation in Medieval Perspective,* also includes other items relevant to this discussion, such as F. Graus on the Hussites, P. Vignaux on Luther and Ockham, B. Moeller on German piety circa 1500, and Ozment on Luther and late medieval theology. Further contributions on the theme appear in F. F. Church and T. George, eds., *Continuity and Discontinuity* (Leiden, 1979).

150. *Archiv für Reformationsgeschichte* (Gütersloh, 1903–).

151. J. T. McNeill, *The History and Character of Calvinism* (New York and London, 1954).

152. R. H. Bainton, *Here I Stand: A Life of Martin Luther* (New York, 1950); *Studies on the Reformation* (Boston, 1963); *Hunted Heretic: The Life and Death of Michael Servetus* (Boston, 1960).

153. Wilhelm Pauck, *The Heritage of the Reformation* (Glencoe, Ill., 1950). A complete bibliography of Pauck's published writings is contained in the festschrift volume Pelikan, *Interpreters of Luther.*

154. See, for instance, *New Catholic Encyclopedia,* VIII, 1085–91; II, 1087–90; XII, 180–190.

155. An up-to-date survey of current research on the Reformation is to be found in Steven Ozment, ed., *Reformation Europe: A Guide to Research* (St. Louis, 1982).

156. On this point see Mansfield, "Erasmus, Luther, and the Problem of Church History."

9. Rediscovered Dimensions

1. Williams, *Radical Reformation,* p. xix.

2. For a survey of the early historiography see H. S. Bender, "The Historiography of the Anabaptists," *Mennonite Quarterly Review,* 31 (1957), pp. 88–104; see also F. H. Littell, *The Origins of Sectarian Protestantism,* 3rd ed. (New York, 1964), chap. 5. A comprehensive bibliography is H. J. Hillerbrand, *A Bibliography of Anabaptism, 1520–1630* (Elkhart, Ind., 1962), which contains over 4,600 titles and was followed by *A Bibliography of Anabaptism, 1520–1630: A Sequel, 1962–1974* (St. Louis, 1975).

3. Tieleman Jans van Braght, *Het Bloedig Tooneel* (Amsterdam, 1685).

4. W. C. Braithwaite, *The Beginnings of Quakerism* (London, 1923), p. 193.

5. For Voltaire's view of the Anabaptists see A. R. Epp, "Voltaire and the Anabaptists," *Mennonite Quarterly Review,* 45 (1971), pp. 145–151. Jacques, the most creditable character in *Candide,* was presented as an Anabaptist.

6. J. L. von Mosheim, *Institutes of Ecclesiastical History,* trans. J. Murdock (London, 1868), p. 689.

7. J. A. Starck, *Geschichte der Taufe und Taufgesinnten* (1789); Herman Schijn, *Geschiednis der Mennoniten* (1743–1745).

8. C. A. Cornelius, ed., *Berichte der Augenzeugen über das münsterische Wiedertäufer-reich* (Münster, 1855–1860), a series of eyewitness accounts.

9. J. E. E. D. Acton, *The History of Freedom and Other Essays* (London, 1907), p. 157.

10. Albrecht Ritschl, *Geschichte des Pietismus* (Bonn, 3 vols., 1880–1886). Ritschl's important "Prolegomena" to this work is translated in his *Three Essays,* ed. P. Hefner (Philadelphia, 1972), pp. 53–147. On Ritschl see also Chapter 8.

11. Ritschl, "Prolegomena," p. 70.

12. Ibid., p. 58.

13. Ibid., pp. 77, 80–83.

14. Ibid., p. 83.

15. Ibid., pp. 77–78.

16. Beck edited *Die Geschichts-Bücher der Wiedertäufer in Oesterreich-Ungarn* (Vienna, 1883); Loserth's works include *Doctor Balthasar Hubmaier und die Anfänge der Widertäufer in Mähren* (Brno, 1893) and an edition of Pilgram Marbeck's *Vermahnung* (1542), published in 1929.

17. Ludwig Keller, *Die Reformation und die älteren Reformparteien* (Leipzig, 1885); see also his *Johann Staupitz und die Anfänge der Reformation* (Leipzig, 1888).

18. Alfred Hegler, *Geist und Schrift bei Sebastian Franck* (Freiburg im Breisgau, 1892).

19. Emil Egli, ed., *Aktensammlung zur Geschichte der Züricher Reformation in den Jahren 1519–1532* (Zurich, 1879).

20. Jules Frederichs, *De Secte der Loisten of Antwerpesche libertijnen* (Ghent, 1891). On the Loists see Williams, *Radical Reformation*, pp. 351–354.

21. Froude, *History of England*, II, 257–258.

22. Charles Beard, *The Reformation of the Sixteenth Century in Its Relation to Modern Thought and Knowledge* (London and Edinburgh, 1885). For the subsequent passages see pp. 223–224. On Beard see also Chapter 8.

23. E. Belfort Bax, *The Rise and Fall of the Anabaptists* (London, 1903), p. 389. On Bax see Chapter 10.

24. Preserved Smith, *The Age of the Reformation* (London, 1920), p. 99.

25. G. P. Fisher, *The Reformation* (London, 1873), p. 311.

26. R. A. Knox, *Enthusiasm* (Oxford, 1950), p. 131.

27. G. R. Elton, *Reformation Europe 1517–1559* (London, 1963), pp. 94, 103.

28. Lindsay, *History of the Reformation*, II, 439, 441.

29. *Cambridge Modern History*, vol. II: *The Reformation* (Cambridge, 1903), p. 223.

30. Williston Walker, *The Reformation* (Edinburgh, 1900), p. 355.

31. A. H. Newman, *A History of Anti-Pedobaptism* (Philadelphia, 1897).

32. H. C. Vedder, *The Reformation in Germany* (New York, 1914), p. 345.

33. H. E. Dosker, *The Dutch Anabaptists* (Philadelphia, 1921).

34. Cited in H. E. Ford, ed., *Rufus Jones Speaks to Our Time* (New York, 1951), p. 8; see also E. C. Vining, *Friend of Life* (London, 1959).

35. R. M. Jones, *Studies in Mystical Religion* (London, 1909), p. 369.

36. R. M. Jones, *Spiritual Reformers in the Sixteenth and Seventeenth Centuries* (London, 1914), pp. 14–16.

37. R. M. Jones, *The Flowering of Mysticism: The Friends of God in the Fourteenth Century* (London, 1939).

38. Max Weber, *The Protestant Ethic and the Spirit of Capitalism*, trans. Talcott Parsons (New York, 1930; rpt. ed. 1958).

39. Ernst Troeltsch, *The Social Teaching of the Christian Churches*, trans. Olive Wyon (London, 2 vols., 1931), II, 691. For a broad modern presentation

see R. Morgan and M. Pye, eds., *Ernst Troeltsch: Writings on Theology and Religion* (London, 1978), which contains a translation of his important essay "Religion and the Science of Religion" (1906).

40. William James, *The Varieties of Religious Experience* (1902); Modern Library ed. (New York, n.d.), p. 397.

41. Troeltsch, *Social Teaching*, I, 331, 743.

42. Ibid., p. 799.

43. Ernst Correll, *Das Schweizerische Mennonitentum, Ein soziologischer Bericht* (Tübingen, 1925).

44. H. S. Bender, "The Anabaptist Vision," *Church History*, 13 (1944), pp. 23–24.

45. Cornelius Krahn, *Menno Simons, 1496–1561, Ein Beitrag zur Geschichte und Theologie der Taufgesinnten* (Karlsruhe, 1936).

46. R. H. Bainton, "Changing Ideas and Ideals in the Sixteenth Century," *Journal of Modern History*, 8 (1936), pp. 417–443.

47. R. H. Bainton, *David Joris, Wiedertäufer und Kämpfer fur Toleranz im 15. Jahrhundert* (Leipzig, 1937).

48. R. H. Bainton, *Hunted Heretic: The Life and Death of Michael Servetus, 1511–1553* (Boston, 1953); and "Sebastian Castellio, Champion of Religious Liberty," in *Studies on the Reformation* (London, 1964), pp. 139–181.

49. R. H. Bainton, "The Anabaptist Contribution to History," in *Studies on the Reformation*, p. 199.

50. R. H. Bainton, "The Left Wing of the Reformation" (originally in *Journal of Religion*, 1941), in *Studies on the Reformation*, p. 121.

51. J. T. McNeill, "Left-Wing Religious Movements," in A. G. Baker, ed., *A Short History of Christianity* (Chicago, 1940), pp. 127–132.

52. Robert Friedmann, "Recent Interpretations of Anabaptism," *Church History*, 24 (1955), pp. 132–151.

53. H. S. Bender, "The Anabaptists and Religious Liberty in the Sixteenth Century," *Archiv für Reformationsgeschichte*, 44 (1953), p. 34.

54. Robert Kreider, "Anabaptism and Humanism," *Mennonite Quarterly Review*, 26 (1952), pp. 123–141; see also K. R. Davis, "Erasmus as Progenitor of Anabaptist Theology and Piety," ibid., 47 (1973), pp. 163–178.

55. F. H. Littell, *The Origins of Sectarian Protestantism*, 3rd ed. (New York, 1964), p. xvii.

56. F. H. Littell, "The Importance of Anabaptist Studies," *Archiv für Reformationsgeschichte*, 58 (1967), p. 17.

57. H. J. Hillerbrand, "Anabaptism and the Reformation: Another Look," *Church History*, 29 (1960), p. 418.

58. Williams, *Radical Reformation*.

59. Ibid., p. xxxi.

60. Ibid., p. xxiv.

61. Ibid., p. xxv.

62. Ibid, p. 861.

63. A. G. Dickens, *Reformation and Society in Sixteenth Century Europe* (London, 1966), pp. 135, 137.

64. A. G. Dickens, "The Radical Reformation," *Past and Present*, 27 (1964), p. 124.

65. Norman Cohn, *The Pursuit of the Millennium*, rev. ed. (London, 1970), pp. 252–286; quotations on pp. 253, 254.

66. William Klaassen, "The Nature of the Anabaptist Protest," *Mennonite Quarterly Review*, 45 (1971), p. 311.

67. Paul Peachey, *Die Soziale Herkunft der schweizer Täufer in der Reformationszeit* (Karlsruhe, 1954); see also his "Social Background and Social Philosophy of the Swiss Anabaptists, 1525–1540," *Mennonite Quarterly Review*, 28 (1954), pp. 102–127.

68. A. L. E. Verheyden, *Anabaptism in Flanders, 1530–1650* (Scottsdale, Pa., 1961). J. S. Oyer, "Anabaptism in Central Germany; I. The Rise and Spread of the Movement; II. Faith and Life," *Mennonite Quarterly Review*, 34 (1960), pp. 219–248; 35 (1961), pp. 5–37.

69. C.-P. Clasen, "Medieval Heresies in the Reformation," *Church History*, 32 (1963), pp. 392–414; and "The Sociology of Swabian Anabaptism," ibid., pp. 150–180.

70. Clasen, "Sociology of Swabian Anabaptism," pp. 150–151.

71. Ibid., p. 173.

72. Ibid., p. 175.

73. C.-P. Clasen, *Anabaptism: A Social History, 1525–1618* (Ithaca and London, 1972), p. 209.

74. Ibid., pp. 324–334.

75. Review by Paul Miller, *Mennonite Quarterly Review*, 47 (1973), pp. 364–367.

76. Karl Holl, "Luther und die Schwärmer," in his *Gesammelte Aufsätze zur Kirchengeschichte*, I, 420–672.

77. See R. Friedmann, "Thomas Muentzer's Relation to Anabaptism," *Mennonite Quarterly Review*, 31 (1957), pp. 75–87.

78. E. W. Gritsch, "Thomas Müntzer and the Origins of Protestant Spiritualism," *Mennonite Quarterly Review*, 37 (1963), pp. 172–194; citation on p. 191.

79. Williams, *Radical Reformation*, p. 45; pp. 59–84.

80. E. W. Gritsch, *Reformer without a Church: The Life and Thought of Thomas Müntzer, 1488(?)–1525* (Philadelphia, 1967).

81. Annemarie Lohmann, *Zur geistigen Entwicklung Thomas Müntzers* (Leipzig, 1931); Carl Hinrichs, *Luther und Müntzer* (Berlin, 1952).

82. Walter Elliger, *Thomas Müntzer* (Berlin, 1960); see also L. H. Zuck, "Fecund Problems of Eschatological Hope, Election Proof and Social Revolt in Thomas Müntzer," in F. H. Littell, ed., *Reformation Studies* (Richmond, Va., 1962), pp. 239–250.

83. Williams, *Radical Reformation*, p. 387.

84. Thomas Nipperdey, "Theologie und Revolution bei Thomas Müntzer," *Archiv für Reformationsgeschichte*, 54 (1963), pp. 145–181.

85. E. G. Rupp, "Thomas Müntzer, Hans Huth, and the 'Gospel of All Creatures,' " *Bulletin of the John Rylands Library*, 43 (1961), pp. 492–519.

86. E. G. Rupp, "Word and Spirit in the First Years of the Reformation," *Archiv für Reformationsgeschichte*, 49 (1958), pp. 13–14.

87. Ibid., p. 25. See also Rupp's extended treatment of Münzer in *Patterns of Reformation* (London, 1969), pt. 3.

88. Marjorie Reeves, *The Influence of Prophecy in the Later Middle Ages* (Oxford, 1969).

89. I. B. Horst, *The Radical Brethren: Anabaptism and the English Reformation to 1558* (Nieuwkoop, 1972), p. 179. On another Netherlandish-English sect see A. Hamilton, *The Family of Love* (Cambridge, 1980).

90. For example, in East Germany see *Historische Forschungen in der DDR, 1960–1970* (Berlin, 1970), p. 344.

91. Domenico Caccamo, *Eretici Italiani in Moravia, Bolonia, Transilvania* (Florence and Chicago, 1970); Antonio Rotondo, *Studi e Richerche di Storia Ereticale* (Turin, 1974). For detailed guidance see Williams, *Radical Reformation*, chaps. 24–31. Recent research in the Socinian field is well represented by J. A. Tedeschi, ed., *Italian Reformation Studies in Honor of Laelius Socinus* (Florence, 1965).

92. K. H. Kirchoff, *Die Täufer in Münster, 1534–35: Untersuchungen zum Umfang und zur Sozialstruktur der Bewegung* (Münster, 1973).

93. James M. Stayer, *Anabaptists and the Sword* (Lawrence, Kans., 1972).

94. Steven Ozment, *Mysticism and Dissent: Religious Ideology and Social Protest in the Sixteenth Century* (New Haven and London, 1973), p. 247.

95. Lucien Febvre, "The Origins of the French Reformation: A Badly-Put Question?" translated from the French in P. Burke, ed., *A New Kind of History* (London, 1973), p. 88.

10. Materialist Perspectives

1. Troeltsch, *Social Teaching*, II, 1004; on Troeltsch see Chapter 11.

2. Ibid., pp. 1002.

3. Karl Marx, "Contribution to the Critique of Hegel's Philosophy of Right," in *Marx and Engels on Religion*, introduced by Reinhold Niebuhr (New York, 1964; rpt. from 1957 ed., Foreign Languages Publishing House, Moscow), p. 41.

4. Ibid.

5. Bruno Bauer, *Kritik der Evangelien und Geschichte ihres Ursprungs* (Berlin, 1850–1852).

6. Karl Marx, Preface to *A Contribution to the Critique of Political Economy* (Berlin, 1859); see also Friedrich Engels, *Ludwig Feuerbach and the End of Classical German Philosophy*, in *Marx and Engels*, pp. 213–268.

7. D. F. Strauss, *Das Leben Jesu* (Tübingen, 2 vols., 1835); English translation, *The Life of Jesus, or a critical examination of his history* (Birmingham, 4 vols., 1842–1844).

8. See D. McLellan, *Karl Marx: His Life and Thought* (London, 1973), p. 372.

9. See H. Lefebvre, *The Sociology of Karl Marx,* trans. N. Guterman (London, 1971), p. 80.

10. *Marx and Engels,* p. 41.

11. See Istvan Meszaros, *Marx's Theory of Alienation* (London, 1970), p. 65.

12. Karl Marx, "Theses on Feuerbach," in *Marx and Engels,* pp. 71–72.

13. Karl Marx, "Critique of Hegel," in *Marx and Engels,* p. 51. Marx did make a few other references to Luther, notably in his response to Feuerbach's *Essence of Christianity* and in *Capital,* where a number of times he used Luther's harsh attacks on usury (for instance, III, bk. 3, pt. 5, chap. 24). None of these references, however, betokens any serious and sustained interest in Luther for his own sake.

14. Marx, "Critique of Hegel," p 51.

15. Ibid.

16. Friedrich Engels, *The Condition of the Working-Class in England,* trans. and ed. W. O. Henderson and W. H. Chaloner, 2nd ed. (Oxford, 1971).

17. Friedrich Engels, *Anti-Dühring (Herrn Eugen Dührings Revolution in Science)* (London, 1935) and *The Origins of the Family, Private Property, and the State* (Chicago, 1902).

18. Friedrich Engels, *The German Revolutions,* ed. Leonard Krieger (Chicago, 1967), introduction, pp. xxiii–xxiv, xxvii.

19. Ibid., p. xxxii.

20. Friedrich Engels, "Der Deutsche Bauernkrieg," *Neue Rheinische Zeitung* (Cologne, 1850); English translation in *The German Revolutions,* pp. 3–119 (all quotations are from this edition); and *Germany: Revolution and Counter-Revolution,* in ibid., pp. 123–240.

21. Preface to the second edition of *The Peasant War in Germany,* in *The German Revolutions,* p. 3.

22. Wilhelm Zimmermann, *Geschichte des grossen deutschen Bauernkrieges* (Stuttgart, 3 vols., 1841–1843). Abraham Friesen's comprehensive study of Marxist historiography of the Reformation, *Reformation and Utopia* (Wiesbaden, 1974), considers Zimmermann's work pivotal in the development of Marxist thought about the Reformation.

23. Engels, *Peasant War,* p. 3.

24. See Abraham Friesen, "The Marxist Interpretation of the Reformation," *Archiv für Reformationsgeschichte,* 64 (1973), pp. 34–54; "Philip Melanchthon (1497–1560), Wilhelm Zimmermann (1807–1878), and the Dilemma of Müntzer Historiography," *Church History,* 43 (1974), pp. 164–182.

25. See Meszaros, *Marx's Theory of Alienation,* p. 33.

26. Engels, *Peasant War,* p.36.

27. Ibid., p. 33.

28. Ibid., p. 41.

29. Ibid., p. 43.

30. Ibid., pp. 46–47.

31. Ibid., p. 52.

32. Engels seemed to believe that Münzer had an official presiding role in the

Mühlhausen "eternal Council." However, this was shown later not to be the case, and although this does not necessarily preclude Münzer's exercise of a leading influence through his presence and advice, Kautsky concluded that he had no such impact.

33. Engels, *Peasant War*, p. 104.

34. Ibid., pp. 107–108, 114.

35. Ibid., p. 52.

36. Ibid., p. 118.

37. See Abraham Friesen, "Thomas Müntzer in Marxist Thought," *Church History*, 34 (1965), pp. 306–327, 316.

38. Engels, *Dialectics of Nature*. Extract in *Marx and Engels*, pp. 152–193; quotation on p. 152.

39. Ibid., pp. 152, 154.

40. Ibid., p. 154. |

41. *Ludwig Feuerbach*, in *Marx and Engels*, pp. 213–268, 264; see also Gibbon's view of the Albigensians (or Cathars) in Chapter 6.

42. Ibid., p. 265; see also *Juristic Socialism* (1887)—wherein Engels declared that "the flag of religion waved for the last time in seventeenth-century England"—in *Marx and Engels*, p. 270.

43. *Ludwig Feuerbach*, p. 266.

44. Friedrich Engels, *Socialism: Utopian and Scientific (Anti-Dühring)*. Extract in *Marx and Engels*, pp. 287–315.

45. Ibid., pp. 300–305. From this point, of course, the fortunes of the bourgeoisie were dramatically affected by the Industrial Revolution (pp. 307–308).

46. Engels, Letter to Josef Bloch, in *Marx and Engels*, pp. 276–277.

47. The issues raised by this letter recall those canvassed more recently by E. P. Hobsbawm in reference to "vulgar Marxism." See his "Karl Marx's Contribution to Historiography," in R. Blackburn, ed., *Ideology and Social Science: Readings in Critical Social Theory* (London, 1972), chap. 12.

48. August Bebel, *Der Deutsche Bauernkrieg* (Brunswick, 1876).

49. Karl Kautsky, *Die Vorläufer des neueren Sozialismus* (Stuttgart, 1894). Translated by J. L. and E. G. Mulliken as *Communism in Central Europe in the Time of the Reformation* (New York, 1953). According to Hobsbawm, "Karl Marx's Contribution," Kautsky provides an example of how Marxist views were assimilated to contemporary non-Marxist perspectives, particularly to evolutionary and positivist views.

50. Karl Kautsky, *The Foundations of Christianity* (London, 1925), pp. 354, 419.

51. Kautsky, *Communism in Central Europe*, pp. 10–11, 71–72.

52. Ibid., p. 108. Kautsky made this judgment knowing that Engels's account was based on Zimmermann and was therefore not strictly independent. However, he noted that Engels had elaborated his material independently and had given many new glimpses into the causes of the Peasants' War which were "of the utmost importance."

53. Ibid., pp. 109–110.

54. Ibid., p. 117. A case in point was Münzer's alleged "disdain" of the Bible—

which Kautsky insisted was true "only in so far as it is not supported by the voice of interior revelation."

55. Kautsky, *Communism in Central Europe*, pp. 101–102, 128–129.

56. Ibid., p. 141.

57. Ibid., pp. 148–149, 151–153. Kautsky's recognition of scholars' unfortunate dependence for information about Reformation radicals on the accounts of hostile witnesses found its counterpart among non-Marxist scholars at this time. See Chapter 9.

58. Ibid., p. 146.

59. On this point see Abraham Friesen, "The Marxist Interpretation of Anabaptism," in Carl S. Meyer, ed., *Sixteenth-Century Essays and Studies* (St. Louis, 1970), I, 23–24.

60. Kautsky, *Communism in Central Europe*, p. 291. The reference here is to Keller.

61. Ibid., pp. 292–293.

62. William Morris, *A Dream of John Ball* (London, 1888) and *News from Nowhere* (London, 1891).

63. Ernest Belfort Bax, *The Religion of Socialism* (London, 1887) and *The Ethics of Socialism* (London, 1889).

64. E. P. Thompson, *William Morris: Romantic to Revolutionary* (New York, 1955; rev. ed., 1977), pp. 438–439.

65. Ernest Belfort Bax, *German Society at the Close of the Middle Ages* (London, 1894); *The Peasants' War in Germany, 1525–1526* (London, 1899); *The Rise and Fall of the Anabaptists* (London, 1903).

66. Ernest Belfort Bax, *Reminiscences and Reflections of a Mid and Late Victorian* (London, 1918), p. 159.

67. Günther Franz, *Der deutsche Bauernkrieg*, 4th ed. (Darmstadt, 1956).

68. Bax, *German Society*, p. vii.

69. Ibid., p. 92.

70. Bax, *Peasants' War*, p. 19.

71. Ibid., p. 280.

72. Ibid., p. 349.

73. Ibid., p. 234.

74. Bax, *Anabaptists*, pp. 389–391.

75. Marx, however, in reviewing Guizot's book on the English Revolution of the 1640s, pointed out links between the emergence of Protestantism and the rise of the gentry. See D. Fernbach, ed., *Surveys from Exile* (London, 1973), p. 253.

76. Max Beer, *A History of British Socialism* (London, 2 vols., 1919–1920), I, 32.

77. Karl Kautsky, *Thomas More and His Utopia*, trans. H. J. Stenning (London, 1927). Hobsbawm, "Karl Marx's Contribution," says of this work that "there is nothing particularly Marxist about the choice of subject, and its treatment is 'vulgar-Marxist' " (p. 271).

78. Frederic Seebohm, *The Oxford Reformers* (London, 1896); R. W. Chambers, *Thomas More* (London, 1935), p. 257. Some recent views of *Utopia* have

confirmed Chambers's opinion that More intended to emphasize the failings of the Christian Europeans by depicting the superior civilization of a race which lived merely by reason, without the inestimable benefits of Christ. J. H. Hexter rejects the notion of More as a proto-Marxist but places him in the beginnings of an English humanitarian tradition based on equality. He reveals More as a "social environmentalist" who was essentially optimistic about the prospects of humanity and considers his thought truly radical for this reason. (Introduction to *Utopia*, Yale edition of More's works [New Haven and London, 1965], IV, cxix, cxxiii). So a vision of More the radical has survived, and the picture of More the bourgeois propagandist put forward by R. Ames in *Citizen Thomas More and His Utopia* (Princeton, 1949) has gained little favor.

79. A. L. Morton, *A People's History of England* (London, 1938), p. 176.

80. Ibid.

81. A. L. Morton, *The English Utopia* (London, 1952), p. 58.

82. Maurice Dobb, *An Outline of European History* (London, 1925), pp. 11–12.

83. Maurice Dobb, *Studies in the Development of Capitalism* (London, 1946), pp. 9–10.

84. H. J. Laski, *A Grammar of Politics* (London, 1925); *The State in Theory and Practice* (London, 1935); *Communism* (London, 1927), p. 13.

85. Roy Pascal, *The Social Basis of the German Reformation: Martin Luther and His Times* (London, 1933), p. vii.

86. E. G. Rupp, "Luther and Government," in *The Righteousness of God*, p. 287.

87. Pascal, *Social Basis*, pp. 1, 92.

88. Ibid., p. 115.

89. Ibid., pp. vii–viii, 124, 241–242.

90. Ibid., pp. 177–178.

91. Ibid., pp. 242.

92. See L. Kolakowski, *Main Currents of Marxism* (Oxford, 3 vols., 1978), II, chap. 52.

93. Franz Mehring, *Deutsche Geschichte vom Ausgang des Mittelalters* (Berlin, 1910; 6th ed., 1952).

94. Ernst Bloch, *Thomas Münzer als Theologe der Revolution* (Munich, 1921; Berlin, 1960), p. 26; and "Blick in den Chiliasmus des Bauernkrieges und Wiedertäufertums," *Genius, Zeitschrift für Werdende und alte Kunst*, 1 (1920), pp. 310–313.

95. Friesen, *Reformation and Utopia*, p. 183.

96. M. M. Smirin, *Die Volksreformation des Thomas Müntzer und der grosse Bauernkrieg* (Berlin, 1952).

97. Ibid., p. 276. Engels's approval of Kautsky's view is indicated in Benedict Kautsky, ed., *Friedrich Engels Briefwechsel mit Karl Kautsky* (Vienna, 1955), pp. 434–435.

98. Smirin, *Die Volksreformation*, pp. 83–87.

99. Ibid., pp. 296–324.

100. M. M. Smirin, *Deutschland vor der Reformation* (Berlin, 1955).

101. On this point see Friesen's discussion, *Reformation and Utopia*, pp. 193–201. Epstein held the notion of a bourgeois revolution without a bourgeoisie. Macek argued that the Peasants' War was a form of bourgeois revolution quite distinct from bourgeois movements in the cities.

102. Leo Stern, *Gegenwartsaufgaben der deutschen Geschichtsforschung* (Berlin, 1952) and *Für eine kämpferische Geschichtswissenschaft* (Berlin, 1954).

103. Leo Stern, "Probleme der Reformation im Spiegel Ihrer Jubiläum," in Leo Stern and Max Steinmetz, eds., *450 Jahre Reformation* (Berlin, 1967), pp. 22–23.

104. Max Steinmetz, *Deutschland von 1476 bis 1648 (Von der frühbürgerlichen Revolution bis zum Westfälischen Frieden)*, Lehrbuch der deutschen Geschichte, 3 (Berlin, 1967), p. 90.

105. Ibid., pp. 80–90.

106. Ibid., pp. 98–106.

107. Max Steinmetz, "Reformation und Bauernkrieg in der Historiographie der DDR," *Zeitschrift für Geschichtswissenschaft*, 8 (1960), pp. 160 ff.

108. Gerhard Brendler, ed., *Die frühbürgerliche Revolution in Deutschland* (Berlin, 1961). See Friesen's discussion, *Reformation and Utopia*, pp. 201–204.

109. Josef Macek, *Husitské revolucni hnuti* (Prague, 1952); Robert Kalivoda, *Das huttische Denken im Lichte seiner Quellen* (Berlin, 1969). This work is discussed by Bernard Töpfer; see n. 111.

110. Leo Stern, *Martin Luther und Philipp Melanchthon* (Berlin, 1953).

111. Bernard Töpfer, "Fragen der hussitischen revolutionären Bewegung," *Zeitschrift für Geschichtswissenschaft*, 11 (1963), p. 149.

112. Gerhard Brendler, "Reformation und Fortschritt," in Stern and Steinmetz, *450 Jahre Reformation*, pp. 65–70.

113. Karl Kleinschmidt, *Martin Luther* (Berlin, 1953), p. 50.

114. Stern, *Martin Luther*, pp. 15–17.

115. Günther Fabiunke, *Martin Luther als Nationalökonom* (Berlin, 1963).

116. Rosemarie Müller-Streisand, *Luthers Weg von der Reformation zur Restauration* (Halle, 1964).

117. Gerhard Zschäbitz, *Martin Luther: Grosse und Grenze* (Berlin, 1967), I. The author's death prevented the completion of volume II of this work.

118. Ibid., pp. 72, 130, 208.

119. See Manfred Bensing, *Thomas Münzer und der Thüringer Aufstand, 1525* (Berlin, 1966), p. 198, where Luther is seen as defending his own Reformation rather than as acting out of political motives. See Friesen's discussion in *Reformation and Utopia*, pp. 219–220.

120. Gerhard Zschäbitz, *Zur Mitteldeutschen Wiedertäuferbewegung nach dem grossen Bauernkrieg* (Berlin, 1958), p. 37.

121. For example, Töpfer and Steinmetz. See discussion in Friesen, *Reformation and Utopia*, pp. 212–214.

122. Ernst Werner, "Messianische Bewegungen im Mittelalter," *Zeitschrift für Geschichtswissenschaft*, 10 (1962), pp. 370–396 and 598–622. Bensing, *Thomas Münzer*, pp. 57–61; see also Friesen, "Marxist Interpretation of the Reformation," p. 51.

123. On this question see Friesen, "Marxist Interpretation of Anabaptism," pp. 17–34.

124. Zschäbitz, *Wiedertäuferbewegung*, p. 12.

125. Bensing, *Thomas Müntzer*, p. 133. Zschäbitz, *Wiedertäuferbewegung*, pp. 73–87, 118, 162, 166; see also his "Die Stellung der Täuferbewegung im Spannungsbogen der deutschen frühbürgerlichen Revolution," in Brendler, *Frühbürgerlichen Revolution*, pp. 152–162.

126. Cited in Friesen, "Marxist Interpretation of Anabaptism," p. 33.

127. Josef Macek, *Der Tiroler Bauernkrieg und Michael Gaismair* (Berlin, 1965).

128. Johannes Schildhauer, *Soziale, politische und religiöse Auseinandersetzung in den Hansetädten—Stralsund, Rostock und Wismar—im ersten Drittel des 16 Jahrhunderts* (Weimar, 1959). This work is listed in Friesen's book under Marxist literature, but not discussed, presumably because it does not overtly demonstrate clearly "Marxist" characteristics.

129. R. W. Scribner, "Is There a Social History of the Reformation?" *Social History*, no. 4 (1977), pp. 483–503, esp. pp. 489–491.

130. Rainer Wohlfeil, ed., *Reformation oder frühbürgerliche Revolution?* (Munich, 1972).

131. Rainer Wohlfeil, *Der Bauernkrieg, 1524–1526: Bauernkrieg und Reformation* (Munich, 1975).

132. Tom Scott, "The Peasant War: A Historiographical Review, Pt. 1," *Historical Journal*, 22 (1979), pp. 693–720, esp. p. 693. Part 2 appeared in the following issue, 22 (1979), pp. 953–974.

133. The *New Cambridge Modern History*, in sharp contrast to the earlier *Cambridge Modern History*, devotes only four paragraphs to the Peasants' War in its volume on the Reformation; R. W. Scribner and Gerhard Benecke, *The German Peasant War, 1525: New Viewpoints* (London, 1979), p. 1.

134. Max Steinmetz, ed., *Der deutsche Bauernkrieg und Thomas Müntzer* (Leipzig, 1976).

135. See Gerhard Heitz, Adolf Laube, Max Steinmetz, and Günter Vogler, eds., *Der Bauer im Klassenkampf: Studien zur Geschichte des deutschen Bauernkrieges und der bäuerlichen Klassenkämpfe Spätfeudalismus* (Berlin, 1975), which includes some essays of this type.

136. Peter Blickle, *The Revolution of 1525*, trans. H. C. E. Midelfort and T. A. Brady (Baltimore, Md., 1982); see also "Thesen zum Thema—Der Bauernkrieg als Revolution des 'Gemeines Mannes,' " *Historische Zeitschrift*, supplement 4, 1975, pp. 127–131; translated in Scribner and Benecke, *German Peasant War*, pp. 19–22.

137. Janos Bak, ed., *The German Peasant War of 1525* (London, 1976; originally a special issue of the *Journal of Peasant Studies*, 3, no. 1 [October 1975]).

138. Scribner and Benecke, *German Peasant War*, pp. 1–8.

139. Among recent positive signs of a more flexible approach developing in East German Marxist circles were some contributions to discussion at the Sixth International Congress of Luther Research in Erfurt, August 1983, which avoided the standard formulas of the past and expressed genuine interest in investigating

Luther's theology in its own terms. The same tendency is evident in a recent biography by Gerhard Brendler, *Martin Luther: Theologie und Revolution* (Berlin, 1983).

11. Models and Patterns

1. Raymond Aron, *Main Currents in Sociological Thought*, trans. Richard Howard and Helen Weaver (Harmondsworth, 2 vols., 1965).

2. Some idea of the range of this discussion is given in R. W. Green, ed., *Protestantism and Capitalism: The Weber Thesis and Its Critics* (Boston, 1959).

3. Cobbett, *History of the Protestant Reformation*, A. W. N. Pugin, *Contrasts* (London, 1836).

4. Max Weber, *Wirtschaft und Gesellschaft* (Tübingen, 1922). Translation edited by G. Roth and C. Wittich as *Economy and Society* (New York, 1968).

5. Max Weber, "Die Protestantische Ethik und der Geist von Kapitalismus," in *Archiv für Sozialwissenschaft und Sozialpolitik* (1904–1905), XX, sec. 1; XXI, sec. 1. Reprinted in *Gesammelte Aufsätze zur Religionssoziologie* (Tübingen, 3 vols., 1920–1921), I, 17–206. Translated by Talcott Parsons as *The Protestant Ethic and the Spirit of Capitalism* (New York, 1958).

6. Weber, *The Protestant Ethic*, p. 13.

7. T. B. Bottomore and M. Rubel, eds., *Karl Marx: Selected Writings in Sociology and Social Philosophy* (Harmondsworth, 1963), p. 58n.

8. Letter to Rickert, cited in H. H. Gerth and C. Wright Mills, eds., *From Max Weber: Essays in Sociology* (London, 1948), pp. 18–19.

9. Ibid., p. 309.

10. Weber, "The Protestant Sects and the Spirit of Capitalism," in ibid., p. 321.

11. The idea of the "spirit of Capitalism" had already been propagated by the economic historian Werner Sombart, a coeditor with Weber of the journal in which Weber's essay was first published.

12. Weber, *The Protestant Ethic*, p. 76.

13. Ibid., p. 153.

14. For example, ibid., pp. 48–50, 64, 71.

15. H. M. Robertson, *Aspects of the Rise of Economic Individualism* (London, 1933).

16. M. M. Knappen, *Tudor Puritanism* (Chicago, 1939), p. 513.

17. C. H. George and Katherine George, *The Protestant Mind of the English Reformation, 1570–1640* (Princeton, 1961), p. 146.

18. A. E. Sayous, "Calvinisme et capitalisme: L'éxperience génevoise," *Annales d'histoire économique et sociale*, 7 (1935), p. 244.

19. André Biéler, *La Pensée économique et sociale de Calvin* (Geneva, 1959).

20. Norman Birnbaum, "The Zwinglian Reformation in Zurich," *Past and Present*, 15 (1959), pp. 27–45.

21. For instance, see A. Fanfani, *Catholicism, Protestantism and Capitalism* (London, 1939).

22. G. R. Elton, *Reformation Europe* (Collins, 1962), pp. 311–318; Dickens, *Reformation and Society in Sixteenth Century Europe*, pp. 178–180.

23. Christopher Hill, "Protestantism and the Rise of Capitalism," in F. J. Fisher, ed., *Essays in the Economic and Social History of Tudor and Stuart England* (London, 1961), pp. 15–39.

24. Hugh Trevor-Roper, *Religion, the Reformation and Social Change* (London, 1967), p. 6.

25. Ibid., p. 27.

26. See n. 4.

27. Max Weber, "Die Protestantischen Sekten und der Geist des Kapitalismus," in *Gesammelte Aufsätze zur Religionssoziologie*, I, 207–236. Translated as "The Protestant Sects and the Spirit of Capitalism," in Gerth and Mills, *From Max Weber*, pp. 302–322.

28. Weber, "Protestant Sects," p. 312.

29. Max Weber, *Die Stadt* (1921). Translated by D. Martindale and G. Neuwirth as *The City* (Glencoe, Ill., 1958).

30. R. H. Tawney, Foreword to *The Protestant Ethic*, pp. 1a–11 (London, 1930).

31. Carlyle, *On Heroes*, lecture 4. On Carlyle see Chapter 7.

32. F. D. Maurice, *Three Letters to the Reverend R. W. Palmer*, 2nd ed. (London, 1842), pp. 16–17; see Chapter 8.

33. Charles Gore (1853–1932) provided a prefatory note to the first edition of Tawney's book.

34. R. H. Tawney, Introduction to Max Beer, *History of British Socialism* (London, 1919–1920), pp. xv, xviii.

35. R. H. Tawney, *Religion and the Rise of Capitalism* (London, 1926; Harmondsworth, 1937).

36. Ibid., p. 26.

37. Tawney, *Religion and the Rise of Capitalism* (1937 ed.), p. xii.

38. Ibid., p. 48.

39. Ibid., p. 169.

40. Ibid., p. 199.

41. Ibid., p. 238.

42. Ibid., p. 251. The reference is to Samuel Smiles (1812–1904), and especially to his book *Self-help* (1859).

43. R. H. Tawney, *The Agrarian Problem of the Sixteenth Century* (London, 1912); *Business and Politics under James I* (Cambridge, 1958).

44. R. H. Tawney, *The Acquisitive Society* (London, 1921) and *Equality* (London, 1931).

45. Tawney, *Religion and the Rise of Capitalism* (1937 ed.), pp. 226, 238.

46. Troeltsch, *Social Teaching* (rpt. ed., Chicago, 2 vols., 1976).

47. Ibid., I, 25.

48. H. Richard Niebuhr, Introduction to *Social Teaching* (1976 ed.), pp. 8–9.

49. Ibid.

50. Ernst Troeltsch, *Der Historismus und seine Probleme*, published in Berlin in 1923, but written earlier.

51. Troeltsch, *Social Teaching,* II, 993.

52. Ibid., pp. 993–994.

53. Ibid., I, chap. 2.

54. Ibid., II, chap. 3, pp. 2, 3.

55. Ibid., pp. 607, 620.

56. Ibid., p. 702.

57. Ibid., p. 820. On Troeltsch's understanding of sectarianism see also Chapter 9.

58. H. R. Niebuhr, *Christ and Culture* (London, 1952).

59. Ibid., p. 14.

60. Ibid., pp. 53–57.

61. H. R. Niebuhr, *The Social Sources of Denominationalism* (New York, 1957).

62. Werner Stark, *The Sociology of Religion: A Study of Christendom* (London, 5 vols., 1966–1972). Volume I, *Established Religions;* volume II, *Sectarian Religions;* and volume III, *The Universal Church,* are described as the "Macrosociology of Religion," as distinguished from the "Microsociology of Religion" covered in volume IV, *Types of Religious Men,* and volume V, *Types of Religious Culture.*

63. Stark, in fact, did not even recognize that Troeltsch employed a threefold model and spoke of Church and sect as being for Troeltsch an "all-embracing alternative"; *Sociology of Religion,* III, 1.

64. Ibid., I, 3–4.

65. Ibid., II, 16, 108, 182; III, 373–374; IV, 323.

66. Michael Walzer, *The Revolution of the Saints* (London, 1966), p. 309.

67. Norman Cohn, *The Pursuit of the Millennium* (London, 1957). Significantly, Cohn's other major works, *Warrant for Genocide* (London, 1967) and *Europe's Inner Demons* (London, 1975), dealing respectively with Nazism and witchcraft, are both studies of mass psychology.

68. Guenther Lewy, *Religion and Revolution* (New York, 1974), pt. 2, chap. 5.

69. Keith Thomas, *Religion and the Decline of Magic* (London, 1971). See Chapter 12 for a more detailed discussion.

70. Preserved Smith, *Luther's Table Talk: A Critical Study* (New York, 1907).

71. Paul Reiter, *Martin Luthers Umwelt, Charakter und Psychose* (Copenhagen, 1937–1941).

72. Ibid., pp. 573–574.

73. Oscar Pfister, *Christianity and Fear* (London, 1948), pp. 344–345.

74. Oscar Pfister, *Die psychoanalytische Methode* (Leipzig and Berlin, 1913). Translated by C. R. Payne as *The Psychoanalytic Method* (London, 1917).

75. Erik Erikson, *Young Man Luther,* 2nd ed. (New York, 1962).

76. Erik Erikson, *Childhood and Society* (New York, 1950).

77. For example, R. H. Bainton, "Psychiatry and History: An Examination of Erikson's *Young Man Luther*"; and L. W. Spitz, Jr., "Psychohistory and History: The Case of *Young Man Luther*"; both in R. A. Johnson, ed., *Psychohistory and Religion: The Case of Young Man Luther* (Philadelphia, 1977).

78. See also Heinrich Bornkamm, "Luther and His Father," in P. Homans, ed., *Childhood and Selfhood: Essays on Religion and Modernity in the Thought of Erik Erikson* (Brunswick, N.J., 1978).

79. See A. G. Dickens, *Martin Luther and the Reformation* (London, 1967), pp. 13–14.

80. For instance, John Osborne, *Luther* (London, 1961).

81. Norman O. Brown, *Life against Death: The Psychoanalytic Meaning of History* (Middletown, Conn., 1959), chap. 14.

82. Roland Dalbiez, *L'Angoisse de Luther: Essai psychologique* (Paris, 1974).

83. Guy Swanson, *Religion and Regime: A Sociological Account of the Reformation* (Ann Arbor, 1967).

84. Guy Swanson, *The Birth of the Gods* (Ann Arbor, 1960).

85. Swanson, *Religion and Regime*, pp. 247–252.

86. Ibid., p. 58.

87. See, for example, *Journal of Interdisciplinary History*, 1 (1970–1971), pp. 379–446.

88. See, for instance, the review by R. M. Kingdon in *American Sociological Review*, 33 (1968), p. 843.

89. Ibid. See also reviews by W. Bouwsma in *Comparative Studies in Society and History*, 10 (1967–1968), pp. 486–491; L. W. Spitz, Jr., in *Political Science Quarterly*, 75 (1970), pp. 129–130.

90. Steven Ozment, *The Reformation in the Cities* (New Haven, 1975).

91. Bernd Moeller, *Reichstadt und Reformation* (Gütersloh, 1962). Translated by H. C. E. Midelfort and M. U. Edwards as *Imperial Cities and the Reformation* (Philadelphia, 1972). See Chapter 12.

92. Review by Spitz (cited in n. 89).

93. N. Z. Davis, "Deforming the Reformation," *New York Review of Books*, 10 April 1969, pp. 35–38; R. L. Colie, in *American Historical Review*, 73 (1968), pp. 1132–34.

12. The Secular Setting

1. On this subject we are chiefly indebted to Peter Burke, ed., *A New Kind of History from the Writings of Febvre* (London, 1973). The editor's introduction is followed by a dozen substantial passages from Febvre's works, translated by K. Folca.

2. Lucien Febvre, *La Terre et l'évolution humaine* (Paris, 1922).

3. Lucien Febvre, "Une Question mal posée: Les origines de la Réforme française et le problème général des causes de la Réforme," *Revue historique*, 161 (1929), pp. 1–73; reprinted in Febvre's *Au coeur religieux du XVIᵉ siècle* (Paris, 1957); translation in Burke, *Febvre*, pp. 44–107.

4. Lucien Febvre, *Un Destin: Martin Luther* (Paris, 1928; 3rd ed., 1951).

5. Augustin Renaudet, *Préréforme et humanisme à Paris pendant les premières guerres d'Italie, 1494–1517* (Paris, 1916); Henri Hauser, *Etudes sur la Réforme*

française (Paris, 1909); Febvre also cites his *Les Sources de l'histoire de France: XVIe siècle* (Paris, 4 vols., 1906–1916).

6. Dermot Fenlon, "*Encore Une Question:* Lucien Febvre, the Reformation and the School of Annales," *Historical Studies,* 11 (1974), pp. 65–81.

7. Marcel Bataillon, *Erasme et l'Espagne: Recherches sur l'histoire spirituelle du XVIe siècle* (Paris, 1937).

8. Pierre Imbart de la Tour, *Les Origines de la Réforme,* vol. I: *La France moderne* (Paris, 1905); vol. II: *L'Eglise catholique: La crise et la renaissance* (1909); vol. III: *L'Evangelisme, 1521–1538* (1914); vol. IV: *Calvin et l'Institution chrétienne* (1935).

9. See Dermot Fenlon, *Heresy and Obedience in Tridentine Italy: Cardinal Pole and the Counter Reformation* (Cambridge, 1972), pp. 14–23; E. M. Jung, "On the Nature of Evangelism in Sixteenth Century Italy," *Journal of the History of Ideas,* 14 (1953), pp. 511–527.

10. See references in Fenlon, "*Encore Une Question,*" nn. 12–32.

11. Lucien Febvre, *Le Problème de l'incroyance au XVIe siècle: La religion de Rabelais* (Paris, 1942).

12. Heinrich Bullinger, *Histoire ecclésiastique des Eglises réformées* (Antwerp, 1580; Paris, 3 vols., 1883–1889); see Chapter 1.

13. For instance, E. Cabié, *Guerres de religion dans le Sud-Ouest de la France* (1906); G. Clément-Simon, *Tulle et le Bas-Limousin pendant les guerres de religion* (Tulle, 1887); G. Lambert, *Histoire des guerres de religion en Provence, 1530–1598* (Toulon, 1870); J. D. Long, *La Réforme et les guerres de religion en Dauphiné de 1560 à l'édit de Nantes* (Paris, 1856); E. Clouard, *Les Gens d'autrefois: Riom aux XVe et XVIe siècles* (Paris, 1910); J. J. Vaissète and C. de Vic, *Histoire générale de Languedoc* (the best edition, much modernized, is Toulouse, 16 vols., 1872–1905; S. Mours, *Le Protestantisme en Vivarais et en Velay des origines à nos jours* (Valence, 1949). P. Wolff, ed., *Histoire du Languedoc* (Toulouse, 1977).

14. For example, L. Grégoire, *La Ligue en Bretagne* (Paris and Nantes, 1856); R. D'Estaintot, *La Ligue en Normandie* (Paris and Rouen, 1862); H. Drouot, *Mayenne et la Bourgogne* (Paris, 2 vols., 1937).

15. Hauser, *Etudes;* also *La Naissance du Protestantisme* (Paris, 1940). Emile Léonard, *Histoire générale du Protestantisme,* vol. I: *La Réformation* (Paris, 1961). Translation edited by H. H. Rowley, *A History of Protestantism,* vol. I: *The Reformation* (London, 1965). Samuel Mours, *Le Protestantisme en France au XVIe siècle* (Paris, 1959) and other works.

16. Jean Delumeau, *Naissance et affirmation de la Réforme* (Paris, 1965).

17. Fernand Braudel, *La Méditerranée et le monde mediterranéen a l'époque de Philippe II* (Paris, 1949). Translated by S. Reynolds as *The Mediterranean and the Mediterranean World in the Age of Philip II* (London, 2 vols., 1972–1973).

18. Janine Garrison-Estèbe, *Tocsin pour un massacre: La saison des Saint-Barthélemy* (Paris, 1968) and *Protestants du midi, 1559–1598* (Toulouse, 1980). Natalie Davis, *Society and Culture in Early Modern France* (Stanford and Lon-

don, 1975); some of these essays were published in journals at earlier dates: see p. x. See also N. Z. Davis, "The Sacred and the Body Social in Sixteenth-Century Lyon," *Past and Present,* 90 (1981), pp. 40–70. Compare also in this field P. Benedict, *Rouen during the Wars of Religion* (Cambridge, 1981); J. H. M. Salmon, *Society in Crisis: France in the Sixteenth Century* (London, 1975); Joan Davies, "Persecution and Protestantism: Toulouse, 1562–1575," *Historical Journal,* 22 (1979), pp. 31–51; Nancy L. Roelker, "Les Femmes de la noblesse huguenote," in *Actes du colloque: L'amiral de Coligny et son temps* (Paris, 1974); and similar articles in *Journal of Interdisciplinary History,* 2 (1972), pp. 391–418; and *Archiv für Reformationsgeschichte,* 63 (1972), pp. 168–195; N. M. Sutherland, *The Huguenot Struggle for Recognition* (New Haven, 1980); H. A. Lloyd, *The State, France and the Sixteenth Century* (London, 1983), chap. 5.

19. Details on this and most of the later-cited local histories, including Francis Drake's *Eboracum,* are readily available in Conyers Read, ed., *Bibliography of British History: Tudor Period, 1485–1603,* 2nd ed. (Oxford, 1959).

20. *Victoria History of the Counties of England* (London, 1900–1934; Oxford, 1935–). The early volumes contain useful summaries of ecclesiastical history from pre-Conquest times, besides accounts of all religious houses, some of which include useful references to the dissolution. Only a few have any significant mention of early Protestantism; yet little relevant research had occurred anywhere before about 1950.

21. Rachel R. Reid, *The King's Council in the North* (London, 1921).

22. The standard work is still M. H. Dodds and R. Dodds, *The Pilgrimage of Grace, 1536–1537, and the Exeter Conspiracy, 1538* (Cambridge, 2 vols., 1915). For references to some subsequent works see A. G. Dickens, *Reformation Studies* (London, 1982), p. 59; and especially C. S. L. Davies in *Past and Present,* 41 (1968), pp. 54–76; M. E. James in ibid., 48 (1970), pp. 3–78; Christopher Haigh, *The Last Days of the Lancashire Monasteries and the Pilgrimage of Grace* (Manchester, 1969); G. R. Elton, "Politics and the Pilgrimage of Grace," in B. C. Malament, ed., *After the Reformation* (Manchester, 1980); M. Bowker, "Lincolnshire 1536: Heresy, Schism or Religious Discontent?" *Studies in Church History,* 9 (1972), pp. 195–212.

23. A. L. Rowse, *Tudor Cornwall: Portrait of a Society* (London, 1947).

24. A. G. Dickens, *Lollards and Protestants in the Diocese of York,* 2nd ed. (London, 1982). Numerous other Yorkshire items appear in his *Reformation Studies.*

25. Christopher Haigh, *Reformation and Resistance in Tudor Lancashire* (Cambridge, 1975).

26. J. E. Oxley, *The Reformation in Essex to the Death of Mary* (Manchester, 1965); Peter Clark, *English Provincial Society from the Reformation to the Revolution: Religion, Politics and Society in Kent, 1500–1640* (Hassocks, 1977); Margaret Bowker, *The Secular Clergy in the Diocese of Lincoln, 1495–1520* (Cambridge, 1968) and *The Henrician Reformation: The Diocese of Lincoln under John Longland, 1521–1547* (Cambridge, 1981).

27. K. G. Powell, "The Beginnings of Protestantism in Gloucestershire," *Bristol and Gloucestershire Archaeological Society Transactions,* 90 (1971), pp. 141–

157; "The Social Background to the Reformation in Gloucestershire," ibid., 92 (1973), pp. 96–120; *The Marian Martyrs and the Reformation in Bristol* (Bristol, 1972). See also A. G. Dickens, "Early Protestantism and the Church in North-amptonshire," *Northamptonshire: Past and Present*, 8 (1983–1984), pp. 27–39; and, on London, Susan Brigden, "Religion and Social Obligation in Early Six-teenth-Century London," *Past and Present* 103 (1984), pp. 67–112.

28. Even, for instance, the great collection in the Lincoln Diocesan Registry; see Bowker, *Henrician Reformation*, p. 181.

29. Foxe, *A and M*, VIII, 407.

30. At the time of writing only one volume is published: *A Biographical Register of Early English Protestants*, pt. I: A–C (Abingdon, n.d.). We have inspected the whole text by Dr. Fines's courtesy. The occupational figures compare with those given by Geisendorf for Protestant fugitives to Geneva (1549–1560), of whom 68 percent were artisans and 3 percent peasants. See Delumeau, *Naissance et affirmation*, p. 267.

31. C. H. Garrett, *The Marian Exiles: A Study in the Origins of Elizabethan Puritanism* (Cambridge, 1938), offers biographies of about 800 exiles, mainly of the upper-middle class and gentry.

32. Susan Brigden, "Youth and the English Reformation," *Past and Present*, 95 (1982), pp. 37–67.

33. G. W. O. Woodward, *The Dissolution of the Monasteries* (London, 1966); Joyce Youings, *The Dissolution of the Monasteries* (London, 1971).

34. Patrick Collinson, *The Elizabethan Puritan Movement* (London, 1967). Others include A. F. Scott Pearson, *Thomas Cartwright and Elizabethan Puritanism, 1535–1603* (Cambridge, 1925); M. M. Knappen, *Tudor Puritanism: A Chapter in the History of Idealism* (Chicago, 1939); George and George, *Protestant Mind of English Reformation*.

35. J. E. C. Hill, *Economic Problems of the Church: From Archbishop Whitgift to the Long Parliament* (Oxford, 1956).

36. John Bossy, *The English Catholic Community, 1570–1850* (London, 1975).

37. Peter Heath, *The English Parish Clergy on the Eve of the Reformation* (London and Toronto, 1969); Rosemary O'Day, *The English Clergy: The Emergence and Consolidation of a Profession, 1558–1642* (Leicester, 1979).

38. Felicity Heal, *Of Prelates and Princes: A Study of the Economic and Social Position of the Tudor Episcopate* (Cambridge, 1980).

39. See n. 24 and R. Houlbrooke, *Church Courts and the People during the English Reformation, 1520–1570* (Oxford, 1979).

40. For example, Felicity Heal and Rosemary O'Day, eds., *Church and Society in England: Henry VIII to James I* (London, 1977); Jennifer Loach and R. Tittler, eds., *The Mid-Tudor Polity, c. 1540–1560* (London, 1980).

41. Dickens, *English Reformation*.

42. Claire Cross, *Church and People, 1450–1660: The Triumph of the Laity in the English Church* (Hassocks, 1976); several shorter works listed in Ozment, *Reformation Europe: A Guide*, pp. 289–290; D. M. Loades, *The Reign of Mary Tudor* (London, 1979); *Two Tudor Conspiracies* (Cambridge, 1965); *The Oxford Martyrs* (London, 1970).

43. G. R. Elton, *Policy and Police: The Enforcement of the Reformation in the Age of Thomas Cromwell* (Cambridge, 1972).

44. Michael Lynch, *Edinburgh and the Reformation* (Edinburgh, 1981).

45. Gordon Donaldson, *The Scottish Reformation* (Cambridge, 1960); but his researches are widely scattered in journals and record publications, such as those of the Scottish Record Society and the Scottish History Society.

46. Glanmor Williams, *The Welsh Church from Conquest to Reformation* (Cardiff, 1962) and *Welsh Reformation Essays* (Cardiff, 1967).

47. Janssen, *Geschichte des deutschen Volkes,* translated by Mitchell and Christie as *History of the German People.* (For a complete citation, see chap. 8 n. 13.)

48. Leopold von Ranke, *History of the Reformation in Germany,* trans. S. Austin (London, 1905), pp. 668–672.

49. Leopold von Ranke, *Die Chroniken der deutschen Städte vom 14 bis 16 Jahrhundert* (Leipzig, 36 vols., 1862–).

50. Ferdinand Frensdorff, *Dortmunder Statuten und Urteile* (Halle, 1882); G. F. von der Ropp, *Göttinger Statuten* (Leipzig and Hanover, 1907).

51. J. D. W. von Winterbach, *Geschichte der Stadt Rothenburg . . . und ihres Gebietes* (Rothenburg, 2 pts., 1826–1827); Leonard Ennen, *Geschichte der Reformation im Bereiche der alten Erzdiözese Köln* (Cologne and Neuss, 1849) and *Geschichte der Stadt Köln, meist aus den Quellen des Kölner Stadt-Archivs* (Neuss, 5 vols., 1863–1880).

52. Ferdinand Roth, *Die Einführung der Reformation in Nürnberg, 1517–1528* (Würzburg, 1885) and *Augsburgs Reformationsgeschichte* (Munich, 4 vols., 1901–1911).

53. Axel Vorberg, *Die Einführung der Reformation in Rostock* (Halle, 1897); Eugen Nübling, *Die Reichsstadt Ulm am Ausgange des Mittelalters, 1378–1556* (Ulm, 2 vols., 1904–1907).

54. Karl Schottenloher, *Bibliographie zur deutschen Geschichte im Zeitalter der Glaubensspaltung, 1517–1585* (Leipzig, 6 vols., 1933–1939); volume VII (Stuttgart, 1962) covers the years 1938–1960. Erich Keyser, *Bibliographie zur Städtegeschichte Deutschlands* (Cologne and Vienna, 1969).

55. Uvo Hölscher, *Die Geschichte der Reformation in Goslar* (Hanover and Leipzig, 1902); Kurt Beckey, *Die Reformation in Hamburg* (Hamburg, 1929); Leonhard Theobald, *Die Reformationsgeschichte der Reichsstadt Regensburg* (Munich, 1936).

56. Hans von Schubert, *Lazarus Spengler und die Reformation in Nürnberg* (Leipzig, 1934).

57. Joseph Lortz, *The Reformation in Germany,* trans. R. Walls (London and New York, 2 vols., 1968), I, 46, 47. The German edition was published in 1939–1940 in Freiburg im Breisgau.

58. Hans Baron, "Religion and Politics in the German Imperial Cities during the Reformation," *English Historical Review,* 52 (1937), pp. 405–427, 614–633.

59. Bernd Moeller, *Reichsstadt und Reformation,* Schriften des Vereins für Reformationsgeschichte, no. 180, vol. 9 (Gütersloh, 1962). Translated by H. C. E. Midelfort and M. U. Edwards as *Imperial Cities and the Reformation:*

Three Essays (Philadelphia, 1972). For an able conspectus of recent research see Basil Hall, "The Reformation City," *Bulletin of the John Rylands Library,* 54 (1971), pp. 103–148.

60. Moeller, *Imperial Cities,* p. 49.

61. Franz Lau, "Der Bauernkrieg und das angebliche Ende der lutherischen Reformation als spontaner Volksbewegung," *Luther Jahrbuch,* 26 (1959), pp. 109–134.

62. Moeller, *Imperial Cities,* p. 67.

63. Ibid., p. 103.

64. Ibid., p. 112.

65. Steven Ozment, *The Reformation in the Cities: The Appeal of Protestantism to Sixteenth-Century Germany and Switzerland* (New Haven and London, 1975), p. 8.

66. Paul Kalkoff, *Die Reformation in der Reichsstadt Nürnberg nach den Flugschriften ihres Ratschreiber's Lazarus Spengler* (Halle, 1926); Adolf Engelhardt, *Die Reformation in Nürnberg,* Mitteilungen des Vereins für Geschichte der Stadt Nürnberg, 33 (Nuremberg, 2 vols., 1936–1937).

67. Gerald Strauss, *Nuremberg in the Sixteenth Century* (New York, 1966), chap. 4; see also his article "Protestant Dogma and City Government: The Case of Nuremberg," *Past and Present,* 36 (1967), pp. 38–58.

68. Gottfried Seebass, "The Reformation in Nuremberg," in L. P. Buck and W. Zophy, eds., *The Social History of the Reformation* (Columbus, Ohio, 1972). Also important on Nuremberg is Harold J. Grimm, "The Role of Nuremberg in the Spread of the Reformation," in F. F. Church and T. George, eds., *Continuity and Discontinuity in Church History: Essays Presented to G. H. Williams* (Leiden, 1979). Documents are in G. Pfeiffer, ed., *Quellen zur Nürnberger Reformationsgeschichte* (Nuremberg, 1968).

69. Strauss, *Nuremberg in the Sixteenth Century,* p. 160; P. N. Bebb, "The Lawyers, Dr. Christoph Scheurl, and the Reformation in Nuremberg," in Buck and Zophy, *Social History,* pp. 52–72.

70. See C. E. Daniel, "Hard Work, Good Work, and School Work: An Analysis of Wenzeslaus Linck's Conception of Civil Responsibility," in ibid., pp. 41–51.

71. The patriciate itself was by no means always harmonious. See J. Spielvogel, "Patricians in Dissension: A Case Study from Sixteenth-Century Nuremberg," in ibid., pp. 73–90.

72. See E. Jane Dempsey Douglass, *Justification in Late Medieval Preaching: A Study of John Geiler of Kaisersberg* (Leiden, 1966).

73. T. W. Röhrich, *Geschichte der Reformation im Elsass und besonders im Strassburg* (Strasbourg, 3 vols., 1830–1832).

74. Charles Schmidt, *Histoire littéraire de l'Alsace à la fin du XVᵉ et au commencement du XVIᵉ siècle* (Paris, 2 vols., 1879).

75. François Wendel, *L'Eglise de Strasbourg: Sa constitution et son organisation, 1532–1535* (Paris, 1942).

76. Miriam U. Chrisman, *Strasbourg and the Reform: A Study in the Process of Change* (New Haven and London, 1967).

77. Ibid., p. 164.

78. R. Kreider, "The Anabaptists and the Civil Authorities of Strasbourg, 1525–1548," *Church History,* 24 (1955), pp. 99–118.

79. Chrisman, *Strasbourg,* p. 176.

80. T. A. Brady, *Ruling Class, Regime and Reformation at Strassburg, 1520–1555* (Leiden, 1977). For the southwest as a whole see M. Hannemann, *The Diffusion of the Reformation in Southwestern Germany* (Chicago, 1975).

81. Miriam U. Chrisman, *Lay Culture, Learned Culture: Books and Social Change in Strasbourg, 1480–1599* (New Haven and London, 1982).

82. Schildhauer, *Soziale, politische und religiöse Auseinandersetzungen;* see also Chapter 10.

83. Wilhelm Jannasch, *Reformationsgeschichte Lübecks vom Petersablass bis zum Augsburger Reichstag, 1515–1530,* Veröffentlichungen zur Geschichte der Hansestadt Lübeck, 16 (Lübeck, 1958). For other works by Jannasch on the Reformation in Lübeck, see Schottenloher, *Bibliographie zur deutschen Geschichte,* VI, 275.

84. Rolf Kiessling, *Bürgerliche Gesellschaft und Kirche in Augsburg im Spätmittelalter* (Augsburg, 1971). Roth, *Augsburgs Reformationsgeschichte,* has the early Reformation period in volume I. For a modern account largely based on manuscript sources see P. Broadhead, "Politics and Expediency in the Augsburg Reformation," in P. N. Brooks, ed., *Reformation Principle and Practice: Essays in Honour of A. G. Dickens* (London, 1980).

85. R. W. Scribner, "Reformation, Society and Humanism in Erfurt, c. 1450–1530" (Unpublished Ph.D. dissertation, London University, 1972); see also his "Civic Unity and the Reformation in Erfurt," *Past and Present,* 66 (1975), pp. 29–60; and A. G. Dickens, *The German Nation and Martin Luther* (London, 1974), pp. 169–176.

86. R. W. Scribner, "Why Was There No Reformation in Cologne?" *Bulletin of the Institute of Historical Research,* 49 (1976), pp. 217–241.

87. C. von Looz-Corswarem, "Die Kölner Artikelserie von 1525: Hintergründe und Verlauf des Aufruhrs von 1525 in Köln," in F. Petri, ed., *Kirche und gesellschaftlicher Wandel in deutschen und niederländischen Städten der werdenden Neuzeit* (Cologne and Vienna, 1980). Along with these numerous urban studies H.-C. Rublack has made important contributions to the history of a special group: the capitals of prince-bishops, for instance, Würzburg and Bamberg. See *Jahresberichte für deutsche Geschichte,* no. 3563 (1976–1977); ibid., nos. 2946, 3302, 3565 (1978–1979).

88. Ozment, *Reformation in the Cities* (see n. 65).

89. Steven Ozment, *The Age of Reform, 1250–1550* (New Haven and London, 1980), p. 192.

90. Ibid., pp. 292–294. Note the reference to Iserloh, p. 292n105; but when one considers the circumstances of image breaking in the 1520s, it remains by no means easy to imagine it as executed or even controlled by Nominalists.

91. See Dickens, *The German Nation;* chaps. 1 and 2 outline this presentation of the problem.

92. *The Cambridge History of the Bible,* III (Cambridge, 3 vols., 1963), p. 432; see also Foxe, *A and M,* III, 718–722; IV, 252–253.

93. G. W. Panzer, *Annalen der älteren deutschen Literatur* (Nuremberg, 2 vols., 1788, 1805); Ranke, *History of the Reformation in Germany*, pp. 284–285.

94. Oscar Schade, *Satiren und Pasquille aus der Reformationszeit* (Hannover, 3 vols., 1856–1858); O. C. Clem, *Flugschriften aus den ersten Jahren der Reformation* (Leipzig and New York, 4 vols., 1907–1911).

95. Henri Gravier, *Luther et l'opinion publique* (Paris, 1943).

96. Elizabeth L. Eisenstein, *The Printing Press as an Agent of Change* (Cambridge, 2 vols., 1979). These volumes largely subsume her earlier articles.

97. Keith Thomas, "Women and the Civil War Sects," *Past and Present*, 13 (1958), pp. 42–62; Patrick Collinson, "The Role of Women in the English Reformation," in *Studies in Church History*, 2 (London and Edinburgh, 1965), pp. 258–272.

98. R. H. Bainton, *Women of the Reformation in Germany and Italy* (Minneapolis, 1971); *Women of the Reformation in France and England* (Minneapolis, 1973); *Women of the Reformation from Spain to Scandinavia* (Minneapolis, 1977).

99. Miriam U. Chrisman, "Women and the Reformation in Strassburg," *Archiv für Reformationsgeschichte*, 63 (1972), pp. 143–168; Charmarie Jenkins Blaisdell, "Renée de France between Reform and Counter-Reform," ibid., pp. 196–226; Nancy L. Roelker, "The Role of Noblewomen in the French Reformation," ibid., pp. 169–195; and "The Appeal of Calvinism to French Noblewomen," *Journal of Interdisciplinary History*, 2 (1972), pp. 391–418.

100. N. Z. Davis, "City Women and Religious Change," in *Society and Culture in Early Modern France* (London, 1975), pp. 65–95, esp. p. 81.

101. Steven Ozment, *When Fathers Ruled: Family Life in Reformation Europe* (Cambridge, Mass., 1983).

102. Keith Thomas, *Religion and the Decline of Magic* (London, 1971). Other scholars were simultaneously reviewing related fields in terms of social anthropology; for example, Alan Macfarlane, *Witchcraft in Tudor and Stuart England: A Regional and Comparative Study* (London, 1970), which deals mainly with evidence from Essex.

103. For instance, H. C. E. Midelfort, *Witch-Hunting in Southwestern Germany, 1562–1684* (Stanford, 1972). The recent bibliography of witchcraft is surprisingly large; see Ozment, *Reformation Europe: A Guide*, pp. 183–209.

104. Gerald Strauss, *Luther's House of Learning: Indoctrination of the Young in the German Reformation* (Baltimore and London, 1978).

105. Ibid., pp. 288–291.

106. John Bossy, "The Counter Reformation and the People of Catholic Europe," *Past and Present*, 47 (1970), pp. 51–70.

107. Strauss, *Luther's House of Learning*, p. 299.

108. Max Rumpf, *Das gemeine Volk*, vol. II: *Religiöses Volkskunde* (Stuttgart, 1933). Another "early" strand appears in Gabriel Le Bras, *Etudes de sociologie religieuse* (Paris, 2 vols., 1955–1956), a successor to work he was already doing around 1930. See detail in Bossy, "The Counter Reformation," p. 52n1.

109. The following German examples are taken from R. W. Scribner, "Ritual

and Popular Religion in Catholic Germany at the Time of the Reformation," *Journal of Ecclesiastical History*, 35 (1984), pp. 47–77. For popular religion and superstitions in England see H. Maynard Smith, *Pre-Reformation England* (London, 1938), chaps. 3, 4.

110. Jacques Toussaert, *Le Sentiment religieux en Flandre à la fin du Moyen Age* (Paris, 1963).

111. Jean Delumeau, *Le Catholicisme entre Luther et Voltaire* (Paris, 1971). English translation *Catholicism between Luther and Voltaire* (London, 1977).

112. Bossy, "The Counter Reformation." The other articles are listed in Ozment, *Reformation Europe: Guide to Research*, p. 313. Bossy's major and very original work, *The English Catholic Community, 1570–1850* (London, 1976), is much more concerned with the later history of the English Catholics.

113. Delumeau, *Catholicism*, chap. 5; Pierre Chaunu, *Le Temps des Réformes* (Paris, 1975), pt. 2.

114. This reference occurs in Jean Wirth, "Against the Acculturation Thesis," Kaspar von Greyerz, ed., *Religion and Society* (London, 1984).

115. Peter Burke, *Popular Culture in Early Modern Europe* (London and New York, 1978). On Protestant "gravity" and reformism see pp. 213–228. Burke also pointed out that printing undermined the oral cultures and that reformism can already be observed in Sebastian Brant and Geiler von Kaysersberg.

116. Robert Muchembled, *Culture populaire et culture des élites dans la France moderne* (Paris, 1978). Compare the same author's *La Sorcière au village: XVe–XVIIIe siècles* (Paris, 1979), together with his "Lay Judges and the Acculturation of the Masses," in von Greyerz, *Religion and Society*, pp. 56–65.

117. Muchembled, "Lay Judges."

118. See R. W. Scribner's review in *History Workshop*, issue 14 (1982), p. 14; and his review article in *European Studies Review*, 13 (1983), pp. 89–105.

119. R. C. Trexler, *Public Life in Renaissance France* (New York, 1980); W. A. Christian, *Local Religion in Sixteenth-Century Spain* (Princeton, 1981).

120. Lionel Rothkrug, *Religious Practices and Collective Perceptions: Hidden Homologies in the Renaissance and Reformation* (Waterloo, Ontario, 1980).

121. Ibid., chaps. 4, 5.

122. Ibid., chap. 3.

123. Commentaries on Rothkrug's work by H. C. E. Midelfort and G. H. Williams are in ibid., pp. 255–264. Midelfort had further points of detail; Williams (p. 263) pointed out a moral in favor of Rothkrug's theory: that the Reformation in fact began by rejecting a peculiar system of salvation for souls in Purgatory and then repudiated saints' intercessions because Luther had proclaimed that salvation was already achieved by election and experienced in faith.

124. Heinz Schilling, "Die politische Elite nordwestdeutscher Städte in der religiösen Auseinandersetzungen des 16. Jahrhunderts," and R. W. Scribner, "The Reformation as a Social Movement," both in *Stadtbürgertum und Adel in der Reformation* (see n. 131).

125. A competent account of his activities is in J. Brodrick, *Saint Peter Canisius, S.J., 1521–1597* (London, 1935).

126. Rainer Wohlfeil, *Einführung in die Geschichte der deutschen Reformation* (Munich, 1982).

127. Ozment, *Reformation Europe: A Guide,* has the most useful bibliographies of very recent work on, for example, humanism and the Reformation (pp. 33–57), the Peasants' War (pp. 107–133), and witchcraft and magic (pp. 183–209).

128. R. W. Scribner, *For the Sake of Simple Folk: Popular Propaganda for the German Reformation* (Cambridge, 1981). On art in general see Ozment, *Reformation Europe: A Guide,* pp. 249–270; and especially C. C. Christensen, *Art and the Reformation in Germany* (Athens, Ohio, and Detroit, 1979).

129. For instance, H. A. Lloyd, *The State, France and the Sixteenth Century* (London, 1983); A. Duke, "Salvation by Coercion: The Controversy Surrounding the 'Inquisition' in the Low Countries on the Eve of the Revolt," in P. N. Brooks, ed., *Reformation Principle and Practice* (London, 1980), pp. 135–156.

130. H.-J. Köhler, ed., *Flugschriften als Massenmedium der Reformationszeit* (Stuttgart, 1981).

131. *The Urban Classes, the Nobility and the Reformation;* alternative German title: *Stadtbürgertum und Adel in der Reformation: Studien zur Sozialgeschichte der Reformation in England und Deutschland,* ed. W. J. Mommsen for the German Historical Institute, London (Stuttgart, 1979).

132. Von Greyerz, *Religion and Society.*

Appendix

1. Gooch, *History and Historians,* pp. 92–93n., 430–433.

2. Howard Kaminsky, *A History of the Hussite Revolution* (Berkeley and Los Angeles, 1967); Matthew Spinka, *John Hus: A Biography* (Princeton, 1968); F. G. Heymann, *John Zižka and the Hussite Revolution* (Princeton, 1955); R. R. Betts, *Essays in Czech History* (London, 1969); Peter Brock, *The Political and Social Doctrines of the Unity of Czech Brethren in the Fifteenth and Sixteenth Centuries* (The Hague, 1957). The best short account in English is in D. M. Lambert, *Medieval Heresy: Popular Movements from Bogomil to Hus* (London, 1977), chaps. 16–18.

3. J. K. Zeman, *The Hussite Movement and the Reformation in Bohemia, Moravia and Slovakia, 1350–1650: A Bibliographical Study-Guide* (Ann Arbor, 1977); Č. Zíbrt, *Bibliografie České Historie* (Prague, 5 vols., 1900–1912); F. Seibt, *Bohemica: Probleme und Literatur seit 1945,* Historische Zeitschrift, 4 (Munich, 1970).

4. Janusz Tazbir, *A State without Stakes: Polish Religious Toleration in the Sixteenth and Seventeenth Centuries* (Panstwowy Instytut Wydawniczy, 1967). On toleration in Poland see also Lecler, *Toleration,* I, bk. 5, pp. 385–423.

5. See A. Gieyztor et al., eds., *History of Poland* (Warsaw, 1967), chaps. 7, 8; and, for example, Maria Bogucka, "Towns in Poland and the Reformation," *Acta Poloniae Historica,* 40 (1979), pp. 55–74, which contains up-to-date parallels with other countries.

6. See, for instance, E. Pamlényi, ed., *A History of Hungary* (London, 1975), chaps. 1–4 by Laszló Makkai, the leading Protestant church historian in that country.

7. H. A. Enno van Gelder, *The Two Reformations in the Sixteenth Century: A Study of the Religious Aspects and Consequences of Renaissance and Humanism* (The Hague, 1964).

8. Werner Elert, *Morphologie des Luthertums* (Munich, 1931). Translated by W. A. Hansen as *The Structure of Lutheranism* (St. Louis, 1962), p. 418n4.

9. John Dillenberger, *Protestant Thought and Natural Science* (London, 1961); B. A. Gerrish, "The Reformation and the Rise of Modern Science," in J. G. Brauer, ed., *The Impact of the Church upon Its Culture* (Chicago, 1968), pp. 231–265.

10. Edward Rosen, "Calvin's Attitude towards Copernicus," *Journal of the History of Ideas*, 21 (1960), pp. 431–441.

11. Gerrish, "Reformation and Science," pp. 244–245, 247–262.

12. R. K. Merton, "Science, Technology and Society in Seventeenth Century England," *Osiris*, 4 (1938), pp. 414–565; reprinted in G. Basalla, ed., *The Rise of Modern Science* (Boston, 1968), pp. 39–47.

13. Reijer Hooykaas, "Science and Reformation," in Basalla, *Rise of Modern Science*, pp. 55–61; and *Religion and the Rise of Modern Science*, Gunning Lectures, 1969 (Edinburgh and London, 1972), chap. 5.

14. D. S. Kemsley, "Religious Influences in the Rise of Modern Science," in C. A. Russell, ed., *Science and Religious Belief: A Selection of Recent Historical Studies* (London, 1973), p. 82.

15. Ibid., pp. 74–102.

16. For attempts to define Puritanism see, for example, Basil Hall, *Studies in Church History*, 2, ed. G. J. Cuming (Leiden, 1965); C. H. George, "Puritanism as History and Historiography," *Past and Present*, 41 (1968), pp. 77–104; Patrick Collinson, "A Comment Concerning the Name Puritan," *Journal of Ecclesiastical History*, 31 (1980), pp. 483–488. See also many passages in George and George, *Protestant Mind of English Reformation*, and Greaves, *Society and Religion in Elizabethan England*.

17. N. R. N. Tyacke, "Puritanism, Arminianism and Counter-Revolution," in Conrad Russell, ed., *The Origins of the English Civil War* (London, 1973).

18. Thomas, *Religion and Magic*, esp. chaps. 2–9.

19. See especially Samuel Clarke, *Lives of Twenty-Two English Divines* (London, 1662) and *Lives of Ten Eminent Divines . . . and of some other Eminent Christians* (London, 1662); further details in DNB, IV, 441–442.

20. DNB, III, 683–687; his central figure was Richard Baxter, of whom he wrote three biographies.

21. Daniel Neal, *The History of the Puritans, or Protestant Non-Conformists; from the Reformation in 1517 to the Death of Queen Elizabeth* (London, 4 vols., 1732–1738; ed. J. Toulmin, Bath, 5 vols., 1793–1797; ed. J. O. Choules, New York, 2 vols., 1844).

22. Benjamin Brook, *The Lives of the Puritans . . . from the Reformation under Queen Elizabeth to the Act of Uniformity in 1662* (London, 3 vols., 1813).

23. H. W. Clark, *History of English Nonconformity from Wiclif to the Close of the Nineteenth Century* (London, 2 vols., 1911–1913). Champlin Burrage, *The Early English Dissenters in the Light of Recent Research, 1530–1641* (Cambridge, 2 vols., 1912), is still a standard work on the Separatists.

24. W. H. Frere and C. E. Douglas, *Puritan Manifestoes* (London, 1907; rpt., 1954); Albert Peel, *The Second Parte of a Register* (Cambridge, 2 vols., 1915).

25. Patrick Collinson, *English Puritanism*, The Historical Association, General Series, 106 (London, 1983), pp. 40–47.

26. Among other works Carlson continued the series of *Elizabethan Nonconformist Texts*, which he had begun with Peel in 1951: it comprises editions of Cartwright, Harrison, Browne, Barrow, and Greenwood; L. J. Trinterud, ed., *Elizabethan Puritanism* (New York, 1971); H. C. Porter, ed., *Puritanism in Tudor England* (London, 1970).

27. See especially Christopher Hill, *Society and Puritanism in Pre-Revolutionary England* (London, 1964) and *The Intellectual Origins of the English Revolution* (Oxford, 1965).

28. M. E. James, *Family, Lineage and Civil Society* (Oxford, 1974); Peter Clark, *English Provincial Society* (Hassocks, 1977); W. J. Sheils, *The Puritans in the Diocese of Peterborough*, Northants Record Society, 30 (Northampton, 1979); Christopher Haigh, *Reformation and Resistance in Tudor Lancashire* (Cambridge, 1975); R. C. Richardson, *Puritanism in Northwest England* (Manchester, 1972); Margaret Spufford, *Contrasting Communities* (Cambridge, 1974); R. B. Manning, *Religion and Society in Elizabethan Sussex* (Leicester, 1969); R. B. Marchant, *The Puritans and the Church Courts in the Diocese of York* (London, 1960); H. C. Porter, *Reformation and Reaction in Tudor Cambridge* (Cambridge, 1958). See also, on Cambridge, P. Lake, *Moderate Puritans and the Elizabethan Church* (Cambridge, 1982). Much regional information also appears in biographies, such as Claire Cross, *The Puritan Earl: The Life of Henry Hastings, Third Earl of Huntingdon* (London, 1966); and Patrick Collinson, *Archbishop Grindal, 1519–1583: The Struggle for a Reformed Church* (London, 1979).

29. Alan Macfarlane, *The Family Life of Ralph Josselin, a Seventeenth-Century Clergyman: An Essay in Historical Anthropology* (Cambridge, 1970). See also L. L. Schuecking, *The Puritan Family: A Social Study from the Literary Sources*, trans. B. Battershaw (London, 1969); from *Die Puritanische Familie* (Leipzig, 1929). E. S. Morgan, *The Puritan Family: Essays on Religion and Domestic Relations in Seventeenth-Century New England* (Boston, 1944; rev. ed., New York, 1966).

30. M. M. Knappen, *Tudor Puritanism: A Chapter in the History of Idealism* (Chicago, 1939; rpt. ed., 1965); George and George, *Protestant Mind of English Reformation;* Patrick Collinson, *The Elizabethan Puritan Movement* (London, 1967; rpt. ed., 1982).

31. William Haller, *The Rise of Puritanism* (New York, 1938; rpt. ed., 1957); Perry Miller, *Orthodoxy in Massachusetts, 1630–1650* (Cambridge, Mass., 1933) and *The New England Mind: The Seventeenth Century* (New York, 1939; rpt. ed., Boston, 1954); Greaves, *Society and Religion in Elizabethan England.*

32. Louis B. Wright, *Middle Class Culture in Elizabethan England* (Chapel Hill, 1935; London, 1964).

33. *New Cambridge Modern History*, XIII, chap. 12.

34. For a good compact account see *New Catholic Encyclopedia*, XIII, 39–42.

35. See B. J. Kidd, ed., *Documents Illustrative of the Continental Reformation* (Oxford, 1911, 1967), pp. 121–124. This selection of documents shows more awareness of the whole problem than its successors: see also pp. 233, 314, 327, 441, 443, 468, 502, 515, 554, 697, some of which concern Scandinavia.

36. From about 1840 to 1938 the German publications are well listed in Schottenloher, *Bibliographie zur deutschen Geschichte*, IV, 549. See also Bruno Gebhardt, *Handbuch der deutschen Geschichte*, 9th ed. (Stuttgart, 2 vols., 1970), II.

37. W. H. Wolff, *Die Säkularisierung und Verwendung der Stifts- und Klosterguten in Hessen-Kassel unter Philipp dem Grossmütigen und Wilhelm IV* (Gotha, 1913); Alfred Hilpert, *Die Sequestration der geistlichen Güter in den kursächsischen Landkreisen Meissen, Vogtland und Sachsen, 1531 bis 1543* (Plauen, 1912).

38. F. L. Carsten, *The Origins of Prussia* (Oxford, 1954, and later eds.), pp. 149–159, after which it is also informative on Prussia itself. The passage is partly based on two important secondary works: F. Grossmann on Mark Brandenburg (1890) and C. J. Fuchs on Neu Vorpommern and Rügen (1888), cited by Carsten, p. 149n1.

39. F. L. Carsten, *Princes and Parliaments in Germany from the Fifteenth to the Eighteenth Century* (Oxford, 1959), p. 437. See the reference in note 1 to the "old view" exemplified by O. Hintze's contribution to F. Hartung, ed., *Staat und Verfassung* (Leipzig, 1941), p. 128.

40. Carsten, *Princes and Parliaments*, p. 437.

41. Gerhard Benecke, *Society and Politics in Germany, 1500–1750* (London and Toronto, 1974), pp. 14–15. On page 165 Benecke describes the aristocratic foundations at Lemgo, which survived both Lutheran and Calvinist regimes.

42. Ibid., p. 6.

43. On the Edwardian processes modern scholarship is represented by Alan Kreider, *English Chantries: The Road to Dissolution* (Cambridge, Mass., and London, 1979).

44. See Michael Sherbrook, "The Fall of Religious Houses," in A. G. Dickens, ed., *Tudor Treatises*, Yorkshire Archaeological Society, Record Series, 125 (1959), pp. 89–142; also the petition of John Hamerton, printed with comments in A. G. Dickens, *Reformation Studies* (London, 1982), pp. 85–91.

45. Henry Spelman, *The History and Fate of Sacrilege* (1698). This still valuable work is now used in the augmented edition by J. Caley, H. Ellis, and B. Bandinel (London, 8 vols., 1817–1830; London, 6 vols., 1846). William Dugdale, *Monasticon Anglicanum* (London, 1655).

46. Cobbett, *History of the Protestant Reformation.* (See Chapter 8.)

47. Gasquet, *Henry VIII;* M. D. Knowles, "Cardinal Gasquet as a Historian," Creighton Lecture in History, University of London, 1956; reprinted in *The*

Historian and Character (Cambridge, 1964), pp. 240–263. The work had already been castigated by G. G. Coulton, *Medieval Studies* (London, 1930), pp. 84–107. See n. 48.

48. David [M. D.] Knowles, *The Religious Orders in England* (Cambridge, 3 vols., 1959), III, has the fullest accounts of late English monasticism, the dissolution, and the attempted restoration by Mary Tudor.

49. Dickens, *English Reformation,* summarizes research to 1964 on the dissolution and its effects; Woodward, *Dissolution;* the select bibliography in Youings, *Dissolution,* p. 254, gives the main recent works; the same author's *Devon Monastic Lands: Particular for Grants,* Devon and Cornwall Record Society, New Series, I (Truro, 1971) is an exceptionally valuable regional contribution; another is G. A. J. Hodgett, *Tudor Lincolnshire* (Lincoln, 1975), chaps. 3, 4.

50. Christopher Kitching, "The Disposal of Monastic and Chantry Lands," in Heal and O'Day, *Church and Society,* chap. 6, pp. 119–136. The earlier works cited in the previous notes should be used with Kitching's additional thoughts.

51. Kreider, *English Chantries.*

52. A. F. Leach, *English Schools at the Reformation, 1546–8* (Westminster, 1896). For criticisms see Joan Simon, "A. F. Leach on the Reformation," *British Journal of Educational Studies,* 3 (no. 2), pp. 128–143; and 4 (no. 1), pp. 32–48 (1955); W. E. Tate, *A. F. Leach as a Historian of Yorkshire Education,* St. Anthony's Hall Publications, 23 (York, 1963).

53. Dickens, *English Reformation,* p. 211. On the background see Kreider, *English Chantries.*

54. P. J. Wallis and W. E. Tate, *A Register of Old Yorkshire Grammar Schools,* University of Leeds, Institute of Education, Researches and Studies, 13 (1956).

55. Dickens, *English Reformation,* pp. 211–213, 354.

56. N. Wood, *The Reformation and English Education* (London, 1931), pp. 181–182. Luther had already demanded girls' schools in his address *To the Christian Nobility of the German Nation* (1520); see E. G. Rupp and B. Drewery, *Martin Luther,* Documents of Modern History (London, 1970), p. 47.

57. Luther himself wrote this in 1530 in his *Sermon on Keeping Children in School* (1530), in Pelikan and Lehmann, *Luther's Works,* XLVI (Philadelphia, 1967), pp. 207–258.

58. *To the Councilmen of All Cities in Germany That They Establish and Maintain Christian Schools* (1524), in *Luther's Works,* XLV (Philadelphia, 1962), pp. 339–378; *Sermon on Keeping Children in School.*

59. H. Rössler and G. Franz, *Sachwörterbuch zur Deutschen Geschichte* (Munich, 2 vols., 1956), II, 1131.

60. This dualism in secondary education was succinctly explained by Friedrich Paulsen, *German Education Past and Present* (London and Leipzig, 1908); translated by T. Lorenz from *Das Deutsche Bildungwesen in seiner geschichtlichen Entwicklung* (Leipzig, 1906), pp. 65–67. On the beneficent princes see Frederick Hertz, *The Development of the German Public Mind* (London, 1957), chap. 23.

61. Compare, for example, the list of works on schools in Schottenloher, *Bibliographie zur deutschen Geschichte,* VII, p. 466, nos. 64036–53, with his list for universities, ibid., pp. 487–492, nos. 64605–713.

62. Friedrich Paulsen, *Geschichte des gelehrten Unterrichts auf den deutschen Schulen und Universitäten vom Ausgang des Mittelalters zur Gegenwart* (Leipzig, 1885); 3rd ed., much revised by R. Lehmann (Leipzig, 2 vols., 1919).

63. Paul Barth, *Die Geschichte der Erziehung in soziologischer und geistes-geschichtlicher Beleuchtung* (Leipzig, 1911; rev. 2nd ed., 1916).

64. Ibid., pp. 261–291: "Der gelehrte Unterricht unter der Einwerkung der Reformation und des deutschen Humanismus"; and pp. 291–317: "Der Volks-unterricht unter der Einwerkung der Reformation."

65. Strauss, *Luther's House of Learning.*

66. H. D. Bürger, *Renaissance, Humanismus, Reformation: Deutsche Literatur in europäischen Kontext* (Bad Homburg, Berlin, and Zurich, 1969).

67. F. I. Borchard, *German Antiquity in Renaissance Myth* (Baltimore and London, 1971).

68. May McKisack, *Medieval History in the Tudor Age* (Oxford, 1971).

69. See n. 60.

70. See n. 41.

71. *Geist und Geschichte der Reformation, Festgabe Hanns Rückert* (Berlin, 1966): articles on Paulinism, Nominalism, Biel, many aspects of Luther, Calvin, humanism, Hooker, Pietism, Spener, and so on; Gerald Strauss, ed., *Pre-Reformation Germany* (London, 1972).

72. Heinrich Boehmer, *Der Junge Luther* (Gotha, 1925); Otto Scheel, *Martin Luther* (Tübingen, 2 vols., 1930); James Mackinnon, *Martin Luther and the Reformation* (London, 4 vols., 1925–1930). An invaluable bibliography of recent and last-generation works on Reformers and Reformation generally is in Léonard, *History of Protestantism*, I, 356–433. Wilhelm Pauck, "The Historiography of the German Reformation during the Past Twenty Years," *Church History*, 9 (1940), pp. 305–340; see also his *The Heritage of the Reformation* (Boston, 1950; enlarged ed., Glencoe, Ill., 1961).

73. These and others are listed in the bibliography of A. G. Dickens, *The German Nation and Martin Luther* (London, 1974), pp. 227–243.

74. Heinrich Bornkamm, *Martin Luther in der Mitte seines Lebens* (Göttingen, 1982); Mark Edwards, *Luther's Last Battles* (Ithaca, N.Y., 1982). Bornkamm's book was translated by E. T. Bachmann as *Luther in Mid-Career* (Philadelphia, 1983).

75. Walter Koehler, *Zwingli und Luther: Ihr Streit über das Abendmahl* (Leipzig, 2 vols., 1924; Gutersloh, 1953). For Koehler's other works on Zwingli see G. R. Potter, *Zwingli* (Cambridge, 1976), p. xiv. On the broader aspects see G. W. Locher, *Die Zwinglische Reformation im Rahmen der europäischen Kirchengeschichte* (Göttingen and Zurich, 1979).

76. Oscar Farner, *Huldrych Zwingli, der schweizerische Reformator* (Emmishofen, 4 vols., 1917, 1949; English trans., London, 1952). Details of Farner's works are given in Potter, *Zwingli*, p. xiii. The key to Zwingli studies is now Ulrich Gäbler, *Huldrych Zwingli im 20. Jahrhundert* (Zurich, 1975), a report on research with a huge descriptive bibliography.

77. Emile Doumergue, *Jean Calvin: Les hommes et les choses de son temps* (Lausanne, 7 vols., 1899–1927).

78. R. N. C. Hunt, *Calvin* (London, 1933); François Wendel, *Calvin: The Origins and Development of His Religious Thought*, trans. P. Mairet (London and New York, 1963; original French ed., Paris, 1950). For recent work on Calvin and Calvinism see D. Kampff, ed., *A Bibliography of Calviniana, 1959–1974* (Leiden, 1975); and Basil Hall's review article "From Biblical Humanism to Calvinist Orthodoxy," *Journal of Ecclesiastical History*, 31 (1980), pp. 331–343.

79. J. T. McNeill, *History and Character of Calvinism* (New York, 1954); E. W. Monter, *Calvin's Geneva* (New York, 1967).

80. For similar reasons we have not embarked on an analysis of that extensive genre of works known as college texts, including both collections of documentary sources in translation and general surveys of history of the Reformation. Among the surveys, those by R. H. Bainton, Owen Chadwick, A. G. Dickens, G. R. Elton, H. J. Hillerbrand, S. Harrison Thompson, and L. W. Spitz, Jr., deserve particular recognition for having made the results of scholarly inquiry available to a wider circle of readers.

81. A bibliography of Bainton's prolific writings to the year 1972 is in *Archiv für Reformationsgeschichte*, 64 (1973), pp. 6–12. See also Chapter 12.

82. Bainton, *Here I Stand*.

83. Ibid., p. 41.

84. Ibid.

Index

Aarts, Jan, 208
Acculturation, 313–315
Aconzio, Jacopo, 50
Acton, John Emerich Edward Dalberg
  (Lord Acton), 194, 196; and Catholic
  records, 57; and Ranke, 168, 174, 175;
  on Reformation radicals, 216
Adiaphora doctrine, 60–61, 62, 63; and
  Melanchthon, 34, 60, 61; and Thirty-
  nine Articles, 65; and Jewel, 66; and Cart-
  wright, 69
Adrian VI (pope), Hume on, 140
Agricola, Johannes, 33
Agricola, Peter, 51
Albani, Johannes, 205
Albigensians: in Crespin's martyrology,
  43; in Bossuet's view, 110; in Macau-
  lay's account, 156; Engels on, 242
Albrecht of Brandenburg-Ansbach, secu-
  larization by, 341–342
Aleandro, Girolamo, 22, 206
Alexander VI (pope): Voltaire on, 121;
  Mosheim on, 132; in Robertson's ac-
  count, 144
Alfield, Thomas, 55
Algermissen, Konrad, 205
Alienation, Marx on, 236, 239
Allen, William, 55

Allerton, Ralph, 293
Amerbach, Bonifacius, 33
American Protestantism, in nineteenth
  century, 198
American Society for Reformation Research, 211
"Anabaptist," as epithet, 62, 214, 232
Anabaptists and Anabaptism, 213, 214–
  215, 223–230, 231–233; predecessors
  of, 1; in Sleidan's history, 15, 16; Bullinger on, 20–21; Foxe pleads for, 47;
  and Haemstede, 50; martyrologies by,
  51; and Thirty-nine Articles, 65;
  Hooker on, 69; as threat, 69; Bayle on,
  115; Voltaire on, 123; Mosheim on,
  133–134; in Macaulay's account, 159;
  Ritschl on, 187; Lindsay on, 197; modern historiography of, 215–219; and
  Catholicism, 216, 226, 227; social
  background of, 218, 228–229; American historical treatment of, 219–221,
  223, 230, 232–233; Weber and
  Troeltsch on, 221–222; Mennonite
  scholars on, 223, 228, 230, 232; divisiveness of, 229; and Münzer, 230, 246,
  260; Marxist interpretation of, 230,
  259–260; in England, 232; Kautsky on,
  246; Steinmetz on, 257; in Febvre's

423